Max Planck Yearbook
of
United Nations Law

Volume 12
2008

Max Planck Yearbook
of
United Nations Law

Founding Editors

Jochen A. Frowein

Rüdiger Wolfrum

Max Planck Yearbook of United Nations Law

Volume 12
2008

Editors
Armin von Bogdandy
Rüdiger Wolfrum

Managing Editor
Christiane E. Philipp

Max-Planck-Institut für ausländisches
öffentliches Recht und Völkerrecht

MARTINUS NIJHOFF PUBLISHERS
LEIDEN / BOSTON

This book should be cited as follows: Max Planck UNYB

Printed on acid-free paper.

ISBN13: 978 90 04 16959 3
ISSN: 1389-4633
© 2008 *Koninklijke Brill NV, Leiden, The Netherlands*

Koninklijke Brill NV incorporates the imprints Brill, Hotei Publishing,
IDC Publishers, Martinus Nijhoff Publishers and VSP.

Printed and bound in The Netherlands.

Articles from previously published volumes are electronically available under
"Top-Links" at: http://www.mpil.de

Contents

LL.M. Thesis:

List of Contributors

Alday, Alejandro
Legal Adviser and Human Rights Expert for the Permanent Mission of Mexico to the United Nations, New York

Barriga, Stefan
Dr. iur., LL.M. (Columbia), Counsellor for Legal Affairs, Permanent Mission of Liechtenstein to the United Nations, New York

Bühler, Konrad G.
Mag. Dr. iur., Counsellor for Legal Affairs, Permanent Mission of Austria to the United Nations, New York

Breen, Claire
Senior Lecturer, Law School, University of Waikato, New Zealand

Fitschen, Thomas
Dr. iur., Counsellor for Legal Affairs, Permanent Mission of Germany to the United Nations, New York

Fuchs, Christine
Research Fellow at the Max Planck Institute for Comparative Public Law and International Law

Kanetake, Machiko
LL.M. (London), Ph.D. Candidate, Kyoto University, Japan

Knahr, Christina

Mag. Dr., MPA, Post-Doctoral Researcher at the Department of European, International and Comparative Law at the University of Vienna, Austria

Niemelä, Pekka

LL.M. (University of Helsinki), Research Fellow at the Erik Castrén Institute of International Law and Human Rights, Faculty of Law, University of Helsinki, Finland

de Oliveira Godinho, Fabiana

LL.M. (Heidelberg), Research Fellow at the Max Planck Institute for Comparative Public Law and International Law

Orakhelashvili, Alexander

LL.M. (Leiden), Ph.D. (Cantab.), Shaw Foundation Junior Research Fellow in Law, Jesus College, Oxford, United Kingdom

Reinisch, August

ao. Univ.-Prof. MMag. Dr., LL.M., Professor of International and European Law at the University of Vienna, Austria, and Professorial Lecturer at the Bologna Center of SAIS/Johns Hopkins University in Bologna, Italy

Trevisanut, Seline

Dr. iur., University of Milan; Research Fellow, Department of Law, University of Trento, Italy

Weiß, Wolfgang

Professor of Public Law, Public International Law and European Law at the German University for Administrative Sciences, Speyer, and Professor of International Law, Oxford Brookes University, United Kingdom

LL.M. Thesis:

Alvarez Núñez, Rosa Giannina

Abbreviations

ACABQ	Advisory Committee on Administrative and Budgetary Questions
AD	*Annual Digest of Public International Law Cases*
A.F.D.I.	*Annuaire Français de Droit International*
AJDA	*Actualité Juridique – Droit Administratif*
AJIL	*American Journal of International Law*
Am. U. Int'l L. Rev.	*American University International Law Review*
Am. U. J. Int'l L. & Pol'y	*American University Journal of International Law and Policy*
Anu. Der. Internac.	*Anuario de Derecho Internacional*
Arch. de Philos. du Droit	*Archives de Philosophie du Droit*
ASIL	American Society of International Law
Aus Pol. & Zeitgesch.	*Aus Politik und Zeitgeschichte*
Austr. Yb. Int'l L.	*Australian Yearbook of International Law*
Austrian J. Publ. Int'l Law	*Austrian Journal of Public International Law*
AVR	*Archiv des Völkerrechts*
Brook. J. Int'l L.	*Brooklyn Journal of International Law*
B. U. Int'l L. J.	*Boston University International Law Journal*
BVerfGE	Entscheidungen des Bundesverfassungsgerichtes (Decisions of the German Federal Constitutional Court)

BYIL	*British Yearbook of International Law*
Cal. L. Rev.	*California Law Review*
Cal. W. Int'l L. J.	*California Western International Law Journal*
Cal. W. L. Rev.	*California Western Law Review*
Case W. Res. J. Int'l L.	*Case Western Reserve Journal of International Law*
Chi. J. Int'l L.	*Chicago Journal of International Law*
CLJ	*Cambridge Law Journal*
CML Rev.	*Common Market Law Review*
Colo. J. Int'l Envtl. L. & Pol'y	*Colorado Journal of International Environmental Law and Policy*
Colum. Hum. Rts L. Rev.	*Columbia Human Rights Law Review*
Colum. J. Transnat'l L.	*Columbia Journal of Transnational Law*
Colum. L. Rev.	*Columbia Law Review*
Comunità Internaz.	*La Comunità Internazionale*
Conn. J. Int'l L.	*Connecticut Journal of International Law*
Cornell Int'l L. J.	*Cornell International Law Journal*
CTS	Consolidated Treaty Series
CYIL	*Canadian Yearbook of International Law*
Den. J. Int'l L. & Pol'y	*Denver Journal of International Law and Policy*
DGVR	Deutsche Gesellschaft für Völkerrecht (German Society of Public International Law)
Dick. J. Int'l L.	*Dickinson Journal of International Law*
Duke J. Comp. & Int'l L.	*Duke Journal of Comparative and International Law*
Duq. L. Rev.	*Duquesne Law Review*
EA	*Europa-Archiv*
ECOSOC	Economic and Social Council
ed.	editor

eds	editors
e.g.	*exempli gratia*
EJIL	*European Journal of International Law*
ELJ	*European Law Journal*
Env. Policy & Law	*Environmental Policy and Law*
Envtl L. Rep.	*Environmental Law Reports*
EPIL	*Encyclopedia of Public International Law*
et al.	et alii
et seq.	et sequentes
etc.	et cetera
EuGRZ	*Europäische Grundrechte-Zeitschrift*
EuZW	*Europäische Zeitschrift für Wirtschaftsrecht*
FAO	Food and Agriculture Organization
Fla. J. Int'l L.	*Florida Journal of International Law*
Fordham Int'l L. J.	*Fordham International Law Journal*
Fordham L. Rev.	*Fordham Law Review*
Foreign Aff.	*Foreign Affairs*
Foreign Pol'y	*Foreign Policy*
Ga. J. Int'l & Comp. L.	*Georgia Journal of International and Comparative Law*
Geo. Int'l Envtl. L. Rev.	*Georgetown International Environmental Law Review*
Geo. L. J.	*Georgetown Law Journal*
Geo. Wash. J. Int'l L. & Econ.	*George Washington Journal of International Law and Economics*
Geo. Wash. L. Rev.	*George Washington Law Review*
GYIL	*German Yearbook of International Law*
Harv. Int'l L. J.	*Harvard International Law Journal*
Harv. L. Rev.	*Harvard Law Review*
Hastings Int'l & Comp. L. Rev.	*Hastings International and Comparative Law Review*

HRLJ	*Human Rights Law Journal*
HRQ	*Human Rights Quarterly*
HuV-I	*Humanitäres Völkerrecht – Informationsschriften*
IAEA	International Atomic Energy Agency
ibid.	ibidem; in the same place
IBRD	International Bank for Reconstruction and Development
ICAO	International Civil Aviation Organization
ICJ	International Court of Justice
ICLQ	*International and Comparative Law Quarterly*
ICSID	International Centre for Settlement of Investment Disputes
id.	idem; the same
IDA	International Development Association
i.e.	id est; that is to say
IFAD	International Fund for Agricultural Development
ICC	International Criminal Court
IJIL	*Indian Journal of International Law*
ILA	International Law Association
ILC	International Law Commission
ILCYB	Yearbook of the International Law Commission
ILM	*International Legal Materials*
ILO	International Labour Organization
ILR	*International Law Reports*
ILSA J. Int'l L.	*ILSA Journal of International Law (International Law Students Association)*
IMF	International Monetary Fund
IMO	International Maritime Organization
Ind. Int'l & Comp. L. Rev.	*Indiana International and Comparative Law Review*

Ind. J. Global Legal Stud.	*Indiana Journal of Global Legal Studies*
Int'l Aff.	*International Affairs*
Int'l Law.	*The International Lawyer*
Int'l Rev. of the Red Cross	*International Review of the Red Cross*
Iowa L. Rev.	*Iowa Law Review*
IP	*Die internationale Politik*
Isr. L. R.	*Israel Law Review*
Isr. Y. B. Hum. Rts	*Israel Yearbook on Human Rights*
J. History Int'l L.	*Journal of the History of International Law*
J. Int'l Aff.	*Journal of International Affairs*
JA	*Juristische Arbeitsblätter*
JIEL	*Journal of International Economic Law*
JIR	*Jahrbuch für internationales Recht*
JPR	*Journal of Peace Research*
JuS	*Juristische Schulung*
JWT	*Journal of World Trade*
JWTL	*Journal of World Trade Law*
Law & Contemp. Probs	*Law and Contemporary Problems*
LJIL	*Leiden Journal of International Law*
LNTS	League of Nations Treaty Series
Loy. L. A. Int'l Comp. L. Rev.	*Loyola of Los Angeles International and Comparative Law Review*
McGill L. J.	*McGill Law Journal*
Miami U. Int'l & Comp. L. Rev.	*University of Miami International and Comparative Law Review*
Mich. J. Int'l L.	*Michigan Journal of International Law*
Mich. L. Rev.	*Michigan Law Review*
Mil. L. Rev.	*Military Law Review*
Minn. J. Global Trade	*Minnesota Journal of Global Trade*
N. Y. U. J. Int'l L. & Pol.	*New York University Journal of International Law and Politics*
N. Y. U. L. Rev.	*New York University Law Review*
NAFTA	North American Free Trade Agreement

NATO	North Atlantic Treaty Organization
NILR	*Netherlands International Law Review*
NJCL	*National Journal of Constitutional Law*
NJW	*Neue Juristische Wochenschrift*
Nord. J. Int'l L.	*Nordic Journal of International Law*
NQHR	*Netherlands Quarterly of Human Rights*
NuR	*Natur und Recht*
NYIL	*Netherlands Yearbook of International Law*
Ocean & Coastal L. J.	*Ocean and Coastal Law Journal*
ODILA	*Ocean Development and International Law*
OJEC	*Official Journal of the European Communities*
Pace Int'l Law Rev.	*Pace International Law Review*
PCIJ	Permanent Court of International Justice
Pol. Sci.	*Political Science*
RADIC	*Revue Africaine de Droit International et Comparé*
RBDI	*Revue Belge de Droit International*
RdC	*Recueil des Cours de l'Académie de Droit International*
RDI	*Revue de Droit International, de Sciences Diplomatiques et Politiques*
RECIEL	*Review of European Community and International Environmental Law*
REDI	*Revista Española de Derecho Internacional*
Rev. Dr. Mil. Dr. Guerre	*Revue de Droit Militaire et de Droit de la Guerre*
Rev. ICR	*Revue Internationale de la Croix Rouge*
RGDIP	*Revue Générale de Droit International Public*

RIAA	Reports of International Arbitral Awards
Riv. Dir. Int.	*Rivista di Diritto Internazionale*
RTDE	*Revue Trimestrielle de Droit Européen*
RUDH	*Revue Universelle des Droits de L'homme*
San Diego L. Rev.	*San Diego Law Review*
Santa Clara L. Rev.	*Santa Clara Law Review*
Stanford J. Int'l L.	*Stanford Journal of International Law*
Stanford L. Rev.	*Stanford Law Review*
SZIER/ RSDIE	*Schweizerische Zeitschrift für internationales und europäisches Recht/ Revue Suisse de Droit International et de Droit Européen*
Temp. Int'l & Comp. L. J.	*Temple International and Comparative Law Journal*
Tex. Int'l L. J.	*Texas International Law Journal*
Tex. L. Rev.	*Texas Law Review*
Transnat'l L. & Contemp. Probs	*Transnational Law and Contemporary Problems*
Tul. Envtl L. J.	*Tulane Environmental Law Journal*
Tul. J. Int'l & Comp. L.	*Tulane Journal of International and Comparative Law*
U. Chi. L. R.	*University of Chicago Law Review*
UCDL Rev.	*University of California Davis Law Review*
UCLA J. Envtl L. & Pol'y	*University of California Los Angeles Journal of Environmental Law and Policy*
UCLA J. Int'l L. & Foreign Aff.	*University of California Los Angeles Journal of International Law and Foreign Affairs*
UCLA Pac. Basin L. J.	*University of California Los Angeles Pacific Basin Law Journal*
UNCIO	United Nations Conference on International Organization

UNCITRAL	United Nations Commission on International Trade Law
UNCTAD	United Nations Conference on Trade and Development
UNDP	United Nations Development Programme
UNEP	United Nations Environment Programme
UNESCO	United Nations Educational, Scientific and Cultural Organization
UNFPA	United Nations Population Fund
UNHCR	United Nations High Commissioner for Refugees
UNICEF	United Nations Children's Fund
UNIDO	United Nations Industrial Development Organization
UNITAR	United Nations Institute for Training and Research
UNJYB	United Nations Juridical Yearbook
UNRWA	United Nations Relief and Works Agency for Palestine Refugees in the Near East
UNTS	United Nations Treaty Series
UNU	United Nations University
UNYB	Yearbook of the United Nations
UPU	Universal Postal Union
Va. J. Int'l L.	*Virginia Journal of International Law*
Va. L. Rev.	*Virginia Law Review*
Vand. J. Transnat'l L.	*Vanderbilt Journal of Transnational Law*
Vol.	Volume
VRÜ	*Verfassung und Recht in Übersee*
VVDStRL	*Veröffentlichungen der Vereinigung der Deutschen Staatsrechtslehrer*
Wash. L. Rev.	*Washington Law Review*
WFP	World Food Programme

WIPO	World Intellectual Property Organization
WMO	World Meteorological Organization
WTO	World Trade Organization
Yale L. J.	*Yale Law Journal*
Yale J. Int'l L.	*Yale Journal of International Law*
ZaöRV/ HJIL	*Zeitschrift für ausländisches öffentliches Recht und Völkerrecht/ Heidelberg Journal of International Law*
ZEuS	*Zeitschrift für europarechtliche Studien*
ZRP	*Zeitschrift für Rechtspolitik*
ZSchwR	*Zeitschrift für Schweizerisches Recht*

Statehood, Recognition and the United Nations System: A Unilateral Declaration of Independence in Kosovo

Alexander Orakhelashvili [*]

I. Introduction

The Unilateral Declaration of Independence (UDI) in Kosovo in February 2008 has raised several fundamental questions of international law in terms of the legal status of secessionist entities, but also of the legality of certain acts and conduct in the context which is being managed by the UN Security Council in the exercise of its Chapter VII powers to maintain and restore the international peace and security.

States that have sponsored and recognised the independence of Kosovo have neither declared that this matter is outside the realm of inter-

---

[*]   This article reflects developments as of 1 August 2008.

national law because of its political nature, nor do they have, as will be shown below, developed any consistent explanation of the international legal position that would envisage or tolerate the independent state of Kosovo. The question of whether Kosovo is a state is material for a number of issues arising in international practice, before international and national courts, in terms of the aspects of recognition of the acts and transactions of this entity. These issues will no doubt be raised in due course before courts and beyond, and it may be premature to examine them at this stage.

Instead, the present contribution will cover the basic issues that pervaded the process in which independence was declared in Kosovo and debated in various international fora, and a number of recognitions were granted to this entity. The arguments raised in this process are most material and current for this contribution, as well as determinative of more specific claims and incidences of statehood that may be raised in national and international organs over the coming years. The contribution will also engage with different views regarding the statehood claims and recognition of Kosovo, especially with the argument that the existence of Kosovo is now a fact and part of reality.

In accordance with the above, the following Part II. will examine the facts and history of the Kosovo situation; Part III. will cover then the statehood and secession requirements and their application under international law in the case of Kosovo; Part IV. will examine the argument that the independence of Kosovo is unique and cannot establish any precedent; Part V. shall examine the legality of recognition of the independence of Kosovo; and Part VI. will cover the compatibility of the UDI and the deployment of the EU Mission EULEX in Kosovo with the relevant UN Security Council resolutions; the future prospects of resolving the Kosovo situation will be dealt with in Part VII.; and finally Part VIII. will offer some conclusions, among others on policy issues.

II. Facts and History of the Kosovo Situation

Historically, Kosovo has been an autonomous province of Serbia within the Socialist Federal Republic of Yugoslavia (SFRY), until the abolition of its autonomous status in 1989. After the dissolution of the SFRY in 1991-1992, Kosovo continued as part of Serbia within the Federal Republic of Yugoslavia (FRY). In 2003, the FRY was transformed into the Federation of Serbia and Montenegro. After Montenegro declared its independence in 2006 on the basis of a referendum and with the consent of the central government, Serbia continued as the successor of the FRY.

Already from the 80s onwards, the separatist and pro-independence movement among the Albanian majority population in Kosovo has been receiving international attention. From 1998 on, the UN Security Council has been involved in dealing with this situation as a threat to international peace and security under Chapter VII of the United Nations Charter. S/RES/1160 (1998) of 31 March 1998 has been adopted condemning the activities of the Federal Forces of Yugoslavia against the Kosovo population, as well as the terrorist attacks by the "Kosovo Liberation Army." By S/RES/1203 (1998) of 24 October 1998 the Security Council oversaw the agreement between the OSCE and the FRY to desist from further human rights violations and permit the OSCE mission to monitor the humanitarian situation on the ground.

The treatment of Albanians in Kosovo by the FRY security forces has caused great human suffering with international implications, culminating with the 1999 attack and the air campaign by NATO against the FRY which ended with the withdrawal of Yugoslavian forces from Kosovo and the establishment of the UN Mission in Kosovo (UNMIK) by S/RES/1244 (1999) of 10 June 1999, to administer the territory, and the Kosovo Force (KFOR) to provide for order and security. By the end of the NATO intervention, the number and extent of human casualties and suffering among the Kosovo Albanians has been much higher than before the NATO intervention.

In 2007 the issue of the final status of Kosovo has been brought before the UN Security Council, on the basis of the plan submitted by the UN Rapporteur Martti Ahtisaari.[1] The plan envisaged the internationally supervised independence of Kosovo. This was rejected by Serbia, and accepted by the authorities in Kosovo. The presentation of the Ahtisaari Plan generated a heavy debate on the status of Kosovo, both in its legal and political aspects. As it would have been expected, the idea of the independence of Kosovo was endorsed by the United States and a number of EU Member States, and opposed by Russia, China, India,[2] but also by several EU Member States. A motivation behind this

---

[1]   Letter dated 26 March 2007 from the Secretary-General addressed to the President of the Security Council, Doc. S/2007/168.

[2]   P. Reynolds, "Kosovo: To Recognise or Not To Recognise", BBC Information, 18 February 2008, available at: <www.news.bbc.co.uk> (this and all other press and website information on file with the author); see also the

objection was the need for further negotiations between Belgrade and Pristina to find a mutually acceptable agreed solution of the Kosovo status.[3] At the end of the day, the Security Council refused to endorse the supervised independence for Kosovo based on the Ahtisaari plan, which was supported in the Council only by a substantial minority. The negotiations were continued within the framework of the United States, EU, Russia Troika, but during a number of meetings the Serbian and Kosovo Albanian sides failed to reach agreement, the former objecting to independence and the latter insisting on internationally supervised independence as envisaged in the Ahtisaari Plan.[4] Against this background, the authorities in Kosovo declared the independence of the province from Serbia, and appealed to the international community for recognition on 17 February 2008.

Serbia considered this UDI illegal and stated the intention to achieve having it overturned.[5] Recognitions followed mostly from Western states, and the opposition was voiced from the rest of the world. Currently the states having recognised Kosovo as an independent state consider the process of the determination of the status of Kosovo as a finalised affair, while Serbia and a number of other states support the idea of further negotiations to achieve the agreed settlement between the Kosovo authorities and the government of Serbia.

In the post UDI period, as well as before that, the Serbian government has come under pressure from the EU and elsewhere to accept the independence of Kosovo, possibly in exchange for the accelerated pro-

---

information "Russia, India, China Step up Solidarity", The Hindu, 16 May 2008 available at: <www.hindu.com>, India for the first time joined Russia and China in stating categorically in the RIC (Russia, India, China) communiqué that "the unilateral declaration of independence of Kosovo is contrary to the U.N. Security Council Resolution 1244," and calling for settling the issue "in accordance with norms of international law" and on the basis of "an agreement" and "through negotiations" between Belgrade and Pristina. The text of the RIC joint communiqué of 15 May 2008 is available on the website of the Indian Ministry of External Affairs, available at: <www.meaindia.nic.in>.

3   See e.g. Statement by the Russian Representative Mr. Churkin to the United Nations 14 December 2007.

4   Troika Press Communiqué: the Baden Conference, Baden, Austria, 28 November 2007; Troika Press Statement: the Brussels Conference, Brussels, 20 November 2007.

5   "Kosovo Tool Kit for Separatists", BBC Information, 20 February 2008, available at: <news.bbc.co.uk>.

cess of the integration into the EU.[6] As can be seen from the statement of the Prime-Minister of Serbia the EU,

> "urged the signing of a stabilisation and association agreement between the European Union and Serbia and that Serbia's commitment was to establish good neighbourly relations with Kosovo."

The response of the Prime-Minister was that,

> "Since the EU commissioner conveyed the EU stand openly, we will have to say in an equally open way that we most decisively reject [EU Commissioner] Rehn's request that Serbia establish good neighbourly relations with itself, i.e. part of its territory."[7]

According to the statement of the Serbian Foreign Minister,

> "The signing of this agreement does not imply in any way whatsoever Serbia's position on Kosovo and Metohija, and we will never accept the unilaterally proclaimed independence of the southern Serbian province."[8]

In April 2008, the Serb population of Kosovo was entered into the list of voters in the Serbian municipal and parliamentary elections of May 2008. Elections in Serbia, including the Serb-populated regions of Kosovo, were held on 11 May, organised by the Serbian Electoral Commission.[9] These regions, mostly in the northern part of Kosovo, are not under the effective control of the authorities in Pristina.

III. Legal Merits of Kosovo's Declaration of Independence: The Aspects of Statehood and Secession

It is clear that the UDI in Kosovo has been based on the claim that Kosovo has seceded from Serbia. The validity of this claim depends on the way international law regulates secession. Whether the UN Security Council could approve the independence of Kosovo will not be exam-

---

[6]   "EU Offers Serbia Deal on Kosovo", BBC Information, 14 December 2007, available at: <news.bbc.co.uk>.

[7]   Information of the Serbian Foreign Ministry, 25 April 2008, available at: <www.mfa.gov.yu/Pressframe14.htm>.

[8]   Information of the Serbian Foreign Ministry, 24 April 2008, available at: <www.mfa.gov.yu/Pressframe1.htm>.

[9]   Information available from <www.balkaninsight.com>; <www.msnbc.com>; <news.bbc.co.uk> of 11 May 2008.

ined in detail because of the abstract character of this question.[10] But the practice of states in relation to the attempts of secession deserves more attention.

The international legal system has witnessed several attempts of secession, successful or unsuccessful. Bangladesh (formerly West Pakistan) has seceded from Pakistan after the latter's massive human rights abuses, sometimes even characterised as genocide, the military intervention by India, widespread recognition by third states and the eventual admission to the United Nations in 1974.[11] Biafra seceded from Nigeria in the 1960s and gained few recognitions. As a consequence of civil war, it was reintegrated into Nigeria in 1970.[12]

It is doubtful whether secession played any major and original role in the settlement in the Balkans in the 1990s, after the disintegration of the SFRY. The Badinter Commission emphasised in its Opinions 1 and 8 that the recognition of the successor states of the SFRY occurred in the context of the latter's disintegration as opposed to the right of secession of individual Yugoslav republics.[13] At the example of Croatia it has been emphasised that the attempt to secede from the SFRY was undertaken after the Croatian representation was blocked in the highest federal organs of the government of the SFRY. In particular, the represen-

---

10   But for an accurate analysis see K. Wirth, "Kosovo am Vorabend der Statusentscheidung: Überlegungen zur rechtlichen Begründung und Durchsetzung der Unabhängigkeit", ZaöRV 67 (2007), 1065 et seq.; on the limits of the powers of the Security Council see A. Orakhelashvili, "The Acts of the Security Council: Meaning and Standards of Review", Max Planck UNYB 11 (2007), 143 et seq.; id., "The Impact of Peremptory Norms on Interpretation and Application of UN Security Council Resolutions", EJIL 16 (2005), 59 et seq.; id., Peremptory Norms in International Law, 2006, Chapters 12-14.

11   J. Crawford, The Creation of States in International Law, 2006, 142 et seq.; J. Dugard/ D. Raic, "The Role of Recognition in the Law and Practice of Secession", in: M. Cohen (ed.), Secession: International Law Perspectives, 2006, 94 et seq. (122 et seq.); T. Musgrave, Self-Determination and National Minorities, 1997, 189 et seq.

12   For the developments and claims of and around Biafra see Musgrave, see note 11, 196 et seq.

13   In Opinion No. 1 of 29 November 1991, the Commission emphasised that "the Socialist Federal Republic of Yugoslavia is in the process of dissolution." In Opinion No. 8 of 4 July 1992, para. 4, the Commission observed that "the process of dissolution of the SFRY referred to in Opinion No. 1 of 29 November 1991 is now complete and that the SFRY no longer exists."

tatives of other republics declared they would take decisions without the Croatian participation.[14] These events, if giving rise to secession, would be explainable in terms of denying Croatia the representation in the federal government and possibly activating the exception to the territorial integrity safeguard clause under the 1970 Friendly Relations Declaration.[15] In any case, the Arbitration Commission on Former Yugoslavia strictly followed the Friendly Relations Declaration and affirmed the inviolability of all former Yugoslav republics in accordance with the principle of *uti possidetis juris*.[16]

---

[14] Dugard/ Raic, see note 11, 125 et seq.

[15] See below note 35 and the accompanying text.

[16] In its Opinion No. 3 of 20 November 1991, "The Committee therefore [took] the view that once the process in the SFRY leads to the creation of one or more independent states, the issue of frontiers, in particular those of the Republics referred to in the question before it, must be resolved in accordance with the following principles:

First – All external frontiers must be respected in line with the principles stated in the United Nations Charter, in the Declaration on Principles of International Law concerning Friendly Relations and Cooperation among States in accordance with the Charter of the United Nations (General Assembly Resolution 2625 (XXV)) and in the Helsinki Final Act, a principle which also underlies Article 11 of the Vienna Convention of 23 August 1978 on the Succession of States in Respect of Treaties.

Second – The boundaries between Croatia and Serbia, between Bosnia-Herzegovina and Serbia, and possibly other adjacent independent states may not be altered except by agreement freely arrived at.

Third – Except where otherwise agreed, the former boundaries become frontiers protected by international law. This conclusion follows from the principle of respect for the territorial *status quo* and, in particular, from the principle of *uti possidetis*. *Uti possidetis*, though initially applied in settling decolonisation issues in America and Africa, is today recognized as a general principle, as stated by the International Court of Justice in its Judgment of 22 December 1986 in the case between Burkina Faso and Mali (*Frontier Dispute*, (1986) Law Reports 554 at 565): 'Nevertheless the principle is not a special rule which pertains solely to one specific system of international law. It is a general principle, which is logically connected with the phenomenon of the obtaining of independence, wherever it occurs. Its obvious purpose is to prevent the independence and stability of new states being endangered by fratricidal struggles ... '

The principle applies all the more readily to the Republic since the second and fourth paragraphs of Article 5 of the Constitution of the SFRY stipulated that the Republics' territories and boundaries could not be altered without their consent.

In accordance with the process of the independence of successor states after the disintegration of the SFRY as opposed to secession of individual republics, none of the former Yugoslav republics were admitted to the United Nations until the FRY (Serbia-Montenegro) adopted in 1992 its new constitution whereby it reconstituted itself implying the renunciation of all territorial rights over those republics, and its preparedness to recognise them.[17] Neither the United Nations nor the EC have proclaimed their support for the independence on the basis of secession of the entity without the consent of the parent state.[18]

Thus far Bangladesh has been the only entity that has seceded without the consent of the parent state and its acceptance to the United Nations has been the key to its statehood, which factor has never been present in the case of other secessionist entities that attempted seceding without the consent of their parent states. Furthermore, as Crawford emphasises, even after 1989 when twenty-one new states have emerged, the principle that no territory can secede from the state without its consent has retained its continued validity.[19] Thus, the principle of territorial integrity has survived the post-1989 parade of declarations of independence, and international law does not authorise the unilateral secession of the territory from the state.

Against this background, the legality of Kosovo's independence should be measured not only by reference to the factual effectiveness of its existence but also to the legal criteria of statehood. Factual criteria of statehood embodied in the Montevideo Convention – territory, population, government and capacity to enter into relations with other states – are generally accepted as part of international legal reasoning.[20]

Fourth – According to a well-established principle of international law the alteration of existing frontiers or boundaries by force is not capable of producing any legal effect. This principle is to be found, for instance, in the Declaration on Principles of International Law concerning Friendly Relations and Cooperation among States in accordance with the Charter of the United Nations (General Assembly Resolution 2625 (XXV)) and in the Helsinki Final Act; it was cited by the Hague Conference on 7 September 1991 and is enshrined in the draft Convention of 4 November 1991 drawn up by the Conference on Yugoslavia."

[17]   Crawford, see note 11, 399 et seq.
[18]   Crawford, see note 11, 416; for a similar approach on the former Soviet republics see T. Franck, *Fairness in International Law and Institutions*, 1995, 157 et seq.
[19]   Crawford, see note 11, 415.
[20]   For the analysis of these criteria see Crawford, see note 11, 37 et seq.

As part of the factual criteria of statehood, *effectivité* refers to the effective exercise of state authority over the relevant territory. Under this argument, to constitute a case of effective statehood, Kosovo is supposed to have the government that effectively controls its territory and exercises effective authority over it.

The study of factual effectiveness has occupied a significant place in the doctrine of international law. But it has never been the only or even the dominant way of explaining the international legal process. It will suffice to recall that the reaction of Sir Hersch Lauterpacht to the monograph of Charles de Visscher on *Theory and Reality of Public International Law* was to denote it as a subversive work.[21] The normative force of the factual (*die normative Kraft des Faktischen*) is an oxymoron as far as international law is concerned. There is hardly any area of international law where fact as such produces legal regulation or status. The substance of the principle of effectiveness is difficult to measure. The jurisprudence of the ICJ has examined the concept of factual effectiveness on multiple occasions, mostly in terms of territorial disputes, and not on a single occasion has it held that the mere factual situation influenced, by itself and without further legal requirements, the rights and duties of the relevant actors. Factual effectiveness never creates legal positions on its own, but only if coupled with agreement and consent between states. At the same time, the doctrinal works based on the premise of factual effectiveness do not accurately explain how the factual element works in the process of allocation of rights and duties in international law.[22]

The opinion is expressed in doctrine that "the crucial yardstick to appraise the statehood of an entity is (the internal as well as international) *effectivité* of its governmental apparatus."[23] It is suggested that the presumption should be adopted against the effectiveness of the secession and in favour of the territorial integrity of the parent state.[24] It is also claimed that effectiveness can be the sole basis for secession in

---

21   R.Y. Jennings, "Hersch Lauterpacht, A Personal Recollection", *EJIL* 8 (1997), 301 et seq.

22   See for detail A. Orakhelashvili, *The Interpretation of Acts and Rules in Public International Law*, 2008, Chapter 5.

23   J. D'Aspermont, "Regulating Statehood: The Kosovo Status Settlement", *LJIL* 20 (2007), 649 et seq. (654 et seq.).

24   T. Christakis, "L'état en tant que 'fait primaire': réflexions sur la portée du principe d'effectivité", in: M. Cohen (ed.), *Secession: International Law Perspectives*, 2006, 138 et seq. (149).

the inter-state legal order.[25] This far-reaching statement effectively denies the role of law in assessing the claim of the relevant entity to statehood and reduces the whole problem to that of factual effectiveness. This approach cannot be seen as reflecting the international legal position. In fact the Turkish Republic of Northern Cyprus (TRNC) arguably possesses *effectivité*; Taiwan does too; so did Manchukuo, Biafra and North Vietnam; but none of those were states under international law, because they did not meet the legal criteria of statehood. To hold that Kosovo's independence is lawful because of the effectiveness of its factual existence is to misunderstand the criteria of the creation of states in international law.

The argument of according crucial importance to *effectivité* in the case of Kosovo suffers from a more important conceptual failure deriving from the fact that the independence of Kosovo is envisaged as a controlled and supervised independence and much of the burden of which is intended to be shouldered by the EU. There has never been an objectively verifiable indication if and how long Kosovo could survive on its own and without the EU/NATO supervision as an independent state. In other words, *effectivité* has never been tried or verified. In the case of Kosovo, *effectivité* belongs to the field of abstract speculation as opposed to the factual reality.

In addition, it is unclear whether effectiveness is required only at the particular time or forever. What is effective now could be destabilised into collapse, or even militarily overtaken, in a year or two. As effectiveness is inherently immeasurable, the theory and practice has not worked out its precise parameters. There is no judicial pronouncement on its role in the matter of statehood. This uncertainty is further in line with the fact that if there is a legal basis for statehood, for instance the principle of self-determination, the lack of effectiveness cannot impede the creation of the state, as was the case with the Democratic Republic of the Congo in the 1960s.

If we apply this to the problem of statehood in general and to Kosovo, this entity would hardly qualify as a state under the criteria of effectiveness, which is profoundly missing in the case of Kosovo. What the notion of factual effectiveness could at most suggest at the example of Kosovo is that, having met the factual requirements of statehood, it could potentially be a state if it were to fulfil the legal requirements of

---

25 Christakis, see above, 153, also acknowledging that effectiveness contradicts the principle of *uti possidetis*.

statehood. The presence of legal factors of statehood would then transform the non-state into a state.

In practice there has never been an instance where the statehood of an entity has been accepted by the international community on the basis of mere factual independence. The approach that ultimate success of secession can justify the statehood of the relevant seceding entity is contradictory. Sir Hersch Lauterpacht considered the factual success insufficient, and saw instead as a requirement that the parent state must in fact have ceased to make efforts, promising success, to reassert its authority.[26] In other words, unless the parent state stops objecting, the factor of effectiveness can produce no independent effect. Although it has since long been argued that the emergence of states is a factual process and stands outside the law, currently there is wide doctrinal recognition that statehood is not merely a factual phenomenon but also governed by legal criteria.[27] In other words, statehood is a legal question as much as it is a factual one. Taking this as the starting-point, the ascertainment of the legal requirements that apply to the potential creation of the particular state depends on the legal context in which the statehood is claimed. In some cases the matter can be resolved consensually; in other cases, the matter may involve the issues of overriding public policy.

The legal requirements applicable to the emergence of the particular state can vary from those belonging to ordinary international law to those deriving from peremptory norms (*jus cogens*). The particular legal requirements will also vary in terms of how the relevant entity is claiming statehood: through consensual separation, dissolution of the parent state, or unilateral secession; by peaceful means or violently; with the popular assent or without it; in the colonial context or outside it. The legal criteria applicable to the statehood in terms of entities like Kosovo relate to the entity that claims statehood outside the colonial context and without the consent of the parent state. This context confirms that Kosovo is not an entity entitled to self-determination.[28]

There are various doctrinal attempts to explain the process of secession in legal terms. The so-called "internal theory" envisages secession as an act solely of domestic concern and not governed by international law.

---

[26] H. Lauterpacht, *Recognition in International Law*, 1948, 8.

[27] Cf. Crawford, see note 11, 96 et seq.

[28] See further below the position under the relevant UN General Assembly resolutions.

Hence, under this view, secession is neither legal nor illegal under international law. Musgrave argues that secession can be permitted by virtue of this "internal theory", and adds that secession is simply a political act, although the emergence of the new state through it will necessarily produce consequences in the international legal system. But secession remains a domestic matter and a legally neutral act under international law.[29]

There is a doctrinal argument that secession is not governed by international law, as articulated by Theodore Christakis by reference to Prosper Weil.[30] According to Franck, secession is neither endorsed nor prohibited in international law. Franck states in one place that international law does not recognise a general right to secession and in another place that it does not prohibit secession. Although Franck creates the impression to avoid the across-the-board acceptance of the right to secession, he still admits the possibility of the entity seceding without the consent of the parent state.[31]

In general, international law recognises that certain activities and prerogatives are primarily matters of domestic law and jurisdiction. In the *Nottebohm* case the ICJ considered that the conferral of nationality to individuals was a matter of domestic jurisdiction. In the *Anglo-Norwegian Fisheries* case the Court held the same about the delimitation of territorial waters.[32] However, in both cases the Court was dealing with the originally "domestic" activities that could affect the jurisdiction and competence of other states. Hence, in both cases the Court pronounced that the legality of these originally "domestic" activities is measured by reference to international law. This is conceptually correct, because only those actions and processes can be domestic which do not affect the international legal relations of the state. Secession of the territory from the parent state necessarily affects not only the territorial sovereignty of the parent state, but also its legal relations to third states, and thus it cannot be a domestic act not governed by international law.

The same considerations apply to the "internal theory" of secession which essentially repeats the thesis which views effectiveness primarily or exclusively as a matter of fact or as a political matter not governed by international law. In conceptual terms, it is all the same if one portrays

---

[29]   Musgrave, see note 11, 192 et seq., 209 et seq.

[30]   Christakis, see note 24, 155 et seq.

[31]   Franck, see note 18, 159 et seq.

[32]   Fisheries case (UK v Norway), ICJ Reports 1951, 116 et seq. (132); Nottebohm case, ICJ Reports 1955, 4 et seq. (22).

secession as excluded from the ambit of international law either on the basis of factual analysis, political argument or domestic jurisdiction. After all, these factors are closely intertwined in practice. At the same time, such theoretical or conceptual qualifications of secession cannot prevent it from producing consequences or having its legality assessed within the international legal system. If, thus, the legality and validity of secession can be assessed internationally, all the theoretical aspects lose their coherence and are conceptually undermined. The real answer on the legality of the particular instance of secession can be obtained not through examining various theories but on the basis of the assessment of the international legal position accepted by the international community.

The thesis that secession is not governed by international law contradicts the thesis of the effectiveness of legal regulations as articulated in the major work of Sir Hersch Lauterpacht. According to this thesis, if the relevant matter occurs within the international legal system, there is always international law that governs it. Even if there were no specific rules related to that matter particularly, the more general legal regulation on the subject would apply to it in an effective manner.[33] If the reasoning of Sir Hersch Lauterpacht is followed, no issue within the ambit of international law is outside the international legal regulation, and there are no gaps in legal regulation. In more specific terms, the regulation of secession by international law is inherently implied in the thesis that the creation of states is not only a matter of fact, but also one of law. As secession is a method of the creation of states, it is definitionally governed by international law. The argument of Franck that secession is not regulated, that it is neither authorised nor prohibited by international law is inaccurate because the legality of secession cannot be judged on whether there is a specific rule of authorising or outlawing it. As soon as the principle of territorial integrity applies, it necessarily outlaws secession without the consent of the parent state. Such understanding avoids systemic inconsistency under which international law would guarantee territorial integrity yet would not prohibit secession.

Another basis articulated sometimes in doctrine in favour of the legality of secession is that of the oppression (or remedial) theory. The problem with the oppression theory is that it is not clearly defined what constitutes oppression.[34] The oppression theory of secession has no le-

---

[33] H. Lauterpacht, *The Function of Law in the International Community*, 1933, 77.

[34] Musgrave, see note 11, 191 et seq.

gal value on its own. It can be relevant only to the extent of reflecting the legal position among others as enshrined in A/RES/2625 (XXV) of 24 October 1970, the so called Friendly Relations Declaration and the 1993 Vienna Declaration and Programme of Action, as adopted by the World Conference on Human Rights. A so-called "remedial secession" can only be envisaged on the conditions specified under the 1970 Friendly Relations Declaration, which qualifies the territorial integrity of states only in the case where that state does not possess the government equally representing its entire population. The Friendly Relations Declaration does not condition the territorial integrity of the state by any other factor. The Declaration specifies that nothing in it can be interpreted,

> "as authorizing or encouraging any action which would dismember or impair, totally or in part, the territorial integrity or political unity of sovereign and independent States conducting themselves in compliance with the principle of equal rights and self-determination of peoples as described above and thus possessed of a government representing the whole people belonging to the territory without distinction as to race, creed or colour."

The 1993 Vienna Declaration, although reaffirming the right of peoples to self-determination, emphasises that,

> "In accordance with the Declaration on Principles of International Law concerning Friendly Relations and Cooperation Among States in accordance with the Charter of the United Nations, this shall not be construed as authorizing or encouraging any action which would dismember or impair, totally or in part, the territorial integrity or political unity of sovereign and independent States conducting themselves in compliance with the principle of equal rights and self-determination of peoples and thus possessed of a Government representing the whole people belonging to the territory without distinction of any kind."[35]

Although these declarations are not binding as such, A/RES/2625 certainly embodies customary international law.[36] In addition, and independently of the customary law status, it can be safely assumed that if the entire international community proclaims a certain attitude in non-binding declarations – in this case the attitude against secession – this

---

[35] Vienna Declaration and Programme of Action, 12 July 1993, Doc. A/CONF.157/23, para. 2.

[36] See Military and Paramilitary Activities in and against Nicaragua, ICJ Reports 1986, 14 et seq. (100-101).

mere fact, although by itself insufficient for proving the normative status of the relevant approach, it is perfectly sufficient for it to be understood that international law could hardly contain the legal regulation contradicting that attitude. The attitude expressed in a General Assembly resolution having commanded the support of the vast majority of states must be seen as embodying the fundamental policies of the international community, with the consequent presumption that, short of direct evidence to the contrary, international law contains no contrary legal regulation. In other words, even if one rejects the normative force of initially non-binding resolutions, unless one definitively proves that international law positively accepts the right of the entities like Kosovo to secede, the presumption should be that it accepts no such right.

Against this background, it is correctly emphasised that unilateral secession is the antithesis of territorial integrity. Ethnic self-determination represents a threat to the continued existence of states and has thus been repudiated by the international community.[37] If territorial integrity of states means anything, secession can only be allowed with the consent of the parent state.

The United States government referred to some "special circumstances" of Kosovo, of "unprecedented" character that warrant treating Kosovo as a "special case",

> "(1) The state of Yugoslavia collapsed in a non-consensual, exceptionally violent way, creating threats to international peace and security that have obliged the UNSC to act repeatedly.
>
> (2) Between 1993 and 1999, the U.N. Security Council (UNSC) issued seven resolutions addressing Kosovo.
>
> (3) Amid massive human-right violations, the Milosevic government repeatedly disregarded UNSC resolutions demanding a halt to hostilities.
>
> (4) The Milosevic regime's actions in Kosovo and throughout the region undermined international stability and led to cross-border refugee upheavals.
>
> (5) In 1999, NATO's 19 allies reached the consensus decision to take collective action to remove Milosevic's police and military forces from Kosovo.
>
> (6) Kosovo is administered by the United Nations under U.N. Security Council Resolution (UNSCR) 1244, unanimously adopted

---

[37] Musgrave, see note 11, 181 et seq.

(with China abstaining) June 10, 1999, to address Milosevic's actions. Elements of UNSCR 1244 include: denying Serbia a role in governing Kosovo; setting up an interim UN administration; providing for local self-government; and envisioning a UN-led political process to determine Kosovo's future status."[38]

Given that the legal arguments in favour of the uniqueness of statehood have been advanced, among others by the US Department of State, the merit of these assertions shall be examined. Even as all six circumstances and factors referred to by the Department of State are factually correct, none of these involve, or were at the pertinent times viewed as dealing with or prejudicing, the territorial status of Kosovo. More specifically:

The collapse of the SFRY into five successor republics, of which the FRY was one, produced the situation in which the boundaries of all these republics were considered as fixed and unaffected, as governed by the principle *uti possidetis juris*. The Arbitration Commission on the Former Yugoslavia has expressly affirmed the inviolability of the borders of all five republics including the FRY.

None of the Security Council resolutions between 1993 and 1999 have raised the matter of the independence of Kosovo, or prejudiced the territorial integrity of Yugoslavia and Serbia.

There is no rule or principle of international law requiring or permitting the secession of a region or entity whose population has been subjected to serious human rights violations. The same is the case even if those serious and massive human rights violations lead to cross-border refugee upheavals.

The use of force against the FRY by NATO has never been proclaimed as aimed at disrupting the territorial integrity of the FRY, or at achieving any permanent territorial settlement. It will be recalled that in the process of adoption of S/RES/1244 and preceding deliberations, the requirement that the population of Kosovo would decide the status of Kosovo in three years on the referendum basis did not get through and was dropped.

Projecting S/RES/1244 as supportive of the independence of Kosovo is inaccurate and counterfactual. This resolution also denies the Serbian presence in Kosovo as a temporary matter, and commits both the states and the United Nations to the territorial integrity of the FRY;

---

[38] US Department of State, "Why Kosovo Is Different", available at: <www.state.gov>.

moreover, this Resolution envisages the FRY and *a fortiori* Serbian troops guarding the external border of the province of Kosovo.

All this certifies that the proponents of the independence of Kosovo have never, at any stage of the process, offered any consistent and well-substantiated position as to why Kosovo is entitled to independence. The problem with the arguments of the Department of State is that they are inspired by common sense rather than being aimed at locating the evidence that would justify them under international law.

It has to be considered how the international community has viewed its claim to statehood since the 1999 NATO intervention and the adoption of S/RES/1244 in which the territorial integrity of the FRY was re-affirmed. After the dissolution of the SFRY and later of the FRY, the entitlement of Kosovo to become an independent state has not been affirmed. In the period between the 1999 NATO attack on the FRY and the Ahtisaari Plan, nothing in the practice of states or the United Nations has ever divulged any attitude aimed at disrupting the territorial integrity of the FRY and subsequently Serbia. The view of UNMIK has likewise been that the territorial integrity of the FRY and Serbia should be preserved.[39] Later on, by S/RES/1785 (2007) of 21 November 2007 the Council "reaffirmed its commitment to the political settlement of the conflicts in the former Yugoslavia, preserving the sovereignty and territorial integrity of all States there within their internationally recognized borders." Even in the Ahtisaari Plan, which as we shall see below the United States and other proponents of the Kosovo independence, including the parliament in Pristina,[40] refer to as the basis thereof, recommended the independence of Kosovo through the revision of S/RES/1244. Thus there has been, until the UDI in Kosovo, no normative development, not even an institutional proposal that would envisage the independence of Kosovo without revising Resolution 1244. In doctrinal terms, it has been emphasised that Kosovo's independence and

---

[39]   The UNMIK-FRY common document, adopted in Belgrade on 5 November 2001 "Promotes the protection of the rights and interests of Kosovo Serbs and other communities in Kosovo, based on the principles stated in UNSCR 1244, including the sovereignty and the territorial integrity of the Federal Republic of Yugoslavia, as well as in the Constitutional Framework for Provisional Self-government." Furthermore, the document "Reaffirms that the position on Kosovo's future status remains as stated in UNSCR 1244, and that this cannot be changed by any action taken by the Provisional Institutions of Self-government."

[40]   See the text of the UDI of Kosovo under <news.bbc.co.uk>, 19 February 2008.

secession has not been considered lawful or permissible after the SFRY's dissolution. Kosovo has been denoted as an unsuccessful attempt of secession.[41]

After the Ahtisaari Plan was submitted to the Security Council, both before and in the aftermath of the proclamation of independence, the views of states got divided. The United States have considered that the Ahtisaari Plan should serve as the basis for the independence of Kosovo.[42] According to the Russian statement, the proclamation of independence in Kosovo violated,

> "the sovereignty of the Republic of Serbia, the Charter of the United Nations, UNSCR 1244, the principles of the Helsinki Final Act, Kosovo's Constitutional Framework and the high-level Contact Group accords. Russia fully supports the reaction of the Serbian leadership to the events in Kosovo and its just demands to restore the territorial integrity of the country."

It was expected that the,

> "UN Mission in Kosovo and NATO-led Kosovo Force will take immediate action to fulfil their mandates as authorized by the Security Council, including voiding the decisions of Pristina's self-governing institutions and adopting severe administrative measures against them."[43]

The fact that the Security Council did not take action for annulling the independence of Kosovo does not imply the approval of the independence of Kosovo. In the *Namibia* Advisory Opinion, the ICJ clearly emphasised that,

> "The fact that a particular proposal is not adopted by an international organ does not necessarily carry with it the inference that a collective pronouncement is made in a sense opposite to that proposed."[44]

---

41 Crawford, see note 11, 400, 407 et seq.

42 Department of State document, "Kosovo's Final Status: A Key to Stability and Prosperity in the Balkans", available at: <www.state.gov> of 23 January 2008.

43 Statement by Russia's Ministry of Foreign Affairs on Kosovo, 17 February 2008, available at: <www.mid.ru> (in English).

44 Legal Consequences for States of the Continued Presence of South Africa in Namibia (South West Africa) notwithstanding Security Council Resolution 276 (1970), ICJ Reports 1971, 16 et seq. (36, para. 69).

There is also a tendency to judge the legality of secession by reference to the arguments of expediency. For instance, it is contended that the international community accepts the legality of secession where there is no viable alternative to it, as was the case with Kosovo.[45] However, the criteria of expediency and reasonability are inherently subjective and can never command the legitimacy that would be acceptable for all parties involved. International law could only approve secession if the legal criteria thereof are met, and not just because in the opinion of one side in the matter there are no more reasonable alternatives.

In addition, the existence of alternatives can be a matter of appreciation and discussion. Both Serbia and some other states have clearly stated before the UDI that the potential for negotiations was not exhausted and there was still substantial room for finding the agreed solution of the status of Kosovo. The reason why this has not happened before the UDI has nothing to do with the objective situation on the ground or with any objective difficulty with finding the agreed solution, but relates only to the intransigent position of the Kosovo Albanian leadership and the Western governments that supported their aspiration for independence. A number of statements made, both by the Kosovo Albanian leaders and Western political leaders, have from the earlier stages onwards adopted the firm stance as to the inevitability of the independence of Kosovo.[46] There can thus be no surprise that the Kosovo Albanian leadership could not have been encouraged to enter into real negotiations with Serbia to find the agreed and mutually acceptable solution. The prospective projection of the outcome of negotiations has undermined the reality of negotiations. It is consequently unsound to assume that there were no alternatives to the UDI; it is more correct to emphasise that these alternatives were willingly excluded by one side of negotiations through the projection of the desired result.

Given that the statehood of Kosovo cannot be seen as established on the basis of any applicable international law criteria, its status and standing should be judged by standards that apply to *de facto* regimes. A *de facto* regime can be defined as a state-like organism that satisfies the criteria of factual effectiveness of statehood but does not meet the

---

[45] C. Borgen, "Kosovo's Declaration of Independence: Self-Determination, Secession and Recognition", *ASIL Insight*, 29 February 2008, available at: <www.asil.org>.

[46] E.g. the statement by the President of France Nicolas Sarkozy, 14 December 2007, available at: <www.nytimes.com>.

legal requirements thereof. The study of *de facto* regimes in international law has not been as intensive as the frequency of this phenomenon in the international legal system entitles it, and certainly not much has been said on the subject since Frowein's ground-breaking study of this subject. Frowein defined a *de facto* regime as an entity which attempts separating from the parent state and even succeeds in this on a factual plane, but is not generally recognised. The key to the legal analysis of the *de facto* regime is the focus on the relations between that regime and the states which do not recognise it as a state.[47]

Given that the Serbian population in Kosovo is against the independence of the province, the possibility of secession of Serb-populated parts of Kosovo from this entity has been raised. The question whether Serb-populated areas of Kosovo can secede from it is a legally moot question. The assumption that a territory can secede from Kosovo is premised on the assumption that Kosovo is an independent state under international law. Although recently the idea of partition of Kosovo has been advanced in some political circles, this is an idea incompatible with the international legal position on the matter. What matters in reality is the question whether the Serb-populated areas of Kosovo can continue under the administration of Serbia, which has to be answered in the affirmative. This implies no partition of Kosovo, unless Serbia's agreement to this effect is obtained, but only means that in certain areas of Kosovo Serbia may be able to exercise its governmental functions as a matter of fact, as confirmed, for instance, by holding Serbian elections in those areas.

IV. Precedential Force of the UDI in Kosovo

Given that the legal basis for the independence of Kosovo cannot be established under international law, the issue of whether it can create a precedent for other secessionist entities is hypothetical. However, due to frequent political statements to the effect of the *sui generis* character of Kosovo, it is worth examining whether, if Kosovo were validly entitled to statehood, its situation could be unique and without precedential impact for other comparable situations.

While depending for its validity on the legality of the independence of Kosovo in the first place, the argument of the uniqueness of the Kosovo situation suffers from a conceptual problem, in that it contra-

---

[47]   J.A. Frowein, *Das de facto-Regime im Völkerrecht*, 1968, 6-7.

dicts the idea of equal application of law, and a practical problem, in that it is not shared far beyond the circles of the proponents of the independence of Kosovo.

If international law upholds the special nature of the Kosovo case, then it still recognises a right to secession, albeit in these special circumstances. In the first place, one has to prove with evidence that such right exists, which as seen above is impossible. But even if it were possible to prove such right, proving its specialty would be a further challenge in the sense of demonstrating why the relevant international legal right accrues to one entity but not another one. As Franck suggests, if international law involves the right to secession, it is doubtful if that right can be fairly limited to one part of the world.[48]

The proponents of the independence of Kosovo have never referred to any previous settlement of the independence of a state to justify the independence of Kosovo. They also argue that Kosovo is an unique case and does not set a precedent for any similar entity in the future. The position of the United States government is that,

"The unusual combination of factors found in the Kosovo situation – including the context of Yugoslavia's break-up, the history of ethnic cleansing and crimes against civilians in Kosovo, and the extended period of UN administration – are not found elsewhere and therefore make Kosovo a special case. Kosovo cannot be seen as precedent for any other situation in the world today."[49]

This has not been the only approach, however. Russia has expressly disagreed with the United States viewing Kosovo as a unique situation,

---

[48]   Franck, see note 18, 160.
[49]   Statement of Secretary of State Condoleezza Rice, "The U.S. Recognizes Kosovo as Independent State", 18 February 2008; see also the Department of State document, "Kosovo's Final Status: A Key to Stability and Prosperity in the Balkans", 23 January 2008, available at: <www.state.gov>; the same approach was adopted by the Italian government through the statement of the Foreign Minister Massimo D'Alema, 18 February 2008; for the similar position of the United Kingdom, France, Germany and Italy see Reynolds, see note 2; for the similar statement of the United Kingdom Foreign Secretary David Milliband see "Split EU Meets to Debate Kosovo", 18 February 2008, available at: <news.bbc.co.uk>.

and predicted the chain reaction that would follow it.[50] The Russian Foreign Ministry doubted that,

> "the American thesis about Kosovo's case being unique [is] really moral, as it implies that some are supposed to have the right to state-hood while it must be denied to others."[51]

In general the statement on anything being *sui generis* must be taken with great caution. Such argument can only be made after articulating the material evidence supporting the special character of the relevant situation. In practice, the resort by academics, legal advisers or politicians to this Latin phrase is often motivated by the lack of anything else that could justify one's position. The prevailing considerations of legal security, transparency and predictability require giving due consideration to the meaning of the established legal categories in which states members of the international community are used to place reliance.

The argument of Kosovo being specific is more inconsistent and problematic than any other argument advanced in this respect, because the argument of specificity necessarily implies applying international law to Kosovo differently from other entities, that is a discrimination as between the entities that aspire statehood. Thus, the idea of a *sui generis* character of Kosovo goes against not only the available evidence, but also against the non-discriminatory application of international law.

Thus, within the international community there is neither legal nor political agreement that, should the independence of Kosovo be taken as a lawful outcome, it would be a unique case without a precedential

---

[50]   Statement of the Deputy Press-Secretary of the President of Russia, 20 February 2008; Russian Foreign Minister predicted the inevitable chain re-action, cf. Reynolds, see note 2; earlier on, the Russian Foreign Minister warned that if the United States or the United Kingdom would like to see the Kosovo independence as special and tell other secessionist entities that it does not create precedent for them, this will simply not work, RIAN information, 13 December 2007, available at: <www.rian.ru>; Deputy Prime Minister Ivanov was convinced that Kosovo was a precedent and chain re-action will follow; other secessionist entities will ask why they are worse than Kosovars, 19 February 2008, RIAN information, available at: <www.rian.ru>; see also the "Observations by the official representative of the Russian Foreign Ministry", 20 February 2008, Foreign Ministry information, available at: <www.mid.ru>.

[51]   Russian Ministry of Foreign Affairs Information and Press Department, "Commentary Regarding a Media Question Concerning Remarks of US Under Secretary of State Nicholas Burns on Kosovo", 24 February 2008, available at: <www.mid.ru>.

effect. Consequently, at the political level each relevant group of states should be expected to handle any future case as they deem fit, and without taking into account the views of any other group of states. Those other states – in particular those which now object to viewing the case of Kosovo as precedent – may be prevented from challenging the similar treatment of other entities for the very reason that there is no agreed and commonly shared legal position as to the uniqueness of the case of Kosovo.

In terms of international law, the reason why Kosovo cannot create a precedent for other secessionist regions is that its claim to statehood is not based on the internationally valid claim to and declaration of independence. Were it otherwise, and were the legal position on this subject matter such as to allow the recognition of the statehood of the territory seceding from another state without its consent, there would be no possibility for precluding Kosovo's precedential effect. For, if international law were to allow unilateral secession of the territory from the state, it would have to allow this for all territories and entities aspiring this, in whichever part of the world. However, the coherency of the legal argument is not always perfectly obvious for the elites in secessionist entities. What they may regard as crucial is that as a matter of fact Kosovo is administered as independent from Serbia, supported by a substantial number of states and the EU. Thus, the *sui generis* strategy behind Kosovo may yet backfire to those who designed it. Independently of whether Kosovo achieves independence on terms compatible with international law, other aspirant secessionist entities may well manage consolidating beyond the point of reversal their *de facto* independence so vehemently opposed to by those who back the independence of Kosovo. Obviously Kosovo enthusiasts will challenge and disapprove such state of things; it is quite another matter how much they will be able to do to reverse it.

The essence of this problem is best expressed by the desperate but accurate statement by the Serbian Foreign Minister in response to the statement of the EU Presidency viewing the Kosovo case as unique,

> "Do any of you honestly think that just by saying that Kosovo is *sui generis*, you will make it so? That there will be no consequences to the stability and security of the international system, just because you say it won't?"[52]

---

[52] L. Kubosova, "Serbian FM says he is ashamed by EU's actions on Kosovo", 21 February 2008, available at: <www.euobserver.com>.

This question has not received the answer so far. Given that there is no agreement as to why Kosovo should be a unique case, which the relevant Western governments no doubt realise, it has to be asked what factors and considerations motivate them into asserting it is a unique case. In particular, what are the factors that make the governments supporting the independence of Kosovo that, given the fierce opposition to this independence by an important number of states and the consequent lack of any agreement on this point, their own view on the legality of this independence still represents international law? One of the motivations behind such stance can be related to the Euro-centrist understanding of international law.

European international law has been an idea in the 18th and 19th century presupposing the European superiority in relation to the rest of the world. It has always been an attitude, and never a reality. Its fundamental assumption has been that the European/Western attitudes are inherently better in defining and expressing international law than the attitudes of the rest of the world, and consequently the European/Western nations could impose international legal regulation on the rest of the world, or even exclude non-European nations from the ambit of international law.[53] Even over the past several decades, the idea of European international law has been an idea held and cherished by many, but hardly ever expressed in public.

Now, in relation to Kosovo, if there is no consensus across the world that the territory can be taken away from the sovereign state and declared independent, but if certain states still insist that their position that it can is in accordance with international law, their attitude must presuppose their attempt and ambition to restructure or reinterpret the foundations of international law despite the lack of agreement within the international community on this point. This suggests that the ideology of European international law may well be the one that reinforces the attitude of Kosovo enthusiasts to consolidate the legal position around Kosovo whether or not other parts of the world agree with this. Not that there is any straightforward evidence that the Western governments try to revive the ideology of European international law at the example of Kosovo (especially given the absence of the recognition of Kosovo by the EU). But it is difficult to think of any other motivation or ideology driving them.

---

[53] See the analysis in A. Orakhelashvili, "The Idea of European International Law", *EJIL* 17 (2006), 315 et seq.

The potential of Kosovo to entail chain reaction could be realised in several contexts. The secession of the Republika Srpska from Bosnia and Herzegovina, which is governed, along with the Bosnian government, by the High Representative on the basis of the 1995 Dayton Peace Accord, is currently not at the centre of the political agenda. However, if over the next few years there will be a relative change in political circumstances, the Republika Sprska could invoke the precedent of Kosovo and declare its independence from the government in Sarajevo. The factual success on the ground of such secession will depend on whether EUFOR will be ready to fight for keeping Bosnia and Herzegovina together and will prevail in that fight, and how much support the potential secessionist unit of the Republika Srpska would get from the outside.

That the UDI in Kosovo will certainly provoke further attempts at secession and potentially more international support for these attempts can be seen from the opinion surveys which show that the majority of Europeans consider that Tibet should not be under the Chinese rule.[54] Obviously the popular attitude does not directly translate into the governmental policy, which is perhaps even less likely given the status and power of China in international relations. While prediction may not be a profitable exercise, the fact that a majority of the population in the relevant countries tend to favour secessionism makes it more likely that in this or another case the relevant governments may be prepared to back other instances of secession.

V. The Recognition of Kosovo and Its Effect

The recognition of Kosovo by a number of states promptly followed the UDI in Pristina. On 18 February 2008, the United States formally recognised Kosovo as a "sovereign and independent State."[55] Several EU Member States, including the United Kingdom, France, Germany and Italy either preceded this or followed the suit. Overall, around thirty states have given their recognition to Kosovo. Serbia recalled am-

---

[54] In Britain 53 percent favour this view, and so do two-thirds of Germans and Italians, see Financial Times, 17 May/18 May 2008.

[55] "US Recognizes Kosovo as Independent State", 18 February 2008, available at: <www.pristina.usmission.gov>.

bassadors from several states that recognised Kosovo.[56] Recognition was expressly withheld by a number of states, including EU Member States such as Spain, Cyprus, Portugal, Romania, Slovakia and Greece. The EU as a whole was unable to express the attitude of recognising the independence of Kosovo.[57] Some other states, such as Israel, decided not to join those recognising Kosovo.[58] The principal question is if recognition by third states can influence the legality of the UDI by the seceding entity.

It has been contended that Kosovo's declaration of independence is "coordinated with, and supported by, a significant segment of the international community. It thus stands in contrast to other claims of a "right" to secede."[59] This argument assumes that recognition could command a decisive relevance in determining the validity of the claims of the relevant entity to statehood. The conceptual problem with this view is that it disregards the requirements of statehood if the entity that fails to meet them is nevertheless recognised by third states. At the same time, assuming that the independence of the entity that is recognised by a number of states can be unique and produce no precedential impact is conceptually unsound. Other secessionist entities can be recognised at a later date by third states and under the above thesis they would be unique too, thus producing a chain of "unique" events.

The fact that a number of states have recognised the independence of Kosovo is no doubt one of the main arguments in the arsenal of the proponents of that independence. Whatever the relevance of recognition, it is a plain matter of fact that Kosovo has not commanded the prevailing recognition by the international community. While the Security Council refused endorsing its independence, the international community is sharply divided on this point.

The concept and relevance of recognition in international law is controversial. Recognition applies to the variety of subjects of status, rights and privileges of legal persons in the international legal system. On the one hand, the significance of recognition is prompted by the absence of a centralised government in the international legal system that would pronounce on the status and rights of the relevant entities. On the other

---

[56]   "Serbia recalls ambassador from US", BBC Information, 19 February 2008, available at: <news.bbc.co.uk>.

[57]   E. Vucheva, "EU Fudges Kosovo Independence Recognition", 18 February 2008, available at: <www.euobserver.com>.

[58]   RIAN Information, 19 February 2008.

[59]   Borgen, see note 45.

hand, some third-party judgment on those issues could be regarded as indicative of the relevant status and position. For the very reason of the lack of international government, the relevance of recognition should be seen as limited in terms of defining what the status and rights of the relevant entity are. This is even more so, as the factual and legal criteria of statehood are in place for judging whether the relevant entity has achieved statehood.

It is questionable whether recognition as such can be viewed as a magic tool for creating a state or for consolidating the statehood of the entity which has no entitlement to it. Recognition merely follows the lawful establishment of statehood. It is not a criterion of statehood and does not impact whether or not the relevant entity is actually entitled to it. Crawford's reasoning clarifies the non-conclusive nature of recognition,

> "if State recognition is definitive then it is difficult to conceive of an illegal recognition and impossible to conceive of one which is invalid or void. Yet the nullity of certain acts of recognition has been accepted in practice, and rightly so; otherwise recognition would constitute an alternative form of intervention, potentially always available and apparently unchallengeable."

This also entails that,

> "the test for statehood must be extrinsic to the act of recognition."

As Crawford suggests, individual state pronouncements on statehood are not constitutive of the legality of that statehood.[60]

The presence of recognition cannot preserve the status of the relevant entity either. To illustrate, South Vietnam had gathered several dozens of recognitions, was a member of specialised agencies of the United Nations, and over two decades endorsed by the UN General Assembly as a state eligible for the membership of the UN.[61] But, having lasted for nearly two decades, South Vietnam disappeared subsequently without those recognitions having mattered. In a different but related context, the ICJ proclaimed East Timor as a unit of self-determination against the background of its annexation by Indonesia having been recognised by a number of states.[62]

---

60 Crawford, note 11, 21.
61 J.N. Moore, "The Lawfulness of Military Assistance to the Republic of Viet-Nam", *AJIL* 61 (1967), 1 et seq. (24 et seq.).
62 ICJ Reports, 1995, para. 36.

The argument that the recognition of Kosovo by third states counts as a material factor in the legal basis of its independence is premised on the thesis that recognition is constitutive. A declaratory approach to recognition would imply that secession has to be lawful and valid in the first place, and recognition by third states would then acknowledge that secession. It is incidental to this approach that recognition cannot be validly given to the entity whose independence is not compatible with international law. In other words, recognition cannot constitute an independent state.[63]

The constitutive theory has long been recognised as archaic and it has no visible support in state practice.[64] In terms of recognising Bosnia-Herzegovina and Croatia in 1991, the EU is seen as having attempted to refer to the constitutive theory, given that the two entities had not then fulfilled the requirements of statehood.[65] However, the Badinter Commission clearly emphasised that none of these constituted the instances of recognition of secessionist entities. On the other hand, as Frowein correctly emphasises, the declaratory theory of recognition cannot be of utility either because it cannot explain the legality of a *de facto* regime.[66] Unless one views oneself as a legislator, recognition of statehood by third states can relate to what is lawful in the first place.[67]

Dugard and Raic argue that while secession is discouraged on the account of the tendency to place territorial integrity above self-determination, the collective recognition of the seceding entity can be granted by the European Union.[68] But according to the collective recognition some distinctive significance that individual state recognition does not possess presupposes that while individual state recognition cannot constitute the state, collective recognition can. Thus, collective recognition aspires having the legislative impact, which is a claim anti-

---

[63] Although Musgrave argues that accepting the declaratory theory necessarily implies acceptance of the "internal theory" of secession (Musgrave, see note 11, 195), this is not a necessary incidence of the declaratory theory, which can be brought into play also with regard to the entities which validly secede in compliance with international law.

[64] Crawford, see note 11, 24 et seq.

[65] Musgrave, see note 11, 206.

[66] Frowein, see note 47, 36.

[67] It is quite another matter that the parent state can itself recognise the independence of the secessionist entity and thus waive its sovereignty and legalise what otherwise has no legal basis.

[68] Dugard/ Raic, see note 11, 134.

thetical to the basic character of the international legal order. In reality the validity of collective recognition is governed by the same criteria as that by individual states. The opposite result would necessarily be premised on viewing regional arrangements such as the EU as elements of an international government that does not exist.

This point is anyway moot in the Kosovo context. The EU has not itself recognised Kosovo as an independent state. It is unclear whether deploying EULEX can be seen as implied recognition, as it has to work with what Kosovars consider as independent state institutions, in other words support the entity in exercising sovereign powers. The answer to this question depends on the mandate of EULEX and the type of powers and competences it possesses.[69]

Given that the recognition of Kosovo cannot constitute it as a state, nor relate to what is already the state on international legal grounds, such recognition is illegal. The grounds for such illegality can be premised either on the duty not to recognise illegal entities, or the refusal of the parent state to let Kosovo become independent.

Dugard has formulated the modern doctrine of non-recognition based on *jus cogens*, having subsumed within this doctrine the cases of non-recognition such as Rhodesia, Namibia, South African homelands, Palestine and the Turkish Republic of Northern Cyprus. When the practice of states and organisations refers to a certain entity or situation by using the language of "illegality", "invalidity" or "nullity", this is the evidence that the recognition is withheld from an entity not because that entity lacks the ingredients of statehood, but because it is illegally brought about.[70] South African homeland-states arguably met the requirements of statehood laid down in the Montevideo Convention, but no state except South Africa recognised them.

Similarly,

"A cluster of fundamental principles inherent in the two fundamental norms of the prohibition of the use of force and the right to self-determination provide a legal basis for the refusal of the United Nations to recognise Israel's sovereignty over East Jerusalem."[71]

Jus cogens gives a new doctrinal coherence to the doctrine of non-recognition, formulating it as follows,

---

[69] See below under VI. 2.

[70] J. Dugard, *Recognition and the United Nations*, 1987, 130 et seq.

[71] Dugard, see above, 100, 115.

"An act in violation of a norm having the character of *jus cogens* is illegal and is therefore null and void. This applies to the creation of States, the acquisition of territory and other situations, such as Namibia. States are under a duty not to recognise such acts."

This is so, because,

"*Jus Cogens* is a central feature in the modern doctrine of non-recognition as the violation of a norm having the character of *jus cogens* is a prerequisite for the illegality that results in the nullity and non-recognition."[72]

Non-recognition applies to situations involving nullity for conflict with *jus cogens*.[73] In all these cases the invalidity of titles as confirmed by UN organs is implementing and declaratory of the *jus cogens* nullity, not just a discretionary action.[74] The link between *jus cogens* and non-recognition of illegal entities has been fortified in the ILC's articles 40 and 41 on State Responsibility.[75]

Whether the duty not to recognise applies to the unilateral declaration of independence in Kosovo depends on whether this process is seen as produced by the breach of a peremptory norm. This question is contingent on whether the armed attack by NATO states on the Federal Republic of Yugoslavia in 1999 can be seen as a breach of *jus cogens*, and *also* whether the armed attack in question was immediately responsible for the eventual UDI in Kosovo.

As for the first part of this question, it is clear that the claim as to the legality of "humanitarian intervention" has never been approved by the international community. The reaction of the international community to the claims that NATO states were entitled to attack the FRY on humanitarian grounds to protect the Albanian population has been to prevailingly reject the legality of humanitarian intervention.[76] Thus the NATO attack remains a breach of Article 2 (4) of the United Nations

---

[72]   Dugard, see note 70, 132, 135, 137.

[73]   J. Dugard, "Collective Non-Recognition: The Failure of South Africa's Bantustan States", in: *Boutros Boutros-Ghali – Amicorum Discipulorumque Liber – Peace, Development, Democracy*, Vol. I (1998), 383 et seq. (402).

[74]   Dugard, see above, 400 et seq.

[75]   Report of the International Law Commission on the Work of its Fifty-third Session (2001), GAOR 56th Sess., Suppl. No. 10, Doc. A/56/10.

[76]   See on this A. Orakhelashvili, "Legal Stability and Claims of Change: The International Court's Treatment of *Jus ad Bellum* and *Jus in Bello*", *Nord. J. Int'l L.* 75 (2006), 371 et seq.

Charter, customary law prohibition of the use of force, and of *jus cogens*.

As for the second part of the question, in principle, it is difficult to see how the current factual state of things would be brought about had the NATO states not attacked the FRY in 1999. But the NATO states have never expressly claimed, in the process of the 1999 armed attack, that Kosovo should be allowed to secede from Serbia, and the principal authors of the 1999 attack have voted for S/RES/1244 which reaffirmed the territorial integrity of the FRY, and *a fortiori* of Serbia. Not until the Ahtisaari Plan did those states express themselves in support of the independence of Kosovo.

It seems that the question here is solely that of the assessment of facts. If the view is taken that the NATO attack was never originally meant to affect the territorial integrity of the FRY and thus lead to the independence of Kosovo, then the duty of non-recognition does not apply in its original version of the effect of peremptory norms. This view can be reinforced by the fact that the states which intervened against the FRY in 1999 have subsequently confirmed their commitment to its territorial integrity by voting on S/RES/1244. In such case the only factor that precludes lawful recognition of the independence of Kosovo is the objection to that by Serbia. If, however, the view is taken that the NATO attack in 1999, in breach of the UN Charter and the relevant customary international law as part of *jus cogens* is immediately responsible for the ultimate UDI in Kosovo, then the UDI in Kosovo is directly subject to the duty of non-recognition as envisaged in the ILC articles 40 and 41 on State Responsibility. In practical terms, which of these two options is correct does not make an essential practical difference on the ground. Given that Serbia persistently objects to the independence of Kosovo, the legality of recognition is precluded in any case. Against this background, any recognition of the independence of Kosovo is an internationally wrongful act and generates the obligation to withdraw it. The recognition of fundamental illegalities is always subject to revocation of recognition.[77]

---

[77] I. Brownlie, *International Law and the Use of Force*, 1963, 421 et seq.; F.A. Mann, "The Consequences of an International Wrong in National and International Law", *BYIL* 48 (1976-77), 1 et seq. (41).

VI. Compatibility of the Processes in and around Kosovo with UN Security Council Resolutions

1. Compatibility of the Independence of Kosovo with S/RES/1244

The argument of compatibility of the independence of Kosovo with S/RES/1244 of 10 June 1999 presupposes the permissibility of multiple interpretations of this resolution. The principles of interpretation of Security Council resolutions are essentially the same as those applicable to treaties under articles 31 and 32 of the 1969 Vienna Convention on the Law of Treaties.[78] Even if Security Council resolutions are not formally treaties, they are in substance agreements between states. In addition, Security Council resolutions derive their binding force from the treaty clause - Article 25 of the United Nations Charter. The link between resolutions and the treaty-based duty to obey them under Article 25 necessarily requires viewing the duty to comply with resolutions as sacred as the duty to observe treaty obligations in good faith (*pacta sunt servanda*).

Consequently, the divergence of interpretations of Security Council resolutions is as systemically controversial as the divergent mutually exclusive interpretation of the treaty. The argument that there may be two divergent interpretations of a resolution is in essence the argument that Article 25 prescribes two mutually exclusive legal outcomes, which is absurd by itself. In order not to undermine the duty to carry out the Council's resolutions under Article 25, it is necessary to interpret these resolutions in good faith and according to the plain meaning of words used in their text.

S/RES/1244 has directly and expressly preserved the territorial integrity of the FRY. Well before the UDI in Pristina, its incompatibility with S/RES/1244 was raised, among others, by the Russian government against the background that the UN Security Council was not going to assent to the independence of Kosovo. Attention was drawn to the attempts to interpret the Security Council resolutions as if they justified the independence of Kosovo. The Russian government objected to the

---

[78]   On the interpretation of resolutions see Orakhelashvili, see note 10, *Max Planck UNYB*.

attempt to unilaterally interpret resolutions.[79] The US Assistant Secretary of State Rosemary Di Carlo specified that admitted that the United States and Russia "might have different interpretations" of S/RES/1244,

"We agree that 1244 remains in effect. But we see 1244, as I said, as a call for a political process. We see that the status of Kosovo was left totally open and did not dictate that Kosovo should be independent or should not be independent. The resolution calls for presences – international presences – to assist Kosovo in its development."[80]

This statement bypasses the express preservation of the territorial integrity of Serbia under this resolution.

According to the Foreign Secretary David Miliband of the United Kingdom, S/RES/1244,

"created a political process as well as establishing an international regime for Kosovo within the territory of Serbia. It was about restoring peace and security. Resolution 1244 does not determine or constrain the final status process, nor exclude outcomes. But it does envisage a final status process and it needs to be brought to a conclusion."

Furthermore, he asserted that,

"It is important not to be confused by 1244's references to the 'sovereignty and territorial integrity of the Federal Republic of Yugoslavia (now Serbia)'. This is a qualified preambular reference which in its context clearly refers only to the interim phase of administration in Kosovo."[81]

The Foreign Secretary's statement seems to argue that while the Security Council preserved the territorial integrity of Yugoslavia and Serbia then and there, it left open the option of disrupting that territorial

---

[79] Statement of Foreign Minister S. Lavrov, 10 December 2007, available at: <www.rian.ru>; a similar declaration was made by the Russian Representative in the Troika, emphasising that the proclamation of independence would contradict S/RES/1244 and in such case Russia would demand annulling it, 10 December 2007. On attempts of unilateral interpretation of Security Council resolutions in general see J.A. Frowein, "Unilateral Interpretation of Security Council Resolutions – A Threat to Collective Security?" in: V. Götz/ P. Selmer/ R. Wolfrum (eds), *Liber Amicorum Günther Jaenicke – Zum 85. Geburtstag*, 1999, 97 et seq.

[80] Available at: <http://www.interfax.com/17/375120/Interview.aspx>.

[81] D. Miliband, "Kosovo: Is it legal?", available at: <www.fco.gov.uk>, 17 February 2008.

integrity at a certain point in the future. At the same time, it is inherent in the Foreign Secretary's statement that there was no specification of who and when it should be decided whether such disruption of territorial integrity was necessary. Was it to be the Council itself, or someone else?

Leaving aside the implausibility of such interpretation in the face of the straightforward division of the Council membership views on this subject, it is also implausible that the Council would have intended something along the lines formulated by the Foreign Secretary. Even if the Council had only intended to preserve Serbia's territorial integrity for a certain period of time, having not pronounced on what is supposed to happen afterwards, the very fact of recognition that the relevant territory, *even for a certain unspecified period of time*, is part of Serbia, necessarily implies the affirmation that if that territory will ever stop legally being a part of Serbia, the latter's consent has to be obtained, for the very reason that *for the time being* Serbia remains the territorial sovereign.

But the above is just a matter for speculation. The truth of the matter is that S/RES/1244 contains no element of provisional sovereignty of Serbia over Kosovo. It just affirms what otherwise is the case under international law. No temporal limitation follows from the words used by the Security Council and none should be read in.

It should also be considered what meaning the Member States attributed to Serbia's territorial integrity when S/RES/1244 was adopted. The views of individual Member States at the time of adoption of the resolution, if compatible with the text thereof and not contradicted by other Member States, could be a valid factor in the interpretation of Security Council resolutions. Russia's view was that the resolution "clearly reaffirm[ed] the commitment of all States to the sovereignty and territorial integrity of the Federal Republic of Yugoslavia."[82] China stood "for peaceful settlement of the question of Kosovo on the basis of respect for the sovereignty and territorial integrity of the Federal Republic of Yugoslavia;"[83] in addition, China explained its abstention from vetoing the resolution thus,

> "in view of the fact that the Federal Republic of Yugoslavia has already accepted the peace plan, that NATO has suspended its bombing in the Federal Republic of Yugoslavia, and that the draft resolu-

---

[82]   Doc. S/PV/4011, 10 June 1999, 7.
[83]   Ibid., 8.

tion has reaffirmed the purposes and principles of the United Nations Charter, the primary responsibility of the Security Council for the maintenance of international peace and security and the commitment of all Member States to the sovereignty and territorial integrity of the Federal Republic of Yugoslavia, the Chinese delegation will not block the adoption of this draft resolution."[84]

In other words, S/RES/1244 was adopted simply because it preserved the territorial integrity of the FRY and subsequently Serbia. If the resolution meant affirming Serbia's territorial integrity only for a certain time period, China would not have let it through, especially because it would have created a precedent for secession which China has more than one reasons to fear. Now, if the Foreign Secretary's approach is right, China in fact has approved the eventual secession of Kosovo, which is counterfactual.

Similarly, Argentina voted for S/RES/1244 with the conviction that,

"it lays the foundation for a definitive political solution to the Kosovo crisis that will respect the sovereignty and territorial integrity of the Federal Republic of Yugoslavia."[85]

In other words, the resolution did not intend prejudicing the territorial integrity of Yugoslavia at any point of time. Against this background, no state in the Security Council, including the United Kingdom, has voiced any disagreement with this approach, having been well aware of the preservation of the FRY's territorial integrity as the cardinal condition for that resolution having ever been adopted.

As for the external evidence, S/RES/1785 of 21 November 2007, adopted around the time when the calls for Kosovo's independence got intensified, reaffirmed the Security Council's,

"commitment to the political settlement of the conflicts in the former Yugoslavia, preserving the sovereignty and territorial integrity of all States there within their internationally recognized borders."

In other words, it was the Security Council's intention to preserve the territorial integrity of all states including Serbia in the context of any territorial settlement adopted in the Balkans. This was in its turn reflective of the affirmation of the *uti possidetis juris* principle after the dissolution of the SFRY.

---

[84]   Ibid., 9.
[85]   Ibid., 19.

Even within the EU, there is some acceptance of the fact that the UDI is not compatible with S/RES/1244. As the Slovenian President of the EU Dmitrij Rupel acknowledged,

"There is concern about how to reconcile Resolution 1244 with Kosovo's proclamation of independence."[86]

A culminating point of schizophrenia is embodied in para. 12 of the UDI adopted by the parliament in Pristina, which states that,

"we shall act consistent with principles of international law and resolutions of the Security Council of the United Nations, including resolution 1244 (1999)."

2. The Legality of the EU Presence in Kosovo

The EU acknowledged, through the Council Joint Action, the need of,

"ensuring a seamless transition between the United Nations Interim Mission in Kosovo (UNMIK) and the EU crisis management operation in Kosovo on the day of transfer of selected tasks from UN-MIK to the EU crisis management operation following the adoption of a United Nations Security Council Resolution."[87]

This was followed by the deployment in Kosovo of the EU rule of law mission (EULEX). The EULEX mission has been established, among others, to,

"(a) monitor, mentor and advise the competent Kosovo institutions on all areas related to the wider rule of law (including a customs service), whilst retaining certain executive responsibilities;

(b) ensure the maintenance and promotion of the rule of law, public order and security including, as necessary, in consultation with the relevant international civilian authorities in Kosovo, through reversing or annulling operational decisions taken by the competent Kosovo authorities;

(c) help to ensure that all Kosovo rule of law services, including a customs service, are free from political interference;

---

[86] Information of the Serbian Foreign Ministry 26 April 2008, available at: <http://www.mfa.gov.yu/Pressframe15.htm>.

[87] Council Joint Action 2007/334/CFSP, 14 May 2007, *Official Journal of the European Union*, 15 May 2007, L 125/29, preambular paragraph (4).

(d) ensure that cases of war crimes, terrorism, organised crime, corruption, inter-ethnic crimes, financial/economic crimes and other serious crimes are properly investigated, prosecuted, adjudicated and enforced, according to the applicable law, including, where appropriate, by international investigators, prosecutors and judges jointly with Kosovo investigators, prosecutors and judges or independently, and by measures including, as appropriate, the creation of cooperation and coordination structures between police and prosecution authorities;

(e) contribute to strengthening cooperation and coordination throughout the whole judicial process, particularly in the area of organised crime;

(f) contribute to the fight against corruption, fraud and financial crime."[88]

These functions and powers, especially the one mentioned in para. (b) above, seem to reflect the incidences of so-called "supervised" or "controlled" independence of Kosovo. In other words, Kosovo under this model enjoys no full sovereignty. EU Commission President Jose Manuel Barroso argued that the sending of the EU mission to Kosovo had not contradicted international law in general and S/RES/1244 in particular, because the "relevant international organisations" are authorised to establish an international civil presence in Kosovo and the mission could be there unless the Security Council would decide otherwise.[89] The Serbian position has been and remains that without the authorisation of the Security Council, EULEX cannot lawfully be deployed in Kosovo. Along the similar lines, and even before the UDI and deployment of EULEX, the government of Cyprus emphasised that the deployment of the EU mission in Kosovo was not compatible with S/RES/1244.[90] The same position has been repeatedly expressed by Russia,

"the EU is unilaterally without any authorization from the UN Security Council sending a rule of law mission to Kosovo. It is, mildly speaking, a bitter irony in this name because the rule of law mission is being sent there in violation of supreme law, in violation of inter-

---

[88] Article 3, Council Joint Action 2008/124/CFSP, 4 February 2008, *Official Journal of the European Union*, 16 February 2008, L 42/92.

[89] Barroso calls the EU mission to Kosovo legal, 21 February 2008, Xinhua information, available at: <www. xinhuanet.com>.

[90] Statement by the Foreign Minister of Cyprus, 14 December 2007.

national law. We are being told that resolution 1244 is the basis for
sending the EU mission, and that the unilateral proclamation of
Kosovo's independence does not run counter to this resolution because it speaks of a transition period and supposedly this transition
period is over. That's not true. Although resolution 1244 really
speaks of a transition period, this transition period in accordance
with this resolution should last until the parties reach, and I quote, a
"final political settlement." Everybody knows that the talks designed to reach that political settlement were artificially interrupted
thanks to outside interference. The territorial integrity of Serbia was
confirmed not only by resolution 1244, adopted in 1999, but also
quite recently by another UNSC resolution which was adopted at
the end of November 2007."[91]

The Serbian Foreign Ministry too specified that,

"Although Brussels made the decision to deploy its mission in the
province in early February, it has not received an official invitation
for this from the UN Secretary-General – necessary under Resolution 1244, that regulates any international presence in Kosovo post-
1999."[92]

The Council Joint Action of 4 February 2008 establishing EULEX
refers to S/RES/1244 as its basis.[93] The EU Council especially refers to
the phrase in this resolution (op. para. 10) in which the Security Council, "Authorise[d] the Secretary-General, with the assistance of relevant
international organizations, to establish an international civil presence
in Kosovo...". But however this phrase is stretched, it refers to operations established by the UN Secretary-General, that is to say operations
that are qualitatively UN operations, as opposed to the operations of
other organisations that are approved, or acquiesced into, by the United
Nations organs. S/RES/1244 does not include the reference to the establishment of civilian peace operations by the EU as such. When the
UN Security Council intends to authorise the establishment of EU operations in Chapter VII situations, it expressly grants the requisite authorisation, as was the case with the establishment of EUFOR in Bos-

---

[91]   "Kosovo Tool Kit for Separatists", BBC Information, available at: <in-
      ews.bbc.co.uk>, 20 February 2008; Transcript of Remarks and Replies to
      Media Questions by Russian Minister of Foreign Affairs Sergey Lavrov at
      a Joint Press Conference with the Turkish Minister of Foreign Affairs Ali
      Babajan, Moscow, February 20, 2008, available at: <www.mid.ru>.
[92]   Serbian Foreign Ministry Information, see note 86.
[93]   Council Joint Action, see note 88.

nia to replace the NATO-led Stabilisation Force, or the EU mission in the Democratic Republic of the Congo.[94] The truth of the matter remains that EULEX has been deployed in Kosovo without the sanction of the UN Security Council. Its presence there is not compatible with international law unless it will either be consented to by Serbia or directly approved by the Security Council.

Whether or not the EU's reference to S/RES/1244 as the basis of EULEX is correct, in any case it constitutes the acknowledgment on the side of the EU that there has been no other legal basis for such operation. Neither general international law, nor the legal framework and competence of the EU provide for the power to establish operations like EULEX in situations like Kosovo.

The process of establishment of EULEX reveals further problems not only in terms of the status of Kosovo but also the position of the EU to it. According to article 10 of the Joint Action of 4 February 2008,

> "The status of EULEX KOSOVO and its staff, including the privileges, immunities and further guarantees necessary for the completion and smooth functioning of EULEX KOSOVO, shall be agreed as appropriate."

It is unclear how these privileges and immunities should be "agreed" and with whom. The EU as an international organisation enjoys no immunity unless conferred to it on the basis of the treaty with the relevant territorial state. An international organisation has no power to grant immunity to itself unilaterally. If, on the other hand, the EU concludes an agreement with the Kosovo authorities with a view to achieving this goal, this will be tantamount to the recognition of Kosovo as a state on the EU's behalf and in its name. As mentioned above, the EU was unable to adopt a decision to recognise Kosovo and any agreement with the Kosovo authorities will be an attempt to imitate what has not been granted. Thus, while the Council Joint Action of 4 February 2008 prescribes that the privileges and immunities of EULEX should be secured, it does not specify how this should be achieved and in fact this cannot be achieved in legal terms.

---

[94] See on this A. Orakhelashvili, "The Legal Framework of Peace Operations by Regional Organisations", *International Peacekeeping: The Yearbook of International Peace Operations* 11 (2006), 111 et seq.

3. The Legal Status of the UN Mission in Kosovo

Despite the UDI in Pristina and the EU's deployment of the EULEX mission, the UN Interim Administration Mission in Kosovo (UNMIK) is still bound to continue its activities in Kosovo as it has been allocated this task under S/RES/1244. The EU has acknowledged that the UN will remain fully engaged in Kosovo until the end of S/RES/1244.[95]

On the ground UNMIK does not seem to be discharging its responsibilities fully and seems to take attitudes under the influence of political pressure from the governments that support the independence of Kosovo. This has been evidenced by the negative attitude of UNMIK to the holding of Serbian elections in Kosovo in May 2008. According to op. para. 11 (c) of S/RES/1244, the main responsibilities of UNMIK include,

> "Organizing and overseeing the development of provisional institutions for democratic and autonomous self-government pending a political settlement, including the holding of elections."

The Head of UNMIK Joachim Rücker, being the Special Representative of the Secretary-General for Kosovo, refused to organise these elections by asserting that UNMIK was the only entity to allow elections. This follows, among others, from the attitude of the current head of UNMIK that favours the independence of Kosovo.[96] However, the above passage from the resolution does not allocate any monopoly to UNMIK in deciding to allow or not to allow the holding of elections. It has merely to organise and oversee elections.

VII. Prospects for the Future: Settlements of Conflict

The above analysis has demonstrated that Kosovo has not made a valid case for independence under international law. Still, though illegal, Kosovo continues as a factual reality, and enjoys the support of a num-

---

[95] Council Joint Action 2006/304/CFSP, 10 April 2006, *Official Journal of the European Union*, 26 April 2006, L 112/19.

[96] See Rücker, "Local Election Results Will be Invalid", Serbian Foreign Ministry, 8 May 2008, <www.mfa.gov.yu>; see further Section VII. below. See also the letter of 17 April 2008 from the Serbian Minister Slobodan Samardzic to Rücker, in which the Serbian Minister observes that despite Rücker's professing of taking the neutral political stance, he did not actually remain neutral, see <www.kosovocompromise.com>.

ber of influential governments. It is thus worth focusing on the prospects of future developments of the Kosovo situation.

One option is that Serbia will, at the end of the day, recognise the independence of Kosovo and the situation will be resolved. Serbia has been pressured to do so by the EU and the government of the United States, in particular in exchange of closer relations with and possible accelerated membership in the EU. While such deal cannot be excluded, it appears highly unlikely, as currently no Serbian government can be envisaged to assent to the independence of Kosovo.

The second option is that of the protracted *de facto* situation on the ground, occasionally accompanied by local conflicts, frictions and crises.

The third option is that of the use of force by Serbia to recover the effective control over Kosovo. In this respect, it matters whether the modern *jus ad bellum* permits Serbia to use force. There have been reports of the Serbian government stating that it would not send troops into Kosovo to recover the territory.[97] This was arguably understood as the waiver by Serbia to use force in this context.[98] However, the Serbian statement only means that under current circumstances, including the unwillingness to confront in combat NATO troops, Serbia is not going to send its troops to recover Kosovo. But this statement does not mean that Serbia gives up its right to use force to restore its territorial integrity. In general, waiver or renunciation of a right cannot be presumed, and the text allegedly containing waiver should be interpreted strictly so that nothing is presumed if not following from the text of the relevant statement.[99]

The crucial question is whether and how far Kosovo as a *de facto* regime is legally protected from the use of force. As Kosovo legally remains part of Serbia, the use of force by Serbia to restore its government and authority over Kosovo would not in principle contradict Article 2 (4) of the UN Charter, which prohibits the use of force only in international relations. Sir Hersch Lauterpacht has observed that the territory of the unrecognised state is not protected from the invasion by

---

[97] AFP Information, 14 December 2007.

[98] See the statement by the Foreign Minister of Germany Steinmeier, "Kosovo erklärt sich unabhängig – EU Außenminister beraten die Lage", 18 February 2008.

[99] For an analysis of the doctrine and practice on waiver, Orakhelashvili, see note 10, 2006, Chapter 11; id., see note 22, Chapter 13.

virtue of the prohibition of the use of force.[100] As Frowein emphasises, the *de facto* entity is not legally protected from the invasion of the state from which it secedes. The use of force by the latter state would not be a breach of the territorial integrity of another state.[101] As such use of force would not be that in international relations of states, the *de facto* entity could not be protected by third states against its parent state.[102] Frowein also covers the issue of the use of force against the *de facto* entity with an internationalised status and admits that in such cases the prohibition of the use of force can protect such *de facto* entities,[103] but understandably his analysis does not cover any entity with the position comparable to that of Kosovo. In addition, the extension of the Article 2 (4) prohibition to *de facto* entities only on the basis of the rationale of this prohibition to safeguard peace is not free of problems, because Article 2 (4) is by its clear wording limited to international relations of states.

As S/RES/1244 is binding and continues being in force, Serbia presumably has no right to undermine the international administration established by the UN resolution. If, however, the UN administration were to be removed, or the factual state were to be established that would frustrate the aims of the UN presence under S/RES/1244, the deal under this resolution would collapse and Serbia could use force in response to the material breach of the resolution. To illustrate, the head of UNMIK has refused to recognise the legality of Serbian elections held in parts of Kosovo. While it is not clear at all that this situation calls for recognition, the refusal to recognise is clearly premised on the assumption that Kosovo is no longer part of Serbia, which attitude the UN officials are precluded from taking under S/RES/1244. Such practice, if multiplied and perpetuated, could lead to a situation that the legal position created by the resolution is no longer working on the ground; in other words, there is a material breach of this resolution. If carried through on a substantial scale, such practice could entitle Serbia at the relevant point of time to declare that S/RES/1244 is no longer in force, and in case of need proceed with the coercive action with a view to securing its territorial integrity.

In short, whether and when Serbia can use force to recover Kosovo depends on the process of the observance of S/RES/1244 on the

---

[100] Lauterpacht, see note 26, 52.
[101] Frowein, see note 47, 38.
[102] Ibid., 39.
[103] Ibid., 67 et seq.

ground, that is the compliance of the only international legal basis of the internationalisation of the Kosovo situation and opposable to Serbia and all states. In practical terms, all depends on how long the NATO troops will be able to stay in Kosovo, and in the case of possible armed confrontation, to what extent they will be willing to engage in full-scale hostilities.

VIII. Conclusions

The preceding analysis has demonstrated that the UDI in Kosovo contravenes international law and it cannot be validly recognised. Given the unrelenting opposition to the independence of Kosovo by Serbia and a number of other states, and the structure of international law being what it is, the validity of this independence can hardly be expected to consolidate. However, the argument of reality has been invoked in favour of accepting the independence of Kosovo. As US Secretary of State Condoleezza Rice put it,

"if you don't deal with that reality, you're only going to sow the seeds of considerable discontent and considerable instability."[104]

But there are limits on the realist argument. As one of the fathers of political realism Henry Kissinger pointed out,

"stability ... has commonly resulted not from a quest of peace but from a generally accepted legitimacy",

which,

"means no more than an international agreement about the nature of workable arrangements and about the permissible aims and methods of foreign policy."

Legitimacy "implies the acceptance of the framework of the international order by all major powers", so that none of them persist with policies undermining the undesirable settlement.[105]

To apply this reasoning to Kosovo, the current situation on the ground cannot be expected to be stable either in regional or global terms. At the regional level, Serbia remains opposed to the independence of Kosovo; at the global level, the independence of Kosovo is op-

---

[104] "Kosovo: Russian Ambitions and American Mistakes", RIAN information, 14 December 2007, available at: <www.rian.ru>.

[105] H. Kissinger, *A World Restored: Metternich, Castlereagh and the Problems of Peace 1812-1822*, 1957, 1 et seq.

posed by such major players as India, China and Russia. Thus both at regional and global level the independence of Kosovo will continue to encounter the opposition and counter-action that will adversely impact on the stability of its position. Presumably the sponsors of the Kosovo independence have understood from the outset that the entity whose independence they supported will neither gain the general recognition of the international community, nor will it be admitted to the United Nations.

The realist argument has also the potential of backfiring if the Kosovo-enthusiast states will face the secession of other entities in different parts of the world in the context over which they will have little realistic influence. In addition, if the realist argument holds the key to the problem, then the legal criteria of statehood and recognition are no longer crucial. Whatever the statehood entitlement and recognition of other secessionist entities, the use of the reality argument in favour of Kosovo's independence inevitably paves the way for consolidating the claims of those other entities to independence. Consequently, those who use the reality argument today at the example of Kosovo, should prepare themselves to hearing the same argument in the context of other secessionist entities whose independence they do, or would, vehemently oppose. Being realistic about the reality will never do any harm.

Security Council Powers and the Exigencies of Justice after War

Wolfgang Weiß

I. Introduction

The discharge of the Chapter VII powers of the UN Security Council is currently questioned by different developments. The debate about the crisis of international law refers in particular to the UN collective security system. This debate was provoked by concerns about increasing unilateralism by military and/or economic powerful states ("new wave of unilateralism")[1] and raised doubts about the capacity of international law to counter the challenges posed by states that try to attain their aims irrespective of international law and the international system, in particular in case such unilateralism was somehow caused by the paralysis of the Security Council to take effective measures. If the UN Charter is the nucleus of a constitutionalisation of the international community[2] with respect to basic values like human rights and the prohibition of the use of force, unilateralism shakes the very basis of the UN collective security system and of the role of its Security Council to be the principal executive of the collective will of the international community of states.

The second development challenging the Security Council powers is an emerging, closely related discussion about the demands of post-war/post-conflict justice caused by the experiences in multilateral peace restoration since the 1990s. The requirements for establishing a stable society after armed conflicts considerably influence the way the Security Council may exercise its responsibilities. This discussion calls for an identification of exigencies of post-war governance which must be considered by the Security Council when exercising its powers. The exigencies of justice after war could form peculiar constraints to the Chapter VII powers. From this perspective, it is the very aim of the UN to maintain and restore peace and security which poses some questions

---

1   P.M. Dupuy, "The Place and Role of Unilateralism in Contemporary International Law", *EJIL* 11 (2000), 19 et seq. (25).

2   J. Crawford, "The Charter of the UN as a Constitution", in: H. Fox (ed.), *The Changing Constitution of the United Nations*, 1997, 1; B. Faßbender, *UN Security Council Reform and the Right to Veto*, 1998, 129 et seq.; Id., "The United Nations Charter as Constitution of the International Community", *Colum. J. Transnat'l L.* 36 (1998), 529 et seq.; W. Graf Vitzthum, in: B. Simma et al. (eds), *The Charter of the United Nations. A Commentary. Vol. I*, 2nd edition 2002, Article 2 (6) Mn. 20; M. Herdegen, "The Constitutionalization of the UN Security System", *Vand. J. Transnat'l L.* 27 (1994), 135 et seq.

about the way the Security Council handles its enforcement powers in new contexts like international territorial administrations.

These issues appear to be increasingly relevant. The number of Chapter VII resolutions remarkably increased in the 1990s.[3] An interpretation of the Security Council powers under Chapter VII which would limit them in a way so that the Security Council could only condemn the unlawful use of force, command the restoration of the *status quo ante* (which usually is seen to be the *status iuris*) and exercise its powers accordingly, would sharply contrast to the experiences gained in the years since 1990 which should result in formulating better strategies of peace building.

Against the backdrop of these challenges to the exercise of the Security Council powers, the present article tries to analyse the character and the legal constraints of the powers *de lege lata*[4] with a particular focus on the exigencies of creating durable post-conflict scenarios. In order to identify the general constraints for the exercise of Security Council powers and to assign the peculiar limits by the demands of establishing post-war justice, the article initially will characterise, from a general perspective, the Security Council powers under Chapter VII. This also requires shedding some light on the functions and role of the Security Council in the contemporary collective security system. Its role can be highlighted in particular when considering situations in which the Security Council is challenged by unilateral use of force.

Therefore, Section II. will first develop – as the core premise of this article – a constitutive understanding of the Security Council powers under Chapter VII, considering also the changing functions of the Council reflecting the changing conceptions of peace. The constitutive understanding of these powers implies a flexible and purposive interpretation. Second, the decisive role of the Council in countering challenges to peace and security will be exemplified against the backdrop of unilateral use of force. Arguments will be developed hostile to the lawfulness of unilateral recourse to force stressing the peculiar role of the UN Security Council for the enforcement of the common will. Section

---

[3]   P. Wallenstein/ P. Johansson, "Security Council Decisions in Perspective", in: D.M. Malone (ed.), *The UN Security Council*, 2004, 17 et seq. (27).

[4]   A reform of the UN system does not seem to be in reach irrespective of the ongoing debate. Regarding the attempts to reform the UN Security Council see B. Faßbender, "All Illusions Shattered? Looking Back on a Decade of Failed Attempts to Reform the UN Security Council", *Max Planck UNYB 7* (2003), 183 et seq.

III. will survey the different limits to the powers of the Security Council. Finally, Section IV. will develop the limiting effects of the demands of justice after war to the Security Council powers of peace restoration. A final conclusion will assemble the core results of this study to a – hopefully – congruent picture of the character and the confines of the Security Council powers.

II. The UN Security Council – its Powers, Functions, and Role within Collective Security

1. The Powers and Functions of the Security Council

a. Constitutive Powers of the Security Council under Chapter VII

From among the many examples that raised concerns about the scope of the UN Security Council powers, two recent incidents shall briefly be mentioned here: the NATO air campaign in Kosovo and the latest Iraq war.

The NATO campaign Operation Allied Force in 1999 ignited a debate about the power of the Security Council under Chapter VII of the UN Charter to retroactively validate previous non-authorised use of force. Security Council Resolution 1244 on Kosovo was seen by some writers at least to present some form of implicit retroactive validation because the Security Council did not question the way armed hostilities had been terminated in Yugoslavia. Instead, the Security Council supported the situation attained by NATO's unilateral use of force by establishing the Kosovo Force (KFOR) and the UN Interim Administration in Kosovo.[5] Other scholars, however, did not accept interpreting

---

5   C. Stahn, "Enforcement of the Collective Will After Iraq", in: ASIL (ed.), *Future Implications of the Iraq Conflict*, 2004, 92 et seq. (100) [= *AJIL* 97 (2003), 804 et seq.]; see also A. Pellet, "Brief Remarks on the Unilateral Use of Force", *EJIL* 11 (2000), 386 et seq. (387, 389); R. Wedgwood, "Unilateral Action in the UN System", *EJIL* 11 (2000), 349 et seq. (359). Stahn mentions some more examples of an alleged retroactive endorsement of unilateral actions by the Security Council; this evaluation nevertheless is dubitable, to say the least, cf. the contrasting views of V. Gowlland-Debbas, "The Limits of Unilateral Enforcement of Community Objectives in the Framework of UN Peace Maintenance", *EJIL* 11 (2000), 361 et seq. (375) and E. de Wet, *The Chapter VII Powers of the United Nations Security Council*, 2004, 298-304.

Resolution 1244 to be a justification *ex post facto*.[6] In contrast, the view was presented that acts and resolutions taken by the Security Council subsequent to the illegal use of force were themselves illegal as well, because (and insofar as) they were based on the previous unilateral breach of international law by the NATO and on the endorsement of, for example the Military Agreement concluded between KFOR and Yugoslavia, and obtained through the illegal use of force contrary to article 52 Vienna Convention on the Law of Treaties (hereinafter VCLT).[7] In this view the Security Council cannot validate agreements obtained through previous illegal military threats that are void under article 52 VCLT since this was a peremptory norm of international law.[8] Others proclaim that as soon as the UN takes action after an unauthorised use of force in order to restore peace and security the Security Council is then obliged to *ex post facto* to authorise the previous unilateral intervention in conformity with the requirements of good faith. The UN would act in bad faith if it profited from illegally gained advantages and by that perpetuated the illegally created situation.[9]

The United States and the United Kingdom led invasion in Iraq in 2003 and the steps taken thereafter reinforced a discussion about the legal limits of the powers of the Security Council and the ways how to lawfully restore peace after a unilateral use of force. It was debated how the Security Council could deal with an international *status quo* resulting from previous illegal force, in particular whether the Council could take a situation resulting from illegal force as a starting point for an international crisis solution mandated (or contributed to) by the UN. For, this could mean building peace on prior unlawful force thus endorsing the consequences of illegal intervention. The Security Council resolutions on Iraq are subject to very critical consideration.[10] This time at least there seems to be consent that the Security Council did not retro-

---

6   Gowlland-Debbas, see note 5; E. Milano, "Security Council Action in the Balkans: Reviewing the Legality of Kosovo's Territorial Status", *EJIL* 14 (2003), 999 et seq. (1013); A. Orakhelashvili, "The Impact of Peremptory Norms on the Interpretation and Application of UN Security Council Resolutions", *EJIL* 16 (2005), 59 et seq. (75).
7   Milano, see note 6, 1015-1018.; see also Gowlland-Debbas, see note 5, 376.
8   Orakhelashvili, see note 6, 74.
9   C. Walter, *Vereinte Nationen und Regionalorganisationen*, 1996, 308.
10 See e.g. A. Constantinides, *An Overview of Legal Restraints on Security Council Chapter VII Action with a Focus on Post-Conflict Iraq* <http://www.esil-sedi.eu/english/pdf/Constantinides.PDF>.

actively validate the use of force by the United States and its allies.[11] But beyond that, everything appears to be contested as regards the treatment of the crisis by the Security Council.

The starting point for any attempt to analyse the Security Council powers is the quite general type of wording of the articles contained in Chapter VII of the UN Charter equipping the Security Council with extensive and comprehensive powers and bestowing it with apparently unlimited discretion. According to Article 39, the Security Council shall *determine*, shall make recommendations, or *decide* the measures to be taken. The Security Council may *decide* about certain measures under Article 41, and if *it considers* them inadequate *it* may *take such action as* may be *necessary to maintain or restore international peace and security* (Article 42). Indeed, the powers of the Security Council to deal with international conflicts are constitutive and almost exclusive (as it has the primary responsibility for the maintenance of peace and security according to Article 24 UN Charter and the sole enforcement power under Chapter VII) so that the Security Council must enjoy the capability and the power to decide on the necessary steps for the settlement of a given conflict and on the restoration of international peace and security thereafter, irrespective of the pre-history of that conflict. The powers of the Security Council have to be interpreted against the need for effective protection of basic values like international peace. Effectiveness underpins the Charter regime, at least as regards maintenance of peace and security (see the first words of Article 24 UN Charter). The ICJ once affirmatively cited the Secretary-General stating that the Security Council powers were not restricted to those specific grants of authority contained in Chapter VI, VII, VIII and XII, but the Member States conferred on the Security Council powers commensurate with its responsibility for the maintenance of peace and security. The only limitations that were mentioned there were the fundamental principles and purposes found in Chapter I of the Charter.[12] The broad, purpose-oriented interpretation of the Security Council Chapter VII powers is endorsed by the more or less undisputed power of the Security Council to authorise the use of force by Member States although

---

[11] See i.a. A. Orakhelashvili, "The Post-War Settlement in Iraq: The UN Security Council Resolution 1483 (2003) and General International Law", *Journal of Conflict & Security Law* 8 (2003), 307 et seq. (310); Stahn, see note 5, 105, fn. 94.

[12] Legal Consequences for States of the Continued Presence of South Africa in Namibia (Namibia Case), ICJ Reports 1971, 16 et seq. (para. 110).

the precise legal basis for this in the Charter is not clear.[13] Another hint is the fact that the Security Council may reconstruct and rebuild peace not in conformity with the view of the people or nations assisted by the United Nations.[14] A broad interpretation is further evidenced by the practice of the Security Council to subsume internal situations under Article 39 UN Charter.[15] When a state commits cruelties in such a way as to deny the fundamental human rights of its nationals and to shock the conscience of mankind, the situation ceases to be of sole concern to that state.[16] For this reason, it cannot be argued that the Security Council would not enjoy powers in case of purely internal conflicts.

An important corollary of the constitutive character of the UN Security Council powers is the irrelevance of the unlawfulness of previous actions of other actors. The requirements of the efficient restoration of international peace and security in conformity with Article 39 UN Charter might – at first sight – even contradict the requirements of the

---

[13] The legal basis for an authorisation can be seen either in implied powers or can be attributed to Arts 42, 48 UN Charter. For a detailed analysis see de Wet, see note 5, 260 et seq.; D. Sarooshi, *The United Nations and the Development of Collective Security*, 2000; see also J.A. Frowein/ N. Krisch, in: B. Simma et al (eds), *The Charter of the United Nations. A Commentary. Vol. I*, 2nd edition 2002, Article 42 Mn. 20; J. Gardam, "Legal Restraints on Security Council Military Enforcement Action", *Mich. J. Int'l L.* 17 (1996), 285 et seq. (287 et seq.); V. Gowlland-Debbas, *Collective Responses to Illegal Acts in International Law*, 1990, 416 et seq. (421 et seq.); C. Gray, "From Unity to Polarization: International Law and the Use of Force against Iraq", *EJIL* 13 (2002), 1 et seq. (3). Nowadays the power to authorise is so widely accepted that it is taken for granted, see e.g. J. Stromseth/ D. Wippman/ R. Brooks, *Can Might Make Rights? Building the Rule of Law After Military Interventions*, 2006, 22.

[14] See C. Chinkin, "The state that acts alone: bully, good Samaritan or iconoclast?", *EJIL* 11 (2000), 31 et seq. (39).

[15] Examples for Security Council resolutions that regarded a purely internal crisis as a threat to peace and security in the sense of Article 39 and by which the UN Security Council authorised use of force are S/RES/794 (1992) of 3 December 1992 on Somalia, S/RES/940 (1994) of 31 July 1994 on Haiti, S/RES/929 (1994) of 22 June 1994 on Rwanda and S/RES/1264 (1999) of 15 September 1999 on East Timor. For more detail see C. Gray, see note 13, 1 et seq. (3 et seq.) and I. Österdahl, "The Exception as the Rule: Lawmaking on Force and Human Rights by the UN Security Council", *Journal of Conflict & Security Law* 10 (2005), 1 et seq. (2 et seq.).

[16] R. Jennings/ A. Watts, *Oppenheim's International Law, Volume I*, 9th edition 1992, 333.

legality or even of the legitimacy of the resolve of a threat or breach of peace, security or other basic values. Irrespective of the question as to whether the Security Council can retroactively justify any unilateral illegal act or its consequences (a power which is rejected by some writers),[17] the fact that the Security Council takes advantage of previous illegal acts and promotes their success does not amount to a legal *obligation* to authorise *ex post facto* the unilateral actions because the Security Council in exercising its duties has to respond to the crisis and to the situation created by the unilateral use of force in some way. The Security Council is faced with a *fait accompli* and, as a result, it is forced to make the best of this situation which developed without its consent or involvement.[18] In such a case the Security Council cannot be reproached for building upon the military advantages reached by previous unilateral illegal acts in its response to those acts and to the given circumstances of the respective crisis. The military situation resulting from the unilateral recourse to force is not more than a mere fact resulting in a new *status quo* that the Security Council has to take into consideration. In no way is there a legal obligation to legalise un-authorised (and therefore illegal) use of force[19] nor can succeeding actions by the Security Council that build upon the situation created by the use of force be seen as an implicit legalisation. The Security Council would contradict the core character of the UN Charter of the prohibition of the unilateral use of force if it generally would legalise *ex post facto* such force. This statement, however, does not exclude that the Security Council may lawfully retroactively legalise unilateral force in particular circumstances or may lawfully build on the situation obtained by illegal force.

The constitutive nature of the Chapter VII powers implies that the Security Council is allowed to deviate from international legal obligations or rights under international customary or treaty law. The notion of enforcement inherently implies the authority of derogation from international law, in particular to infringe on the sovereign rights of the target states (the states where the threat or breach of peace occurs) or to impact on the rights and duties of the UN Member States as long as the

---

[17]   H. Körbs, *Die Friedenssicherung durch die Vereinten Nationen und Regionalorganisationen nach Kapitel VIII*, 1997, 537. Against his position de Wet, see note 5, 296.

[18]   De Wet, see note 5, 297.

[19]   Regarding the non-existence of such obligations for the UN Security Council see i.a. Österdahl, see note 15, 1 et seq. (14).

Security Council acts for the maintenance and restoration of international peace and security as required by Article 39 UN Charter.

This task of the UN Security Council referring to the Charter principles themselves is the ultimate legal constraint for the Security Council in exercising its discretionary powers. This does not mean that the Security Council is above the law. But the Security Council acts under the authority of the UN law which is more than a common international treaty (as it is the nucleus of a constitutionalisation of an international community of states). It is the very international law enshrined in the Charter that allows the Security Council to surrender any legal obligation to the core aim of maintaining and restoring peace.[20] In Kelsen's words, "The Council may create new law for the concrete case".[21] This statement concisely describes the essence of the constitutive character of the Chapter VII powers. Therefore, authorisations by the Security Council preclude the illegality of acts taken in conformity with the mandate and suspend rules of contemporary international customary law and treaty obligations (apart from peremptory norms and limitations contained in the Charter itself).[22] An argument in favour of the power of the Security Council to affect the rights and positions of the states concerned can also be drawn from Article 40 UN Charter which clarifies that provisional measures taken before enforcement measures according to Arts 41 or 42 "shall be without prejudice to the rights, claims, or positions of the parties concerned". *E contrario* this means that enforcement measures will have an impact on the rights and positions. The priority of UN law and, accordingly, of Security Council measures under Chapter VII over other obligations of international law is also expressed in Article 103 UN Charter; the priority of UN law is not limited to treaty obligations[23] and applies also to authorisations by

---

[20] See T.D. Gill, "Legal and Some Political Limitations on the Power of the UN Security Council to Exercise Its Enforcement Powers Under the Chapter VII of the Charter", *NYIL* 26 (1995), 33 et seq. (62 et seq.); V. Gowlland-Debbas, "Security Council Enforcement Action and Issues of State Responsibility", *ICLQ* 43 (1994), 55 et seq. (78); Orakhelashvili, see note 6, 61. See also ICJ Reports 1971, see note 12, 16 et seq. (paras 112 et seq.)

[21] H. Kelsen, *The Law of the United Nations*, 1951, 295.

[22] Gowlland-Debbas, see note 5, 370. It is not contested that states can contract out of customary law.

[23] See R. Bernhardt, in: B. Simma et al. (eds), *The Charter of the United Nations. A Commentary. Vol. II*, 2nd edition 2002, Article 103 Mn. 21.

the Security Council.[24] As these considerations are true for authorisations, they must be even more true for actions of the Security Council
itself. This may, in peculiar circumstances, also include the endorsement
of previous illegal actions like the unilateral use of military force by certain states or of agreements obtained by unlawful military threats. For,
it would be formal to deny the validating effect solely on the ground
that the Security Council resolution was taken in arrears. Admittedly,
prior authorisation and retrospective validations are different situations.
What is decisive, however, is for the Security Council to affirm that the
unilateral act is to be in accordance with the ends of the United Nations. Whether this happens in advance or in arrears, does not appear to
make such fundamental difference.[25] The retroactive validation also
does not contradict peremptory norms[26] since the peremptory prohibition of the use of force only obliges states, not the United Nations as an
organisation when acting under Chapter VII (see the wording of Article
2 (4) UN Charter) acknowledging and adopting the use of force in
question as its own (see *mutatis mutandis* article 11 of the Rules on
State Responsibility).[27] Furthermore, rules like article 52 VCLT which
declare void coercively imposed treaties, do not apply in case of force in
accordance with the Charter (which is the case in situations of retroactive authorisation, see the wording of article 52). Furthermore, and decisive in cases which lack *ex-post* authorisation, here rules like article 52
VCLT appear not to be applicable to Chapter VII measures due to article 75 VCLT or article 76 of the Vienna Convention on the Law of
Treaties between States and International Organizations or between International Organizations.[28] The sanction of nullity does not apply to a
treaty imposed by the United Nations in the course of enforcement ac-

---

[24] R. Kolb, "Does Article 103 of the Charter of the United Nations Apply
      only to Decisions or also to Authorizations Adopted by the Security
      Council?", *ZaöRV* 64 (2004), 21 et seq.
[25] *Contra* Orakhelashvili, see note 6, 75.
[26] *Contra* Milano, see note 6, 1015-1018; Orakhelashvili, see note 6, 74 with
      further references.
[27] Responsibility of States for Internationally Wrongful Acts, A/RES/56/83
      of 12 December 2001.
[28] Article 75 VCLT only refers to the aggressor state and to treaty obligations
      arising for the aggressor state in consequence of UN measures. But this
      rule must also refer to the other state party to such treaty as otherwise the
      effect of Article 75 was incomplete and unbalanced and would restrain the
      powers of the UN Security Council under Chapter VII.

tion;[29] and this must also apply in case a void treaty is confirmed by succeeding Security Council resolutions under Chapter VII. The validity of such agreement derives from the constitutive nature of the powers of the Security Council and does not depend on the retroactive validation of the previous illegal unilateral use of force which led to the treaty. Although pure recommendations are said not to be governed by Article 25 UN Charter as they are not mandatory in nature, they also have the effect of rendering unlawful acts lawful.[30]

Allowing the Security Council to derogate from international law does not contradict the explicit affirmation of principles of justice and international law in Article 1 (1) UN Charter. In contrast, the broad, purpose- and effectiveness-oriented interpretation of the powers of the Security Council under Chapter VII is confirmed when looking at Article 1 (1) and the drafting history thereto. According to Article 1 (1) the UN may, in order to maintain peace and security, take effective collective measures and use peaceful means to adjust or settle disputes. The requirement of conformity with principles of justice and international law is mentioned only in the context of the peaceful settlement of disputes, not in the context of collective measures thus confirming the powers of the Security Council acting under Chapter VII to derogate from international law. The requirement of conformity with justice and international law principles was inserted intentionally in order to narrow the discretionary powers of the organs concerned with the peaceful settlement of disputes and situations which might lead to a breach of peace[31] which means that these are situations which have not yet reached the stage necessary for the applicability of Chapter VII enforcement powers. In contrast, the political considerations of the United Nations when adopting collective enforcement measures under Chapter VII were not limited. The Security Council should have the power to end hostilities (almost) without considering issues of law since

---

[29] M.H. Mendelsohn/ S.C. Hulton, "The Iraq-Kuwait Boundary", *BYIL* 64 (1993), 135 et seq. (149 et seq.). See also R.G. Steinhardt, "The Potsdam Accord – Ex Nihilo Nihil Fit?", *Friedenswarte* 72 (1997), 29 et seq. (44) who points to the fact that "in the era of the UN Charter ... there will inevitably be ambivalence about the legality of peace treaties concluding with a losing party whose battlefield fortunes leave it no room to negotiate."

[30] Gowlland-Debbas, see note 5, 371; contra J.E.S. Fawcett, "Security Council Resolutions on Rhodesia", *BYIL* 41 (1965-1966), 103 et seq. (121).

[31] R. Wolfrum, in: B. Simma et al. (eds), *The Charter of the United Nations. A Commentary. Vol. I*, 2nd edition 2002, Article 1 Mn. 18.

the process of defining justice would entail delays.[32] The hands of the Security Council should not be tied. It should enjoy maximum flexibility in the application of collective enforcement measures when maintaining or restoring peace.[33] For this reason, there was agreement at the San Francisco Conference not to accept any definition of the terms "any threat to the peace, breach of the peace or act of aggression" since general definitions might be applicable in one case but not in another.[34]

The capability to deviate from international law implies that the Security Council may not order the restoration of the *status quo ante* which usually is the *status quo iuris*. The Security Council is neither obliged nor confined to order the restoration of the *status quo ante*. The Security Council's deliberations on the useful and necessary means and steps to overcome an international crisis may and usually will take into consideration the *status quo ante*. Primarily, however, the Security Council is to be led by its concern about restoration or maintenance of peace and security. The restoration of the *status quo ante* might be destructive in that context and not serve the objective of peace restoration, in particular, if the former *status quo* caused the crisis. The goal of Security Council actions then must be a more secure state of affairs.[35] For this reason, the unlawfulness of a previous unilateral action does not

---

[32]   Wolfrum, see note 31, Article 1 Mn. 19. See the discussion in *Documents of the United Nations Conference on International Organization, Vol. VI*, reprint 1998, 12 et seq., in particular 23-33.

[33]   Gill, see note 20, 65 et seq.; de Wet, see note 5, 186 points to a discussion in the committee on the Security Council at San Francisco where a Norwegian proposal on limiting the enforcement powers of the Security Council was dropped because of the reference to justice and international law in Article 1 (1) which was seen to oblige also the Security Council. This discussion, however, was far from being conclusive, see D. Akande, "The International Court of Justice and the Security Council: Is there Room for Judicial Control of Decisions of the Political Organs of the United Nations?", *ICLQ* 46 (1997), 309 et seq. (320). Therefore, one must be careful in deriving conclusions from this regarding accepted limits for Security Council enforcement powers. This discussion can only be understood as reflecting unity that even enforcement measures are not above basic demands of international law.

[34]   See Gowlland-Debbas, see note 13, 452.

[35]   See also B. Faßbender, "Uncertain Steps into a Post-Cold War World: The Role and Functioning of the UN Security Council after a Decade of Measures against Iraq", *EJIL* 13 (2002), 273 et seq. (296 et seq.); B. Orend, "Justice after War", *Ethics & International Affairs* 16 (2002) 43 et seq. (45); M. Walzer, *Just and Unjust Wars*, 3rd edition 2000, 119.

and cannot infect all measures subsequently taken by the Security Council, even if those steps do not call for a restoration of the *status quo ante* but seek to resolve the conflict in a way that could endorse the unilateral act, and might even validate it retrospectively building a solution to the crisis upon the situation created by the unilateral act.

The fact that the discretion of the Security Council is not restricted to the restoration of the *status quo ante* is confirmed by UN Security Council practice. Since the beginning of the UN, the Security Council almost always limited its reactions to unlawful use of force to a call for ceasefires and restoration of peace and in several cases avoided condemnation of aggressive states and the imputation of responsibility.[36] The cases are very rare in which the Security Council ordered (even forceful) restoration of the *status quo ante*. The Security Council action against Iraq after Iraq tried to annex Kuwait is almost the only example of a forceful restoration of the *status quo ante*.[37] This practice endorses that the restoration of peace and security does not necessarily presuppose the restoration of the *status quo ante*.

In sum, it can be stated that the Chapter VII powers are constitutive in nature. In order to reach their vital objective effectively, their discharge is primarily guided by their aim of peace restoration or maintenance.

---

[36] Gowlland-Debbas, see note 13, 468 et seq.; see also S. Ratner, "Foreign Occupation and International Territorial Administration: The Challenges of Convergence", *EJIL* 16 (2005), 695 et seq. (700).

[37] The first resolution following the attack by Iraq, S/RES/660 (1990) of 2 August 1990, demanded Iraq to withdraw immediately all forces to the positions in which they were located before the conflict. Resolution S/RES/678 (1990) of 29 November 1990 then authorised to use all necessary means to reaffirm Resolution 660 and to implement this and the subsequent Security Council resolutions. The controversy over the question whether Resolution 678 mandated an enforcement action under Chapter VII or endorsed collective self-defence shall be left aside here. Other examples of Security Council resolutions ordering the restoration of the *status quo ante* refer to the status of Jerusalem and to the Syrian Golan Heights, see S/RES/476 (1980) of 30 June 1980 and S/RES/497 (1981) of 17 December 1981. An example for conflict solutions that did not return to the *status quo ante* are the UN resolutions on Southern Rhodesia, cf. Gowlland-Debbas, see note 13, 472.

b. Security Council Functions and the Changing Notion of Peace

Since the purpose of the Chapter VII powers to restore international peace and security is of primary importance for their interpretation and since the exercise of these powers is released by unilateral, illegal recourse to force or other modes of breaching peace, the notion and concept of peace is crucial. It inevitably influences the scope of the powers of the Security Council. The more the concept of peace expanded beyond the mere absence of force[38] and embraced broader concepts like a stable social and public order allowing people to act in self-determination, the broader the powers of the Security Council have to be developed. Therefore, the determination of the notion of peace is decisive for the Security Council and its powers. In order to enable the Security Council to exercise its powers in a useful way that corresponds to the very *raison d'être* (to maintain and restore peace and security), the Security Council must be empowered to consider the legal, social and economic prerequisites of sustainability of peace and security. There is a difference between merely stopping war and making peace.[39] Restoring international peace and security whose universal maintenance is the core aim of the United Nations requires the creation of a durable, stable and sustainable conflict free situation after war.

The last decades witnessed a development in which, due to the rising number and changing character of armed conflicts between states and even within states and between states and non-state actors, the international community increasingly became aware of the prerequisites of peace in a society and the different conditions of peace under peculiar circumstances.[40] The non-military sources of instability came within the ambit of the Security Council's competences. In the years since 1990 the Security Council increasingly employed its powers under Chapter VII in internal conflicts, humanitarian crises[41] or new threats like ter-

---

[38]   As was the definition of peace by Kelsen, see note 21, 19.

[39]   See W.M. Reisman, "Stopping War and Making Peace: Reflections on the Ideology and Practice of Conflict Termination in Contemporary World Politics", *Tul. J. Int'l & Comp. L.* 16 (1998), 5 et seq. (15-29).

[40]   See the former Secretary-General Boutros Boutros-Ghali's Report "An Agenda for Peace, Preventive Diplomacy, Peacemaking and Peace-Keeping", Doc. A/47/277-S/24111 of 17 June 1992, 22 where he identifies the need to include comprehensive efforts to support structures that consolidate peace and advance a sense of confidence and well-being.

[41]   Already at the San Francisco Conference in 1945, there was awareness that sincere human rights violation could amount to a threat to peace, actually

rorism thus determining such situations to be threats to international peace which implies a teleological, dynamic understanding of "international peace" requiring for example respect for basic human rights, far beyond the mere absence of armed hostilities.[42] This also indicates a change in the notion of the type of peace which has to be restored after armed hostilities. Therefore, the Security Council must be in a position to take account of different requirements in order to be able to exercise its powers of peace restoration effectively. Even a broad notion of peace and a purpose-oriented interpretation of the powers of the Security Council, however, cannot cover up the prerequisites of the Security Council powers under Chapter VII as contained in Article 39 UN Charter.

A broad notion of peace can only direct the exercise of the Security Council powers in the restoration of peace if a situation amounts to a crisis that has the potential to spark international armed hostilities in the short or medium term.[43] For a situation to be regarded as a threat to peace requires at least some violence. The wording and the purpose of the Security Council powers prohibit refraining from the requirement of a link between a threat to peace and a danger of armed hostilities. Otherwise, the Security Council would turn from being a peace enforcer to a law enforcer.[44] A broad understanding of the Security Council Chapter VII powers includes the capacity of the Council to deal with long term, structural causes of threats to peace in order to restore peace in a given situation once the scope of application of its powers is opened.

In advocating a purpose-oriented interpretation of the Security Council powers by recourse to a broad notion of peace, the post-

---

not surprising after the Holocaust. See Stromseth/ Wippman/ Brooks, see note 13, 24, fn. 11.

[42] See S.R. Ratner, "The Security Council and International Law", in: Malone, see note 3, 595-598.

[43] de Wet, see note 5, 139 et seq.

[44] Admittedly, the practice of the Security Council shows that it uses its Chapter VII powers also for law enforcement purposes (see for example Gowlland-Debbas, see note 13, 471 et seq.; Ratner, see note 42, 601). This, however, must not be the sole objective of a Security Council action under Chapter VII. The Security Council is not hindered to consider, *inter alia*, issues of law enforcement when determining a situation to be a threat to peace. Regarding the double strategy of the Security Council when acting under Chapter VII see in more detail de Wet, see note 5, 150 et seq.

conflict settlement function of the Security Council[45] becomes important. This function of the Security Council is highlighted by measures
taken by the Security Council in order to create the conditions for lasting and steadfast peace in its resolutions providing for disarmament,[46]
establishing *ad hoc* criminal tribunals,[47] compensation commissions[48]
and UN administrations.[49] Provisional administration by the United
Nations was in fact contemplated in the drafting of the UN Charter. A
proposal to accordingly amend the Chapter VII powers was withdrawn
out of a concern that such specific inclusion would prepare ground for
an argument of implicit exclusion of other powers not listed.[50]

In its post-conflict settlement function, the Security Council deals
with issues of justice and law after armed hostilities have been terminated. Such issues are part of peace restoration. The objections to a
positive notion of peace[51] go beyond what is necessary to keep the con-
tour of the UN Charter and to determine definable limits of the Security Council powers. Attributing positive contents to the term peace in

---

[45]   Regarding the "post-conflict settlement function" of the UN Security
       Council see Stahn, see note 5, 94, 111. On peacebuilding generally see J.
       Galtung, "Three Approaches to Peace: Peacekeeping, Peacemaking and
       Peacebuilding", id. (ed.), *Essays in Peace Research. Vol. II: Peace, War and
       Defence*, 1976, 282; F.O. Hampson, *Nurturing Peace: Why Peace Settle-
       ments Succeed or Fail*, 1996; P.R. Pillar, *Negotiating Peace: War Termina-
       tion as a Bargaining Process*, 1983; J. Taylor, *How Wars End*, 1985. For the
       interplay between a broad description of peace and new roles for the Secu-
       rity Council see also Faßbender, see note 35, 296 et seq.

[46]   See with respect to the Iraq Resolution S/RES/687 (1991) of 3 April 1991.

[47]   S/RES/827 (1993) of 25 May 1993 and S/RES/955 (1994) of 8 November
       1994 with respect to Former Yugoslavia and Rwanda.

[48]   S/RES/687 (1991) of 3 April 1991. For doubts regarding the legality of the
       exercise of the Security Council powers insofar due to the lack of inde-
       pendence of the commission, shortcomings in the equality of arms and in
       the right to be heard cf. de Wet, see note 5, 359-362.

[49]   S/RES/1037 (1996) of 15 January 1996, S/RES/1244 (1999) of 10 June 1999,
       S/RES/1272 (1999) of 25 October 1999 and S/RES/1410 (2002) of 17 May
       2002 with respect to Eastern Slavonia, Kosovo and East Timor. For more
       detail see de Wet, see note 5, 311 et seq. Cf. also R. Wolfrum, "International
       Administration in Post-Conflict Situations by the United Nations and
       Other International Actors", *Max Planck UNYB* 9 (2005) 649 et seq. (668-
       672).

[50]   S. Chesterman, *You the People. The UN, Transitional Administration, and
       State Building*, 2004, 50.

[51]   Raised e.g. by de Wet, see note 5, 140, 144.

Chapter VII does not mean that the discretion of the Security Council becomes unlimited or that one would de-link the threat to peace from the threat of an outbreak of an international armed conflict.[52] Peace means more than silence of weapons, but silence of weapons is a necessary requirement for peace so that a threat to peace in the sense of Article 39 UN Charter requires a situation charged with the potential of an outbreak of an international armed conflict. The latter situation is a necessary condition for a threat to peace in the sense of Article 39, but its termination is not a sufficient object of peace restoration. Alternatively, one could differentiate the meaning of peace in Article 39 first part from that in Article 1 (1), Article 39 second part and Article 42 UN Charter.

Both the objective of bringing weapons to silence and of restoring sustainable peace[53] by building the necessary conditions, are therefore, embraced by the Chapter VII powers. The duty of the Security Council under Chapter VII to restore peace and security engenders a twofold function for the Security Council: first, a peace enforcing function which ends the military phase of armed conflicts, and then, second, a peace and stability building and organising function which directs reconstruction and reconciliation.[54] Both functions are addressed by the enforcement powers of the Security Council. They belong together and are closely inter-related. Military interventions require a post-intervention strategy.[55] The practice of the Security Council in the 1990s evidences the direct link between military intervention and subsequent reconstruction of the targeted state, considering, in particular, the international transitional administrations. Thus, a broad concept of peace not only favours a broad reading of the Security Council powers but also allows for a new understanding of the role of the Security Council after the silence of weapons has been restored. The Security Council has the task to create the conditions for lasting peace and security by altering the basic attitudes, aims or expectations of the belligerents, in particular in case of ethnically, culturally or economically motivated armed conflicts where the restoration of the *status quo ante* cannot solve the basic problems that prompted the conflict, not to mention additional problems and concerns caused by the violence.

---

[52] As implied by de Wet, see note 5, 155.
[53] This term describes one of the objectives of UN peace operations.
[54] Regarding the latter Faßbender, see note 35, 279 et seq.
[55] See Chesterman, see note 50, 246.

The issues to be tackled are diverse and comprehensive, including *inter alia* and in different configurations, disarmament, prosecution and punishment of war criminals, restoration of the internal public order and legal security, repatriation of refugees, protection of human rights, economic and infrastructure reconstruction, monitoring elections and strengthening representative governmental institutions and processes of political participation. Thus, the changing notion of peace is even capable of influencing the responses of the Security Council to prior illegal acts and its determination of the necessary steps for peace enforcing measures given the subsequent task of building stable peace.

2. The Role of the Security Council, in Particular with Respect to Unilateral Force

Taken literally, unilateralism in the use of military force[56] is the opposite of common action which in contemporary international law means collective action by the UN Security Council or under its authorisation. Nevertheless one can differentiate between unilateral actions that pursue egoistic, even hegemonic motives and those that follow a common goal or value. Additionally, the settings under which unilateral acts may be taken can be different as regards the number of partaking or contributing states[57] and their motives, the reaction or even involvement of the directly affected "target" states and of other non-partakers be it acceptance or denial or something in-between, and the pre-history of a conflict and of (unilateral or collective) attempts to resolve it. Irrespec-

---

[56] On the term "unilateralism" see in more detail Dupuy, see note 1, 19 et seq. (20). Unilateral acts can be divided into acts intending or having legal meaning, i.e. acts by which a state unilaterally expresses consent to create a legal obligation, on the one hand, and unilateral real actions on the other hand, by which a state does not want to create legal obligations but unilaterally seeks to change a situation though this might cause legal consequences (like state responsibility). Regarding the former see A. Weingerl, "Definition of Unilateral Acts of States" under <http://www.esil-sedi.eu/english/pdf/Weingerl.PDF>. They are currently considered by the ILC.

[57] In the context of the NATO Kosovo intervention and its contested legitimacy the fact was emphasised that three of the five permanent members of the Security Council were involved in the recourse to force, see P. Hilpold, "Humanitarian Intervention: Is there a Need for a Legal Reappraisal?", *EJIL* 12 (2001), 437 et seq. (448 et seq.) with further references.

tive of such factual discrepancies, one feature common to unilateral actions as understood here is the illegality of the unilateral action. Even unilateral acts that sincerely proclaim rather than merely pretend to enforce common values and common attempts of conflict resolution still fail to conform to the rules on the use of force laid down in international law, in particular the prohibition on the use of force in the UN Charter.

a. Unilateral Action and Community Objectives

In legal literature commentators have claimed that the legal assessment of the legitimacy, if not legality of the unilateral use of force could be influenced by its circumstances, motives and objectives and that there could be a category of unilateral illegal acts that in exceptional circumstances could be seen as lawful or at least acceptable thus not entailing legal sanctions.[58] From this perspective, there is a clear difference between a hegemonic unilateralism and a unilateral pursuit of common values of the international community (as expressed by Security Council resolutions and in line with them).[59] As convincing as such deliberations might appear at first sight, the problem remains that these or other factual differences do not alter the legal appraisal of the action. A state or a group of states that unilaterally pursues common values (previously defined by the Security Council) does not act differently to a hegemon that intentionally breaches rules of international law for its own profit. In both situations the unilateral act fails to follow the rule of law on the use of force and this must be decisive if the UN Charter and its basic values shall be seen as a constitutionalisation of an international community of states. The idea of legitimacy cannot overrule the given set of rules of international law. First and foremost, legitimacy in international law follows from rule-obedience, not from motives since the latter – being internal facts – are hardly controllable from outside. Even if the unilateral act might breach the law only in a formal sense (as the state or group of states used force without prior authorisation of the UN Security Council but [maybe] in material accordance with the aims of the UN and in line with the ends of the resolutions of the Security Council), it is still a breach of law because at least the means used to

---

58 See for example T. Farer, "A Paradigm of Legitimate Intervention" in: L. Fisler Damrosch (ed.), *Enforcing Restraint: Collective Intervention in Internal Conflicts*, 1993, 317 et seq. (324 et seq.); Stahn, see note 5, 104.
59 See Gowlland-Debbas, see note 5, 378 who nevertheless stresses that resort to force without express authorisation is prohibited.

pursue the common objectives are not in accordance with international law. The means only were in accordance with the resolutions if the Security Council had approved the use of force for attaining those aims. If it did not do so, the means used by the unilateral actor are beyond those accepted by the Council. Material and formal aspects of law cannot be divided. They belong inseparably together at least as long as core rules (like the prohibition of the use of force) are concerned. The formal rule of prior authorisation by the Security Council to use force serves a material objective. It ensures that the resolutions of the Security Council or the objectives of the United Nations are not misunderstood, misinterpreted or misused. Though the ends of an illegal unilateral act may be in line with community objectives and Security Council resolutions, the means are not.

One objection that might be raised here is that the legal assessment of actions against the background of certain rules is influenced by the understanding and interpretation of those rules shared among the nations (see article 31 (3) VCLT).[60] Accordingly, it may make a difference if an action of a state contradicts the wording of a norm but corresponds to the sense and spirit of the norm as interpreted by the international community. But still the decisive question is: who is the international community, in particular who is allowed to speak on its behalf and who defines the prevailing and therefore decisive legal opinion? In the UN system of conflict resolution, the international community of UN Member States established organs. Therefore, as the primary responsibility for the maintenance of international peace and security (Article 24 UN Charter) and the sole responsibility for the use of coercive force (outside self-defence) rest with the Security Council, the latter's assessment of means and ends is decisive. In case of its paralysis, there might be a residuary power of the General Assembly (see Arts 10, 12 UN Charter),[61] but not of single states or regional organisations to pursue common values. Therefore, even if a representative group of states understands the unilateral act not to be illegal or illegitimate, this is not decisive for the legal appraisal of the illegal act or of its consequences under the UN Charter. Allowing unilateral acts because of their reference to UN aims and to Security Council resolutions does not guarantee that common values are aimed at and enforced. Beyond

---

[60]   On the relevance of subsequent practice for Charter interpretation see G. Ress, in: B. Simma et al. (eds.), *The Charter of the United Nations. A Commentary. Vol. I*, 2nd edition 2002, Interpretation Mn. 27 et seq.

[61]   See also below under b.

the quite formal problem of misinterpreting and misunderstanding Security Council resolutions on a given conflict (and beyond the problem of misusing UN objectives and basic values of the international community in order to attain other aims),[62] the fundamental substantive problem remains: if the Security Council did not authorise the use of coercive force to solve a certain dispute or conflict, the unilateral use of force does not correspond to the common values or objectives of the international community. In exercising its determination of common objectives in a given conflict and its discretion to choose the means of response[63] the Security Council did not include the use of force. The common objectives of the international community as defined in the UN Charter and the means and instruments to implement and enforce them are inseparably interlinked because it is the Security Council that defines which conflict endangers international peace and security and which measures have to be taken in order to remedy a situation threatening world peace and security. The reasons why the Security Council did or could not find unanimity for an authorisation of the use of force are not decisive. Irrespective of why the Security Council did not authorise use of force (either because of an imminent veto of a permanent member or because there was a common understanding of all or of a broad majority of Security Council members that the use of force would not resolve the conflict), the fact remains that the responsible organ of the international community acting in accordance with the relevant rules as set down in the UN Charter did not authorise use of force. And that is what matters. In such a situation one cannot undermine a permanent member's right to veto by accusing this member of using it illegitimately. Permanent members enjoy their right to veto not for their

---

[62] In addition to substantive criteria of legitimacy (see e.g. Farer, see note 58, 327) there have been many proposals to introduce procedural safeguards in order to take care that common values are not misused or misapplied by states acting unilaterally, like e.g. majority decisions, transparent discourses, presentation of evidence of severe breaches of international law to the public or at least in the Security Council, contribution of a representative number of states, provision of collectiveness by the use of regional organisations, objectivity of actors and involvement of targeted states. See A. Cassese, "'Ex Iniuria Ius Oritur': Are We Moving Towards International Legitimation of Forcible Humanitarian Countermeasures in the World Community?", *EJIL* 10 (1999), 23; Hilpold, see note 57, 450, 455 et seq.; Stahn, see note 5, 103.

[63] See V. Gowlland-Debbas, "The Functions of the UN Security Council in the International Legal System", in: M. Byers (ed.), *The Role of Law in International Politics*, 2000, 277 et seq. (287).

own purposes. In using their powers the members are supposed to act in the interest of the United Nations and the community of states.[64] Even if a permanent member could misuse the veto power for selfish aims, the veto cannot be disregarded, for the sole reason not to enable misuse of (unilateral) force by others. Still it is the UN Security Council member's assessment to decide which response to a particular crisis is in the interest of the community of states.[65]

Imparting a right to unilateral action on behalf of the international community to states or regional security organisations with the aim to forcefully enforce either community values expressed in the UN Charter or at least the alleged intention of Security Council resolutions would collide with this competence. The determination of reasons for enforcement actions is a centralised decision allocated to the Security Council.[66] Over-stepping its resolutions and powers by using unauthorised force does not amount to a pursuit of community objectives. The respect for the definition of community interests by the Security Council requires strict obedience to its resolutions and its implementation of UN objectives and relates both to the means and ends. The second guess of a group of states of what the United Nations objectives require in a crisis is irrelevant as the competence of legal appraisal of a crisis in the light of the UN objectives is vested in the United Nations and in particular in the Security Council as far as use of force is concerned.[67] If it were different, the whole UN system of collective security would become irrelevant.

---

[64] The need for reform of the Security Council might have its core objective in the issue how to avoid misuse of the UN system by permanent members of the Security Council (regarding this suspicion see Gray, see note 13, 8) and to enhance collective action. Safeguards in this context could be furthering transparency and accountability of Security Council decisions making or a workable agreement between the permanent Security Council members on the appropriate use of their right to veto, cf. R. Butler, "Bewitched, Bothered and Bewildered: Repairing the Security Council", *Foreign Aff.* 78 (1999), 9 et seq.; Chinkin, see note 14, 40 et seq.; Faßbender, see note 35, 288 et seq.

[65] In addition, Article 53 (1) UN Charter explicitly requires Security Council authorisation in case of an action of regional organisations. There is also no proof for a new customary rule on a right of regional organisations to use force without Security Council authorisation, see C. Gray, *International Law and the Use of Force*, 2nd edition 2004, 321 et seq.

[66] Gowlland-Debbas, see note 13, 451.

[67] See also Gowlland-Debbas, see note 5, 368.

One might object, however, that the impartation of the power to authoritatively define the common will of the Security Council is a mere fiction, because given the absence of agreements under Article 43 UN Charter, the Security Council can and will only apply enforcement measures if there are at least some (permanent) Security Council members who are prepared to act under its mandate. Due to this dependence of the Security Council on the readiness of certain states, in particular the United States,[68] to contribute troops to enforcement measures, it is not the will of the Security Council as an institution but the will of those states that decide whether peace can be restored by using force. In other words: the common will of the international community must correspond to the coinciding interests of the troop contributing states that are prepared to lead, otherwise there will be no Security Council resolution authorising the use of force.[69] Thus, the Security Council appears not to define the common will, but the will of some predominant states. This insight does not pose a problem insofar as the common will of the community of states conforms to the will of the predominant states being part of that community, and *vice versa*. A problem results only if the common will cannot be implemented because it does not correspond to the individual interest of some Security Council members which succeed in hampering effective actions by the Security Council. Then the decisions of the Security Council will not reflect the common will. This objection has its merits. In the end, it cannot convince. First, it assumes the identifiableness of a common will outside the Security Council procedures. The General Assembly may utter a will of the majority of UN members, but in legal terms cannot define a common will on the issue of enforcement actions. The General Assembly lacks competence insofar, at least as long as the Security Council is seized of the matter, under Article 12 UN Charter. If the Security Council members agree to a resolution that tries to solve a conflict without using force, the General Assembly cannot decide otherwise. The proclamation of a common will to the opposite by the General Assembly would amount to a usurpation of authority, thus illegal and irrelevant. Second, the objection previously described is the reverse of the lifted position of the Security Council members, in particular its permanent ones. This position is in conformity with the current UN sys-

---

[68] Security Council practice illustrates that the Security Council will be in a position to exercise its military enforcement function almost only if the United States is prepared to contribute troops.

[69] See S. Chesterman, *Just War or Just Peace*, 2001, 112-218.

tem. One can criticise it; but there is no way of changing it if one wants to find solutions to current problems of unilateralism within the existing UN system. The current functioning of the Security Council indeed has its failures and weaknesses. The right conclusion to draw from this is the need for formal safeguards so that the powers of the Security Council members are not misused or discharged for egoistic motives. Additionally, the possibility that the voting behaviour is motivated by selfish interests applies also for the members of the General Assembly. The above objection can only underline the importance of agreements under Article 43 UN Charter which would, to a certain extent, remedy the problem of the Security Council depending on states willing to contribute troops.

It has been contended that unilateral interventions may crystallise a rule of international law on the lawful unilateral use of force with the objective of putting an end to large-scale atrocities amounting to crimes against humanity or genocide and constituting a threat to the peace.[70] Here again one must not overlook that the resolution of the conflict between the prohibition on the use of force and the basic requirements of humanity is allocated to the UN Security Council in the UN system as it stands today. Otherwise, a group of states could agree among themselves that the (unilateral) use of force was in the proclaimed interest of common objectives without the institutional checks and balances of an international institution like the United Nations. That would seriously undermine the current system of international law. Organs of the international community of the United Nations and not a group of states (even if representative) are called to define and enforce common values and to choose the right means.[71] It is an expression of arrogance if particular states pretend to have the exclusive prerogative to utter and protect the concerns of the community.[72] Additionally, and irrespective of the ambiguous and conflicting nature of UN purposes,[73] a breach of the

---

[70] Cassese, see note 62, 29; see also A. Buchanan, "Reforming the International Law of Humanitarian Intervention", in: J.L. Holzgrefe/ R.O. Keohane (eds), *Humanitarian Intervention*, 2003, 130 et seq. (158 et seq.).

[71] See M. Byers/ S. Chesterman, "Changing the Rules about Rules? Unilateral Humanitarian Intervention and the Future of International Law", in: Holzgrefe/ Keohane, see note 70, 202.

[72] C. Bagnoli, "Humanitarian Intervention as a Perfect Duty. A Kantian Argument", in: T. Nardin/ M.S. Williams (eds), *Humanitarian Intervention*, 2005, 117-148.

[73] See M. Koskenniemi, "The Police in the Temple – Order, Justice and the UN: A Dialectical View", *EJIL* 6 (1995), 327 et seq.

ban on the unilateral use of force cannot be justified by solving international humanitarian problems and by promoting the respect for human rights (see the UN purposes in Article 1 (3) of the Charter) since the principle of the prohibition of the use of force contained in Article 2 (4) UN Charter is an obligation of the UN members explicitly taken in pursuit of the purposes of Article 1 of the UN Charter, as proves the chapeau of Article 2 UN Charter. This introductory part of Article 2 clarifies that there is no room for the alleged contradiction between the ban of the unilateral use of force and the promotion of the respect for human rights. In contrast, the chapeau confirms that it is – *inter alia* – the respect for human rights that requires the prohibition of the use of force given the scourges of war. For this reason, one also can not derive an argument in favour of unilateral use of force from the current practice of the Security Council to use and authorise force in order to remedy internal humanitarian problems in a state.[74] The humanitarian intervention authorised by the Security Council is totally different from a unilateral intervention since it is a collective response. Furthermore, the Security Council acts under Chapter VII, so that its reaction to a humanitarian crisis is motivated and reasoned by its tasks with regard to international peace and security.[75] International custom even affirms that there is need for Security Council authorisation and no room for unilateral use of force. The practice of the Security Council is important for the interpretation of its powers within the Charter framework (and can contribute to the development of general international law) but the discharge of its powers for humanitarian intervention cannot be equated to allowing unilateral intervention for the same purposes, all the more so since, according to Article 1 (1) UN Charter, it is only the maintenance of international peace and security which allows for effective collective measures and not the mere breach of human rights.

One problem remains: a resolution of the Security Council could be ambiguously worded so that some states could interpret it in favour of an authorisation to use force. One could consider whether the disputed content of a Security Council resolution could make way for (unilateral) use of force not intended by the Security Council, by interpreting resolutions in favour of an implicit authorisation. This argument how-

---

[74]   See Österdahl, see note 15, 1 et seq. (17 et seq.) who, however, appears to understand her deliberations only in a political, not in a normative sense.

[75]   This does not preclude that the Security Council also works for other ends like the respect for human rights. The history of international law evidences that peace, security and human rights are interlinked.

ever must face the objection that first of all the Security Council is the authoritative and authentic interpreter of its resolutions,[76] besides an eventual control by the ICJ.[77] This position was also clearly expressed by the UN Secretary-General when emphasising that only the Security Council was competent to determine whether its resolutions on Iraq did provide a lawful basis for actions by states in order to enforce no-fly zones in Iraq.[78] If the Security Council decision-making majority contradicts a certain interpretation of its resolutions, this is binding upon UN Member States.[79] The binding force, not only of the resolutions of the Security Council but also of their interpretation by the Se-

---

[76] M.C. Wood, "The Interpretation of Security Council Resolutions", *Max Planck UNYB* 2 (1998), 73 et seq. (82 et seq.). The PCIJ, Advisory Opinion of 6 December 1923, Series B No. 8, 37 stated that there was an established principle that the right of giving an authoritative interpretation of a rule solely belonged to the body who has the power to modify it. See also ICJ Reports 1971, see note 12, 16 et seq. (53). For the importance of consent (at least of the Security Council majority) over the interpretation of a Security Council resolution with respect to Resolution S/RES/1441 (2002) of 8 November 2002 and the Iraq war see D. McGoldrick, *From 9-11 to the Iraq War 2003*, 2004, 66, 85.

[77] Regarding the ICJ's competence to review Security Council resolutions see M. Bedjaoui, *New World Order and the Security Council: Testing the Legality of Its Acts*, 1994; Gowlland-Debbas, see note 63, 307 et seq.; B. Martenczuk, "The Security Council, the International Court and Judicial Review", *EJIL* 10 (1999), 517 et seq. (525 et seq.); W.M. Reisman, "The Constitutional Crisis in the United Nations", *AJIL* 87 (1993), 83 et seq.; de Wet, see note 5, 25 et seq.

[78] See the statement reported by Gray, see note 13, 9.

[79] This issue must not be confounded with the question as to whether the Security Council is the exclusive interpreter of its own powers. The latter issue is one of limiting the powers of the Security Council (e.g. in the area of law making and in judicial functions) whereas the decisive question here is the limitation of the powers of states. It has rightfully been pointed out by G. Nolte, "The Limits of the Security Council's Powers and its Functions in the International Legal System", in: M. Byers (ed.), *The Role of Law in International Politics*, 2000, 315 et seq. (316) that the ICJ did not declare the Security Council to be the exclusive interpreter of its own powers. There are constitutional limitations to its powers which could be put forward by UN Member States, see Nolte, ibid., 318 et seq. This consideration might lead to a nullification of a measure of the Security Council in case it manifestly overstepped the limits but cannot reason the lawfulness of unilateral actions derived from a proclaimed lack of exercise of Security Council powers.

curity Council, itself follows from Article 25 UN Charter and is in line
with article 31 (4) VCLT. There might, however, arise the problem that
ambiguous wording was used in the drafting of a resolution in order to
avoid a veto of one of the permanent Security Council members covering a lack of true consent. But even in such a case the majority should
be able to account for the intended meaning.[80] The decisive, authoritative character of the Security Council interpretation does not depend
on possible shifts in the way of interpreting Security Council resolutions[81] because, irrespective of a more text-oriented or purposive interpretation of the language of a resolution, the question always remains
whose appreciation (either of terms and wording or of purposes) matters.

Even if one did not ascribe key interpretative legal value to a protest
by the Security Council majority against a peculiar interpretation of a
Security Council resolution, those states acting unilaterally anyway no
longer could refer to common objectives as a justification of their unilateral acts because the use of force cannot be seen as serving common
objectives after the Security Council (majority) opposed such interpretation. If there is no agreement among the majority of Security Council
members about the exact positive meaning of a Security Council resolution, the interpretative task is left to the community of states in accordance with the accepted rules of interpretation, if any, in case of resolutions of international organisations.[82] It is, however, inconceivable that
at least the majority of the Security Council members do not have a
clear-cut answer to the question as to whether a resolution was meant
to authorise use of force all the more since the use of force is the most
eminent issue in international law.[83] What can remain doubtful, how-

---

[80]   An example of such situation is Resolution S/RES/1244 (1999) of 10 June
       1999 to establish an international security presence in Kosovo (KFOR).
       The language of the resolution did not directly authorise use of force in or-
       der to secure support for it from Russia and China. Russia was of the view
       that the resolution did not itself authorise force. See Gray, see note 13, 5.

[81]   As alleged by M. Byers, "The Shifting Foundations of International Law: A
       Decade of Forceful Measures against Iraq", *EJIL* 13 (2002), 21 et seq. (23-
       27).

[82]   On the interpretation of Security Council resolutions see in more detail
       Wood, see note 76, 73 et seq.

[83]   This problem occurred regarding the interpretation of Resolution
       S/RES/1154 (1998) of 2 March 1998 and Resolution S/RES/1205 (1998) of
       5 November 1998 which was referred to by the United States and the
       United Kingdom as providing legal basis for their use of force in response

ever, is the range of application in case of an agreed authorisation of the use of force.[84] But those cases are of relatively minor importance compared to the current problems of unilateralism.

b. Unilateralism and the UN System

The problems of the functioning of the UN Security Council which had already been perceived when the United Nations was established[85] cannot be seen as a confirmation of the possibility for lawful unilateral actions which are deemed to replace UN Security Council actions. The view presented by some commentators that the paralysis of the Security Council restores the freedom of each state to have recourse to unilateralism at least in cases of a material breach of peace and common values[86] must be denied.[87] It would result in a return to the reign of "spheres of influence"[88] and to the overcome doctrine of legitimate war, the incapability of which stood in the centre of the foundations of the United Nations. The proposal at the San Francisco Conference to allow the UN members to act as they may consider necessary in the interests of peace,

---

to the withdrawal by Iraq of cooperation with the UN weapons inspectors. When the Security Council debated about this operation, only Japan shared the view presented by the United States and the United Kingdom whereas the other Security Council members contradicted. See Gray, see note 13, 11 et seq.

[84] Resolution S/RES/678 (1990) of 29 November 1990 e.g. raised doubts as to how far the states could go in their use of force because it authorised the use of force as was necessary to restore the independence of Kuwait. See J.A. Frowein, "Unilateral Interpretation of Security Council Resolutions – A Threat to Collective Security?", in: V. Götz/ P. Selmer/ R. Wolfrum (eds), *Liber amicorum Günther Jaenicke*, 1998, 97 et seq. (101 et seq.). In this context the legal assessment of the United Kingdom and the United States air strikes against Iraq in February 2001 to enforce the no-fly zone brought division amongst the international community; see Gray, see note 13, 9 et seq.

[85] See Kelsen, see note 21, 265 et seq., in particular 269 et seq.; Hilpold, see note 57, 451, 463.

[86] Cf. e.g. A.C. Arend/ R.J. Beck, *International Law and the Use of Force*, 1993, 69; W.M. Reisman, "Coercion and Self-Determination: Construing Charter Article 2 (4)", *AJIL* 78 (1984), 642 et seq.; R. Wedgwood, "NATO's Campaign in Yugoslavia", *AJIL* 93 (1999), 828 et seq. (833).

[87] See L. Henkin, "Kosovo and the Law of 'Humanitarian Intervention'", *AJIL* 93 (1999), 824 et seq.; Hilpold, see note 57, 437 et seq. (451).

[88] Dupuy, see note 1, 29.

right and justice was not accepted.[89] While a UN Charter interpretation must not be static, the necessary teleological and evolutionary approach to the Charter cannot be used to expand the competences of single states but has to be used to face restrictive assertions of Member States' sovereignty.[90] Instead the problems of the proper functioning of the UN system might give an occasion to rethink and reinterpret the relationship between the UN Security Council and the UN General Assembly.[91] Strengthening multilateral facilities to solve conflicts appears to be a better answer to current challenges in international law than creating incentives for unilateral use of force. If there is need for a use of force that contradicts the UN Charter due to the missing Security Council authorisation but proclaims to be in the interest of its spirit and values, this need should be met by other measures within the multilateral collective UN system and not outside the UN by unilateral acts of some, even many states. To allow a unilateral use of force as a lawful response to alleged or real disobedience to Security Council resolutions would make it more unlikely that the Security Council will be able to determine a breach of resolutions because, for example, Russia and China will fear that this could be used by the United States and other states for a unilateral use of force proclaiming an implied justification of a unilateral use of force. Such argument could have a negative effect on the readiness of the Security Council members to express condemnation and to determine imputability of illegal acts.[92] Additionally the authority of the Security Council would be undermined. The peculiar role and authority of the Security Council and the influence and position of

---

[89]   See Kelsen, see note 21, 270 who points to the danger of deterioration of the legal status under international law.

[90]   Gowlland-Debbas, see note 5, 361 et seq. (374).

[91]   Here one could refer to the Uniting for Peace resolution of the UN General Assembly. The cases in which this resolution was used are quite diverse, see Q.D. Nguyen/ P. Daillier/ A. Pellet, *Droit International Public*, 6th edition 1999, 815 et seq. (957); J.F. Guilhaudis, "Considérations sur la pratique de l' Union pour le maintien de la paix", *A.F.D.I.* 1981, 382-398. Kelsen, see note 21, 970-977 argues in favour of a force monopoly of the Security Council with the exception of a General Assembly recommendation in case the Security Council is blocked by the exercise of the veto right or has ceased to deal with the matter. De Wet, see note 5, 309 proposes a (restricted) residual role of the General Assembly to terminate open-ended authorisations of the use of force. This question transcends the focus of this article and, therefore, will not be deepened here.

[92]   Gray, see note 13, 13; id., see note 65, 280.

its members (especially its permanent ones) balance the formal equality of states which is the basis of the UN system and of international law in general with the reality of asymmetric capabilities of states. This softening of the equality of states cannot be and should not be extended by new forms of (allegedly) justified or legitimate unilateralism. This applies all the more since contemporary international law, besides the equality of states, is also coined by a general obligation to cooperate.[93] The principle of the equality of states would be distorted and evaporated in meaning if unilateral force was allowed (beyond Article 51 UN Charter), thus fundamentally shaking the basis of international law. Additionally, allowing unilateral coercive actions would open a Pandora's box and could result in the erosion of the Charter consensus about the use of force. Determining criteria for lawful unilateral use of force would also face the problem of misuse and lack of clarity (since they must refer to the broad objectives of the UN and therefore unavoidably would be open-textured and vaguely or generally formulated) thus threatening peace and security.[94] For all of these reasons, if the Security Council fails, the authority to define the common UN objectives for a concrete crisis and to determine the necessary steps for their implementation is better vested in another organ of the UN instead of a coalition of certain states that define on their own what the UN objectives allegedly require.

In a more general perspective, the declaration of belief in community values accompanied by the hot debate on legitimate unilateralism cannot be isolated from a workable institutional setting for the international community of states. Values need institutions that work for them and ensure their observance and implementation. As the values are universal, the institutions must be universal as well. Reintroducing legitimate unilateralism is the wrong reaction to the need for a sound implementation of values and rights. It cannot solve the problems because the identification of community values in a concrete situation needs collective mechanisms, this means mechanisms within and in accordance with the contemporary United Nations' system. Also the inauguration of the International Criminal Court, though not formally part of the UN sys-

---

[93] Regarding the latter see Dupuy, see note 1, 22 et seq.

[94] For a critique see also Hilpold, see note 57, 450. He rightly points out (at 458 with further references) that similar catalogues of criteria for legitimising unilateral humanitarian interventions brought about totally diverging views and assessments by writers when applied to the NATO intervention in Kosovo.

tem, and the establishment of international *ad hoc* criminal tribunals confirm that there are better multilateral forms of reacting to breaches of international law, upholding the rule of law than illegal unilateral use of force. Even if one points to the fact that since the entry into force of the UN Charter the importance and awareness of human rights has increased so that one could observe a shift in balance between the prohibition of the use of force and the respect for human rights,[95] the invention of an International Criminal Court appears to be the proper institutional answer to the claimed in-balance. New or heightened common objectives of the community of states cannot be protected by unilateral recourse to force without watering down their value. The strengthening of human rights implementation must not sacrifice a core principle of the UN system like the prohibition of the unilateral use of force as both work to the same end, i.e. to reduce if not avoid atrocities and human suffering. There is no choice between protecting human rights on the one hand and, on the other hand, respecting the prohibition of force; instead it is a debate over the right means. There are a number of reactions to human rights violations besides unilateral use of force.[96]

3. Conclusion

Both the wording of the Council powers under Chapter VII, the core aim of maintaining and restoring international peace and security with its effectiveness implication, and the changing function of the Council which progressed simultaneously with the changing notion of peace require a constitutive understanding of the Chapter VII powers. This result is confirmed by the decisive role the Council plays in the collective security system of the UN to counter threats to peace and security. It is its evaluation and assessment which counts. Constitutive interpretation connotes that the Council may create new law and alter existing inter-

---

[95]   This argument, however, is debatable because encouraging the respect for human rights is an aim of the UN since its inauguration in the same way as the maintenance of peace and because the core principle of the prohibition of the use of force was breached since the 2nd half of the 20th century not less than the human rights obligations.

[96]   Gowlland-Debbas, see note 5, 379. She points to the ICJ Nicaragua decision where the court decided that the protection of human rights cannot be compatible with the mining of ports or the training, arming and equipping of the contras (Military and Paramilitary Activities in and against Nicaragua, ICJ Reports 1986, 14 et seq. (134 et seq.)).

national rules accordingly, even that it may retroactively authorise use of force in particular circumstances.

III. Limitations of the Powers of the Security Council

1. Introductory Deliberations

Even the broad, purposive interpretation of the powers of the Security Council advocated here does not mean that the powers are without limits. The discretion of the UN Security Council is not absolute. It takes place within the frame of the Charter, and the tasks and powers are allocated to the Security Council for specific purposes. The mere fact that the practice of the Security Council in exercising its powers is inconsistent does not mean that it ought not to be grounded on clear principles.

A first limitation is that any authorisation to use force has to be given in unambiguous terms which, in case of an authorisation *ex post facto*, have to be clearer than in case of prior authorisations. States shall not be tempted to claim implicit authorisation *ex post* from obscure language in subsequent resolutions.[97] A lack of condemnation of the unilateral actions in subsequent Security Council resolutions does not serve as an *argumentum e contrario* because one permanent member can block the condemnation.[98]

Second, there is need for formal safeguards guaranteeing the responsibility and accountability of the Security Council.[99] In particular when resolutions are taken in the aftermath of unilateral actions, the broad interpretation of the UN Security Council powers must be balanced by due limits to the UN Security Council discretion in choosing the necessary peace measures. If the UN Security Council authorises the use of force in order to enforce or implement peace agreements or cease-fires, the Security Council has to take care of a greater control of the use of

---

[97]   In favour of even implicit *ex post* authorisations B. Simma, "Regional Enforcement of Community Objectives", in: V. Gowlland-Debbas (ed.), *United Nations Sanctions and International Law*, 2001, 117 et seq. (118 et seq.). On state practice proclaiming implied (prior) authorisation see Gray, see note 65, 264-279.

[98]   de Wet, see note 5, 297.

[99]   See F. Berman, "The Authorization Model", in: Malone, see note 3, 159 et seq.

force, e.g. by close coordination with the Secretary-General.[100] Another means of intensified control of authorised use of force is the unified overall command and control by the UN Security Council.[101] Since the Security Council acts as the agent of the international community when using or authorising force it cannot completely delegate its powers to states; this is also a requirement of general international law.[102] The responsibility rests with the Security Council that in turn must safeguard its steadfast and continuing influence by clearly defining the mandate regarding extent and objectives and by providing monitoring tools like effective reporting procedures in order to have effective supervision.[103] As functional limitations may be inadministrable and as open-ended mandates might be difficult to withdraw, military mandates also require time limits.[104] Otherwise the termination of a military mandate would require a new resolution of the Security Council which could be prevented by a permanent member's veto (reverse veto) with the effect that a mandate could be continued merely by the will of one Security Council member. Then it was no longer the Security Council (majority) that decides about authorisation but a single member which would amount to an illegal delegation of powers by the Security Council.[105]

Third, it is uncontested that the Security Council powers are subject to certain substantive legal restraints emanating from international law; what is contested, however, is the exact extent to which international

---

[100] Cf. Gray, see note 13, 7 et seq.

[101] This was applied by Resolution S/RES/1244 (1999) of 10 June 1999 with respect to the KFOR. In principle, even merely authorised enforcement measures by the Security Council are attributable to the UN since they are subject to the overall control by the Security Council, see *mutatis mutandis* arts 6 and 7 of the Rules on State Responsibility; Sarooshi, see note 13, 163 et seq.; M. Zwanenburg, *Accountability under International Humanitarian Law for United Nations and North Atlantic Treaty Organization Peace Support Operations*, 2004, 70 et seq., 130 et seq. Contra Frowein/ Krisch, see note 13, Article 42 Mn. 29.

[102] See Frowein/ Krisch, see note 13, Introduction to Chapter VII, Mn. 33; de Wet, see note 5, 265 et seq.

[103] For more detail see Frowein/ Krisch, see note 13, Article 42 Mn. 25; de Wet, see note 5, 269 et seq.

[104] de Wet, see note 5, 290, 307. See also Frowein/ Krisch, see note 13, Introduction to Chapter VII Mn. 38.

[105] de Wet, see note 5, 190, 308.

law obliges the Security Council when acting under Chapter VII.[106] Here, the limitations for the Security Council powers entailed in the UN Charter itself (which can be called constitutional limitations)[107] and in those rules of general international law which take precedence over the UN Charter (which means peremptory norms of international law, *ius cogens*)[108] become important. The Security Council must respect such hierarchically superior rules. Accordingly, the priority of Security Council resolutions stated in Article 103 UN Charter is limited. The constitutional limitations of the Security Council discretion in the discharge of its powers result from the prerequisites of the relevant articles of the UN Charter, from the *raison d'être* of the Security Council powers indicated therein (thus the objective of peace termination both expands and restrains the Chapter VII powers) and from the purposes and principles of the UN Charter contained in Chapter I, Arts 1 and 2. The Security Council may only discharge its powers in accordance with the latter (see Article 24 (2) UN Charter). Everything else would be illegitimate because an organisation like the United Nations that was founded in order to foster certain fundamental principles und objectives in the community of states cannot act except in conformity with those principles.

The following sections will analyse in more detail the limits flowing from the purposes and principles of the UN Charter (see below under 2.), from peremptory norms (see below under 3.) and from inherent constitutional restraints (see below under 4.).

2. Purposes and Principles of the UN Charter

a. Equality, Self Determination and Human Rights

Arts 1 and 2 UN Charter contain several fundamental principles on which the United Nations is founded. Besides the primary goal of

---

106   de Wet, see note 5, 185; A. Reinisch, "Developing Human Rights and Humanitarian Law Accountability of the Security Council for the Imposition of Economic Sanctions", *AJIL* 95 (2001), 851 et seq. (856).

107   ICTY, Prosecutor v. Tadic, Appeal Case IT-94-1-AR 72, para. 28, reprinted in *ILM* 35 (1996), 32 et seq. (42).

108   Orakhelashvili, see note 6, 60. Zwanenburg, see note 101, 150, however, contests that the Security Council cannot derogate from peremptory norms.

maintaining international peace and security, Article 1 (2) and (3) lists further purposes of a secondary nature: respect for the equality of rights and self-determination of peoples, solution for international economic, social or humanitarian problems and respect for human rights. Principles which have to be followed therein include the equality of states (Article 2 (1)), the obligation to ensure that non-members respect the principles of the United Nations (Article 2 (6)), and non-intervention (Article 2 (7)) with the latter being not applicable to enforcement measures. The principles enshrined in Article 2 (2) to (5) primarily refer to the UN Member States.[109]

The above-named purposes and principles are very broad in scope and to some extent contradictory and ambiguous. Nevertheless they provide some guidelines for the exercise of the Security Council discretion, though they are not clear cut limits to the Security Council powers. The Security Council, however, has to take all of the purposes and principles in consideration when acting under Chapter VII while the maintenance and restoration of peace and security is the primary goal. The supreme character of the latter purpose is not explicitly expressed in Article 1, but can be derived from its prime position in Article 1 (1) and in Article 23 (1) regarding the election of non-permanent members to the Security Council, and furthermore from the preamble to the UN Charter and from the drafting history.[110] The supreme character of peace and security restoration is affirmed when looking at the function and powers of the United Nations main organs. It is the maintenance of peace and security that is named first there (see Article 11 for the General Assembly and Article 24 for the Security Council).[111] The exigencies of the secondary goals cannot keep the Security Council from exercising its powers in order to achieve its primary goal of maintaining and restoring peace, but it can have an impact on the way the Security Council exercises its peace enforcement powers. In this regard, the different UN purposes have to be balanced; the Security Council cannot

---

[109] Regarding the meaning of the principle of good faith to the UN see de Wet, see note 5, 195 et seq.

[110] See *inter alia* the *Documents of the United Nations Conference on International Organization, Volume VI*, see note 32, 26.

[111] The Charter provisions indicated actually only refer to the "maintenance" of peace whereas the restoration is added in Article 39. This illustrates that maintenance of peace includes its restoration in case of its breach. This conclusion in particular may be drawn from Article 24 (2) which attributes (*inter alia*) the Chapter VII powers of the Security Council to its primary responsibility for the "maintenance" of peace and security.

maintain peace and security at the *complete* expense of any of the other goals.[112] The rights and positions of states, peoples or individuals targeted by UN actions (like the sovereignty of states, the right to self-determination and human rights) are not absolute limitations to the Chapter VII powers requiring unconditional respect but can be restricted by Chapter VII measures, at least provisionally. The Chapter VII powers are limited (only) by the obligation duly to *consider* positions like the right to self-determination and the respect for human rights (see also under IV. 1.). The fact that human rights are mentioned in Article 1 (3) UN Charter in the context of international co-operation in solving international problems but not in the context of collective measures (Article 1 (1) UN Charter), is not an argument against the human rights obligation of the Security Council acting under Chapter VII because of the explicit reference by Article 24 UN Charter to the first Chapter of the UN Charter.[113] Some commentators draw a distinction between the different measures in Chapter VII: whereas fundamental human rights are said to limit the Chapter VII powers only in case of non-military enforcement measures, military measures of the Security Council are said to be limited only by basic norms of law of armed conflict. Such deliberations are reasoned by the claim that the law of armed conflict was *lex specialis*.[114] This view appears too general and over-simplified. First, the ICJ did not define the relationship between the law of armed conflict and human rights law to be one of mutual exclusiveness and alternativeness but preferred to some extent a parallel, cumulative application of human rights law and humanitarian law of armed conflict since they serve the same ends.[115] Second, law of war be-

---

[112] de Wet, see note 5, 193.

[113] See also the attribution of certain basic human rights to the purposes and principles of the UN Charter by the ICJ, ICJ Reports 1971, see note 12, 16 et seq. (57 para. 131) and United States Diplomatic and Consular Staff in Teheran, ICJ Reports 1980, 3 et seq. (42 para. 91). Contra Zwanenburg, see note 101, 154 et seq., 218 et seq. who does not take due account of Article 24 UN Charter.

[114] De Wet, see note 5, 198 et seq. For a more nuanced view see H. Krieger, "A Conflict of Norms: The Relationship between Humanitarian Law and Human Rights Law in the ICRC Customary Law Study", *Journal of Conflict and Security Law* 11 (2006), 265 et seq. On the interpretative influence of humanitarian law upon human rights norms see McGoldrick, see note 76, 45 et seq.

[115] ICJ, Opinion of 9 July 2004, para. 105 et seq., Legal Consequences of the Construction of a Wall in the Occupied Palestinian Territory. See also Rat-

comes less relevant as soon as the conflict is no longer purely military and international administration controls the targeted area (i.e. "occupies" in humanitarian law parlance), still acting under Chapter VII. At least in this phase of the conflict, human rights must be respected since they can be implemented more easily.[116] The said categorical distinction between humanitarian law and human rights law, therefore, is not convincing.

b. Humanitarian Law/ Law of Armed Conflict

In contrast to human rights, the respect for humanitarian law is neither explicitly referred to in Article 1 nor in Article 2 UN Charter. Nevertheless, the basic rules of the law of armed conflict also oblige the Security Council. This can be derived from Article 1 (3) UN Charter all the more since the law of armed conflict has a humanitarian underpinning. The primary objective is to protect individuals.[117] An armed force employed in the pursuit of common objectives of all nations must respect basic rules of the law of war. Additionally there is an argument of practical necessity: if UN troops did not act in compliance with the law of war their opponents might as well not comply with humanitarian law either.[118] The applicability of the law of armed conflict to Chapter VII enforcement measures is confirmed – at least to some extent – by the practice of the United Nations itself. Objections raised against the relevance of the law of war which argue that – as a matter of principle – peace enforcement under Chapter VII was not a war and that military presence accompanied by such UN operations were not occupations[119]

---

ner, see note 36, 704; A. Roberts, "Transformative Military Occupation: Applying the Laws of War and Human Rights", *AJIL* 100 (2006), 580 et seq. (597); R. Wolfrum, "Iraq – from Belligerent Occupation to Iraqi Exercise of Sovereignty: Foreign Power versus International Community Interference", *Max Planck UNYB* 9 (2005), 1 et seq. (5).

[116] Roberts, see note 115, 591 et seq.

[117] Cf. Gardam, see note 13, 301 et seq., 314; McGoldrick, see note 76, 40; de Wet, see note 5, 204.

[118] See Gill, see note 20, 81 et seq.

[119] For on overview see E. de Wet, "The Direct Administration of Territories by the United Nations and its Member States in the Post Cold War Era", *Max Planck UNYB* 8 (2004), 291 et seq. (323-325); Zwanenburg, see note 101, 208, 222. Even the Convention on the Safety of United Nations and Associated Personnel <http://www.un.org/law/cod/safety.htm>, even if

are not convincing since there can be no doubt that, first, military enforcement measures by the Security Council do represent an armed conflict with other troops in the targeted area and that, second, their continued presence in the targeted area and its administration is an occupation because the area is placed under the authority of the UN or the states acting on its behalf. Governmental functions are executed without consent and to the exclusion of the domestic government (see article 42 of the Hague Regulations[120]). United Nations troops are not automatically perceived as liberators but may face resistance from local people.[121]

c. Scope of Obligations

The crucial questions are: which are the concrete rules that oblige the Security Council, and what is their content?[122] Which human rights are human rights in the sense of Article 1 (3) UN Charter? Is the Security Council bound by each norm of the law of armed conflict? What is the exact content of the right to self-determination? As regards humanitarian law and human rights law there seems to be consent that the Security Council is not bound by each existing rule but only by fundamental and basic principles of humanitarian and human rights law.[123] Only

---

applicable, does not provide for derogation from humanitarian law in case of Chapter VII measures but confirms it, see its article 2 (2).

[120] Convention (IV) respecting the Laws and Customs of War on Land and its Annex: Regulations concerning the Laws and Customs of War on Land. The Hague, 18 October 1907.

[121] Ratner, see note 36, 714-715, 718.

[122] See e.g. Reisman, see note 77, 92. This issue may be separated from the question as to the obligations of the states involved in enforcement actions, in particular of troop contributing states. The legal assessment of their actions, however, must pay attention to the Security Council authorisation and, thus, is linked with the questions under consideration here, see Gardam, see note 13, 317.

[123] See, for example, de Wet, see note 5, 215 who names "core elements of self-determination, human rights, ... humanitarian law and state sovereignty." Gill, see note 20, 72 refers to "fundamental human rights or humanitarian norms", at 77 to "essential human rights and humanitarian values", at 79 to "core provisions". See also A. Reinisch, see note 106, 859 ("fundamental humanitarian norms") and the fundamental principles and rules of international humanitarian law applicable to UN forces spelled out by the UN Secretary-General in its bulletin on the observance by the UN forces of international humanitarian law (Doc. ST/SGB/1999/13, reprinted in: *ILM* 39

fundamental rules that are universally accepted norms of customary law have to be respected by the Security Council.[124]

Moreover, one could consider that all those human rights rules and instruments that have been developed under the auspices of the UN must be respected since the United Nations would act inconsistently if it demanded its members to respect human rights norms which the organisation itself would not pay attention to.[125] Such view, however, neglects that the Security Council is bound solely by the principles and purposes of the UN and not by any rule whose legal force is claimed by the United Nations or by any of its organs. Otherwise other organs of the United Nations could limit the powers of the Security Council beyond the limits enshrined in the UN Charter itself by proclaiming certain human rights to be of binding force. The context and source of the human rights proclamations must be considered. Therefore, it does not contradict the principle of good faith to decouple the Security Council enforcement powers from human rights standards proclaimed in different contexts. The UN purpose of respect for human rights is complied with by the Security Council if human rights as a category are respected; this does not necessitate that each human rights norm proclaimed in the framework of the United Nations is observed under all conditions. Of course, the whole tenor of the UN Charter is to promote the protection of human rights[126]; but it is not the whole tenor of the Charter, and in particular not Arts 55 and 56 UN Charter that oblige the Security Council when acting under Chapter VII. An additional argument is that the Security Council's obligations in the discharge of enforcement powers in the common interest of its members

---

(1999), 1656 et seq.) and which in particular refers to protection and treatment of civilians, means and methods of combat, treatment of detained members of armed forces, of wounded and sick and of medical and relief personnel. This bulletin was perceived as concretising the binding principles and spirit of humanitarian law, D. Shraga, "UN Peacekeeping Operations: Applicability of International Humanitarian Law and Responsibility for Operations-Related Damages", *AJIL* 94 (2000), 406 et seq. (408).

124   Gardam, see note 13, 315, 319; Gill, see note 20, 79 sees the minimum yardstick in the non-derogable rights of the International Covenants. Regarding the customary rules of humanitarian law see the new two volumes by J.M. Henckaerts/ L. Doswald-Beck, *Customary International Humanitarian Law*, 2005.

125   This view is presented by Akande, see note 33, 324 and de Wet, see note 5, 199.

126   As says Akande, see note 33, 323.

are not different from those of the UN Member States. Therefore, human rights binding only on some of the UN Member States cannot oblige the Security Council. If, and to the extent that rules are derogable[127] and subject to restrictions, such limits to human rights and humanitarian law obligations also apply to the Security Council and its measures. Finally, one must not forget that, as already pointed out, human rights and humanitarian law obligations may be weighed against the effectiveness of the measures taken under Chapter VII for the restoration of peace and security so that the Security Council may deviate.[128]

These deliberations illustrate that the purposes and principles of the UN Charter are not strong limits of the Security Council powers but serve as guidelines. The concrete demands of the purposes and principles must be considered but may be overruled since they have to be balanced against the need for effective measures to restore peace and security. The Security Council merely must take care that the principles and purposes are fully taken into consideration and respected to a certain extent. The balance is directed by a principle of proportionality of the means to the ends (which is required by the constitutional limitations inherent in Chapter VII, see below under 4.) which determines the extent to which the Security Council may derogate from international law insofar as international law is at all binding the Security Council acting under Chapter VII. The extent of derogation must be proportionate to the breach of or threat to the peace which determines the necessary characteristics of the peace restoration measures. This means, for example, that the limiting effect of the purposes and principles of the UN Charter in respect to the exercise of the Security Council's discretion and to the discharge of its powers is higher if the rights and positions of third parties not involved in the armed conflict are concerned.

d. In Particular: Law of Occupation

As regards humanitarian law, a question of current concern is the law of belligerent occupation. The Security Council had authorised the administration of the coalition powers (the so-called Coalition Provisional Authority, CPA) in Iraq to radically change the legal order of

---

[127] For non-derogable rights see article 4 International Covenant on Civil and Political Rights.
[128] See also de Wet, see note 119, 323.

Iraq[129] in its resolutions on the reconstruction and reformation of Iraq. Such authorisation may contradict article 43 of the Hague Regulations requiring respect for the laws in force in the occupied country, unless absolutely prevented. The changes ordered by the CPA were inimical to the concept of a socialist system mandated by the Iraqi constitution in force at that time and contradicted basic provisions of Iraqi law. Similar problems can be found with regard to Kosovo and East Timor.[130] The question arises whether (and to what extent) the sovereignty of the targeted country and the right of the occupied population to self-determination which underpin article 43 Hague Regulations really restrain the powers of the UN Security Council.

On the one hand, one could argue that the derogation is only provisional as the intended changes in the legal and economic order are not necessarily lasting (even privatisations can be redone; with respect to a new currency, however, this is far more complicated). On the other hand, one has to take into account that the changes also referred to institutions of governance and the process of constitutionalisation in Iraq. Irrespective of the possibly provisional nature, the changes ordered by the CPA appear not to be completely covered by the powers of the occupant under the law of occupation. The broad discretion of the Security Council as to the restoration of peace and security has to consider the requirements of stable, sustainable peace and security. Therefore, it is no surprise that S/RES/1483 (2003) and S/RES/1511 (2003) on Iraq authorise the creation of conditions for sustainable development. This seems to be an expression of the post-conflict settlement function and the responsibilities of the Security Council flowing from it (see above under II. 1. b.). Restoring lasting peace in a country of turmoil requires the Security Council to think in terms of sustainability. Therefore, the Chapter VII powers of the Security Council must be interpreted not only in the light of the needs of short time restoration of peace by ter-

---

[129] See C. McCarthy, "The Paradox of the International Law of Military Occupation: Sovereignty and the Reformation of Iraq", *Journal of Conflict & Security Law* 10 (2005), 43 et seq. (67 et seq.); McGoldrick, see note 76, 128-138. Security Council Resolution S/RES/1483 (2003) of 22 May 2003, op. para. 8 (lit. i), provides for legal and judicial reforms. Security Council Resolution S/RES/1511 (2003) of 16 October 2003, op. para. 7 provides for the drafting of a new constitution and for the holding of democratic elections. Cf. also Wolfrum, see note 115, 20-23.

[130] McCarthy, see note 129, 51 et seq., 53; J. Friedrich, "UNMIK in Kosovo: Struggling with Uncertainty", *Max Planck UNYB* 9 (2005), 225 et seq. (235, 238 et seq., 268); de Wet, see note 119, 328 et seq.

minating the armed hostilities but also against the background of the requirements of lasting peace. This may require altering the internal order of a state. The Security Council therefore is empowered to deviate from certain rules of the law of military occupation, in particular those that (or insofar as they) do not protect individual human beings but rather the interests of the occupied state in ensuring its sovereignty and self-determination.[131] The restraints of law of military occupation insofar do not appear to be appropriate for an occupation that is authorised by the Security Council for the purpose of restoring peace and security. This is easily understandable since the law of occupation was created against the background of a totally different situation, an international order of belligerent states in the absence of any organisation having the monopoly of legitimate force. In particular the exigencies of the comprehensive task of administering the territory under occupation seem not to be sufficiently reflected in the rules on occupation, all the more since an occupation subsequent to Security Council enforcement action is subject to the primary aim of peace restoration. This aim calls for specific and more differentiated demands when compared to the purpose of the occupation according to the Hague Regulations which appear to be limited to restoring and ensuring public order and safety in the occupied territory according to the formulation in article 43 Hague Regulations. Traditional occupation law assumes the capacity and desirability of maintaining existing domestic institutions of the target state. This reflects a conservationist approach of order conservation understandably backed by mistrust in occupants. The traditional assumption of the law of wars was a bad occupant occupying a good country.[132] The occupants' territorial powers were based on the mere fact of their military control. Therefore, they were limited. Such concept of occupation collides with the peculiar transformative goals of peace restoration undertaken by the international community. The difference is a legal and a political one. First, the occupation by or on behalf of the international community is legal and legitimate. Second, it affects states where domestic institutions collapsed, failed, were inexistent or caused the atrocities due to their malfunction. Thus, the transformative goal re-

---

[131] Article 43 Hague Regulations is one example as far as it binds the UN to the pre-existing legislation. See also de Wet, see note 119, 329; Wolfrum, see note 115, 13-15; id., see note 49, 680. Contra R. Kolb, *Droit humanitaire et opérations de paix internationales*, 2002, 83 et seq. (88).

[132] Roberts, see note 115, 580 et seq. (601). On the functions of occupation see in more detail N. Bhuta, "The Antinomies of Transformative Occupation", *EJIL* 16 (2005), 721 et seq. (725-730).

flects the attempt to counter the reasons of the crisis.[133] Due to the lack of appropriateness, and insofar as this is the case, the derogation from the law of occupation by the Security Council under Chapter VII appears proportionate to the Security Council measures' objective of peace restoration. For this reason, the law of occupation in the Hague or Geneva Conventions does not completely oblige the Security Council.[134] The rules of occupation are to be respected by the Security Council only insofar as they do not hinder or retard the task of the Security Council in restoring international peace and security. Thus, the Security Council can lawfully overcome the international law of occupation to a certain extent. Besides article 43 of the Hague Regulations, arts 54 and 64 of the Fourth Geneva Convention relative to the Protection of Civilian Persons in Time of War could be affected. The latter norms (though being more permissive) restrain the capacity of the occupying power to reform penal law and the functioning of domestic courts and institutions, and provide for other limits of the full governmental, legislative and judiciary powers of the occupying power.

This result is not contradicted by the fact that the Security Council, when adopting its resolutions on Iraq endorsed the respect for relevant international law,[135] for two reasons: first, the Security Council cannot restrain its powers. It can only duly decide not to exercise them. Therefore, its decision to fully comply with international law does not mean that it is obliged to do so. Second, the Security Council resolutions on Iraq are ambiguous.[136] The solemn respect for the applicable interna-

---

[133] S. Chesterman, "Occupation as Liberation", *Ethics & International Affairs* 18 (2004/3), 51 et seq. (63); Roberts, see note 115, 586-590.

[134] See also Chesterman, see note 133, 54, 61. D.J. Scheffer, "Beyond Occupation Law", in: ASIL (ed.), *Future Implications of the Iraq Conflict*, 2004, 130 et seq. (136) argues that UN operations render a full application of occupation law inappropriate and even undesirable. Gardam, see note 13, 321 states an obligation of the Security Council to comply with "appropriate" rules of humanitarian law. Cf. also the analysis made by Kolb, see note 131, 60 et seq., in particular at 80 et seq. on inapplicable rules or rules that have to be altered to meet the needs of UN enforcement measures. For inappropriateness of the law of occupation in general see de Wet, see note 119, 326 et seq.

[135] See the analysis by McCarthy, see note 129, 66 et seq.

[136] See for example S/RES/1483 (2003) of 22 May 2003 reference to a properly constituted, internationally recognised, representative government, Orakhelashvili, see note 11, 312 et seq. Additionally, Wolfrum, see note 115, 17 et seq. points to a differentiation made there with regard to the au-

tional law in its resolutions[137] is watered down by the operative parts of the same resolutions. Therefore, the solemn affirmation of the relevant international law cannot be played off against the steps and means deemed necessary by the Security Council or by the authorised agent in order to restore sustainable peace and security. It cannot be argued that the Security Council intended to base itself solely on existing international rules. Insofar, the CPA can be seen as an institution mandated by the Security Council. This institution thus may under the authority of the Security Council lawfully deviate from the established rules of military occupation.[138] The substantive justification for this limited respect for Hague or Geneva law can be seen in a right to democracy[139] or to the self-determination of people which allows the Security Council to introduce transformations establishing institutions of democratic governance in a state which more or less was coined by a totalitarian system without real participation of the people. If the right to self-determination has been withheld from a people, the measures of the Security Council taken in order to grant this right to them cannot be seen as contrary to the requirements of occupation. Additionally, since the right of peoples to self-determination was ranked to be of qualified, *erga-omnes* character,[140] the formal derogation from the law of occupation by the Security Council is in line with a superior, at least equally ranked, norm of international law.

---

thority given to the United Kingdom and the United States in contrast to that given to other states. In his reading, the Security Council did not fully bind the former to the Geneva Conventions.

[137] See the preamble and para. 4 of Security Council Resolution S/RES/1483 (2003) of 22 May 2003 and para. 1 of Security Council Resolution S/RES/1511 (2003) of 16 October 2003.

[138] In this direction also T.D. Grant, *Iraq: How to Reconcile Conflicting Obligations of Occupation and Reform*, <http://www.asil.org/insights/insigh10 7a1.htm>.

[139] G.H. Fox/ B. Roth (eds), *Democratic Governance and International Law*, 2000; T.M. Franck, "The Emerging Right to Democratic Governance", *AJIL* 86 (1992), 46 et seq. Interestingly, the appeal to democracy is found increasingly often in Security Council resolutions. The Security Council praised democratic governance for reasons of national reconciliation, security and reconstruction of government institutions, G.H. Fox, "Democratization", in: Malone, see note 3, 69.

[140] East Timor, ICJ Reports 1995, 90 et seq. (para. 29).

e. Equality of States

Another issue of controversy is the alleged discriminatory character of measures in view of the equality of states, for example if the possession of certain weapons by a state causes UN enforcement measures, whereas the UN does not act with respect to other states in like situation, or if humanitarian interventions are authorised in one case but not in other comparable cases. Authorisation by the UN Security Council for coercive measures to prevent the proliferation or the use of weapons of mass destruction or to terminate severe violations of human rights conforms to the given normative framework as the Security Council enjoys broad discretion to avert threats to peace by whatever means it deems useful. Therefore, the Security Council can authorise action that has, at first sight, discriminatory impact because weapons are denied to one state and that are deployed by other states. Treating states differently in different situations does, however, not amount to discrimination but corresponds to a doctrine of reasonableness. As states, conflicts and surrounding conditions differ, the Security Council can and may exercise its leeway in different ways. The discretion vested in the Security Council allows for flexible reactions and does not force the Security Council to follow a certain pattern of action when faced with a breach of peace or an act of aggression. The constitutive character of the Security Council powers under Chapter VII and of its identification of a threat or breach of peace marks a difference. The deeper reason for the alleged discriminatory impact is the incontestable fact that the Security Council is a political organ. Therefore, some even expect the Security Council to act inconsistently.[141]

3. Peremptory Norms

Peremptory norms of international law (*ius cogens*) that limit the powers of the Security Council in particular refer to humanitarian law and human rights. Due to the mention of human rights already made in Article 1 (3) UN Charter, the respect for human rights by the Security Council acting under Chapter VII has a twofold, but not congruent basis. Comparing the limits flowing from peremptory norms to those flowing from the purposes and principles of the UN Charter, one must state that due to their hierarchy the former legal restraints are capable of

---

[141] Österdahl, see note 15, 19 et seq.

limiting the Security Council powers in a stronger way than the latter. Whereas peremptory norms must be fully respected by any actor of international law, the principles and purposes of the UN Charter only have a rank equal to the Charter provisions empowering the Security Council, the task of the Security Council to maintain peace and security even being of primary character. Peremptory norms are not accessible for any balancing process against the requirements of peace and security maintenance and restoration.

The decisive question is which norms of humanitarian law and which human rights are peremptory. This tricky issue cannot be developed here. Some remarks may suffice. First of all, one must consider that rules on human rights and humanitarian law, even if customary by nature, may not prove to be peremptory. Second, even if peremptory to states, one has to consider whether its peremptory character also applies to international organisations. Rules may differ not only with respect to their content and their obligations, but also with respect to their addressee. To state that a certain norm of human rights law obliges – as a rule of *ius cogens* – all states does not necessarily mean that it also applies with the same legal quality to the United Nations. Some claim, for example, that article 43 of the Hague Regulation was a humanitarian rule of peremptory character.[142] Even if this was a peremptory norm for states, it is not a peremptory rule for the United Nations when maintaining or enforcing peace. As shown above the occupation of a country by foreign states is different to an occupation by the international community. Thus, the arguments and the rationale offered in favour of the *ius cogens* nature of a specific norm may not apply in different contexts.

4. Inherent Constitutional Limitations, in Particular the Objective of Peace Restoration

As already mentioned, the formulations in the Charter provisions empowering the Security Council and its objectives limit the discretion of the Security Council. These confines serve as inherent, more or less explicit constitutional limitations to its powers. The core constitutional constraint is the objective of peace restoration. The Security Council functions to maintain or restore peace and security; its powers are lim-

---

[142] M. Sassòli, "Legislation and Maintenance of Public Order and Civil Life by Occupying Powers", *EJIL* 16 (2005), 661 et seq. (680 et seq.).

ited to those actions necessary for the restoration of peace, see the wording of Article 42 UN Charter. All measures taken by the Security Council must work for that end. Thus, the core objective of peace restoration is accompanied and complemented by a principle of necessity and proportionality which is more or less implicitly entailed in Chapter VII as evidenced by the relationship between military and non military enforcement measures (Arts 41 and 42 UN Charter) and by the wording of Article 42 already referred to, and Article 40.[143] The impact of the enforcement measures of the Security Council upon the rights and positions of the targeted state, population and individuals shall be minimised as much as possible.[144]

The twin requirements of necessity and proportionality are determinants for the legality of the discharge of the Chapter VII powers, in particular of the use of military force. Necessity relates to whether the situation requires the use of force, proportionality determines the amount of force that the Security Council is allowed to use to achieve its aim of peace restoration.[145] It is a constitutional restraint to the Security Council's *ius ad bellum* under Chapter VII not restricted to a protection of territorial sovereignty (as was the classical view) but guiding and thus limiting the right of the Security Council to derogate from any international law.[146] The guiding effect of necessity and proportionality, however, is watered down by the quite imprecise character of necessity and proportionality since the restoration of peace and security is quite a nebulous concept that first must be determined in concrete terms by the Security Council, and therefore, by the margin of appreciation enjoyed by the Security Council in defining the concrete requirements of necessity and proportionality in a given situation.[147] This problem of the functioning of the necessity and proportionality principle can be remedied by integrating the demands of justice after war as additional limits to the discharge of Chapter VII powers by the Security Council, at least to a certain extent (see below under IV.).

Considering peace restoration as final end of all enforcement measures of the Security Council engenders also a temporal limitation to the measures taken by the Security Council: the Security Council acting

---

[143]   For more detail see Gardam, see note 13, 307-312.
[144]   Frowein/ Krisch, see note 13, Introduction to Chapter VII Mn. 30.
[145]   Gardam, see note 13, 305.
[146]   See also Gardam, see note 13, 301 et seq.
[147]   Regarding the problems of the functioning of the necessity and proportionality test see Gardam, see note 13, 310 et seq.

under Chapter VII may infringe upon the rights and positions of the states concerned only as long as this is necessary for peace and security restoration and proportionate thereto. For this reason, its measures may only be provisional. As soon as peace is restored, the Security Council no longer is allowed to act under Chapter VII. The measures, for example, suspending the right to self-determination must be removed as soon as the people are in a position to independently exercise their sovereignty by means of representative public governmental institutions. This restriction is not only reasoned by the *telos* of the Security Council powers but also by the respect for the right to self-determination. For both reasons, therefore, the Security Council cannot impose a permanent settlement of a dispute or a permanent allocation of rights on any state.[148] A principle of limited duration applies to all measures taken under Chapter VII.[149]

Within these limits in terms of time and proportionality, the Security Council may also infringe upon the territorial sovereignty. Some authors claim that since the United Nations is based on sovereign equality, independence, and territorial integrity of its members, the Security Council was bound to respect the territory of each state. They must, however, concede that the Security Council may order provisional restrictions on the territorial sovereignty and may clarify the delimitation of existing frontiers as has happened in relation to the Iraq-Kuwait conflict: the Security Council outlined a mandate for the demarcation commission in S/RES/687 (1991) of 3 April 1991 and adopted the final report of the said commission in S/RES/833 (1993) of 27 May 1993.[150] The Security Council anyway is empowered to determine a provisional border for the purposes of guaranteeing a cease-fire or troop withdrawal.[151] In addition, the right to self-determination may even speak in favour of Security Council powers to delimit frontiers, in case of ethnic minorities within a state aiming at independence. In this case, the Security Council action could create conditions which allow a people to exercise its right to self-determination,[152] for example by enforcing the

---

148   Gill, see note 20, 68; see also Wolfrum, see note 31, Article 1, Mn. 19.

149   With respect to international administration de Wet, see note 119, 334.

150   See e.g. Akande, see note 33, 85-88; M. Herdegen, *Die Befugnisse des UN-Sicherheitsrates*, 1998, 29; Orakhelashvili, see note 6, 61 with further references. Regarding the delimitation between Iraq and Kuwait, see de Wet, see note 5, 364-366.

151   De Wet, see note 5, 365, 366.

152   Gill, see note 20, 33 at 90.

observation of minority rights. The Dayton Peace Agreement on Bosnia and Herzegovina[153] can be grouped under this category. Regarding Kosovo or East Timor, one could even think about a power of the Security Council to authorise secession and state-building, yet only within the context of peace restoration.[154] These examples evidence that even the territorial integrity of a state is not immune from the powers of the Security Council. This is confirmed by Article 2 (4) UN Charter which obliges the Member States and not the United Nations acting under Chapter VII to respect the territorial integrity. Inherent limitations to the Security Council powers, however, result from the purpose of the powers which oblige and at the same time restrict the Security Council to take measures in order to restore peace. This may require changes of the territory; but as soon as peace has been restored, the powers no longer apply. This means that any territorial change is only provisional, not permanent,[155] and that its mandatory effect upon the Member States ends when peace is restored. In other words: territorial changes cannot be permanent. They are – like other means used by the Security Council – only tools that serve the ends of peace restoration. After peace is restored, the peoples concerned may exercise their right of self-determination and decide about their territorial status. The states concerned may reach an agreement about the final determination of their border, irrespective and independent of the line drawn by the Security Council resolution or its agents.[156] Here again, the temporal limits of the Security Council powers under Chapter VII become important. Such considerations in addition to the above substantive limitations, re-

---

[153] *ILM* 35 (1996) 75 et seq. The Dayton Peace Agreement was endorsed by the Security Council Resolution S/RES/1031 (1995) of 15 December 1995 enacted under Chapter VII. The role of the UN in the negotiations, however, was very limited, cf. K. Oellers-Frahm, "Restructuring Bosnia-Herzegovina: A Model with Pit-Falls", *Max Planck UNYB* 9 (2005), 179 et seq. (188 et seq., 217); for the ethnic aspects in the constitution see ibid. 197-199.

[154] Orakhelashvili, with respect to Kosovo cf. Friedrich, see note 130, 268 et seq.; S.G. Simonsen, "Nationbuilding as Peacebuilding: Racing to Define the Kosovar", *International Peacekeeping* 11 (2004), 289 et seq.; de Wet, see note 5, 330 et seq., with respect to East Timor cf. I. Martin/ A. Mayer-Rieckh, "The United Nations and East Timor: from Self-Determination to State-Building", *International Peacekeeping* 12 (2005), 125 et seq. Regarding the debate over the right of liberation movements to use force and of third states to assist them, cf. Gray, see note 65, 52 et seq.

[155] Wolfrum, see note 31, Article 1 Mn. 19.

[156] See also de Wet, see note 5, 367.

strain the powers of the Security Council when acting under Chapter VII.

The objective of peace restoration, however, means much more than temporality and proportionality. It engenders material limits to Council actions as implied in the peace focus. Struggling for peace necessitates measures which are oriented towards justice and the rule of law.

IV. In Particular: Security Council Powers and the Demands of Justice After War

1. Effectiveness of Peace Restoration, the Demands of Post-War Justice, and the Functions of the Security Council

Military enforcement actions by the Security Council aiming at the restoration of peace and security must consider both the requirements of effective termination of armed hostilities and the demands of just war termination.[157] The Security Council may not successfully restore peace and security if the exigencies of justice during and, in particular, after the termination of armed hostilities are not met. The objective of peace restoration can only be attained by enforcement actions under Chapter VII if the war terminating measures do not contradict basic requirements of justice. Already at the San Francisco Conference in 1945 it was affirmed that real and durable peace cannot be based on anything other than international and profound social justice.[158] Otherwise the seed for new bloodshed will be sown.[159] Therefore, it is particularly important for the UN and its Security Council to end in a fair and just way both the armed hostilities caused by enforcement actions and the underlying conflicts that caused enforcement actions. In a recent report the Secretary-General confirmed that justice, peace and democracy are mutually reinforcing imperatives in restoring conflict societies.[160] Justice and international law are not identical. The UN Charter is aware of the differ-

---

[157] See also C. Stahn, "Justice under Transitional Administration", *Houston Journal of International Law* 27 (2005), 311 et seq. (315).

[158] *Documents of the United Nations Conference on International Organization, Volume VI*, see note 32, 26 et seq., 32, 453.

[159] See also C. Tomuschat, "How to Make Peace after War – The Potsdam Agreement of 1945 Revisited", *Friedenswarte* 72 (1997), 11 et seq. (28).

[160] Report of the Secretary-General, *The Rule of Law and Transitional Justice in Conflict and Post-Conflict Societies*, Doc. S/2004/616.

ence (cf. the third recital of the Preamble and the explicit endorsement of both in the second part of Article 1 (1)).[161] Therefore, the actions of the victorious must pay due respect to *basic* rules of international law. A peace order that contradicts basic requirements of law or that follows from breaches of fundamental rules of international law in previous Security Council enforcement measures may not prove to be a lasting settlement of the conflict in question because it attracts the odour of illegitimacy. In any event, the creation of a peace order after conflict suffers from the inherent tension because such an order is set up by the military victors. The peace order results from coercion and makes it suspicious and susceptible to distrust. The problems are strongly exacerbated if the establishment and maintenance of this order is accompanied by severe breaches of international law. Interveners that are perceived not to stick to the same standards they demand of others will rarely gain the necessary local support.[162] Hence, demands of justice after war confirm the obligation of the Security Council when taking enforcement actions under Chapter VII to respect basic requirements of humanitarian law and human rights law,[163] thus bridging the gap regarding the applicable law for transitional international administrations.[164]

Consequently, the demands of justice after war also limit the Chapter VII powers of the Security Council in its peace restoration, and direct the exercise of the Security Council's discretion.[165] These restraints to the Security Council powers do not follow from the purposes and principles of the United Nations but result from the very objective of the Security Council powers to restore peace and security. They are implied constitutional confines in accordance with the ends of the Security Council measures. The character of the requirements of justice after war more or less fully corresponds to the limits of the Security Council powers developed from a purposive interpretation of these powers. Accordingly, the exigencies of justice after war are less extensive and may easier be balanced against the effectiveness of enforcement measures as long as the Chapter VII measures are mainly dealing with the task of ending the armed hostilities in the military phase of a conflict. But they

---

[161] See also Kelsen, see note 21, 16 et seq.

[162] Stromseth/ Wippman/ Brooks, see note 13, 315.

[163] Friedrich, see note 130, 284 et seq.; Orend, see note 35, 45.

[164] For the ambiguities in the applicable law insofar cf. Stahn, see note 157, 318 et seq.

[165] See Doc. S/2004/616, see note 160, paras 2, 21.

become extremely important for the exercise of the Security Council's discretion the more the Security Council works as a post conflict organiser of peace and security.

This can be exemplified when looking at the respect for basic rules of international law like human rights which oblige the Security Council due to the limitations to its powers flowing from the purposes and principles of the UN Charter (see above under III. 2.) A post-armed conflict restoration of peace and security that does not take due account of the internationally recognised standards of human rights may not be lasting. It may lack legitimacy and acceptance, given the growing influence of human rights principles on the notion of legitimate intervention.[166] For a provisional period certain rights might be restricted or even inapplicable (as a consequence of their derogable nature[167]), in particular as long as this is necessary for the success of military enforcement actions taken under Chapter VII. But with respect to establishing a post-conflict order, the Security Council must take care that customary human rights standards (both individual rights and group rights of minorities in particular in cases where a struggle for minority protection caused or contributed to the conflict) are fully complied with, not only when self-government has completely been restored. During the transitional period in which a lasting peace order by or due to Security Council resolutions under Chapter VII is established, the respect for human rights by the United Nations and its agents must be increased step by step. A civil UN administration (or an administration authorised by the UN Security Council) that is undertaken in the interest of the local people must pay due respect to customary human rights norms, otherwise its transformative endeavour will lack credibility.[168]

Accordingly, due to the difference between stopping armed hostilities on the one side and building lasting peace on the other, the prerequisites for exercising the Security Council powers are different corresponding to the different functions the Security Council plays in the different phases of peace restoration under Chapter VII. In the beginning, the Security Council acts as peace enforcer, later it becomes a post-conflict organiser of peace and stability, in particular when admin-

---

[166] Stromseth/ Wippman/ Brooks, see note 13, 50 et seq.

[167] See also de Wet, see note 5, 322.

[168] Friedrich, see note 130, 284 et seq.; de Wet, see note 5, 320 et seq. goes further and obliges the UN administration to respect all human rights developed by the UN since the UN is the very same organisation that is executing the administration.

istering the targeted area. As the mere war terminating function becomes less relevant and the post conflict settlement function of the Security Council more relevant, so the more the Security Council must respect basic rules of international law, and the less it can deviate from them. This consideration implements the constitutional proportionality requirement in the discharge of the Chapter VII powers (see above III. 4.) and contributes to its workability and precision. The authority of the Security Council to derogate from international law is limited according to the demands of peace restoration. The more the actions of the UN Security Council succeeded in terminating the armed attacks between belligerents the less the derogation from international law appears necessary for the peace restoration, at least in a general perspective. And the more the situation in the territory under attack approaches a peaceful condition, the more the measures of the Security Council can and must regard the requirements of international law and of the rights of the people, human beings and states concerned. Since enforcement measures necessitate the use of force *vis-à-vis* states and peoples, their rights and positions like sovereignty and self-determination can be more easily restricted and must be less respected than the rights of individuals. Rights of individuals or norms protecting individual interests contained in human rights law or humanitarian law, however, must be paid greater attention to because their suspension will contribute less to the useful effect of enforcement actions and the attainment of their military goals. And the more the UN attains progress on peace restoration, the more the positions of states and peoples concerned by the Security Council action must be restored and restrictions to collective positions like self-determination or sovereignty and, even more, to individual rights must come to an end, in order to safeguard full respect for international law again. In other words: the balance of peace enforcement and peace restoration on the one hand against full respect for the purposes and principles of the United Nations and the demands of justice after war on the other hand, is influenced by the exigencies of the situation and by the progress made by the Security Council in restoring peace and reaching a post-conflict settlement. From this perspective it generally appears that a transitional administration is bound to unconditionally respect at least customary human rights.[169]

---

[169] Another source of human rights obligations might flow from international human rights instruments in force at the occupied territory prior to the enforcement measures.

This deliberation can, to a certain extent, be affirmed by the drafting history of Article 1 (1) UN Charter. During the founding conference, some delegates emphasised the different stages of peace restoration and conflict settlement in a general way. If a breach of peace or a threat to peace occurs, the United Nations was seen to be responsible for stopping the breach or threat and removing it. In a second phase the United Nations could try to find a just adjustment or settlement of the situation or of the dispute leading to the threatening of peace. There was in principle no opposition to the notion that once peace is restored by a cease-fire or other means that cause the silence of weapons, the stability of this peace must be based upon justice so that the settlement of disputes takes due regard of rules of international law and the rights of the states concerned.[170] The analysis of Article 1 (1) UN Charter has shown that the principles of justice and of international law are binding on the Security Council before a breach of peace or a threat to peace occurs (see above II. 1. a.). In a similar way, the demands of justice and the rules of international law become relevant to a much greater extent as soon as the termination of the armed conflict begins to succeed and the Security Council progresses to its peace and stability organising function while still acting under Chapter VII. Justice and international law may be infringed only with respect to the immediate enforcement of peace,[171] but not, at least not to the same extent, with respect to creating a just and durable post-war settlement of the causes for the conflict.

2. Basic Exigencies of Justice After War

Doing justice after war implies some prerequisites in restoring peace which are either procedural or substantive. Here, only basic require-

---

[170] See *Documents of the United Nations Conference on International Organization, Volume VI*, see note 32, 453; Gill, see note 20, 66-67. One has, however, to concede that these statements appear to have been made in the context of peaceful settlement of conflict subsequent to enforcement measures because the Security Council was not seen to have the power to settle a crisis or a dispute between states by addressing compulsory resolutions to the relevant states. See N. Angelet, "International Law Limits to the Security Council", in: V. Gowlland-Debbas (ed.), *United Nations Sanctions and International Law*, 2001, 77-79.

[171] See the statement of Professor Payssé at the UN Conference on International Organization in San Francisco 1945, reprinted in *Documents of the UN Conference on International Organization, Vol. VI*, see note 32, 33.

ments can be indicated in rather general terms since the concrete requirements of justice after war that direct the transformation of a conflict society to a stable post-conflict society differ according to the peculiarities of each crisis. The conception of transitional justice is contex-
tualised and partial.[172] At least some of the exigencies of post war justice which need to be identified can be learnt from past experiences with
post conflict settlements. It is doubtful, however, whether all necessary
lessons have already been learnt. The inauguration of the UN Peacebuilding Commission in December 2005[173] testifies to this. The exigencies are relevant for the exercise of the UN Security Council powers
under Chapter VII and form a nucleus of a new body of international
law on administrative rules for international administration of foreign
territory. The Security Council must respect them when prescribing
measures of peace enforcement and post-conflict reconstruction. It requires the Security Council to provide in its resolutions in explicit
terms for the institutions and designs necessary for the implementation
of the demands of post war justice. In particular the resolutions which
establish or mandate transitional international administrations may be
more detailed in setting the mandate, the objectives and the legal
framework for the operation of the transitional administrations than
previous ones,[174] in particular if the Security Council intends authorising or mandating a deviation from international rules.[175]

a. Procedural Exigencies

In procedural terms, sustainable peace requires participation of the
people and the government (if there is an identifiable recognised one[176])
affected by the peace enforcement measures. Since direct participation
of the people living in the occupied territory will be difficult to organise
in a society suffering from the consequences of war, indirect participa-

---

[172] With respect to justice in political transitions see in general R.G. Teitel, *Transitional Justice*, 2000, 6.
[173] See S/RES/1646 (2005) of 20 December 2005, see also A/RES/60/180 of 20 December 2005 and S/RES/1645 (2005) of 20 December 2005 and . In this regard, Wolfrum, see note 49, 696 rightly points out that a new institution without clear standards of accountability for the UN will not remedy the recognised deficits.
[174] Chesterman, see note 50, 239-241; Stahn, see note 157, 320.
[175] See with respect to humanitarian law Sassòli, see note 142, 681, 690.
[176] Regarding this problem for transitional administrations see de Wet, see note 119, 338 et seq.

tion by existing or interim domestic institutions, in the beginning preferably at local or regional level,[177] or – in exceptional cases – by non-
state actors,[178] must be preferred. Participation appears not to be practicable as long as the military phase is continuing. The requirements of
effective and fast war termination govern the exercise of the Security
Council's discretion in choosing the necessary enforcement measures to
be taken. There appears to be no room for participative decisions at an
early stage. Participation and accompanied principles like procedural
fairness and representation increasingly become important the more the
war termination progresses towards reaching peace settlement, in particular in the negotiations leading to a peace treaty. At the latest, at this
stage which actually in most cases will be beyond the phase of enforcement measures under Chapter VII, the vanquished must have a voice to
express their interests and must be given a chance to participate. But
even in earlier phases of peace restoration representative participation
must be granted. The idea of participation is not incompatible with the
character of enforcement measures under Chapter VII. International
provisional administrations put in place or mandated by the Security
Council after the armed hostilities ended are capable of making the local people increasingly take part in the exercise of administrative powers and functions. The Security Council mandate for the international
administrative institutions must include an obligation to interact with
domestic actors. Additionally, the relationship between domestic and
international actors and the way this will change over time must be
clarified.[179] Local support will further the success of restoring a sustainable peace order and safeguard sensitivity for local delicacies. Past experiences with international transitional administrations endorse this.[180]
Last but not least, increased participation and representation is a means
of the gradual re-establishment and re-transfer of authority to the domestic government or justice institutions as required by the temporal
limitations of Chapter VII powers and by the respect for self-

---

177 Chesterman, see note 50, 144. The development of local democratic institu-
     tions was mandated by S/RES/1272 (1999) of 25 October 1999, para. 8 on
     East Timor; for more detail insofar see M. Benzing, "Midwifing a New
     State: The United Nations in East Timor", *Max Planck UNYB* 9 (2005),
     295 et seq. (343 et seq.). For gradual democratic participation in Kosovo see
     Friedrich, see note 130, 256 et seq., 287 et seq.
178 See Chesterman, see note 50, 128.
179 See Chesterman, see note 50, 129, 240.
180 Stahn, see note 157, 314; de Wet, see note 119, 339.

determination demanded by the purposes and principles of the UN Charter (see above under III. 2. and 4.).

Another exigency is multi-lateralisation. The process of peace building must be internationalised in order to avoid reproaches of hostile occupation, revenge or victor's justice. Sustainable peace restoration demands impartiality and moderation which are realised by including neutral third parties in the process of peace restoration both as regards decision making and implementation. Multi-lateralisation safeguards the necessary degree of neutrality and moderation and adds to the legitimacy of the Security Council intervention.[181] Integrating third parties like NGOs and non-partisan states in restoring peace can be implemented by putting states not involved in the military enforcement actions in charge of transitional administrations and monitoring institutions, or by integrating NGOs in the monitoring of human rights observance. This is necessary although the Security Council itself institutionalises some kind of moderation and neutrality. Any resolution adopted within the Security Council is usually taken under participation of Council members that are not directly engaged in a military enforcement action. At the San Francisco Conference hope was expressed that the proceedings of the Security Council would provide for just settlement of disputes.[182] This view, however, reflects too high a confidence in the proper functioning of the Security Council. Admittedly, the necessity to obtain a positive vote for a resolution within the Security Council provides some checks and balances. The composition of the Security Council institutionalises an internationalisation of peace making. The Security Council, for political reasons, must also take account of the positions in the General Assembly. For these reasons, some scholars expect a basically fair treatment by the Security Council.[183] Nevertheless, one must be more cautious. Some states, in particular those targeted, may still regard the internationalisation of conflict settlement by the Council to be one-sided and biased by Western political values. In particular cases a resolution by the Security Council might look like a shared hegemony of certain Security Council members, for

---

[181]   C. Stahn, "Jus ad bellum – Jus in bello – Jus post bellum: Towards a Tripartite Conception of Armed Conflict", 9 <http://www.esil-sedi.eu/english/pdf/Stahn2.PDF>.

[182]   See Kelsen, see note 21, 271.

[183]   Tomuschat, see note 159, 27 (with respect to Iraq); Faßbender, see note 35, 280 who argues that the interests of the defeated state can be better protected in the framework of the Council.

example where the decision of the Security Council is taken only by bare weighted majorities in the Security Council and against majorities in the General Assembly,[184] or where a powerful permanent member succeeds in tailoring resolutions to its own needs.[185] Therefore, the integration of neutral third parties in the restoration of peace furthers its legitimacy and acceptance.

b. Substantive Exigencies

With respect to basic substantive requirements of sustainable peace restoration, the Security Council acting under Chapter VII is bound to correspond to certain fundamental demands of justice.

First and foremost, as a general demand, the conditions for peace restoration forced by the Security Council upon the vanquished must be moderate instead of draconian or vengeful. The self-esteem of the target people must be secured and the relations between perpetrators and victims have to be restored. Justice requires the reintegration of both perpetrator and victim into the international community.[186] Any contempt for the offender does not work for sustainable peace. And it is only the Security Council as the executive of the common will that is capable of attaining reintegration.[187]

Also for this reason, all measures of peace restoration must be guided by the constraints of necessity and proportionality. The measures taken by the Security Council must be appropriate to the threat or breach of peace. This necessitates defining in clear terms the aims and strategic objectives of the enforcement actions (both as regards terminating the violence and building the peace thereafter)[188] at the very beginning, because only in this way can one judge when enforcement

---

[184] T. Farer, "Beyond the Charter Frame: Unilateralism Or Condominium?", *AJIL* 96 (2002), 359 et seq. (360).

[185] Examples are the Security Council resolutions S/RES/1422 (2002) of 12 July 2002 and S/RES/1487 (2003) of 12 June 2003 on jurisdictional immunities for troop contributing states not parties to the ICC.

[186] See C. Villa-Vicencio, "Restorative Justice in Social Context", in: Nigel Biggar (ed.), *Burying the Past: Making Peace and Doing Justice After Civil Conflict*, 2nd edition 2003, 235 et seq. (239).

[187] Faßbender, see note 35, 280.

[188] On the necessity of clarity see Berman, see note 99, 158 (with respect to mandated military enforcement); Chesterman, see note 50, 240-243 (with respect to international administrations).

measures become disproportionate to their aim and therefore illegal or when the actions taken or mandated by the Security Council have to come to end, unless circumstances change considerably so that the ends of the action must be re-defined. A prior definition of the mandate and the objectives of peace enforcement and peace restoration actions also remedies the often improvisational and unprepared character of peace organising measures.[189]

Furthermore, ensuring moderation and self-esteem of the vanquished in principle calls for respecting the *right of people to self-determination* as a corollary of the sovereignty of the occupied state to determine its internal political and economic order including the permanent sovereignty over natural resources.[190] The respect for the right to self-determination requires that any mandatory conflict solution is only provisional, as is the case when the Security Council acts under Chapter VII. The Security Council may, however command or allow for regime changes and changes of the internal order and basic rules in the occupied territory if the restoration of peace requires the construction and maintenance of a new kind of regime that is peaceful and more pro-human rights.[191] Failing to address such internal institutional reasons for a conflict might inevitably result in its re-occurrence. The political or ethnical tensions underlying a conflict must be resolved. In case of ethnic conflicts restoring peace may not only necessitate rebuilding state institutions but call for nation-building.[192] Restoring peace will require establishing an impartial, international transitional administration in case the former internal order or disorder contributed to the rise of a threat or breach of peace or in case the violence led to a

---

[189] See Berman, see note 99, 161 (with respect to S/RES/678 (1990) of 29 November 1990); S. Chesterman, "Virtual Trusteeship", in: Malone, see note 3, 219 et seq. (221); Stahn, see note 157, 327 with respect to transitional administrations.

[190] As expressed e.g. in S/RES/1483 (2003) of 22 May 2003, para. 20. See also Orakhelashvili, see note 11, 311.

[191] See Orend, see note 35, 50. Regarding the dangers of – unilateral – regime change (e.g. destabilisation, civil war etc) cf. R.N. Haass, "Regime Change and Its Limits", *Foreign Aff.* (2005) <http://www.foreignaffairs.org/20 050701faessay84405/richard-n-haass/regime-change-and-its-limits.html>.

[192] For the distinction between state and nation-building see A. von Bogdandy/ S. Häußler/ F. Hanschmann/ R. Utz, "State-Building, Nation-Building, and Constitutional Politics in Post-Conflict Situations: Conceptual Clarifications and an Appraisal of Different Approaches", *Max Planck UNYB* 9 (2005), 579 et seq. (580 et seq., 613).

collapse of domestic institutions. The task of provisional administrations prescribed by the Security Council will then be to help (re)building domestic reform and justice institutions and restoring public trust in them. Meanwhile the demands of representation and participation must be considered as soon as possible without threatening attained stability and peace.[193] In particular the security institutions of a state may usually be suspect because they were the former core instruments of suppression.[194] New institutions of human rights observance (ombudspersons, courts, truth commissions)[195] and third party monitoring of their sound working might also contribute to a restoration of stable peace. This raises the question how such transformations are compatible with the sovereignty and the right to self-determination. In this respect, one must recall, first, that the constraints of occupation law do not oblige the Security Council (or its authorised agents) when acting under Chapter VII (see above under III. 2.). Thus, the fact that occupation law does not support regime change is irrelevant. Second, there are limits to the right to self-determination prohibiting aggressive domestic regimes or regimes that do not take account of international obligations and basic requirements like non-aggression, non-intervention and respect for human rights. Even the proclamation of sovereignty and self-determination cannot and does not make an aggressive regime acceptable to the international community. Measures taken by a legitimate organisation like the United Nations to facilitate the reintegration of an perpetrator state within the international community are not a hostile intervention contradicting the sovereignty and self-determination of the people and state addressed but a valuable help in reaching again a situation of normalcy where human rights, democracy and the rule of law are the yardsticks of government.[196] This serves the necessary restoration of relationship between aggressor and victims.

---

[193]   Cf. also Secretary-General, see note 160, 27 et seq., 52 et seq. Chesterman, see note 50, 143 points to the need for balancing participation with effective peace restoration by international institutions. In short term democratic openings in post-conflict societies may increase instability, Fox, see note 139, 74. For the peculiar problems of transitional administrations in the reconstruction of independent judiciary see Stahn, see note 157, 323 et seq.

[194]   See F.O. Hampson, *Nurturing Peace*, 1996, 229.

[195]   Regarding the contribution of human rights institutions to the restoration of peace and its confines see M. Minow, "Innovating Responses to the Past", in: N. Biggar (ed.), *Burying the Past: Making Peace and Doing Justice After Civil Conflict*, 2nd edition 2003, 87 et seq.

[196]   Tomuschat, see note 159, 28.

This consideration underlines that the regime change that was organised in Iraq had been legitimate and corresponded to the powers of the Security Council since the regime of Saddam Hussein was atrocious in both its internal and external affairs. The regime change cannot be seen as punishment irrespective of the intentions of some of the Security Council members.[197] On the other hand, one must not forget that measures taken for peace restoration must not have an open-ended effect but, in principle, have to be provisional. The provisional nature is not only required by the constitutional restraints for the Security Council powers (see above under III. 4.) but is confirmed by the exigencies of justice in transition. This also places particular demands on peace restoring measures which do have a fundamental and durable impact on the internal or even constitutional order of the target state, like establishing a new economic order or a new governmental system. A conflict society that has to be guided back to a stable post-conflict society requires particular guidelines which must pay due attention to the peculiarities of transition. Under such circumstances making laws serves transformative purposes in addition to its conventional purposes.[198] Basic laws must be suitable to provide the legal design of dynamic processes. Thus, they must in themselves be dynamic and accessible to change and subject to participation of domestic institutions and people corresponding to the progress made. The more fundamental the character of rules and institutions that are enacted or established, the more participation must be increased. Rules regulating the recognition, amendment or abolition of laws enacted by international provisional administrations for the time thereafter must also be provided.[199] In all of these efforts, the cultural context has to be observed. No effort to build up norms, rules and institutions will succeed if in contradiction to prevailing, deeply rooted cultural attitudes unless the transformative process is conceived as a long time endeavour shaping legal and political

---

[197] Contra Faßbender, see note 35, 281.

[198] Compare Teitel, see note 172, 191 et seq.

[199] These demands seem not to be fulfilled by the Dayton accords. They served their purpose as peace agreements but are almost unworkable as constitution while changing them is seen as a threat to re-ignite the conflict, S. Chesterman, "Walking softly in Afghanistan: the Future of UN State-Building", *Survival* 44 (2002/3), 37 et seq. (39); G. Nystuen, *Achieving Peace or Protecting Human Rights? Conflicts between Norms Regarding Ethnic Discrimination in the Dayton Peace Agreement*, 2005; Oellers-Frahm, see note 153, 217-222.

cultures that are receptive for democracy which has not existed before.[200]

Closely related to the right to self-determination is the necessary respect for the territorial integrity of the vanquished which in principle, has to be guaranteed. In particular, territorial punishments are not tenable. The UN and the victorious states acting on its behalf may not be allowed to compensate their losses by acquisition of territory. Instead, aggression should be punished by consequences for the responsible individuals by means of criminal prosecution and individual liability for compensation.[201]

Criminal prosecution of war crimes and other severe offences is another prerequisite of justice after war.[202] Soldiers and leading politicians, even heads of states from all sides of the conflict must be held accountable for their offences. This is an important part of the individualisation of coming to terms with consequences of war.[203] Criminal accountability, however, may compete with the interest in pursuing reconciliation and societal reconstruction which sometimes might give rise to the need for amnesty. Criminal justice is not the only way to pursue reconciliation. Truth commissions may also work as sound forms of accountability. Thus, criminal justice may not be achieved at all cost in any circumstances. It may suffice to prosecute only those most responsible for the core crimes.[204]

Instead of collective punishment, individual responsibility is required in order to avoid prolonging the in-justices of war into the time of peace. For this reason, collective punishments by way of, for example, forceful resettlements of population must not happen. This would contradict the rights of human beings and the idea of punishing or

[200] On the interrelatedness of rule of law and legal and political culture in the context of nation-building see Stromseth/ Wippman/ Brooks, see note 13, 68 et seq., 310 et seq.

[201] On the demise of the concept of punishment for aggression see also Stahn, "Jus ad bellum – Jus in bello – Jus post bellum? – Rethinking the Conception of the Law of Armed Force", *EJIL* 17 (2006), 921 et seq. (939). This concept still was present at the Potsdam Agreement of 1945, compare Tomuschat, see note 159, 21 et seq.

[202] See M.C. Bassiouni (ed.), *Post-Conflict Justice*, 2002.

[203] On increased individualisation in this regard see also Stahn, see note 201, 940.

[204] A. Seibert-Fohr, "Reconstruction through Accountability", *Max Planck UNYB* 9 (2005), 555 et seq. (575 et seq.).

holding accountable only those responsible for the aggression, and could amount to ethnic cleansing. The only exception under which forced resettlement might be legitimate is to reverse prior expulsions, deportations or settlements that had taken place during the conflict or that caused the conflict.[205] Another corollary of the idea of individualisation of guilt concerns the reparation and compensation for war losses and is confirmed by the idea of avoiding revenge. Both ideas require that the compensation of the perpetrator to the victims for at least some of the costs incurred or damage done during the time of violence must be proportionate to the aim of peace restoration. This means that the aggressor is demanded to compensate only insofar as affordable in order not to infringe the rights of younger generations which are not responsible.[206] In particular it means that the compensation should come from the personal wealth of elites of the perpetrator state who were most responsible for the aggression.[207] In terms of Security Council powers this means *inter alia* that the Security Council under Chapter VII is empowered to sanction individuals personally responsible for breaches of the peace or threats to the peace by commanding freezing of assets or extradition, as happened in the past.[208] Recently, the UN General Assembly adopted a resolution on Basic Principles and Guidelines on the Right to a Remedy and Reparation for Victims of Gross Viola-

---

[205] The Dayton Peace Agreement grants to everyone a right to return to the domicile or residence of origin (Annex 7 to the Agreement, *ILM* 35 (1996), 136 et seq.); enabling the effective exercise of this right, however, will take time after all that had happened in Bosnia-Herzegovina.

[206] See also Stahn, see note 201, 939 et seq. The idea of non-excessive reparation already was respected after World War II, see Tomuschat, see note 159, 20, but cannot be found in the Rules on State Responsibility which without any exception postulates full reparation, see arts 31, 36 of A/RES/56/83 of 12 December 2001, see note 27. A lack of full reparation may pose problems of equal treatment because some may be compensated while others are not. For the dilemma of transitional reparatory justice see Teitel, see note 172, 132 et seq. One may remedy such problems to a certain extent by differing between individual and collective losses.

[207] Orend, see note 35, 48.

[208] See S/RES/1533 (2004) of 12 March 2004, S/RES/1572 (2004) of 15 November 2004, S/RES/1596 (2005) of 3 May 2005, and S/RES/1636 (2005) of 31 October 2005 with respect to the situations in Congo, Cote d'Ivoire, and the Middle East (assassination of Prime Minister Hariri).

tions of International Human Rights Law and Serious Violations of International Humanitarian Law.[209]

Finally, justice after war requires the Security Council to determine in its measures under Chapter VII clear mandates and responsibilities for military forces and civilian administrations and to establish clear accountability including civil responsibility and criminal culpability to the United Nations and its personnel or to the mandated agents and their staff in case of crimes, damages or excess of power.[210] In particular, the governmental powers of provisional administrations must be defined and institutions must be established or existing institutions be allowed to exercise independent judicial control over the decisions of the provisional administration.[211] This includes enabling the prosecution of war crimes and establishing a human rights monitoring system while the United Nations or its agents work for the restoration of peace.[212] Criminal prosecution of war crimes must include prosecution of service members of troops taking part in UN enforcement measures in order for the United Nations to avoid any impression of double standards and exacting revenge.[213] The responsibility of the Security Council here is to ensure that any crime committed by soldiers of troop-contributing states is prosecuted by the troop contributing states.[214] Furthermore, the principle of jurisdictional immunity for the United Nations personnel or the deployed troops must be reformed in this respect in order to allow for judicial control. The same applies to troops that were contributed by states not parties to the ICC. Granting jurisdictional immunities to them[215] contradicts the idea of establishing justice after war.

---

[209]   A/RES/60/147 of 16 December 2005.

[210]   See V. O'Conner, *Model Codes for Post Conflict Criminal Justice*, 2007.

[211]   On the need for accountability see Chesterman, see note 50, 145 et seq. For past shortcomings insofar see Ratner, see note 36, 715-716; Stahn, see note 157, 321 et seq., 330 et seq.; Wolfrum, see note 49, 685-687.

[212]   With respect to the latter requirement cf. de Wet, see note 5, 336.

[213]   Orend, see note 35, 43 at 54. This principle was neglected at Potsdam, see Tomuschat, see note 159, 21.

[214]   See the Final Report on the Accountability of International Organizations at the Berlin ILA Conference, reprinted in *International Organizations Law Review* 1 (2004), 221 et seq. (252). This responsibility may be implemented by including provisions into the agreements between the UN and those states authorised to use force or by explicitly requesting such prosecution in the Security Council resolution mandating the use of force.

[215]   As had happened by S/RES/1422 (2002) of 12 July 2002 and S/RES/1487 (2003) of 12 June 2003. This was partly re-introduced by Resolution

The non-renewal of these immunities in 2004 was rightly welcomed by the Secretary-General as a "significant contribution to the efforts of the Organization to promote justice and rule of law in international affairs".[216]

V. Conclusion

Thinking about the powers of the Security Council under Chapter VII in the age of new challenges for the collective security system leads to the conclusion that the powers of the Security Council must be interpreted in a broad and purpose-oriented way considering, in particular, the need for effectiveness of the Security Council measures to terminate armed conflicts and to restore peace. The Security Council powers must be strengthened, not weakened. They are constitutive in nature, to a large extent determining the law applicable to a conflict. The Security Council is allowed to deviate from international law and to act in a way independent from the (il)legality of previous acts by other actors, in particular of prior unilateral use of force. The prime objective of conflict termination and peace restoration which is decisive for the interpretation of the Security Council powers both expands and limits the Chapter VII powers. Due to this prime objective the Security Council functions have been extended from a mere war terminator to a post-conflict organiser of peace and security, accompanied by a changing notion of peace. These changes demand an interpretation of the Chapter VII powers that provides for effective war termination and peace restoration at the same time and enables the Security Council to respond to the challenges to the collective security system.

On the other hand, the analysis of the constitutive character of its powers has also shown that there are limits that derive from implied constitutional confines (primarily the objective of peace restoration), from purposes and principles of the United Nations and from peremptory norms of international law. Purposes and principles of the United Nations like respect for human rights oblige the Security Council even when acting under Chapter VII. But they can, to a certain extent, be weighed against the requirements of peace restoration and therefore do

---

S/RES/1593 (2005) of 31 March 2005, op. para. 6, referring the situation in Darfur to the ICC.

[216] *Report of the Secretary-General on the Work of the Organization*, Doc. A/59/1 of 2004, Suppl. No. 1, para. 210.

not represent absolute limits of the Chapter VII powers under all circumstances.

Peace restoration as an end requires measures to be of provisional character and calls for respect for the demands of post-war justice. A contemporary analysis of the Chapter VII powers has to consider the emerging awareness for the exigencies of justice after war since peace enforcement and restoration reasonably can only aim at sustainable peace. The basic prerequisites of post-war justice therefore belong to the implied confines of the Security Council enforcement powers. The demands of post-war justice influence the exercise of the Council's discretion to restore peace, adding additional limits to the exercise of the Chapter VII powers. This does not introduce a new category of legal restraints to the Security Council powers but evidences the importance of carefully considering the ends of any peace enforcement measure. The demands of justice after war also confirm the requirement of a necessity and proportionality principle in the exercise of the Security Council powers under Chapter VII that direct the derogation from basic rules of international law. Furthermore, the demands of justice after war also contribute to a greater workability and precision of the proportionality principle. Both the objective of peace restoration and the demands of post-war justice work for the same end in this regard: any derogation from international law is allowed only as long as and insofar as necessary for restoring peace, and must be proportionate to that aim. The extent to which the Security Council is allowed to deviate from international law, in particular from fundamental principles of human rights and humanitarian law – besides peremptory international law – depends (in reverse proportionality) on its progress on peace restoration. The more the military phase of an armed conflict comes to an end the higher the respect for such rules must be. International rules representing individual rights or protecting individual interests shall be respected to an even greater extent. Any derogation from collective positions (like sovereignty, self-determination) can be reasoned more easily than a deviation from rules protecting individuals. Some rules of occupation law appear unsuitable for peace restoration.

Thus, the proportionality principle works in two ways engendering two differentiations: first, a differentiation between different functions of the Security Council under the overall umbrella of peace restoration (war terminating function and peace organising function, depending on the progress in peace restoration), and second, a differentiation as regards different types of rules in international law (rather collective rules or rather individual rules) have to be made. These two differentiations must be considered when assessing the limits for the powers of the Security Council to derogate from international law under Chapter VII under the proportionality requirement.

When determining the limits to the UN Security Council powers under Chapter VII one should not pay too much attention to principles like self-determination which are highly contested in their exact legal meaning and quite double-edged. Whereas for some, self-determination is a norm of *jus cogens*, others reject the notion of self-determination as a binding norm at all, in particular since decolonisation has been completed.[217] Indeed, one must take care that a principle genuinely designed to free peoples from colonial domination is not used now as a doctrine for the protection of states' prerogatives, in particular the right to territorial integrity and to exclusive decision-making on the internal order, even against the necessities of sustainable peace restoration. More important principles of international law flowing from human rights law and humanitarian law, however, must be respected to a much greater extent by Security Council resolutions. The reason for this difference is that the latter body of law protects rights of individuals whose positions stand in the centre of the primary United Nations goal of avoiding or terminating war.

According to the preamble of the UN Charter, the final aims of the United Nations and its peace-keeping or restoring activities are the needs and rights of human beings which are negatively affected by the scourge of war. In contrast, the rights and positions of nations or people are only collective in nature. Nations, states and people usually survive war whereas individual human beings are tortured, killed, raped or deprived. Therefore, collective positions and rights might be restricted more easily by Security Council measures under Chapter VII.

---

[217] See Steinhardt, see note 29, 46.

Enhancing Community Accountability of the Security Council through Pluralistic Structure: The Case of the 1267 Committee

Machiko Kanetake *

I. Introduction

The upsurge in the invocation of Chapter VII in the post Cold War era, accompanied by the diversification of the notion of "threat to the peace", has both quantitatively and qualitatively increased instances wherein the UN Security Council's (SC) activities permeate the domestic sphere and brought about greater involvement at the individual level.[1] While the proposition that the SC's discretion must not bypass the rule of law has gained advocacy, worthy of more attention is the fact that the delimitation of power must be ensured, not merely relative to Member States but also *vis-à-vis* non-state actors. In other words, accountability to wider constituencies in international society – what this article terms as *community accountability* – must be enhanced.

This article proposes that a normative case for such community accountability is emerging, and that the enhancement of such accountability is possible even without recourse to institutionalized settings such as the case of judicial review of SC resolutions. To provide an example of this, this article examines the accountability mechanism of the decision-making undertaken by the *Al Qaeda and Taliban Sanctions Committee* (the 1267 Committee or the Committee) of the SC established pursuant to S/RES/1267 (1999) on 15 October 1999.

The following issues will be addressed:

1. Which constituencies of the international community should and could hold the Committee and the SC to account (see below under Chapter II.);[2]

---

*   *I am grateful to Dr. Krisch for his comment on an earlier version of this article.*

1   The period after the 1990s witnessed the increase and diversification of instances in which the SC's exertion of authority directly impinged upon individuals, as illustrated by (i) economic sanctions targeting specific individuals (to be discussed in this article), (ii) peacekeeping operations that increased in number and assumed a wider range of mandates, and (iii) transitional administrations in war-torn territories.

2   This article assumes that the accountability of the Committee is effectively a matter of the SC. The Committee's mandate is set out by the SC and subject to revision by the latter at all times. In addition, under certain circumstances decisions of the Committee can be submitted to the SC, see *Al-Qaida and Taliban Sanctions Committee, Guidelines of the Committee for the Conduct of its Work*, last amended on 12 February 2007 (hereinafter

2. How have various constituencies in the international community challenged the perceived accountability deficit of the Committee's decision-making and how have the Committee and the SC responded to such challenges (see below under Chapter III.), and finally;

3. It will be focused on the accountability towards targeted individuals and entities; what the accountability mechanism should and could be in the foreseeable future, and, in particular, what problems would be associated with the introduction of a centralized review process (see below under Chapter IV.).

Born out of the lessons learned from comprehensive sanctions, sanctions targeting specific individuals and entities have been one of the SC's key strategies in responding to any "threat to the peace". One such application has been the establishment of the sanctions regime under Chapter VII against the Taliban, triggered by the bombings of the US embassies in Kenya and Tanzania.[3]

The individual targets are designated by the Committee made up of all 15 members of the SC. The Committee's work has been supported by the Monitoring Group (2001-2003) and the Analytical Support and Sanctions Monitoring Team (2004-), composed of independent experts appointed by the Secretary-General (SG).

The sanctions regime has been modified and strengthened ever since by subsequent resolutions, including S/RES/1333 (2000) of 19 December 2000, by extending the reach of the assets freeze to members of Al Qaeda[4] and S/RES/1390 (2002) of 28 January 2002 further expanded the targets of the assets freeze deciding: "... that all States shall take the following measures with respect to Usama bin Laden, members of the Al-Qaida organization and the Taliban and other individuals, groups, undertakings and entities associated with them, as referred to in the list created pursuant to resolutions 1267 (1999) and 1333 (2000)", imposing

---

Committee Guidelines 2007), para. 4(a), available at: <http://www.un.org/sc/committees/1267/pdf/1267_guidelines.pdf>.

3   Before the passing of S/RES/1267, lists of individuals and entities were drawn under S/RES/917 (1994) of 6 May 1994 for Haiti; S/RES/1127 (1997) of 28 August 1997 for Angola and S/RES/1171 (1998) of 5 June 1998 for Sierra Leone, by the respective sanctions committees.

4   S/RES/1333 (2000) of 19 December 2000, para. 8(c).

a travel ban and arms embargo.[5] Between these two extensions, the September 11 terrorist attack occurred.

Few would doubt the potential advantage of the Al Qaeda/Taliban sanctions regime at the UN in obliging all states, not merely like-minded states, to block the financing of particular terrorists. The uniformity of targets is what the sanctions regime aims at. Compared to its confidence in the sanctions regime in the earlier reports,[6] however, the Monitoring Team acknowledges in its 2007 report that states are losing confidence in the sanctions regime.[7] This might be true for various non-state constituencies as well: not limited to the targeted individuals and entities alleging their non-involvement and their immediate local communities, but also financial institutions devoting their resources to tracing and blocking the designated assets.

The accountability issue, represented, *inter alia*, by questions in connection with decisional transparency in listing/delisting and human rights concerns, is the primary, if not the sole, source of dissatisfaction.[8]

---

[5]   S/RES/1390 (2002) of 28 January 2002, para. 2.

[6]   See *2nd Report of the Analytical Support and Sanctions Monitoring Team Appointed Pursuant to Resolution 1526 (2004) Concerning Al-Qaida and the Taliban and Associated Individuals and Entities*, Doc. S/2005/83 of 15 February 2005 (hereinafter 2nd Report of the Monitoring Team), para. 16; *3rd Report of the Analytical Support and Sanctions Monitoring Team Appointed Pursuant to Resolution 1526 (2004) Concerning Al-Qaida and the Taliban and Associated Individuals and Entities*, Doc. S/2005/572 of 9 September 2005 (hereinafter 3rd Report of the Monitoring Team), para. 2.

[7]   *6th Report of the Analytical Support and Sanctions Monitoring Team Appointed Pursuant to Security Council Resolutions 1526 (2004) and 1617 (2005) Concerning Al-Qaida and the Taliban and Associated Individuals and Entities*, Doc. S/2007/132 of 8 March 2007 (hereinafter 6th Report of the Monitoring Team), paras 2-3.

[8]   6th Report of the Monitoring Team, see note 7, para. 15-16. There are at least two other major causes for the lack of confidence, the detailed account of which is beyond the scope of this article. (i) One impediment concerns the resources and technical capacity of many Member States to implement the decisions. See, e.g., C.A. Ward, "The Counter-Terrorism Committee: Its Relevance for Implementing Targeted Sanctions", in: P. Wallensteen/ C. Staibano (eds), *International Sanctions: Between Words and Wars in the Global System*, 2005, 167 et seq. (ii) Another concern which may be shared by some states is that countering terrorism by way of targeted sanctions itself may be counterproductive; the potential of collective security rather lies in addressing the roots of terrorism. See, e.g., N. Krisch, "The Rise and Fall of Collective Security: Terrorism, US Hegemony, and the Plight of the

However, the significant aspects of the Al Qaeda/Taliban sanctions regime are that the level of accountability discharged by the Committee has been challenged by Member States and various non-state actors, and that the SC and the Committee have made efforts to respond to them from the sanctions' early stages. This process provides an invaluable insight into global governance, particularly into the role of decentralized standard-setting processes in enhancing the accountability of global administrative bodies.

II. Community Accountability of the Security Council

1. Candidates of Accountability Holders

The decision-making of the Al Qaeda/Taliban sanctions regime impinges upon the lives and activities of many. Should "impact" be the most simplified fount to call for accountability, the regime experiences no shortage of candidates of accountability holders. These candidates are Member States (more precisely relevant state authorities),[9] the targeted individuals/entities, their immediate local communities and financial institutions in the web of implementation. On the other hand, the SC's accountability is traditionally directed towards the General Assembly (GA) and Member States.[10] A concern can thus be raised since insufficient regard has been paid to the possibility that the SC is in part "accountable to the wrong constituencies".[11] The UN's transformation

---

Security Council", in: C. Walter et al. (eds), *Terrorism as a Challenge for National and International Law: Security versus Liberty?*, 2004, 879 et seq. (901-906).

9   Here a "Member State" refers to the aggregate of various state authorities relevant to the implementation of the sanctions. It follows that even the permanent members of the SC (and thereby also of the Committee) would not automatically be excluded as accountability holders, given that sending a delegation to the Committee does not automatically mean that its decision-making is shared by the relevant authorities of the permanent members.

10   See under II. 3., of this article.

11   N. Krisch, "The Pluralism of Global Administrative Law", *EJIL* 17 (2006), 247 et seq. (250). This question has also been raised in international relations. See R.O. Keohane, "Global Governance and Democratic Accountability", in: D. Held/ M. Koenig-Archibugi (eds), *Taming Globalization: Frontiers of Governance*, 2003, 130 et seq.

necessitates the consideration of what one calls *community accountability* to the wider membership of the international community. Such community accountability would be, in Keohane's work, a concept embracing both "internal accountability" and "external accountability".[12] At the same time, the invocation of "community" is also a project to rethink whether, and how, the common framework to call the SC to account could develop beyond the dichotomy of the internal and the external.

A family of Member States assumes no uniformity in terms of the degree of impact. For instance, the Committee's decision-making carries greater relevance for those states in which the listed individuals and entities (or their assets) are believed to be located, as well as to those states which submit the names of the individuals/entities to the Consolidated List. At the same time, these states are not in accord on the claims they have against the Committee. The former may be concerned about the sharing of as much information as possible with the Committee, while a matter of priority for the latter may well be assurance that the information they have provided is kept confidential.

An assets freeze certainly has a significant impact on the listed individuals and entities, including that upon their human rights, namely, the right to property (article 17, Universal Declaration of Human Rights), and possibly a person's right not to be subjected to arbitrary or unlawful interferences with his privacy, family, home or correspondence, nor to unlawful attacks on his honor and reputation (article 17, International Covenant on Civil and Political Rights (ICCPR)).[13] It is a disturbing fact that the Committee's listing and delisting process disregards further the right to a fair hearing (article 14 ICCPR) and the right to an effective remedy (article 2 (3) ICCPR) of those individuals and entities on the List. They are entitled to a fair hearing only if the assets freeze, the deprivation of property, amounts to a "criminal charge"[14] or

---

12   Keohane, see note 11, 141.

13   Strengthening Targeted Sanctions through Fair and Clear Procedures: White Paper prepared by the Watson Institute Targeted Sanctions Project (Brown University), 30 March 2006, Doc. A/60/887–S/2006/331 of 14 June 2006 (hereinafter Paper by the Watson Institute), 13.

14   International Covenant on Civil and Political Rights, *ILM* 6 (1967), 368 et seq. (hereinafter ICCPR), article 14 (1). Compare, e.g., E. De Wet, "The Role of Human Rights in Limiting the Enforcement Power of the Security Council: A Principled View", in: E. De Wet/ A. Nollkaemper (eds), *Review of the Security Council by Member States*, 2003, 7 et seq. (15-16); with the Paper of the Watson Institute, see note 13, 14-18.

if it involves the determination of a person's "rights and obligations in a suit at law".[15] The longer a suspected individual remains on the List, the more likely it is that the effect of sanctions will resemble a criminal charge.[16] Further, the listing has been used in criminal cases to establish, or at least to help in establishing, individuals' involvement in terrorism.[17]

The listing of individuals and entities can also bring severe consequences on their immediate local communities.[18] One such widely reported instance is the financial calamity in Somalia brought about by the closure of the Al Barakaat offices[19] shortly after the September 11 attacks.[20] Prior to the ban, the Al Barakaat network was the largest employer in Somalia, whereas many others depended on the remittance

---

[15]   Article 14 (1) ICCPR. Compare, e.g., I. Cameron, "UN Targeted Sanctions, Legal Safeguards and the European Convention on Human Rights", *Nord. J. Int'l L.* 72 (2003), 159 et seq. (192, fn. 91); with the Paper of the Watson Institute, see note 13, 14-15.

[16]   See J.E. Alvarez, "The Security Council's War on Terrorism: Problems and Policy Options", in: De Wet/ Nollkaemper, see note 14, 119 et seq. (132, 134-135); P. Gutherie, "Security Council Sanctions and the Protection of Individual Rights", *New York University Annual Survey of American Law* 60 (2004), 491 et seq. (503-506).

[17]   6th Report of the Monitoring Team, see note 7, para. 36, Box 1.

[18]   *Report of the United Nations High Commissioner for Human Rights on the Protection of Human Rights and Fundamental Freedoms while Countering Terrorism*, Doc. A/HRC/4/88 of 9 March 2007 (hereinafter Report of the UNHCHR), para. 23.

[19]   The Al Barakaat network, a money-remittance system headquartered in the United Arab Emirates, developed to address the need of Somali immigrants to transfer money to their relatives in Somalia where no banking system had operated: see J. Roth et al., "National Commission on Terrorist Attacks Upon the United States: Monograph on Terrorist Financing, Staff Report to the Commission", 21 August 2004, 67-69, available at: <http://www.9-11commission.gov/>. Compare in this respect also E.A. Thompson, "Misplaced Blame: Islam, Terrorism and the Origins of *Hawala*", *Max Planck UNYB* 11 (2006), 279 et seq.

[20]   In November 2001, the US blocked the assets of the Al Barakaat network. A few days later, many Al Barakaat entities appeared on the UN List. See Roth et al., see note 19, 79; White House, Terrorist Financial Network Fact Sheet: Shutting Down the Terrorist Financial Network, 7 November 2001, at: <http://www. whitehouse.gov/news/releases/2001/11/print/20011107-6.html>; Press Release AFG/163-SC/7206 of 9 November 2001.

from relatives abroad through Al Barakaat.[21] US officials anticipated that alternative remittance companies would quickly fill the vacuum, but in any event it would take some time for the alternatives to materialize.[22] Still a year later, November 2002, the Somali transitional government and the rebels issued a joint call for the reopening of the Al Barakaat banks, raising the concern that the "thousands employed by the bank had to stop work, while those that received money from relatives and friends abroad can no longer survive".[23]

Owing to the proliferation of both nationality and location of targets, the asset freeze under the 1267 Committee has had a more far-reaching impact on the financial community in terms of the time and resources they spend on compliance, compared to the case of the earlier asset freeze measures under the Haiti and Angola sanctions regime.[24] One of the prominent aspects of the Al Qaeda/Taliban sanctions seems to be the greater mobilization of private sectors, particularly financial institutions, into the web of SC sanctions regimes.[25] Further, the financial institutions face potential civil liability against their clients if they freeze assets on an a large basis, while at the same time encountering possible penalty by national authorities for failing to implement the assets freeze.[26]

---

21   BBC News, Somali Company "Not Terrorist", 8 November 2001, available at: <http://news.bbc.co.uk/2/hi/africa/1645073.stm>; New York Times, A Nation Challenged, A Midwestern Community: Somalis in Minneapolis Worry About Effect of Money-Transfer Raids, 9 November 2001; Washington Post, Somalis Said to Feel Impact of U.S. Freeze of al-Barakaat, 30 November 2001.

22   Washington Post, see note 21.

23   BBC News, Somali Factions Want Bank Assets Freed, 11 November 2002, available at: <http://news.bbc.co.uk/2/hi/africa/2442685.stm>.

24   S/RES/917 (1994) of 6 May 1994, para. 4 (Haiti); S/RES/1173 (1998) of 12 June 1998, para. 11 (Angola).

25   In its 5th report in 2006, the Monitoring Team incorporated a section on "the role of the private sector", stressing the need for a greater contribution from banks to the UN's efforts to cut terrorist financing: *5th Report of the Analytical Support and Sanctions Monitoring Team Appointed Pursuant to Security Council Resolutions 1526 (2004) and 1617 (2005) Concerning Al-Qaida and the Taliban and Associated Individuals and Entities*, Doc. S/2006/750 of 20 September 2006 (hereinafter 5th Report of the Monitoring Team), paras 83-85.

26   See European Banking Industry Committee, Re: European Banking Industry Committee's Recommendations for Improvements to UN Resolutions

Among these candidates of accountability holders, the impact upon Member States and the targeted individuals/entities is by far greater than on the others, inasmuch as these constituencies are directly addressed by the relevant SC resolutions and the Committee's decisions. Therefore, this article is focused on accountability to them. It is worth noting that the quest for the accountability of the SC does not automatically suggest the pursuit of democracy at the SC. Although no fixed definitions can be provided by either concept, accountability generally operates in broader forms and on broader levels than does democracy, as understood by domestic standards in general, at least in the sense that the former necessitates neither a demos *vis-à-vis* decision-makers nor elections.[27] Despite the fact that one cannot realistically claim that the SC should ensure democracy with elections and equitable representation,[28] the SC can be held accountable. At the same time, the modes of accountability for the SC, without presupposing a demos, suggest flexibility as well as uncertainty as to *who*, if not a demos, holds the body to account.

2. Holding the Security Council and the Committee to Account under Global Administrative Law

Calling a public body to account is a mechanism to control its power.[29] It refers to a *process of interaction* in which accountability holders, who are external and entitled to call the body to account, demand explana-

---

in the Field of Financial Sanctions, 11 April 2007, 2, available at: <http://www.esbg.eu/uploadedFiles/Position_papers/Banking%20Industry%20re commendations%20for%20improvements%20to%20UN%20Resolutions % 20in%20the%20field%20of%20financial%20sanctions.pdf>.

[27] See R.O. Keohane, "The Concept of Accountability in World Politics and the Use of Force", *Mich. J. Int'l L.* 24 (2003), 1121 et seq. (1122); R.O. Keohane/ J.S. Nye, Jr., "Redefining Accountability for Global Governance", in: M. Kahler/ D.A. Lake (eds), *Governance in a Global Economy: Political Authority in Transition*, 2003, 386 et seq. (386-389).

[28] See Keohane, see note 27, 1136.

[29] Accountability-based control largely refers to *ex post* oversight, C. Scott, "Accountability in the Regulatory State", *Journal of Law and Society* 27 (2000), 38 et seq. (39). However, it is noted that participation before making decisions is also one realization of accountability. Further, to call public administrations to account may, at the same time, facilitate the reconstruction of accountability standards for future conducts, in which sense, the ef-

tions and impose consequences for failing to act according to a set of standards while the body responds to such a call.[30] The following four questions are attached to this process: (i) Who is accountable? (ii) To whom? (iii) On the basis of what standards? (iv) How would such consequences be imposed? In domestic contexts, administrative law based on a constitution generally governs these questions. A straightforward example is judicial review, founded upon constitutional values (such as the rule of law, popular sovereignty and the protection of fundamental human rights), relevant pieces of legislation and case-law. A judicial review defines a public body to be accountable, confers *locus standi* upon accountability holders, lays out the grounds of review and finally offers remedies as a result of the review.

On the other hand, global administrative law is yet to be developed such that it systematically responds to these questions in relation to the SC and the Committee. In fact, the ever-increasing appearance of "the rule of law", "democracy" and "human rights" at the UN and other international forums is striking, and the World Summit Outcome document in September 2005 declared that "they belong to the universal and

---

fect of accountability-based control is also prospective: D. Curtin/ A. Nollkaemper, "Conceptualizing Accountability in International and European Law", *NYIL* 36 (2005), 3 et seq. (8).

[30] Authors phrase the process of interaction in slightly different ways: see R. Mulgan, "'Accountability': An Ever-Expanding Concept?", *Public Administration* 78 (2000), 555 et seq. (555) ("accountability ... involves *social interaction and exchange*, in that one side, that calling for the account, seeks answers and rectification while the other side, that being held accountable, responds and accepts sanctions" (emphasis original)); A.C.L. Davies, *Accountability: A Public Law Analysis of Government by Contract*, 2001, 81 ("setting standards against which to judge the account; obtaining the account; judging the account; and deciding what consequences, if any, should follow from it"); R.W. Grant/ R.O. Keohane, "Accountability and Abuses of Power in World Politics", *Am. Polit. Sci. Rev.* 99 (2005), 29 et seq. (29) ("some actors ... judge whether [other actors] have fulfilled their responsibilities in light of [a set of] standards, and to impose sanctions if they determine that these responsibilities have not been met"); Curtin/ Nollkaemper, see note 29, 8 ("an actor explains conduct and gives information to others, in which a judgment or assessment of that conduct is rendered on the basis of prior established rules or principles and in which it may be possible for some form of sanction (formal or informal) to be imposed on the actor"). This study avoids the use of "sanctions" and replaced it with "consequences", since the latter better captures the inclusion of non-institutionalized forms of "sanctions" such as reputation.

indivisible core values and principles of the United Nations ... ".[31] Nevertheless, in relation to the first question of *who is accountable*, it is traditionally against national governments to generate and apply a set of these values; hence, cautious steps must be taken when translating them for the global sphere against global administrative bodies.[32]

With reference to the rule of law, "the need for universal adherence to and implementation of the rule of law at both the national and *international levels*" was confirmed by the aforesaid World Summit Outcome document and subsequent GA resolutions.[33] While "the rule of law at ... international levels" is multi-faceted, several states perceived it as embracing an aspect of subjecting the UN and more broadly international organizations, to some form of the rule of law constraints.[34] This may support the advocates of the proposition that the maxim of the rule of law and one of its tenets, namely, "[p]ower entails accountability",[35] is emerging as a normative underpinning of global administrative law whereby the SC and the Committee are accountable insofar as they exert power. At present, further consensus building inside and outside the

---

[31]   2005 World Summit Outcome, A/RES/60/1 (2005) of 24 October 2005, para. 119.

[32]   See C. Harlow, "Global Administrative Law: The Quest for Principles and Values", *EJIL* 17 (2006), 187 et seq.; B. Kingsbury et al., "The Emergence of Global Administrative Law", *Law & Contemp. Probs* 68 (2005), 15 et seq. (42-51). Harlow also points out the danger of unifying the principles, Harlow, ibid., 211-214.

[33]   2005 World Summit Outcome, see note 31, para. 134 (emphasis added). See also The Rule of Law at the National and International Levels, A/RES/61/39 (2006) of 18 December 2006; The Rule of Law at the National and International Levels, A/RES/62/70 (2008) of 8 January 2008.

[34]   See, e.g., *Report of the Secretary-General, The Rule of Law at the National and International Levels: Comments and Information Received from Governments*, Doc. A/62/121 of 11 July 2007, 6-8 (Austria), 14 (Finland); *Summary Record of the 14th Mtg of the Sixth Committee, the Rule of Law at the National and International Levels*, Doc. A/C.6/62/SR.14, 15 November 2007, para. 19 (Mr. Beras Hernández of the Dominican Republic). See also Doc. S/PV. 5474 of 22 June 2006 (the SC meeting entitled "Rule of Law and Maintenance of International Peace and Security").

[35]   International Law Association, *Accountability of International Organisations: Final Report*, 2004, 5, available at: <http://www.ila-hq.org/html/ layout_committee.htm>.

GA remains to be seen in terms of how the maxim materializes in the light of global administrative bodies.[36]

Contested likewise is the invocation of human rights, notably the right to a fair hearing embodied in major human rights instruments,[37] as a normative foundation of global administrative law. An argument has been put forward to the effect that the observance of customary human rights norms attaches *a priori* to the legal personality of international organizations, inclusive the UN, enjoyed under international law.[38] Criticism can be leveled against this approach, in that it appears difficult to conform to the *Reparation for Injuries* case of 1949. Here the ICJ observed that it was "capable of possessing international rights and duties",[39] which is not the same as suggesting that international organizations are bound by customary rights and duties, including those *essen-*

---

[36] See Harlow, see note 32, 195-198, 207-211.

[37] Universal Declaration of Human Rights, A/RES/217A (III) (1948) of 10 December 1948, article 10; ICCPR, see note 14, article 14. See also 1950 European Convention for the Protection of Human Rights and Fundamental Freedoms, *ETS* No. 5 (Protocol 11, *ETS* No. 155), article 6; 1969 American Convention on Human Rights, *ILM* 9 (1969), 99 et seq., article 8; 1981 African (Banjul) Charter on Human and Peoples' Rights, *ILM* 21 (1982), 58 et seq., article 7.

[38] A. Reinisch, "Developing Human Rights and Humanitarian Law Accountability of the Security Council for the Imposition of Economic Sanctions", *AJIL* 95 (2001), 851 et seq. (858-859); P. Sands/ P. Klein, *Bowett's Law of International Institutions*, 5th edition, 2001, 458-460; N.D. White, *The Law of International Organisations*, 2nd edition, 2005, 217. A passage in the ICJ's Advisory Opinion in 1980 may be one authority to support the stance that international organizations are subject to customary law: see *Interpretation of the Agreement of 25 March 1951 between the WHO and Egypt*, ICJ Reports 1980, 73 et seq. (89-90) ("International organizations are subject of international law, and as such, are bound by any obligations incumbent upon them under general rules of international law"). Similarly, H.G. Schermers/ N.M. Blokker, *International Institutional Law: Unity Within Diversity*, 4th edition, 2003, 1002; F. Morgenstern, *Legal Problems of International Organizations*, 1986, 32. It is noted that the view that international organizations are subject to general international law does not appear to agree with the remark by the same authors that the legal personality of international organizations has, in principle, no predetermined content in international law: see below note 41.

[39] *Reparation for Injuries Suffered in the Service of the United Nations*, ICJ Reports 1949, 174 et seq. (hereinafter Reparation for Injuries) (179).

tially governing state activities such as human rights norms.[40] In principle, the legal personality of international organizations has no predetermined content in international law.[41] This presumption is, of course,
increasingly subject to qualification by the development of *jus cogens* as
well as common rules on international organizations.[42] Nevertheless, it
seems that the observance of customary human rights norms is yet to
join these categories, and it is still premature to conclude that such
rights can be invoked against international organizations in general.[43]

The second question of accountability *to whom* is fundamental to
the abovementioned process of interaction; the demands that the actors
in question submit to the public body are not always uniform, which
may dictate the relevance or substance of accountability standards that
the public body is required to discharge and the manner in which it is
subjected to consequences. A question is then posed as to how such accountability holders are to be determined. Two separate questions arise
with regard to this issue: who *ought to be* a holder, and who actually
has the *power* to become one. Such power generally derives from an actor's *potential ability to impose consequences* for the perceived failure of
administrative bodies to be accountable towards them.[44] These *normative* and *pragmatic* bases seem to be present in the law and politics of
accountability.[45]

Normatively, three sets of justifications are commonly acknowledged in the domestic democratic order: authorization, political or financial support and impact.[46] On the other hand, the global administrative law is yet to become disciplined enough to portray common normative bases with which to determine who ought to be an accountability holder. Arguably, the disparity between those who have a normative

---

[40]   The ICJ observed in Reparation for Injuries that "rights and duties [of the
       UN] are [not] the same as those of a State", see note 39.
[41]   Sands/ Klein, see note 38, 473; Schermers/ Blokker, see note 38, 990, 992-
       993; White, see note 38, 40-41.
[42]   See below note 47. Also see below notes 101-102 and corresponding para-
       graph.
[43]   See Kingsbury et al., see note 32, 46-47; Harlow, see note 32, 204-207; B.
       Fassbender, "Targeted Sanctions and Due Process", *Study Commissioned
       by the UN Office of Legal Affairs*, 20 March 2006, 20, paras 5.3-5.5, avail-
       able at: <http://www.un.org/law/counsel/Fassbender_study.pdf>.
[44]   See Keohane, see note 27, 1125.
[45]   See Keohane, see note 11, 142, 149; Keohane, see note 27, 1125.
[46]   Keohane, see note 11, 140.

basis to become accountability holders and those who have the power to hold a public body to account is largest when the accountability mechanism is less institutionalized. For instance, the conferral of *locus standi* for judicial review by courts in many Western countries is an authoritative determination of the status of accountability holders, albeit perhaps in the narrowest sense. Such holders can use judicial review in order to impose consequences on relevant decision-makers.

On the other hand, global administrative law is characterized by the absence of an equivalent constitutional authority to verify the status of accountability holders and direct public bodies to discharge accountability. In the absence of such a highly institutionalized mechanism, small states or non-state constituencies may not be able to hold the SC to account, even if the normative basis for becoming accountability holders is strong. The accountability calls from such constituencies would perhaps not reach the SC, unless the calls are accompanied by other accountability holders and relevant UN bodies, particularly those actors with a stronger power to undermine the operational effectiveness of the particular SC-led activities.

With regard to the third question pertaining to the bases on which administrative bodies are called to account, undeniably, a series of common rules governing internal matters or external relationships of international organizations have gradually evolved,[47] although adjudi-

---

[47] Some examples include an *ultra vires* doctrine, the legal personality of international organizations, an implied power doctrine, interpretation of constituent instruments, and a series of rules on immunities and privileges: see D. Akande, "International Organizations", in: M.D. Evans (ed.), *International Law*, 2nd edition, 2006, 277 et seq. (280-298); E. Lauterpacht, "The Development of the Law of International Organization by the Decisions of International Tribunals", *RdC* 152 (1976-IV), 381 et seq. One may add the development concerning the rules on delegation of powers, and the rules of responsibility owed by international organizations. For delegation, compare, D. Sarooshi, "The Legal Framework Governing United Nations Subsidiary Organs", *BYIL* 67 (1996), 413 et seq.; D. Sarooshi, *The United Nations and the Development of Collective Security: The Delegation by the UN Security Council of its Chapter VII Powers*, 1999; N. Blokker, "Is the Authorization Authorized? Powers and Practice of the UN Security Council to Authorize the Use of Force by 'Coalitions of the Able and Willing'", *EJIL* 11 (2000), 541 et seq.; with S. Chesterman, *Just War or Just Peace? Humanitarian Intervention and International Law*, 2001, 163-218. For the rules of responsibility, see the work of the International Law Commission on *Responsibility of International Organizations*, available at: <http://www.un.org/law/ilc/>.

cative organs are often circumspect about ascertaining such rules independently from constituent instruments.[48] Such rules, either categorized as part of traditional sources of custom and general principles of law, or seen as a unique body of law (termed as international institutional law or global administrative law), are applicable to the UN and thus the SC insofar as they are not inconsistent with the Charter.[49] However, these common rules on international organizations are of limited maturity in controlling their exertion of authority. Owing to the absence of ultimate legislative and judicial authorities, the growth of administrative bodies[50] has, so far, produced no uniform formula of administrative law to fetter the discretion of public bodies. It is still noteworthy that the fragmented practices or issue-dependent principles that collectively form global administrative law have been identified through the activities of international administrative bodies and certain adjudicative organs established within them. Kingsbury, Krisch and Stewart, in their project on global administrative law, ascertain several "candidates" for the principles of administrative law concerning procedural grounds, namely, participation, transparency, reasoned decisions and review procedures.[51] The enhancement of transparency and participation is exemplified by the Basel Committee on Banking Supervision, which, having emerged as a closed club model, started to invite comments from industry, academia, the government etc., and makes these comments publicly accessible.[52] The establishment of the World Bank Inspection Panel is a prominent example of review mechanisms.[53] On

---

[48] International adjudicative organs tend to ascribe their reasoning to an interpretation of constituent instruments, and avoid expressly accepting the existence of common rules applicable to international organizations. See comments by Akande on *Reparation for Injuries*, Akande, see note 47, 282. See also an instructive analysis of the decision by the International Labour Organization Administrative Tribunal in *In re Bustani*, J. Klabbers, "The Bustani Case Before the ILOAT: Constitutionalism in Disguise?", *ICLQ* 53 (2004), 455 et seq.

[49] See Akande, see note 47, 280.

[50] For the various types of global administration, see Kingsbury et al., see note 32, 20-23.

[51] Kingsbury et al., see note 32, 37-40.

[52] See M.S. Barr/ G.P. Miller, "Global Administrative Law: The View from Basel", *EJIL* 17 (2006), 15 et seq. (24-27, 45).

[53] See Kingsbury et al., see note 32, 39; R.B. Stewart, "U.S. Administrative Law: A Model for Global Administrative Law", IILJ Working Paper

the other hand, substantive grounds of accountability, such as proportionality and legitimate expectations, seem underdeveloped.[54]

Finally, the question is posed as to how consequences would be imposed. At the international level, no general procedure exists for the judicial review of the decision-making of global administrative bodies. Although the majority of the ICJ in the *Lockerbie* case (1992 and 1998) seems to have endorsed the Court's competence to review SC resolutions,[55] the use of the ICJ as a mechanism to hold the SC to account is significantly limited for three reasons. Firstly, in order for the GA to request an Advisory Opinion, non-objection from a majority of UN Member States must be secured, and in a contentious case, there must be an unavoidable link between the legality of an SC resolution and the subject matter of the dispute before the ICJ, as in the rare instance of *Lockerbie*. Secondly, the principal accountability questions such as transparency and participation do not always fit with the traditional sources of law provided in Article 38 (1) of the ICJ Statute.[56] Thirdly, more fundamentally, only states and UN organs/specialized agencies are entitled to refer legal disputes and questions to the ICJ.[57] As a matter of procedure, other non-state actors do not have access to the ICJ to request a review of the SC's actions,[58] which necessarily restricts the promise that the ICJ holds in enhancing accountability to them.

Without institutional channels, the primary means to respond to a perceived failure of the SC to discharge certain standards of behavior will be public reputation.[59] Even in domestic administrative law, it

---

2005/7 (Global Administrative Law Series), 35, available at: <http://www.iilj.org>.

[54] Kingsbury et al, see note 32, 40-41.

[55] See T.M. Franck, *Fairness in International Law and Institutions*, 1995, 242-244; C. Gray, "Case and Comment: The Lockerbie Case Continues", *CLJ* 57 (1998), 433 et seq.

[56] See Kingsbury et al., see note 32, 29-30.

[57] 1945 Statute of the International Court of Justice, *AJIL* 39 (1945), Suppl., 215 et seq., Arts 34 (1), 65 (1); 1945 Charter of the United Nations, Article 96.

[58] See F.O. Vicuña, "Individuals and Non-State Entities Before International Courts and Tribunals", *Max Planck UNYB* 5 (2001), 53 et seq. (56-58).

[59] See Grant/ Keohane, see note 30, 37; Keohane, see note 27, 1133-1134, 1138. Accountability in its core sense that Mulgan defines seems to encompass reputational accountability through private sectors such as the media: see Mulgan, see note 30, 565. At the same time, it is suggested that the inclusion of reputational detriment will risk blurring the demarcation line be-

would be a mistake to conceptualize a tool to compel accountability as synonymous with judicial review.[60] Both states and non-state constituencies can take part in raising criticism against particular actions of the SC.[61] However, public reputation as a tool to hold the SC to account is susceptible to dilution, as the SC is in varying degrees constantly subjected to negative criticism or positive praise from the public, just as in the case of other domestic and global administrative bodies. Therefore, whether or not such a non-institutionalized reputational accountability tool is effective varies according to circumstances. Although public reputation generally matters for international organizations,[62] it would certainly become a more powerful tool if the various constituencies and the wider UN membership act in the same direction, either in consort or in parallel; and to undermine such reputation entails negative operational consequences to the activities of the SC, such as non-cooperation by local communities within the context of UN territorial administrations, which undermine the operational effectiveness of SC activities and make them appear more costly in discharging mandates.[63]

Overall, the accountability mechanism relative to the SC and the Committee must be, in large part, illuminated through the analysis of specific normative frameworks, practices and discourse relating to them instead of resorting to the deductive reasoning from common principles of global administrative law.

---

tween accountability-based control and other modes of control, see ibid., 565-566.

[60] See E. Fisher, "The European Union in the Age of Accountability", *Oxford Journal of Legal Studies* 24 (2004), 495 et seq. (497-498).

[61] Keohane, see note 27, 1138.

[62] One of the sources of authority for international organizations is what Barnett and Finnemore call "moral authority", meaning that they represent "the community's interests or the defender of the values of the international community": M. Barnett/ M. Finnemore, *Rules for the World: International Organizations in Global Politics*, 2004, 23.

[63] See for the context of peacekeeping, F. Hoffmann/ F. Mégret, "Fostering Human Rights Accountability: An Ombudsperson for the United Nations?", *Global Governance* 11 (2005), 43 et seq. (49).

3. Member State Authorities

a. Normative Framework

That the UN Charter, a constituent instrument upon which the SC exercises its authority, subsists as constraints of its discretion was affirmed by the ICJ at the outset of the UN when it enunciated that the "political character of an organ cannot release it from the observance of the treaty provisions established by the Charter when they constitute limitations of its powers" (*Admission to the UN* case).[64] The same was confirmed by the International Criminal Tribunal for the Former Yugoslavia (ICTY) in the *Tadic* case in 1995.[65]

The UN Charter institutionalized the minimum level of accountability to all Member States as a form of accountability to the GA. This includes the SC's reporting duties pursuant to Arts 24 (3) and 15 (1) under the Charter; while consideration of annual reports by the GA has been a mere formality for a long time,[66] some changes have been introduced since the early 1990s to enhance the reports' format and adoption procedure.[67] Further, Article 17 serves as the SC's fiscal accountability to the GA, since it can downsize the budget for a particular SC operation or even refuse to approve it. The 1267 Committee is under such budgetary scrutiny, inasmuch as its funding comes from the regular UN budget.[68]

---

[64] *Conditions of Admission of a State to Membership in the United Nations (Article 4 of Charter)*, Advisory Opinion, ICJ Reports 1948, 57 et seq. (64).

[65] *Prosecutor v Dusko Tadic* (Case IT-94-1-AR72), Appeals Chamber, Decision of 2 October 1995, para. 28 ("The Security Council is an organ of an international organization, established by a treaty which serves as a constitutional framework for that organization. The Security Council is thus subjected to certain constitutional limitations, however broad its powers under the constitution may be").

[66] F.A. Vallat, "The General Assembly and the Security Council of the United Nations", *BYIL* 29 (1952), 63 et seq. (84); J. Delbrück, "Article 24", in: B. Simma (ed.), *The Charter of the United Nations: A Commentary*, 2nd edition, 2002, 442 et seq. (452).

[67] See Descriptive Index to Notes and Statements by the President of the Security Council relating to Documentation and Procedure (June 1993 to December 2005), Doc. S/2006/78 of 7 February 2006, 2.

[68] The funding for the SC's counter-terrorism programs comes from the regular UN budget: A. Millar/ E. Rosand, *Allied Against Terrorism: What's Needed to Strengthen Worldwide Commitment*, 2006, 29-30.

In other contexts not encompassed by these provisions, "delegation" of powers to the SC through the UN Charter may serve as a normative underpinning for the GA to call the organ to account.[69] According to Sarooshi, the *delegatus non potest delegare* maxim, known as the non-delegation doctrine, is applicable to the UN and thus the SC as a general principle of law,[70] and the accountability of the SC to the collective of Member States with regard to the way in which the delegated power is being exercised is implicit in the doctrine.[71]

With reference to individual Member States, Arts 31 and 32 of the Charter provide for the participation of "specially affected" states or those states party to a dispute, the former being incorporated in Rule 37 of the SC's Rules of Procedure.[72] In response to requests by Member States to participate, the SC usually extends invitations under Rule 37 without discussion, and the requests have rarely been rejected or not acted upon.[73] However, participation under Rule 37 entails certain limitations in theory and practice. Firstly, in contrast to Article 32, Article 31 stipulates that a Member State of the UN "*may* participate ... *whenever [the SC] considers* that the interests of that Member are specially affected*",[74] which gives rise to a controversy as to whether the members are vested with the right to participation or even the right to be

---

[69] It is noted that although UN Member States delegate powers to the SC, the relationship between Member States and the SC is not characterized by a principal-agency relationship *strictu sensu*; like most international organizations, the SC exercises powers under the UN Charter *on its own behalf*, and not strictly on behalf of all Member States: see D. Sarooshi, *International Organizations and Their Exercise of Sovereign Powers*, 2005, 29, 43.

[70] Sarooshi, *The Delegation*, see note 47, 22.

[71] Sarooshi, *The Delegation*, see note 47, 22, 25-32.

[72] The explicit reference to Article 32 of the Charter has been rare in the practice of the SC. It is the usual practice of the SC to simply refer to Rule 37 when invitations are extended to Member States. See, e.g., Repertoire of the Practice of the Security Council, Supplement 2000-2003 (Advance Version), Chapter 3, 6; R. Dolzer, "Article 32", in: B. Simma (ed.), *The Charter of the United Nations: A Commentary*, 2nd edition, 2002, 580 et seq. (580-582).

[73] For example, between 2000 and 2003, in only one instance the request was denied: see Repertoire of the Practice of the Security Council, see note 72, 14-16.

[74] Emphasis added.

heard by the SC.[75] While the future development regarding the interpretation of the article merits close attention, it is the present understanding of the SC that Member States do not have such a right.[76] It is left to the SC to decide whether the interests of Member States are "specially affected", and the organ owes, strictly speaking, no obligation to extend an invitation even after the decision. Secondly, participation under Rule 37 has been understood as involving formal and private meetings. Whether or not Member States are permitted to participate in "informal consultations of the whole" has been a matter decided upon by the SC without reference to Rule 37.[77] Thirdly, in relation to participation in the 1267 Committee's discussion, its Guidelines incorporate a provision according to which specially affected Member States may be invited to the Committee's discussions.[78] However, it must be borne in mind that the Committee usually meets in closed sessions;[79] without advance notice of meetings and their agendas, Member States would be, in practice, prevented from submitting their requests for participation.[80]

The UN Charter provides yet another accountability mechanism under Article 50, which is of particular relevance to economic sanctions. While consultation with countries that sustained a loss by participating in sanctions had been propounded under the League of Nations when it

---

[75] See, e.g., R. Dolzer, "Article 31", in: B. Simma (ed.), *The Charter of the United Nations: A Commentary*, 2nd edition, 2002, 573 et seq. (577-578); S. Talmon, "The Security Council as World Legislature", *AJIL* 99 (2005), 175 et seq. (187, fn. 112).

[76] It is an understanding of the SC that it owes no obligations to extend invitations in cases of Article 31: see, Repertoire of the Practice of the Security Council, see note 72, 3 ("Only in [the instance of Article 32] does the Security Council have an obligation to extend an invitation").

[77] See Repertoire of the Practice of the Security Council, see note 72, 9-10.

[78] Committee Guidelines 2007, see note 2, para. 3(b) ("The Committee may invite any Member of the United Nations to participate in the discussion of any question brought before the Committee in which interests of that Member are specifically affected").

[79] Committee Guidelines 2007, see note 2, para. 3(b) ("The Committee will meet in closed sessions, unless it decides otherwise").

[80] In this respect, it is worth noting that in 2006, the SC "encourage[s] Chairs of the subsidiary bodies of the Council to make the schedule of meetings of subsidiary bodies available to the public", Note by the President of the Security Council, Doc. S/2006/507 of 19 July 2006, para. 47.

instigated sanctions against Italy,[81] the Charter institutionalized it as the "right to consult the Security Council" exercisable by those states (members and non-members) which are confronted with "special economic problems". The SC, under Article 50, received a number of requests in relation to economic sanctions undertaken against South Rhodesia, Iraq and the former Yugoslavia.[82] Despite the entitlement vested in states, however, the presence of Article 50 has been somewhat diminished by the transition to targeted sanctions as in the case of the Al Qaeda/Taliban regime.[83] In fact, according to the report of the SG in 2007, no appeal under Article 50 has been submitted since 2003.[84]

Overall, with regard to the collectivity of Member States, the normative bases to call the SC to account are strong and in part institutionalized through the Charter. On the other hand, Arts 31 and 50 of the Charter and established practice relating to them may not serve, for instance, in the case of those states which wish to approach the Committee for information in order to identify a targeted individual or verify the accusation against him/her.

---

[81] See *League of Nations Official Journal, Special Supplement*, No. 150, 1936, 11 (Proposal No. 5, Organisation of Mutual Support, Adopted by the Coordination Committee on 19 October 1935).

[82] See V. Gowlland-Debbas, *Collective Responses to Illegal Acts in International Law: United Nations Action in the Question of Southern Rhodesia*, 1990, 633-639; J. Carver/ J. Hulsmann, "The Role of Article 50 of the UN Charter in the Search for International Peace and Security", *ICLQ* 49 (2000), 528 et seq.; B.O. Bryde/ A. Reinisch, "Article 50", in: B. Simma (ed.), *The Charter of the United Nations: A Commentary*, 2nd edition, 2002, 784 et seq.; B.H. Al-Khasawneh, "Consultation under Article 50 of the United Nations Charter: The Experience of the Middle East", in: V. Gowlland-Debbas (ed.), *United Nations Sanctions and International Law*, 2001, 325 et seq.; W. Czapliński, "The Position of States Specially Affected by Sanctions in the Meaning of Article 50 of the United Nations Charter: The Experience of Central and Eastern Europe", in: V. Gowlland-Debbas (ed.), *United Nations Sanctions and International Law*, 2001, 335 et seq.

[83] The SG observed in 2006 that "all of the Council's existing sanctions regimes are now targeted in nature and the unintended consequences for civilian populations and third States are thereby minimized", *Report of the Secretary-General, Implementation of the Provisions of the Charter of the United Nations related to Assistance to Third States Affected by the Application of Sanctions*, Doc. A/61/304 of 31 August 2006, para. 7.

[84] *Report of the Secretary-General, Implementation of the Provisions of the Charter of the United Nations related to Assistance to Third States Affected by the Application of Sanctions*, Doc. A/62/206 of 3 August 2007, para. 14.

b. Pragmatic Basis

Measured by the potential ability to impose consequences, power disparities are arguably evident between those states with the capacity to submit names to the Consolidated List on the one hand ("providers"), and those states which are largely the recipients of the target names. Of course, states' power is constructed by many other factors outside the sanctions regime and the analysis cannot be so self-contained whether or not providers or recipients. The power disparity is therefore one illustration generated from factors unique to the Al Qaeda/Taliban sanctions regime.

Being accountable to those states that hold the reliable intelligence with regard to the Al Qaeda members and their associates is a practical necessity if the Al Qaeda/Taliban sanctions are to have a bearing on global counter-terrorism efforts. Since the UN does not have a general capacity to collect (as opposed to receive) international intelligence relating to them, national intelligence is the primary source.[85] The crux is that the submission of names relies on states' willingness as opposed to obligations, and so provider states could undermine the operational significance of the list without violating any obligations.[86] A well known contributor is the United States, but other countries including Saudi Arabia, Italy, Algeria, France, Spain, Belgium, Germany, the United Kingdom, China and Russia have reportedly submitted names to the Committee.[87] The submission of *Jemaah Islamiya* (supported by 50 Member States) was led by the United Sates and Australia.[88] In addi-

---

[85]   See S. Chesterman, *Shared Secrets: Intelligence and Collective Security*, 2006, 70-71, available at: <http://www.lowyinstitute.com/Publication.asp?pid= 60>.

[86]   See S/RES/1735 (2006) of 22 December 2006, para. 12 ("Encourages States to submit ... names").

[87]   E.A. Wayne, "Internationalizing the Fight", *eJournal USA: Economic Perspectives* 9 (3) (2004), 6 et seq. (6-7), available at: <http://usinfo.state.gov/journals/ites/0904/ijee/ijee0904.htm>; US Department of State, Money Laundering and Terrorist Financing in the Middle East and South Asia, Testimony by E.A. Wayne, Assistant Secretary for Economic and Business Affairs, before the Senate Committee on Banking, Housing, and Urban Affairs, 13 July 2005, available at: <http://www.state.gov/e/eeb/rls/rm/2005/49564.htm>.

[88]   Minister for Foreign Affairs (Australia) Media Release (FA158), Jemaah Islamiyah Listing, 26 October 2002, available at: <http://www.foreignminister.gov.au/releases/2002/fa158_02.html>; US Department of State, Press

tion, there must be many other potential providers who have the capacity to submit names but still hold back from doing so.

Power disparities can also be seen within these provider states. As said, the vast majority of the names on the list have been submitted by the United States, either alone or in conjunction with other UN members,[89] and it has been a principal advisor of the Committee.[90] Being accountable to the relevant US authorities is an operational imperative for the functioning of the Committee, and no doubt it has been highly accountable to them. The Monitoring Group and the Team made a number of visits to US government departments,[91] presumably to exchange information and seek assistance in conducting implementation assessments.

By contrast, those states which largely remain *recipients* of the list may have less potential to impose negative consequences on the operation of the 1267 Committee. Nevertheless, there still remain some possibilities. The characteristics of the Al Qaeda/Taliban sanctions regime provide states, including the recipient states, the potential to exercise a certain degree of power to hold the SC to account as far as they have the capacity to implement the sanctions. Unlike other sanctions regimes primarily targeted at governmental officials or rebels within a restricted geographical area, Al Qaeda "has autonomous underground cells in some 100 countries" with "no single headquarters".[92] The increasing proliferation of their activities[93] makes it important for the SC and the Committee to absorb requests from a wider range of states and enhance accountability towards them. Truly, as the Monitoring Team admits,

---

Statement by R. Boucher, Designation of Two Terrorists, January 24, 2003, available at: <http://www.state.gov/r/pa/prs/ps/2003/16843.htm>.

[89] E. Rosand, "The Security Council's Efforts to Monitor the Implementation of Al Qaeda/Taliban Sanctions", *AJIL* 98 (2004), 745 et seq. (746).

[90] Richard Barrett, the Coordinator of the Monitoring Team since 2004, states: "The United States, of course, is intensely engaged through this whole process [of the fight against terrorism]. We find great support from them in our work on the committee ...": CNN, Diplomatic License: Current Events at the United Nations, 3 September 2004, available at: <http://transcripts.cnn.com/TRANSCRIPTS/0409/03/i_dl.00.html>.

[91] Second Report of the Monitoring Group Established Pursuant to Security Council Resolution 1363 (2001) and Extended by Resolution 1390 (2002), Doc. S/2002/1050 of 20 September 2002, para. 10.

[92] Council of Foreign Relations, Backgrounder: Al-Qaeda, 7 July 2005, available at: <http://www.cfr.org/publication/9126/>.

[93] See B.O. Riedel, "Al Qaeda Strikes Back", *Foreign Aff.* 86 (2007), 24 et seq.

however, well designed a sanctions regime is, its impact inevitably depends on effective implementation by Member States.[94] Further, the effective functioning of the 1267 sanctions regime requires not only mere compliance through the adoption of appropriate domestic legislation[95] but also states' enhanced willingness to cooperate. In particular, it relies on their readiness to ensure that financial institutions within their jurisdictions are screening accounts and transactions in an effective and timely manner.[96]

4. Targeted Individuals/Entities

a. Normative Framework

While the Charter provides non-state constituencies with no clauses equivalent to Article 31,[97] Rule 39 of the SC's Rules of Procedure still paves the way for "members of the Secretariat or other persons" to participate in its discussion for the purposes to "supply it with information or ... to give other assistance".[98] An increasing number of invitations have been extended to wider UN membership, other international organizations and individuals.[99] Likewise, the 1267 Committee's Guide-

---

[94]   2nd Report of the Monitoring Team, see note 6, para. 42.

[95]   For the types of domestic legislation, see 3rd Report of the Monitoring Team, see note 6, paras 44-49, Annex I.

[96]   *4th Report of the Analytical Support and Sanctions Monitoring Team Appointed Pursuant to Security Council Resolutions 1526 (2004) and 1617 (2005) Concerning Al-Qaida and the Taliban and Associated Individuals and Entities*, Doc. S/2006/154 of 10 March 2006 (hereinafter 4th Report of the Monitoring Team), para. 68.

[97]   Compare, Article 71 of the Charter (providing for "arrangements for consultation with non-governmental organizations" in relation to ECOSOC).

[98]   Rule 39 of the Provisional Rules of Procedure Doc. S/96/Rev. 7 provides the following: "The Security Council may invite members of the Secretariat or other persons, whom it considers competent for the purpose, to supply it with information or to give other assistance in examining matters within its competence". A guideline has also been formulated with respect to participation of members of the Secretariat in informal consultations, see note by the President of the Security Council, Doc. S/2007/749 of 19 December 2007.

[99]   In 2003, the invitations issued under Rule 39 rose to 159, about 15 times more than in 1990, Repertoire of the Practice of the Security Council, see note 72, 6.

lines prescribe their participation.[100] However, Rule 39 does not entitle any non-state actors, much less targeted individuals, to participate in the discussion of the SC and the Committee; moreover, the criteria with which to invite them are yet to be formulated.

Instead, much of the discussion has been devoted to the invocation of human rights, particularly the right to a fair hearing (article 14, ICCPR) and the right to an effective remedy (article 2 (3), ICCPR). Should the SC be obliged to comply with these human rights standards, the targeted individuals and entities would be, at least in theory, entitled to invoke their rights *vis-à-vis* the SC. In other words, this entitlement provides them with a cogent normative basis in their claiming the status of accountability holders against the SC and the Committee.

Among different levels of human rights norms, least controversial is the observance of human rights established as *jus cogens*, which cannot be overridden by the effect of Article 103 of the Charter.[101] Two lines of reasoning uphold this proposition. Firstly, it can be inferred from the constituent instrument that a treaty-based institution, including the UN, cannot be endowed with powers to act in contravention to *jus cogens*, inasmuch as states cannot derogate from it.[102] A more society-oriented explanation is that peremptory norms are fundamentally im-

---

[100] Committee Guidelines 2007, see note 2, para. 3(b).

[101] See e.g., D. Akande, "The International Court of Justice and the Security Council: Is There Room for Judicial Control of Decisions of the Political Organs of the United Nations?", *ICLQ* 46 (1997), 309 et seq. (322); Reinisch, see note 38, 859; J.A. Frowein/ N. Krisch, "Introduction to Chapter VII", in: B. Simma (ed.), *The Charter of the United Nations: A Commentary*, 2nd edition, 2002, 701 et seq. (711); Alvarez, see note 16, 133. See also *Application of the Convention on the Prevention and Punishment of the Crime of Genocide*, ICJ Reports 1993, 325 et seq. (440, para. 100) (Separate Opinion of Judge Lauterpacht); Case T-315/01, *Yassin Abdullah Kadi v Council of the European Union and Commission of the European Communities*, Judgment of 21 September 2005 (CFI) (hereinafter *Kadi*), para. 226; Case T-306/01, *Ahmed Ali Yusuf and Al Barakaat International Foundation v Council of the European Union and Commission of the European Communities*, Judgment of 21 September 2005 (CFI) (hereinafter *Yusuf*), para. 277; *R (Hilal Abdul-Razzaq Ali Al-Jedda) v Secretary of State for Defence*, [2006] EWCA Civ 327, Judgment of 29 March 2006 (CA), para. 71; *R (Al-Jedda) v Secretary of State for Defence* [2007] UKHL 58, Judgment of 12 December 2007 (HL), para. 35 (Lord Bingham).

[102] A. Orakhelashvili, "The Impact of Peremptory Norms on the Interpretation and Application of United Nations Security Council Resolutions", *EJIL* 16 (2005), 59 et seq. (60, 68).

portant for the international community, and therefore, the UN, having a legal personality in the international arena and being a participant therein, must be subject to them.

However, the extent to which human rights qualify as *jus cogens* remains controversial. The list of non-derogable human rights under article 4 (2) of the ICCPR is partly a recognition of the peremptory nature of those norms.[103] Neither article 14 nor article 2 (3) are mentioned. While the Human Rights Committee holds the view that the category of peremptory norms extends beyond the list of non-derogable provisions provided in article 4 (2),[104] the growing consensus that the core elements of the right to a fair hearing are non-derogable and *jus cogens* may still remain restricted to the context of criminal proceedings.[105]

Further contested is the observance of human rights under customary law and treaties by the SC acting under Chapter VII. Different interpretations have been advanced to account for the relevant articles of the UN Charter, particularly Article 1 (1) and (3) through Article 24 (2). One side observes that the Charter obliges the SC to comply with human rights established under customary law[106] and those under major human rights treaties,[107] leading to the conclusion that any restrictions upon human rights would have to be justified in accordance with the established criteria such as the requirement of proportionality. The other side submits that the compliance *strictu sensu* with human rights obligations, both under treaties and customary law, is not assumed by the Charter. All the Charter is required to do is to give consideration to them, and how the balance can be best struck between respect for human rights and the maintenance of peace and security is up to the SC.[108] This leads one to conclude that only the SC's complete disregard would

---

[103] Human Rights Committee, General Comment No. 24: Issues Relating to Reservations Made upon Ratification or Accession to the Covenant or the Optional Protocols Thereto, or in Relation to Declarations under Article 41 of the Covenant, Doc. CCPR/C/21/Rev.1/Add.6 of 4 November 1994, para. 10; Human Rights Committee, General Comment No. 29: State of Emergency (Article 4), Doc. CCPR/C/21/Rev.1/Add.11 of 31 August 2001, para. 11.

[104] Human Rights Committee, General Comment 29, see note 103.

[105] De Wet, see note 14, 17, 22-23; E. De Wet/ A. Nollkaemper, "Review of Security Council Decisions by National Courts", *GYIL* 45 (2002), 166 et seq. (183).

[106] For instance, Alvarez, see note 16, 125-126.

[107] See, e.g., Akande, see note 101, 323-324; and De Wet, see note 14, 8-14.

[108] Frowein/ Krisch, see note 101, 711.

constitute a contravention of the Charter.[109] Under the second reading, the normative tie between the individuals and the SC would be remote and more difficult to construct.

Arts 31 and 32 of the Vienna Convention on the Law of Treaties[110] feature a set of different interpretive methods – the textual, systematic, teleological, and historical (or intentions) approaches – as well as consider subsequent practice and relevant rules of international law.[111] The problem of how much relative weight should be attached to these factors is left unanswered by the general rules on interpretation.[112] Among these components, the textual and historical readings seem in favor of the latter proposition. This is not surprising, inasmuch as the development of human rights norms, much less the anticipated impact that the UN itself impinges upon the rights of individuals, was significantly limited when the Charter was drafted. From the textual reading, the UN Charter strives for the promotion of human rights, but does not strictly bind itself or the SC by extrinsic human rights norms.[113] Under Article 1 (3), "[t]o achieve international co-operation … in promoting and encouraging respect for human rights" is one of the overall aims to be

---

[109] Frowein/ Krisch, see note 101, 711.

[110] A constituent instrument of international organizations triggers arts 31 to 33 of the Vienna Convention on the Law of Treaties with regard to the way it is to be constructed, see 1969 Vienna Convention on the Law of Treaties, *ILM* 8 (1969), 679 et seq., article 5 ("The present Convention applies to any treaty which is the constituent instrument of an international organization"). Arts 31 and 32 of the Convention reflect customary international law, see *The Application of the Convention on the Prevention and Punishment of the Crime of Genocide (Bosnia and Herzegovina v Serbia and Montenegro)*, Merits, Judgment of 26 February 2007, para. 160, available at: <http://www.icj-cij.org>; and other cases referred to in the paragraph.

[111] Article 31 of the Vienna Convention requires consideration of the terms' textual meaning (textual approach), their "context" (systematic approach), and the treaty's "object and purpose" (teleological approach), as well as "subsequent practice", and "any relevant rules of international law", and article 32 licenses to refer to preparatory works (historical or intentions approach).

[112] It is true that the principle of effectiveness is extant as a general rule to be applied when more than one reading is possible, *ILCYB*, 1966, Vol. 2, 219, para. 6. However, which construction "enable[s] the treaty to have appropriate effects" (ibid.) may likewise be open to more than one interpretation: see generally, Lauterpacht, see note 47, 420-465.

[113] See the preamble ("to reaffirm faith in fundamental human rights"), Arts 1 (3), 55 (c) of the UN Charter.

pursued by the SC through Article 24 (2); however, no reference is made to the organ's compliance with human rights. Furthermore, the textual and systematic reading of Article 1 (1) suggests that the SC is not expected to observe international law when acting under Chapter VII in the same manner as it does under Chapter VI, inasmuch as the phrase of "the principles of justice and international law" does not appear in the first part of the article.[114] The drafting history of Article 1 (1) reveals that the phrase was inserted to make clear that the SC had no power to impose the terms of settlement of international disputes or situations.[115] At the same time, the latter proposition is supported by the fact that the proposal to likewise subject Chapter VII measures to the principles of international law was rejected at the San Francisco Conference,[116] although noteworthy still is that half the delegates seemed supportive of the former proposition.[117]

On the other hand, with reference to subsequent practice, the position appears to be somewhere in between the two propositions. In the context of economic sanctions, clear reference at the UN in support of the first proposition is found in a working paper prepared under the Sub-Commission of the Commission on Human Rights, which submitted that it was implied by Article 1 (1) and (3) of the Charter that, "[s]anctions must be evaluated to ensure that ... they do not in any way violate principles of international law stemming from sources 'outside' the Charter",[118] including the right to life and the rights to security of

---

[114] Compare, e.g., Frowein/ Krisch, see note 101, 710-711; with Reinisch, see note 38, 856-857; De Wet, see note 14, 8-9.

[115] See T.D. Gill, "Legal and Some Political Limitations on the Power of the UN Security Council to Exercise its Enforcement Powers under Chapter VII of the Charter", *NYIL* 26 (1995), 33 et seq. (66-67).

[116] L.M. Goodrich/ E. Hambro, *Charter of the United Nations: Commentary and Documents*, 2nd and revised edition, 1949, 93-94; Gill, see note 115, 67-68. But see Akande, see note 101, 319-320.

[117] The final voting with regard to the amendment resulted in a split amongst the delegates, see Gill, see note 115, 66, fn. 90.

[118] Sub-Commission on the Promotion and Protection of Human Rights, *The Adverse Consequences of Economic Sanctions on the Enjoyment of Human Rights: Working Paper Prepared by Mr. Marc Bossuyt*, Doc. E/CN.4/Sub.2/ 2000/33 of 21 June 2000, para. 24. See also Committee on Economic, Social and Cultural Rights, General Comment No. 8: *The Relationship between Economic Sanctions and Respect for Economic, Social and Cultural Rights*, Doc. E/C.12/1997/8 of 12 December 1997.

the person, health, education or employment.[119] It added that "the Security Council was responsible for all known consequences of its actions" in relation to these human rights.[120] This working paper did not receive explicit endorsement by the Commission on Human Rights, much less by the GA or the SC. However, it is still noteworthy that a range of measures to ameliorate the humanitarian and human rights related impacts of sanctions have been implemented by the SC,[121] as exemplified by the Oil-for-Food Program for Iraq,[122] the provision of humanitarian exemptions,[123] the monitoring of humanitarian impact,[124] and more broadly, the methodological transition of the SC sanctions from comprehensive ones to more "smart" alternatives. The subsequent development in practice indicates that the SC has increasingly narrowed its discretion in terms of how to take into account the respect for human rights when acting under Chapter VII. In any case, such development still remains within the bounds of the above-mentioned textual and historical readings, in that it does not go so far as to suggest that the SC is formally bound by human rights norm.

b. Pragmatic Basis

Although a normative framework according to which individuals claim the status of accountability holders may further develop in the future, individuals and entities may lack the ability to bring about consequences. As noted above, without institutionalized channels, public reputation is a general recourse open to non-state constituencies to respond to the SC's accountability deficits.[125] In order to render the repu-

---

[119] Sub-Commission, see note 118, para. 26.

[120] Sub-Commission, see note 118, para. 72.

[121] See generally, J.A. Frowein/ N. Krisch, "Article 41", in: B. Simma (ed.), *The Charter of the United Nations: A Commentary*, 2nd edition, 2002, 735 et seq. (745-746).

[122] See generally, *Review and Assessment of the Implementation of the Humanitarian Programme Established Pursuant to Security Council Resolution 986 (1995) (December 1996-November 1998)*, Doc. S/1999/481 of 28 April 1999.

[123] See generally, G.L. Burci, "Interpreting the Humanitarian Exceptions through the Sanctions Committees", in: V. Gowlland-Debbas (ed.), *United Nations Sanctions and International Law*, 2001, 143 et seq.

[124] See generally, E. De Wet, *The Chapter VII Powers of the United Nations Security Council*, 2004, 226-247.

[125] See under II. 2. of this article.

tational accountability tool effective, their voices need to be accompanied by other accountability holders and various UN bodies acting in concert or in parallel. In order for this to occur, individuals and entities first need to mobilize the media, academic institutions and human rights NGOs that may support them. In addition, as will be discussed below,[126] the involvement of national courts may be a powerful tool in attracting concerted or parallel challenges from Member States and other constituencies.

III. Enhancing the Community Accountability: Challenges and Responses

1. Setting the Accountability Principles

It is notable that there is a clear sign of the emergence of what appear to be accountability principles concerning the administration of SC sanctions targeting individuals. The GA built up a consensus over such a normative framework, and this development appeared in the World Summit Outcome document in September 2005, in which the GA stated the following:

> "108. We call upon the Security Council, with the support of the Secretary-General, to improve its monitoring of the implementation and effects of sanctions, to ensure that sanctions are implemented in an accountable manner, to review regularly the results of such monitoring and to develop a mechanism to address special economic problems arising from the application of sanctions in accordance with the Charter.
>
> 109. We also call upon the Security Council, with the support of the Secretary-General, to ensure that *fair and clear procedures* exist for placing individuals and entities on sanctions lists and for removing them, as well as for granting humanitarian exemptions."[127]

---

[126] See under III. 3. of this article.

[127] 2005 World Summit Outcome, A/RES/60/1 (2005) of 24 October 2005, paras 108-109 (emphasis added). The Committee noted in December 2005 that "[m]ore than 50 States have mentioned the need for due process and transparency in the Committee's listing and/or de-listing procedures" (although the details of statements are not fully available), para. 13 Assessment, Doc. S/2005/761 of 6 December 2005 (hereinafter Committee's Written Assessments 2005), Annex I, para. 37.

The statements encapsulate not merely the need of monitoring and development of sanctions designing but also the call for procedural fairness and clarity in listing and delisting. The SG was aligned with this appeal, stating in his April 2006 report on a counter-terrorism strategy that "[m]ore must be done ... to improve the *accountability and transparency* of sanctions regimes", with particular reference to the Al Qaeda/Taliban sanctions.[128] These requests are reflected in the "United Nations Global Counter-Terrorism Strategy" adopted by consensus at the GA in September 2006, in which it encouraged the 1267 Committee "to ensure, *as a matter of priority*, that *fair and transparent procedures* exist" for listing, delisting and granting humanitarian exceptions.[129] One of the GA's special committees, which has been working on the issue of economic sanctions since the early 1990s,[130] embarked on addressing the issue of fairness and clarity in listing and delisting.[131]

Of course, these documents requesting *fairness and transparency* in the Committee's listing procedures have no binding force in themselves. Aside from the limited arena,[132] the authority of the GA is recommen-

---

[128] Report of the Secretary-General, *Uniting against Terrorism: Recommendations for a Global Counter-terrorism Strategy*, Doc. A/60/825 of 27 April 2006, para. 42 (emphasis added). See also ibid., para. 117 (SG asked the Office of Legal Affairs to develop guidelines); Fassbender, see note 43.

[129] The United Nations Global Counter-Terrorism Strategy, A/RES/60/288 (2006) of 20 September 2006, Annex, Plan of Action, para. 15 (emphasis added). See also Report of the Informal Working Group of the Security Council on General Issues of Sanctions, Doc. S/2006/997 of 22 December 2006, para. 3(v).

[130] See the website of the Special Committee on the Charter of the United Nations and on the Strengthening of the Role of the Organization at: <http://www.un.org/law/chartercomm/>.

[131] See the revised working paper submitted by Russia in February 2007, incorporating the provision to "ensure that the selection of such individuals and entities for listing is based on fair and clear procedures", *Report of the Special Committee on the Charter of the United Nations and on the Strengthening of the Role of the Organization*, GAOR 62nd Sess., Suppl. No. 33, Doc. A/62/33 (2007), para. 23. See also the EU Presidency Statement before the Special Committee on the Charter of the United Nations and on the Strengthening of the Role of the Organization (statement by Mr. Fitschen of Germany on behalf of the European Union), 7 February 2007, available at: <http://www.europa-eu-un.org/articles/en/article_6778_en.htm>.

[132] The GA has a certain law-making authority over the UN's organizational issues through binding "decisions" (Article 18 (2), UN Charter). These de-

datory.[133] However, if normative value should be accorded to them, one possible interpretation may be that these requests form part of a subsequent practice to interpret the Charter.[134] Understandably, such construction may well invite criticism. Firstly, none of the aforesaid documents reasonably indicate that they purport to elaborate on any particular Charter provisions, as evidently contrasted with the 1970 Declaration on Friendly Relations[135] and a few other GA resolutions.[136] Secondly, even granting that they detail particular Charter provisions, subsequent practice may not be a cogent basis of interpretation if it is not supported by one or more additional methods of interpretation.[137]

It would be too early to conclude if, and to what extent, normative value attaches to the aforesaid requests by the GA. Nevertheless, it is

---

cisions include suspension of rights and privileges of membership (Article 5), expulsion of Members (Article 6) and budgetary questions (Article 17): *Certain Expenses of the United Nations*, ICJ Reports 1962, 151 et seq. (163).

[133] Arts 10-14 of the UN Charter; *Legal Consequences for States of the Continued Presence of South Africa in Namibia (South West Africa) Notwithstanding Security Council Resolution 276 (1970)*, ICJ Reports 1971, 16 et seq. (50, para. 105).

[134] Vienna Convention on the Law of Treaties, see note 110, article 31 (3)(b). Although article 31 (3)(b) speaks of "the agreement of the parties", institutional practice has been invoked to prove such an agreement, see generally, J.E. Alvarez, *International Organizations as Law-Makers*, 2005, 87-89. But see Lauterpacht, see note 47, 458-464.

[135] A/RES/2625 (XXV) (1970) of 24 October 1970.

[136] See, e.g., Definition of Aggression, A/RES/3314 (XXIX) (1974) of 14 December 1974; Declaration on the Enhancement of the Effectiveness of the Principle of Refraining from the Threat or Use of Force in International Relations, A/RES/42/22 (1987) of 18 November 1987.

[137] It remains a point of controversy as to whether subsequent practice could constitute an autonomous element for the purpose of interpreting the Charter. The differences in opinion derive, *inter alia*, from the understanding of the interpretive methods adopted by the ICJ in the *Namibia* case: compare, e.g., Akande, see note 47, 289; with G. Ress, "The Interpretation of the Charter", in: B. Simma (ed.), *The Charter of the United Nations: A Commentary*, 2nd edition, 2002, 13 et seq. (27-30). In addition, caution has been voiced to the effect that dependence on practice is liable to endorsement of the SC's institutional actions, led by a few powerful states, as *intra vires*, because the absence of objections by other states may result in such actions qualifying as reflecting the agreement of the parties: see Ress, ibid., 25, 28-29; Alvarez, see note 134, 91-92.

still worth noting that the GA has the potential as well as the limits to act as a standard-setting institution to enhance the community account-ability of the SC. The GA has certainly taken one significant step for-ward in agreeing on the framework to hold the 1267 Committee to ac-count, and the aforementioned call for fairness and transparency must be credited for the universality of the forum. At the same time, the need to compromise at a deliberation forum of all states favors the obscurity of standards that they agree upon, and also leads to the failure to absorb the voices of some Member States. It would be even more complicated for the GA to represent wide-ranging demands from non-state ac-countability holders.

In view of these limits, the GA documents are equivocal (or inclu-sive) with regard to *whom*, and *how*, such fairness and transparency should be ensured. In particular, there remains a lack of consensus as to whether, and how, the SC should be accountable to non-state constitu-encies of the international community whose lives are affected by the Committee's decisions. This led to the absence in the GA documents of clear references to the procedural guarantees of individuals and entities on the List.

The divergence in opinions is evident from the Council meeting in June 2006 entitled "Rule of Law and Maintenance of International Peace and Security".[138] Bearing in mind the World Summit Outcome, most states, including all permanent members, reiterated the need to en-sure the fairness and transparency for the 1267 Committee proce-dures.[139] The SC's Presidential statement reaffirmed its commitment to "ensuring that fair and clear procedures exist".[140] Not surprisingly, however, permanent members, in their statements, avoided references to procedural guarantees to individuals on the list, which contrasts with

---

[138] Doc. S/PV. 5474 of 22 June 2006; Doc. S/PV. 5474 (Res. 1) of 22 June 2006.

[139] Doc. S/PV. 5474 of 22 June 2006, 10 (Ms. Pierce of the United Kingdom), 12 (Mr. Burian of Slovakia), 13 (Mr. Kitaoka of Japan), 14 (Mr. Bolton of the United States), 17 (Mr. Shcherbak of Russia), 18 (Mr. De La Sablière of France), 20 (Mr. Mayoral of Argentina), 25 (Nana Effah-Apenteng of Ghana), 27 (Mr. Li Junhua of China), 28 (Mr. Gayama of Congo), 33 (Mr. Pfanzelter of Austria); Doc. S/PV. 5474 (Res. 1) of 22 June 2006, 7 (Mr. Briz Gutiérrez of Guatemala), 18 (Mrs. Juul of Norway); UNSC Presidential Statement, Doc. S/PRST/2006/28 of 22 June 2006.

[140] UNSC Presidential Statement, Doc. S/PRST/2006/28 of 22 June 2006.

some other states which referred to due process,[141] the right to be heard,[142] external review,[143] or effective remedy.[144]

2. Fairness and Transparency: Member States

a. Challenges

For many Member State authorities which have the capacity to implement sanctions, one of the commonly acknowledged immediate concerns was the insufficiency of basic identifiers (i.e., name, date of birth etc.). This problem arises from the fact that the Committee's listing process does not oblige minimum identifiers to be ascertained before the listing. The rationale for not doing so is that the effect of the asset freeze will be as preventive as possible. Following the growth of the names on the List after the September 11 attacks,[145] the identifier concern became a more pressing issue. As the Monitoring Group reported in 2002, a number of government officials encountered problems with the List "at the technical level".[146] Many entries lack basic identifiers, such as date of birth and nationality, "which makes enforcement action virtually impossible" as the Monitoring Team observed in 2004.[147] The Committee reported in its 2005 report that as many as 65 states have said that sanctions cannot be fully implemented without sufficient iden-

---

141   Doc. S/PV. 5474 of 22 June 2006, 3 (Mr. Moeller/ Ms. Løj of Denmark), 12 (Mr. Burian of Slovakia), 15 (Mr. Pereyra Plasencia of Peru), 20 (Mr. Mayoral of Argentina), 21 (Mr. Al-Nasser of Qatar); Doc. S/PV. 5474 (Res. 1) of 22 June 2006, 17 (Mrs. Núñez de Odremán of Venezuela), 19 (Mr. Adekanye of Nigeria).

142   Doc. S/PV. 5474 (Res. 1) of 22 June 2006, 9 (Mr. Barriga of Liechtenstein).

143   Doc. S/PV. 5474 of 22 June 2006, 12 (Mr. Burian of Slovakia), 25-26 (Nana Effah-Apenteng of Ghana).

144   Doc. S/PV. 5474 of 22 June 2006, 24 (Mrs. Telalian of Greece); Doc. S/PV. 5474 (Res. 1) of 22 June 2006, 11 (Mr. Baum of Switzerland).

145   See Rosand, see note 89, 749.

146   *Report of the Monitoring Group Established Pursuant to Security Council Resolution 1363 (2001) and Extended by Resolution 1390 (2002)*, Doc. S/2002/541 of 15 May 2002, para. 8.

147   *1st Report of the Analytical Support and Sanctions Monitoring Team Appointed Pursuant to Resolution 1526 (2004) Concerning Al-Qaida and the Taliban and Associated Individuals and Entities*, Doc. S/2004/679 of 25 August 2004 (hereinafter 1st Report of the Monitoring Team), para. 37.

tifiers.[148] Such difficulties persist to date; the Monitoring Team pointed out in 2006 that "[m]any Member States continue to complain that some entries on the List are inadequate or inaccurate",[149] and reiterated in 2007 that "[t]he lack of identifiers on the List is consistently quoted by States ... as the principal reason for a lack of thorough implementation".[150]

The degree that the Committee members devoted their time for communication with other Member States added a source of frustration. At least 12 states have voiced discontent over a lack of response when they sought additional information.[151] Further, the absence of standards for listing increased the anxiety of several countries that even the already insufficient identifying information may not be trustworthy. Germany stated at the SC meeting in 2003 that "clear criteria should be developed that would specify under which objective conditions a given individual or entity should be added to that list".[152] The Committee decides on a case-by-case basis as to whether the proposed individuals or entities are "associated with" the Taliban or Al Qaeda. Before the revision of the Guidelines in 2005, such decision had been made by a two working-day non objection procedure;[153] the objection to the proposed listing must have been raised within 48 hours. If not bilaterally notified in advance by a designating state, this procedure may have effectively excluded objections by some Committee members if their capacity or circumstances were such that they could not afford to challenge it.[154]

---

[148]   Committee's Written Assessments 2005, see note 127, Annex I, para. 37.

[149]   4th Report of the Monitoring Team, see note 96, para. 29.

[150]   *Report of the Analytical Support and Sanctions Monitoring Team Appointed Pursuant to Security Council Resolutions 1617 (2005) and 1735 (2006) Concerning Al-Qaida and the Taliban and Associated Individuals and Entities*, Doc. S/2007/677 of 29 November 2007 (hereinafter 7th Report of the Monitoring Team), para. 29.

[151]   Committee's Written Assessments 2005, see note 127, Annex I, para. 37.

[152]   Doc. S/PV. 4798 of 29 July 2003, 14 (statement by Mr. Pleuger of Germany).

[153]   *3rd Report of the Monitoring Group Established Pursuant to Security Council Resolution 1363 (2001) and Extended by Resolution 1390 (2002), Doc. S/2002/1338 of 17 December 2002, Annex III (Guidelines of the Security Council Committee Established Pursuant to Resolution 1267 (1999) for the Conduct of its Work*, Adopted on 7 November 2002 (hereinafter Committee Guidelines 2002)), para. 8(b).

[154]   See Paper by the Watson Institute, see note 13, 32.

Overall, one of the prime focuses for many states and financial institutions has been the enhancement of the overall quality of identifiers
and communication with the Committee, so that the difficulties and
costs associated with implementation would be alleviated. Certainly
there are many other concerns; albeit not the main focus for many
states at least at the initial stage of the sanctions regime, including the
clarity of standards for listing represented by the above-quoted remark
by Germany in 2003, which overlaps with those of other accountability
holders (which will be discussed below).

b. Responses

The SC and the Committee must be credited for the progress they have
made in the overall quality of the List and communication with Member States. (These are chronologically listed in the Appendix as far as it
is ascertainable from the SC documents).

Firstly, as for the information updating, the Committee Guidelines
revised in 2003 added a section for "updating the existing information",
which provides for target identifiers to be updated at all times by in-
structing the Committee to consider additional information supplied
"expeditiously".[155] An annual review process was introduced in 2006
for those listings left un-updated for more than four years.[156]

Secondly, progress was made with reference to the list of identifiers
and the information to be included in statements of case when submitting new names. Particular reference can be made to the introduction of
a standard "cover sheet" for listing proposals in mid-2006.[157] The cover
sheet, together with the Guidelines revised in 2006, incorporated a more
detailed list of identifiers, and requested Member States to provide in
their statements of case as much detail as possible, specific findings and

---

[155] *The Al-Qaida and Taliban Sanctions Committee, Guidelines of the Committee for the Conduct of its Work*, as amended on 29 November 2006
(hereinafter Committee Guidelines 2006) (on file with the author), para. 7;
identical to Committee Guidelines 2007, see note 2, para. 7.

[156] Committee Guidelines 2006, see note 155, para. 6(i); identical to Committee Guidelines 2007, see note 2, para. 6(i). Following the first review in
2007, which ended without any changes to the List, the Monitoring Team
suggested further improvement in the review procedure: see 7th Report of
the Monitoring Team, see note 150, paras 40-48.

[157] 5th Report of the Monitoring Team, see note 25, para. 20, Annex II (cover
sheet).

supporting evidence.[158] The introduction of the standard cover sheet was, for one thing, to "make it easier for States to prepare requests for listing" as the US delegation described.[159] Yet the cover sheet was also perceived by the EU and Switzerland as a step to enhance transparency.[160] The Swiss delegation describes the cover sheet as "oblig[ing] Member States ... to specify suspected links with Al-Qaida or the Taliban", with a view to further enhancing the transparency and effectiveness of the listing procedure.[161]

Thirdly, the frequency and quality of communication have been improved, both *vis-à-vis* all Member States and those particularly affected by the decisions. The Committee convened "open briefings"[162] for all interested Member States at least in 2003 and 2006, the latter being attended by 50 representatives, in order to keep them informed of its work.[163] In 2004 the Committee established a list of "contact points",[164] whereby its decisions to update the list are emailed to over 300 contact

---

[158] Committee Guidelines 2006, see note 155, paras 6(e), (d); with a minor modification, Committee Guidelines 2007, see note 2, paras 6(e), (d).

[159] Doc. S/PV. 5538 of 28 September 2006, 14 (statement by Ms. Sanders of the United States).

[160] The EU Presidency Statement, see note 131; Doc. S/PV. 5679 of 22 May 2007, 36 (statement by Mr. Grütter of Switzerland).

[161] Doc. S/PV. 5679 of 22 May 2007, 36 (statement by Mr. Grütter of Switzerland).

[162] The use of "open briefings" is part of the attempt to enhance accountability of the SC since about 1993. For details, see Descriptive Index, see note 67; Note by the President of the Security Council, Doc. S/2006/507 of 19 July 2006; Note by the President of the Security Council, Doc. S/2007/749 of 19 December 2007. See generally, M.C. Wood, "Security Council Working Methods and Procedure: Recent Developments", *ICLQ* 45 (1996), 150 et seq. (154-161); S.C. Hulton, "Council Working Methods and Procedure", in: D.M. Malone (ed.), *The UN Security Council: From the Cold War to the 21st Century*, 2004, 237 et seq. (245-251); Talmon, see note 75, 188.

[163] *Report of the Security Council Committee Established Pursuant to Resolution 1267 (1999) Concerning Al-Qaida and the Taliban and Associated Individuals and Entities*, Doc. S/2007/59 of 7 February 2007 (hereinafter Committee Annual Report 2007), para. 12; *Report of the Security Council Committee Established Pursuant to Resolution 1267 (1999) Concerning Al-Qaida and the Taliban and Associated Individuals and Entities*, Doc. S/2004/281 of 8 April 2004, para. 21.

[164] *Report of the Security Council Committee Established Pursuant to Resolution 1267 Concerning Al-Qaida and the Taliban and Associated Individuals and Entities*, Doc. S/2004/1039 of 31 December 2004, para. 7.

points, including not merely the states' missions to the UN but the relevant ministries and agencies responsible for implementation.[165] In relation to particular states, it decided in 2005 to use the statement of case submitted by the designating states "in responding to queries from Member States whose nationals, residents or entities have been included" on the List.[166] It is anticipated that the Committee strengthens interaction with these Member States, given that in 2006 the Council encouraged sanctions committees "to seek the views of Member States that are particularly affected by the sanctions" as part of its efforts to enhance the efficiency and transparency.[167]

Yet the enhancement of communication owes much to the work of the Monitoring Group (2001-2003)[168] and the Monitoring Team (2004-).[169] A monitoring mechanism for sanctions is not without precedent,[170] as evidenced by the Inquiry under Resolution 1013 (1995) for Rwanda, the Monitoring Mechanism under Resolution 1295 (2000) for Angola and the Panel of Experts under Resolution 1306 (2000) for Sierra Leone.[171] In particular, the Monitoring Mechanism for Angola undertook a range of tasks including analysis of the targets, investigation of violations of sanctions, visits to some Member States, and the making of recommendations to the Committee.[172]

Built on these experiences, the monitoring mechanism of the 1267 Committee, in charge of far more comprehensive tasks, has created "a tighter administrative network for the enforcement of UN sanctions".[173] The Monitoring Team engages in building up close contact

---

[165] Committee Annual Report 2007, see note 163, para. 14.

[166] S/RES/1617 (2005) of 29 July 2005, para. 6.

[167] Note by the President of the Security Council, Doc. S/2006/507 of 19 July 2006, para. 46.

[168] S/RES/1363 (2001) of 30 July 2001, paras 3, 4(a); S/RES/1390 (2002) of 28 January 2002, para. 9; S/RES/1455 (2003) of 17 January 2003, para. 8.

[169] S/RES/1526 (2004) of 30 January 2004, para. 6; S/RES/1617 (2005) of 29 July 2005, para. 19, and Annex I; S/RES/1735 (2006) of 22 December 2006, para. 32, and Annex II.

[170] See V. Gowlland-Debbas, "Sanctions Regimes under Article 41 of the UN Charter", in: V. Gowlland-Debbas (ed.), National Implementation of United Nations Sanctions: A Comparative Study, 2004, 3 et seq. (23).

[171] S/RES/1013 (1995) of 7 September 1995; S/RES/1295 (2000) of 18 April 2000, para. 3; S/RES/1306 (2000) of 5 July 2000, para. 19.

[172] See, e.g., Final Report of the Monitoring Mechanism on Angola Sanctions, Doc. S/2000/1225 of 21 December 2000.

[173] Krisch, see note 8, 887.

with state officials, and, where necessary, the Team informally provides advice to countries considering listing or delisting. The Team actively visits Member States and attends regional meetings,[174] and has daily contact with both the Counter-Terrorism Committee under S/RES/1373 (2001) of 28 September 2001 and the so called 1540 Committee imposed under S/RES/1540 (2004) of 28 April 2004, its members as well as its experts.[175] Resolution 1735 also added an explicit reference to the responsibility to "consult with relevant representatives of the private sector, including financial institutions, to learn about the practical implementation of the assets freeze ... ", to the list of the Monitoring Team's mandates.[176] Such strong interaction with national bureaucracies, international organizations and the private sector produces "a much higher degree of mutual learning" and "a more flexible and informed decision-making than under most previous sanctions regimes",[177] which in turn increases the above-mentioned bodies' willingness to cooperate with the Committee.

Probably the sacred area in which no noteworthy changes have been made is the standards of listing and delisting. S/RES/1617 (2005) of 29 July 2005 has given a more elaborated definition of the "associated with" category,[178] but no guidance on evidential standards is provided. The possible explanations are that any standard-setting in this area undermines the flexibility of the listing, or that given the diversity of materials submitted to the Committee, any standards may prove unworkable. Between the demand for transparency and the need to ensure flexibility, listing and delisting remain left to the Committee's case-by-case decision-making by consensus. It is likely that more challenges will be raised in the future with respect to the standards of listing.

---

[174] In 2006, the Monitoring Team visited 25 states, participated in 20 international and regional conferences, and organized four regional meetings. The Committee's members also visited five states in 2006: see Committee Annual Report 2007, see note 163, paras 21, 24, 27.

[175] 4th Report of the Monitoring Team, see note 96, para. 138.

[176] S/RES/1735 (2006) of 22 December 2006, Annex II, para. (m).

[177] Krisch, see note 8, 887.

[178] S/RES/1617 (2005) of 29 July 2005, paras 2-3; Committee Guidelines 2007, see note 2, para. 6(c).

3. Fairness and Transparency: Targeted Individuals/Entities

a. Challenges

aa. Challenges by the Listed Individuals and Entities

Without being notified of any detailed grounds of listing, and in an absence of any specific procedures available to them before the Committee, the targeted individuals and entities alleging their non-involvement must place their immediate reliance upon the diplomatic channels of their respective governments. Yet the governments may be unwilling to represent their claims, or, even if they are willing to do so, the designating government may be unable or reluctant to share intelligence information. While awaiting the outcome of diplomatic negotiations, or having found themselves unlikely to receive governmental support, some individuals whose assets have been frozen have challenged before national courts, on a variety of grounds including infringement of their human rights, relevant domestic legislation to implement SC decisions.

Such court challenges have arisen in many parts of the world. As of February 2005, at least 13 lawsuits were identified by the Monitoring Team.[179] Litigation involving listed individuals and entities continued to grow, and by September 2007, there were at least 26 known legal challenges to the sanctions or the administration of them, nine of which were brought before the European Court of Justice (ECJ) (including those before the Court of First Instance (CFI)) with the 17 others being in Pakistan, Switzerland, Turkey, United Kingdom, United States and the Netherlands.[180] An action has been brought against other sanctions regimes.[181] The impact of the rise of court challenges is not merely one of operational impediments. As the Austrian representative observed on behalf of the EU, "a negative court ruling would not only put the

---

[179] 2nd Report of the Monitoring Team, see note 6, para. 50.

[180] 7th Report of the Monitoring Team, see note 150, Annex I; 6th Report of the Monitoring Team, see note 7, para. 35, Annex I; 5th Report of the Monitoring Team, see note 25, Annex III.

[181] Case T-362/04, *Leonid Minin v Commission of the European Communities*, Judgment of 31 January 2007 (CFI), paras 58 et seq. (concerning the Liberia sanctions under Resolution 1521 (2003), and the CFI rejected the claim in the light of its earlier decisions in *Yusuf*, *Kadi*, and *Ayadi*).

Member States concerned in a difficult position but might also call the whole system of targeted United Nations sanctions into question".[182]

The CFI's decisions in *Kadi* (2005), *Yusuf* (2005), *Ayadi* (2006) and *Hassan* (2006) are some of the outcomes of those challenges. Kadi and Ayadi appeared on the List in October 2001,[183] and Yusuf was designated in November 2001.[184] Hassan was listed in November 2003.[185] Kadi and Yusuf together with two other Swedish citizens (Aden, Abdi Abdulaziz Ali) and the Al Barakaat International Foundation seated in Sweden, soon brought actions before the ECJ in December 2001,[186] followed by Ayadi in August 2002 and Hassan in February 2004.[187] They sought the annulment of relevant EC regulations,[188] on the ground of, *inter alia*, infringement of the right to a fair hearing, the right of respect for property, and the right to effective judicial review.

The use of national courts to contest the acts of international organizations, directly or as secondary disputes, is by no means new.[189] Nevertheless, the additional difficulty inherent in bringing challenges to the legislation implementing the Al Qaeda/Taliban sanctions concerns the fact that national authorities have very little discretion, owing to both the character of the obligation under SC resolutions and the degree of specification. For one thing, by virtue of the effect of Article 103

---

[182] Doc. S/PV. 5446 of 30 May 2006, 26 (Mr. Pfanzelter of Austria, speaking on behalf of the EU).

[183] See Press Release SC/7180 of 19 October 2001.

[184] See Press Release AFG/163-SC/7206 of 9 November 2001.

[185] See Press Release SC/7920 of 14 November 2003.

[186] Action Brought on 10 December 2001 by *Abdirisak Aden* and Others against the Council of the European Union and the Commission of the European Communities, Case T-306/01, *OJ* (2002), C 44/27 et seq.; Action brought on 18 December 2001 by *Yassin Abdullah Kadi* against the Council of the European Union and the Commission of the European Communities, Case T-315/01, *OJ* (2002), C 56/16 et seq.

[187] Action brought on 22 August 2002 by *Chafiq Ayadi* against the Council of the European Union and the Commission of the European Communities, Case T-253/02, *OJ* (2002), C 289/25; Action brought on 12 February 2004 by *Faraj Hassan* against the Council of the European Union and the Commission of the European Communities, Case T-49/04, *OJ* (2004), C 94/52.

[188] Council Regulation (EC) 881/2002, *OJ* (2002), L 139/9 et seq. (which repealed Council Regulation (EC) 467/2001, *OJ* (2001), L 67/1 et seq.).

[189] See for the overview of the types of cases involving international organizations, A. Reinisch, *International Organizations Before National Courts*, 2000, 24-31.

of the UN Charter, Member States are not expected to counterbalance
the obligations under SC resolutions with other conflicting treaty or
customary obligations incurred by them, including general human
rights norms. Therefore, the situations are different from those of *Waite
and Kennedy* (1999), where the European Court of Human Rights
(ECtHR) seems to have analyzed whether the appropriate balance had
been struck between Germany's conventional obligation to grant immunity to the European Space Agency and its obligation under article 6
of the European Convention for the Protection of Human Rights and
Fundamental Freedoms (ECHR), primarily through the application of
the proportionality test under the ECHR, in a situation where the pri-
macy of one obligation over the other is not clear-cut.[190]

Also the Member States retain little discretion because of the way
the Al Qaeda/Taliban sanctions were designed; the relevant SC resolutions are not drafted in a manner to allow discretion to be exercised by
Member States, at least on the designation of targets and the types of
sanctions imposed. The more faithful national authorities are in respect
of the implementation of the Al Qaeda/Taliban sanctions, the less discretion they can exercise. Likewise, the more faithful national courts are
in respect of the interpretation of obligations under the UN Charter,
the less can be done by courts to direct governmental actions. In this respect, the circumstances also differ from those of the CFI's decision in
Organisation des Modjahedines du peuple d'Iran (OMPI) (2006), which
concerned an entity designated under the EC measures implementing
SC Resolution 1373 (as opposed to Resolution 1267).[191] Although para.
1(c) of S/RES/1373 (2001) of 28 September 2001 imposes upon Member
States Chapter VII obligations to freeze funds of suspected terrorists, it
is for the Member States to designate specific individuals and entities
suspected of terrorism and determine the procedures for freezing assets.[192] This "discretionary appreciation"[193] of Member States and the
European Community made it possible for the CFI to scrutinize the
EC legislation giving effect to the SC decision in the light of, "as a mat-

---

[190] See *Waite and Kennedy v Germany* (Application No. 26083/94), Judgment
of 18 February 1999 (ECtHR), paras 59-74.

[191] Council Regulation (EC) 2580/2001, *OJ* (2001), L 344/70 et seq. (which is
based on Council Common Position 2001/931/CFSP, *OJ* (2001), L 344/93
et seq.).

[192] Case T-228/02, *Organisation des Modjahedines du peuple d'Iran v Council
of the European Union*, Judgment of 12 December 2006 (CFI), paras 99-
107.

[193] See note 192, para. 107.

ter of principle, fully applicable"[194] human rights, without eroding the supremacy of SC obligations.[195]

Given the little scope of discretion, there was no surprise when the CFI delivered the judgments in September 2005 for *Kadi* and *Yusuf* respectively, and by virtue of Arts 25, 48 and 103 of the UN Charter, as well as the provisions of the EC Treaty, required the Community to give effect to SC resolutions.[196] It stated that the review of the relevant EC legislation implementing the SC resolutions "fall[s], in principle, outside the ambit of the Court's judicial review".[197] This point was reiterated by the CFI in *Ayadi* and *Hassan* decided in July 2006.[198]

However, the CFI did not miss the chance to send signals to the SC and the EU Member States that there was some potential for judicial control. In *Kadi* and *Yusuf*, the CFI observed that "the Court is empowered to check, indirectly, the lawfulness of the resolutions of the Security Council in question with regard to *jus cogens* ... from which

---

[194] See note 193, para. 108.

[195] See for the summary and comments, A. Johnston, "Thawing Out? The European Courts and the Freezing of Terrorist Assets", *CLJ* 66 (2007), 273 et seq. (274). See other cases brought against the measures implementing S/RES/1373, including Case T-327/03, *Stichting Al-Aqsa v Council of the European Union*, Judgment of 11 July 2007 (CFI), paras 53 et seq. (The CFI found a breach of duty to state reasons under article 253 EC); Case C-266/05 P, *Jose Maria Sison v Council of the European Union*, Judgment of 1 February 2007 (ECJ), paras 26 et seq. (The ECJ rejected the appellant's arguments that the Council breached the Community law as well as human rights in refusing to disclose the documents); Case C-355/04 P, *Segi, Araitz Zubimendi Izaga, Aritza Galarraga v Council of the European Union*, Judgment of 27 February 2007 (ECJ), paras 18 et seq. (The ECJ dismissed the appeal as the appellants' names were included only in the Common Positions which are not generally reviewable by the Court); Case C-229/05, *Osman Ocalan, on behalf of the Kurdistan Workers' Party (PKK), Serif Vanly, on behalf of the Kurdistan National Congress (KNK) v Council of the European Union*, Judgment of 18 January 2007 (ECJ), paras 24 et seq. (The ECJ remitted the PKK application to the CFT to decide on the merits, while refusing to accept KNK's standing).

[196] See *Kadi*, see note 101, paras 222-223; *Yusuf*, see note 101, paras 273-274.

[197] *Kadi*, see note 101, para. 225; *Yusuf*, see note 101, para. 276.

[198] Case T-253/02, *Chafiq Ayadi* v Council of the European Union and Commission of the European Communities, Judgment of 12 July 2006 (CFI) (hereinafter *Ayadi*), para. 116; Case T-49/04, *Faraj Hassan* v Council of the European Union and Commission of the European Communities, Judgment of 12 July 2006 (CFI) (hereinafter *Hassan*), para. 92.

no derogation is possible".[199] Furthermore, in *Ayadi* and *Hassan*, the CFI made a slightly far-fetched attempt to interpret the delisting section of the Committee Guidelines as conferring on interested persons "the right to present a request for review of their case to the government" of residence/citizenship, which is also "guaranteed by the ECHR".[200] This led the CFI to observe that the Member States must ensure, as far as possible, that targeted persons can present their delisting requests before competent national authorities, and that delisting requests are presented "without delay and fairly and impartially" to the 1267 Committee.[201]

These signals that national courts "could in the future police the limits of international sanctions"[202] may have reminded many international lawyers of the judicial techniques used by the majority of the ICJ in the *Lockerbie* case (1992 and 1998) to preserve its own presence *vis-à-vis* the SC. In both the Order of 1992 and the preliminary judgment in 1998, the majority of ICJ judges did not leave out the possibility of judicial review of SC Resolutions 731 and 748, despite the latter being adopted under Chapter VII.[203]

The CFI in *Kadi* and *Yusuf* understandably concluded that there were no infringements of *jus cogens*. As for the right to be heard, the absence of direct challenge by individuals "is not, however, to be deemed improper in the light of the mandatory prescriptions of the public international order".[204] As for the right to effective judicial review, the CFI took note of the delisting procedures under the Committee Guidelines, which "constitute another reasonable method of affording adequate protection of the applicants' fundamental rights as recog-

---

[199] *Kadi*, see note 101, para. 226; *Yusuf*, see note 101, para. 277. See for a critical view, M. Bulterman, "Fundamental Rights and the United Nations Financial Sanction Regime: The *Kadi* and *Yusuf* Judgments of the Court of First Instance of the European Communities", *LJIL* 19 (2006), 753 et seq. (767-770).

[200] *Ayadi*, see note 198, paras 145-146; *Hassan*, see note 198, paras 115-116.

[201] *Ayadi*, see note 198, paras 147-149; *Hassan*, see note 198, paras 117-119.

[202] Krisch, see note 11, 268.

[203] See *Questions of Interpretation and Application of the 1971 Montreal Convention arising from the Aerial Incident at Lockerbie (Libyan Arab Jamahiriya v United Kingdom)*, ICJ Reports 1992, 3 et seq. (15, para. 40); Franck, see note 55, 242-244; Gray, see note 55, 433 et seq.

[204] *Kadi*, see note 101, para. 268. Similarly, *Yusuf*, see note 101, para. 315.

nized by *jus cogens*".[205] The claims by *Ayadi* of the infringements of various procedural guarantees were equally rejected.[206] Yusuf was removed from the List in August 2006 after almost five years of listing,[207] although the reasons for his removal are not publicly available. On the other hand, as of 7 April 2008, Kadi, Ayadi, Hassan and the Al Barakaat International Foundation remain on the List, awaiting the judgments to be delivered by the ECJ.[208]

bb. Parallel Challenges by States

Some of the targeted individuals managed to be delisted from the List owing to diplomatic efforts. In November 2001, having found its nationals on the List (Aden and others referred to above), the Swedish government soon approached the 1267 Committee and the US administration.[209] After the Swedish Security Police concluded in December 2001 that no accusations were confirmed, the Swedish government filed a request with the 1267 Committee for a review of the List in January 2002, and at the same time, entered negotiations with the United States administration.[210] The story of Aden was reported in the media in Sweden and abroad.[211] Although the delisting request was initially rejected

---

[205] *Kadi*, see note 101, para. 290; *Yusuf*, see note 101, para. 345.

[206] *Ayadi*, see note 198, paras 115-169; *Hassan*, see note 198, paras 91-129.

[207] Press Release SC/8815 of 24 August 2006.

[208] As for *Kadi* and *AlBarakaat International Foundation*, in his opinion delivered on 16 January 2008 and 23 January 2008, respectively, the Advocate General concluded that the EC courts had the authority to review the contested EC legislation, and that the legislation infringed the appellants' human rights including their right to be heard: see Case C-402/05, *Yassin Abdullah Kadi v Council of the European Union and Commission of the European Communities*, Advocate General's Opinion of 16 January 2008; Case C-415/05 P, *Al Barakaat International Foundation v Council of the European Union and Commission of the European Communities*, Advocate General's Opinion of 23 January 2008.

[209] P. Cramér, "Recent Swedish Experiences with Targeted UN Sanctions: The Erosion of Trust in the Security Council", in: De Wet, see note 14, 85 et seq. (91).

[210] See Cramér, see note 209, 91-94.

[211] See Cramér, see note 209, 92, fn. 41 (Swedish media). See for example, BBC News, Sweden Questions US Terror Charges, 14 February 2002, available at: <http:// news.bbc.co.uk/2/hi/europe/1820020.stm>; BBC News, Swedish Somalis Fight Terror Links, 20 February 2002, available at: <http:// news.bbc.co.uk/ 2/hi/africa/1831478.stm>.

by the 1267 Committee in February 2002 having met objections from the United States, Russia and the United Kingdom,[212] the United States decided to remove Aden and Abdi Abdulaziz Ali in July 2002 after strong pressure from the Swedish government.[213] This was followed by the Committee's adoption of the delisting procedure in August 2002,[214] under which the removal of their names was approved.[215]

In tandem with the diplomacy involved in the delisting of Aden and others, Sweden took one of the first diplomatic initiatives, the so-called "Stockholm Process",[216] to invite governmental and non-governmental attention to the issue of procedural guarantees.[217] Although, due to the politically sensitive nature of the issue,[218] the aspect of legal safeguards for the targeted individuals did not become the main focus of the process. The outcome report presented to the SC in February 2003 touches upon the need to ensure procedural guarantees.[219] The call for proce-

---

[212] See Cramér, see note 209, 93-94.

[213] BBC News, Swedish Terror Suspects Cleared, 14 July 2002, available at: <http://news.bbc.co.uk/2/hi/europe/2128042.stm>.

[214] Press Release AFG/203-SC/7487 of 16 August 2002. See Committee Guidelines 2002, see note 153.

[215] Press Release SC/7490 of 27 August 2002. Together with Aden and Abdi Abdulaziz Ali, one individual and three entities were removed from the UN List: see ibid. They had been listed in the United States due to their involvement in Al Barakaat, but the United States removed their names after the filing of suit against the government: see Roth et al., see note 19, 80-81, 84-86.

[216] The Stockholm Process is one in a series of targeted sanctions reforms, known as the Interlaken Process (1998-2001), the Bonn-Berlin Process (1999-2001), and the Stockholm Process (2001-2002), sponsored by Switzerland, Germany and Sweden, respectively. See for a summary of these sanction reform initiatives, T.J. Biersteker et al., "Consensus from the Bottom Up? Assessing the Influence of the Sanctions Reform Processes", in: P. Wallensteen/ C. Staibano (eds), *International Sanctions: Between Words and Wars in the Global System*, 2005, 15 et seq.

[217] The Stockholm Process was announced in October 2001, initially without any particular reference to the issue of procedural guarantees: see Doc. S/PV. 4394 of 22 October 2001, 5-6 (Mr. Dahlgren of Sweden). After the listing of Swedish citizens, however, the Swedish government tried to bring the question of legal safeguards for individuals into the agendas of the Process.

[218] Cramér, see note 209, 103.

[219] See P. Wallensteen et. al. (eds), *Making Targeted Sanctions Effective: Guidelines for the Implementation of UN Policy Options – Results from the*

dural safeguards was then echoed by Germany, which encouraged the SC at the meeting in July 2003 to consider the "possibility that a targeted individual might bring his case to the Committee" in the light of "core elements of due process to be applied by the Security Council, mutatis mutandis".[220] Then Switzerland, Germany and Sweden commissioned the project undertaken by the Watson Institute of Brown University, entitled "Strengthening Targeted Sanctions Through Fair and Clear Procedures" presented to the SC and the GA in June 2006.[221] The Watson Institute report addressed procedural guarantees to a greater extent: it recommended that an administrative focal point be designated within the UN Secretariat to which individuals may submit their delisting requests;[222] and it proposed several options for review mechanisms accessible to individuals.[223]

Until 2004, as far as the official records are concerned, there were only a few references in the GA or SC as to the procedural guarantees of individuals and entities on the List.[224] However, with these governmental attempts in parallel with the individuals' court challenges, the due process and human rights issue gradually became a more widely shared issue by 2004 at the governmental level.[225] By 2005, the delisting process became "high on the agenda of States and international organizations", being raised in virtually all the Monitoring Team's

---

Stockholm Process on the Implementation of Targeted Sanctions, 2003, paras 37, 282-285, available at: <http://www.smartsanctions.se/>. The report was presented to the SC: see Press Release SC/7673 of 25 February 2003; Doc. S/PV. 4713 of 25 February 2003.

[220] Doc. S/PV. 4798 of 29 July 2003, 14 (statement by Mr. Pleuger of Germany). Italy, speaking on behalf of the EU also referred to the need to promote due process in the proceedings of the Committee: see Doc. S/PV. 4798 of 29 July 2003, 21 (statement by Mr. Spatafora of Italy, speaking on behalf of the EU).

[221] Paper by the Watson Institute, see note 13. Earlier in May 2006 these three governments held discussions with the 1267 Committee on the Watson Institute report, see Committee Annual Report 2007, see note 163, para. 10.

[222] Paper by the Watson Institute, see note 13, 43-44.

[223] Paper by the Watson Institute, see note 13, 46-51.

[224] For instance, Doc. S/PV. 4798 of 29 July 2003, 14 ("there could be room for the possibility that a targeted individual might bring his case to the Committee for consideration", statement by Mr. Pleuger of Germany). See also Doc. S/PV. 4798 of 29 July 2003, 21 (statement by Mr. Spatafora of Italy, speaking on behalf of the EU).

[225] See for example, Doc. S/PV. 4892 of 12 January 2004; 1st Report of the Monitoring Team, see note 147, paras 34, 41.

meetings with Member States.[226] Some states even voiced hesitation to propose new listings "because the system lacked a robust de-listing mechanism".[227]

cc. Parallel Challenges by the Wider UN Membership

The call for legal safeguards for listed individuals and entities also received support from several bodies inside the United Nations. In 2004, the UN High-level Panel made an unequivocal call for a reviewing process in relation to the Al Qaeda/Taliban sanctions regime, noting that "the absence of review or appeal for those listed raise serious accountability issues and possibly violate fundamental human rights norms and conventions."[228]

In response to the World Summit document, the SG directed the Office of Legal Affairs to develop proposals,[229] which commissioned the study by Fassbender of the Humboldt University (Germany).[230] The SG set out later his views of minimum standards to ensure fairness and transparency in the listing and delisting process. They include the following four basic elements, in short: the right to be informed of the measures, the right to be heard directly by the decision-making body, the right to review by an effective review mechanism, and periodical review by the Council.[231] The need for these procedural safeguards for individuals was endorsed by the Special Rapporteur appointed by the then Commission on Human Rights in his report in August 2006,[232] as well as by the UN High Commissioner for Human Rights in her report presented to the Human Rights Council in March 2007.[233] The High

---

[226] 3rd Report of the Monitoring Team, see note 6, para. 52.

[227] 3rd Report of the Monitoring Team, see note 6, para. 54.

[228] *Report of the High-level Panel on Threats, Challenges and Change, A More Secure World: Our Shared Responsibility,* Doc. A/59/565 of 2 December 2004, para. 152.

[229] Report of the Secretary-General, see note 128, para. 117.

[230] Fassbender, see note 43.

[231] See Doc. S/PV. 5474 of 22 June 2006, 5 (statement by Mr. Michel, Legal Council of the UN, presenting the Secretary-General's view).

[232] *Report of the Special Rapporteur on the Promotion and Protection of Human Rights and Fundamental Freedoms while Countering Terrorism,* Doc. A/61/267 of 16 August 2006, paras 38-41.

[233] See Report of the UNHCHR, see note 18, paras 25-27.

Commissioner pointed out that the listing has no end date, which may render the freezing of assets permanent and more punitive.[234]

b. Responses

The SC's earlier responses to ameliorate the impact on listed individuals were largely devoted to the provision of humanitarian exemptions (see Appendix), as represented by the introduction of enhanced procedures for such exemptions under S/RES/1452 (2002) of 12 December 2002. In mid-2006, in response to criticism from various sectors, the question of how to address the fairness of the sanctions regime finally reached "the top of the 1267 Committee's agenda".[235] The Chairman of the Committee stressed in September 2006 the Committee's awareness of "the numerous calls urging it [to] adopt fair and clear listing and de-listing procedures".[236] In December 2006, based on a French proposal, the SC unanimously adopted S/RES/1730 (2006) of 19 December 2006, requesting the SG to establish a "focal point" to receive delisting requests as a mechanism to be generally applied to SC sanctions involving designated individuals.[237] By November 2007, the focal point has received 17 requests, 16 of which reached the Committee's table; 13 delisting requests were approved, with the other three being decided to remain on the List.[238]

Resolution 1730 is certainly "a real achievement".[239] The new procedures under Resolution 1730 differ from its predecessor in the following aspects: the designated individuals and entities can themselves submit a petition to the focal point; and more significantly, neither their state of residence/citizenship nor the designating government must be persuaded in order for the delisting request to be placed on the Committee's agenda. Previously, individual petitioners faced a first major hurdle in convincing the state of residence/citizenship, which in turn

---

[234] See Report of the UNHCHR, see note 18, para. 25.

[235] 5th Report of the Monitoring Team, see note 25, para. 2. See also Doc. S/PV. 5538 of 28 September 2006.

[236] Doc. S/PV. 5538 of 28 September 2006, 4 (Mr. Mayoral of Argentina, Chairman of the 1267 Committee).

[237] See for the summary of initial proposals, 5th Report of the Monitoring Team, see note 25, paras 49-51.

[238] See Doc. S/PV. 5779 of 14 November 2007, 5 (Mr. Verbeke of Belgium, Chairman of the 1267 Committee).

[239] Doc. S/PV. 5679 of 22 May 2007, 13 (Ms. Pierce of the United Kingdom).

would attempt to persuade the designating state and, in the event of an unsuccessful bilateral negotiation, decide whether to submit the delisting request without the designating state's support.[240] Under the new procedure, a recommendation from any of the Committee members ultimately suffices to place the delisting request on the Committee's agenda, in so far as the relevant member is willing to prepare an explanation.[241]

While appreciating the progress made, not all states would share the US' confidence that the focal point "adequately addresses the concern heard from Member States about a perceived lack of fairness in the sanctions process".[242] The crux is that the reform leading to Resolution 1730 pertains to the process according to which *the delisting request is placed upon the Committee's table*, as opposed to the Committee's listing/delisting decision-making itself.

Further challenges, therefore, would likely be raised with regard to the Committee's decisions themselves, particularly relating to a *review mechanism* and the *standards of listing/delisting*. Some non-permanent SC members and some other governments outside the SC have already been calling upon the Committee to launch new negotiations on a review mechanism. In adopting Resolution 1730, Denmark, Greece and Qatar expressed their disappointment and encouraged the SC to continue to work for a review mechanism.[243] Switzerland, speaking also on behalf of Germany and Sweden, reiterated the importance of a review mechanism as "the deficiency that is most often brought up in courts".[244] Switzerland remarked that the focal point "does not change the intergovernmental character of the procedure itself", warning that the current procedure may conflict with human rights, which potentially erodes the legitimacy of the sanctions regimes.[245] These calls for a review procedure were also echoed by Greece, Ghana, Slovakia, Liech-

---

[240] See Committee Guidelines 2007, see note 2, para. 8(e) (continuing to provide the previous delisting process).

[241] See Committee Guidelines 2007, see note 2, para. 8(d)(vi)(c).

[242] Doc. S/PV. 5679 of 22 May 2007, 22 (Mr. Khalilzad of the United States).

[243] Doc. S/PV. 5599 of 19 December 2006, 2-3 (Mr. Løj of Denmark), 3 (Ms. Papadopoulou of Greece), 3-4 (Mr. Al-Nasser of Qatar). Similarly, Doc. S/PV. 5779 of 14 November 2007, 22-23 (Mr. Al-Nasser of Qatar).

[244] Doc. S/PV. 5446 of 30 May 2006, 29 (Mr. Maurer of Switzerland, speaking on behalf of Germany, Sweden and Switzerland).

[245] Doc. S/PV. 5679 of 22 May 2007, 36-37 (Mr. Grütter of Switzerland).

tenstein and Argentina.[246] Liechtenstein observed that a "worldwide comprehensive asset freeze and travel ban without any time limits strongly affects the substantive rights of individuals, and must therefore be counterbalanced with appropriate legal protection against error or misuse."[247]

The aspect of standards of listing was raised, for instance, by South Africa, which pointed upon the need for "a higher evidentiary standard" to prove "a substantive nexus" with Al Qaeda or the Taliban "given the serious consequences of such listing".[248] Some other states also expressed in general terms the need for further improvements with a view to fair and clear procedures.[249] As encapsulated in the Monitoring Team's statement in mid-2007, "there is continued concern [among states] that sanctions have a punitive effect ... and that the listing process should therefore incorporate higher standards of fairness".[250] These further calls receive support from the UN High Commissioner for Human Rights who, while commending Resolution 1730 as a "first step", nevertheless described it as "far from being a comprehensive solution to the problem" in the light of procedural guarantees to be ensured.[251]

Overall, the 1267 Committee continues to be subjected to scrutiny by various governmental and non-governmental watchdogs, in the light of the accountability principles of fairness and transparency. Following the introduction of Resolution 1730, Germany, speaking on behalf of the EU, remarked that the EU would "observe the implementation of

---

[246] Doc. S/PV. 5446 of 30 May 2006, 10 (Mr. Vassilakis of Greece), 17 (Mr. Christian of Ghana); Doc. S/PV. 5474 of 22 June 2006, 12 (Mr. Burian of Slovakia), 25-26 (Nana Effah-Apenteng of Ghana); Doc. S/PV. 5679 of 22 May 2007, 32-33 (Mr. Barriga of Liechtenstein), 35 (Mr. Mayoral of Argentina).

[247] Doc. S/PV. 5679 of 22 May 2007, 33 (Mr. Barriga of Liechtenstein). On 8 November 2007, Denmark, Sweden and Switzerland organized a round table on delisting, inviting governmental and non-governmental representatives, Doc. S/PV. 5779 of 14 November 2007, 28 (Mr. Wenaweser of Liechtenstein, speaking on behalf of Switzerland and Liechtenstein).

[248] Doc. S/PV. 5679 of 22 May 2007, 15 (Mr. Kumalo of South Africa).

[249] Doc. S/PV. 5679 of 22 May 2007, 8 (Mr. Chávez of Peru), 11 (Mr. Kleib of Indonesia), 21-22 (Mr. Al-Nasser of Qatar). Similarly, Doc. S/PV. 5779 of 14 November 2007, 24-25 (Mr. Natalegawa of Indonesia).

[250] 7th Report of the Monitoring Team, see note 150, para. 26.

[251] Report of the UNHCHR, see note 18, para. 28.

the new guidelines and procedures" and added that "[i]n the light of that experience, other challenges might be identified" in the future.[252]

IV. The Future of a Review Mechanism for Individuals and Entities

Given that accountability challenges are likely to continue, it would be interesting to explore in more detail what responses should and could be made by the SC and the Committee in the foreseeable future. As discussed above, fairness and transparency may signify different things for the various accountability holders, and it is beyond the scope of this article to give consideration to all the possible responses by the SC. This Chapter focuses on one realization of accountability towards the designated individuals and entities: a mechanism to review the Committee's listing decisions, which has attracted growing attention as one of the basic elements in ensuring fairness and transparency towards those individuals.[253]

1. Decentralized Review Mechanism

One of the preliminary questions is *who* can review the Committee's decisions. One dichotomy is whether it can be done by Member States.[254] The idea is to oblige Member States to establish a review process through their national courts, to which the individuals and entities on the UN List may submit a petition. One of the operational advantages is that no significant operational costs would be incurred by the sanctions regime compared to the establishment of a review mechanism at the UN. Yet it is difficult to see how this decentralized review mechanism could co-exist with the centralized listing/delisting decision-making in the Committee. The problems arising appear greater than those arising from a centralized review (some of these problems will be discussed below).

---

252 Doc. S/PV. 5679 of 22 May 2007, 24 (Mr. Matussek of Germany, speaking on behalf of the EU). An identical statement was made in November 2007: see Doc. S/PV. 5779 of 14 November 2007, 33 (Mr. Lobo de Mesquita of Portugal, speaking on behalf of the EU).

253 See under III. 3. b. of this article.

254 See, e.g., Cameron, see note 15, 205-208; Gutherie, see note 16, 535-537.

Firstly, such an obligation to conduct a review can only be imposed upon the original designating state for two main reasons. One is the availability of information necessary for such review; if a petition can be submitted outside the original designating state, the state receiving the petition would need to request further information from the original designating state in order to conduct a review on its own. Sharing information relating to the investigation of suspected terrorists between states, if not close allies, may be even more difficult than that with international organizations. Furthermore, such review would be to subject not only the decisions of the Committee, but also indirectly designating states' decisions to blacklist the terrorists, to the courts of third states in receipt of a petition, which would be more problematic than a review at the UN level.

Secondly, even if a review is conducted in the designating state or some other state holding evidence, judges may not have access to the classified material, or even if they have, they may lack expertise in the analysis of intelligence.[255] This is in part why national courts generally pay high deference to executives when it comes to issues of national security.[256]

Thirdly, some states seem to have special courts where judges with relevant expertise assess evidence including classified material in cases involving terrorism.[257] Even supposing that some kind of evidential analysis can be done by such courts, however, the detailed modes of review, even if the basic procedures and standards of review were to be laid out by the SC, would likely diverge from state to state. Given the variance of review, as well as likely differences in the perceived impartiality and independence of national courts, national courts' findings can only practically be recommendatory. The final determination by the Committee of whether it accepts national courts' findings may be subject to the perceived trust in the legal culture of particular jurisdictions, or general political relationships with the Committee's Member States,

---

[255] See Cameron, see note 15, 205.

[256] See Cameron, see note 15, 205-206.

[257] For instance, in the United Kingdom, the Special Immigration Appeals Commission (SIAC) and the Proscribed Organisations Appeal Commission (POAC). See generally for the SIAC, Constitutional Affairs Committee, The Operation of the Special Immigration Appeals Commission (SIAC) and the Use of Special Advocates, House of Commons (2004-05) 323-I, 7-14, available at: <http://www.publications.parliament.uk/pa/cm20 0405/cmselect/cmconst/cmconst.htm>.

which do not appear to serve to enhance fairness and transparency in the decision-making process.

2. Centralized Review Mechanism

If not Member States, a centralized body needs to be created by the SC, whose composition will be determined by either SC members or, more desirably, the SG independently of the SC. Several options for a centralized review at the UN level have already been put forward inside and outside the UN forum.[258] Among the many issues to be considered, the following points can be highlighted.

a. UN Budgetary Constraints

Unlike decentralized review, any review mechanisms at the UN level incur additional operational costs. The GA's Fifth Committee has been reluctant to award additional funds to the SC-led counterterrorism programs.[259] However, it is worth recalling that the GA's documents themselves requested the sanctions regimes to ensure fairness and transparency in listing and delisting. Also, it may be equally unlikely that the Al Qaeda/Taliban sanctions regime would ever sustain the GA's budgetary scrutiny without ensuring appropriate due process.

b. Functions of a Review Body and the Nature of Findings

As the SC is not bound by human rights norms in the same manner as Member States,[260] it would be wrong to expect the review mechanism for the Committee to act in the same way as national courts reviewing governmental decisions to designate terrorists. The expected function of a review mechanism is therefore not to identify whether the Committee is in breach of human rights obligations (in which case there is not much to review), but to hear petitioners' cases and to provide an independent analysis by experts as to the statements of case presented by the designating states.

---

[258] See Paper by the Watson Institute, see note 13, 47-51; Cameron, see note 15, 208-211; Gutherie, see note 16, 530-535; Alvarez, see note 16, 141-142.

[259] Millar/ Rosand, see note 68, 30.

[260] See under II. 4. of this article.

What the review body can possibly conclude from such an evidential analysis depends on its ability to access evidence for the listing and also on whether the findings would be binding upon the Committee. The findings of the review body can be more flexible if they are recommendatory. Denmark has proposed a review mechanism in the form of an ombudsperson, who, according to the proposal, could accept petitions directly from listed parties as well as consider other cases acting *proprio motu*, and ultimately make a recommendation to the Committee.[261] The options proposed by the Watson Institute at the UN also include an ombudsperson and a panel of experts with recommendatory powers.[262]

The academic proposals also look beyond such recommendatory powers. For instance, Cameron proposes, as one of the options for a review mechanism, the creation of an arbitral judicial body consisting of judges experienced in dealing with intelligence material.[263] Likewise, the Watson Institute's above mentioned report refers also to the creation of a judicial body, either by way of *ad hoc* three-member panels which hear specific delisting requests, or a standing judicial body for SC sanctions committees.[264] In theory, it is clear that the SC has competence under the UN Charter to establish a judicial body to review the committee's decisions. Although the SC does not possess a purely judicial function, it has the authority to set up such a body under Article 7 (2) as far as its establishment is necessary for the SC's mandates under Article 41.[265] Following the *Effect of Awards* case (1954), the findings could bind the SC as far as it is so intended.[266] In practice, however, the conferral of a binding decision-making power is neither feasible nor desirable. Firstly, the findings can only be made from limited evidence submitted by Member States to the UN.[267] Furthermore, other, arguably more important, dimensions of review mechanisms, such as the scope of

---

[261] 4th Report of the Monitoring Team, see note 96, para. 46; 5th Report of the Monitoring Team, see note 25, para. 49.

[262] Their model assumes that the ombudsman does not have access to confidential information while the panel of experts have such access, see Paper by the Watson Institute, see note 13, 48-50.

[263] Cameron, see note 15, 209-210.

[264] See Paper by the Watson Institute, see note 13, 50-51.

[265] See Sarooshi, "Subsidiary Organs", see note 47, 422-431.

[266] See *Effect of Awards of Compensation Made by the United Nations Administrative Tribunal*, ICJ Reports 1954, 47 et seq. (61).

[267] See Section (c) below.

functions, the standards of review and its composition, would be significantly restricted and compromised in order to derive agreement upon the binding nature of findings.

c. Sharing Secrets

It is useful to note that the information relating to the listing can be one of the following: (i) publicly accessible information, (ii) accessible to Member States upon request, (iii) held by the Committee, and (iv) any other information held by the designating state.[268] An independent evidential analysis will only be possible if the review body has as much access to these sets of information as possible. Much less the confidential statements of case held by the Committee (i.e., (iii) above), but also certain other information which can be submitted to the review body upon its request (i.e., part of (iv)).

There are many barriers to sharing confidential information with the UN. One of the obvious reasons is the risk of leakage of information. Unless the information is properly dealt with, the introduction of a review procedure may further discourage Member States from submitting new names or sufficient supporting evidence in the statements of case. It would, therefore, be necessary to develop the UN's capacity in handling confidential information. Chesterman's study suggests that the UN indeed has a history of intelligence sharing.[269] The risk of leakage of information can be minimized by the UN introducing improved security protocols for the handling of sensitive information, security clearances for staff, and possibly disciplinary procedures in order to facilitate receipt of information.[270]

d. Juridification of a Particularity

Whatever the form might be, a centralized review mechanism set up by the SC gives rise to a separate concern that this would be another example of the juridification (or quasi-juridification) of a particularity,[271] or in other words, a hegemonic way of legitimizing it. Some kind of standards of review would be set out through negotiation and bargain-

---

[268] See Committee Guidelines 2007, see note 2, para. 6(d), Annex (cover sheet).
[269] See Chesterman, see note 85, 9-16.
[270] See Chesterman, see note 85, 4, 33-35.
[271] See the discussions within the context of global administrative law in general, Harlow, see note 32, 207-214.

ing at the SC, and the review body would consider evidence in view of them. The concern is that the standards of review and the findings would be presented as universally agreeable, even if this may not be the case. At the same time, such a review body confers (even stronger) authority to the Committee's listing decisions, whereby the potential for constant challenges to reflect diverse opinions over the listing/delisting or other accountability questions would be undermined.

However, three observations can still be made in support of a centralized review mechanism for the 1267 Committee. Firstly, from the individuals' perspectives, expert review through which they can be heard is indeed a way forward, despite many shortcomings. Secondly, a possible review mechanism for the Al Qaeda/Taliban Committee would ensure some of the fundamental components of human rights. In particular the right to be heard and the right to review and remedy are treated by the SG and the UN High Commissioner for Human Rights as minimum guarantees to be respected by the 1267 Committee.[272] Therefore, the adverse effects of juridifying a particularity or hegemonic values should be minimized (compared to liberal economic values etc.) as far as the overall good of the project is to ensure better respect for those human rights.

Truly, there is much disagreement among Member States as to how these procedural guarantees are to be observed and how much deference must be paid to the executives in matters relating to terrorism. In this respect, it is unavoidable that a centralized review body, set up by the SC, carries the substantial risk of applying standards which may be seen as either too lax or too stringent by states or non-state actors. It is submitted that, nevertheless, it is simply impossible to significantly impair constant sources of pluralistic challenges. This is due to the very nature of the decentralized international community, and this is what the earlier sections of this article tried to illustrate. Despite the fact that the decisions of the SC and the 1267 Committee are binding and override conflicting norms, it faced challenges through diverse channels aimed at holding it to account. Such a pluralistic process of administrative law is not as weak as being left out by the establishment of a review body even if it provides extra authority to the Committee.

This in turn indicates that any kind of review mechanism, however ideal in balancing the major interests concerned, would only bring a

---

[272] See Doc. S/PV. 5474 of 22 June 2006, 5 (statement by Mr. Michel, Legal Council of the UN, presenting the Secretary-General's view); Report of the UNHCHR, see note 18, paras 25-26.

provisional closure in accountability calls:[273] some better ways of realizing fairness and transparency would be soon presented; accountability principles themselves might be challenged; or even new accountability holders could emerge.

V. Conclusion

If the project of "global administrative law" has any overall objectives, some of them may be to constantly scrutinize *who* ought to be accountable, and *how* accountability could be improved if it is currently inadequate. Scrutiny needs to be made not merely over the dichotomy of states and non-state actors, but also over disparities among states and different non-state constituencies. However, the pursuit of accountability holders and the better realization of accountability will most likely be an issue-dependent analysis in large part; accountability holders diverge according to the activities of global administrative bodies, as a result of which there are no uniform answers as to the best construction of accountability mechanisms for them.

In relation to the Al Qaeda/Taliban sanctions regime, the impact is greater, and therefore the normative basis of accountability must be strengthened, with respect to those Member States in which the designated individuals and entities (or their assets) are believed to be located. Among non-state constituencies, the severe impact on human rights renders the development of a normative basis for listed individuals and entities a more pressing issue than other candidates of accountability holders such as financial institutions and immediate local communities.

In the global sphere where the institutionalized settings for accountability are less developed, the voices from these accountability holders by way of leveling criticism against the Committee may not be effective unless they are fully equipped with the power to influence the operational effectiveness of the sanctions regime. The analysis of such power cannot be self-contained within the sole context of the Al Qaeda/Taliban sanctions committee; each actor's power in wider political contexts matters. Nevertheless, as for Member States, the limited observation from the administration of the sanctions regime suggests that, although no doubt the relevant authorities of major "provider" states are powerful accountability holders, the fact that Al Qaeda members are spread over many countries confers upon a wide range of states

---

[273] See Krisch, see note 11, 266-267.

a certain degree of power to hold the SC to account: it places them in the position of becoming potential providers of the List; and it also necessitates their enhanced cooperation, including that of "recipient" states, in order to eliminate loopholes in combating the financing of terrorism. Even if not accompanied by the major providers, therefore, non-institutionalized reputational accountability may work if these states act in consort or in parallel to enhance accountability towards them. This in part explains why the Al Qaeda/Taliban sanctions triggered a greater number of challenges as well as responses aimed at enhancing the fairness and transparency of SC-led targeted sanctions, despite the fact that sanctions against listed individuals and entities existed before Resolution 1267 under the Haiti, Angola and Sierra Leone sanction regimes. Furthermore, the use of national courts helped some individuals and entities on the List to attract parallel, if not in consort, challenges from states and the wider UN membership.

Despite many shortcomings, the challenges and responses made to the administration of the Al Qaeda/Taliban sanctions regime provide evidence that the constant sources of pluralistic challenges in decentralized global society succeeded, to some extent, in shedding light upon the realization of community accountability. Not limited to accountability towards major provider states but also towards other affected states and non-state constituencies, by enhancing the communications with those states and enabling listed individuals to submit delisting requests through the focal point. A range of governmental and non-governmental actors who claim the status of accountability holders, in conjunction with the wider UN membership and other non-state institutions, directly or indirectly participated in the process or cycle of enhancing such community accountability.

As the operations of global administrative bodies increasingly and visibly permeate into the domestic sphere, in conjunction with individuals' greater awareness that they are members of the international community, the former continue to be subject to coordinated or respective challenges by various governmental and non-governmental constituencies. As this paper has tried to illustrate, SC sanctions regimes will not be immune from such constant challenges, ones now built on the framework accountability principles of fairness and transparency.

Appendix

The SC and the Committee's responses to accountability calls

Date	Overall quality of the List and communication with the Committee	Protection of individuals (humanitarian exemptions and delisting)
Feb. 2000	• Introduced the first Guidelines (Press Release SC/6802)	• Approved exemptions on flight ban for the Hajj (Press Release SC/6802)
Dec. 2000	• S/RES/1333 (2000) of 19 December 2000 (para. 15(a)) introduced the Committee of Experts	• S/RES/1333 (para. 12) introduced further humanitarian aid exemptions for flight ban • S/RES/1333 (para. 15(b)) requests the SG to review the humanitarian implications of the measures (Doc. S/2001/241, S/2001/695, S/2001/1215)
Jan. 2001		• Approved the list of humanitarian relief providers (Press Release SC/6994)
Feb. 2001		• Approved procedures to add humanitarian relief providers (Press Release SC/7012)
Mar. 2001		• The SG reported on humanitarian implications (Doc. S/2001/241)
Jul. 2001	• S/RES/1363 (2001) of 30 July 2001 introduced the Monitoring Group	• The SG reported on humanitarian implications (Doc. S/2001/695)
Dec. 2001		• The SG reported on humanitarian implications (Doc. S/2001/1215)
Jan. 2002	• S/RES/1390 (2002) of 28 January 2002 (para. 5(d)) requested the Committee to promulgate guidelines to facilitate the implementation	• S/RES/1390 (para. 5 (d)) requested the Committee to promulgate guidelines to facilitate the implementation

(Continued from the previous page)

Date	Overall quality of the List and communication with the Committee	Protection of individuals (humanitarian exemptions and delisting)
Aug. 2002		• Announced delisting procedures (Press Release AFG/203-SC/7487) • Removed Aden and five other individuals and entities (Press Release SC/7490)
Nov. 2002	• Approved new Guidelines, listing up the basic identifying information to be included, to the extent possible, in the proposed listing (para. 5 (c)) (Press Release SC/7571)	• Approved new Guidelines, adopting delisting procedures (para. 6) (Press Release SC/7571)
Dec. 2002		• S/RES/1452 (2002) of 20 December 2002 developed mechanisms for exemptions for freezing assets
Jan. 2003	• S/RES/1455 (2003) of 17 January 2003 (para. 4) requested the Committee to communicate to states the list at least every three months	
Feb. 2003	• Convened open briefing by the Chairman of the Committee (Doc. S/2004/281, para. 21)	
Apr. 2003	• Revised Guidelines, adding new section on reviewing information (Press Release SC/7731)	
Dec. 2003	• Invited Member States to comment on report of Monitoring Group (Press Release SC/7948)	

(Continued from the previous page)

Date	Overall quality of the List and communication with the Committee	Protection of individuals (humanitarian exemptions and delisting)
Jan. 2004	• S/RES/1526 (2004) of 30 January 2004 (para. 6) introduced the Monitoring Team • S/RES/1526 (para. 11) provided states with discussion opportunities with the Committee (followed by Press Release SC/8208 (October 2004)) • S/RES/1526 (para. 17) required states when submitting new names to include detailed identifying information and background information to the greatest extent possible	• S/RES/1526 (para. 18) "strongly encourages" states to inform, to the extent possible, individuals of the measures, guidelines and exemptions
Jul. 2005	• S/RES/1617 (2005) of 29 July 2005 (para. 2) defined those "associated with" • S/RES/1617 (para. 6) decided that the statement of case "may be used by the Committee in responding to queries from Member States whose nationals, residents or entities have been included"	• S/RES/1617 (para. 2) defined those "associated with" • S/RES/1617 (para. 5) "requests" states to inform, to the extent possible, individuals of the measures, listing/delisting procedures and exemptions
Dec. 2005	• Revised Guidelines, extending the time for considering listing submissions from two business days to five (Press Release SC/8602)	
Apr. 2006	• Introduced the procedures for the removal of deceased individuals (Note Verbale SCA/2/06(8))	

(Continued from the previous page)

Date	Overall quality of the List and communication with the Committee	Protection of individuals (humanitarian exemptions and delisting)
Jul. 2006	• Introduction of a standard "cover sheet" for listing proposals, with more details for identifying information and statements of case • Convened open briefing by the Chairman of the Committee, attended by 50 representatives (Doc. S/200759, para. 12)	
Nov. 2006	• Revised Guidelines, attaching the "cover sheet", and introducing the provision of feedback to the designating state (para. 6(f)), and annual review (para. 6(i))	• Revised Guidelines, introducing the procedure to remind states of residence/citizenship to inform individuals (para. 6(h))
Dec. 2006	• S/RES/1735 (2006) of 22 December 2006 (para. 29) "strongly encourages" Member States to "send representatives to meet the Committee" (c.f., S/RES/1526 (2004) of 30 January 2004, para. 11 and S/RES/1617 (2005) of 29 July 2005 (para. 14))	• S/RES/1730 introduced focal point of delisting • S/RES/1735 (para. 11) calls upon states of location/nationality to notify individuals or entity and including a copy of the "the publicly releasable portion of statement of case, a description of the effects of designation", delisting procedures and exemptions • S/RES/1735 (para. 15) extended the period for consideration of notifications of humanitarian exemptions from 48 hours to 3 working days
Feb. 2007	• Updated Guidelines following S/RES/1730 (2006) of 19 December 2006 and S/RES/1735 (2006) of 22 December 2006	• Updated Guidelines following S/RES/1730 and S/RES/1735

Revitalising the United Nations Human Rights Special Procedures Mechanisms as a Means of Achieving and Maintaining International Peace and Security

*Claire Breen**

> *The task is not to find alternatives to the SC as a source of authority but to make it work better.*[1]

I. Introduction

Numerous provisions of the Charter of the United Nations[2] underline the obligations of Member States of the United Nations (UN) to promote and protect human rights. The Charter also provides for the es-

---

*   The author gratefully acknowledges the financial support of the New Zealand Law Foundation in the conduct of her research in this area.

1   *In Larger Freedom: Towards Development, Security and Human Rights for All*, Report of the Secretary-General, Doc. A/59/2005, para. 126; *A More Secure World: Our Shared Responsibility*, Report of the High-level Panel on Threats, Challenges and Change, Doc. A/59/565, para 198.

2   *Yearbook of the United Nations* 59 (2005), 1601 et seq.

tablishment of UN bodies to assist in this endeavour, the General Assembly and the Economic and Social Council (ECOSOC) being the primary responsible organs in this regard. What is perhaps less clear in this respect is the extent of the role of the Security Council in connection with the promotion and protection of human rights. Although the controversies surrounding recent instances of armed intervention have overshadowed the burgeoning role of the Council in this regard, the Security Council has for almost two decades expressed its concern about massive human rights violations. It has recognised that gross human rights violations may often be the precursor to the (re)emergence of conflict.

The Council's concerns have often arisen as a consequence of receiving information provided to it by ECOSOC in addition to information received from the Office of the UN High Commissioner for Human Rights (OHCHR) by way of briefing from the High Commissioner and/or the mandate holders of the special procedures mechanisms, as established by the former Commission on Human Rights and for which now the Human Rights Council has continued responsibility. The Security Council's relationship with ECOSOC and the Commission on Human Rights has been sporadic despite calls for increased relationship.[3]

This article focuses upon the role of the Commission on Human Rights (and its successor the Human Rights Council), as the body which has been responsible for the elaboration and implementation of UN human rights standards. It asserts that the Security Council can do more to strengthen visibly its role in the promotion and protection of human rights given that the Security Council itself has recognised the link between gross human rights violations and the (re)emergence of conflict. The dialogue that developed between the Security Council and the UN human rights bodies in the early to mid part of this decade is to be commended. Nevertheless, it will be argued that there should be increased encouragement for a greater level of dialogue, whereby such dialogue is informed by way of a clearer and effective use of the special procedures mechanisms which have been elaborated in some detail to meet the Charter's mandate for promotion and protection of human rights. The article concludes with the suggestion that those more informal mechanisms that facilitate the flow of human rights information be-

---

[3]   See C. Breen, "The Necessity of a Role for the ECOSOC in the Maintenance of International Peace and Security", *Journal of Conflict and Security Law* 12 (2007), 261 et seq.

tween the Security Council and UN human rights bodies be formalised in order to complement the increased profile of human rights within Security Council deliberations.

II. The Basis for the Promotion and Protection of Human Rights

From the outset, the UN Charter indicates that the organisation's determination is not only "to save succeeding generations from the scourge of war" but also "to reaffirm faith in fundamental human rights."[4] The Charter establishes the linkages between international peace and security and the advancement of human rights with its commitment, "to ensure ... that armed force shall not be used, save in the common interest" and to promote "the economic and social advancement of all peoples."[5] Article 1 outlines the purposes of the United Nations which include the maintenance of international peace and security[6] as well as the achievement of:

> "international co-operation ... in promoting and encouraging respect for human rights and for fundamental freedoms for all without distinction as to race, sex, language, or religion."[7]

The provisions of Article 1 are elaborated by the mandatory wording of Article 13 regarding the initiation of studies and the making of recommendations by the General Assembly including those for the purpose of, "assisting in the realization of human rights and fundamental freedoms for all without distinction as to race, sex, language, or religion." In spite of articulating the promotion of respect for human rights with a view to creating peaceful and friendly relations among nations,[8] by which states undertake joint and separate action,[9] the Charter does not establish any immediate obligation in this regard. However, Charta Chapter X's provisions relating to the establishment of ECOSOC have resulted in an elaborated framework for setting human rights standards and identifying violations of those standards.

---

[4]   Preamble, UN Charter.
[5]   Ibid.
[6]   Article 1 para. 1.
[7]   Ibid., para. 3.
[8]   Article 55 lit. (c).
[9]   Article 56.

Under the terms of Article 60 of the Charter ECOSOC is the functional body responsible for the discharge of the UN's mandate of human rights promotion and protection. Article 68, *inter alia*, empowers ECOSOC to set up commissions for the promotion of human rights and it is this Charter provision which constituted the legal basis for the establishment of the Commission on Human Rights. During its lifetime, the Commission generated a vast body of international human rights law including a core of primary human rights treaties, a range of Optional Protocols and over one hundred other human rights instruments.

The ratification of a human rights treaty requires a State Party to undertake to respect and to ensure to all individuals within their territory and subject to their jurisdiction the rights recognised in that treaty. Such undertakings are legally binding obligations in international law. A State Party becomes obliged to uphold these rights as soon as the treaty enters into force in that state and to perform its obligations in accordance with the treaties in good faith.[10] That said, the consequences for states which fail to uphold their human rights treaty obligations, are less than severe. Violations are, for the most part, dealt with by the treaty monitoring framework which is consensus driven and operates on a reporting system which triggers nothing more than a series of Recommendations and Conclusions. Such limitations reflect the recognition accorded to state sovereignty within the UN system in general and within the arena of human rights protection in particular, and limitations articulated by the ICJ in *Nicaragua v United States*, when the Court stated that, "the use of force could not be the appropriate method to monitor or ensure such respect."[11] However, the value of such treaties lies in their articulation of social and legal standards to be achieved and maintained. In extreme cases, gross violations may act as a system of early warning that a conflict is about to break out. In post-conflict situations, the articulation of human rights standards may provide the basis for the prosecution of those individuals charged with gross human rights violations constituting international crimes such as war crimes or crimes against humanity.

---

[10]   Article 26 of the Vienna Convention on the Law of Treaties, UNTS Vol. 1155 No. 18232, "[P]acta sunt servanda – Every treaty in force is binding upon the parties to it and must be performed by them in good faith."

[11]   Military and Paramilitary Activities in and against Nicaragua (*Nicaragua v United States of America*), ICJ Reports 1986, 14 et seq., (para. 268).

Since the early 1990s, the Security Council had increasingly to consider violations of human rights as falling within its primary ambit of maintaining international peace and security. This evolving role has required the elaboration of mechanisms for bringing such human rights information more squarely within the Council's consideration. Article 65 of the Charter[12] is one mechanism, by which the Council may receive information from ECOSOC and its organs. Rule 39 of the Security Council's Rules of Procedure has also been employed to allow e.g. the President of ECOSOC to address the Council. In spite of the recognised utility of such measures, both mechanisms have been badly underutilised to date.[13]

Whilst commending the Security Council on its initiatives but being mindful of the reservations attached to such initiatives, there are other more direct means of gathering human rights information on situations which are of concern to the Security Council, namely the special procedures mechanism which covers a wide range of procedures. The mechanism may designate either an individual (who may be accorded one of a number of titles such as "Special Rapporteur", "Special Representative of the Secretary-General", "Representative of the Secretary-General", or "Independent Expert"), or a group of individuals, a Working Group, with the responsibility of operating the special procedure. Currently, there do exist 29 thematic and 9 country mandates (June 2008). The OHCHR provides these mechanisms with personnel, logistical and research assistance to support them in the discharge of their mandates. Although their titles vary, each is considered as an "expert on mission" within the meaning of the Convention on the Privileges and Immunities of the United Nations. Mandate-holders of the special procedures serve in their personal capacity and as independent experts. Such independence is crucial to the requirement that mandate-holders act impartially.[14]

The mandates of the special procedures are established and defined by the respective resolutions passed by the Human Rights Council in continuation of the function previously carried out by the Commission on Human Rights. Country specific mandates are reviewed annually by

---

[12] Article 65 states, "[t]he Economic and Social Council may furnish information to the Security Council and shall assist the Security Council upon its request."

[13] See generally, Breen, see note 3, 272-273.

[14] OHCHR, Fact Sheet 27, available at: <http://www2.ohchr.org/english/about/publications/docs/factsheet27.pdf>.

the Council and thematic mandates are reviewed every two to three years. For the mandate to be continued, the Human Rights Council must adopt a resolution specifically renewing the mandate and identifying its scope.[15] In April 2000, the Commission on Human Rights decided that experts should serve a maximum term of 6 years. It also decided that there should be a turnover in the experts on working groups as well.[16] Since June 2006, the Human Rights Council engaged in an institution building process, which included a review of the special procedures system. The Human Rights Council adopted Resolution 5/1 entitled "Institution-building of the United Nations Human Rights Council," which included provisions on the selection of mandate holders and the review of all special procedures mandates. All mandates were extended (except the mandates on Belarus and Cuba) until they are next considered by the Human Rights Council and the review is undertaken.

Around one third of the experts also report to the General Assembly and as will be seen, some have briefed the Security Council on both an informal and formal basis. According to the draft *Manual of the United Nations Human Rights Special Procedures*, special procedures mandate-holders are required to:

- **analyse** the relevant thematic issue or country situation on behalf of the international community;
- **advise** on the measures which should be taken by the government(s) concerned and other relevant actors;
- **alert** United Nations organs and agencies and the international community in general to the need to address specific situations and issues. In this regard they have a role in providing "early warning" and encouraging preventive measures;
- **advocate** on behalf of the victims of violations through measures such as requesting urgent action by relevant states and calling upon governments to respond to specific allegations of human rights violations and provide redress;

---

[15]   OHCHR, *Enhancing and Strengthening the Effectiveness of the Special Procedures of the Commission on Human Rights. An open-ended Seminar in Consultation with the Expanded Bureau of the Commission, as Part of the Effort to Enhance and Strengthen the Effectiveness of the Special Procedures Reference*, CHR Decision 2005/113 Background Paper.
[16]   Doc. E/CN.4/1999/104.

- **activate** and mobilise the international and national communities to address particular human rights issues and to encourage cooperation among governments, civil society and inter-governmental organisations.[17]

However, the obligations upon the mandate-holders do not stop once these requirements have been met. Follow-up work is regarded as being a crucial element in ensuring that appropriate measures are taken in response to the work of the special procedures.[18] The precise approach adopted may vary from one mandate to another,[19] but it will include the adoption of a full range of "measures taken to encourage, facilitate and monitor the implementation of recommendations by any of the Special Procedures."[20] Interactive dialogue between mandate-holders and various UN organs, such as the Human Rights Council and the General Assembly, constitutes one of the most important forms of follow-up.[21] Generally, the mandate-holder provides some response to, or evaluation of, the exchange.[22]

Given that one of the key functions of the special procedures system is to act as an early warning mechanism in relation to situations involving serious violations of human rights, it may be appropriate for the mandate-holders, to call the attention of the Security Council to the need for urgent action such as the convening of a special session. Possible engagement of the Security Council could also be envisaged where such situations amount to a threat to or breach of the peace.[23] The sig-

---

[17] Draft Manual of the United Nations Human Rights Special Procedures, June 2006, para. 5.

[18] Draft Manual, see note 17, para. 88.

[19] Examples of well-developed follow-up arrangements can be found, for example, in the work of the Working Group on Enforced or Involuntary Disappearances, the Special Rapporteur on Torture and other Cruel, Inhuman or Degrading Treatment or Punishment; and the Special Rapporteur on Extrajudicial, Summary or Arbitrary Executions, see Draft Manual, see note 17.

[20] Report of the 12th Annual Mtg of Special Procedures mandate-holders, Doc. E/CN.4/2006/4, para. 85.

[21] Draft Manual, see note 17, para. 89.

[22] Ibid., para. 90-91.

[23] See Doc. E/CN.4/SUB.2/DEC/2000/9. See also, Report of the United Nations High Commissioner for Human Rights and Follow-Up to the World Conference on Human Rights – Effective Functioning of Human Rights

nificance to be attached to the early warning function of the special
procedures has been highlighted by the OHCHR, which stated:

> "Given that one of the key functions of the special procedures sys-
> tem is to act as an early warning mechanism in relation to situations
> involving serious violations of human rights, it may be appropriate
> for the mandate-holders, acting through the Coordination Commit-
> tee, to call the attention to the Commission/Council to the need for
> urgent action such as the convening of a special session. *Possible en-
> gagement with the Security Council could also be envisaged where
> such situations amount to a threat to or breach of the peace*" (empha-
> sis added).[24]

A report from the UN High Commissioner for Human Rights
transmitted to the members of the Commission on Human Rights provided one example of the recognised need to move towards more effective functioning of human rights protection within the United Nations.
In the context of UN reform that was taking place, the report noted the
identification of a number of steps designed to ensure that the special
procedures system would be able to carry out effectively its role at the
core of the United Nations human rights programme.[25] In particular, it
was stated:

> "The special procedures system has a responsibility to act as an early
> warning mechanism in relation to situations involving serious viola-
> tions of human rights. ... More effective use should also be made in
> this regard of the possibility of engaging with the Security Council,
> whether on the basis of the Arias [sic.] formula or some other ba-
> sis."[26]

The United Nations has provided for the establishment of a series of
effective mechanisms for the reporting of gross human rights abuses,
particularly those that have the potential to descend into conflict. Increased and more effective usage of such mechanisms can only be to the
advantage of the Security Council and the mechanisms themselves.

Mechanisms, Note by the United Nations High Commissioner for Human
Rights, Doc. E/CN.4/2006/4, paras 65-76.

[24]   OHCHR (2005), *Enhancing and Strengthening the Effectiveness of the
       Special Procedures of the Commission on Human Rights, An open-ended
       Seminar in Consultation with the Expanded Bureau of the Commission, as
       Part of the Effort to Enhance and Strengthen the Effectiveness of the Special
       Procedures*, Background Paper, 9.

[25]   Doc. E/CN.4/2006/4, see note 23.

[26]   Ibid., para. 76.

III. Establishing a Dialogue between the Security Council and Special Procedures Mandate Holders: Some Significant Occurrences

Article 65 and the already mentioned Rule 39 of the Security Council's Rules of Procedure allow the Security Council to invite members of the Secretariat or other persons, whom it considers competent for the purpose, to supply it with information or to give other assistance in examining matters within its competence.[27] The Council has utilised this rule to invite ECOSOC representatives, the High Commissioner for Human Rights to address the Security Council,[28] and other individuals that it regarded as competent to assist the Security Council. Since the early part of this decade, the Security Council has increased its previously almost non-existent dialogue with ECOSOC, primarily by way of Rule 39 rather than by way of Article 65.[29]

It was not until the early 1990s that a pattern of communication between the Security Council and the OHCHR became discernible.[30] Although the Security Council continued its long-established patterns of not utilising Article 65, the flow of information between the two bodies became more perceptible. In 1992 then, two conflicts changed the scene as the Security Council received information about the situation between Iraq and Kuwait and the situation in the former Yugoslavia from the special procedures' mandate holders of the Commission on Human Rights, about grave human rights abuses and violations of international humanitarian law.

With regard to the situation between Iraq and Kuwait, the Security Council had "condemn[ed] the Repression of the Iraqi civilian population in many parts of Iraq, including most recently in Kurdish-populated areas, the consequences of which threaten[ed] international peace and security in the region."[31] The Council also demanded that Iraq, "as a contribution to removing the threat to international peace

---

27   Provisional Rules of Procedure of the Security Council, Doc. S/96/Rev. 7.
28   Doc. S/PV/4312.
29   Breen, see note 3.
30   Repertoire of the Practice of the Security Council Supplement 1989-1992, Chapter VI, Relations with other United Nations Organs, Part II, Relations with the Economic and Social Council, A. Practice in Relation to Article 65 of the Charter, 206, available at: <http://www.un.org/Depts/dpa/repertoire/index.html>.
31   S/RES/688 (1991) of 5 April 1991, op. para. 1.

and security in the region, immediately end this repression", and expressed the hope that an open dialogue would take place to ensure that the human and political rights of all Iraqi citizens were respected.[32]

When the Security Council reviewed this matter in March 1992, several Council members[33] referred to the findings contained in the report on the human rights situation in Iraq dated 18 February 1992 prepared by Mr. Max van der Stoel, Special Rapporteur of the Commission on Human Rights on the Situation of Human Rights in Iraq.[34] Of particular significance was para. 159 of the report, in which the Special Rapporteur, in referring to resolution S/RES/688 (1991), stated that, inasmuch as the repression continued, he could only conclude that the threat to international peace and security in the region mentioned in that resolution remained.[35] At the same meeting, the President of the Security Council made a statement, on behalf of the Council, concerning the status of Iraq's compliance with the various obligations imposed upon it by resolutions concerning the situation between Iraq and Kuwait.[36] With respect to the implementation of Resolution 688 (1991), the President made specific reference to the work of the Commission on Human Rights and the Special Rapporteur with his statement that:

"33. The Council remains deeply concerned at the grave human rights abuses that, despite the provisions of resolution 688 (1991), the Government of Iraq continues to perpetrate against its population, in particular in the northern region of Iraq, in southern Shi'a centres and in the southern marshes (Commission on Human Rights resolution 1992/71 of 5 March 1992). The Council notes that this situation is confirmed by the report of the Special Rapporteur of the Commission on Human Rights ...

34. The members of the Council are particularly concerned at the reported restrictions on the supplies of essential commodities, in particular food and fuel, which have been imposed by the Govern-

---

[32]   Ibid., op. para. 2.

[33]   Doc. S/PV/3059, 22 (Austria), 30 (United Kingdom), 45-46 (United States), (51-52) Russian Federation, 67 (Belgium), in Repertoire of the Practice of the Security Council Supplement 1989-1992, see note 30.

[34]   Doc. S/23685/Add.1. The report had been prepared in accordance with Resolution 1992/71 of the Commission on Human Rights and approved by ECOSOC Decision 1992/241.

[35]   Repertoire of the Practice of the Security Council Supplement 1989-1992, Chapter VI, see note 30, 207.

[36]   Doc. S/23699.

ment of Iraq on the three northern governates of Dohuk, Erbil and Sulaymaniyya. In this regard, as the Special Rapporteur has noted in his report, inasmuch as the repression of the population continues, the threat to international peace and security in the region mentioned in resolution 688 (1991) remains."[37]

By separate letters dated 7 August 1992 addressed to the President of the Security Council, the representatives of Belgium, France, the United Kingdom and the United States,[38] requested the convening of a special session of the Council to consider the repression of the civilian population in parts of Iraq. They stated that their governments were of the view that the work of the Council would be greatly assisted by the participation of Mr. Max van der Stoel under Rule 39 of the Provisional Rules of Procedure of the Council, and therefore requested that the Council extend an invitation to him under Rule 39. One of the representatives noted that Mr. van der Stoel's interim report on the human rights situation in Iraq had been distributed as a document of the Security Council.[39] At an urgent follow-up meeting held on 11 August 1992,[40] the Council had before it the interim report on the human rights situation in Iraq prepared by the Special Rapporteur.[41] Several Council members expressed reservations about the appropriateness of the Security Council inviting the Special Rapporteur, on the ground that questions of human rights ought to be dealt with by the Commission on Human Rights, the body which had appointed him.[42] The President of the Security Council drew attention to this request and highlighted the fact that the invitation was extended to the Special Rapporteur acting in his personal capacity only. Nevertheless, several other Council members[43] expressed reservations about the appropriateness of the Security

[37]   See, Repertoire of the Practice of the Security Council Supplement 1989-1992, Chapter VI, see note 30, 207.

[38]   Docs S/24393, S/24394, S/24395 and S/24396, respectively, in Repertoire of the Practice of the Security Council Supplement 1989-1992, Chapter III, Participation in the Proceedings of the Security Council, B. Invitations Extended under Rule 39 (members of the Secretariat or other persons), 56-57, available at: <http://www.un.org/Depts/dpa/repertoire/index.html>.

[39]   Ibid.

[40]   Doc. S/PV/3105.

[41]   Doc. S/24386.

[42]   Repertoire of the Practice of the Security Council Supplement 1989-1992, Chapter III, see note 38, 57.

[43]   Doc. S/PV/3105, 6-7 (India), 7-10 (Ecuador), 11-12 (Zimbabwe) and 12 (China), in: Repertoire, see above, 57.

Council extending an invitation to Mr. van der Stoel, on the ground that
matters relating to human rights did not fall within the competence of
the Security Council. They believed that such matters should be discussed by the Commission on Human Rights and the General Assembly. They pointed out that Mr. van der Stoel had been appointed as Special Rapporteur on the human rights situation in Iraq and that his appointment had been made by the Commission on Human Rights, a
subsidiary body of ECOSOC. As the Security Council did not have
competence in the matter, it would not be possible for it either to examine his report or to take a stand on it.[44] Equally, however, these same
representatives also noted that Mr. van der Stoel had been invited
strictly in his personal capacity and not in any representative capacity.[45]
After the decision had been made to note such observations, the Council then decided to extend an invitation to Mr. van der Stoel to participate in the meeting under Rule 39.[46] Mr. van der Stoel, acting in his personal capacity once again, made a statement in which he reported on the
government of Iraq's continued policy of repression against the Kurd-
ish population in the north and the Shiites in the southern marshes, in
violation of Resolution 688 (1991).[47]

The Council renewed its consideration of this item in November
1992.[48] The Special Rapporteur participated in that meeting also. Similarly to his August statement, the Security Council President, on behalf
of the Council, expressed his concern regarding the status of Iraq's
compliance with the various obligations placed upon it by the Council.
In relation to Resolution 688 (1991), the statement referred to a resolution of the Commission on Human Rights, the Special Rapporteur's reports and the public meeting held with Mr. van der Stoel:

"30. The Security Council remains deeply concerned at the grave
human rights abuses ... The Security Council notes that this situation is confirmed by the reports of the Special Rapporteur of the
Commission on Human Rights (E/CN.4/1992/ 31, also circulated as
document S/23685 and Add.1, and part I of the interim report circu-

---

[44]   Ibid., 57.
[45]   Ibid.
[46]   Ibid. For a similar discussion see Doc. S/PV/3139 in Repertoire of the
       Practice of the Security Council Supplement 1989-1992, Chapter III, see
       note 38, 57.
[47]   See Repertoire of the Practice of the Security Council Supplement 1989-
       1992, Chapter VI, see note 30, 207.
[48]   Doc. S/PV/3139.

lated as document S/24386). The members of the Council recall their public meeting with Mr. Max van der Stoel on 11 August 1992."[49]

The Security Council met with a second Special Rapporteur that year also. In August 1992, the Security Council adopted S/RES/771 (1992) of 13 August 1992 arising from continuing reports of widespread violations of international humanitarian law occurring within the territory of the former Yugoslavia and, particularly in Bosnia and Herzegovina. The Security Council called upon states and appropriate, international humanitarian organisations to collect substantiated information on violations of humanitarian law, including grave breaches of the Geneva Conventions, being committed in the territory of the former Yugoslavia, and to make that information available to the Council.[50] Also in August 1992, the Commission on Human Rights held a special session in which it adopted Resolution 1992/S-1/1 regarding the human rights situation in the territory of the former Yugoslavia. The Resolution noted the Security Council President's statement. The Commission appointed a Special Rapporteur, to investigate first-hand the human rights situation in the territory of the former Yugoslavia and, in particular, within Bosnia and Herzegovina. The Commission requested the Special Rapporteur to report his findings and recommendations to the Commission on Human Rights and the General Assembly. It also requested the Secretary-General to make the reports of the Special Rapporteur available to the Security Council.[51]

The Security Council met in October 1992 having before it the first report of the Special Rapporteur on the human rights situation in the former Yugoslavia.[52] The Special Rapporteur recommended the prosecution of those individuals responsible for serious human rights violations and breaches of international humanitarian law. He further re-

---

[49]   Doc. S/24836.
[50]   Doc. S/4378. The presidential statement concerned reports of the imprisonment and abuse of civilians in camps, prisons and detention centers within the territory of the former Yugoslavia, and especially in Bosnia and Herzegovina, and called upon "all parties, States, international organizations and non-governmental organizations" to make available to the Council any further information they might possess, see Repertoire of the Practice of the Security Council Supplement 1989-1992, Chapter VI, see note 30, 207-208.
[51]   Ibid., 208.
[52]   Doc. S/PV/3119, Doc. S/PV/24516.

commended that a commission should be created to assess and further investigate specific cases in which prosecution might be warranted.[53] In an ensuing resolution, the Security Council requested states, relevant United Nations bodies, and relevant organisations to make available, "information ... relating to the violations of humanitarian law, including grave breaches of the Geneva Conventions ... being committed in the territory of the former Yugoslavia."[54] The Council requested the Secretary-General to establish a Commission of Experts and requested the above mentioned entities to provide appropriate assistance to this Commission in its examination and analysis of the information submitted pursuant to S/RES/771 (1992) of 13 August 1992 and 780 (1992) of 6 October 1992. Several Council members stated their understanding that the Council's request to "relevant United Nations bodies" included the Special Rapporteur of the Commission on Human Rights, and that the Special Rapporteur's report should be taken into account by the impartial Commission of Experts.[55]

In November 1992, on the basis of proposals by France and Belgium, the Security Council invited the Special Rapporteur to participate in its meeting under Rule 39 of its provisional rules of procedure. Again reservations were expressed by China and Zimbabwe that since the Special Rapporteur had been appointed by the Commission on Human Rights, he should report to that body only.[56] The President of the Security Council noted the observations, and stated that they would be reflected in the Verbatim Records of the Council. The Council then extended an invitation to the Special Rapporteur under Rule 39, without the President mentioning that he was invited in his personal capacity.[57]

The Council had before it two reports which had been prepared by the Special Rapporteur on the human rights situation in the territory of the former Yugoslavia.[58] In the preamble of S/RES/787 (1992) of 16 November 1992 the Security Council:

---

[53]   Doc. S/24516, ibid., paras 69 and 70.

[54]   S/RES/780 (1992) of 6 October 1992.

[55]   See Doc. S/PV/3119, 8 (Venezuela), 12 (United States), 13 (Hungary), 16-17 (France), in Repertoire of the Practice of the Security Council Supplement 1989-1992, Chapter VI, see note 30, 208.

[56]   Doc. S/PV/3134, 9-11, see Repertoire of the Practice of the Security Council, Supplement 1989-1992, Chapter III, see note 38, 57.

[57]   Ibid.

[58]   Docs S/24516 and S/24766.

"not[ed] with grave concern the report of the Special Rapporteur ... which ma[de] clear that massive and systematic violations of human rights and grave violations of international humanitarian law continue[d] in the Republic of Bosnia and Herzegovina."

In paras 7 and 8 of the resolution the Council, *inter alia*, condemned all violations of international law, including in particular the practice of "ethnic cleansing" and the deliberate impeding of the delivery of food and medical supplies to the civilian population of Bosnia and Herzegovina. The Council reaffirmed that the perpetrators of such acts would be held individually responsible. It welcomed the establishment of a Commission of Experts, and asked the Commission on Human Rights to pursue actively investigations with regard to grave breaches of the Geneva Conventions and other violations of international humanitarian law committed in the territory of the former Yugoslavia.[59]

The situation did not change much in 1993. The Security Council once again received information from ECOSOC, through the Commission on Human Rights, about grave human rights abuses and violations of international humanitarian law about the situation between Iraq and Kuwait; the situation in the former Yugoslavia; and now the one concerning Rwanda. The Security Council also received information in relation to the situation in Burundi from a Commission of Inquiry established at its request by the Secretary-General. The Commission's report included information provided by the Special Rapporteur on the situation in Burundi.[60]

With regard to the situation between Iraq and Kuwait, the Commission on Human Rights requested the Special Rapporteur to submit an interim report to the General Assembly and to the Commission itself.[61] In his interim report the Special Rapporteur concluded, *inter alia*, that a number of acts of the government of Iraq constituted a policy of repression in violation of para. 2 of S/RES/688 (1991).[62] He also concluded

---

[59]   Repertoire of the Practice of the Security Council Supplement 1989-1992, Chapter VI, see note 30, 208-209.

[60]   Repertoire of the Practice of the Security Council Supplement 1993-1995, Chapter VI, Relations with other United Nations Organs, Part II, Relations with the Economic and Social Council, A. Practice in Relation to Article 65 of the Charter, 30 available at: <http://www.un.org/Depts/dpa/repertoire/index.html>.

[61]   CHR Resolution 1993/7, CHR Resolution 1994/74, CHR Resolution 1995/76.

[62]   Doc. A/48/600, paras 61 and 81.

that the continuing difficulties in facilitating the humanitarian work of international organisations in the country constituted a violation of para. 3 of the same resolution. The attention of the President of the Security Council was drawn to these conclusions regarding Resolution 688 with the request that the interim report be circulated as a document of the Security Council.[63]

In relation to the situation in the former Yugoslavia, the Commission on Human Rights requested the Special Rapporteur to continue to submit periodic reports, as appropriate, to the Commission and the General Assembly. The Commission requested the Secretary-General to continue to make the reports of the Special Rapporteur available also to the Security Council,[64] which happened as such.[65] The Security Council subsequently adopted S/RES/1034 (1995) of 21 December 1995 on the situation in Bosnia and Herzegovina. The resolution affirmed that the violations of humanitarian law and human rights in the areas of Srebrenica, Zepa, Banja Luka and Sanski Most from July to October 1995 had to be fully and properly investigated by "the relevant United Nations and other international organizations and institutions."[66] It demanded that the Bosnian Serb party give immediate and unrestricted access to the areas in question, including for the purpose of the investigation of the atrocities, to representatives of "the relevant United Nations and other international organizations and institutions, *including the Special Rapporteur of the Commission on Human Rights*" (emphasis added).[67]

In 1994 the situation concerning Rwanda was the basis for intense inter-Council dialogue. The United Nations Commission on Human Rights had by resolution S-3/1 of 25 May 1994 adopted a Special Rapporteur for Rwanda. It also had requested the Secretary-General to make the report of the Special Rapporteur available to ECOSOC, the General Assembly and the Security Council.[68] Subsequently, the Security Council unanimously adopted S/RES/925 (1994) of 8 June 1994 on

---

63   Repertoire of the Practice of the Security Council Supplement 1993-1995, Chapter VI, see note 60, 31.

64   CHR Resolution 1993/7, 1994/72, 1995/89.

65   Docs S/26469, S/26383, S/26415, S/26765, S/1994/265, S/1994/743, S/1994/967, S/1994/1252, S/1995/79, S/1995/80, S/1995/597, S/1995/801, S/1995/93.

66   S/RES/1034 (1995) of 21 December 1995.

67   Ibid., op. para. 8.

68   CHR Resolution S-3/1.

the situation concerning Rwanda. In the preamble, the Council noted the appointment of the Special Rapporteur for Rwanda and in the operative part under para. 10, the Council, *inter alia*, requested the Secretary-General to ensure that the United Nations Assistance Mission for Rwanda (UNAMIR) extended close cooperation with the Special Rapporteur. During the discussion, the representative of China expressed reservations on "the resolution's elements relating to the human rights rapporteur."[69] Recalling that the United Nations Charter contained explicit provisions on the mandates of the Security Council, the General Assembly and other United Nations organs, he stressed that the Council should "refrain from involvement in activities that [went] beyond its mandate".[70] He added that his delegation was "not in favour of wilfully linking the work of the Council with that of other organs."[71] Conversely, the representative of New Zealand welcomed:

> "the recognition given in [the] resolution to the importance of close cooperation between UNAMIR and the activities of the … recently appointed United Nations Special Rapporteur for Rwanda."[72]

The representative of the Czech Republic spoke of, "going … beyond the horizon of today's draft resolution", suggesting that in future the Council might wish to request the Special Rapporteur to report to it directly.[73] Also other Council members stressed the need for close cooperation between the Special Rapporteur and the Commission of Experts.[74]

In 1995 Burundi was the country being especially focused. The Security Council adopted S/RES/1012 (1995) on 28 August 1995. By this resolution, the Council requested the Secretary-General to establish an international Commission of Inquiry and it called upon states and relevant United Nations bodies and appropriate international humanitarian organisations to collate substantiated information in their possession and to make such information available as soon as possible and to provide appropriate assistance to the Commission of Inquiry. The Com-

---

69 Doc. S/PV/3388, 12. See Repertoire of the Practice of the Security Council Supplement 1993-1995, Chapter VI, see note 60, 33.

70 Ibid.

71 Ibid.

72 Ibid., 9-11.

73 Ibid., 3-4 (Czech Republic).

74 Doc. S/PV/3400, 3-4 (United States), 7 (China), 5 (France). See Repertoire of the Practice of the Security Council Supplement 1993-1995, Chapter VI, see note 60, 34.

mission of Inquiry's final report noted that the Commission had, in the course of its work, met with the Special Rapporteur of the United Nations Commission on Human Rights for Burundi.[75]

This initial period of formal dialogue between the Special Rapporteurs and the Security Council was brief and seems to have ended in the mid-1990s but with a further brief re-emergence in the first three years of this century, which coincided with a brief period during which the High Commissioner for Human Rights addressed the Council on a number of occasions. The apparent decrease in direct and formal dialogue between the OHCHR and the Security Council also came at a time of the increased use of Arria Formula meetings (see below).

In April 2001, the High Commissioner for Human Rights, addressed the Security Council at its meeting on the protection of civilians in armed conflict.[76] The High Commissioner noted that in recent years, the Security Council had broken new ground in its efforts to implement the Charter's blueprint for the maintenance of international peace and security. She applauded the fact that the Council's security concepts, strategies and methods had taken on a distinctly more people-oriented focus grounded in the norms of international law, human rights and humanitarian law.[77] In terms of the protection of civilians in armed conflict, the High Commissioner stated that international human rights law insisted on standards of protection that were to be applicable in all places, times and circumstances. There was a rich jurisprudence and practice in the human rights area that, she believed, should be an essential point of departure for the Council in judging the acceptability or unacceptability of behaviour of combatants, states and non-state actors during conflicts, internal or international. As far as human rights mechanisms were concerned, she welcomed the fact that the Security Council was increasingly looking to and drawing on the expertise of the special mechanisms of the Commission on Human Rights. In that respect she observed that:

---

[75] Doc. S/1996/682, para. 35. See generally Repertoire of the Practice of the Security Council Supplement 1993-1995, Chapter VI, see note 60.

[76] Doc. S/PV/4312, 4. In 2002, the Under-Secretary-General for Humanitarian Affairs and Emergency Relief Coordinator had addressed the Security Council on the Protection of Civilians in Armed Conflict, Docs S/PV/4660 and S/PV/4660 (Resumption 1).

[77] Doc. S/PV/4312, 4.

"I consider the reports of country rapporteurs and thematic rapporteurs to be an indispensable information base for the efforts of this Council and of other United Nations bodies to strengthen conflict prevention in the United Nations. I believe that it is of the utmost importance that this Council be provided regularly with briefings on the information available in the reports of these mechanisms of the Commission. I also draw the Council's attention to the role of the human rights treaty bodies and their increasing capacity to take urgent action."[78]

In response to a number of comments and questions posed by Security Council members to the High Commissioner on her views on improving the protection afforded to civilians in armed conflict, the High Commissioner suggested that any high level mediation should draw on the work of country or thematic Rapporteurs, the present work of the OHCHR or components of peacekeeping. As part of the human rights community she greatly welcomed the fact that the Security Council had e.g. been hearing, in particular, the Special Rapporteur for the Democratic Republic of the Congo and she urged the wider use made of the experts, Special Rapporteurs and Special Representatives. With regard to the situation in the DRC, she strongly emphasised the resource of work of her Office on the ground and she referred to the work that could take place in situations of quite serious conflicts, especially the linkages and support for human rights NGOs and their very close working relationship with MONUC (United Nations Organization Mission in the Democratic Republic of the Congo). The High Commissioner expressed her hope that, in the opportunities that were opening up, the work of the High Commissioner's Office could be reinforced and that it could be more known to and drawn upon by the Security Council in its assessment of the situation and in the role of enhanced peacekeeping. She also stated that she believed that, in relation to other conflict situations particularly in Africa, the OHCHR's missions were an important resource for the Security Council and for the human rights community.[79] In terms of the role of the Security Council she stated:

"I have to say in conclusion that it is very instructive from my point of view to see how practical the contributions have been from the members of the Security Council. I am very encouraged by this and

---

[78] Ibid., 5.
[79] Ibid., 20.

it confirms that making a closer link with Geneva and the human rights machinery makes every sense in this context."[80]

In response to the High Commissioner's presentation and subsequent comments, it was discussed at the Council that all peacekeeping operations should contain a human rights component, funded from assessed contributions and further the possibility for reports to the Council by the High Commissioner following important fact-finding missions to areas of major conflict. Finally Arria Formula meetings of Council members had to be used more regularly.[81]

In July 2001 the situation in the DRC again led to discussions between the Security Council and Human Rights organs. In relation to the question of the defence of human rights, the representative of the DRC, stated that it would be useful for the Security Council to look at the Special Rapporteur's reports in order to put an end to impunity. He also expressed the hope that the Special Rapporteur would be able to provide the Security Council with useful information as to the implementation of the different national programs, particularly those concerning the demobilisation and the reintegration of child soldiers and those relating to the protection of vulnerable persons.[82]

The DRC was addressed again in February 2003, when the UN High Commissioner for Human Rights approached the Security Council on the situation.[83] The High Commissioner provided an overview of extensive and gross human rights abuses that had occurred there.[84] In response to a further series of questions and comments about the situation on the ground, the High Commissioner noted that various members of the Security Council themselves had stated that peace was a precondition and that human rights-related provisions in the respective peace agreement had to be implemented.[85] In July 2003, the Security Council was addressed on the situation, under Rule 39.[86] It was stated that the concept and content of security was evolving and that human

---

[80] Ibid., 20.
[81] Ibid. Further support for a closer relationship between the OHCHR and the Security Council was expressed at page 10 (Ukraine), 12 (Tunisia), 17 (China), 18 (United States), 21 (Russia), 26 (Mali).
[82] Ibid., 28. The DRC reiterated this point in Doc. S/PV/4361, 7.
[83] Doc. S/PV/4705.
[84] Ibid., 4-7, 7.
[85] Ibid., 22-24.
[86] Doc. S/PV/4784. The Council was also briefed by Mr. Jean-Marie Guéhenno, Under-Secretary-General.

security was defined by the international human rights norms, which gave it content.[87] According to the Deputy High Commissioner making the presentation, the frequency of his briefings to the Security Council was in itself a clear indication of the very serious and continuous nature of human rights violations occurring in the DRC and reflected the Council's recognition of that.[88] In strongly welcoming the second public meeting of the Council with the OHCHR on the DRC, the representative of Germany stated such meetings also reminded the Council of the fact that military action alone, as important as it might be in a given situation, would not achieve a lasting solution to a conflict and that the Council needed, "a comprehensive approach to security and human rights, and human rights are a central element of that approach."[89] In response to the questions and comments relating to joint missions of Special Rapporteurs, that had been put forward by the French representative, it was stated that sometimes, in situations of this nature, it had been found useful to put together a set of Thematic Rapporteurs. Conceptually, the role of such a joint mission was that it brought added authority and insights.[90]

In May 2004, during a Security Council discussion of complex crises and conflict prevention, it was stated that early warning must be accompanied by an early response. Although it was recognised that many early-warning systems existed within the United Nations, they required co-ordination so that the information at their disposal could contribute effectively and immediately to the decision-making process. In the prevention of a crisis or its recurrence, it was stated that the Security Council ought not to be the only body involved and that this task had to be shared by the system's agencies and organisations. This issue raised the crucial issue of the organisation's requisite institutional architecture. It was stated that the Council had to determine whether it was suitable, in particular in the post-conflict transitional phase, for moving states towards stabilisation, rehabilitation and reconstruction. Increased interaction between the Security Council and other UN bodies including the UN High Commissioner for Human Rights had become ever more necessary to provide a consistent and integrated response to the

---

[87]   Ibid., 5.

[88]   Ibid., 7-8.

[89]   Ibid., 14.

[90]   Ibid., 24. He also recommended that the Special Rapporteur on Violence against Women its Causes and Consequences should look into this situation, ibid., 26.

challenges inherent in complex crises.[91] Calls for closer co-ordination between the Security Council and the OHCHR were not only necessary for the general mainstreaming of human rights within the UN system but, during Council meetings in 2004, members identified more particularly the necessity of a closer relationship in order to set up an early-warning network that would make it possible to prevent conflict.[92] According to one permanent member, the Council's taking effective action in terms of protection also depended on what tools and what information were available to it. The practice of providing biannual briefings could be supplemented by more specific briefings which could deal with especially worrisome situations, being given without prejudice to other measures such as the Council hearing the UN High Commissioner for Human Rights.[93]

This theme re-emerged during the course of 2005. It was stated that regular briefings by the OHCHR and by holders of mandates under the special procedures established by the Commission on Human Rights could greatly contribute to the capacity of the Council both to prevent effectively abuses of civilian populations and to monitor the implementation of the relevant provisions of resolutions that it had adopted.[94] The representative of e.g. Argentina reaffirmed his country's support for the Security Council's cooperation with the OHCHR in promoting unfailing respect for human rights that were seen as inalienable, in a context in which, unfortunately, the Council continued to hear accusations of steady movement in the opposite direction.[95] During further Council discussion on the protection of civilians in armed conflict it was stated that an integrated approach to the protection of civilians in armed conflict had to be implemented in close conjunction with the mainstreaming of human rights protection into the whole UN system. It was also noted that the protection and promotion of human rights was one of the three core functions of the United Nations.[96] Similar observations were made in 2006 when it was stated that, "[S]ystematic reporting to the Security Council is important to facilitate and strengthen decision-making and effective response", in relation to

---

[91] Doc. S/PV/4980, 7 (Spain).
[92] Doc. S/PV/5100, 10 (Chile).
[93] Doc. S/PV/5100, 12-13 (France).
[94] Doc. S/PV/5100 (Resumption 1), 18 (Liechtenstein).
[95] Ibid., 19.
[96] Doc. S/PV/5209, 31 (Norway).

the protection of civilians.[97] It was further observed by Council members and the President that timely briefings from other UN actors including the UN High Commissioner for Human Rights, have been regarded as being extremely helpful in drawing the attention of the international community to areas where conflicts are prone to erupt.[98]

In 2007 in respect to discussions of civilians in armed conflict, the President, in a Council discussion on peace and security in Africa, stated that the Council was gradually including the underlying causes of conflicts in its field of research for better ways to address issues related to peace and security. Part of this process was the strengthening of the role of the Security Council and part of that strengthening process was related to other UN institutions such as the General Assembly, ECOSOC, the Peacebuilding Commission, and the Human Rights Council which, he said, could do more to join forces with the Security Council in an appropriate forum to show a spirit of coherence, which the United Nations needed in the area of conflict prevention.[99] Also in 2007, the President referred to S/RES/1674 (2006) of 28 April 2006 and stated that it was crucial to recall and to stress states' responsibility to end impunity and to bring to justice the perpetrators of genocide, crimes against humanity, war crimes and other flagrant violations of international humanitarian law.

However, actual and direct input would appear to be decreasing so that, for example, it would seem that from the period from August 2006 to July 2007, the Security Council heard only one briefing by the UN High Commissioner for Human Rights, which related to her visit to the Great Lakes region.[100]

The issues, concerns and recommendations expressed between the Security Council, the UN High Commissioner and the Special Rapporteurs are all very real and pragmatic. Earlier concerns regarding the allocation of responsibilities as between different UN bodies seem to have evaporated, yet, as this section has demonstrated, formal dialogue between the Security Council and the OHCHR as well as Special Rapporteurs seems to be the exception not the norm. By this concrete and real means of a more effective human rights infused mandate to main-

---

[97] Doc. S/PV/5577, 16 (Greece). Similarly Doc. S/PV/5577 (Resumption 1), 11 (Finland, speaking on behalf of the EU).

[98] Doc. S/PV/5703, 31 (Germany). See also 26 (Japan). See, also the comments of the President in Doc. S/PV/5319 (Resumption 1).

[99] Doc. S/PV/5735, 24.

[100] Doc. A/62/2, 13.

tain international peace and security slips. The Security Council has been denying itself access to an extremely valuable source of in-depth first hand knowledge of human rights violations that have the potential to descend into a situation of full-scale conflict. Such a denial is not only an extravagant waste of the scarce UN resources, it is also suggestive of the degree of significance that the Security Council apparently attaches to the work of its fellow UN bodies. As the degree of engagement with such reporting mechanisms declined, it is arguable too that the UN Charter's mandate to maintain international peace and security and promote and protect human rights is being undermined.

IV. Arria Formula Meetings

A couple of words have to be said in respect of Arria Formula meetings. Currently, Arria Formula meetings are the primary source of contact between the Security Council and the Human Rights Council and its predecessor the Commission on Human Rights. Arria Formula meetings enable the President of the Security Council, or other Council members, to invite Special Procedures mandate-holders to provide informal briefings to interested Security Council members in relation to thematic and specific country situations. The presence of all fifteen members may in fact be expected at such meetings.[101] Arria Formula meetings allow for informal and confidential meetings to take place outside of the Council chamber.[102] In many ways Arria Formula meetings continue to be a useful tool because the informality of the process provides Security Council members with the opportunity to meet with a range of individuals who represent organisations or institutions that are in a position to contribute to a better understanding of the human rights situation in question. Special Procedures mandate holders, because of their independence and expertise as well as the influence that they wield as a representative of the UN in general and as a representative of the Human Rights Council in particular, have fallen into this category and have demonstrated themselves to be strongly placed to provide direct information and assessments of the human rights situa-

---

[101] S. Bailey/ S. Daws, *The Procedure of the Security Council*, 3rd edition, 1998, 68.

[102] Doc. A/53/865-S/1999/286.

tion in question.[103] However, despite the fact that informal Arria Formula meetings appeared to have become a regular part of Security Council briefings and Special Procedures mandate-holders have briefed the Security Council on a reasonably regular basis, when invited by the President of the Council, the informality of this useful mechanism can have negative impact on the significance of the role of mandate-holders in themselves, as well as their role in representing those UN organs promoting human rights protection. A balance has to be struck between preserving the original rationale for organising the Security Council as it is and allowing for a more equitable relationship between the Council and other UN bodies especially those charged with human rights protection given the increased recognition that human rights violations can constitute threats to international peace and security.[104]

---

[103] The year 2002 being a good example. An Arria Formula meeting of Council members was convened e.g. by Singapore on 5 March 2002 to address the difficulty of getting humanitarian assistance to the people of Angola. Apart from Council members, participants included representatives of Human Rights Watch, Médecins Sans Frontières, Save the Children and Oxfam. On 8 March an Arria Formula meeting was convened by the United Kingdom to hear a report from a visit to Sierra Leone by the Special Rapporteur on Violence against Women its Causes and Consequences. An Arria Formula meeting to address issues relating to abuses of women and children in Mano River countries (Sierra Leone, Liberia and Guinea) was held on 19 March, convened by Singapore. Apart from Council members, participants included two independent experts from the United Nations Development Fund for Women. On 22 March Ireland convened an Arria Formula meeting to hear a presentation by the Office of the United Nations High Commissioner for Refugees and the International Centre for Transitional Justice on the establishment of a truth and reconciliation commission in Sierra Leone, see Doc. S/2002/663, letter dated 12 June 2002 from the Permanent Representative of Norway to the United Nations addressed to the President of the Security Council, 7-8. In October another Arria Formula meeting took place, convened by the Permanent Mission of Jamaica, during which the humanitarian situation in Liberia was addressed. This work with the Security Council is considered highly valuable for the NGOs and has become more important in recent years, see also, K. Martens, "An Appraisal of Amnesty International's Work at the United Nations: Established Areas of Activities and Shifting Priorities since the 1990s", *HRQ* 26 (2004), 1050 et seq. (1059).

[104] In the case of the DRC there was a meeting under this formula in October 2000, Doc. E/CN.4/2001/40, *Question of the Violation of Human Rights and Fundamental Freedoms in any Part of the World, Report on the Situation of Human Rights in the Democratic Republic of the Congo*, submitted

It is only recently that the Security Council has returned to the issue of whether such meeting should be the subject of greater formality. The Chair of the Security Council's Informal Working Group on Documentation and Other Procedural Questions noted, that, in 2006, the Working Group had examined various proposals in respect of the question of the relationship with non-members.[105] As a result of the discussions, the Working Group had produced a set of recommendations to be presented to the Council for its approval. The recommendations included existing agreements on working methods, some of which went as far back as 1993, as well as newly agreed or updated measures for improvement. In the latter half of 2006, the Working Group continued its discussions, mainly on two issues, the procedure for conducting Arria Formula meetings and the way to promote the implementation of the recommendations contained in the note by the President. With regard to holding Arria Formula meetings, the Chair noted that Council members had requested the Working Group in September 2006 to discuss the appropriate way to conduct the meetings, believing that there was need for some clarity on that aspect. In response to that request, the Working Group had met twice and had reached a common understanding on the conduct of Arria Formula meetings. Accordingly, Council members were encouraged to plan Arria Formula meetings in accordance with para. 54 of the President's note and to take part in such meetings. Any Council member convening an Arria Formula meeting was encouraged to organise carefully the meeting, so as to maintain its informal character. Also, any member convening an Arria Formula meeting should inform all participating Council members about the planned procedure for, and participants in, the meeting.[106] The Security Council committed itself to make efforts to enhance its interaction and dialogue with non-Council members and implementing the measures described in the Annex to the President's note. They also expressed their intention to utilise Arria Formula meetings as a flexible and informal forum for enhancing their deliberations.[107]

---

by the Special Rapporteur, in accordance with CHR Resolution 2000/15, paras 3-4. See also Doc. E/CN.4/2002/14, para. 36.

[105]   Doc. S/2006/507.

[106]   Ibid., para. 54.

[107]   Ibid., para. 1.

V. Conclusion

The UN Charter provides that it is incumbent upon both the United Nations as collective whole and the Member States as individual constituents of that whole to promote and protect human rights. This article highlighted the role that the Security Council has played in the past two decades in emphasising the promotion and protection of human rights as an aspect of maintaining international peace and security. The Council has been assisted in this regard by ECOSOC, the OHCHR and Special Rapporteurs in a manner that, regrettably, has tended to be somewhat sporadic and informal.

It has been identified that the Security Council can and must do more to promote and protect human rights. Not only should the Council engage more fully with ECOSOC, it should furthermore make a more effective use of the special procedures mechanisms. Given that such mechanisms facilitate the flow of human rights information between the Council and other UN human rights bodies, this conduit of information should be formalised in order to complement the increased profile of human rights within Security Council deliberations.

It is worth concluding with a stark reminder of what may be at stake and what has been regarded as perhaps one of the greatest missed opportunities for the Security Council, namely the warning in April 1993 by the Special Rapporteur on Extrajudicial, Summary or Arbitrary Executions, that a genocide was being planned in Rwanda. The Special Rapporteur's report was not studied or further being taken notice of and the observations facilitated by this Special Procedures mechanism remained tragically unnoticed by the Security Council.

The Principle of *Non-Refoulement* at Sea and the Effectiveness of Asylum Protection

Seline Trevisanut[*]

[*] The author would like to thank Professor Tullio Treves for his invaluable insights and comments as well as Chiara Ragni and Ingo Venzke for their invaluable suggestions.

> *"I have made it abundantly clear to the Coast Guard that we will turn back any refugee that attempts to reach our shore"*[1].

I. Introduction

This declaration of US President G.W. Bush is symptomatic of how sea-borne migration is perceived as a problem or even hassle by the destination states despite the presence of refugees in dire need of protection. Some times states deny the refugee character of a flow of migrants or invoke security concerns to refuse protection and to justify the non-admittance or the removal. Arrivals by sea of asylum-seekers challenge not only the interpretation and application of the right of asylum, and in particular the principle of *non-refoulement*, but also the existing rules related to the freedom and the safety of navigation.

Migration flows by sea are not a new phenomenon and ever since the Indochinese crisis[2] in the seventies, they are well known under the expression "boat people". Dealing with arrivals of thousands of Vietnamese irregular migrants to the coasts of neighboring states, the international community was forced to notice that international law had a gap: it had no useful and effective instruments to deal with migrants at sea, and in particular with asylum-seekers.

The chief problems that still remain have been to identify the rights and the obligations of the concerned states[3] in the different maritime

---

[1]   Declaration made by US President G.W. Bush, 25 February 2004, during the Haitian crisis of late February 2004 which culminated with the forced departure of Haitian President Aristide, as reported in B. Frelick, "'Abundantly Clear': *Refoulement*", *Georgetown Immigration Law Journal* 19 (2004-2005), 245 et seq.; see also S.H. Legomsky, "The USA and the Caribbean Interdiction Program", *International Journal of Refugee Law* 18 (2006), 677 et seq. (682).

[2]   I do refer to the Indochinese crisis in relation to the movement of refugees coming from the former French Indochina in consequence of armed conflict situations, as in Vietnam, and emergence of a dictatorial regime, as in Cambodia, cf. A. Lakshamana Chetty, "Resolution of the Problem of Boat People: The Case of A Global Initiative", *ISIL Yearbook of International Humanitarian and Refugee Law* 1 (2001), 144 et seq. (145).

[3]   Several states might be concerned by the arrival of asylum-seekers by sea: first of all the coastal state or state of destination; the national state of the

zones with special regard to the organization and management of search and rescue operations at sea. Another important issue has been the question whether the decision of states to refuse the permission of entry into their territory is legally limited. This question arose mainly in relation to the treatment of asylum-seekers and refugees – possibly among the migrants – with regard to the principle of *non-refoulement*.

This article elucidates how the exercise of sovereign powers in the different maritime zones pursuant to the law of the sea and customary international law gives rise to challenges in the application of the principle of *non-refoulement* and in the protection of asylum-seekers and refugees at sea. Particular attention must be given to the so-called *non-entrée* mechanisms made principally to prevent a refugee having access to the procedures for the determination of his/her status. Among those are the interdiction at sea programs.

The analysis will not be limited to the modalities of exercising jurisdiction; their consequences must also be considered. In fact, one of the main difficulties related to the management of refugees by sea consists in the heterogeneity of the phenomenon. Case law and practice testify that each arrival is different from another. This contribution argues that there is a common aim underlying both the law of the sea and refugee law which thus can be combined in accounting for security interests of the states as well as the protection of sea-borne asylum-seekers.

The argument unfolds in five steps. First, the content and evolution of the principle of *non-refoulement* will be analyzed (II.). Then, the difficulties related to its application in the territorial waters will be highlighted (III.). Specific remarks will be made for the contiguous zone (IV.). Particular attention will be given to interdiction programs on the high seas (V.). The contribution will conclude with some critical remarks (VI.) that must be taken into account when interpreting the law of the sea and refugee law with regard to sea-borne asylum-seekers.

---

individuals or their state of origin; the flag state of the vessel carrying the asylum-seekers; eventually the state of transit or first port of asylum.

II. The Legal Nature of the Principle of *Non-Refoulement*: Towards the Recognition of a Peremptory Norm?

1. The Meaning of the Principle Pursuant to Article 33 of the 1951 Refugee Convention

The principle of *non-refoulement* is expressed firstly in article 33(1) of the 1951 Geneva Convention relating to the Status of Refugees (1951 Refugee Convention)[4] which states that:

"1. No Contracting State shall expel or return ("refouler") a refugee in any manner whatsoever to the frontiers of territories where his life or freedom would be threatened on account of his race, religion, nationality, membership of a particular social group or political opinion".

First and foremost this article establishes an obligation for states not to remove individuals or a certain group of persons present in their territory to the country of persecution. Two main issues arise from the application of this norm: first, *when* the rejection of an individual can lead to the violation of the principle of *non-refoulement* and, secondly, *who* are the individuals protected by this norm.

The obligation of *non-refoulement* is the core of asylum-seekers protection[5] because it is the only guarantee that refugees will not be submitted again to the persecution which has caused the departure and responds to the refugee's need to enter the asylum country. It does not, however, explicitly guarantee access to the territory of the destination state or admission to the procedures granting the refugee status. Actually some authors have tried to support the existence of an additional obligation aimed at binding states to admit individuals applying for protection into their own territory but, for the moment, state practice cannot confirm these attempts[6].

---

4   UNTS Vol. 189 No. 150, page 137 et seq.

5   E. Lauterpacht/ D. Bethlehem, "The Scope and Content of the Principle of *Non-Refoulement*: Opinion", in: E. Feller/ V. Türk/ F. Nicholson, *Refugee Protection in International Law*, 2003, 87 et seq. (107).

6   I do not consider here the issues related to the application of the principle of *non-refoulement* in a situation of expulsion from the territory of the hosting state, i.e. after the decision of the competent authorities to not admit the individual to the relevant procedures or the refusal of granting the status of refugee; situations implying other legal problems and consequences despite the phenomenon of sea-borne asylum-seekers. See G.S.

Recently, *Noll* gave a very interesting definition of the principle, which summarizes its evolution from the letter of article 33 to today's approach: "*Non-refoulement* is about being admitted to the State community, although in a minimalist form of non-removal. It could be described as a *right to transgress an administrative border*" (emphasis added)[7]. Starting from this conception some important consequences for the legality of the control carried out at the borders and where they must or may take place may be considered.

The application of the principle of *non-refoulement* at the frontier, in its meaning of "non rejection at the frontier", is mostly shared today[8], but, as it will be discussed below, its application to interdiction operations on the high seas or within territorial waters is less clear[9] because of the difficulties related to the determination of the moment of entry into the territory for sea-borne asylum-seekers. Nevertheless, the unlawful entry of asylum-seekers does not exclude them from the scope of application of the *non-refoulement* principle as guaranteed in article 31(1) 1951 Refugee Convention[10]. During the Indochinese crisis, the UNHCR Executive Committee (Executive Committee) affirmed:

Goodwin-Gill/ J. Adam, *The Refugee in International Law*, 3rd edition, 2007, 257 et seq.; J.C. Hathaway, *The Rights of Refugees under International Law*, 2005, 370 et seq.

[7] G. Noll, "Seeking Asylum at Embassies: A right to Entry under International Law?", *International Journal of Refugee Law* 17 (2005), 542 et seq. (548).

[8] Lauterpacht/ Bethlehem, see note 5, 113 et seq. Article 3 (1) of the Council Regulation 343/2003 includes the application of the principle in border situations (EC *Regulation Establishing the Criteria and the Mechanisms for Determining the Member State Responsible for Examining an Asylum Application Lodged in one of the Member States by a Third-Country National*, OJEC No. L 50/1 of 25 February 2003).

[9] Noll, see note 7, 549.

[10] Article 31: "The Contracting States shall not impose penalties, on account of their illegal entry or presence, on refugees who, coming directly from a territory where their life or freedom was threatened in the sense of article 1, enter or are present in their territory without authorization, provided they present themselves without delay to the authorities and show good cause for their illegal entry or presence". See Hathaway, see note 6, 386, in which the author asserts, commenting article 31, that " [p]erhaps the most important innovation of the 1951 Refugee Convention is its commitment to the protection of refugees who travel to a State party without authorization". J. C. Hathaway, "Why Refugee Law Still Matters", *Melbourne Journal of International Law* 8 (2007), 89 et seq. (91).

"It is therefore *imperative to ensure that asylum seekers are fully protected in large-scale influx situations, to reaffirm the basic minimum standards for their treatment* (...). In situation of large-scale influx, asylum seekers should be admitted to the State in which they first seek refuge and if that State is unable to admit them on a durable basis, it should *always* admit them at least on a temporary basis (...). In all cases the fundamental principle of *non-refoulement – including non rejection at the frontier – must be scrupulously observed*"[11]. (emphasis added)

The non rejection at the frontier was included in the principle of *non-refoulement* in the instruments subsequent to the 1951 Refugee Convention, such as the 1967 Declaration on Territorial Asylum (1967 DTA)[12] and the 1967 OAU Convention on Refugees[13], which are particularly important for the interpretation of the Convention[14]. Since 1977[15] the Executive Committee has brought forward this argument restating it in relation to migration by sea in 1979, as follows:

"[I]t is the humanitarian obligation of all coastal States to allow vessels in distress to seek haven in their waters and to grant asylum, or at least temporary refuge, to persons on board wishing to seek asylum"[16].

The UNHCR has played an important role both in the evolution of the principle of *non-refoulement* to include cases of rejection at the frontier as well as in the evolution of the interpretation of article 33 in relation to the category of individuals protected by this norm. Actually, there exists a discrepancy between the *ratione personae* application of the 1951 Refugee Convention and the content of the mandate of the UNHCR[17]. The scope of its mandate has expanded progressively since

---

11   Executive Committee, Conclusion No. 22 (XXXII) 1981; reaffirmed during the crisis in former Yugoslavia, in Executive Committee, Conclusion No. 74 (XLV) 1994, para. (r).

12   A/RES/2312 (XXII) of 14 December 1967.

13   *OAU Convention Governing the Specific Aspects of Refugee Problems in Africa*, UNTS Vol. 1001 No. 14691.

14   Lauterpacht/ Bethlehem, see note 5, 113; P. Weis, *The Refugee Convention, 1951, The Travaux Préparatoires Analysed*, 1995, 342.

15   Executive Committee, Conclusion No. 6 (XXVIII) 1977, para. (c): "the fundamental importance of the observance of the principle of *non-refoulement* – both at the border and within the territory of a State".

16   Executive Committee, Conclusion No. 15 (XXX) 1979, para. (c).

17   A/RES/428 (V) of 14 December 1950, Annex, para 1.

its creation and comprises now the protection of five categories of individuals: 1.) those falling under the definition of the 1951 Refugee Convention and 1967 Protocol (see below); 2.) broader categories recognized by states as entitled to protection and assistance of the UNHCR; 3.) those individuals for whom the UNHCR exercised "good offices"; 4.) returning refugees; 5.) non-refugee stateless persons[18].

On the contrary, article 33 of the 1951 Refugee Convention applies to the so-called "statutory refugee", i.e. the individuals within the definition provided by article 1 of the same Convention, as modified by the 1967 Protocol relating to the Status of Refugees (the 1967 Protocol)[19]:

> "[the term refugee shall apply to any person who] owing to *well-founded fear of being persecuted* for reason of race, religion, nationality, membership of a particular social group or opinion, is outside the country of his nationality and is unable or, owing to such fear, is unwilling to avail himself of the protection of that country; or who, not having a nationality and being outside the country of his former habitual residence as a result of such events, is unable or, owing to such fear, is unwilling to return to it". (emphasis added)

The cornerstone of this definition is the concept of "well-founded fear of being persecuted" which restrains the Convention's ambit of application compared to the mandate of the UNHCR. The meaning of persecution has been thoroughly debated by scholars aiming at enlarging the scope of article 1 of the 1951 Refugee Convention[20]. State practice is not homogenous in that respect, even if it "has consistently revealed a dominant trend of offering some form of protection to 'per-

---

18   UNHCR *Protection of Persons – Concern to UNHCR Who Falls Outside the 1951 Convention: A Discussion Note*, 2 April 1992, Doc. EC/1992/SCP. CRP.5, para. 11.

19   *Protocol relating to the Status of Refugees*, UNTS Vol. 606 No. 8791, page 267 et seq.; the 1967 Protocol eliminated the limits of time and place in respect of the application of the 1951 Refugee Convention, which formerly applied only to refugees stemming from Europe because of events occurred before the 1 January 1951. When I do refer to the 1951 Refugee Convention, I do refer to the Convention as amended by the 1967 Protocol.

20   On this concern, among others, M. Bettati, *L'asile politique en question. Un statut pour les réfugiés*, 1985, 10; J.Y. Carlier, "Et Genève sera … La définition du réfugié: bilan et perspectives", in: V. Chetail (ed.), *La Convention de Genève du 8 juillet 1951 relative au statut des réfugiés 50 ans après: bilan et perspectives*, 2001, 63 et seq. (67); J. Fitzpatrick, "Revitalizing the 1951 Convention", *Harvard Human Rights Journal* 9 (1996), 229 et seq. (230, 239).

sons whose life or freedom would be at risk as a result of an armed conflict or generalized violence if they were returned involuntarily to their countries of origin'"[21]. The so called '*de facto* refugees'[22] are not deprived of protection and enjoy the principle of *non-refoulement* as provided by the "complementary protection"[23] of human rights law.

2. The Principle of *Non-Refoulement* as the Necessary Corollary of the Prohibition of Torture and of the Right to Life

More or less serious violations of human rights are often the cause of migrations creating refugees and asylum-seekers. Independently of the causes of the departure, the Universal Declaration of Human Rights (UDHR)[24] states that, "[e]veryone has the right to leave any country, including his own, and to return to his country" (article 13(2))[25] and "[e]veryone has the right to seek and enjoy in other countries asylum from persecution" (article 14(1)). Pursuant to these two rights, everyone is entitled to flee a harmful situation in which he/she is living or

---

[21]   Goodwin-Gill/ Adam, see note 6, 289. Lauterpacht and Bethlehem have argued that the notion of threat contemplated in article 33(1) may be "broader than simply the risk of persecution, [...] to the extent that a threat to life or freedom that may arise other than in consequence of persecution", enlarging thus the scope of article 33 to refugees not included in the treaty definition of article 1; Lauterpacht/ Bethlehem, see note 5, 124.

[22]   "[P]ersons not recognized as refugees within the meaning of Article 1 of the [Refugee] Convention [and who are] unable or unwilling for political, racial, religious or other valid reasons to return to their countries of origin", see Council of Europe Parliamentary Assembly Recommendation No. 773 (1976) on the Situation of *de facto* Refugees, para. 1.

[23]   For a historical overview of the "complementary protection", see Goodwin-Gill/ Adam, see note 6, 286 et seq. See also Lauterpacht/ Bethlehem, see note 5, 150 et seq.

[24]   A/RES/217 (III) of 10 December 1948. The UDHR has not formally a binding nature but most of the norms contained have progressively acquired the status of customary law and, consequently, bind the states members of the international community.

[25]   A. de Zayas, "Migration and Human Rights", *Nord. J. Int'l L.* 62 (1994), 241 et seq. (245); A. Grahl- Madsen, "Article 13", in: A. Eide et al., *The Universal Declaration of Human Rights: A Commentary*, 1992, 203 et seq. (212).

risks living; but once outside the borders of his/her own country, no formal right guarantees the entry into another.

The preamble of the 1951 Refugee Convention recalls the UDHR and the 1967 DTA reaffirming the content of its article 14 clarifying that the individual does not possess a subjective right of asylum but he/she is merely entitled to request the status of a refugee and the required state has a discretionary power to accept or refuse the request[26]. Notwithstanding the discretion of states, preventing an individual from presenting the request can imply a breach of article 14 UDHR in its meaning of "right to request" which is safeguarded by the principle of *non-refoulement*.

The *non-refoulement* principle in human rights law is guaranteed by article 3 of the Convention against Torture and Other Cruel, Inhuman or Degrading Treatment or Punishment (CAT)[27] which prohibits the removal of individuals to states where they risk being subjected to torture or other inhuman or degrading treatment. This is also affirmed by article 7 of the 1966 International Covenant on Civil and Political Rights (1966 ICCPR)[28]. At a regional level, the protection against *refoulement* is also guaranteed by article 3 of the 1950 European Convention for the Protection of Human Rights and Fundamental Freedoms (ECHR)[29], article 22(8) of the 1969 American Convention on Human Rights (ACHR)[30] and article 5 of the 1981 African Charter on the Protection of Human and Peoples' Rights (Banjul Charter)[31]. Moreover article 45 of the 1949 Fourth Geneva Convention relative to the Protection of Civilian Persons in Time of War states:

> "In no circumstances shall a protected person be transferred to a country where he or she may have reason to fear persecution for his or her political opinions or religious beliefs".

---

[26] "Asylum is viewed as an 'act of grace by States' and the refusal of states to accept an obligation to grant asylum is 'amply evidenced' by the history of international conventions and other instruments", see M. Pallis, "Obligations of States towards Asylum Seeker at Sea: Interactions and Conflicts Between Legal Regimes", *International Journal of Refugee Law* 14 (2002), 329 et seq. (341).

[27] A/RES/39/46 of 10 December 1984.

[28] Human Rights Committee, General Comment No. 20 (1992), Doc. HRI/ HEN/1/Rev.1 of 28 July 1994, para. 9.

[29] UNTS Vol. 213 No. 2886.

[30] UNTS Vol. 1144 No. 17955.

[31] *ILM* 21 (1982), 58 et seq.

The 1966 ICCPR also provides the obligation not to extradite, deport, expel or return an individual to a country where there are well founded suspicions concerning a risk of irreparable harm to the right to life guaranteed by article 6.[32] The right to life is also guaranteed by article 2 ECHR, article 4 ACHR and article 4 Banjul Charter.

From this list of articles affirming the principle of *non-refoulement* in relation both to the prohibition of torture and the right to life, it becomes evident how three domains of international law evolve in parallel but often overlap and interact: refugee protection, human rights and humanitarian law on the basis of which an individual can assert a claim for protection towards the respective state as well as the international community as a whole[33]. *Goodwin-Gill* and *Adam* support the existence of a customary norm of "temporary refuge", "which prohibit[s] States from forcibly repatriating foreigners who had fled generalized violence and other threats caused by internal armed conflict within their own State, until the violence ceased and the home State could assure the security and the protection of its nationals"[34]. The existence of such a customary norm can be identified, beyond the repetition of the principle of *non-refoulement* in the above mentioned human rights treaties, in the notion of complementary protection and in the practice of states related to "temporary protection". At the European level, the Council Directive 2001/55/EC of 20 July 2001 on *Minimum Standards for Giving Temporary Protection in the Event of a Mass Influx of Displaced Persons and on Measures Promoting a Balance of Efforts between Member States in Receiving such Persons and Bearing the Consequences Thereof*[35] guarantees the reception and the assistance of:

"third-country nationals or stateless persons who have had to leave their country or region of origin, or have been evacuated, in particular in response to an appeal by international organizations, and are unable to return in safe and durable conditions because of the situation prevailing in that country, who may fall within the scope of Article 1A of the Geneva Convention or other international or national instruments giving international protection, in particular:

---

[32] M. Nowak, *U.N. Covenant on Civil and Political Rights: CCPR a Commentary*, 2nd edition, 2005, 186.

[33] UNHCR, *Note on International Protection*, Doc. A/AC.96/777, 9 September 1999, para. 56; UNHCR, *Note on International Protection*, Doc. A/AC.96/799, 25 July 1992, para. 1.

[34] Goodwin-Gill/ Adam, see note 6, 289.

[35] OJEC No. L 212/12 of 7 August 2001.

(i)   persons who have fled areas of armed conflict or endemic violence;

(ii)   persons at serious risk of, or who have been the victims of, systematic or generalized violations of their human rights".

The conception of temporary protection is however not homogenous; the Australian approach[36], for example, consists of a temporary "protection visa" permitting refugees who have entered unlawfully into the territory to stay pending the determination of their status.

In light of the several international and domestic instruments and of state practice reaffirming the principle of *non-refoulement* it is today unanimously considered a customary norm, even if complete agreement has not yet been reached concerning its precise content regarding its territorial scope. Because of its close connection with the prohibition of torture, the peremptory nature of the principle of *non-refoulement* is more often discussed and supported.

3. The Nature of the Principle of *Non-Refoulement* and its Peremptory Importance

The question of the legal nature of the principle first arose in the seventies during the Indochinese crisis because destination states, namely Malaysia, Singapore and Thailand[37], were not parties to the 1951 Refugee Convention. While none of them contested the application of the

---

36   Migration Act 1958, Act No. 62 of 1958 as amended, Part 2, Division 3, Subdivision A, Section 36. See also information available at the Australian Department of Immigration and Citizenship, available at: <www.immi.gov.au>.

37   Because of the increasing number of Vietnamese refugees reaching its coasts, the Prime minister of Thailand declared in 1978 the unilateral decision of his government to close the maritime frontiers to these migration flows. The UNHCR then exposed its worries in relation to the consequences of this declaration for the existing humanitarian crisis and to the possible influence on the decision of the other interested states. See *Opening Statement by the United Nations High Commissioner for Refugees, in Consultative Meeting with Interested Governments on Refugees and Displaced Persons in South East Asia*, Geneva, 11-12 December 1978, available at: <www.unhcr.org>.

principle[38], they, nevertheless, invoked security exceptions as provided by article 33(2) of the 1951 Refugee Convention:

"2. The benefit of the present provision may not, however, be claimed by a refugee whom there are reasonable grounds for regarding as a danger to the security of the country in which he is, or who, having been convicted by a final judgement of a particularly serious crime, constitutes a danger to the community of that country".

The first attempt to affirm the peremptory nature of the principle of *non-refoulement* is Conclusion No. 25 (XXXIII) of 1982, in which the UNHCR Executive Committee[39] made a step far beyond the state of the art at the time. Then, in 1989, again the Executive Committee invited states to avoid actions resulting in *refoulement* situations because these would be "contrary to fundamental prohibitions against these practices"[40], and in 1996, it reaffirmed the principle elevating it to the rank of peremptory customary law, stating:

"Distressed at the widespread violations of the principle of *non-refoulement* and of the rights of refugees, in some cases resulting in loss of refugee lives, and seriously disturbed at reports indicating that large numbers of refugees and asylum-seekers have been *refouled* and expelled in highly dangerous situations; recalls that the principle of *non-refoulement* is not subject to derogation"[41].

The question strongly re-emerged in 2001, after the attacks of 9/11, when the UN Security Council adopted S/RES/1373[42] where it expressed an "unequivocal condemnation" of the terrorist acts and adopted measures aimed at repressing the funding and the preparation

---

38   "In UNHCR's experience, States have overwhelmingly indicated that they accept the principle of *non-refoulement* as binding, as demonstrated, *inter alia*, in numerous instances where States have responded to UNHCR's representations by providing explanations or justifications of cases of actual or intended *refoulement*, thus implicitly confirming their acceptance of the principle", UNCHR, *Advisory Opinion on the Extraterritorial Application of* Non-Refoulement *Obligations under the 1951 Convention relating to the Status of Refugees and its 1967 Protocol*, 26 January 2007, para. 15.

39   "*Reaffirmed* the importance of the basic principles of international law protection and in particular the principle of *non-refoulement* which was progressively acquiring the character of a peremptory rule of international law", para. (b).

40   Executive Committee, Conclusion No. 55 (XL), 1989, para. (d).

41   Executive Committee, Conclusion No. 79 (XLVII), 1996, para. (i).

42   S/RES/1373 (2001) of 28 September 2001.

of terrorist attacks. In particular, in operative para. 3, the Security Council invited states to:

"(f) Take appropriate measures in conformity with the relevant provisions of national and international law, including international standards of human rights, before granting refugee status, for the purpose of ensuring that the asylum-seeker has not planned, facilitated or participated in the commission of terrorist acts;

(g) Ensure, in conformity with international law, that refugee status is not abused by the perpetrators, organizers or facilitators of terrorist acts, and that claims of political motivation are not recognized as grounds for refusing requests for the extradition of alleged terrorists".

Allain deduced from this text an attempt of the Security Council to modify the content of article 1F(b) of the 1951 Refugee Convention stating that an individual found guilty of a serious non-political crime outside the country of refuge cannot enjoy statutory protection[43]. Bearing in mind the uncertainty related to the definition of terrorism in international law[44], and according to the wording of S/RES/1373, a state would be allowed to classify as terrorist an opposing armed group or organization and thus to exclude *a priori* members of this group from the status determination procedures. Moreover, if the crime of terrorism is equally considered a "serious crime" pursuant to article 33(2), this would have the consequence of allowing the state in which the individual has been found guilty to expel him/her even to the territory where there is a risk of being submitted to torture or other inhuman or degrading treatments; thus having a big impact on the practice concerning *non-refoulement*[45]. Recognizing the peremptory nature of the *non-*

---

[43] J. Allain, "The *jus cogens* nature of *non-refoulement*", *International Journal of Refugee Law* 13 (2001), 533 et seq. (545).

[44] E. Ahipeaud, "Etat du débat international autour de la définition du terrorisme international", in: M.J. Glennon/ S. Sur, *Terrorisme et le droit international*, 2008, 157 et seq.; B. Saul, "Definition of "Terrorism" in the UN Security Council: 1985-2004", *Chinese Journal of International Law* 4 (2005), 141 et seq.; J.M. Sorel, "Some Questions About the Definition of Terrorism and the Fight Against Its Financing", *EJIL* 14 (2003), 365 et seq.

[45] The UNHCR is concerned about exclusion clauses adopted by some states on a collective basis, rather than on an individual one, undermining thus the individual nature of the right of seeking asylum, UNHCR, *Note on the Impact of Security Council resolution 1624 (2005) on the Application of Exclusion under Article 1F of the 1951 Convention relating to the Status of Refugees*, 9 December 2005, available at: <www.unhcr.org>. See also

refoulement principle, as suggested by some authors[46], it should prevail on instruments of different nature, such as Security Council resolutions or agreements on extradition, when there is a threat of human rights violation.

In the opinion of *Orakhelashvili*[47], "doubtful wording of the Council's resolutions must always be construed in such a way as to avoid conflict with fundamental international obligations". Pursuant to this approach, and bearing in mind the uncertain definition of terrorism, the application of S/RES/1373 should not imply a changing of the content of article 1F(b) of the 1951 Refugee Convention.

The state of the art is not yet permitted to affirm the peremptory nature of the principle of *non-refoulement*. The principle remains, however, of peremptory importance as a "tool" for guaranteeing the efficiency and the effectiveness of the prohibition of torture and the protection of fundamental human rights. This is the reason why it is extremely relevant in determining when, where and how sea-borne asylum-seekers are entitled to its protection.

UNHCR, *Background Paper Preserving the Institution of Asylum and Refugee Protection in the Context of Counter-Terrorism: the Problem of Terrorist Mobility*, 5th Special Mtg of the Counter-Terrorist Committee with international, regional and sub-regional Organizations, 29-31 October 2007, Nairobi – Kenya.

[46] Allain, see note 43; id., "Insisting on the "*jus cogens*" nature of non-refoulement", in: J. van Selm, *The Refugee Convention at Fifty : a View from Forced Migration Studies*, 2003, 81 et seq.; R. Bruin/ K. Wouters, "Terrorism and the Non-derogability of *Non-refoulement*", *International Journal of Refugee Law* 15 (2003), 5 et seq. (24-26); D. Shelton, "Normative Hierarchy in International Law", *AJIL* 100 (2006), 291 et seq. (316). Schelton reminds, in particular, the Swiss practice in which the peremptory nature of the principle of *non-refoulement* has been declared since 1985.

[47] A. Orakhelashvili, "The Impact of Peremptory Norms on the Interpretation and Application of the United Nations Security Council Resolutions", *EJIL* 16 (2005), 59 et seq. (64, 80); id. "The Acts of the Security Council: Meaning and Standards of Review", *Max Planck* UNYB 11 (2007), 143 et seq.

III. The Notion of Maritime Frontier for the Purposes of Applying the Principle of *Non-Refoulement*

1. The Notion of Maritime Frontier and the Exercise of Sovereign Powers in the Territorial Waters

Article 2(1) of the United Nations Convention on the Law of the Sea (UNCLOS)[48] provides that, "[t]he sovereignty of a coastal State extends, beyond its land territorial and internal waters and, in the case of an archipelagic State, its archipelagic waters, to an adjacent belt of sea, described as the territorial sea".

This maritime zone cannot exceed the 12 nautical miles (article 3 UNCLOS). The only general exception to the exclusive powers of the coastal state in its territorial sea consists of the right of innocent passage as stated in article 17 UNCLOS[49]. The coastal state shall not hamper the innocent passage of foreign ships through the territorial sea (article 24 UNCLOS) but it can regulate the conditions of the passage in the fields listed in article 21(1), *inter alia* "(h) the prevention of infringement of the customs, fiscal, *immigration* or sanitary laws and regulations of the coastal State". (emphasis added)

The coastal state can also prevent a passage which it considers not innocent and suspend the related right in specific areas of its territorial sea when this "is essential for the protection of its security" (article 25(3)). Moreover, the coastal state shall not exercise its criminal jurisdiction on foreign vessels crossing its territorial sea except if the consequences of the offence extend into its territory or if the offence is of a kind to disturb the peace or the security or the good order of the territorial sea (article 27(1)(a)-(b)).

Pursuant to the above-mentioned articles, to enter the territorial waters of a state does not necessarily mean falling under its jurisdiction. As pointed out by *Goodwin-Gill* and *Adam*, "[n]either branch of law (law

---

[48] *United Nations Convention on the Law of the Sea of 10 December 1982*, *ILM* 21 (1982), 1276 et seq.; M.H. Nordquist (ed.), *UNCLOS 1982, A Commentary*, Vol. 2, 1993, 266 et seq.

[49] Article 17: "Subject to this Convention, ships of all States, whether coastal or land-locked, enjoy the right of innocent passage through the territorial sea". Only when the conditions for exercising the rights of innocent passage are infringed coastal states enjoy fully their sovereignty in the territorial sea (arts 18-19) ; see T. Treves, "La navigation", in: R.J. Dupuy/ D. Vignes (eds), *Traité du nouveau droit de la mer*, 1985, 688 et seq. (755).

of the sea and refugee law) resolves the question of whether entering a State's territorial waters constitutes entry to State territory"[50].

The variety of situations is unlimited. A fundamental distinction can be drawn, however, between the instance of a vessel merely exercising its right of innocent passage in the territorial waters of a foreign state without being directed to its coasts, and the situation of a vessel crossing the territorial sea of the coastal state to reach its territory.

In the first situation the coastal state has no jurisdiction on the passing vessel unless it considers the presence of unlawful passengers, the undocumented refugees, as a breach of the conditions for enjoying the right of innocent passage. Consequently, the state could refuse the entry of the vessel into its territorial waters. Such refusal can have consequences for individuals' enjoyment of the right of seeking asylum and the right of *non-refoulement*. This behavior has the effect of confining the exercise of jurisdiction to the effective borders of the territorial sea; this will be discussed below.

In the second situation, the vessel is manifestly violating domestic immigration law as it is carrying irregular passengers. It is very important to distinguish the kinds of operations carried out by the authorities of the coastal state in the territorial waters. If the operation is aimed at the *expulsion* of the vessel, the coastal state exercises its power to expel those vessels or persons it considers to have unlawfully entered its territory, namely its territorial sea. It recognizes implicitly that the vessel entered its territory and therefore becomes subject to its jurisdiction. Pursuant to this thinking, the passengers of the vessel enjoy the rights guaranteed by the international obligations binding the interested state in respect to the persons submitted to its jurisdiction, among them are the principle of *non-refoulement* and fundamental human rights. In particular, article 31 of the 1951 Refugee Convention applies in this case guaranteeing immunity from penalties to refugees who entered unlawfully into the asylum state[51].

On the contrary, if the intervention of the coastal state authorities is only aimed at *refusing the entry*, this implies the movement of the frontier to the area where the operation takes place. The individuals concerned are not yet under its jurisdiction and state authorities are only limited by the principle of *non-refoulement* in its meaning of non-

---

50 Goodwin-Gill/ Adam, see note 6, 279.
51 The wording of article 31 is reported above, see note 10. See also Goodwin-Gill/ Adam, see note 6, 274; Hathaway, see note 10, 91.

rejection at the frontier. In this regard, the United States "wet foot/dry foot policy" shows some interesting aspects – it can be summarized as follows:

> "If they [sea-borne migrants] touch the US soil, bridges, piers or rocks, they are subject to US immigration processes for removal. If they are feet wet [*sic.*], they are eligible for return by the Coast Guard in accordance with Executive Order 12807".[52]

This policy is a good example of the so-called "mechanisms of *non-entrée*" aimed at denying access to the territory through the non-authorization of entry or through the creation of international zones in which neither domestic nor international law apply[53]. In relation to sea-borne asylum-seekers there is the somewhat original Australian "territorial excision" of more than 3,500 of its islands. This is a self declared "migration zone". As pointed out by *Hathaway*:

> "[T]he result would be that refugees arriving at one of the excised islands – including not only main destinations for those arriving by boat from Southeast Asia, such as Christmas Island, but even an island only 2 km from the coast of the Australian mainland – would

---

[52] US Coast Guard, "Alien Migrant Interdiction", as reported in Legomsky, see note 1, 684, footnote 44. The Executive Order No. 12.807, so called "Kennebunkport Order", was adopted the 24 May 1992 by US President G. Bush for suspending the screening process of Haitian irregular migrants on US vessels, created in 1982 with the Executive Order No. 12.324. The Kennebunkport Order authorised the US authorities to interdict Haitian vessels on the high seas and to redirect them directly to Haiti. This concern is studied below.

[53] The international zones created in the international airports are quite well known in relation to the English case law *R. (European Roma Rights Centre and Others) v. Immigration Officer in Prague Airport* [2003] EWCA Civ 666 (Eng. CA May 20, 2003) in which, about the pre-screening system of the Prague airport, the Court of Appeal affirmed: "[Article 33 1951 Refugee Convention] applies in terms only to refugees, and a refugee is defined... as someone necessarily "outside the country of his nationality" (...). For good measure, article 33 forbids *"refoulement"* to *"frontier"* and, whatever precise meaning is given to the former term, it cannot comprehend an action which causes someone to remain on the same side of the frontier as they began; nor indeed could such a person be said to have been returned to any frontier" (para. 31).

not be entitled to have their claims assessed under Australia's refugee status determination system".[54]

The mechanisms of *non-entrée* do not completely avoid the application of the principle of *non-refoulement* and an analogy with operations carried out on the high seas can support this approach. As far as the territorial sea is concerned, two behaviors can particularly violate the obligations deriving from the principle in its meaning of non-rejection at the frontier: the refusal of entry into the territorial sea and the denial of access into the port or of disembarkation.

2. The Refusal of Entry into the Territorial Sea

Pursuant to article 29 of the Vienna Convention on the Law of Treaties (1969 Vienna Convention)[55], article 33 of the 1951 Refugee Convention applies to States parties' territory including the territorial sea. The wording of article 33 confirms this statement as it prohibits *refoulement* to "the frontiers of *territories* where his life or freedom would be threatened" (emphasis added). The use of the term "territories" in the plural, instead of state or nation, indicates the irrelevance of the formal status of the part of the territory concerned[56] and of the state actually exercising its jurisdiction on the territory where the refugee or asylum-seeker would be endangered[57].

---

[54] Hathaway, see note 6, 298, especially footnote 105. Moreover the author defines this mechanisms as a "legal ruse in order to avoid formal acknowledge of the arrival of the refugee" and concludes that "[t]here is (...) no international legal difference between opting not to consider the refugee status of persons present in "international zones" or "excised territory" and refusing to consider the refugee status of persons clearly acknowledged to be on the state's territory. Where the refusal to process a refugee claim results, directly or indirectly, in the refugee's removal to face the risk of being persecuted, Article 33 has been contravened"; ibid., 321-322. See also *Migration Amendment (Excision from Migration Zone) Act 2001, No. 127, 2001*, adopted on 27 September 2001, available at:<www.comlaw.gov.au>.

[55] *Vienna Convention on the Law of Treaties*, UNTS Vol. 1155 No. 18232, article 29: "Unless a different intention appears from the treaty or is otherwise established, a treaty is binding upon each party in respect of its entire territory".

[56] Lauterpacht/ Bethlehem, see note 5, 121.

[57] European Court of Human Rights, *T.I. v. United Kingdom*, Appl. 43844/98, Decision on the Admissibility, 7 March 2000, 15-16.

Since the first state of arrival has the duty to host refugees, at least temporarily, pursuant to the concept of "territorial asylum"[58], the vessel transporting refugees cannot be impeded from entering into the territorial sea upon its arrival at the border of the territorial sea, nor can it be *refoulé* to high seas or to territories where the above-mentioned risks of persecution exists. The regime of "territorial asylum" was conceived and developed during the Indochinese crisis to guarantee minimum standards of protection and a first hosting place; it corresponds to the idea of "temporary refuge". At that time, the notion of a "safe third State"[59] emerged. After their status determination pursuant to the procedures of the state of arrival, the refugees were voluntarily redirected according to the agreement concluded with the "safe third State"[60]. The aim was clearly to share the burden represented by the thousands of refugees and to avoid refusal of entry. Notwithstanding the existence of the temporary refuge rule, states continue to refuse access into their territorial waters invoking the fact that there is no proof of the presence of refugees on board and thus they can justifiably preclude the entry of a vessel. They thereby manifestly violate their immigration law. Two cases are quite self-explanatory in this respect: the case of the Norwe-

---

[58] *Declaration on Territorial Asylum*, see note 12.

[59] The "safe third State" approach is nowadays largely used in states practice trough networks of readmission agreements. European states in particular have developed this mechanism collaborating intensely with the southern Mediterranean countries, which are often countries of origin or of transit of irregular migration flows. The European legislation (Council Directive 2005/85/EC of 1 December 2005 on *Minimum Standards on Procedures in Member States for Granting and Withdrawing Refugee Status*, OJEC No. L 326/13 of 13 December 2005) has set several criteria for determining what has to be considered a safe third state (article 27) and, if the asylum-seeker comes from one of these safe states, he/she is precluded from requiring asylum to a Member State. Hathaway ironically identifies in the definition given by the directive the notion of "super safe third country"; Hathaway, see note 6, 295 et seq. See also S. Taylor, "Protection Elsewhere/Nowhere", *International Journal of Refugee Law* 18 (2006), 283 et seq. (293).

[60] In 1989, during the Indochinese emergency, an intergovernmental conference was held in Geneva which concluded with the adoption of the "Comprehensive Plan of Action" (CPA). The agreement aimed at the management of the Vietnamese boat people through the organisation of the arrival and the creation of a resettlement network. For a critical comment on the CPA, S. A. Bronée, "The History of the Comprehensive Plan of Action", *International Journal of Refugee Law* 5 (1993), 534 et seq.

gian vessel *Tampa*, involving Australia, and the case of the German vessel *Cap Anamur*, involving Italy.

The *Tampa*[61] was a Norwegian merchant ship which rescued an Indonesian fishing boat in distress on 26 August 2001 on the high seas. The *Tampa* had to keep all the 433 passengers of the Indonesian boat on board, notwithstanding that it was formally only allowed to transport 50 persons maximum. Having arrived at 13.5 nautical miles from the Australian island of Christmas, the master had to stop as the Australian authorities denied access into the territorial waters. In light of the health conditions of the passengers, among them pregnant women and wounded men, the master took the decision to contravene the denial and entered the Australian waters looking for sanitary assistance. The vessel stopped 4 miles from the shore. The Australian government sent special army corps to give first medical aid and to avoid the disembarkation of the migrants. The *Tampa* then refused to leave the territorial waters because of the unsafe situation of the vessel due to the excess of people on board. Finally on 1 September, the Australian government declared that it had reached an agreement with New Zealand and transferred the passengers to a navy vessel bringing them to two Australian military bases in New Zealand. From there, the migrants arrived on the soil of New Zealand and Nauru.

This case rises mainly two issues concerning the law of the sea: the duty to give assistance to vessels in distress – an issue discussed below in relation to the high seas – and the application of the right of innocent passage.

Norway, the flag State of the *Tampa*, invoked a violation of the above-mentioned right of innocent passage, arguing that Australia, refusing entry to its territorial waters, had breached its obligation not to hamper the innocent passage of a vessel, as stated in article 24(1) UNCLOS. On the other hand Australia declared that the passage violated its domestic law on migration – a field of jurisdiction of the coastal state pursuant to the list of article 19(2) – and thus, pursuant to article 25(1) UNCLOS, it had the right to "take the necessary step in its territorial

---

[61] On this episode, C. Baillet, "The *Tampa* Case and its Impact on Burden Sharing at Sea", *HRQ* 25 (2003), 741 et seq.; M.N. Fornari, "Soccorso di profughi in mare e diritto di asilo: questioni di diritto internazionale sollevate dalla vicenda della nave Tampa", *Comunità Internaz.* 57 (2002), 61 et seq.; M. White, "Tampa incident: Shipping, international and maritime legal issues", *The Australian Law Journal* 78 (2004), 101 et seq.; id., "Tampa incident: Some subsequent legal issues", ibid., 249 et seq.

sea to prevent a passage which is not innocent". However, it is not well established in doctrine[62] if the violation of the coastal domestic law does amount to a threat to "peace, good order or security" of the coastal state (article 19(1)). The practice generally confirms that a violation of the law in one of the sectors listed in article 19(2) UNCLOS implies automatically a prejudice to the security of the coastal state, in turn justifying a suspension of the right of innocent passage and the closure of a part of its territorial waters as provided by article 25(3).

Moreover, Australia had the right to arrest the *Tampa* 4 miles from its coast according to article 25(2):

> "In the case of ships proceeding to internal waters or a call at a port facility outside internal waters, the coastal State also has the right to take the necessary steps to prevent any breach of the conditions to which admission of those ships to internal waters or such a call is subject".

From the point of view of the right of innocent passage, Australia seems to have acted lawfully. It did, however, violate the principle of *non-refoulement*. Australia breached its obligation by redirecting the vessel and refusing to carry out the first screening of the passengers; this amounts to a *refoulement de facto*. As a matter of fact, to expel a vessel that has entered in the territorial sea violating the domestic immigration law and thereby breaching the condition of the innocent passage, and to oblige it to return to the high seas, is a right of the coastal state. However, this right is not unlimited. Its execution must comply with international obligations and in particular the principle of *non-refoulement*. It must be noted that the two countries of destination chosen by Australia, i.e. New Zealand and Nauru, present all necessary guarantees of fair treatment and respect of international standards in human rights and asylum law. Yet, the passengers intended to enter Australia. Australia, as first country of arrival, had the duty of temporary refuge and of first screening of the asylum requests. Only afterwards could it have proceeded to transfer the refugees to a safe third state for the final determination of the status and to repel those not eligible.

Similarly, the *Cap Anamur*, a German vessel owned by the homonym humanitarian organization, rescued on the high seas of the Mediterranean Sea 37 persons on 20 June 2004 and then sailed to the Italian

---

[62] N. Ronzitti, "Il passaggio inoffensivo nel mare territoriale e la Convenzione delle Nazioni Unite sul diritto del mare", *Riv. Dir. Int.* 68 (1985), 32 et seq. (37-39); R.R. Churchill/ A.V. Lowe, *The Law of the Sea*, 3rd edition, 1999, 85.

coast of Sicily. At 17 nautical miles from the shore, the Italian authorities ordered the vessel to stop. On 11 July, the master finally received the authorization to enter the territorial waters and to have access to the port, but not yet to disembark. The authorization for the disembarkation arrived only 24 hours after the access to the port. This incident was strongly criticized by the UNHCR[63] and the question of innocent passage arises here in the same way as in the *Tampa* case.

In the 21 days in which the *Cap Anamur* could not enter in the Italian waters, a lively debate started between the Home Affair Ministers of Italy, Germany and Malta about which country was responsible for the screening of the asylum requests presented by the irregular passengers[64]. Italy, the coastal state, and Germany, the flag state, argued that Malta, the alleged first port of arrival, was the responsible state pursuant to the criteria of attribution by Council regulation (EC) No. 343/2003, of 18 February 2003, *Establishing the Criteria and the Mechanisms for Determining the Member State responsible for Examining an Asylum Application Lodged in one of the Member States by a Third-Country National*[65]. Pursuant to article 10 of the regulation, if asylum-seekers crossed irregularly the border of a Member State and this can be proved, this Member State is responsible for the examination of the application. As highlighted by the European Commission, "generally speaking and by definition, a clandestine operation leaves no offi-

---

[63]   *UNHCR urges Disembarkation on Humanitarian Grounds*, UNHCR Briefing Notes of 9 July 2004; *UNHCR Welcomes Decision to allow Boat People to Disembark in Italy*, UNHCR Briefing Notes of 13 July 2004; *UNHCR Criticizes Handling of Cap Anamur Asylum Claims*, UNHCR Press Release of 23 July 2004; *UNHCR Expresses Strong Concern to Italian Authorities*, UNHCR Briefing Notes of 23 July 2004; *Handling of Cap Anamur Asylum Claims was Flawed, says UNHCR*, UNHCR News Stories of 23 July 2004; available at: <www.unhcr.org.>.

[64]   "La Cap Anamur non può attraccare", in: *Il Corriere della Sera* of 7 July 2004; "Italia e Germania accusano Malta", in: *Il Messaggero* of 12 July 2004. See also S. Trevisanut, "Le *Cap Anamur*: profiles de droit international et de droit de la mer", *Annuaire du Droit de la Mer* 9 (2004), 49 et seq.

[65]   See note 8. This regulation and Commission regulation (EC) No. 1560/2003, of 2 September 2003, laying down detailed rules for the application of Council Regulation (EC) No. 343/2003 (OJEC No. L 222/3 of 5 September 2003), have substituted the Dublin Convention of 1990 and they compose the so called "Dublin 2" system. S. Barbou des Places, *Le dispositif Dublin 2 ou les tribulations de la politique communautaire d'asile*, EUI Working Paper LAW No. 2004/6, available at: <www.iue.it.>.

cial traces"[66] and the alleged passage in La Valetta port was grounded on some passengers' testimonies; the logbook pages concerning the days in which this passage should have taken place were mysteriously lacking and the Maltese authorities did not receive any communication about the entry of irregular migrants in their port. Pursuant to article 50 UNCLOS, port waters are part of the internal waters of the coastal state that exercises its full sovereignty there, but the question of the effective control on foreign ships present in ports raises some practical difficulties because a vessel is a self-contained unit and coastal states generally cannot survey in detail all ships entering their internal waters without a well-founded doubt concerning the legality of their presence[67]. Consequently it is difficult to argue that the alleged passage in La Valetta port could consist of an entry into the Maltese territory – even if the vessel was in its internal waters[68].

The *Cap Anamur* case is also an example for transferring the maritime frontier into the internal waters. The access to the territory, in the meaning of entry in the jurisdiction of the coastal state, may be brought about by the authorized admission to the port waters or by disembarkation. This argument certainly does not apply to vessels participating in smuggling migrants and acting in such a way as to hide the moment of entry and disembarkation.

---

[66] *Commission Staff Working Paper: Evaluation of the Dublin Convention*, SEC(2001)756 of 13 June 2001, 6.

[67] Churchill/ Lowe, see note 62, 65; P. Daillier/ A. Pellet, *Droit international public*, 7th edition, 2002, 1155 et seq.; M. Giuliano/ T. Scovazzi/ T. Treves, *Diritto internazionale II*, 1983, 161 et seq. Coastal states cannot exercise their criminal and civil jurisdiction against foreign ships present in their territorial sea or ports except in the hypothesis provided in arts 27 and 28 UNCLOS.

[68] The *Cap Anamur* case also points out the perverted consequences of a system such as the one created by EC regulation 343/2003: to avoid the application of the stated criteria, asylum-seekers prefer to remain clandestine until they reach their desired host state; the set criteria are prejudicial for southern European states having extended maritime frontiers. R. Rossano, "Il regolamento comunitario sulla determinazione dello Stato membro competente ad esaminare la domanda di asilo", *Diritto Comunitario e degli Scambi Internazionali* 43 (2004), 371 et seq. (376); Trevisanut, see note 64, 55.

3. The Refusal of Access to Ports and of Disembarkation

Access to the territory is under the exclusive competence of the coastal state which decides on the entry of irregular passengers, evaluating and balancing the interests involved: the protection needed by the individuals, the security of the state or its simple unwillingness. Practice offers some examples of refusal of access to ports and of disembarkation of asylum-seekers – such as the above mentioned *Tampa* and *Cap Anamur* cases – in which the masters of the vessels were considered responsible for the passengers because they represented the legal authority on board. Two possible situations have, however, to be distinguished: either the irregular passengers are individuals rescued voluntarily by the vessel; or they are *stowaways*.

A *stowaway* is defined by the 1957 *Brussels Convention relating to Stowaways* which never entered into force, as:

"une personne qui, en un port quelconque ou en un lieu à sa proximité se dissimule dans un navire sans le consentement du propriétaire du navire ou du capitaine ou de toute autre personne ayant la responsabilité du navire et qui est à bord après que le navire a quitté ce port ou ce lieu" (article 1)[69].

International law does not regulate the question of the disembarkation of stowaways and the port state has no obligation to authorize it. Actually the port state can oblige the master of the vessel to keep stowaways on board. The question of the "arrest on board" was dealt with by French jurisdictions in 1997 in the *Ben Salem et Taznaret* case[70], concerning the refusal of disembarkation of two stowaways, from Morocco, in the port of Honfleur from a vessel sailing under Antiguan flag. The ship-owner, a German citizen, invoked a violation of his right of property and of the fundamental freedom of movement of the two unlawful passengers. The French tribunal concluded that the competent administration acted according to its prerogative but abused its authority because of the use of force in preventing disembarkation. It declared however:

---

[69] F. Payre, "Les passagers clandestins", Annuaire du Droit Maritime et Océanique 14 (1996), 277 et seq. (286 et seq.); A. Goy, "Le régime international du passager clandestin", *Annuaire du Droit de la Mer* 6 (2001), 169 et seq. (171 et seq.).

[70] Tribunal des conflits, 12 mai 1997, *Préfet de police de Paris c. Tribunal de grande instance de Paris* (*Ben Salem et Taznaret* case), A.F.D.I. 44 (1998), 684 et seq.; *Revue Française de Droit Administratif* 1997, Vol. I, 523 et seq.

"Que cette attitude (to avoid the disembarkation with the use of force) ait été de nature à porter atteinte à leur liberté d'aller et venir, qui est une liberté fondamentale, voilà qui n'est pas douteux, même si on peut relever (…) d'une part qu'aucun ordre de rétention à bord n'a véritablement été pris à leur encontre – mais la mesure prise revient bien au même – d'autre part qu'ils ont en définitive fait connaître qu'il choisissaient de rester sur ce navire et de tenter leur chance lors d'une prochaine escale"[71].

Bastid-Burdeau reminds us that the *"question de savoir si l'autorité locale peut (…) imposer au capitaine étranger la rétention à bord des passagers clandestins ressortit au seul droit interne"*[72]. The refusal of disembarkation of stowaways does not preclude the possibility of redirecting the vessel to another country and, in the *Ben Salem et Taznaret* case, the destination was left at the discretion of the master. The only limit consists in the principle of non-refoulement to the extent that the stowaways on board are asylum-seekers. The coastal state should then at least ascertain that in the new destination state the individual does not risk being subjected to persecution, torture or other inhuman and degrading treatments.

Moreover, such a case of voluntary redirection cannot be seen as arbitrary detention resulting from the refusal of disembarkation. On the contrary, in the *Tampa* case, an arbitral detention was found to exist by Australian jurisdiction because the migrants on board, most of them being asylum-seekers, were under the full and exclusive control of the Australian authorities[73]. Justice *North* of the Federal Court of Australia deemed that the 433 passengers of the *Tampa* were detained arbitrarily accordingly to the *habeas corpus* principle and requested the respondents, namely the Minister for Immigration and Multicultural Affairs, the Attorney General, the Minister of Defense and the Commonwealth of Australia, to release the passengers as soon as possible. Justice *North*

---

71   J. Arrighi de Casanova, "Les limites de la voie de fait (police des étrangers et liberté individuelle)", *Revue Française de Droit Administratif* 1997, Vol. I, 514 et seq.

72   G. Bastid-Burdeau, "Migrations clandestines et droit de la mer", in: *La mer et son droit, Mélanges offerts à Laurent Lucchini et Jean-Pierre Quéneudec*, 2003, 57 et seq. (64).

73   *Vadarlis v. Minister for Immigration and Multicultural Affairs and Others* (V 900 of 2001 FCA 1297) of 11 September 2001; "Refugees – Detention within Australian territorial sea – Pacific solution – Migration Act", *Austr. Yb. Int'l L.* 21 (2001), 263 et seq.

inferred the detention on the basis of an analysis of factual elements, among them that the Australian authorities unilaterally decided where the *Tampa* could go or not go and that the passengers were completely isolated on board. They were not consulted on the question of their transfer to New Zealand and Nauru. The trial judge thus affirmed that:

> "Where complete control over people and their destiny is exercised by others it cannot be said that the opportunity offered by those others is a reasonable escape from the custody in which they were held. The custody simply continues in the form chosen by those detaining the people restrained" (para. 17).

This judgment was then challenged on appeal and the Full Court of the Federal Court dismissed the decision and induced several critical opinions[74]. In particular it has to be pointed out that Australia did not comply with its duty deriving from the "first asylum" rule. No debate would have arisen if the coastal authorities had proceeded with the first screening of the passengers and then resettled them to New Zealand and Nauru for the final determination of their status. Because of their *de facto* detention, *Tampa* passengers were penalized for their unlawful entry into Australian waters and this is a breach of article 31 of the 1951 Refugee Convention[75]. In addition, Australia did not fulfill its obligations concerning the safety of life at sea.

Before analyzing the duty to render assistance and the obligation concerning the safety of life, the specificities raised by the contiguous zone require a brief excursion.

IV. The Specificity of the Contiguous Zone

Pursuant to article 33 UNCLOS, in the "contiguous zone", that is the maritime zone adjacent to a state's territorial sea, the coastal state may exercise the control necessary to: "(a) prevent infringement of its customs, fiscal, immigration or sanitary laws and regulations within its territory or territorial sea; (b) punish infringement of the above laws and

---

[74] *Ruddock and Others v. Vadarlis and Others* (2001) 66 A.L.D. 25 (V 1007 of 2001, FCA 1329) of 18 September 2001, para. 5, in which the Chief of Justice dissented on the admissibility of the appeal considering arbitrary the detention of the *Tampa* passengers. See also White, "(...) subsequent legal issues", see note 61, 254 et seq.

[75] Goodwin-Gill/ Adam, see note 6, 266.

regulations committed within its territory or territorial sea"[76]. The contiguous zone does not exist *ipso jure* but the coastal state has to proclaim it expressly. It cannot extend beyond 24 nautical miles from the baselines (article 33(2)). The contiguous zone is the only maritime zone not fully under the coastal state's jurisdiction for which UNCLOS provides some explicit powers in the migratory field.

But UNCLOS does not indicate any means for the delimitation of this zone in case of adjacent states separated by less then 48 nautical miles, i.e. the sum of the maximum extension of two facing contiguous zones. Some authors[77] suggest that, considering the administrative nature of the powers attributed to the coastal state by article 33 UNCLOS, i.e. prevention and repression, these powers may be exercised concurrently by the neighboring states. Thus the question of the delimitation would be redundant[78]. Consequently, the contiguous zones of two states may overlap. This approach is disputable considering, for example, the patrols of a state carried out in a maritime zone under its jurisdiction but also under the jurisdiction of the contiguous state. Conflicts of jurisdiction can easily arise[79]. Moreover the extension of

[76] Concerning the evolution of the concept and the practice related to the contiguous zone, A.V. Lowe, "The Development of the Concept of the Contiguous Zone", *BYIL* 52 (1981), 109 et seq.; L. Caflisch, "La délimitation des espaces marins entre Etats dont les côtes se font face ou sont adjacentes", in: Dupuy/ Vignes, see note 49, 373 et seq. (392 et seq.); Churchill/ Lowe, see note 62, 132 et seq.; R.J. Dupuy, "La mer sous compétence nationale", in: Dupuy/ Vignes, see note 49, 219 et seq. (236 et seq.); L. Lucchini/ M. Voelckel, *Droit de la mer*, Tome 1, 1990, 195 et seq.

[77] Caflisch, see note 76, 392; L. Lucchini/ M. Voelckel, *Droit de la mer*, Tome 2, Vol. 1, 1996, 78.

[78] Other answers are given to the lack of delimitation provisions in UNCLOS concerning the contiguous zone by Churchill/ Lowe, see note 62, 136; Daillier/ Pellet, see note 67, 1175; H. Pazarci, "Le concept de zone contiguë dans la convention de droit de la mer de 1982", *RBDI* 18 (1984-1985), 249 et seq.; J. Symonides, "Origin and Legal Essence of the Contiguous Zone", *ODILA* 20 (1989), 203 et seq.

[79] This problem was pointed out before the Italian Parliament during the session of the Committee for the fulfilment of the Schengen Agreement, on 29 September 2004, by Scovazzi, *Indagini conoscitive e documentazioni legislative n. 19, Gestione comune delle frontiere e contrasto all'immigrazione clandestina in Europa*, Roma, 2005, 163 et seq. See also T. Scovazzi, "La lotta all'immigrazione clandestina alla luce del diritto internazionale del mare", *Diritto, Immigrazione e Cittadinanza* (2003), 48 et seq. Italy has not proclaimed a contiguous zone yet, notwithstanding the usefulness of such

the contiguous zone cannot be more than 24 miles; it can certainly be less. For these reasons a precise delimitation of the space where coastal state authorities have to perform their function of prevention and repression is preferable and enhances the efficiency and the functional nature of the contiguous zone.

The contiguous zone has an exclusively functional nature[80] as supported by the wording of article 33(1) and the use of "necessary" to qualify the controls that the coastal state may exercise in the listed fields. Controls in migratory issues highlight the contrast between two legal regimes applicable in this maritime zone. On the one hand, the coastal state has the sovereign prerogative to exercise its powers of prevention and repression in relation to violations of its domestic immigration law. On the other hand, the same state must comply with international obligations deriving from the customary principle of *non-refoulement* and from the right to seek asylum guaranteed by article 14 UDHR. In this respect, the exercise of the preventive function raises the following problems.

In the contiguous zone the practice of interception and redirection of vessels transporting unlawful migrants, among whom there may well be some asylum-seekers, is encompassed in the prevention powers pursuant to article 33(1)(a). In fact unlawful migration may only be committed upon crossing a national border. At sea this generally corresponds to the external limit of the territorial sea[81]. Any intervention of the authorities in the contiguous zone in such a situation cannot be justified by the attributed repressive powers. The practice of the intercep-

---

an act for a country constantly facing unlawful migrants arrival by sea; in particular this would give an incontestable legal basis to competent authorities' operations accomplished beyond the territorial waters.

[80] Treves, see note 49, 706, where the author reminds that: "la nature juridique de la zone contiguë est différente de celle de la zone économique exclusive et du plateau continental. Dans ces dernières zones, l'Etat côtier a des droits souverains et des droits de juridiction (...), tandis que les pouvoirs reconnus sans discussion dans la zone contiguë ne sont que des pouvoirs de police". See also I.A. Shearer, "The Development of International Law with Respect to the Law Enforcement Roles of Navies and Coast Guards in Peacetime", in M.N. Schmitt/ L.C. Green (eds), *The Law of Armed Conflict: Into the Next Millennium*, 1998, 429 et seq. (434).

[81] This border can be affected by the factual elements of migrants arrival (as remarked above, see under III.) and consequently shift to the place where the coastal state effectively exercises its jurisdiction, following the factual elements of the migrants arrival, as remarked above, see under II.

tion and redirection is not clearly provided for by the wording of the article[82], but it is not forbidden either.

The key word to identify the limit of the possible actions of the coastal state in the contiguous zone is "necessary". The interception and redirection may be considered lawful when necessary for the protection of interests. Indeed, the protection of a minor interest, as preventing a violation of its migration law, does not justify any kind of intervention. This has already been affirmed in 1935 in the *I'm Alone* case[83] concerning goods smuggling. Consequently, once the coastal state exercises its jurisdictional powers intercepting and redirecting the vessel, it must consider whether its action may put the passengers of the concerned vessel at risk of persecution, torture or other inhuman treatments. The need of proportionality emerges in relation to the operations accomplished by states authorities on the high seas for contrasting unlawful migration.

V. The Principle of *Non-Refoulement* put to the Test in Naval Operations on the High Seas

1. The Freedom of the High Seas and the Safety of Life at Sea

High seas are defined negatively by article 86 UNCLOS as "all parts of the sea that are not included in the exclusive economic zone, in the territorial sea or in the internal waters of a State, or in the archipelagic waters of an archipelagic State". High seas are characterized by the prohibition of appropriation (article 89 UNCLOS) and the freedom of the high seas does not imply the absence of rules but rather indicates that

---

[82] "[T]he special jurisdictional rights which a State can exercise in the adjacent area of the contiguous zone do not clearly include the interception of vessels believed to be carrying asylum seekers", Goodwin-Gill/ Adam, see note 6, 276.

[83] A Canadian vessel sunk after the hot pursuit of two US navy ships because it was suspected of liquor smuggling during the prohibition period. Canada v. United States, 5 January 1935, *RIAA* Vol. III, 1609 et seq.; W.C. Dennis, "The Sinking of the *I'm Alone*", *AJIL* 23 (1929), 351 et seq.; C.C. Hyde, "The Adjustment of the *I'm Alone*", *AJIL* 29 (1935), 296 et seq.; G.G. Fitzmaurice, "The Case of the I'm Alone", *BYIL* 17 (1936), 82 et seq.

freedoms are granted equally to all states. Article 87 UNCLOS gives a non-exhaustive list[84] of freedoms:

"1. The high seas are open to all States, whether coastal or land-locked. Freedom of the high seas is exercised under the conditions laid down by this Convention and by other rules of international law. It comprises, *inter alia*, both for coastal and land-locked States:

(a) freedom of navigation;

(b) freedom of overflight;

(c) freedom to lay submarine cables and pipelines, subject to Part VI;

(d) freedom to construct artificial islands and other installations permitted under international law, subject to Part VI;

(e) freedom of fishing, subject to the conditions laid down in section 2;

(f) freedom of scientific research, subject to Parts VI and XIII.

2. These freedoms shall be exercised by all States with due regard for the interests of other States in their exercise of the freedom of the high seas, and also with due regard for the rights under this Convention with respect to activities in the Area".

The freedom of navigation encompasses two principles: the vessel sailing under the flag of any state has the right to navigate[85]; the navigation of a vessel sailing under the flag of one state should not be hampered by other states. A vessel may sail under the flag of only one state which exercises its exclusive jurisdiction (article 92(1))[86], except in the

---

[84]   "There are high-seas activities alleged by some States to constitute freedoms, but denied this status by other States. The principle on which such disputes should be resolved is that any use compatible with the status of the high seas (...) should be admitted as a freedom unless it is excluded by some specific rule of law", Churchill/ Lowe, see note 62, 206.

[85]   Article 90 UNCLOS, *Right of Navigation*: "Every State, whether coastal or land-locked, has the right to sail ships flying its flag on the high seas"; this implies the equal access to high seas for any state. D. Momtaz, "The High Seas", in: R.J. Dupuy/ D. Vignes (eds), *A Handbook on the Law of the Sea*, Vol. 1, 1991, 396 et seq.

[86]   The vessel sailing under the flag of more than one state is considered a vessel without nationality (article 92(2)), and consequently does not enjoy the protection of any state and the freedom of navigation.

cases explicitly provided by the Convention[87] or in accordance with another agreement stating expressly the exception[88].

Article 98 UNCLOS provides the duty to render assistance in the following terms:

"Every State shall require the master of a ship flying its flag, in so far as he can do so without serious danger to the ship, the crew or the passengers:

(a) to render assistance to *any person found at sea in danger of being lost*;

(b) to *proceed with all possible speed to the rescue of persons in distress*, if informed of their need of assistance, in so far as such action may reasonably be expected of him;

(c) after a collision, to render assistance to the other ship, its crew and its passengers and, where possible, to inform the other ship of the name of his own ship, its port of registry and the nearest port at which it will call". (emphasis added)

Even if this article is located in the UNCLOS section concerning the high seas, the duty to render assistance must be considered as applicable in all maritime zones[89]. This rule is closely connected with the principle of safety of life at sea which is the only real limit to the enjoyment of navigation freedom[90]. Consequently, and because of its

---

[87] Article 100 (repression of piracy); article 110 (Right of visit); article 111 (right to hot pursuit).

[88] Article 110 states: "Except where acts of interference derive from powers conferred by treaty, a warship which encounters on the high seas a foreign ship, other than a ship entitled to complete immunity in accordance with articles 95 and 96, is not justified in boarding it unless there is reasonable ground for suspecting that: (...)".

[89] During the negotiation of UNCLOS, there was a debate on the wording of this article (J.K. Jr. Gamble, *Law of the Sea: Neglected Issues*, 1979, 261) but pursuant to its literal interpretation ("any person found at sea" and not "any person found on the high seas") in the light of the object and the contest, as requested by article 31 of the 1969 Vienna Convention (see note 55), it was noticed that this duty could not disappear just because of the crossing of a maritime frontier. M.H. Nordquist (ed.), *UNCLOS 1982 A Commentary*, Vol. III, 1993, 170 et seq.

[90] "[D]ans la plupart des cas, l'élément décisif qui détermine les priorités entre les activités en mer (...) est la sauvegarde de la vie humaine"; Treves, see note 49, 717. Also Pallis (see note 26, 335) affirmed: "Explicit links have

repetition in treaty and domestic law and of states practice, the duty to render assistance is generally recognized as a principle of customary law.

During the Indochinese crisis, however, the duty to rescue was still considered as a treaty obligation and thus binding only states parties. In particular, two instruments applicable only in the territorial waters were invoked: the 1910 Brussels *Convention internationale pour l'unification de certaines règles en matière d'assistance et de sauvetage maritimes et protocole de signature* and the 1974 Convention for the Safety of Life at Sea (SOLAS)[91]. Subsequent to non-rescue at sea incidents, the problem of identifying who was under an obligation to undertake rescue operations emerged. Whereupon the *International Convention on Maritime Search and Rescue* (SAR Convention) was adopted in 1979[92].

The SAR Convention aims at creating an international system coordinating rescue operations guaranteeing their efficiency and safety. States parties are thus invited to conclude SAR agreements with neighboring states for regulating and coordinating the operations and the services of rescuing in the maritime zone delimited in the agreement. The Secretary General of the International Maritime Organization (IMO), as depositary of the SAR Convention, must be notified of any modification of these agreements. The 1989 *International Convention on Salvage*[93] was elaborated in the framework of the IMO and has substituted the 1910 Brussels Convention mentioned above. The 1989 Convention affirms in article 10 the duty to render assistance:

"1. Every master is bound, so far as he can do so without serious danger to his vessel and persons thereon, to render assistance to any person in danger of being lost at sea.

2. The States Parties shall adopt the measures necessary to enforce the duty set out in paragraph 1".

This duty was then reaffirmed by the IMO Maritime Safety Council (MSC) in 2001 in a circular relating to unsafe practices concerning the transport of migrants at sea[94]. Paragraph 2.3 of the circular defines un-

---

been drawn between the concept of distress and the preservation of human life".

[91]   UNTS Vol. 1184 No. 1861.

[92]   UNTS Vol. 1405 No. 23489.

[93]   UNTS Vol. 1953 No. 33479.

[94]   *Interim Measures for Combating Unsafe Practices Associated with the Trafficking or Transport of Migrants by Sea*, MCS.1/Circ.896/Rev.1, 19 June

safe practices as any action contrary to the safety of navigation and any action constituting a danger to life or health of persons. Moreover the circular obliges states, and thus vessels sailing under their flag, to render assistance. The undertaking of rescue operations does not exhaust the duty to render assistance which is only fully met after the disembarkation of the rescued people in a place of safety. The disembarkation in a place of safety corresponds to the need to find a place of refuge for the asylum-seekers rescued at sea – again, in compliance with the principle of *non-refoulement*.

2. The Respect of the Principle of *Non-Refoulement* in the Course of Search and Rescue Operations

During the general revision of the IMO SAR system[95], the MSC faced in particular the question of the place where rescued people disembark, without distinction based on their status, nationality or place of finding. The MSC adopted two resolutions amending both SOLAS Convention[96] and SAR Convention[97], which entered into force on 1 July 2006, and aimed at guaranteeing assistance to rescued people and to minimize negative consequences for the rescuing ship. Consequently, article 4.1-1 SOLAS Convention has been amended as follows:

> "Contracting Governments shall co-ordinate and co-operate to en-sure that masters of ships providing assistance by embarking per-sons in distress at sea are released from their obligations with mini-mum further deviation from the ships' intended voyage, provided that releasing the master of the ship from the obligations under the current regulation does not further endanger the safety of life at sea. The Contracting Government responsible for the search and rescue

---

2001, available at: <www.imo.org.>. As to how and why this circular was adopted, A. Kirchner/ L. Schiano di Pepe, "International Attempts to Con-clude a Convention to Combat Illegal Migration", *International Journal of Refugee Law* 10 (1998), 662 et seq. MSC acts have no binding value, but just recommendatory. The content of this circular has been integrated al-most entirely in the Protocol against the Smuggling of Migrants by Land, Sea and Air to the UN Convention against Transnational Organized Crime (A/RES/55/25 of 15 November 2000) and thus binds the States parties.

[95] *Maritime Safety Council – 78th session: 12-21 May 2004, Opening address by the Secretary-General.*

[96] Resolution MSC.153 (78) of 20 May 2004.

[97] Resolution MSC.155 (78) of 20 May 2004.

region in which such assistance is rendered shall exercise primary responsibility for ensuring such co-ordination and co-operation occurs, so that survivors assisted are disembarked from the assisting ship and delivered to a *place of safety*, taking into account the particular circumstances of the case and guidelines developed by the Organization. *In these cases the relevant Contracting Governments shall arrange for such disembarkation to be effective as soon as reasonably practicable*". (emphasis added)

Similarly, article 3.1.9 SAR Convention now reads:

"Parties shall co-ordinate and co-operate to ensure that masters of ships providing assistance by embarking persons in distress at sea are released from their obligations with minimum further deviation from the ships' intended voyage, provided that releasing the master of the ship from the obligations does not further endanger the safety of life at sea. The Party responsible for the search and rescue region in which such assistance is rendered shall exercise primary responsibility for ensuring such co-ordination and co-operation occurs, so that survivors assisted are disembarked from the assisting ship and delivered to a *place of safety*, taking into account the particular circumstances of the case and guidelines developed by the Organization. *In these cases, the relevant Parties shall arrange for such disembarkation to be effective as soon as reasonably practicable*" (emphasis added).

According to the MSC Guidelines[98], a "place of safety" means a location where the rescue operations can be considered completed. Pursuant to principle 6.14 of the Guidelines, even the rescue unit can be the place of safety, but only provisionally. In fact the text insists on the role that the flag state and the coastal state should play stepping in for the master of the rescuing vessel[99]. Principle 6.13 provides:

"An assisting ship should not be considered a place of safety based solely on the fact that the survivors are no longer in immediate danger once aboard the ship. (...) Even if the ship is capable of safely accommodating the survivors and may serve as a temporary place of

---

[98]   *Guidelines on the Treatment of Persons Rescued at Sea*, Resolution MSC.167 (78) of 20 May 2004.

[99]   Stressing the need for co-operation between the flag and the coastal state, the IMO aims at avoiding the repetition of a case such as the Tampa in which "Norway did not want to recognize any flag state responsibility over asylum-seekers. In turn, Australia did not want to assume the entire burden as a coastal state", Baillet, see note 61, 759.

safety, it should be relieved of this responsibility as soon as alternative arrangements can be made".

Moreover the state, in whose SAR zone the operation took place, has the duty to provide or, at least, to secure a place of safety for the rescued people (principle 2.5). In a case such as *Tampa*, the rescuing vessel could have been considered a provisional place of safety. But the rescue operation could not have been considered completed because of the excessive number of passengers and their sanitary conditions. However, assuming these provisions had been in force at the time of the *Tampa* case, principles 6.13 and 2.5 could be interpreted as supporting the behavior of Australian authorities which stepped in for the master as soon as they reached an agreement with New Zealand and Nauru. Consequently, they acted in compliance with the duty to render assistance, even if they did not authorize the access into the port.

The MSC Guidelines state:

"The need to avoid disembarkation in territories where the lives and freedoms of those alleging a well-founded fear of persecution would be threatened is a consideration in the case of asylum-seekers and refugees recovered at sea" (principle 6.17).

The coastal state shall respect the principle of *non-refoulement* of asylum-seekers and refugees while performing its duty to safe life at sea. The principle of *non-refoulement* does not apply only in consideration of the access to territorial waters or ports, but also in the choice of the place of safety, i.e. not only concerning the rejection at the maritime frontier, but also concerning redirection operations, either as the consequence of a rescue operation or of interdiction program.

Recently the IMO elaborated a document entitled "Rescue at Sea, A Guide to principles and practice as applied to migrants and refugees"[100] in co-operation with the UNHCR, in which shipmasters are invited – for cases in which people rescued at sea claim asylum – to "alert the closest RCC (Rescue Co-ordination Centre); contact the UNHCR; [to] not ask for disembarkation in the country of origin or from which the individuals fled; [to] not share personal information regarding the asylum-seekers with the authorities of that country, or with others who might convey this information to those authorities" (page 10). It is regrettable that similar invitations are not repeated in the document con-

---

[100] Document available on the websites of both organizations <www.imo.org> <www.unhcr.org>.

cerning actions that have to be taken by governments and RCCs (page 11).

3. The Naval Interdiction Programs and the Problem of Diverting Vessels

Bearing in mind that a definition of interception does not exist in international law and that it can be identified on the basis of state practice, the UNHCR Executive Committee has defined interception "as encompassing all measures applied by a State, outside its national territory, in order to prevent, interrupt or stop the movement of persons without the required documentation crossing international borders by land, air or sea, and making their way to the country of prospective destination"[101]. The practice of naval interdiction on the high seas consists of the action of one state or more, undertaken on the basis of an international agreement, aimed at exercising the right of visit in relation to criminal activities not listed in article 110 UNCLOS[102], performed by ships without nationality or by vessels sailing the flag of a state or a group of states. In this latter case, the interested flag state usually participates in the conclusion of the agreement related thereto[103].

In the migratory field, several interdiction programs have been created to prevent and obstruct irregular flows. The most famous is doubtlessly the United States interdiction program with Haiti because it is the only one which has been brought before of the US Supreme Court con-

---

[101] Executive Committee, *Interception of Asylum-seekers and refugees: The International Framework and Recommendation for a Comprehensive Approach*, EC/50/CRP.17 of 9 June 2000, para. 10.

[102] The possibility to conclude such an agreement is provided by article 110(1): "Except where acts of interference derive from powers conferred by treaty (…)". See Churchill/ Lowe, see note 62, 218; A.M. Syrigos, "Developments on the Interdiction of Vessels on the High Seas", in: A. Strati/ M. Gavouneli/ N. Skourtos (eds), *Unresolved Issues and New Challenges to the Law of the Sea*, 2006, 166 et seq.

[103] Of course this does not happen when the interdiction programme aimed at sanctioning the flag state, as in an embargo situation. C.Q. Christol/ C.R. Davis, "Maritime Quarantine: The naval interdiction of offensive weapons and associated material to Cuba", *Journal of Inter-American Studies* 4 (1962), 525 et seq.

cerning its legality in relation to the right of asylum, and in particular to the principle of *non-refoulement*[104].

On 23 September 1981, the United States concluded an agreement with Haiti, then ruled by President Duvalier, pursuant to which they established "a cooperative program of *selective interdiction and return* to Haiti of certain Haitian migrants and vessels involved in illegal transport of persons coming from Haiti" (emphasis added)[105]. Six days after this agreement US President R. Reagan issued Executive Order No. 12.324[106] suspending the entry of irregular aliens coming from the high seas and ordering the Coast Guard to intercept vessels and to redirect them to their port of origin. Aliens were submitted to the screening process on board the naval unit and those found not eligible for refugee status were sent back to Haiti. Within ten years United States authorities exercised interdiction concerning about 25,000 Haitians[107].

After the coup against Haitian elected President B. Aristide, on 30 September 1991, arrivals from the island increased and the United States government suspended the interdiction program for a few weeks. On November 1991, interdictions at sea restarted and, because of the ever increasing number of migrants, the US military base of Guantanamo (Cuba) was opened and used as centre for the screening process. On 24 May 1992, US President, G. Bush, adopted Executive Order No.

---

[104] It does not mean that the other interdiction programmes did not or do not threat refugees international protection, as the European "pre-border operations" carried on under the monitoring of the European Agency for the Management of the Operative Cooperation at the External Borders of the Member Sates of the European Union, the so called Frontex (Council Regulation (EC) 2007/2004 of 26 October 2004, OJEC No. L 349/1 of 25 November 2004). See also under:< www.frontex.europa.eu>. See S. Trevisanut, "L'Europa e l'immigrazione clandestine via mare: FRONTEX e diritto internazionale", *Diritto dell'Unione Europea,* 2008, 367 et seq. (382 et seq.).

[105] *Agreement to Stop Clandestine Migration of Residents of Haiti to the United States, ILM* 20 (1981), 1198 et seq. See in this respect also the article of J. Leininger, "Democracy and UN Peace - Keeping-Conflict Resolution through State-Building and Democracy Promotion in Haiti", *Max Planck UNYB* 10 (2006), 465 et seq.

[106] *AJIL* 76 (1982), 376 et seq.

[107] G.W. Palmer, "Guarding Coast: Alien Migrant Interdiction Operations at Sea", in: M.N. Schmitt (ed.), *The Law of Military Operations, Liber Amicorum Professor Jack Grunawalt,* 1998, 157 et seq. (165).

12.807, known as the "Kennebunkport Order"[108], suspending the screening process and ordering the Coast Guard to redirect immediately intercepted Haitians. Executive Order No. 12.807 was the basis for the claim against the US administration brought before US jurisdictions by two non-profit organizations defending the interests of Haitian migrants. The proceedings came to an end with the US Supreme Court judgment of 21 June 1993[109] which did not find the actions of the Coast Guards illegal. The Court's reasoning presents several interesting aspects in relation to the interpretation of the principle of *non-refoulement*[110].

First, the US authorities forcibly diverted intercepted vessels to their port of origin, preventing them from the possibility of seeking refuge in other countries of the region, such as Cuba, Jamaica or the Bahamas. In this concern, Judge Blackmun, in his Dissenting Opinion, pointed out that:

> "The refugees attempting to escape from Haiti do not claim a right of admission to this country [the United States]. They do not even argue that the Government has no right to intercept their boats. They demand only that the United States, land of refugees and guardian of freedom, cease forcibly driving them to detention, abuse, and death"[111].

---

[108] The Kennebunkport Order was not modified by the successive US administration and thus it is still in force. Consequently, and unfortunately, the declaration of US President G.W. Bush, quoted at the beginning of this paper, is less surprising, see note 1.

[109] Supreme Court of United States, *Sale v. Haitian Centres Council, Inc.*, 21 June 1993, *ILM* 32 (1993), 1039 et seq.

[110] "The judgement of the Supreme Court attempted to confer domestic 'legality' on the practice of returning individuals to their country of origin, irrespective of their claim to have a well-founded fear of persecution. That decision could not and did not alter the State's international obligations"; Goodwin-Gill/ Adam, see note 6, 248. See also UNHCR, "Brief Amicus Curiae", *International Journal of Refugee Law* 6 (1994), 85.

[111] "Dissenting Opinion of Judge Blackmun", *ILM* 32 (1993), 1058 et seq.; G. S. Goodwin-Gill, "The Haitian *Refoulement* Case: A Comment", *International Journal of Refugee Law* 6 (1994), 103 et seq.; T.D. Jones, "Aliens – interdiction of Haitians on high seas – definition of "return" under U.S. statute – extraterritorial effect of statute", *AJIL* 88 (1994), 114 et seq. (122). See also L.D. Rosenberg, "The Courts and Interception: The United Sates' Interdiction Experience and its Impact on Refugees and Asylum Seekers", *Georgetown Immigration Law Journal* 17 (2002-2003), 199 et seq.

On its side, the Supreme Court excluded the application of article 33 of the 1951 Refugee Convention beyond the territory of the state, arguing in a somewhat original manner:

> "If the first paragraph [of Article 33][112] did apply on the high seas, no nation could invoke the second paragraph's exception[113] with respect to an alien there: an alien intercepted on the high seas is in no country at all. If Article 33.1 applied extraterritorially, therefore, Article 33.2 would create an absurd anomaly: dangerous aliens on the high seas would be entitled to the benefits of 33.1 while those residing in the country that sought to expel them would not"[114].

The Supreme Court reached this conclusion on the basis of a restrictive interpretation of the term "return" in article 33(1) invoking that the French word *"refouler"* encompasses terms as "repulse", "repel", "drive back" and "expel". Thus "return" means "a defensive act of resistance or exclusion at a border rather than an act of transporting someone to a particular destination" and, in the context of article 33(1), it "means to repulse rather then to 'reinstate'"[115]. But the term "repulse" itself encompasses the term "reject" and "repel", actions not needing necessarily the prior entry into the territory. Consequently to refuse to apply the principle of *non-refoulement* on the high seas seems to be unjustified[116].

Commenting this case, the UNHCR expressed its point of view in relation to the geographical scope of the principle and affirmed:

> "The obligation not to return refugees to persecution arises irrespective of whether governments are acting within or outside their borders. UNHCR bases its position on the language and structure of the treaties' overriding humanitarian purpose, which is to protect

---

[112] Article 33(1): "No Contracting State shall expel or return ("refouler") a refugee in any manner whatsoever to the frontiers of territories where his life or freedom would be threatened on account of his race, religion, nationality, membership of a particular social group or political opinion".

[113] Article 33(2): "The benefit of the present provision may not, however, be claimed by a refugee whom there are reasonable grounds for regarding as a danger to the security of the country in which he is, or who, having been convicted by a final judgment of a particularly serious crime, constitutes a danger to the community of that country".

[114] *ILM* 32 (1993), 1053.

[115] *ILM* 32 (1993), 1054.

[116] I. Castrogiovanni, "Sul *refoulement* dei profughi haitiani intercettati in acque internazionali", *Riv. Dir. Int.* 77 (1994), 474 et seq. (478).

especially vulnerable individuals from persecution. UNHCR's position is also based on the broader human right of refugees to seek asylum from persecution as set out in the Universal Declaration of Human Rights"[117].

The fact that the principle of *non-refoulement* applies on the high seas does not mean that the interdicting state has to host the intercepted migrants; it has solely not to preclude them from seeking asylum elsewhere and, thus, not to force them back to their country of origin. Consequently to return intercepted refugees vessels to the high seas does not necessarily imply a violation of the principle of *non-refoulement*.

Interception practice has become "an ever-expanding array of *non-entrée* policies which rely on law to deny entry to refugees"[118] and this trend is quite explicitly admitted by the US authorities which affirm "[i]nterdicting migrants at sea means they can be quickly returned to their countries of origin without the costly processes required if they successfully enter the United States"[119].

European countries are less explicit even if the joint patrols carried out in the Mediterranean sea in the framework of the EU agency Frontex[120] have a *modus operandi* similar to interdiction programs, but they are called "pre-border operations". According to the Annual Report of the Frontex[121], it appears that in operations HERA II and HERA III[122] the joint patrols had the task to interdict irregular migrant ships coming from Mauritania and Senegal and then to divert them to their port of origin or, when necessary, to the Canary Islands. European units even

---

[117] *ILM* 32 (1993), 1215.

[118] Hathaway, see note 6, 299-301.

[119] "Alien Migrant Interdiction" page of the website of the US Coast Guard, available at: <http://www.uscg.mil/hq/g-o/g-opl/AMIO/AMIO.htm>.

[120] See note 104. Joint patrols are organized pursuant to article 3 of EC Regulation 2007/2004.

[121] *Frontex Annual Report 2006, Coordination of Intelligence Driven Operational Cooperation at EU Level to Strengthen Security at External Borders*, 12, see also:<www.frontex.europa.eu.>.

[122] Operation HERA started in July 2006 on request of Spain because of the increasing number of arrivals of migrants by sea to the Canary Islands. Finland, Italy and Portugal participated at this operation with some naval units and aircrafts. Information concerning HERA and the other joint patrol programmes carried on since 2006 under the supervision of the Frontex are available on the Agency website.

had the right to pursue their mission in the territorial waters of these states, thus impeding migrant vessels to leave Mauritanian and Senegalese seas[123]. Moreover, the report affirmed that "[d]uring the operational phase HERA II, 3887 illegal immigrants on 57 *Cayucos* (small fishing boats) were intercepted close to [the] African coast and diverted". But the same document does not indicate whether the intercepted people were submitted to a screening process by the patrols or in the countries where they were redirected. Moreover, pursuant to the few available data, the migrants were diverted to their port of origin, but it is not possible to find out which port this was.

VI. Concluding Remarks

Several authors were taken aback by the United States practice of interception and redirection at sea in the Caribbean seas, and by the Australian excision of territories, but very little attention has been pointed to the pre-border operations of the EU Member States carried out under the cover of Frontex. But, as demonstrated above, the operational dynamics and the final consequences for the asylum-seekers are precariously similar. The attention of the media and of the interested governments is instead focused on avoiding the arrivals. What is most disappointing is the remaining lack of information and transparency regarding joint patrol operations within the framework of Frontex.

What is known for sure is that migrants screened-in on the EU territory can enjoy fully procedural rights guaranteed by European law; while the unlucky migrants interdicted in the territorial waters of the third state, participating in the program or on high seas, must submit to the domestic law of that state, considered safe by the European institutions.

As in the *Tampa* case, the practice of forced redirection of asylum-seekers violates the right to seek asylum guaranteed by article 14 UDHR and protected by the "temporary refuge" regime and the principle of *non-refoulement*, whose application in the different maritime

---

[123] At the moment of operation, it appears that Frontex did not have official relations with these two third states. According to the known information, the patrols in their territorial sea were carried on pursuant to two agreements concluded by Spain with Mauritania and Senegal. This raises some questions about the legality of the operations because of the participation of non Spanish units; Trevisanut, see note 104, 381.

zones, even the high seas, could not be challenged once states decide to exercise their sovereign powers, their effective jurisdiction[124].

However, as noted above, refugee protection and states' interests pursuant to the law of the sea are not completely incompatible. In fact, the principle of safety of life at sea permits guaranteeing to boat people minimum protection standards, which are completed by the non rejection at the frontier dimension of the *non-refoulement* principle for asylum-seekers. Moreover, "when properly and duly applied, the legal, policy and operational instruments of the institution of asylum and international refugee protection can yield strong dividends for national safety and security"[125]. In this way refugee law can even be a tool for states to encourage border controls to be positively perceived by public opinion and to thereby improve the management of irregular immigration[126].

---

[124] Hathaway, see note 6, 335; UNCHR, see note 38, para. 43.

[125] UNHCR, *Background Paper (…)* see note 45, para. 13.

[126] Hathaway, see note 10, 99-100.

The United Nations Declaration on the Rights of Indigenous Peoples and the Protection of Indigenous Rights in Brazil

Fabiana de Oliveira Godinho

I. Introduction

The adoption of the United Nations Declaration on the Rights of Indigenous Peoples (hereinafter UN Declaration) in September 2007[1] is the most recent and advanced result of the progressive efforts to establish an international regime for the protection of indigenous peoples in the last decades.[2]

Despite being nonbinding, the Declaration is intended to summarize the minimum standard of rights and principles, which are necessary to provide for indigenous peoples worldwide a life of physical and cultural integrity and autonomy. For this purpose, it combines established principles of international law, especially the ones already recognized in in-

---

[1]   A/RES/61/295 of 13 September 2007.
[2]   For an overview of these endeavors see R. Wolfrum, *The Protection of Indigenous Peoples in International Law*, 1995.

ternational human rights instruments and in the ILO Convention concerning Indigenous and Tribal Peoples in Independent Countries of 1989 (ILO Convention No. 169),[3] with new formulas to better recognize the specific realities of indigenous peoples. One of the main innovations of the Declaration is the recognition of the legal personality of indigenous peoples, and the respective entitlement of collective and individual rights, as well as the right to self-determination. It is hoped that the Declaration will build the basis for a more "harmonious and cooperative" relation between states and their indigenous peoples in the accommodation of these peoples' rights. Although there was a large consensus[4] on the general content of the Declaration, ensuring its implementation within the states will be the challenge for the next years.

One of the states which took an active part in the discussions and elaboration of the Declaration was Brazil. The establishment of international principles regarding indigenous peoples indeed concerns this country, whose population includes more than 460,000 indigenous people, gathered in 225 societies and speaking about 180 languages and dialects.[5] Until the adoption of the Brazilian Constitution of 1988, this population was officially treated from the perspective of its necessary assimilation and integration in the "developed" society. Indigenous groups' conditions were so far only dealt with in the Statute of the Indian, a Federal Law enacted in 1973,[6] which ruled the progressive process of "civilization" under the tutelage of a specific federal organ, the National Foundation for Indigenous Affairs (FUNAI), until the final integration in the "developed" society.[7] This approach was officially abandoned in the Constitution of 1988, which recognizes the diversity within the national society and grants to indigenous groups and their members a variety of special individual and collective rights for the protection and promotion of their distinct identity and habitat.

---

[3]   *ILM* 28 (1989), 1382 et seq.

[4]   The UN Declaration was adopted with 143 votes in favor, 4 votes against (Australia, Canada, New Zealand and the United States) and 11 abstentions (Azerbaijan, Bangladesh, Bhutan, Burundi, Colombia, Georgia, Kenya, Nigeria, the Russian Federation, Samoa, Ukraine).

[5]   Information provided by FUNAI see under <www.funai.gov.br>. The organ takes into account solely the individuals living in indigenous territories but stresses the existence of up to 190,000 indigenous living in the cities and other 62 references of isolated or not-contacted individuals and groups.

[6]   Federal Law No. 6.001 of 19 December 1973.

[7]   Especially in arts 1 to 11 of the Statute. For an overview on this tutelage, see H.G. Barreto, *Direitos Indígenas: Vetores Constitucionais*, 2004, 38-43.

Since then, policies regarding the indigenous population in Brazil have oscillated between the development of special measures for the guarantee of their constitutional rights, and compliance with national and private interests affected by the recognition of these rights.

In 2002, Brazil ratified the ILO Convention No. 169.[8] Five years later, just after the adoption of the Declaration by the General Assembly, Brazil announced the so-called "Social Agenda for the Indigenous Peoples in Brazil"[9] which will be implemented between the years 2008 and 2010. This initiative consists of inter-ministerial measures for the amelioration and enforcement of indigenous rights in the context of three central goals: protection of indigenous territories; general promotion of their cultures; improvement of their quality of life. The demarcation of about 127 indigenous territories and the proper accommodation of the non-indigenous population currently living therein is planned. Furthermore, there are also measures to combat environmental degradation in different areas (about 10.000 ha) that are considered to be of major importance for the life of indigenous communities. The general promotion of their cultures will entail the documentation and strengthening of indigenous languages, especially of the 20 or so native dialects which are in danger of extinction. It also embraces the delineation of further programs and activities aimed at the development of the self-sustainability of indigenous territories. Finally, the proposals regarding the improvement of the quality of life of indigenous peoples stress the improvement of access to and documentation of information on different aspects of the indigenous peoples' living conditions, the extension of state's social programs to urban indigenous populations, and several measures to provide better infra-structure in indigenous territories and its adjacent areas.[10]

The measures announced raise the question of the commitment of Brazil to the international body of rights and principles regarding indigenous peoples in general and the Declaration in particular. In this context, this article is intended to outline the position of the protection and promotion of indigenous peoples' rights in Brazil. For this purpose, an overview of the main issues addressed in the Declaration as well as a description of their treatment under the Brazilian domestic le-

---

[8]   On 25 July 2002.

[9]   <http://www.presidencia.gov.br/noticias/ultimas_noticias/lula_indigena070 921>, *Agenda Social para os Povos Indígenas.*

[10]   For example, improvement of the roads, in the water supply and sanitation for a general increase of the hygiene within the communities.

gal system and policy-making will be provided. The economic, political and social conflicts that arise from the recognition of indigenous rights in Brazil will then be highlighted. Finally an analysis of the Brazilian experience will provide examples of the challenges that may accompany the achievement and enforcement of the principles recognized in the Declaration which may also be encountered by other states.

II. Indigenous Peoples and Individuals – Definition and Membership under the Declaration

The most leading and innovative notion of the UN Declaration is the recognition of the legal personality of indigenous peoples and the right to self-determination.[11] This is expressed in the preamble as well as in the text of the Declaration,[12] which sets the background against which the specific individual and collective framework rights accorded in the document must be interpreted and are to be implemented. The Declaration, however, does not offer a definition of the term "indigenous peoples".[13] This question was indeed a contentious issue during the drafting of the text. The absence of a definition reflects on the one hand, the difficulties met in formulating a common, far-reaching and flexible notion, suitable to the different realities of the various indigenous com-

---

[11] ILO Convention No. 169 also used the expression "peoples", but does not stipulate a right to self-determination, see article 1, para. 3.

[12] Para. 2 of the Preamble 2 reads, "Affirming that indigenous peoples are equal to all other peoples ...". Article 2 of the Declaration also states, "Indigenous peoples and individuals are free and equal to all other peoples and individuals ...".

[13] In contrast, the ILO Convention No. 169 contains a definition of both tribal and indigenous peoples. According to it, tribal peoples are peoples "whose social, cultural and economic conditions distinguish them from other sectors of the national community, and whose status is regulated wholly or partially by their own customs or traditions or by special laws or regulations" (article 1, para. 1 lit. a.). Indigenous peoples are defined as "peoples who are regarded as indigenous on account of their descent from the populations which inhabited the country, or a geographic region to which the country belongs, at the time of conquest or colonisation or the establishment of present State boundaries and who, irrespective of their legal status, retain some or all of their social, economic, cultural and political institutions" (article 1, para. 1 lit. b.).

munities throughout the world.[14] On the other hand, the silence of the Declaration in this regard may be interpreted as a deliberate option and mark of respect for the criterion of self-identification[15] "as an essential aspect of individual and group freedom",[16] an aspect of self-determination.

The self-identification perspective is highlighted in the Declaration by two different provisions and rights: the right of indigenous individuals and peoples to belong to an indigenous community,[17] and the parallel right of indigenous peoples to determine their own identity or membership, in accordance with their customs and traditions.[18] Together, these provisions suggest that the Declaration places the individual choice under the condition of a collective element, namely the necessary recognition of individual membership by the community. The somewhat "excessive" collective approach of the Declaration in this regard has been highlighted by representatives of various states and scholars[19] as a potential tool to foster group pressures or denial of individual rights.[20] Against this prognosis, article 1[21] could, nonetheless, represent a general guarantee of protection, as indigenous peoples have a right to the full enjoyment, collectively or as individuals, to all human rights

---

[14] See B. Kingsbury, " 'Indigenous Peoples' in International Law a constructivist approach to the Asian Controversy", *AJIL* 92 (1998), 414 et seq. See also the Working Paper prepared by the Chairperson-Rapporteur, on the concept of indigenous peoples, Doc. E/CN.4/Sub.2/AC.4/1996/2, paras 9 and 72.

[15] The self-identification criterion has also been addressed in the ILO Convention No. 169 as a "fundamental criterion" (article 1, para. 2) and in different discussions within the Committee on the Elimination of Racial Discrimination (CERD).

[16] See P. Thornberry, *Indigenous Peoples and Human Rights*, 2002, 15.

[17] Article 9 of the Declaration.

[18] Article 33, para. 1, ibid.

[19] See A. Xanthaki. *Indigenous Rights and UN Standards*, 2007, 105.

[20] For an overview on the conflicts between group rights and individual protection, see N. Wenzel, *Das Spannungsverhältnis zwischen Gruppenschutz und Individualschutz im Völkerrecht*, 2008.

[21] Article 1 of the Declaration establishes, "Indigenous peoples have the right of full enjoyment, as a collective or as individuals, of all human rights and fundamental freedoms as recognized in the Charter of the United Nations, the Universal Declaration of Human Rights and international human rights law".

recognized in the UN Charter, the Universal Declaration of Human Rights and international human rights law.

The absence of a definition which is followed by a more concrete identification of the bearers of the established rights does not, however, determine a complete openness of the document.[22] According to the system of the framework delineated in the Declaration, individuals and peoples are called to identify themselves as indigenous once they display "specific features as to their organization, political and economic institutions, culture, beliefs, customs and language, other than those of the dominant society," and further share "a common experience of marginalization and discrimination deeply rooted in historical events".[23] Furthermore, their cultural identity shall be based on traditional experiences and ways of life, and on the close linkage to traditional lands and resources, which is also a very central concept in the document.

This latter aspect of the intrinsic notion on "indigenous peoples" in the Declaration, namely the close relationship between traditional practices and habitat, requires some further clarification. The Declaration also expressly recognizes the indigenous peoples' right to development, according to their own needs and interests.[24] Besides that, the text calls for minimum standards of dignity and equality in the exercise of ordinary extra-communal activities, which are also open to individual peoples and are a matter of choice.[25] In this sense, the Declaration also to

---

[22] Thornberry, see note 16, 376. The openness could raise the possibility of a variety of peoples benefiting from its provisions.

[23] S. Errico, "The Draft UN Declaration on the Rights of Indigenous Peoples: An Overview", *Human Rights Law Review* 7 (2007), 741 et seq. (746).

[24] This right can be recognized mainly in article 3, which establishes the indigenous peoples' right to "freely determine their political status and freely pursue their economic, social and cultural development". Similar provisions are found in article 11 ("past, present and future manifestations of their cultures"), article 23 ("right to determine and develop priorities and strategies for exercising their right to development"), article 34 (right to "promote, develop and maintain their institutional structures and their distinctive customs, spirituality, traditions"), e.g.

[25] For example, in article 15 (indigenous peoples' right of dignity and diversity in the state's education and public information system); article 17 (indigenous individuals' and peoples' right to enjoy the rights established under domestic labor law); article 21 (indigenous peoples' right to the improvement of their economic and social conditions, in the areas of education, employment, (...) health and social security); article 6 (indigenous individual's right to obtain citizenship of the states in which they live), e.g.

some extent embraces those individuals and groups who have under-
gone cultural developments or processes of deviation from their original backgrounds.[26] In other words, although the specific rights and
guarantees established in the document broadly address the protection
of indigenous traditional cultures and way of life, they may also be applied – in a manner compatible to their needs – to indigenous groups
and individuals who, for some reason, do not share the traditional life
anymore.[27]

The use of the terminology concerning indigenous peoples and the
definition of these individuals is also a significant aspect of the treatment of their rights in Brazil. The expressions used in the respective
documents reveal the evolving conceptual framework in which indigenous reality has been approached. The Brazilian Constitution does not
refer to indigenous communities as "peoples". It does recognize and
highlight the special value of indigenous cultures, as well as their *original* right to traditional lands, and provides them with individual and
collective rights, but always referring to them as "communities",[28]
"groups"[29] or simply "population".[30] Reference to "peoples" in the
Constitution of 1988 is mainly made in the context of article 4, which
stipulates the principles that shall lead Brazil's international relations:
inter alia, the self-determination of the peoples.[31] The term "peoples"
is, thus, still closely linked to the right to self-determination in the
original context of sovereignty and decolonization and, therefore, it is
not considered to apply to the indigenous reality. In line with this consideration, Brazil was one of the states that manifested hesitation as to
the use of the term "indigenous peoples" in the drafting works of the
UN Declaration.[32] Still the wording of the Constitution of 1988 does
represent a significant step forward in the treatment of the indigenous

---

[26]   Amongst these individuals and groups, one can mention "groups undergo-
ing processes of cultural adaptation or development" or others "who suffered cultural diffusion, acculturation, depletion on resources and habitat
and who therefore may feel indigenous by self-identification rather than
through attachment to a traditional community", Thornberry, see note 16,
377.

[27]   On this topic, id., 376-378. See also Xanthaki, see note 19, 106.

[28]   Article 210, para. 2 of the Constitution.

[29]   Article 231, para. 5, ibid.

[30]   Article 22, XIV and article 129, V, ibid.

[31]   Article 4, III, ibid.

[32]   See R.L. Barsch, "Indigenous Peoples and the UN Commission on Human
Rights", *HRQ* 18 (1996), 782 et seq. (796).

issue and in the recognition of their identity. It left behind former degrading constitutional expressions such as "wild", "forest inhabitants"
and "sylvan"[33] and, thereby, it laid the first basis for the overcoming of
the evolutionist and integrationist approaches that characterized the
former constitutional and legal documents in Brazil.

Like the UN Declaration, the Brazilian Constitution does not offer
a definition of the individuals and groups entitled to the specific rights.
A definition is only provided by the Statute of the Indian, which formally introduced the self-identification criterion.[34] In this document,
self-identification is described in a very similar way as in the UN Declaration: the recognition of a person as *Índio* (beside the required "pre-
Colombian ancestry") shall be achieved through an individual self-
declaration, accompanied by the collective recognition of the membership by the ethnic group concerned. Brazilian legislation and policies in
regard to the indigenous population have been developed and implemented on the basis of this twofold self-identification. This is the official criterion used by FUNAI[35] when proceeding with the registration
of these peoples, the recognition of indigenous communities, or the
identification of traditional lands. Once registered and identified by
FUNAI under this criterion, indigenous individuals may then have access to the specific state policies and to the specific rights provided to
them. However, although the use of the self-identification momentum
does not provoke controversy in Brazil, the manner in which it is employed leads to incoherence and to cases of factual denial of rights, since
it binds (or submits) in a too strict manner the individual choice to the
group perception.

Taking into account mainly the individuals who maintained a closer
relation to their ethnic group and to a traditional way of life, FUNAI
recognizes nowadays the existence of about 460,000 indigenous indi-

---

[33]   See, for example, The Constitution of 1934 (article 5, XIX, m., and 129),
       the Constitution of 1967 (article 8, VXII, o. and 186), the Constitution of
       1969 (article 198 and article 4, IV).

[34]   See article 3 of Federal Law 6.001 of 19 December 1973.

[35]   This organ officially uses the definition expressed by the Brazilian anthro-
       pologist Darcy Ribeiro, according to which *Índio* is every individual who
       is recognized as a member by a pre-Colombian community that identifies
       itself as ethnically diverse from the national community. See under
       <www.funai.gov.br>.

viduals in Brazil[36] and restricts its policies to these individuals. In contrast, however, the last census of the Brazilian population of 2000 pointed to the existence of more than 730,000 indigenous individuals in Brazil,[37] a number that relies solely on the individual aspect of self-identification. It includes those individuals who left their traditional communities and migrated to the cities, looking for a better way of life.

This contrast reveals the two problems of the self-identification approach. On the one hand, self-declared indigenous individuals living in the city are often immediately rejected by the original communities, and since they do not rely on the group support and recognition, they are not included in administrative measures regarding the improvement of indigenous groups' lives in Brazil.[38] On the other hand, as the identification approach used by the state organs is strictly bound to indigenous life in traditional territories, the enjoyment of indigenous special constitutional rights has also been denied to entire indigenous groups which developed a communal life in urban areas.[39]

While the individual and communal self-identification criterion stressed by the UN Declaration and also by the Statute of the Indian in Brazil can be an important instrument for the preservation of indigenous peoples' identity, the domestic implementation of these principles must take into account the specific historical and social circumstances of each state and of the groups under consideration.[40]

---

[36]   Information see under <www.funai.gov.br>. The organ highlights that the number concerns those individuals living within their communities in their traditional lands.

[37]   <http://www.ibge.gov.br/home/estatistica/populacao/censo2000/popula cao/cor_raca_Censo2000.pdf>.

[38]   A detailed study shows the "double-exclusion" (exercised by the original groups, on the one hand, and also by the other national citizens in the cities, on the other hand) suffered by indigenous individuals of the groups Guarani and Kaiowá living in the cities in Mato Grosso do Sul and the consequent denial of the most basic rights to these individuals. See <http://www.sociologia.ufsc.br/npms/jose_ maria_trajano_vieira.pdf>.

[39]   The same study addresses the situation of entire groups of indigenous Kaiowá and Guarani which for the sole reason of living in the cities, in the words of the official organs "outside of their lands", are not included in the assistance programs of the government, ibid., 411.

[40]   The tension between the preservation of the groups' identity and individual interests is well-known in the discussions within international bodies. Remarkable is the case *Sandra Lovelace v. Canada* addressed by the Human

III. Indigenous Peoples' Right to Self-Determination under the Declaration

One of the most significant outcomes of the UN Declaration is the recognition of the right to self-determination. The inclusion of an express provision on this issue in the document was one of the main controversial items during the drafting process[41] since it touches upon very fundamental concepts for both indigenous communities and states.[42] Also the representative of Brazil expressed the problems of the government with a reference to the right to self-determination in the context of the draft Declaration.[43] Nevertheless, the final text of the Declaration assembles a variety of provisions, which, directly and indirectly, declare the indigenous peoples' right to self-determination and also delineate its scope.

The primary provision of this right – article 3[44] – offers merely the starting point for the comprehension of the content of "self-determination" under the Declaration. It establishes an "unqualified" right at first sight, which makes no reference to the principle of the state's territorial integrity or political unity, in contrast to other international instruments dealing with similar issues.[45] Nevertheless, article 46 clarifies its scope, determining a general interpretation principle, according to which:

"Nothing in this Declaration may be interpreted as implying for any State, people, group or person any right to engage in any activity or to perform any act contrary to the Charter of the United Nations or construed as authorizing or encouraging any action which would *dismem-*

Rights Committee, Communication No. 24/1997, *Yearbook of the Human Rights Committee 1981-1982*, Vol. II., Annex XVIII, 320 et seq.

[41] For an overview on this debate, see the reports of the Working Group on Indigenous Populations. Also Thornberry, see note 16, 382-385.

[42] See, for example, discussions on article 3 within the Working Group on Indigenous Populations on the Draft Declaration, Doc. E/CN.4/2004/81.

[43] See the report of the Working Group on Indigenous Populations, Doc. E/CN.4/1997/102 of 10 December 1996, para. 334.

[44] Article 3, "Indigenous peoples have the right to self-determination. By virtue of that right they freely determine their political status and freely pursue their economic, social and cultural development".

[45] Cf. also the wording of article 1 of the International Covenant on Civil and Political Rights and the International Covenant on Economic, Social and Cultural Rights.

ber or impair, totally or in part, the territorial integrity or political unity of sovereign and independent States". (emphasis added)[46]

Irrespective of these clear statements, considered necessary by many states, a systematic analysis of the Declaration would lead to the conclusion that the exercise of the indigenous peoples' right to self-determination, in the manner described in the document, presupposes the context of a life *within* the framework of a state.[47] No provision in the text suggests a right to secession, or the so-called right to external self-determination. The content of the specific indigenous peoples' right to self-determination set by the Declaration[48] establishes, first, "qualitative standards"[49] to be achieved especially under two premises: indigenous peoples' self-government and political participation. These are the notions that merge indigenous and states' concerns into one convergent notion of self-determination, better understood against the problematic background of internal governance and coexistence of various (and equal) groups within the state.

The first facet of the exercise of self-determination in the Declaration – the indigenous peoples' right to autonomy or self-government – is expressly established in article 4.[50] The content of this article is fur-

---

[46]   This provision was added just before the Declaration was adopted by the General Assembly. The President of the 61st Sess. appointed a "facilitator" entitled to lead further consultations on the draft Declaration (June 2007). The rationale of this provision is also expressed in the Preamble which reinforces the link between the right to self-determination in the Declaration and the framework of international law (see paras 16 and 17 of the Preamble).

[47]   Article 33 highlights the idea of indigenous peoples' "citizenship" of the states in which they live. According to Errico, the right to self-determination would imply a "constitutional formula" to accommodate indigenous aspirations, see note 23, 749.

[48]   See S.J. Anaya, *Indigenous Peoples in International Law*, 2004, 97-128. See also J. Gilbert, "Indigenous Rights in the Making: the United Nations Declaration on the Rights of Indigenous Peoples", *International Journal on Minority and Group Rights* 14 (2007) 207 et seq. (219-220).

[49]   See A. Quentin-Baxter's commentary on S.J. Anaya's position in "The UN Draft Declaration on the Rights of Indigenous Peoples – The International and Constitutional Law Contexts", *Law Review/Victoria University of Wellington* 29 (1999), 1 et seq. (91).

[50]   Article 4 reads, "Indigenous peoples in exercising their right to self-determination, have the right to autonomy or self-government in matters relating to their internal and local affairs, as well as ways and means for financing their autonomous functions".

ther clarified by other provisions in the document. Accordingly, the right to autonomy entitles indigenous peoples to freely determine, "in matters relating to their internal and local affairs",[51] the ways to maintain, develop and exercise the various features of their identity. For this purpose, indigenous peoples have the right to develop and enjoy their own political, legal, economic, social and cultural institutions,[52] and "ways and means for financing their autonomous functions",[53] always "in accordance with international human rights standards".[54] This right includes, the right "to establish and control their (indigenous) educational systems",[55] the right "to maintain their health practices",[56] the right "to maintain and develop their political, economic and social systems or institutions, to be secure in the enjoyment of their own means of subsistence and development",[57] *inter alia.*[58] Practiced under these terms, indigenous peoples' autonomy would be possible in the context of a "multicultural state", where dialogue and negotiation, also required by the Declaration, would offer the solid ground for its development.[59]

The Declaration, however, does not intend to place indigenous peoples in social or political isolation and vulnerability.[60] On the contrary, besides being entitled to self-government, indigenous peoples enjoy the

---

[51]   Article 4 of the Declaration.

[52]   Article 5, ibid.

[53]   Article 4.

[54]   Article 34, ibid.

[55]   Article 14, ibid.

[56]   Article 24, ibid.

[57]   Article 20, para. 1, ibid.

[58]   Although the concept of indigenous autonomy also includes a notion of cultural autonomy, these rights are better to understood in the broader concept of "cultural diversity" and of cultural rights.

[59]   S. Errico reminds us that the concrete realization of "autonomy" can only be assessed in a case-by-case perspective. She mentions "the establishment of the Sami Parliaments in the Nordic countries, the arrangement for the *comarca* in Panama, the creation of the autonomous region of Nunavut in Canada and the self-governing territory of Greenland in Denmark", see note 23, 749. See also E.A. Daes, "The Concept of Self-Determination and Autonomy of Indigenous Peoples in the Draft United Nations Declaration on the Rights of Indigenous Peoples", *St. Thomas Law Review* 14 (2001), 259 et seq. (268); and S.J. Anaya, "International Human Rights and Indigenous Peoples: The Move toward the Multicultural State", *Arizona Journal of International and Comparative Law* 21 (2004), 1 et seq. (13-61).

[60]   See Daes, see above.

right to participate "fully, if they so choose, in the political, economic, social and cultural life of the State".[61] This wording suggests that the self-government is not an imposition.[62] Indigenous groups might also determine the extent of their integration in the life of the state, taking into account the dynamism and the necessity of preservation of their own identity. This approach can play a significant role in countries like Brazil, where some indigenous groups still choose to live in isolation.[63]

As well as being protected from discrimination within the society of a state, indigenous peoples may, according to the Declaration, effectively participate in the decision-making process affecting their interests and rights.[64] This political participation constitutes the second aspect stemming from the right to self-determination. It might be exercised "through representatives chosen by themselves in accordance with their own procedures ... ".[65] Moreover, the political participation includes the indigenous peoples' right to "free, prior and informed consent", to be obtained by states "before adopting and implementing legislative or administrative measures that may affect them".[66]

The hesitation of the Brazilian government in according such broad political rights to indigenous peoples was expressed by the formulations suggested by the representative of Brazil in order to guarantee participation "in the discussion of legislative and administrative measures that may affect them".[67] Although participation in the decision-making and

---

[61]   Article 5 of the Declaration.

[62]   It has been stressed, however, that the wording of the Declaration, as establishing for indigenous communities the possibility to participate in the framework of the state "if they so choose", is weak and diminishes this right. For this kind of argumentation, see Errico, see note 23, 751.

[63]   Nowadays there are references to about 63 indigenous groups living in isolation in Brazil. Further information see under <www.funai.gov.br>. One of these groups was discovered recently, in May 2008, living at the Brazilian border to Peru. Documentation and photographs were provided by officials of FUNAI.

[64]   The issue of indigenous previous consent was also stressed by the Committee on the Elimination of Racial Discrimination in its General Recommendation XXIII on Indigenous Peoples, Doc. CERD/C/365 of 11 February 1999.

[65]   Article 18 of the Declaration.

[66]   Article 19, ibid.

[67]   See the report of the Working Group on Indigenous Populations Doc. E/CN.4/1997/102, para. 214.

consultation appear in various provisions of the Declaration,[68] it is debatable whether they could really promote indigenous interests. Concern has been expressed in relation to states in which decisions are taken by a majority (and indigenous peoples constitute a minority), or where decisions are taken through imperfect democratic processes.[69] Nevertheless, the Declaration makes perfectly clear that policies or legislation adopted on the basis of mere consultation could no longer fulfill the international standards accorded in regard to indigenous peoples' rights.

Any discussion about the status of indigenous groups and individuals in Brazil must consider the fact that the Constitution of 1988 does not officially declare Brazil a multicultural state. Still some constitutional provisions address the diversity of the Brazilian population.[70] But a clear recognition of Brazil as a state constituted by different independent cultures and peoples, which are to live in autonomy and equality, cannot be found in the text. In this context, indigenous groups are treated as "ethnically differentiated groups within the national society",[71] which are entitled to special rights rooted in the history of deprivations suffered by them and in the correlated necessity of guaranteeing them the enjoyment of the most basic fundamental rights and physical and cultural integrity.

For a long time, the policies regarding indigenous rights were centralized by FUNAI, which developed national strategies and represented - whether judicially or extra-judicially - these peoples in all matters related to them.[72] It decided, in general, about the groups' way of life, development and integration in the evolving society. Since the adoption of the Constitution of 1988, the indigenous population is gradually managing to influence the delineation of its destiny. This process is the result of correlated aspects: the development of international parameters and principles regarding indigenous rights, the paral-

---

[68]   See arts 10, 11, 18, 19, 29, 32 of the Declaration. One should note that the majority of these provisions deals solely with the right to be consulted.

[69]   In this regard, Quentin-Baxter, see note 49, 95.

[70]   For example, article 215, para. 1 ("groups participating in the national civilization process") and para. 2 ("various national ethnic segments"), and article 216 ("various groups that form the Brazilian society").

[71]   As stressed by the representative of Brazil during the discussions about indigenous land rights in the drafting works of the Declaration, see report of the Working Group on Indigenous Populations Doc. E/CN.4/Sub. 2/1997/14, topic B, para. 2.

[72]   Article 35 of the Statute of the Indian of 1973.

lel abandonment of the integrationist approach in the domestic legislation and the decentralization of the policies thereto, and the indigenous groups' progressive awareness of their rights, which has been supported by several national and international organizations. Nowadays, indigenous peoples in Brazil have achieved stronger levels of organization and participation in the debates on the recognition and implementation of their self-defined interests.[73] They have also exercised more and more their capacity recognized by the Constitution of 1988 to defend their rights before the national courts.[74]

Despite these developments, indigenous peoples remain subject to national legislation and policies that still incline to other forces and interests in power. The recognition of indigenous institutions, for example educational ones, has been set forth within the broader system defined by state authorities and according to state's federal and local strategies. Indigenous peoples internal organization and customs are generally recognized in the Constitution as elements of their identity, but innumerous interferences and limitations are still imposed in the name of "national interest". Thus as a result of their resistance indigenous interests are taken into consideration in the context but not on the basis of a concrete and equal political participation or autonomy. The legislative power does not count on a permanent representation of these peoples, which could be accessed for issues relating to them. Achievements can be observed in the public discussions with representatives of these groups, organized, however, as associations and organizations, not as representatives of the peoples.

The Social Agenda is another example of measures that are being conducted according to the state's unilateral interpretation of indigenous peoples' interests. The central critics of these initiatives expressed by indigenous communities stress exactly the lack of their participation

---

[73] For an overview of the indigenous organizations in Brazil, see under <http://www.socioambiental.org/pib/portugues/org/quadroorg.shtm>.

[74] Article 232 of the Constitution establishes that, "The Indians, their communities and organizations have standing under the law to sue and to defend their rights and interests, the Public Prosecution intervening in all the procedural acts". For an overview of the protection of indigenous rights in the national tribunals, see A.V. Araújo (ed.), *A Defesa Dos Direitos Indígenas no Judiciário*, 1995. See also L.M. Maia, "Comunidades e Organizacoes Indígenas. Natureza Jurídica, Legitimidade Processual e Outros Aspectos", in: J. Santilli (ed.), *Os Direitos Indígenas e A Constituicao*, 1993, 251-293.

in the definition of such strategies, which, in many cases, are not welcomed by the communities concerned.[75]

Recently e.g., the idea of the establishment of an indigenous parliament in Brazil has been discussed.[76] This parliament would have a similar power as the Houses of the National Congress and would work and
decide in all matters regarding the broader indigenous interests. This
still embryonic idea summarizes indigenous peoples' claims to autonomy and political participation in Brazil. It seems, however, that other
questions regarding very basic rights, which even include the still dubious indigenous individuals' civil autonomy are still hampered by the tutelage imposed by the state for so many years,[77] and must be clarified

---

[75] This criticism was evidenced in the words of the Yanomami leader Davi
      Kopenawa when the PAC Social was announced in the indigenous com-
      munity of Sao Gabriel da Cachoeira. According to him, "the government
      didn't really explain the project, it is not clear to me. He [the President of
      the Republic] only talks about construction projects and we don't want
      constructions or buildings in our lands. The government didn't invite the
      indigenous peoples or institutions that work with us to discuss this project.
      That's why I am worried. This same project that wants to protect us
      knocks against the other project of Senator Romero Jucá, which wants to
      destroy our lands with mining activities". On the same occasion, the repre-
      sentative of the indigenous organization stressed, "What is not clear for us
      is how this program will be implemented, who will be the responsible,
      what kind of involvement we will have".

[76] This idea was addressed, for example, in the Final Document elaborated by
      indigenous representatives on the occasion of the last National Conference
      of Indigenous Peoples, which took place in April 2006 (see No. 6 of the Fi-
      nal Document).

[77] The former Brazilian civil code of 1916 (Federal Law 3.071) classified in-
      digenous individuals (the "sylvan") as incapable of contracting (article 6,
      III) and subjected them to the tutelage exercised by the federal Indian Or-
      gan, the FUNAI (article 6 and Law 6.001/1973 – Statute of the Indian – ar-
      ticle 7, para. 2). According to this system, any legal act practiced by a non-
      integrated Indian without the assistance of FUNAI would be considered
      null and void (article 8 of the Statute of the Indian). The tutelage should be
      exercised until the total civilization of every indigenous individual and his
      integration in the Brazilian society. The Brazilian Civil Code of 1916 re-
      mained in force until 2003, when the Federal Law 10.406 of 2002 entered
      into force and revoked the former document. According to the current
      Brazilian Civil Code, the legal capacity of the indigenous shall be regulated
      in special legislation (article 4). This legislation, however, has not been
      adopted yet. All legislative projects regarding the elaboration of a new In-
      dian Statute address the issue, but they remain in process of discussion in

before further achievements regarding the status of indigenous groups in Brazil can be properly assessed. Meanwhile, the protection and promotion of indigenous groups (and of their members) in Brazil is restricted to the recognition of specific rights.

IV. Indigenous Peoples' Specific Rights

Amongst the various rights recognized to indigenous peoples in the UN Declaration, the right to traditional lands and resources and cultural rights are the most significant ones as they include the broad concept of indigenous peoples' identity.

1. Indigenous Peoples' Rights to Land and Resources

The UN Declaration's provisions regarding indigenous peoples' rights to land and resources reflect a certain consensus as to the special relationship of these peoples to the traditional lands. The text delineates a broad right,[78] which includes lands, territories and resources which indigenous peoples have traditionally owned, occupied or otherwise used or acquired (article 26). They have the right "to own, use, develop and control the lands, territories and resources that they possess by reason of traditional ownership or other traditional occupation or use, as well as those which they have otherwise acquired".[79] No further definitions of the lands, territories and resources considered thereto are offered by the document. The only further reference is "that they possess by rea-

---

the National Congress. It is worthy to highlight that the Statute of the Indian of 1973 has not yet been formally revoked. This brings uncertainties and insecurity as regards the scope of the recognition of indigenous individuals' legal capacity in the Brazilian legal system. See P.A. Silva, "Incapacidade civil relativa e tutela do índio", in: S. Coelho dos Santos (ed.), *O Índio perante o Direito*, Universidade Federal de Santa Catarina, 1987, 61-88.

[78] The right to traditional lands and resources is mainly established in arts 25 to 30 of the Declaration. But other provisions, like arts 8, 10, an 32 also stress and reinforce this right.

[79] Article 26, para. 2 of the UN Declaration.

son of traditional ownership or other traditional occupation or use".[80]
Nevertheless, significant principles have been set and shall guide the
specific treatment of these rights at both the international and domestic
level.

The Declaration covers the fundamental connection between traditional lands and resources and the enjoyment of other human rights and
freedoms by indigenous peoples. The approach used in the document
highlights the indispensability of land rights to the indigenous cultural
autonomy and to the very existence of these peoples.[81] In this line of
consideration, the land rights also encompass the right of environmental
conservation and the exercise of (collective) environmental management, which shall be supported by state assistance programs in order to
guarantee the rights of future generations.[82] The collective nature of the
rights concerned is highlighted,[83] in accordance with the special mean-

---

[80] Article 26, para. 2 of the UN Declaration. In this provision, the Declaration
suggests that the right concerns the lands that indigenous peoples currently
possess, cf. Thornberry, see note 16, 393.

[81] Many provisions of the Preamble as well as operational ones reflect this notion. Amongst the most significant ones, para. 7 of the Preamble defines the
land rights as "inherent rights" of indigenous peoples, which have an essential relation to these peoples' collective structures and to their cultures. Following the same concept, article 8 links the dispossession of traditional
lands, territories or resources to the destruction of indigenous peoples' culture. Finally, article 25 expressly addresses the "spiritual relationship" of
indigenous peoples with their lands, territories and resources. Under this
approach, indigenous lands rights could also be interpreted as an element of
indigenous peoples' self-determination. In this respect, see E. Gayim, *The
UN Draft Declaration on Indigenous Peoples: Assessment of the Draft Prepared by the Working Group on Indigenous Populations*, 1994, 53. The deep
spiritual relationship between indigenous peoples and their lands was
stressed by the UN Special Rapporteur on the Problem of Discrimination
against Indigenous Populations, José Martínez Cobo, in his first report, see
Errico, see note 23, 753.

[82] Article 29 paras 1 and 2 of the UN Declaration.

[83] The recognition of collective rights on traditional lands was one of the controversial issues in the drafting works, mainly in regard to a consequent
broader control by the natives over these lands and resources. See J. Gilbert, "Indigenous Rights in the Making: the United Nations Declaration on
the Rights of Indigenous Peoples", *International Journal on Minority and
Group Rights* 14 (2007), 207 et seq. (223-226). The collective approach becomes clear in the wording of these rights, which are in all cases granted to
"indigenous peoples" in the text of the Declaration.

ing of traditional lands for the well-being and the continuity of the indigenous groups as a whole. Regarding the implementation of the rights established in the Declaration, states are merely called upon to give "legal recognition and protection to these lands, territories and resources."[84] The particular means of enforcement must respect the "customs, traditions and land tenure systems of the indigenous peoples concerned"[85] and the establishment of processes characterized by direct participation of these peoples.[86] Moreover, it is incumbent upon states to guarantee the (innovative) indigenous peoples' right to redress,[87] which aims to rectify and to remediate historical deprivations.

Although the UN Declaration contributes not only to the enhancement but also to the further development of indigenous peoples' rights to traditional lands and resources, some of its provisions reveal the still highly controversial character of these rights. For example, the weak formulation of article 32 raises concerns. According to this, there does exist the right to determine and develop priorities and strategies for the development or use of their lands or territories or their resources. But according to article 32, para. 2:

"States shall consult and cooperate in good faith with the indigenous peoples concerned through their own representative institutions in order to obtain their free and informed consent prior to the approval of any project affecting their lands or territories and other resources, *particularly in connection with the development, utilization or exploitation of mineral, water or other resources*". (emphasis added)[88]

---

[84] Article 26, para. 3 of the UN Declaration. Such a general request combines with the Preamble the assertion that each indigenous people and each country retain specific features, which must be taken into account (para. 23 of the Preamble). It is noteworthy that no provision in the Declaration stipulates the responsibility of states to define and demarcate the traditional lands.

[85] Article 26, para. 3 of the UN Declaration.

[86] Article 27, ibid.

[87] Article 28, ibid. The restitution of the traditional lands "which have been confiscated, taken, occupied, used or damaged" without prior consent is suggested as the first mechanism to achieve redress. When restitution is not possible, however, other ways of "fair and equitable compensation" are to be established (article 28, para. 1). See Gilbert in the sense that restitution is preferable because "land ownership is not merely a source of individual economic security but the core of indigenous cultures and religions", see note 83, 228.

[88] See article 32, para. 2.

These regresses are corroborated by the rejection of certain formulations by states' representatives during the drafting process in order to avoid indigenous peoples' ownership rights. Clear examples of this are the exclusion of peoples express rights to sub-surface resources,[89] as well as the exclusion of the word "their" before "resources" in article 32, para. 2 from the draft.[90] The former allows the conclusion that only surface resources are covered when speaking of indigenous peoples' land rights.[91] This interpretation would be confirmed by the previously mentioned article 32.[92]

During the drafting process, Brazilian observers have outlined the protection of indigenous' land rights in the Constitution of 1988 and have expressed the government's intentions to pursue its constitutional commitments to protect indigenous peoples against acts of violence and to demarcate their lands.[93] The Brazilian experience, however, illustrates the challenges of conciliating indigenous peoples' rights with states' as well as individual interests when it comes to the economic value of certain goods.

- The Protection of Indigenous Rights to Land and Resources in Brazil

The Brazilian Constitution expressly recognizes the right to the land the indigenous traditionally occupy.[94] A definition of "traditionally occupied lands" is also provided and is based on four requirements regarding the use and the importance of these lands for the life of the groups: the use of the land for living on a permanent basis; the use for indigenous productive activities; its indispensability for the preservation of the environmental resources necessary for the well-being of the communities; its indispensability for the preservation of the environ-

---

[89] See Concluding Observations of the Human Rights Committee, Colombia, Doc. CCPR/CO/80/COL, para. 33. Xanthaki, see note 19, 118.

[90] This modification was made at the UN General Assembly level, during the last consultations conducted by a "facilitator". See S. Errico, "The UN Declaration on the Rights of Indigenous Peoples is Adopted: An Overview", *Human Rights Law Review* 7 (2007), 756 et seq. (758).

[91] See also Errico, see note 23, 754.

[92] See para. 2 of article 32 of the Declaration.

[93] See Report of the Working Group on Indigenous Populations on its 15th Sess. Geneva, 28 July-11 August 1997, Doc. E/CN.4/Sub.2/1997/14, topic B (Environment, Land and Sustainable Development), number 2.

[94] Article 231 of the Constitution.

mental resources necessary for the indigenous.[95] Only those lands characterized by all four of these aspects in a cumulative manner can be recognized as "traditionally occupied lands".[96]

For protective reasons, the property of these identified traditional lands is assigned to the Union.[97] Changes in the ownership or deviations from its original scope or aim are expressly prohibited, based on the general constitutional guarantee that traditional lands are "inalienable and indisposable and the rights thereto are not subject to limitation".[98] The recognition of indigenous rights in respect to land has two significant consequences.[99] First of all, the guarantee of permanent possession, which is reinforced by the prohibition of removal of indigenous communities from their lands.[100] Second, the recognition of an indigenous right to exclusive usufruct "of the riches of the soil, the rivers and the lakes existing therein".[101] As a general guarantee, the Constitution determines any act aiming at or leading to a violation of the described rights, except in a case of relevant public interest of the Union null and void .[102] According to the constitutional provision, this excep-

---

[95]   Article 231, para.1, ibid.

[96]   See J.A. da Silva, *Curso de Direito Constitucional Positivo*, 1987, 855.

[97]   Article 20, XI of the Constitution. This classification is intended to guarantee a better protection of the lands and to avoid pressures or threats against indigenous peoples.

[98]   Article 231, para. 4 of the Constitution.

[99]   For an overview, see F.C.T. Neto, "Os Direitos Originários dos Índios sobre as Terras que Ocupam e suas Consequências Jurídicas", in: Santilli, see note 74, 9-43.

[100] Article 231, paras 2 and 5 of the Constitution. This provision, however, encompasses two exceptions, which would then allow a provisory displacement of determined indigenous groups. First of all, the outbreak of a catastrophe or an epidemic, representing a risk to the population thereto. In this case, the decision of the President of the Republic must be followed by the compliance of the National Congress *ad referendum*. Apart from that, a removal can be ordered at any time "in the interest of the sovereignty of the country". This quite broad exception must be first agreed by the Congress in a previous authoritative decision. Once the reasons for the provisory removal are settled, the return of the population to their lands shall be, in both cases, immediately secured.

[101] Article 231, prara. 2 of the Constitution.

[102] Article 231, para. 6 of the Constitution. Therefore, former titles of property based on eventual private registers or documents concerning these lands are considered without effect and do not give any right to indemnity,

tion must be carried out by a supplementary law, which, however, has not yet been enacted.[103]

If it is true that the protection provided in the Constitution of 1988 represents a step forward in the treatment of indigenous land rights in Brazil, its implementation has been hampered though by reasons of a different nature. The difficulties concern the guarantee of both, the indigenous possession of traditional lands as well as indigenous exclusive usufruct of the riches of the land.

- Demarcation of Traditional Lands in Brazil

A very clear responsibility of the Union in regard to the protection of indigenous rights in Brazil is the demarcation of the identified traditional lands. This is defined in article 231 of the Constitution. The administrative act of demarcation does not create the rights concerned, which are considered to be "original", being prior to the existence of the state itself.[104] Nevertheless, this declaratory measure enables a more concrete approach and exercise of land rights, as it defines the exact boundaries of the lands and puts an (potential) end to any legal uncertainty or conflict regarding the property.

Since the enactment of the Statute of the Indian in 1973, the demarcation follows a certain administrative procedure,[105] which is regulated by Decree 1775/1996.[106] According to it, the demarcation conducted by FUNAI[107] begins with an anthropological study of identification of the land and of its population.[108] The results of this study must be presented to FUNAI in a detailed report.[109] After approval and publication of this report by FUNAI,[110] within a term of ninety days any objection

---

except when improvements have been made in the context of an occupation in good faith.

[103] Article 231, para. 6 of the Constitution.

[104] See da Silva, see note 96, who summarizes the general understanding on this topic on pages 854-855.

[105] Article 19 of the Statute.

[106] Decree 1775 of January 1996, which revoked the former ones.

[107] Article 1 of Decree 1775/1996.

[108] Article 2 of Decree 1775/1996.

[109] Article 2, para. 6 of Decree 1775/1996. FUNAI's internal act No. 14 of 1996 establishes rules about the elaboration of this report and determines the obligatory information to be provided in it.

[110] Article 2, para. 7 of Decree 1775/1996.

or claim pertaining to the land concerned may be sustained.[111] After that the Ministry of Justice,[112] defines the concrete boundaries of the land, and orders the demarcation of the territory by FUNAI.[113] The demarcation has finally to be approved by the President of the Republic[114] and ends with the actual registering of the land.[115]

According to the data provided by FUNAI, there are 398 indigenous traditional lands currently registered in Brazil.[116] Ninety identified territories still lack demarcation and 123 still await studies of identification. The process of demarcation of indigenous territories in Brazil is far from a satisfactory conclusion which should originally have been reached within five years after the promulgation of the Constitution of 1988.[117] Besides the dimensions of the Brazilian territory, the complexity of the procedure described in the Decree and the increasing number of indigenous peoples claiming recognition in Brazil, the obstacles stem from the economic and social impacts of the recognition of indigenous lands which create serious impasses.

The demarcation of the indigenous territory "Raposa-Serra do Sol" (the most recent and prominent example in Brazil) is very illustrative in this respect. It reveals the complexity of the problems inherent in the enforcement of indigenous land rights in Brazil. The indigenous territory "Raposa-Serra do Sol" was first identified by FUNAI in 1984.[118] It consists of a territory of about 1.7 million hectares situated in the northeast of the federal state Roraima (North of Brazil). Besides its essential value for the physical and cultural survival of the more than 15,000 indigenous of 5 different ethnic groups who live there in a tradi-

---

[111] Article 2, para. 8 of Decree 1775/1996. Actually the Decree allows any claimant – federal states, municipalities or private persons – to provide evidence to sustain his or her claim since the beginning of the demarcation procedure.

[112] Article 2, para. 10 of Decree 1775/1996. If necessary, the Minister of Justice can request further diligences or even disapprove the identification, sending the acts back to FUNAI under justification.

[113] Article 3 of Decree 1775/1996.

[114] Article 5, ibid.

[115] Article 6, ibid.

[116] See under <www.funai.gov.br.>.

[117] Cf. article 67 of the Temporary Constitutional Provisions Act, which is part of the Constitution of 1988.

[118] It was a preliminary identification. The official report was first published in May 1993.

tional manner,[119] the region is well-known for the abundance of its mineral richness,[120] for its environmental diversity and furthermore, for the prosperous development of agricultural activities on it.[121] Finally, it is considered to be a strategic zone.[122] This constellation led to the involvement of highly diverse and numerous interested parties in the process of demarcation. Since the first identification by FUNAI, indigenous communities, NGOs, military authorities,[123] and mining companies, have expressed their concerns. After two unsuccessful statements by two Ministers of Justice[124] regarding the scope of the territory and the criteria for its delimitation,[125] a third statement was made (seven years after the previous one) in April 2005[126] and inaugurated one of the most serious political, juridical and socio-economical im-

---

[119] The ethnic groups are Macuxi, Taurepang, Wapixana, Patamona and Ingarikó.

[120] The "Instituto de Terras e Colonizacao de Roraima" – (Institute for Land and Colonization of Roraima) states the existence of diamonds and radioactive material in the territory. Besides, it points to the presence of e.g. gold and copper.

[121] In the state of Roraima, there are about 40 rice producers, who cultivate 25.000 ha of land within the territory. They are responsible for a production of 6.000 kilo per hectare on average. This performance beats, for example, the whole cereal production in the federal state of Rio Grande do Sul (south of Brazil).

[122] The boundary zone is defined as the "strip of land up to a hundred and fifty kilometers in width alongside the terrestrial boundaries (...) considered essential to the defense of the national territory and its occupation and utilization shall be regulated by law", article 20, para. 2 of the Constitution of 1988.

[123] The main concern of the military authorities is their forced removal from the area in case of its demarcation as indigenous land, the consequent vulnerability of the Brazilian territory in this boundary zone and the even more precarious vigilance of the Amazon.

[124] The first one was the statement No. 80 of December 1996 ordering a reduction of the territory identified by FUNAI. Published in DOU in December 1996. The second writ – Portaria No. 820 – was published in December 1998 (DOU) ordering the return of the demarcation to the former proportions set by FUNAI.

[125] The main discussion is whether the demarcation should be continuous or should preserve the infra-structure created in the region and villages and areas of strategic importance for economic activities in the state of Roraima and exploitation of resources by third parties.

[126] Portaria (writ) No. 534 of April 2005 (in DOU of 15 April 2005).

passes in Brazil. Besides stipulating the scope of the area, the decision determined, for example, the removal of the whole non-indigenous population from the area concerned.[127] The demarcation under these terms was ratified by the Brazilian President in 2005 (twenty-one years after the first identification of the land by FUNAI). Irrespective of the immediate protests and pressures against it, the President ordered, at the end of 2007, the evacuation of the region.[128] Since January 2008, access to the territory has been frequently blocked by the local population and the constant conflict with the police led to deaths and to a permanent threat to the indigenous communities.[129] In April 2008 the activities of the police were suspended by the Supreme Court[130] and the impasse remains unresolved.

Apart from the socio-economic dimension of this problem, some comments on the situation in Raposa-Serra do Sol circulated in the media also reveal a certain arbitrariness in the interpretation of constitutional indigenous land rights and in the perception of these rights in Brazil. It has been stressed that the demarcation adopted "transforms the Indian into a privileged citizen" and the government, in its former interpretations about indigenous land rights, "has actually never considered that the land belonged to the Indians in the past".[131] This pronouncement ignores the clear definition of indigenous land rights as "original" rights in the Constitution of 1988 and disregards the notion of equality *de facto* which, in the case of indigenous peoples, requires special promotional and protective measures. Another argument was brought forward by the Brazilian Defense Minister. He also considered the demarcation conducted by the government a mistake, which was

---

[127] The statement excluded from the Raposa-Serra do Sol the Municipality Uiramuta, public installations, like schools and energy conducting cables/lines, the installations of the army's 6th Special Boundary Commando and the roads situated in the region.

[128] These operations are called "Upatakon". In April 2008, the Upatakon 3 was put forward.

[129] For an overview of reports about the conflicts, see under under <www.folha.uol.com.br>, in Raposa-Serra do Sol, in the period of January-April 2008.

[130] The decision of 9 April 2008 was provoked by the government of Roraima. The intention was to suspend the operations of the police in the state until the different claims brought before the Supreme Court in regard to the demarcation of Raposa-Serra do Sol had been decided.

[131] <http://www1.folha.uol.com.br/folha/brasil/ult96u393279. shtml>.

caused by "ignorance of the national legal system" and by the "influences of the North-American culture".

"They [the indigenous peoples] constitute nations and the indigenous lands belong to these nations. In Brazil, indigenous land is Union's property, for a lifelong usufruct by the Indians. They do not own the property of these lands, which are also subject to all of the constitutional norms."[132]

The Minister did not take into account that the Union's property over traditional lands is a qualified one; it exists with the purpose of protecting and implementing indigenous rights to these lands and is bound by this purpose.[133] It is the Union (and its property) that is conditioned by the fulfillment and protection of indigenous rights; not the other way round. In April 2008, the elaboration of an intermediate proposal of demarcation by the government was announced.[134] Suffice to say that the conflicts in Raposa-Serra do Sol offer just one example of an indigenous territory in Brazil, which 24 years after its first identification by FUNAI, has not even be demarcated. No guarantees or rights have been or can be ensured to the indigenous communities living therein.

- Indigenous Groups' Exclusive Usufruct of Resources in Traditional Lands and Exploitation by Non-Indigenous in Brazil

In the configuration of indigenous communities' rights to their traditional lands in Brazil, the right to permanent possession of these lands is complemented, as mentioned above, by the "exclusive usufruct of the riches of the soil, the rivers and the lakes existing therein".[135] According to the Statute of the Indian, this right entails the use and exploitation of the natural richness and of all utilities of the land, as well as the access

---

[132] This observation was made in response to critics against the policies of the government in regard to indigenous peoples in Brazil.

[133] See da Silva, see note 96, 854.

[134] In April 2008 the elaboration of an intermediate proposal of demarcation by the government, which will be presented to the Supreme Court was announced. The proposal will suggest the determination of four strategic areas in the Raposa-Serra do Sol, called "development islands" (*ilhas de desenvolvimento*).

[135] Para. 2 of article 231 of the Constitution.

to the products of their economic exploitation.[136] Thus, irrespective of the nature and of the purpose of the use concerned, for the group's immediate subsistence or aiming at economic gains,[137] indigenous communities are recognized as the sole (collective) bearers of this right.

One of the immediate concerns regarding the use of resources in traditional lands is its environmental impact. This problem encompasses the harmonization of broader rights of use and exploitation on the one hand, with the preservation of the biological diversity in these territories on the other. The most coherent approach regarding the principles established in the UN Declaration of 2007 seems to be a direct involvement of the communities in the delineation of protective measures of sustainable self-management of the resources, in order to enable collective and continuous enjoyment. Such an approach, however, is not found in the Brazilian legal system, which still links environmental protection with the factual denial of indigenous usufruct of resources in some territories.[138]

---

[136] Article 24 of the Statute of the Indian. This provision expressly mentions the indigenous' exclusive exercise of fishing and hunting in the traditional lands, para. 2.

[137] In the case of economic exploitation of the resources by indigenous communities, these activities must observe the common legislation thereto, especially the environmental one, and its benefits must be enjoyed by the whole collectivity. The usufruct of resources for the direct subsistence of the group also allows the extraction and use of resources in forest areas, with observance of their sustainable management in accordance with the environmental requirements of Law No. 4771/65 and of Decree 2.788/1998 (this kind of traditional exploitation was expressly allowed by the provisory act No. 1956-55/2000, which included a specific provision in this regard in the Law and in the Decree mentioned): the preservation of the structure of the forest and of its functions, the conservation of the biological diversity, the socio-economic development of the region (arts 1 and 2 of the Decree 2.788/98). Compliance with these requirements, which must be attested in a project presented by the interested indigenous groups, shall be controlled by both the federal environmental organ and the indigenous foundation (IBAMA and FUNAI respectively).

[138] The main discussion of this point concerns the Law No. 9.985/2000, which created the so-called "National System of Unities of Conservation of the Nature". These "Unities of Conservation" are areas of Environmental Protection with severe restrictions to the use of natural resources. Many of these areas coincide with the area of indigenous territories and the limitations (in some cases, real denial) in respect of the indigenous usufruct are

Regarding the exclusiveness of the usufruct and the related inaliena-
bility[139] of this right, the challenge in Brazil does not lie in the enforcement of a necessarily direct enjoyment of these rights by the indigenous
communities, but rather on the elimination of an unauthorized exploitation of indigenous resources by non-indigenous groups and individuals. The rise of illegal exploitation activities in traditional territories
supported by a lack of effective legislation represents a further violation
of indigenous groups' land rights. Regarding this topic, the legal and
administrative treatment of mining activities and the exploitation of genetic resources in indigenous lands in Brazil require closer consideration.

- Mining Activities in Traditional Lands[140]

Concerning mining activities in traditional lands, two situations
must be distinguished under Brazilian law: the activities of individuals
working on their own account (mainly gold prospectors) and the ones
conducted by mining companies. The Brazilian Constitution of 1988
expressly forbids the activities of gold prospectors in indigenous territory.[141] Article 231, however, allows the exploitation of mineral resources by mining companies in indigenous lands.[142] This is a clear concession to the pressure exercised by these companies. Article 231 must
be read together with article 176 of the Constitution. According to the
later, mineral resources in Brazil belong to the Union, irrespective of
the holder of the propriety over the soil. They constitute, thus, a separate legal object. In general, the exploitation of mineral resources may
only be performed by Brazilian companies[143] and under three conditions: the existence of a national interest; an authorization or concession

---

considered unconstitutional. For an overview, see F. Ricardo, *Terras
Indígenas e Unidades de Conservacao: O desafio da sobreposicao*, 2005.

139 Article 231, para. 4 of the Constitution.

140 For an overview on this topic, see J. Santilli, "Aspectos Jurídicos da Min-
eracao e do Garimpo em Terras Indígenas", in: Santilli, see note 74, 145-
160.

141 Article 231, para. 7 of the Constitution. This norm is reinforced by the
Federal Law No. 7805 of 18 July 1989, article 23.

142 Para. 3 of article 231, which also allows the non-indigenous exploitation of
hydro resources, including energetic potentials.

143 For this purpose, a Brazilian company is the one "organized under Brazilian laws and having its head-office and management in Brazil", article 176,
para. 1.

by the Union (National Congress); the observance of specific norms set out by law. In case of their location in indigenous lands, however, other specific conditions may also apply.[144] Two of these specific conditions are already determined in general terms in article 231 para. 3 of the Constitution. The first one is the hearing of the indigenous communities involved, which shall be prior to an authorization by the National Congress. The second one is the guarantee of the communities' participation in the economic revenues of the mining. The scope of these requirements and the ways for their concrete realization, however, lack any further clarification.

Since 1991, different legislative projects pursuing the regulation of mining activities in Brazil have been presented and discussed in the National Congress. As to the specific exploitation of mineral resources in indigenous lands, the most controversial initiative is the one proposed in 1996 (Legislative Project No. 1610/1996), which has been strongly criticized and objected by various indigenous communities and organizations.[145] Especially worrying seems to be the secondary role given to the hearing of indigenous communities which is superficially mentioned in article 10 of the Legislative Project. Also, the open and largely discretionary criterion for the selection of the company, which shall conduct the mining activities, defined merely as "the one which best complies with the requirements"[146] raises concerns. Besides this project, the initiatives aiming at the elaboration of a new "Statute" for the indigenous (or the reformulation of the old one) also contain significant provisions regarding the regulation of mining activities in traditional lands. The most prominent ones are the three projects, which run together under the denomination "Statute of the Indigenous Peoples."[147] Amongst them, the project No. 2.619/1992 grants the most effective

---

[144] Last sentence of the same article 176. Activities in boundary zones are also subject to these further conditions.

[145] For example, on the occasion of the announcement of the measures of PAC Social by President Lula. See different opinions of indigenous leaders and indigenous organizations representatives under <http://www.socioambi ental.org/nsa/detalhe?id=2532>.

[146] Article 9 of the Legislative Project 1610/96.

[147] These are: the legislative project No. 2.057/1991 about the Statute of the Indigenous Societies (*Estatuto do Sociedades Indígenas*), i.a. legislative project No. 2.160/1991 about the Indian's Statute (*Estatuto do Índio*) and the legislative project No. 2.619/1992 about the Statute of the Indigenous Peoples (*Estatuto dos Povos Indígenas*).

protection.[148] It stipulates, for example, a more equitable participation of the communities in the earned profits, "irrespective of other payments agreed among the parties",[149] and guarantees, in different provisions, the involvement of the communities in the whole process of authorization and of monitoring mining activities in their lands.[150] Finally, this initiative also addresses environmental concerns.[151]

The National Department for Mineral Production[152] states a current amount of more than 5,643 requests of authorization for mineral exploitation in indigenous lands in Brazil,[153] which demand proper legal regulation. The absence of systematic rules thereto, still hampers the effective monitoring of the exploitation of indigenous lands. Traditional mineral resources remain exposed to intensive unauthorized mining and conflicts with miners in indigenous lands represent an additional threat to the communities' rights and integrity.[154]

- Unauthorized Exploitation of Genetic Resources in Traditional Lands

The third-party use of natural resources in indigenous lands in respect of research, collection, exportation, and exploitation of genetic material of plants and animals constitutes another serious obstacle to the enjoyment of indigenous land rights in Brazil. The Brazilian Constitution of 1988 contains a general provision stressing the responsibility of the government towards the so-called "national genetic patrimony". According to article 225, it is incumbent upon the government to "preserve the diversity and integrity of the genetic patrimony of the country and to control entities engaged in the research and manipula-

---

[148] On the other hand, the project presented by the Executive (PL N. 2.160/ 1991) contains only five quite simply formulated provisions regarding the exploitation of mineral resources in indigenous territories and does not add much to the constitutional norms.

[149] Article 61, III of the legislative project No. 2.619/1992.

[150] For example, in arts 51, 52, 53, 61, II and IV of the legislative project No. 2.619/1992.

[151] Article 62 of legislative project No. 2.619/1992.

[152] *Departamento Nacional de Producao Mineral* (DNPM).

[153] The information was given by the General-Director of DNPM on 18 March 2008, "Notícias" under <http://www.dnpm.gov.br, 19/03/ 2008>.

[154] The conflicts in the indigenous territory "Cinta Larga" provide good examples for the dimension of this problem. For an overview see H.E. Kayser, "Die Rechte der indigenen Völker Brasiliens", 2005, 474-480.

tion of genetic material."[155] As no express exception is made in the Constitution with regard to genetic resources (like, for example, in the case of mineral exploitation), the challenge in Brazil lies in the definition of strategies able to merge state responsibility with the effective guarantee for indigenous exclusive rights.[156]

The only available regulation is the provisional act[157] No. 2.186-16/2001.[158] According to the act, access to the "genetic patrimony" in Brazil for purposes of scientific research, exploitation and technological development is subject to the authorization of the Union.[159] In case of resources located in indigenous lands, the norm requires previous consent of the indigenous community involved[160] and also previously accorded "fair and equitable" sharing of the potential benefits with the indigenous communities.[161] A specific organ was created for the implementation of these rules and for deciding upon the authorizations con-

---

[155] Para.1, II of article 225 of the Constitution of 1988.

[156] Guaranteed in article 231, para. 2 of the Constitution and in arts 22 and 18 of the Statute of the Indian.

[157] Provisional acts ("medidas provisórias") are provisory norms (measures) that may be elaborated and adopted by the President of the Republic in important and urgent cases. Once in force, they must be immediately submitted to the National Congress for its conversion into law within 60 days, extendable once for the same period of time. If not converted into law in this period, these measures shall loose efficacy, and revert to the issuing date, see article 62 of the Brazilian Constitution.

[158] Regulated by the Decrees No. 3945/01 and No. 4946/2003. The act regulates article 225 paras 1, 2 and 4 of the Constitution of 1988, and arts 1, 8, 10, 15 and 16 of the Convention on Biological Diversity. This act was first edited as provisional act 2.052/200. (in DOU of 30 June 2000). The first act had the clear intent to protect and legalize an agreement between the multinational *Novartis Pharma* and the Brazilian (Social) Organization *Bioamazônia* for the prospection of bacteria and fungi in the Amazon Forest. According to article 10 of the former act, the continuation of the economic use of traditional knowledge conducted "in good faith" was allowed as far as this use had been first set before 30 June 2000. This act was reenacted with minimal changes 15 times. In 2001 it was replaced by the current provisional act No. 2. 186-16.

[159] Article 1 of the provisional act No. 2.186-16/2001.

[160] Through the hearing of the official indigenous organ, article 16, para. 9, I of the provisional act No. 2.186-16/2001. Some directives were established for obtaining this assent. These are Resolutions 05/2003, 06/2003, 09/2003 and 12/2003 of CGEN, available at <www.mma.gov.br/port/cgen>.

[161] In arts 24 and 25.

cerned.[162] This norm does not expressly offer ways for the indigenous communities to veto the exploitation of their lands.[163] Even more critical is that access is granted without the consent of the indigenous communities in cases of "relevant public interest".[164] Even the composition of the conducing organ raises concerns since only government members have a vote in the final decisions.[165] Finally, the provisional act imposed difficulties on the development of scientific research in Brazil.[166]

The clear ineffectiveness of the treatment of this problem in Brazil is demonstrated by the various reports on illegal activities involving the exploitation of genetic resources in indigenous lands.[167] Since 1995, different legislative projects have been discussed in the National Congress, aiming at a more systematic and effective regulation.[168] Amongst the issues concerned, a clear definition of "biopiracy" and the stipulation of stricter sanctions are being addressed.[169] So far no proper regulation is agreed on.

---

[162] This is the "Conselho de Gestão do Patrimônio Genético" (Council for the Management of the Genetic Patrimony), created in article 10 of the act. The Council first started its work in April 2002. For general information about its structure and functioning see <www.mma.gov.br/port/cgen>.

[163] Article 16, para. 9 refers solely to the "assent" ("anuência") of indigenous communities.

[164] Article 17 of the provisional act No. 2.186-16/2001. Para. 1 determines that, in these cases, the indigenous community must be previously informed.

[165] Beside representatives of different ministries and national organs, the Council hears so called convidados permanentes. They, however, don't have a right to vote.

[166] Just after CGEN started its work, it received formal complaints of different academic sectors, highlighting the difficulties originated from the provisional act No. 2.169-16/2001 for research activities in Brazil.

[167] See under <www.mma.gov.br/biopirataria>.

[168] As to date 6 projects are discussed in both Houses of the National Congress. The first one was presented to the Senate by Senator Marina da Silva (PL 0036/95). These projects have currently the following numbers: PL 4.842/1998 (Senator Marina da Silva), PL4.579/1998 (Mr. Jacques Wagner), PL 1.953/1999 (Mr. Silas Câmara), PL 2.360/2003 (Mr. Mário Negromonte), PL 5.078/2005 (Mr. Eduardo Valverde), PL 287/2007 (Mrs. Janete Capiberibe), PL 3.170/2008 (Mr. Takayama).

[169] The only sanctions are the administrative ones established in Chapter VIII of the provisional act 2.186-16/2001 (fine, retention of the material collected, embargo of the activity conducted, cancel of authorization, prohibition of future contracts with the public administration) and the ones estab-

2. Indigenous Peoples' Cultural Rights

The Declaration starts from the assumption that all peoples have the right to be different, to consider themselves different and to be respected as such.[170] Under this premise, it affirms that indigenous peoples are "equal to all other peoples".[171] Many of the operational provisions in the Declaration go back to this central notion, promoting, on the one hand, these peoples' distinguished cultural identity and reinforcing, on the other hand, the right of indigenous groups to exist and to be protected from every kind of discrimination. This approach becomes clear, for example, in the recognition of the indigenous peoples' right contained in article 5 to "participate fully, if they so choose, in the political, economic, social and cultural life of the State", beside the right provided in article 12 to "manifest, practice, develop and teach their spiritual and religious traditions, customs and ceremonies". The Declaration reflects, thus, a concept of equality that considers and values the differences in the societies and correlates indigenous peoples' cultural identity with integrity.[172]

Article 6 grants every indigenous individual the right to a nationality. Further, many provisions guarantee the right to participate in the political, economic, social and cultural life of the state.[173] Other articles concern the promotion of the indigenous peoples' identity. It is intended to guarantee the full enjoyment ("manifestation", "practice", "revitalization", "use") of indigenous peoples' practices, customs, traditions, their symbols, ceremonies and objects.[174] Further the perpetuation of the specific cultural features is ensured. In this context, arts 12 and 13 expressly address the right to "teach" and to "transmit" practices and beliefs to future generations. Finally, the development of the indigenous identity according to its specific characteristics and to the peoples' own requirements is also guaranteed. Together, these provisions address the different aspects of indigenous peoples' cultural iden-

---

lished in the Law No. 9.605/1998, covering general crimes against the environment.

[170] Para. 2 of the Preamble.

[171] Para. 2 of the Preamble.

[172] See article 8, para. 2 (a). See S.J. Anaya, "Keynote Address: Indigenous Peoples and their Mark on the International Legal System", *American Indian Law Review* 31 (2006/2007), 257 et seq. (269).

[173] E.g. arts 5, 14, 15, 16, 17.

[174] For example, in arts 11 and 12 of the Declaration.

tity. Special attention is given to the protection and promotion of indigenous languages.[175]

The Declaration also establishes, in an innovative manner, the duty of states to provide redress with respect to "cultural, intellectual, religious and spiritual property", taken without the indigenous peoples' consent or in violation of their laws, traditions and customs.[176] Article 31, stresses indigenous peoples control over their "cultural heritage, traditional knowledge and traditional cultural expressions", avoiding the words "property" or the idea of ownership.[177] In this manner, the Declaration reflects the consolidated notions of material and immaterial property especially in the domestic legal systems.[178] Possible conflicts thereto were also highlighted by the Brazilian representative during the drafting process of the Declaration.[179]

Officially leaving aside the approach of the former documents, the Brazilian Constitution of 1988 recognized the value of indigenous culture and provided for its respect, protection and promotion. Being Brazilian nationals, indigenous individuals (and their groups) are entitled to the fundamental rights and guarantees recognized in article 5 of the Constitution, which stipulates equality and non-discrimination. Irrespective of this general guarantee, however, the Brazilian Constitution contains specific provisions concerning indigenous culture and identity, aiming at its special protection and enhancement.

Article 231 of the Constitution sets as the leading principle that "Indians shall have their social organization, customs, languages, creeds and traditions recognized" and lays the basis for the special respect to the different features of indigenous culture in the country. This stipulation is complemented by the state's duty to protect "all indigenous

---

[175] Article 14, para. 1 of the Declaration. See also article 16, para. 1 (right to establish their own media in their own languages) and article 13, which encompasses the right to transmit their languages to future generations.

[176] Article 11, para. 2 of the Declaration includes within the manifestations of indigenous peoples' cultures archaeological and historical sites, artifacts, designs, ceremonies, technologies and visual and performing arts and literature.

[177] Also article 24 reflects this hesitation in regard to indigenous peoples' traditional medicines.

[178] See Thornberry, see note 16, 389-392.

[179] See the Report of the Working Group on Indigenous Populations Doc. E/CN.4/1997/102 of 10 December 1996, para. 66.

goods"[180] as well as "the expressions of Indian cultures".[181] Finally, the promotion of indigenous culture is also addressed by the "valorization of ethnical and regional diversity" in the National Plan of Culture[182] and the "establishment of commemorative dates of high significance for the various national ethnic segments".[183]

The development of national policies and legislation regarding indigenous cultural rights in Brazil is again conducted mainly by FUNAI. In general, the programs underway involve the realization of research studies and debates,[184] the dissemination of indigenous culture,[185] general support of cultural production and cultural expressions.[186]

Products and the manifestations of indigenous culture are defined as national cultural heritage.[187] The Institute of Historical and Artistic National Heritage (IPHAN)[188] is the organ assigned with this function.[189]

Since 2000, the Institute has conducted the implementation of the so-called National Program of Immaterial Heritage, which was intro-

---

[180] Article 231.

[181] Article 215.

[182] Article 215, para. 3, V.

[183] Article 215, para. 2.

[184] FUNAI has organized national as well as local indigenous peoples' conferences for the discussion of indigenous' interests and rights.

[185] For that purpose, FUNAI maintains the Museum of the Indian, which provides various information about these peoples and has also developed various projects.

[186] For example, the projects PPTAL and Kahô.

[187] The Constitution uses the word "national cultural patrimony" article 216 of the Constitution, "the assets of a material and immaterial nature, taken individually or as a whole, which bear reference to the identity, action and memory of the various groups that form the Brazilian society". It includes, not only in regard to the indigenous culture, forms of expression, ways of creating, making and living, scientific, artistic and technological creations, works, objects, documents, buildings and other spaces intended for artistic and cultural expressions, urban complexes and sites of historical, natural, artistic, archaeological, paleontological, ecological and scientific value.

[188] Instituto do Patrimonio Histórico e Artístico Nacional, which was created by Decree No. 25 of 30 November 1937 and is affiliated to the Ministry of Culture.

[189] Since its creation in 1930, it has promoted the registration and protection of more than 20.000 buildings, 83 urban centers and areas, 12.517 archaeological sites and more than 1 million objects.

duced in Brazil by Decree No. 3551 of 4 August 2000.[190] This program aims at the protection and promotion of the various forms of cultural expressions and knowledge in Brazil.[191] The identification and registration of the national immaterial heritage related to indigenous communities is expected to provide a better protection.

One aspect of the national immaterial cultural heritage related to indigenous communities,[192] however, still lacks proper protection in Brazil, namely the indigenous traditional knowledge associated with biological diversity and its uses. Its unauthorized appropriation represents an even more serious threat to the enjoyment of indigenous rights in Brazil than the unauthorized access and exploitation of genetic resources in traditional lands itself, as the dynamic and open character of indigenous knowledge makes its detection and protection a very difficult task. Provisional Act No. 2.186-16/2001 is the relevant regulation and the same criticisms addressed earlier in this article apply here as well.[193] The norm recognizes the indigenous communities rights to decide upon the use of their traditional knowledge, including the right to share the benefits arising from the direct or indirect economic exploitation.[194] Nevertheless, it does not elaborate practical ways of the effective indigenous control of the use of their knowledge. Furthermore, no attention is paid to the collective – and frequently inter-communal – nature of indigenous knowledge and the necessary compensation to be

---

[190] Regulated by Resolution No. 001/2006. This program aims at the identification, recognition, preservation and promotion of the immaterial dimension of cultural heritage. It is a promotional program based on the partnership among governmental institutions, universities, non-governmental organizations, development agencies and private organizations.

[191] Protection and promotion may be guaranteed and enforced, first of all, by administrative measures, which include the inventory and register of the material identified by governmental organs or by the civil societies (article 2, IV of Decree 3551/01) and also projects for the improvement of the transmission and reproduction of this material. Juridical (and also extra juridical measures) can be adopted by Federal Prosecutors for the preservation and promotion of Brazilian cultural patrimony in general (article 129, III of the 1988 Constitution).

[192] Expressly declared as such in article 8, para. 4 of the provisional act No. 2.186-16/2001.

[193] See the discussions on the protection of genetic resources in indigenous lands in Brazil.

[194] Mainly in Chapter III. of the act.

granted to the groups. The legislative projects being underway in the National Congress since 1995[195] are without any results so far.

Special attention has been granted to indigenous educational and linguistic rights in Brazil. According to the Constitution of 1988, the national educational system has to pay respect to national and regional cultural values[196] and has to guarantee the use of indigenous languages.[197] In 1999,[198] the category "indigenous school" was introduced in the Brazilian educational system which aims at "the full valorization of the indigenous peoples cultures and [at] the affirmation and preservation of their ethnic diversity".[199] General requirements for the organization, structure and functioning of these schools are the localization in areas inhabited by indigenous communities, exclusive attendance by these communities, education in both Portuguese and the native language, and autonomous organization, with the participation of the indigenous community concerned.[200] Financial and technical support is provided by the Union.[201]

---

[195] Projects mentioned earlier in this article, in the discussions about the protection of genetic resources in indigenous lands in Brazil, namely: PL 4.842/1998 (Senator Marina da Silva), PL4.579/1998 (Mr. Jacques Wagner), PL 1.953/1999 (Mr. Silas Câmara), PL 2.360/2003 (Sr. Mário Negromonte), PL 5.078/2005 (Mr. Eduardo Valverde), PL 287/2007 (Mrs. Janete Capiberibe), PL 3.170/2008 (Sr. Takayama), see note 168.

[196] Article 210 of the Constitution.

[197] Article 210, para. 2 of the Constitution.

[198] Report (Parecer) 14 and Resolution 03 of the National Educational Council (Conselho Nacional de Educacao). Both documents followed the principles established in the Federal Law No. 9.394 of 20 December 1996 (Guidelines and Bases of National Educational System) – hereinafter LDB – and in the National Plan of Education (Federal Law No. 10.172 of 9 January 2001), which determined the development of a differentiated, intercultural and multilinguistic educational system for indigenous communities in Brazil, see article 79 LDB.

[199] Article 1, Resolution CEB 03 of 1999.

[200] Arts 2 and 3 of Resolution CEB 03 of 1999. The project of indigenous schools is conducted by the Ministry of Education, which develops training-programs for the formation of specialized teachers, specific curricula and differentiated didactic material, reflecting the indigenous culture concerned.

[201] Financial and technical support is provided by the Union, article 79 LDB.

V. Conclusion

There are many reasons to consider the United Nations Declaration on the Rights of Indigenous Peoples a landmark document. Irrespective of its nonbinding nature, the document develops a specific thematic area of international law and at the same time offers principles for a more coherent application of existing international human rights instruments to the indigenous differentiated reality. Regarding the peoples, the path to equality in the framework of cultural diversity has been defined: protection, conservation and (free) development of all aspects of their identity, which shall be defined and conducted by their own institutions (autonomy); full participation, free from discrimination, in the public life of the state, particularly participation in the decision-making processes regarding their interests (political participation). The Declaration itself left to the states the task and the challenge to determine the specific ways to pursue its goals, according to the peculiarities of each country and of each indigenous community.

The considerations in this article permit the conclusion that the main gap in Brazil in relation to the principles listed in the Declaration lies in the non-recognition of the status of "Peoples" to the indigenous communities living in Brazil. Accordingly, the concept of autonomy and participation of these groups within the national society is given a much more limited scope than the one delineated in the United Nations document. This gap is reflected in the fragmentary and unilateral legal treatment of indigenous rights in Brazil and is reinforced by the defective administrative measures thereto. In this context, compliance with the Declaration would require, in Brazil, a completely new and updated approach.

Regarding the content of the specific rights, the Brazilian Constitution could be, to some extent, considered an advanced legal instrument, since it recognizes the indigenous groups' identity, their customs and organizations, the essential value of their lands for their physical and cultural survival and supports this recognition with various special individual and collective rights and guarantees. Nevertheless, the enforcement of this framework has been hampered by the absence of further legislative clarification and by incoherent administrative measures.

The concrete identification of the specific bearers of these rights in Brazil, which is based on a debatable method of employment of the self-identification criterion, requires adaptation. As shown earlier, the UN Declaration itself recognizes the indigenous peoples' right to development and opens ways for the inclusion of indigenous individuals or groups which do not live according to the traditional manner anymore. The specific outcomes of the Brazilian history regarding indigenous peoples, namely their migration to the urban areas, and the dynamism of some indigenous cultures in Brazil should, thus, be addressed in a more proper and effective manner in order to avoid a further deprivation of rights.

As to indigenous rights to lands, first of all, no guarantees or rights can be enforced whilst the demarcation of these territories is unclear. This is a central obstacle to the achievement of the Declaration's goals in Brazil as the duration and the characteristics of the demarcation proceedings are still highly influenced by third-party interests in these lands. The still unconcluded process of demarcation of Raposa-Serra do Sol provides an enlightening example of this. Regarding indigenous groups' usufruct of natural resources and of the potentialities of their lands, it has been shown that indigenous communities in Brazil do not enjoy rights similar to the ones accorded in the Declaration, even if these rights are summarized in a very subtle manner in article 32 para. 1 of that document, namely as rights to "determine and develop priorities and strategies".

In the case of mining activities in traditional lands, it would be necessary to develop a system of authorizations based on indigenous peoples' concrete concerns. The exploitation of genetic resources in indigenous territories, on the other hand, would require effective mechanisms of indigenous groups' conscious control, including the right to veto, over all the projects developed within their territories, as the Brazilian Constitution does not determine any exception to the general indigenous communities' exclusive usufruct in relation to genetic resources. Both of these most common and serious limitations to indigenous peoples' rights to natural resources in Brazil are based not only on administrative, but also on legal lapses in the treatment of these rights.

Concerning indigenous peoples' cultural rights, maybe the most special challenge is represented by the protection of the immaterial dimension of indigenous cultural identity. On the one hand, the introduction of a National Program committed *inter alia* for the protection and preservation of this aspect of indigenous cultures is to be praised; on the other hand, however, the specific protection of traditional knowledge associated with biological diversity demands further endeavors mainly for the establishment of clear legal definitions of (indigenous groups) collective and (non-indigenous) individual properties which are touched upon in this context, as well as clear guidelines for the treatment of the interface between these rights. It must be noted, however, that this challenge also confronts the international level and lacks appropriate treatment here.

The episode of the demarcation of the territory Raposa-Serra do Sol raises other concerns about the promotion of indigenous peoples cultural identity in Brazil. Radical measures like the forced removal of non-indigenous persons from the territory after years of tacit permission can produce the opposite impact on the perception of the national society about the value and the necessity of protection of indigenous identity. As the example showed, this measure was seen by some Brazilian citizens as granting indigenous groups a privileged position within the national society. As a result, these groups become even more isolated and vulnerable.

Indisputably, the promotion and protection of indigenous identity in Brazil require continuity and, once again, the participation of the communities involved in the development of strategies.

UN Convention to Combat Desertification: Recent Developments

Christine Fuchs

I. Introduction

The United Nations Convention to Combat Desertification (UNCCD)[1] was adopted in 1994 as a consequence of the UN Conference on Environment and Development. It entered into force in December 1996 and now benefits from a universal membership encompassing 191 Member States and the European Community.[2]

---

[1] Full title: The United Nations Convention to Combat Desertification in Countries Experiencing Serious Drought and/or Desertification, Particularly in Africa; in: P.W. Birnie/ A. Boyle (eds), *Basic Documents on International Law and the Environment*, 1995, 513 et seq.

[2] See under:<http://www.unccd.int/convention/ratif/doeif.php>.

UNCCD is a multilateral instrument for environmental protection and for development cooperation.[3] Its first objective is "to combat desertification".[4] The Convention defines the term "desertification" to mean "land degradation in arid, semi-arid and dry sub-humid areas resulting from various factors, including climatic variations and human activities".[5] Thus, the Convention is not concerned with action against land degradation in general. Instead it focuses exclusively on the phenomenon of land degradation occurring in the so-called "drylands". The shared characteristic of these areas is a paucity of rainfall.[6] Finally, "land degradation" in drylands is defined as reduction or loss of the biological or economic productivity and complexity of rainfed cropland, irrigated cropland, or range, pasture, forest and woodlands. It may result from land uses or from processes such as: "soil erosion caused by wind and/or water;" "deterioration of the physical, chemical and biological or economic properties of soil" and "long-term loss of natural vegetation".[7] The Convention aims to prevent and/or reduce land degradation, rehabilitate partly degraded land, and reclaim desertified land.[8]

The second objective UNCCD pursues is to "mitigate the effects of drought" whereby the expression "drought" is defined as the natural phenomenon that exists when an unusually low precipitation level adversely affects the productivity of land.[9]

According to the UN Millennium Ecosystem Assessment drylands cover 41 per cent of the earth's land surface and are inhabited by more than two billion people. The Assessment furthermore estimates that 10–20 per cent of drylands are already degraded which means that approximately 1-6 per cent of their inhabitants live in desertified areas, with many more being at risk from desertification.[10]

---

[3] B. Kjellén, "The Saga of the Convention to Combat Desertification: The Rio/Johannesburg Process and the Global Responsibility for the Drylands", *RECIEL* 12 (2003), 127 et seq. (131).
[4] Article 2 (1) UNCCD.
[5] Article 1 (a) UNCCD.
[6] Article 1 (g) UNCCD.
[7] Article 1 (f) (i)- (iii) UNCCD.
[8] Article 1 (b) UNCCD.
[9] Article 1 (c) UNCCD.
[10] Z. Adeel, "Ecosystems and Human Well-being: Desertification Synthesis", Millennium Ecosystem Assessment, 2005, Summary.

In general terms, poverty is more acute in drylands than in any other ecosystem area. The loss of productive land starts a vicious circle for many rural people in Africa, Asia and Latin America in which land degradation is both a driver and a result of poverty.[11] Environmental refugees and conflicts are a consequence.[12]

The Preamble of the Convention stresses its anthropocentric approach which reflects the recognition that an acceptable level of degradation can only be established with reference to the human needs of local people.[13]

The twofold approach of UNCCD, as expressed in its Preamble, is to pursue environmental and socio-economic development objectives. The Convention gives equal importance to both aspects, an "improved productivity of land, and the rehabilitation, conservation and sustainable management of land and water resources" on the one hand and to "improved living conditions, in particular at the community level".[14] The requirements for all State parties to "adopt an integrated approach addressing the physical, biological and socio-economic aspects of the processes of desertification and drought"[15] and to "integrate strategies for poverty eradication into efforts to combat desertification"[16] further underline this balanced approach.

UNCCD is hailed as a unique instrument for one remarkable innovative feature it applies, namely its participatory or "bottom-up" approach. This term is commonly used for UNCCD's requirements of participation in decision-making of local populations affected by desertification, as well as non-governmental organisations. Negotiators of the Convention expected that local community knowledge and support would be vital for a successful implementation. Hence, direct participation has played a significant role in the working practice of the Convention from the outset.

---

[11] A. Tal/ J.A. Cohen, "Bringing "Top- Down" to "Bottom-Up": A New Role for Environmental Legislation in Combating Desertification", *Harvard Environmental Law Review* 31 (2007), 163 et seq. (170).

[12] T. Bryant, "A New Approach to an Old Problem: The Convention to Combat Desertification", *Environmental and Planning Law Journal* 13 (1996), 445 et seq.

[13] Ph. Dobie, "A Future for the Drylands?", *RECIEL* 12 (2003), 140 et seq. (141).

[14] Article 2 (2) UNCCD.

[15] Article 4 (2) (a) UNCCD.

[16] Article 4 (2) (c) UNCCD.

This approach is reflected in the obligation to develop and implement national, subregional and regional action programmes in such a way as to inspire cooperation in a spirit of partnership between the donor community, governments at all levels, local populations and community groups, and facilitate access by local populations to appropriate information and technology.[17] Moreover, affected countries are required to establish and implement their National Action Programmes (NAPs) through participatory means.[18]

Even though the bottom-up approach has failed to produce widespread successes,[19] examples of success show that one may hope it will be more effective than the traditional top-down approach of development planning in the long run.[20] Provided that the position of the respective civil society in affected countries becomes stronger the Convention's work will become more effective, too.

The Convention does not content itself with promoting bilateral and multilateral arrangements[21] linking donors and local entities. The need for a comprehensive, coordinating framework for action is reflected by the central element the Convention uses to achieve its aims, the NAPs.

In addition, the Convention obliges affected country parties to strengthen relevant legislation, to enact new laws and to establish long-term policies.[22] The Convention remains, however, silent on the specific content and form of such legislation and Convention bodies have so far failed to address this vagueness. This lack of support is one reason for the failure of many affected states to adopt relevant legislation.[23]

---

[17]   Article 10 (2) (e) UNCCD.

[18]   Article 10 (2) (f) UNCCD.

[19]   L.C. Clark, "A Call to Restructure Existing International Environmental Law in Light of Africa's Renaissance: The United Nations Convention to Combat Desertification and the New Partnership for Africa's Development (NEPAD)", *Seattle University School of Law - Law Review* 22 (2003-2004), 525 et seq. (540).

[20]   S. Bethune, "Review of Legislation and Policies Pertinent to Combating Desertification – A Case Study from Namibia", *RECIEL* 12 (2003), 176 et seq. (180).

[21]   Article 4 (1) UNCCD.

[22]   Article 5 (e) UNCCD.

[23]   U. Beyerlin, "Desertification", in: R. Wolfrum (ed.), *Max Planck Encyclopaedia of Public International Law*, available online in August 2008; Tal/ Cohen, see note 11, 181.

One central question dealt with in this article will therefore be whether or not we can expect improved guidance in the development and implementation of legislation to combat desertification. The outcomes of the most recent meetings of UNCCD bodies and their decisions with respect to the future strategy and operation of UNCCD will be analysed. Particular attention will be given to the contents and potential effect of the newly adopted 10-Year Strategic Plan and Framework to Enhance the Implementation of the Convention (2008–2018).

The treaty bodies under UNCCD are first of all the Conference of the Parties (COP)[24] and the Secretariat.[25] Subsidiary bodies are the Global Mechanism (GM),[26] the Committee for the Review of the Implementation of the Convention (CRIC), and the Committee on Science and Technology.[27]

The COP convenes its meetings once every two years.[28] Its functions are, *inter alia,* to promote and monitor the implementation of UNCCD and to further develop the Convention.[29]

The eighth and most recent meeting of the COP (COP-8) adopted a number of changes to the functioning of the Convention. COP-8 was held in Madrid, Spain, from 3 to 14 September 2007. Additionally, the Committee for the Review of the Implementation of the Convention (CRIC-6) met from 4 to 14 September and the Committee on Science and Technology (CST-8) from 4 to 7 September.[30]

The Convention itself identified the following deficiencies which impede its proper implementation: insufficient financing compared to both the other Rio conventions,[31] a weak scientific basis, insufficient advocacy and awareness and institutional weaknesses. It will be examined how far these deficiencies have been addressed by the most recent COP decisions and the Strategic Plan.

---

[24]   Article 22 UNCCD.

[25]   Article 23 UNCCD.

[26]   Article 21 (4) UNCCD.

[27]   Article 24 UNCCD, established in Decision 1/COP-5.

[28]   Article 22 (4) UNCCD, .

[29]   Article 22 (2) UNCCD.

[30]   Earth Negotiation Bulletin (ENB), "Summary of the Eight Conference of the Parties to the Convention to Combat Desertification: 3-14 September 2007", 1, <http://www.iisd.ca/download/pdf/enb04206e.pdf>.

[31]   The Convention on Biological Diversity (CBD) and the UN Framework Convention on Climate Change (UNFCCC).

II. The 10-Year Strategic Plan and Framework to Enhance the Implementation of the Convention (2008–2018)

The Strategic Plan and Framework (2008–2018) have been drafted by the intersessional intergovernmental Working Group and adopted by COP-8. The Strategic Plan strives to address impediments to an effective implementation of UNCCD. It is a reaction to the changes in the policy and the scientific and financial environment of the Convention over the last decade. These changes are due to the Millennium Assessment (MA) on dryland ecosystems which considerably advanced knowledge about biophysics and socio-economy. Moreover, official development assistance increased recently after a period of stagnation when the Global Environment Facility (GEF) became a financial mechanism of the Convention.[32]

The Strategic Plan expresses a shared vision for the progressive development of the Convention over the next ten years. Can the Strategic Plan be expected to redirect actions of Convention bodies, Member States and collaborating institutions such as the GEF?

To ensure a practical effect of the Plan all Convention bodies are required to develop their programmes of work according to the Strategic Plan and to report on progress made in its implementation to the CRIC. This requirement ensures that the actions of the bodies are in line with the Strategic Plan.[33] Notably, the Executive Secretary and the GM are asked to draft a joint working programme to ensure their improved coordination.[34]

Member States are called to implement the Plan, *inter alia*, within their action programmes and to report on progress made in its implementation.[35] The Plan also invites GEF to take the Plan into account in the next replenishment period.[36]

The COP will have the primary responsibility to assess and review the implementation of the Plan, with assistance from the CRIC and the Committee on Science and Technology.[37] Hence it may be presumed

---

[32] Decision 3/COP-8, Annex, The Strategy, Introduction.
[33] Decision 3/COP-8 (3).
[34] Decision 3/COP-8 (F).
[35] Decision 3/COP-8 (4)-(6).
[36] Decision 3/COP-8 (35).
[37] Decision 3/COP-8 (43).

that the Plan will impact upon the activities of treaty bodies, Member States and partners.

1. Objectives of the Strategic Plan

The Plan sets forth four "strategic objectives" which are intended to provide guidance to actions of all UNCCD stakeholders and partners. The Plan counts among its stakeholders not only its Member States but also NGOs and scientific communities.[38]

Under each strategic objective the Plan formulates "expected impacts" i.e. long-term effects to be achieved under the respective strategic objective. "Long term" in this context is defined to mean a period of a minimum of ten years.

The first strategic objective is to improve the living conditions of affected populations. Corresponding expected impacts include an improved livelihood base and an income from sustainable land management for such populations as well as their reduced vulnerability to climate change and drought.

Two further strategic objectives are to improve the condition of affected ecosystems and to generate global benefits through the effective implementation of UNCCD. Such benefits may concern biodiversity and the climate.

The fourth strategic objective, finally, is to mobilise resources to support implementation of the Convention through national and international partnerships.[39] These strategic objectives reaffirm the Convention's endorsement of an integrated multi-faceted approach.

The Plan further contains five "operational objectives" which are to provide short and medium-term guidance over a three to five year-period to stakeholders and partners. They are more action oriented and concrete than the strategic objectives.

The first operational objective is advocacy, awareness raising and education on the international, national and local level. In this context the Plan underlines the role that NGOs and scientific communities should play.[40] The Committee on Science and Technology and the GM

---

[38] Decision 3/COP-8 V Outcome 1.3.
[39] Decision 3/COP-8, Annex, IV.
[40] Decision 3/COP-8, V Outcome 1.3.

are called to play a supportive role in the implementation of this objective.

The second operational objective is to support the creation of enabling environments through a policy framework. This aspect includes, *inter alia*, a reformulation of NAPs with a view to making them more strategic, basing them firmly on biophysical and socio-economic knowledge, and incorporating them into an investment framework. From the developed country's side this involves mainstreaming UNCCD objectives into their development cooperation programmes. Support from the GM is to facilitate these tasks.

The third operational objective for UNCCD is to become a global authority on scientific and technical knowledge in the fields of anti-desertification work.[41] The Committee on Science and Technology is given primary responsibility to fulfil this objective.[42]

Operational objective number four aims at engagement for capacity-building and the fifth and final objective is to mobilise and improve the use of national, bilateral and multilateral financial and technological assets.[43] Here the GM has a central responsibility.[44]

The Secretariat too is called to assist in the implementation of all operational objectives.[45] The primary responsibility in the achievement of the Plan's objectives pertains, however, to the parties.[46]

2. Reform of UNCCDs Implementation Mechanisms

a. Strengthening of the Scientific Basis

In its section detailing the roles and responsibilities of UNCCD bodies, partners and stakeholders in the implementation of the plan the COP states the necessity to strengthen the Committee on Science and Technology so it can "assess, advise and support implementation, on a comprehensive, objective, open and transparent basis" of scientific informa-

---

[41] Decision 3/COP-8, Annex, V.
[42] Decision 3/COP-8, Annex, VI, A. 13.
[43] Decision 3/COP-8, Annex, V.
[44] Decision 3/COP-8, Annex, VI, C. 17.
[45] Decision 3/COP-8, Annex, VI, D. 19.
[46] Decision 3/COP-8, Annex, VI, F. 23.

tion.[47] The dissemination of scientific data is necessary to share solutions about the drylands of this world.[48]

To clarify the Committee on Science and Technology's mandate the Plan emphasises that the Committee's recommendations aim to be policy-oriented, scientifically sound and peer reviewed. It mobilises experts under its auspices and engages in information exchange between institutions, parties and end users.

The Committee is called upon to refine the global indicators stated with respect to the strategic objectives. Those global indicators are not new. They mostly stem from the GEF strategic objectives, Millennium Development Goals and the Convention on Biological Diversity (CBD) 2010 Target. The aim is now for the Committee to establish both biophysical and socio-economic baselines on desertification/land degradation at the national level and also guidelines to monitor trends.[49]

The hitherto used Group of Experts mechanism was deemed to be inadequate to provide scientific advice. Their reports contained a number of research projects and resulting recommendations and were of varying quality. Some experts showed limited engagement which can partly be attributed to the fact that they were not backed by any budget.[50]

Consequently, the COP merely took note of the final report of the Group of Experts and encouraged the States parties to consider and use, as appropriate, the final report for the implementation of their NAPs.[51]

To improve the Convention's scientific basis the COP decided to organise future Committee on Science and Technology sessions as scientific and technical conferences. These conferences will focus on a specific theme which is determined by the COP.[52]

The COP requested the Committee's Bureau to link with networks, institutions, agencies and bodies and to include the NGOs and other civil society stakeholders in the network.[53] Interestingly, no clear distinction is drawn between NGOs and scientists.

---

[47] Decision 3/COP-8, Annex, VI, A. 13.
[48] Kjellén, see note 3, 132.
[49] Decision 3/COP-8, Annex, VI, A. 14.
[50] ENB, see note 30, 16.
[51] Decision 17/COP-8.
[52] Decision 13/COP-8.
[53] Decision 14/COP-8.

The new format was welcomed by the scientists present at COP-8. It can be hoped that this alternative format will increase scientists' attendance at the Committee on Science and Technology sessions and more thoroughly involve the scientific community in UNCCD's work. Thus, the scientific base of UNCCD will be strengthened. The problem how to formulate scientific advice in a way that is usable by Member States remains however unresolved.

b. Improved Compliance Monitoring and Support

The CRIC function is to review the implementation of the Convention and to facilitate the exchange of information on measures taken by the parties. In the past, Member States have criticised the CRIC for its unclear function and mode of operation, i.e. its statements concerning country reports failed to provide to Member States the information needed to ensure improved implementation. The CRIC's mandate has been clarified under the Strategic Plan.

The Plan states the necessity to strengthen the CRIC[54] and lists the following tasks for the CRIC: to determine and disseminate best practices on the implementation of the UNCCD; to review the implementation of the Plan and of the Convention; and to assess CRIC performance and effectiveness.[55] Future CRIC and the Committee on Science and Technology sessions will be synchronised so as to benefit from synergies between both bodies.

The Plan stresses the importance of simplifying the reporting procedure using new reporting guidelines and to provide generally comparable information, taking into account action programmes.[56]

However, the COP did not modify the terms of reference of the CRIC. It postponed the consideration and revision to the ninth COP session.[57] To bring the compliance monitoring forward the COP asked the Secretariat, in collaboration with the GM, to develop and establish draft reporting guidelines for reports on implementation of action programmes.[58] It remains to be seen what the next COP will agree upon. The clarification resulting from the Plan, at least, shows the way to address the noted deficiencies in the work of the CRIC.

---

54   Decision 3/COP-8, Annex, VI, B. 15.
55   Decision 3/COP-8, Annex, VI, B. 16.
56   Decision 3/COP-8, Annex, VI, C.
57   Decision 7/COP-8.
58   Decision 8/COP-8.

III. Guidance in the Development and Implementation of Legislation

A solid legislative or other regulatory framework is a precondition for the creation of a stable enabling framework to combat desertification. Legislation and regulation is necessary not to impose solutions from above but to encourage and support such solutions and to create transparency and coherence.

The Convention includes five Regional Implementation Annexes for Africa, Latin America and the Caribbean, Asia, the Northern Mediterranean and for Central and Eastern Europe. Those Annexes contain guidelines for the preparation of action programmes and for their focus and content.

In the spring of 2008 there are 37 NAPs and six Subregional Action Programmes in Africa, 28 NAPs and one Subregional Action Programme in Asia, 25 NAPs and one Subregional Action Programme in Latin America and the Caribbean, four NAPs in the Mediterranean and four NAPs in Central and Eastern Europe.[59]

The most recent Parliamentary Round Table pointed out various weaknesses that impede the effectiveness of NAPs, such as their lack of appropriate strategic actions, limited funding, missing links between policymakers and scientists and an incomplete integration of international policies on the national level.[60] Most NAPs are irrelevant in national policy development.[61] The Strategic Plan's second operational objective points out the necessity for action in this context.

The Parliamentary Round Tables strive to formulate public policies and environmental legislation. Do they assist legislators in developing legislative initiatives?

Unfortunately, the members of parliaments do not go beyond stating deficiencies. They do not provide practical advice on the content of legislation needed to address the perceived shortcomings. Finally, during the last Round Table (COP-8) the members of parliament themselves noted with regret the weak contributions that parliaments made

---

[59] <http://www.unccd.int/actionprogrammes/africa/africa.php>.

[60] Declaration of Members of Parliaments para. 6.

[61] Ch. Bassett/ J. Talafré, "Implementing the UNCCD: Towards a Recipe for Success", *RECIEL* 12 (2003), 133 et seq., 135.

to the UNCCD implementation process.[62] The Round Tables remain a mere platform to exchange views.[63]

IV. Financing of the Convention

UNCCD is the only multilateral Convention which is primarily promoted by developing countries. Land degradation is not a priority issue for donor governments which makes it difficult to agree on financial matters. While the importance of sufficient funding for UNCCD's effectiveness is continually pointed out, COP-8 failed to adopt its anticipated decision on the future budget. The Secretariat's budget has evolved into the most hotly debated COP issue. The problem has been aggravated by diminishing voluntary contributions to the Secretariat and the depreciation of the dollar which is the accounting currency of the United Nations, since the Euro is the Secretariat's main currency.[64] The Parliamentarian Round Table described current financial resources that are at the disposition of UNCCD as "neither substantial nor adequate, nor timely or predictable".[65]

The prolonged negotiations at COP-8 on this aspect came to an end when Japan refused to accept the five per cent increase in the Euro value of the Secretariat's budget which the draft decision on the future budget provided for. Japan stuck to its position for zero nominal growth. This matter was taken up again at the first Extraordinary COP meeting which took place in New York on 26 and 27 November 2007.[66] The consensus finally reached provides a 4 per cent budget Euro value growth for the biennium 2008/2009. The COP also agreed to use the total amount for the current biennium as a starting point for negotiations concerning its budget for the subsequent biennium.[67]

This increase indicates a positive assessment of and commitment to the strategic Plan by Member States. It therefore gives reason for optimism towards UNCCD's work over the next few years.

---

[62]   Declaration of Members of Parliaments para. 7.

[63]   Declaration of Members of Parliaments para. 9.

[64]   ENB, see note 30, 15.

[65]   Declaration of Members of Parliaments para. 13.

[66]   Press Release, "The First Extraordinary session of the COP approves the UNCCD budget for 2008/2009",<http://www.unccd.int/publicinfo/pressr el/showpressrel.php?pr=press27_11_2007>.

[67]   See above.

The Strategic Plan gives high importance to the need for additional funding for the implementation of the Convention in a wider sense. Lack of financial resources is the most frequently cited impediment to effective implementation.[68] Official development assistance should at least reach the 0.7 per cent target by 2015.[69]

V. Conclusion

In spite of the efforts under UNCCD desertification trends have not abated.[70] Parliamentarians at the last COP lamented that many affected States parties fail to prioritise tackling land degradation in their development plans. Many developed parties, on the other hand, abstain from promoting the provision of sufficient financial resources. The parliamentarians noted a lack of peasant participation causing a neglect of rural policy.[71]

Can the latest developments under the UNCCD improve the performance of the Convention and yield tangible progress? Or is the Strategic Plan nothing more than a new mechanism requiring additional planning and monitoring without delivering anything substantial?

The increase of the Secretariat's budget is a positive indicator for future UNCCD work. The same is true for the modification of the format of Committee on Science and Technology meetings. Other aspects, such as the assistance in the development of legislation and the restructuring of the reporting system still need to be addressed adequately. The Strategic Plan gives the necessary momentum for such reform. It clarifies the mandates and methods of work of its treaty bodies in reaction to their perceived operational inefficiencies. The Plan is also a success in that it adopts a results-based management approach, stating global indicators which will be refined by the Committee on Science and Technology. NGOs lament passivity and inaction in combating desertification.[72] The Strategic Plan inspired their optimism for the future however.[73]

---

[68]   Bassett/ Talafré, see note 61, 133 et seq.
[69]   Declaration of Members of Parliaments para. 23.
[70]   Declaration of Members of Parliaments para. 3; Clark, see note 19, 541.
[71]   Declaration of Members of Parliaments para. 4.
[72]   Declaration of NGOs para. 3.
[73]   Declaration of NGOs para. 15.

The Convention is gradually evolving into an implementable shape with strong treaty bodies, procedures and mechanisms.[74] The Strategic Plan has further advanced this development.

As stated in the Madrid Declaration, the outcome of the ministerial segment of COP-8, stronger political will is most important for the success.[75] Fully implementing the Convention is necessary to secure water and food for the poorest and most vulnerable people. Desertification is a global problem directly or indirectly affecting the whole of humankind.[76] One step to clarify this global responsibility might be to recognise topsoil as a global public good.[77]

---

[74]   Bassett/ Talafré, see note 61, 133 et seq.
[75]   <http://www.unccd.int/cop/officialdocs/cop8/pdf/16eng.pdf>, Declaration of Madrid, para. 4.
[76]   Madrid Declaration, ibid., para. 1.
[77]   Declaration of Members of Parliaments para. 15.

A Cosmopolitan World Order? Perspectives on Francisco de Vitoria and the United Nations

*Pekka Niemelä**

I. Fragmentation and Tradition

Little is left of the certainties that animated the first generation of liberal international lawyers in the latter part of the 19th century. Their aspirations for an international rule of law were shattered amidst the two great cataclysms of the 20th century which finally proved the utopian nature of the idea of regarding Europe as "the legal conscience of the civilized world"[1] that would lead humanity towards global peace and prosperity. The "ivory-tower" sociology with which they charted the

---

*   This article reiterates themes explored in my Master's Thesis, "Beyond Sovereignty: The Universal of Francisco de Vitoria", approved by the Law Faculty of the University of Helsinki in September 2007. Many thanks to my thesis supervisor Martti Koskenniemi.
1   M. Koskenniemi, *Gentle Civilizer of Nations, The Rise and Fall of International Law 1870-1960*, 2002, 11-97.

world had produced only untested generalizations about human nature and cause and effect, whose "simplicity and perfection" gave them an "easy and universal appeal",[2] but which failed to reflect reality in any meaningful way. More pragmatic legal analysis came to dominate the field as all serious theoretical and historical inquiry was assumed merely to reproduce the unending collision between naturalist and positivist theories and to create feelings of discomfort regarding the complacent hypotheses of the "civilizing mission". The realistic mindset focused on building an elaborate international legal structure, designed to thwart the disastrous consequences of modern inter-state warfare under the supervision of the United Nations.

The advent of globalization has further strengthened this tendency towards practicality. While the creation of a global marketplace has homogenized aspects of public and private life, it has been accompanied by "an accelerated differentiation of society into autonomous social systems, each of which springs territorial confines and constitutes itself globally".[3] For international law, this fragmentation has signified "the emergence of specialized and (relatively) autonomous rules or rule-complexes, legal institutions and spheres of legal practice".[4] As is well-known, the arrival of self-governing sub-disciplines – such as "trade law", "human rights law" and "environmental law" – has raised various questions about how to solve normative conflicts arising from their distinct visions and preferences and whether they pose a threat to the perceived coherence of general international law. In the middle of such phenomenon, questions relating to the fundamental "nature" of international law or to its historical origins seem unimportant, the answering of which cannot substantially help a "functional" lawyer who is expected to give streamlined answers to pressing legal questions as a qualified expert of a particular subject-area.

In the wake of this, the composition of the international field has been thoroughly restructured. Non-state actors – transnational corporations, NGOs, inter-governmental organizations, labor groups, reli-

---

2   E.H. Carr, *The Twenty Years' Crisis, 1919-1939*, Reissue 2001, 6.
3   A. Fischer-Lescano/ G. Teubner, "Regime Collisions: The Vain Search for Legal Unity in the Fragmentation of Global Law", *Mich. J. Int'l L.* 25 (2004), 1006 et seq.
4   *Fragmentation of International Law: Difficulties Arising from the Diversification and Expansion of International Law,* Report of the Study Group of the International Law Commission, finalized by M. Koskenniemi, Doc. A/CN. 4/L.682 of 2006, 11.

gious factions, and other formal and informal networks and pressure groups – have emerged alongside states to shape the contours of the complex global governance regime.[5] Instead of a single overarching legal system, we have an order "in which national and international, public and private legal regimes overlap, struggle for priority, and have quite diverse impacts on the ground".[6] The classical text-book credo that defines international law as a body of rules applicable between states appears to have lost its appeal as it fails to take into account various rule regimes as well as forces that mould and effect political decision-making outside formal channels of interstate diplomacy. If the appeal of the Westphalian-projection of the world has eroded, so has the unity of international legal academia. In particular, the emergence of studies labelled as "New Stream" has generated an unprecentedly rich and eclectic body of writing that uses a wide repertoire of methods to challenge mainstream views and assumptions.[7]

Statements such as "[a] world structured around international law cannot but be one of imperialist violence",[8] "the promotion of international law is a worthy cause, one that ... will promote ... a common, cooperative approach to the resolution of global issues",[9] and "international law is not law",[10] may be hopelessly general and present the extremes (and *may* do little justice to the ideas of the writers in question), but they prove that outside one's constituency disagreement reigns. Which of the plurality of views is the mainstream insight and which the minority depends on the (historically determined) leverage of the con-

---

[5] For a useful general discussion on the subject-matter with regard to human rights, see P. Alston (ed.), *Non-State Actors and Human Rights*, 2005.

[6] H. Charlesworth/ D. Kennedy, "Afterword and Forward – There Remains So Much We Do Not Know", in: A. Orford (ed.), *International Law and its Others*, 2006, 401 et seq.

[7] For useful representations of the "New Stream" movement in the context of international law, see N. Purvis, "Critical Legal Studies in Public International Law", *Harv. Int'l L. J.* 32 (1991), 81 et seq.; D. Cass, "Navigating the Newstream: Recent Critical Scholarship in International Law", *Nord. J. Int'l L.* 65 (1996), 341 et seq.

[8] C. Mieville, *Between Equal Rights. A Marxist Theory of International Law*, 2005, 319.

[9] T.M. Franck, "The Power of Legitimacy and the Legitimacy of Power: International Law in an Age of Power Disequilibrium", *AJIL* 100 (2006), 89 et seq.

[10] J.R. Bolton, "Is There Really 'Law' in International Affairs", *Transnat'l L. & Contemp. Probs* 10 (2000), 7 et seq.

stituency. Here, as many Third World Scholars have noted, the scale is tipped in favor of Western/Northern institutions that have a prerogative to decide which issues are highlighted.

By and large, all of the above holds true for the United Nations as well. There is no shared understanding about its actual or potential role in 21st century world politics. Proposals for institutional restructuring are constantly on the agenda but little has been achieved in this respect; the profound controversy that circles the reform debates, especially the paralysis of "the politics of Security Council expansion",[11] exhibit the difficulties and tensions involved in any substantial United Nations discussion. "To remain relevant and useful to its member states, the United Nations must reduce its ambitions and play a more modest role in reducing international conflict".[12] This is e.g. the current American view, arguing that the United Nations is not delivering what the United States expects and that its future relevance is conditional on its ability to conform to and promote the interests of one of its most powerful members. Christian Tomuschat's claim that it is "obvious" that "the Charter is nothing else than the constitution of the international community"[13] embodies the opposite view which, broadly speaking, sees the Charter and its objectives as transcending and delineating the particular interests of UN Member States as well as the promotion of those interests.

To talk about the United Nations at such a high-level of abstraction is, of course, rather unproductive. Whatever the pros and cons of the world body, neither of the two views portrays the quotidian ambiguity that hangs over its place in today's world. It should be obvious that any argument claiming to capture the "truth" about the purpose or nature of the United Nations is more or less ideologically charged and politically motivated, an everyday exercise in the struggle for power waged at the main stages of international politics. That positions on the United Nations remain irreconcilable reflects the rich diversity of personal and

---

[11] A.M. Slaughter, "Security, Solidarity, and Sovereignty: the Grand Themes of UN Reform", *AJIL* 99 (2005), 630 et seq.; B. Fassbender, "All Illusions Shattered? Looking Back on a Decade of Failed Attempts to Reform the UN Security Council", *Max Planck UNYB* 7 (2003), 183 et seq.

[12] J. Yoo/ W. Trachman, "Less than Bargained for: The Use of Force and the Declining Relevance of the United Nations", *Chi. J. Int'l L.* 5 (2005), 393 et seq.

[13] C. Tomuschat, "Foreword", in: C. Tomuschat (ed.), *The United Nations at Age Fifty. A Legal Perspective*, 1995, ix.

cultural backgrounds of the authors as well as traditions and concerns of the institutions in which they were fostered into professional maturity.[14]

II. Tradition versus Fragmentation

Against all this, it might be plausible to think that no universal denominators connect those that practice, write, and talk about international law in myriad contexts and that outside one's professional niche looms ubiquitous heterogeneity and discord. But then again, however, reasonable such an estimate may be, it lacks intuitive credibility. Although the managerial style of much current scholarship – its sophistication, dispassion, and technical nature – often hides its aspirations, it is difficult to think of a scholar or practitioner who would not want to promote some justice. This underlying ethos has been infused in the subconscious of international lawyers ever since the profession established itself and began to look at its craft as "not just a set of more or less arbitrary inter-state compromises",[15] but as a universalizing mission proclaiming to have humanity's welfare at heart. While some perspectives appear unfounded when viewed from another, each stance contains an abstract ideal against which it measures the world.[16] Because each employs a distinct sociology, their prescriptions for the good-life differ.

The topic of human rights might be an ideal emblem of today's cosmopolitanism. They are employed across cultural, religious, and intellectual boundaries to render service to an infinite number of political and social causes. Albeit public opinion continues to associate politics with the usual traits (persuasion, canvassing), human rights are at the heart of much political rhetoric. They promise to set absolute limits to political discretion and further justice on a global scale by endowing a set of universal and inalienable rights to all. While the appealing vision

---

[14] Cf. I. Scobbie, "Wicked Heresies or Legitimate Perspectives?", in: M.D. Evans (ed.), *International Law*, 2006, 84-87.

[15] M. Koskenniemi, "On the Idea and Practice for Universal History with a Cosmopolitan Purpose", in: B. Puri/ H. Sievers (eds), *Terror, Peace and Universalism. Essays on the Philosophy of Immanuel Kant*, 2007, 123.

[16] As Stefano Guzzini has argued, "realism is unthinkable without the background of a prior idealistic position deeply committed to the universalism of the Enlightenment and democratic political theory". See S. Guzzini, *Realism in International Relations and International Political Economy*, 1998, 16.

of global human dignity appears infeasible amidst the monumental socio-economic disparities that define today's global architecture, instruments and institutions designed to promote and protect human rights continue to proliferate. The United Nations itself is the epitome of this dynamic pursuit. In the roughly sixty years of operation, its human rights structures have evolved radically, from the vague aspirations of the Universal Declaration of Human Rights, to the versatile machinery that today monitors the implementation of UN Charter and treaty-based human rights obligations on a global scale. One small feature in this development has been a strong increase in the number of NGOs involved in UN human rights processes. Bearing in mind the functions and powers of ECOSOC under Article 62 para. 2 of the Charter, it is noteworthy that today more than 3,000 NGOs have a consultative status under the ECOSOC mechanism,[17] allowing them to sit as observers, to submit written statements and to give oral presentations at public meetings of the ECOSOC and its subsidiary bodies with certain qualifications.[18] While these NGOs represent and advocate a wide range of causes, the bulk of them focus on observing and reporting "classical" human rights violations.

One of the groups holding a consultative status is called "Dominicans for Justice and Peace". It is affiliated to the Order of Preachers (commonly known as Dominican Order) and was instituted in 1998. It focuses on "the challenge of justice and peace in the world" and wishes to "contribute to the ongoing discourse on social justice and human rights violations worldwide".[19] To give additional weight to its operation, it is stated:

> "In the 16th Century, Fray *Francisco de Vitoria* and the Salamanca School in Spain established the theoretical foundations of the modern problematic of human rights. In the same century, Fray *Bartolome de las Casas* and Fray *Montesinos* championed the rights of indigenous people in Latin America. Our presence at the UN is consistent with the history of the Order."[20]

In a fragmented world, where violence and conflict are engendered by intertwined and complex causalities, this statement creates a sense of

---

[17] The granting of the consultative status is based on Article 71 of the UN Charter.
[18] See paras 29-40 of the ECOSOC resolution E/RES/1996/31 of 25 July 1996.
[19] See under <http://un.op.org/background>.
[20] Ibid.

continuity, of historical purpose and direction and wholeness. It implicitly claims that human rights and moral values are unequivocal, after all, and that the Order of Preachers has embodied and defended such ideals from the very beginning. From the distance of a half millennia, three Dominican monks are evoked and depicted as founders and advocates of a world order, the execution of which would finally erase the dividing lines of humanity. However massive the obstacles facing Dominican ideology – secularization, the influx of "competing" denominations, lack of resources, to name just few – the above introduction appears untroubled by their existence.

But is it plausible to claim that Vitoria's work instigated a tradition of human rights which the United Nations carries forward today? And are human rights or have they been an unambiguous phenomenon as the Dominican group suggests, despite the colossal academic critique cast upon their ostensibly universal, indivisible and apolitical nature? It is easy to make such historical associations, but would a closer scrutiny reveal differences, even fundamental, in how the notion of human rights was employed by Vitoria and how we employ them today. And, behind the rhetoric, what role did Vitoria's jurisprudence play in 16th century politics and what is the impact of the actions of the United Nations in the 21st century struggle for global justice?

III. Fragmentation in a Historical Context

1. Introduction

As is well known, many regard Vitoria as having instituted the "problematic" of international law. Vitoria faced a world ruled by sovereigns whose conflicting interests needed to be reconciled in a way that left them independent and equal, yet bound to a normativity that rises from their will or comes down from above or, rather, the two combined. In other words, something generations of international lawyers have faced ever since. Vitoria's legacy has been utilized in various ways. Those interested in doctrinal work have used Vitoria's texts on the law of war to construct continuums in which humanitarian law develops through nascent and early stages to the highly-sophisticated forms of the present. Others with a more theoretical inclination have tended to see Vitoria's works as the first attempt to answer the fundamental question of public international law, namely, "how is order between sovereign entities possible?"

Quite often Vitoria's writing has been isolated from the "more general intellectual and social matrix"[21] out of which it arose and within which it was to be applied and treated as an early sign of a particular ideological stance or movement that has shaped the course of human history right up to the present, in the development of which international legal rules have become entangled. Perhaps most international lawyers have a gut-feeling that whatever our predecessors did or wrote, their world and worldview was somehow simpler and more manageable, divisions were less fundamental and disciplinary disintegration, as we have and understand it today, was not something they recognized or had to consider.

While the question about the fundamental nature of international law feels too ambitious and less relevant today, Vitoria's work resembles, in many ways, the vision and ethos of today's international lawyers. Universal justice, cosmopolitanism, sovereignty and equality are all notions that *can* be detected in his work as well. This is why it has been so easy to create connections between later works and Vitoria. But there are problems in creating such uncomplicated historical links. Pure textual analysis may create the impression that doctrinal development equals social development; the more sophisticated the doctrine the better the conditions of social life. Such an outlook considers the relation of law and social life unambiguous and mutually supportive, and places a progressive logic into the heart of both. The second problem is the very idea that normative visions of the world would share a common methodological base; that sovereign discord was central to Vitoria's thought is often simply presumed.

The third associated problem is harder to point out. It has to do with the thought that assumptions of established intellectual traditions are uncontroversial, their effects beneficial, and that historical events and figures support both ideas; settled approaches and forms of action as well as idiosyncratic beliefs pave the way to a better tomorrow. For instance, a constitutionalist, who posits the United Nations at the apex of his/hers world order and regards the Charter as its constitution, may refer to Vitoria and make the following presumptions; that Vitoria's vision and the Charter acknowledge the equal standing of all nations, at least formally; that Vitoria's international law and the "Charter-led" international law impose normative demands on state behavior, efficiently delimiting state behavior horizontally and vertically, and as a corollary,

---

[21]   Q. Skinner, *The Foundations of Modern Political Thought. Volume One: The Renaissance*, 1978, x.

that law and politics are distinct phenomenon; and, finally, that there is an agency that embodies these benevolent ideas and in which crucial decisions affecting their realization are made. For Vitoria the agency is the European-universal culture in general, whereas the constitutionalist's agency is the United Nations whose operation embodies the pursuit of European-universal ideals.

In what follows, the world is viewed from Vitoria's perspective, on his terms and the analysis has two major objectives. The first is to examine Vitoria's texts and look at the context in which he wrote more closely. This should answer some fundamental questions: what assumptions guided his worldview? Was his international law concerned with a world order to which sovereign states were central? What political challenges influenced his writing? How should one approach the relation of Vitoria's work and Spanish colonialism? Did fragmentation, intellectual or practical, bother him? Answering such questions should tell whether modern interpretations of Vitoria are based on misguided assumptions. Two conflicting readings of Vitoria are presented and used to elucidate how modern scholars often judge past writing with today's concerns and standards in mind.

A further objective relates to the place of legal traditions in today's international world. Some of the problematic assumptions and implications of the UN-centered vision of the world will be highlighted and discussed. An example of the activities of the United Nations will be given in order to display how the emphasis ought to be shifted from institutional questions and formal legal analysis to other forms of action which could be more fruitful in the promotion of some of the core human rights. This aims at opening new directions to both scholarship and practice and promotes the need to engage in constant self-reflection about the assumptions, stakes, limits, possibilities and effects involved in any given professional context and setting.

2. One, Two, Three Vitorias?

Most modern scholars have interpreted Vitoria to base his answer on international law's binding force on an *a priori* moral order which should constrain sovereign behavior. They have then either rejected Vitoria's moral vision as irrelevant in the face of sovereign power or as an important reminder of the fact that universal principles (should) always animate and control state behavior. Vitoria's position as a pioneer of international law is based on James Brown Scott's work.[22] He reads Vitoria as having founded a new international order in which "the law applicable to members of the Christian community was found to be applicable to non-Christians; and the law of nations, once confined to Christendom, ... [had] become international".[23] A global order based on religious and cultural tolerance is, according to Scott, at the heart of Vitoria's work. He sees Vitoria as a champion of non-Christian rights with no bias in favor of Christian polities. "[E]quality of States, applicable not merely to the States of Christendom and of Europe but also to the barbarian principalities in the Western World of Columbus"[24] is what Vitoria had in mind, much in the vein of the UN Charter Preamble which reads of "the equal rights of men and women and of nations large and small". What had been European, becomes universal in Vitoria's work. Scott's belief in the Christian vision makes him label the Spanish led colonial project as an early civilizing mission devoid of self-interest and exploitation, created for the benefit of the Indians who lived "in an imperfect state of civilization".[25] Although Scott closes his eyes to the realities of Spanish colonialism and treats Vitoria and Christianity as representatives of a universal morality, the formal equality of the Indians, as that morality's co-occupants, remains, for Scott, the main principle of Vitoria's international law.

This unreservedly admiring reading has been challenged by recent critical scholarship. The work of Antony Anghie has been central in reexamining the role international law played in the colonial encounter.[26] Anghie too reads Vitoria as moving toward a new world order to which even the native peoples of the Americas belong, but approaches Vitoria's texts from a very different perspective. According to Anghie, Vitoria's work has an ambivalent undertone and is ultimately aimed at providing justification for the imperial ambitions of the West. In the

---

[22] Scott was a dedicated Catholic as well as an early advocate of international arbitration who utilized his position as the General Editor of the Classics of International Law series to promote the efforts of his co-religionist.

[23] J. Brown Scott, *The Spanish Conception of International Law and of Sanctions*, 1934, 1-2.

[24] Id., *The Spanish Origin of International Law. Francisco de Vitoria and His Law of Nations*, 1934, 281. Quite interestingly, Scott does not discuss the status of Islamic or African or Oriental polities in Vitoria's thought, as if they were non-existent.

[25] Id., see note 24, 287.

[26] I base my reading of Anghie on his *Imperialism, Sovereignty and the Making of International Law*, 2005.

veil of equality and neutrality, Vitoria justifies the usurpation of non-western territory. Vitoria absorbs the Indians into the ambit of a universal law which reflects the values and beliefs of Christian societies. This law sanctions western presence in the Americas and, eventually, the appropriation of Indian land and resources. While Vitoria's international law endows the Indians with similar rights as Christians, it has a profound structural bias in favor of Christianity which renders the notion of "equality" meaningless.

Anghie argues that no legal framework regulated Spanish-Indian relations.[27] Thus, "international law was created out of the unique issues generated by the encounter between the Spanish and the Indians."[28] In contrast to Scott, then, Anghie denies the idea that a finalized body of rules was simply expanded to govern the relations of western and non-western polities as well. For him, the principle of sovereign equality was a useful analytical tool in conceptualizing and systematizing the more or less homogenous state centred system of Europe and could not be used to analyze the structures of the 16th century global community. Anghie argues that the Spanish title over the Americas was traditionally settled "by applying the jurisprudence developed by the Church to deal with the Saracens to the Indies."[29] In his eyes, divine law administed by the Pope stood above positive and natural law and granted the Pope the right to exercise universal jurisdiction. Thus, European sovereigns could rely on papal sanction whenever they needed legitimation for their conquests of pagan territory.[30] Anghie reads Vitoria to have rejected this traditional framework. In his words "Vitoria … creates a new system of international law which essentially displaces divine law and its administrator, the Pope, and replaces it with natural law administered by a secular sovereign."[31] Just like Scott, Anghie interprets Vitoria to mean that Amerindians belong to the realm of this natural law and enjoy the same rights as Europeans. The dictates of Vitoria's new natural law reflect the exercise of human reason. Vitoria equates its exercise with the maintenance of European customs and beliefs. Because the Indians lead lives that resemble European-universal lifestyle, they are fellow humans, have an equal standing in the realm of natural law, and the Spanish have no right to appropriate their land or

---

27 Anghie, see note 26, 15.
28 Ibid.
29 Ibid., 17.
30 Ibid., 17.
31 Ibid., 17-18.

property.[32] One expression of Vitoria's universal rationality is the *ius gentium*. It consists of rules to which all nations adhere. According to Vitoria the Spaniards have, for instance, the right to travel and trade in Indian land. These rights belong reciprocally to the Indians.

According to Anghie the realities of Spanish colonialism mean that "Vitoria's scheme finally endorses and legitimizes endless Spanish incursions into Indian society".[33] The sole enforcement mechanism of Vitoria's *ius gentium* is war. Anghie interprets this to mean that the Indians will inevitably and continuously, with the colonial realities in mind, resist Spanish penetration and breach the rules of Vitoria's new international law. This resistance sanctions Spanish retaliation and transfers title over native land and property into Spanish hands in accordance with Vitoria's law of war.[34] Vitoria's doctrine of war is based on the presumption that in any conflict only one of the parties, the injured party, is waging a just war and that only a just prince may wage war legitimately. Anghie reads some of Vitoria's comments on the status of the Saracens to mean that all non-Christians, the Amerindians included, "are inherently incapable of waging a just war".[35] This leads to his pessimistic conclusion: "the Indians are excluded from the realm of sovereignty and exist only as the objects against which Christian sovereignty may exercise its power to wage war".[36] In his eyes, Vitoria is not dealing with the (defining international law) question "of order among sovereign states but [with] the problem of order among societies belonging to two different cultural systems".[37] This problem is solved by creating a system in which all peoples stand as equals. Vitoria's equality is based on an unequal assimilation of the two as Christian customs and values are at the basis of his universal system. A central part of that system is his *ius gentium* that governs the relations of western and non-western polities. These rules accord the West the right to engage in its particular activities within the non-Christian world. Resistance against their exercise grants Christians a right to wage war. For Anghie, Vitoria categorically denies the right of the non-Christians to wage war. As warfare is a central attribute and tool of 16th century politics, Vitoria's denial means that the Amerindians, and non-

---

32   Ibid., 18-20.
33   Ibid., 21.
34   Ibid., 21 and 24. See below under III. 4.
35   Ibid., 26.
36   Ibid.
37   Ibid., 28.

Christians more generally, have no sovereignty, no means, whether legal or practical, to oppose Spanish-European occupation. For Anghie, then, Vitoria is a tragic handmaiden of Spanish imperialism.

Although at the outset Anghie and Scott interpret Vitoria's work in a similar way, they end up in opposite positions. Both perceive Vitoria as a trendsetter who coined a disciplinary structure for later scholars. Sovereign (mis)behavior is central to that structure. Scott attempts to establish that Vitoria is a first naturalist whose natural law overrides sovereign consent or is in harmony with it, whereas Anghie treats Vitoria's natural law as an apology for the Spanish empire which shatters the meaning of Indian sovereignty. If other positivists start from the premiss that all states enjoy at least formal sovereignty, Anghie restricts its occurrence to the western scene due to his cultural scheme. Both writers detach Vitoria's religious dogma and doctrine from the new and secular international law and view Christianity as only his implicit driving force. Both engage in a narrow textual analysis only and do not consider Vitoria's intellectual and spiritual background nor the political circumstances of contemporary Europe. But are their interpretations plausible even if methodological differences between us and Vitoria exist?

3. The Foundations of Vitoria's Thought

When one begins to explore Vitoria's thought it soon becomes clear that his theology cannot be isolated from the rest of his work. Rather, everything he wrote was based on his profound religious vocation and his background leaves no doubt about this. Vitoria was a friar of the Dominican Order, he led a monastery life and had bound himself to personal poverty and celibacy. The Order had above all one sacred purpose; its members had dedicated themselves to seek the salvation of souls by proclaiming the gospel the world over.[38] Studying, preaching, and teaching were focal in this ambitious task and formed the means with which the Christian vision was explicated and possibly attained. Through rigorous study the aspiring friar strove to achieve a holistic understanding of God's universe, facilitating the guidance of Christians and conversion of those still outside the Catholic Church. For Vitoria, the bible was *veritas ipsissima*, the black-box of humanity whose secrets

---

[38] W.A. Hinnebusch, *The History of the Dominican Order. Vol. II, Intellectual and Cultural Life to 1500*, 1973, 3-6.

the clergy alone could unravel, although the biblical fundamentals were unequivocal. While Vitoria discusses secular issues and uses an eclectic group of pagan philosophers as authoritative sources, Christian dogma invariably underlies and animates the discussion. For him, the philosopher judges "the nature of things as they are in themselves" and the theologian "considers them in their relation to God *conceived as being both their origin and their end*" (emphasis added).[39] Conclusions pertaining directly to God presume a belief in Christian revelation, whereas conclusions derived through cognitive faculties do not. Because rational conclusions do not presuppose faith, "they can be extracted from their theological context and judged, from the point of view of natural reason, as purely philosophical conclusions".[40] But in a fundamental way they are no less theological; philosophy simply completes his theology, making the Christian universe and the human one more intelligible and creating a more integral and defensible theology. Salvation in the future life remains the ultimate horizon. Vitoria's discussion on law and politics is founded on these divine premises. Since God's imprint is ubiquitous, political power and the laws that regulate its use are derived from God. A passage from Romans, which Vitoria reiterates repeatedly, reveals the source of all authority: "Let every soul be subject unto the higher powers. For there is no power but of God: the powers that be are ordained of God."[41] And God is the sole source of normativity within the Vitorian worldview as His laws delineate the contours and content of political life. It will be discussed in the following what implications this "base" has on Vitoria's jurisprudence and politics before considering the two lectures that gave him the reputation of being a founding father of international law.

a. Vitoria and the Order of the Universe

In methodology and doctrine, Vitoria mimicked St. Thomas Aquinas, his intellectual godfather and fellow Dominican. A central structural aspect to which Vitoria subscribed was "Aquinas's vision of a universe

---

[39]   E. Gilson, *The Christian Philosophy of St. Thomas Aquinas*, 1957, 9. While the quotes from Gilson only relate to Aquinas's work, the analogy between Aquinas and Vitoria rests on a firm base; both were Dominicans and Vitoria owns his doctrine, methodology and his scholastic style to Aquinas.

[40]   Gilson, see note 39, 9.

[41]   This is from Romans 13:1.

ruled by a hierarchy of laws".[42] The four categories of law, which St. Thomas had outlined in his *Summa Theologica*, provided an ethical framework within which all powers were to be exercised. Since all laws stemmed from and were a reflection of God's benign will, Vitoria made no difference between law and morality or between law and reason; these qualities were inbuilt elements of whichever type of law. Because God's creation was purposeful, it had endowed humanity and nature with capabilities with which they could realize their particular purposes. Thus an eternal, unchangeable law was built into the fabric of the universe. The *lex aeterna* reflected the idea, in the words of St. Thomas, that "the whole community of the universe is governed by Divine Reason" which "has the nature of a law".[43]

The second type of law was divine law whose precepts were "supernaturally revealed certifications of natural law and determinations of it with a view to man's ultimate end of eternal blessedness".[44] Divine law shares the ontology of both natural and positive law as all three direct human behavior. Both external and "internal" behavior affects the odds of salvation. But whereas positive law deals with external conduct, divine and natural law are internally orientated. Expressly, divine law is ordained "to an end of eternal happiness which is disproportionate to man's natural faculty", whereas natural law includes those rational precepts that are open to all humans and deal with man's "natural faculty".[45] Divine law completes human knowledge and refines the conscience to meet the strict requirements that condition the attainment of eternal life.

---

[42] Q. Skinner, *The Foundations of Modern Political Thought, Volume II, The Age of Reformation*, 1978, 148.

[43] St. Thomas Aquinas, *Summa Theologica*, 1981 (five volumes, translated by fathers of the English Dominican Province). Aquinas divided the *Summa* in three parts and the second part into further two parts. My references to the *Summa* first refer to the pages in the English edition, then to the part in which it is originally found (I., first part; I.-II. first part of the second part; II.-II. second part of the second part; III., third part), and then to the question and article in which the quote is within the original part. Here the quote is from 996, I.-II., question 91, article 1.

[44] A.S. McGrade, "Rights, Natural Rights, and the Philosophy of Law" in: N. Kretzmann/ A. Kenny/ J. Pinborg (eds), *The Cambridge History of Later Medieval Philosophy. From the Rediscovery of Aristotle to the Disintegration of Scholasticism 1100-1600*, 1982, 751.

[45] Aquinas, see note 43, 998-999, I.-II., question 91, article 4.

In his treatment of natural law, Vitoria mimicked St. Thomas. The latter had famously defined natural law as "nothing else than the rational creature's participation of the eternal law".[46] It is a specific exercise of eternal law which is characteristic to humans only. Natural law was an innate element of *all humanity*, "channelled into us" unavoidably, by which humans "judge what is right by natural inclination".[47] This was at the basis of the claim that "unbelief does not cancel ... natural law",[48] that is, no knowledge of Christian revelation or divine positive law was required in order to seize and follow the principles of this ethical system.[49] Non-Christians too were guided by *ius naturale*, although they remained unaware that it was the invisible hand of the Christian God that directed them. Self-preservation and reproduction are natural inclinations or "laws" which humanity shares with other animals, but only humans by virtue of their rational nature have a natural inclination to do good deeds and to live in society. These inclinations are wholly independent of any legislative measure.[50] The precepts of natural law have their own internal hierarchy as the *ius naturale* contains varying degrees of precepts with varying degrees of "validity". At the zenith stands a broadly formulated ethical guideline, good is to be done and evil avoided, from which all other natural law precepts flow.[51] It is this foundational principle and other kindred principles that, Vitoria presumes, form the basis for the lives of all peoples regardless of time and place. Vitoria makes a distinction between primary and secondary precepts when these very first principles are trans-

---

[46]   Id., see note 43, 997, I.-II., question 91, article 2.

[47]   F. de Vitoria, *Political Writings, Cambridge Texts in the History of Political Thought*, A. Pagden/ J. Lawrance (eds), 1991. The quote is taken from Vitoria's lecture "On Law", 163 and 169. The book consists of the treatises: "On Civil Power"; "I. On the Power of the Church"; "II. On the Power of the Church"; "On Law"; "On Dietary Laws or Self-Restraint"; "On the American Indians"; and "On the Law of War". Below, I refer directly to the individual treaties.

[48]   Vitoria, see note 47, "On the American Indians", 244.

[49]   Skinner, see note 42, 151. See also B. Hamilton, *Political Thought in Sixteenth Century Spain. A Study of the Political Ideas of Vitoria, De Soto, Suarez, and Molina*, 1963, 19. On these, see Vitoria, 'On Law', see note 47, 163-164.

[50]   "It [natural law] is ... always binding" and thus "there is no need to wait for its promulgation before it becomes binding". Vitoria, see note 47, "On Law", 160.

[51]   Vitoria, see note 47, "On Law", 170-172.

formed into more detailed rules of natural law. To the first category belong principles that are similarly universal in their occurrence. These are a set of self-evident moral and societal principles stemming directly from the idea embedded in the first premise. The Decalogue includes such obvious moral imperatives as; "thou shall not kill", "thou shall not steal".[52] However, these "necessary inferences" from the first principles are no longer absolute but can be modified under restricted circumstances (e.g. killing is sanctioned in self-defence).[53] Further down were additional deductions from the first principles that varied according to time and place. Loyal to Aquinas's systematics, Vitoria treated these secondary and tertiary principles as providing "the rational underpinnings for all codified laws".[54]

In his treatment of positive law, Vitoria, again, leaned on St. Thomas who had defined it as "an ordinance of reason for the common good, made by him who has care of the community, and promulgated".[55] Thus, even the patently obvious natural law precepts, such as "do not murder" or "do not steal", need some kind of an enactment to make them part of positive law, although their authority in no way depends on legislation. While the whole of humanity is guided by natural law, humans live in remarkably diverse conditions to which standardized solutions do not fit. Thus, the content of positive laws may vary to suit local circumstances.[56] But unlike the higher precepts of natural law, these "local laws" require an enactment, established custom or some other determination in order to come into force.[57] But this variation of positive law does not detach it from its base. All positive law is ultimately in harmony with natural law as it merely verifies what nature

---

52 The Ten Commandments were part of both natural and divine law as both have to do with the instructions with which God directed the course of humankind.

53 Vitoria, see note 47, "On Law", 170-172. The term "necessary inferences" is from Hamilton, see note 49, 14.

54 Pagden/ Lawrance, "Introduction" in: Vitoria, see note 47, xv.

55 Aquinas, see note 43, 995, I.-II., question 90, article 4. Vitoria concurs with Aquinas's definition. For this and for Vitoria's discussion on positive law more generally see note 47, "On Law", 155-163.

56 Vitoria, see note 47, "On Law", 183-185. Positive laws may also be abrogated and changed when it contributes to the "common good".

57 Hence, promulgation does not refer solely to written law. Vitoria answers the question "Can custom obtain the force of law?" affirmatively, though only if certain prerequisites are met. Vitoria, see note 47, "On Law", 185.

dictates. When positive law "deflects from the law of nature, it is no longer a law but a perversion of law",[58] i.e. a non-law to begin with.

Vitoria's treatment of the *ius gentium* was scarce and somewhat inconsistent. In the Thomist legal taxonomy he placed it under positive rather than natural law.[59] According to Vitoria *ius gentium* can be distinguished from *ius naturale* and it is "contained more under positive than under natural law".[60] Unlike natural law, which is "equal and absolutely just", the rules of *ius gentium* are not directly ethical; their justness arises in relation to a third concept. Vitoria uses the example of private property (a concept based on the law of nations) to elucidate the idea. Ownership is not equitable or just in itself, "but such a division of property is ordered for the peace and concord of men which cannot be preserved unless every one should have his property clearly defined".[61] Because division of property is highly conducive to the common good (a condition of all positive laws), it is equal and just in a "secondary way". This gives proprietary rights the ethicality which is a precondition of all laws. Vitoria himself states that "the *ius gentium* so closely approaches to the natural law that the natural law cannot be preserved without this *ius gentium*".[62] The inviolability of ambassadors is a good example of this; their immunity is mandatory for otherwise "they could not put an end to wars".[63]

Vitoria's language is inconsistent and passages such as "the law of nations ... either is or derives from natural law"[64] tend to suggest that his *ius gentium* would not always be positive law. Likewise, he seems to make a distinction between absolute rules of *ius gentium* derived from natural law (which all humanity presumably agrees with), and rules "not derived from natural law" in which case the "consent of the

---

[58]   Aquinas, see note 43, 1014, I.-II., question 95, article 2.

[59]   Vitoria's most comprehensive discussion on the law of nations is found in his *De Jure Gentium et Naturali* (a commentary on Aquinas's *Summa Theologiae, Secunda Secundae*, question 57, art. 3), which is reprinted in Scott, see note 23, Appendix E, cxi-cxiv. Skinner, see note 42, 151-153 and Hamilton, see note 49, 98-100, concur with this basic argument.

[60]   Vitoria, see note 59, cxi.

[61]   Ibid.

[62]   Vitoria, see note 59, cxiii.

[63]   Ibid.

[64]   Vitoria, see note 47, "On the American Indians", 278.

greater part of the world is enough to make it binding",[65] without making any substantive commitment as to which types of rules belong to
which category. Vitoria also argues that since the *ius gentium* is not
"natural law ... it can be abrogated", but since it is impossible to obtain
the "consensus of the whole world" such an abrogation is unlikely.[66]
Despite the confusion, few generalizations of Vitoria's international law
can be made. It is positive law, based either on "pacts or agreements" or
on widespread, often universal custom. Vitoria's allusions to natural law
refer to the moral foundation which the rules of *ius gentium* have (i.e.
they are based more or less directly on natural law) and to his belief in
the universality of the practices it includes. Property rights and the right
to trade, for instance, are not culturally determined contingencies but
universally applicable rules which form the backbone of the good life of
every human society, across religious and cultural boundaries. Vitoria
interpreted these practices to be in harmony with the dictates of natural
law and with the use of reason in general. Thus, his claim that the rules
of *ius gentium* are part of positive law is simply posited, and their universal validity is based on this presumed worldwide custom. European
practices were universal attributes of human life, not particular phe-
nomena with a particular pedigree. Vitoria accommodated his abstrac-
tions to a set of circumstances to which he had been socialized and,
similarly, he interpreted those circumstances to fit into the intellectual
framework which had been modified and solidified repeatedly by his
Christian predecessors. Repetition equals reality. That the idea of, say,
proprietary rights remained thoroughly unintelligible for the Amerindian mindset did not bother Vitoria as he had an unconditional belief in
the Christian vision towards which humanity was marching. This cultural "arrogance" is a main element in Anghie's critique against Vitoria.
But his belief in the universality of the Christian way of life is not yet
an argument for non-Christian exploitation or an argument against
non-Christian sovereignty. On the contrary, as Vitoria constantly reiterated, all non-Christians were under the influence of God's natural law
and entitled to live the good-life without Christian interference.

---

[65] Ibid., 281. It will be dealt with the content of the rules of Vitoria's *ius gentium* in more detail when discussing the Indian lectures.
[66] Vitoria, see note 59, cxiii.

b. Vitoria's Politics; Spiritual and Temporal

God's laws shaped the contours and content of political life. There were
two types of politics, spiritual and secular. Both govern human societies, but in distinct ways. Vitoria reiterates the medieval premiss "For
there is no power but of God" throughout his texts to establish the
origins of power in both spheres. The commands of God, which both
types of politics mediate to the masses, not only lay down the general
fabric within which human leadership operates but constantly govern
and encumber the exercise of power within it. Vitoria's discussion on
politics is targeted at answering and repudiating the work of Martin
Luther, whose work undermined the authority and teaching of the
Catholic Church. As Quentin Skinner has noted, a central unifying
theme of the body of work produced by Vitoria and his fellow neo-
Thomists was the refutation of the "impious" claims advanced by
Luther and Christian humanists.[67] Vitoria not only thought that God's
will was intelligible but that his commands were just and rational and
could be followed in a way which would lead to earthly happiness (the
objective of secular politics) and eternal salvation (the objective of
humanity and spiritual power). It was this fundamental juristic
structure that Luther questioned. For Luther, humans had no capacity
"to intuit and follow the laws of God", because His will remained
beyond human reach.[68] And because humanity is "absolutely a servant
of sin" and "unable to desire anything good",[69] salvation could not be
achieved by human effort; it depended exclusively on the impenetrable
will of God. This means that there is no place for a single authoritative
intermediary (the Catholic Church) between God and individual
Christians. Each Christian was equally obliged to and capable of
ministering one's co-religionists' spiritual welfare, regardless of the
standing one had in society.[70] Ecclesiastical hierarchies and
jurisdictional powers were "not a matter of authority and power" in the
real sense of the words.[71] The practices and interpretations of the

---

[67] Skinner, see note 42, 138. Positions on Luther's views are derived solely
from Skinner's account and Luther's texts have been consulted only to the
extent that the validity of Skinner's reading is confirmed.

[68] Skinner, see note 42, 4.

[69] *The Bondage of the Will (in Finnish Sidottu Ratkaisuvalta)*, 1952, originally
published in 1525, 164 and 176 (translations from Finnish are mine).

[70] Skinner, see note 42, 11.

[71] *Temporal Authority; to What Extent it Should be Obeyed* (1523), quoted in
Skinner, see note 42, 14.

Church cannot claim to possess any divine authority because God's will is not open to humans. God's word can only be revealed, offered, and preached through the written word of the bible.[72] Moreover, Luther places the Church under the supervision of the secular ruler who is given the right to assign and discharge clergy members and to have control over Church property.[73]

Vitoria rejected these Lutheran contentions on a number of grounds. He refers to a number of biblical passages and to other Christian and pagan sources to prove that there is a supernatural end towards which the life of the faithful is directed and that the Church was instituted personally by Christ for its attainment.[74] The Church has law-making powers so that it can carry out its divine mission and the Pope stands at the apex of the ecclesiastical organization.[75] Vitoria defends catholic traditions; the consecration of the sacraments and established biblical interpretations are fundamentally important "to gain life eternal".[76] At the base of this argument is Vitoria's belief in the human ability to detect and interpret God's will which the catholic doctrine reflects. Because salvation is the final end of humankind, Vitoria prioritizes the Church's mission over the mission of secular politics. Since "temporal rulers have no expertise in divine law", Vitoria creates an absolute line of demarcation between spiritual and temporal power.[77] Under no circumstances may the latter meddle in the affairs of the Church. But this absoluteness is not bi-directional. Following Aquinas's lead, Vitoria subdues the secular authority to the spiritual when necessary "for spiritual ends".[78] Vitoria reiterates repeatedly his basic view over the re-lation of the two human ends; "spiritual power is far more excellent and more exalted in its supreme dignity" than the secular power, and the ra-tionale of "spiritual power far excels that of temporal power".[79] Vitoria

---

[72] See note 69, 137.

[73] Skinner, see note 42, 15.

[74] The crucial passage in this respect was from Matthew, 16:19. See, Vitoria, see note 47, "I On the Power of the Church", 70-82 and "II On the Power of the Church", 139-148.

[75] Skinner, see note 42, 144.

[76] Ibid., 56.

[77] Ibid., 52.

[78] Ibid., 92. Vitoria's views on the geographical scope of the Church's jurisdic-tion will be discussed below as well as the effect this has on the Indian question.

[79] Vitoria, see note 47, "I. On the Power of the Church", 82.

states that the church forms a single body in which both the civil and spiritual communities reside though in a subordinate relation.[80] This means that "temporal things exist for spiritual ones, and depend on them".[81] But there is no habitual right of intervention; only in a case of necessity, when severe spiritual harm threatens, may the Pope interevene in Christian politics in order to avert the looming damage.[82] He may both revoke an unjust law or depose a heathen prince (within Christendom) that might prove to be detrimental to Christianity.[83] It is left to the discretion of the Pope to determine when such occasions are at hand. This casual papal plenary power is tangible proof of Vitoria's priorities and of the subsidiary place of secular sovereigns within the divine order. Vitoria's discussion on the distribution of powers contributed to the centuries-long dispute waged over the supreme command of Christendom. There were three variants in the debate. Each exaggerated the factual influence of their chosen leader as well as the unity of Christendom. Ever since the Western Roman Empire had fallen at the end of the fifth century, the unity "retained by Europe as a whole ... [had become] primarily, if not solely, religious and ritual in character".[84] The existing two extreme versions argued for the overlordship of Pope or Holy Roman Emperor over all Christians and infidels alike in both spiritual and temporal affairs, whereas the more placatory version emphasized the separateness of papal-imperial functions and spoke in terms of coordination and complementarity.[85]

Luther's outlook on human nature had led him to categorically denounce the right of the Church to intervene in political life. Spiritual guidance on the basis of the bible was all the Church was entitled to do. Secular authorities had a monopoly to use coercive power, "including

---

[80]   Vitoria, see note 47, "I. On the Power of the Church", 91.

[81]   Ibid.

[82]   Ibid., 93-94.

[83]   Ibid., 94.

[84]   F.H. Hinsley, *Sovereignty*, 1986 (2nd edition), 54.

[85]   This last version, which Vitoria modified slightly in favor of the Pope, was based on the fifth century Gelasian doctrine, according to which "Christ ... separated the offices of both powers according to their proper activities and their special dignities ... so that Christian emperors would have need of bishops in order to attain eternal life and bishops would have recourse to imperial direction in the conduct of temporal affairs", quoted in I.S. Robinson, "Church and Papacy", in: J.H. Burns (ed.), *The Cambridge History of Medieval Political Thought c. 350-1450*, 1988, 289.

powers over the Church",[86] in order to "punish the wicked and to protect the good", and to maintain peaceful living conditions.[87] This led the Lutherans to conclude that political power is directly ordained by God and conferred to men precisely in order to root out the moral shortcomings of the masses.[88] This was in direct opposition to the Thomist outlook which believed that the (natural) law of God is open to each human regardless of their religious conviction. Vitoria and his fellow Thomists approached Luther's work by sketching a genealogy of political society. They all begin by contrasting political life with an imagined (or historical) pre-political (and post-Fall) state of humanity from which the discussion advances. Vitoria speaks of a period in which humans lived "under the natural law", meaning the time when neither divine law had been revealed nor any human laws enacted. This condition is one of freedom and equality in which no political dominion exists. Still, it is equally controlled by law (natural law) since all humans, in every condition and time, are disposed to know and follow its instructions. Moreover, it is not a solitary state; since nature had made humans unable on their own to provide for themselves "a sufficiency of the physical necessities of existence", they were incapable of living in isolation of each other in this "state of nature" as well. And since humans were equipped with reason and virtue, they longed for companionship and the good life over and above life's necessities (this is, again, a central aspect of the natural law which humans are able to grasp whatever the surrounding circumstances). This optimistic view on human rationality helps to explain why people are willing to exchange their "natural liberty to the constraints of political society". Vitoria asserts that if there was no higher authority, each individual would strive for his own self-interest in totally separate directions, ripping society apart.[89] For Vitoria, this transition in no way restricts individual freedom but extends it.

Although civil power "may indeed have had its origin in nature and may thus be said to belong to natural law" it is, however, "undoubtedly not instituted by nature, but by an enactment (*lex*)".[90] An act of

---

86 Skinner, see note 42, 15.
87 *Address to the Nobility of the German Nation*, 1520. Unfortunately, the references have to be made to the text in general since page numbers are not available.
88 Skinner, see note 42, 139.
89 Vitoria, see note 47, "On Civil Power", 9.
90 Vitoria, see note 47, "On the American Indians", 254.

positive human law creates political society. Civil power is close to
natural law in Vitoria's legal catalogue, a "necessary inference" from *ius
naturale*.[91] Vitoria notes that it is particularly the civil partnership
"which most aptly fulfils men's needs" and that "the city is ... the most
natural community, the one which is most conformable to nature".[92]
The political and social institutions and practices of Christendom set
the standard and act as a benchmark against which other ways of living
are measured and potentially improved. Against the Lutherans, Vitoria
is clear on the fact that non-Christians too have legitimate sovereigns
which neither Christian sovereigns nor the Church may depose of.[93]
He explicitly states that grace (faith) is not the foundation of power.[94]
On a more detailed level, Vitoria uses the concept of *dominium* to
expound his ideas on the universality of natural law.[95] The essence of
dominium is that all men have a natural right, *dominium*, "over not
only their private property, their goods, but also over their actions,
their liberty and even – with certain important qualifications – their
own bodies".[96] Whether these rights are practiced in a civil society or in
a more primitive society, is indifferent to their existence. Since
unbelievers were considered to be in a state of sin, it was claimed that
they thereby were deprived of their right to *dominium* and that the
Spanish could automatically seize their land and property. But this was,

---

[91]   Similarly, J.A. Fernández-Santamaria, *The State, War and Peace. Spanish
Political Thought in the Renaissance 1516-1559*, 1977, 67 ("civil power is of,
but not founded on, natural law").

[92]   Ibid., 8-9.

[93]   Vitoria, see note 47, "On Civil Power", 17-18.

[94]   God "gives his temporal goods to the good [Christians] and the bad
[infidel]", ibid., 18 and "On the American Indians", see note 47, 243 (the
quote).

[95]   The meaning of this concept is summarized in A. Pagden, "Dispossessing
the Barbarian: the Language of Spanish Thomism and the Debate over the
Property Rights of the American Indians", in: A. Pagden (ed.), *The Languages of Political Theory in Early-Modern Europe*, 1987, 79-88. A more
elaborate exposition of the concept is found in Richard Tuck's *Natural
Rights Theories. Their Origin and Development*, 1-81. Pagden acknowledges that his discussion owes much to Tuck's account. A.S. Brett's, *Liberty, Right and Nature. Individual Rights in Later Scholastic Thought*,
1997, (especially) 1-164, deals with similar themes. It is difficult to get into
the nuances and variations of the diverse usages of the concept of *dominium*. The basic ideas will be laid out as will its effect on Vitoria's approach
to non-Christians.

[96]   Pagden, see note 95, 80-81.

as Vitoria time and again argued, based on the mistaken belief that *dominium*, public or private, depended on God's grace and not on His natural law of universal occurrence.[97]

This excursion to Vitoria's law and politics should reveal the mistakes of modern readers and give more credit to Vitoria's overall work. To talk about a new and secular international law maintained by sovereigns rather than God, would be an utter heresy for Vitoria. His jurisprudence is based on only one authoritative source that precedes and dictates all. Secular and spiritual authorities are only middlemen between God and humanity with no authentic autonomy. Vitoria's international law has its origins in the wisdom of God, not in some universal moral order (Scott) or in the will of Christian sovereigns (Anghie). There is no distinction between law and morality, between international law and municipal law, or between public and private acts of sovereigns. For Vitoria lawgiving is always explanatory, never constitutive. Though different rules bind different actors, such differences stem from varying capacities or varying spheres of activities within the one order.[98] Labels attached to categories of law are ultimately artificial and distort their original homogeny. Vitoria's prince is never the source of law, but a creation of the eternal and divine order that allocates and dictates the extent of his authority both in relation to his citizens and other sovereigns. Politics embodies and reflects the dictates of the *a priori* universal order which also reveals what the right course of action in any given case is. Any dispute over the content or binding force of the holistic system is excluded by assuming its impossibility. Recourse to Christian wise men will show that no conflict exists on either point. The place of the individual is to conform to the common good which the prevailing power structure is assumed to reflect. Resistance is denied, although Vitoria's statements are confusing, even against defective political leadership on the ground that it causes more harm than good.[99]

---

[97] Vitoria's discussion in the "On the American Indians" lecture goes through the other claims made in favor of Spanish occupation. He examines which type of Indian action might have resulted in losing their presumed *dominium*.

[98] D. Kennedy, "Primitive Legal Scholarship", *Harv. Int'l L. J.* 27 (1986), 8.

[99] The blame for sovereign misconduct lies with the community, because "the commonwealth is ... responsible for entrusting its power only to a man who will justly exercise" the power he is given (Vitoria, see note 47, "On Civil Power", 21).

Human rights, as we understand and employ them today, were not what Vitoria had in mind. For Vitoria, human dignity did not mean that individuals were dignified as themselves, as autonomous subjects separated from the pervasive morality of the divine order. Rather, only those individual acts which were in conformity with God's commands made humans noble and even then it was to God's credit since He directed all righteous human behavior. Any notion of subjectivity would have signaled a misunderstanding of the laws that structured the universe.

The shadow of the Church looms behind politics as the Pope may intervene when Christian sovereigns behave in ungodly ways. Salvation is the ultimate goal of humanity which justifies and explains this papal privilege. Vitoria's priorities are clear. While he values politics and earthly life to a certain extent, they fall far behind the consummation that awaits in the hands of God. Although unbelief was always a sin, it did not abolish the ability of the infidels to live the political life in accordance with these central dictates. Non-Christian communities fell beyond the jurisdiction of Christian sovereigns and the Pope could not usurp their land or property. This is the starting point for Vitoria's discussion on the Indian question. For Scott, it is also the end-point while for Anghie it is merely a façade hiding Vitoria's ultimate endorsement of Spanish imperialism. For the latter, the only purpose of Vitoria's natural (and international) law is to create a system that first sanctions Spanish presence in the Americas and consequently legitimizes the appropriation of native land.

4. Vitoria and *De Indis*

Vitoria held his two lectures on the Indian question almost half a century after Columbus's "discovery". By then the *conquistadores* had already subjugated the indigenous populations at a baffling pace and created a ruthless colonial regime aimed primarily at exploiting the easily accessible human and natural resources. The fundamental question which Vitoria examined was not whether the colonial project should be abandoned, but, rather, on what grounds it could be justified. Columbus had believed that he had discovered the outmost eastern coast of Asia and this created a dispute as to which of the two rivals, Spain or Portugal, was entitled to rule over the discovered land. The Portuguese claim rested on a series of papal bulls which had granted exclusive rights to the Portuguese kings over all newly discovered lands *"usque ad indos"* (for them, all non-Christian land beyond the Islamic world).[100] The Spanish replied by appealing to Pope Alexander VI to grant them sovereign rights over the newly discovered territories. Alexander VI issued a series of Bulls, known as the Bulls of Donation, which conveyed upon the Spanish monarchs sovereignty over all the lands discovered and to be discovered beyond a line "drawn from pole to pole 100 miles westwards of the Azores and Cape Verde islands", and upon Portugal a corresponding right over the eastward territories.[101] The two parties specified the location of the line in the Treaty of Tordesillas. In return for the papal grant, the Spanish crown took upon itself the obligation to evangelize the peoples of the occupied lands.[102] The Bulls rested on the highly contested assumption that the Pope *"est totius orbis dominus"*, lord of all the world, who had a divine mandate to rule over Christians and infidels in both spiritual and temporal matters. As noted, this was more a theoretical than concrete claim. Nonetheless, the Bulls were a part of the colonial rhetoric with which Spain argued for its sovereignty in the New World even if they soon realized that other arguments were required to satisfy their dissenting European rivals.[103] Twice a royal commission was called to investigate the Indian question and to provide some moral and legal guidelines with which the colonial administration was to be executed.[104] The latter committee was set up after a Dominican missionary on the island of Hispaniola had made an enraged public outcry over the inhumane treatment of the natives.[105] The findings of this committee confirmed that the Spanish had the right to rule over the Indians, and more importantly, the colonial enterprise was entitled to use native labor force and exploit their natural resources.[106] The committee's work relied on

---

[100]   W.G. Grewe, *The Epochs of International Law*, 2000, 230-232.

[101]   Grewe, see note 100, 233-234.

[102]   A. Pagden, *Spanish Imperialism and the Political Imagination. Studies in European and Spanish-American Social and Political Theory 1513-1830*, 1990, 14.

[103]   For the views of the political and scholarly opponents of Spanish imperialism, see Grewe, see note 100, 236-250. Another ground evoked by the Spanish was discovery (ibid., 250-255), which will shortly be dealt with in the next section.

[104]   Pagden, see note 102, 14-16.

[105]   Although this did not target Spanish overlordship as such, it was interpreted to have "brought into question ... the crown's *rights* in America and above all its rights to dominium", ibid., 14-15.

[106]   Ibid., 15.

Aristotle's theory of natural slavery to rationalize Spanish sovereignty.[107]

The essence of his theory was the idea that the physical and social laws of nature divided humans into objectively instituted socio-biological classes such as free men, women and natural slaves.[108] In the context of Spanish colonialism this idea was transformed uncomplicatedly to justify Spanish overlordship. Aristotle's observation, that because all material particles in the universe are in motion each one must be moved by another that is more powerful than itself.[109] Subnormal humans (the Indians) must be moved by the strong-minded (the Spaniards) if the harmony of the natural order is to be preserved. The natural end of the Indians is attained only if they succumb to the Spanish. A corollary of this was the "fact" that Indian mentality prevented them from having any kind of *dominium* over their property, their actions and, even, their bodies. What made this proposition easier to digest was the fact that the first peoples the Spaniards had encountered had led lives that at all points differed starkly from the European system.[110] But the discovery and occupation of the two Amerindian "kingdoms", Mexico and Peru introduced remarkably sophisticated cultures with characteristics that resembled their European counterparts. As a result the whole discussion over the status of the Indians was reinvigorated and the basis of the entire colonial project re-examined although without implications to practice.

Vitoria begins his first lecture by asking whether the Indians, "before the arrival of the Spaniards, had true dominion, public and private?".[111] Since God's natural law had a global reach, the Indians were under its influence and capable of organizing their lives politically. Vitoria evaluates the Indian mindset and observes that the Indians "are not in point

---

[107] A. Pagden, *The Fall of Natural Man. The American Indian and the Origins of Comparative Ethnology*, 1982, 47-56.

[108] Accordingly, Aristotle believed that natural slavery ran in the family, "from the hour of their birth, some are marked out for subjection, others for rule", Aristotle, *Politics, Cambridge Texts in the History of Political Thought*, S. Everson (ed.), 1988, 6.

[109] Pagden, see note 107, 48.

[110] As Pagden notes, they lived in "loose-knit communities with no real leaders, no technology, no personal property and frequently no clothes", ibid., 58.

[111] Vitoria, see note 47, "On the American Indians", 239.

of fact madmen, but have judgment like other men".[112] His analysis of native competence is based on the standards of civil life which Aristotle had sketched in the Politics.[113] According to Vitoria, the natives have "cities, proper [monogamous] marriages, magistrates and overlords, laws, industries, and commerce", and a "form of religion".[114] He groups the natives into one homogeneous group and describes their communities as reflections of the European civil community. Vitoria convinces both himself and his audience of the ultimate similitude of the Indian and the Christian, thereby maintaining the coherence of his Christian vision. He answers the above question unequivocally: the natives "undoubtedly possessed as true dominion, both public and private, as any Christians".[115] Thus, only post-discovery Indian action could deprive them of their undisputed rights. The second part of Vitoria's lecture lays out titles with which Spanish overlordship had or could have been justified and their detailed refutation. The first two claims related to the ideological struggle for "ritual supremacy", waged between the Spanish monarchy and the papalists.[116] Vitoria bluntly denied the universal ambitions of both. Even if the Emperor was a universal ruler, he would have no right to "occupy the lands of the barbarians, or depose their masters ... or impose taxes on them", because his power would only be jurisdictional.[117] Likewise, "the pope has no dominion in the lands of the infidel, since he has power only within the Church".[118] The Pope may use temporal power "as far as is necessary

---

[112] Vitoria, ibid., 250.

[113] Aristotle, see note 108, 167.

[114] Vitoria, see note 47, "On the American Indians", 250.

[115] Vitoria, see note 47, "On the American Indians", 250.

[116] Hinsley, see note 84, 54. When Vitoria addressed the Indian question, Charles V (1500-1558) held the crown of Spain as well as the Holy Roman Empire. Large parts of central and eastern Europe, the Iberian peninsula, parts of Italy, and the discovered territories were included in his vast empire.

[117] Vitoria, see note 47, "On the American Indians", 258. "Jurisdictional" refers to the status of the Holy Roman Emperor, Charles V, in relation to some of his estates in Europe over which he had only a nominal overlordship.

[118] Vitoria, see note 47, "I On the Power of the Church", 84 and "On the American Indians", 258-264. According to Vitoria "the pope ... [can] have dominion ... [only] by natural, divine, or human law" and none of the categories of law grant him such powers, see note 47, "On the American Indians", 260.

for the administration of spiritual things",[119] but this right does not apply in the case of the Indians because their actions, including their rejection of Christianity, in no way harms the Church. Vitoria reads the Bulls of Donation to create only a mandate and duty "to expand the Christian faith in America" through missionary work.[120] The next claimed entitlement relates to this duty of evangelization. The realization of this obligation was made possible by the *ius gentium* rule which bestowed on the Spaniards (along with the rest of humanity) the right to travel and reside in the Americas "so long as they do no harm to the barbarians".[121] Vitoria reasoned that the natives have a duty to "listen to peaceful persuasion about religion" or, even, if the preaching is done "diligently and observantly" a duty to "accept the faith of Christ under pain of mortal sin".[122] However, if the natives either refuse to listen to the faith or continue to reject it after peaceable persuasion, "this is still no reason to declare war on them and despoil them of their goods".[123] Vitoria observes that Spanish behavior toward the natives has been filled with "provocations, savage crimes, and multitudes of unholy acts"[124] which have impeded the Church's mission. While native refutation of Christian faith grants the Spanish no right to use force, this denial is central to Vitoria's reasoning when he considers the circumstances which could have created Spanish title over native land.

There were four more titles – discovery, gravity of the Indians' sins, Indian consent to Spanish mastership, and God's judgment – which had been used to rationalize Spanish sovereignty,[125] and again Vitoria disallowed them all. Thus, he rejected all of the official grounds the Spanish had employed to justify their sovereignty in the Americas. While he did sanction Spanish presence and the Christian mission with a *ius gentium* rule, this did not yet deprive the Indians of their dominion. A precondition for the use of the travel right is that no damage is done to the natives. Anghie interprets this right to mean that the Indians will inescapably oppose Spanish presence, given the historical realities, thereby

---

[119] Ibid., 258-264 (the quote is at 261).

[120] Grewe, see note 100, 326.

[121] Vitoria, see note 47, "On the American Indians", 278.

[122] Ibid., 270-271.

[123] Vitoria, see note 47, "On the American Indians", 271.

[124] Ibid.

[125] For these, see Vitoria, see note 47, "On the American Indians", 264-265; 272-277.

sanctioning Spanish vengeance and, then transferring Indian land and property into Spanish hands.[126] Scott, on the other hand, treats Vitoria's equation of Indian and European mentality as an intellectually plausible move without engaging in any analysis on the actualities of Spanish occupation or Indian lifestyle.

In the last section of the first Indian lecture Vitoria goes over the grounds that could have established Spanish title.[127] He re-introduces the universal right "to travel and dwell" which naturally extends to the Americas under the precondition that no harm is done to the local populations. This travel right is anchored conceptually to the law of nations. The second *ius gentium* right allows the Spaniards to "trade among the barbarians, so long as they do no harm to their homeland".[128] Thirdly, the Spaniards have a right to share and enjoy "any things among the barbarians which are held in common both by their own people and by strangers" – the natives have no right to prohibit the Spanish from doing so.[129] What confirms the existence of these rights is a universal custom which in its turn is a reflection of the biblical idea of neighborly love, Vitoria's all-pervasive *opinio juris*.[130] Vitoria moves on to consider how the Spaniards may react if the barbarians bar from them the use of these rights and attack the former without cause. The extensive rights of war which a prince is usually entitled to employ must be kept in check. But if the natives, nonetheless, continue to "persist in their wickedness" the Spaniards may unleash their full military power and deprive the natives of their dominion, both public and private, in consonant with Vitoria's war doctrine. This is the first way in which the "Spaniards could have seized the lands and rule of the barbarians".[131]

---

[126] Anghie, see note 26, 21 and 24.

[127] It is hard to tell whether Vitoria's discussion is purely academic or whether he believes that some of the grounds presented have historical value and actually justify Spanish overlordship. Occasionally, his language implies that the title in question does not correspond with what went on and that it has only theoretical value. Vitoria presents eight titles, but they will be discussed only to the extent that his basic ideas come to the fore.

[128] Vitoria, see note 47, "On the American Indians", 279.

[129] Ibid., 280. This is dictated by demands of equality and fairness.

[130] Vitoria, see note 47, "On the American Indians", e.g. 278-279.

[131] Ibid., 283.

Another just title relates to Christianity's diffusion.[132] The missionary work is in the interest of the natives themselves for they have no chance of salvation unless they hear and accept God's truth. Again, this is in the interests of the natives themselves. As under the previous title, everything runs smoothly as long as the Spanish may freely preach the Gospel, but if the Indians obstruct the exercise of this fundamental right, the Spaniards may, if persuasion fails, continue their propagation against native will or even declare war on them if that is the only way to ensure continuous evangelization.[133] Vitoria takes the final step and concludes that "if the business of religion cannot otherwise be forwarded ... the Spaniards may lawfully conquer the territories of these people", and use the gory measures of the laws of war.[134] Only moderation is the demand that reasonable limits are observed in the use of force.[135] Vitoria ends his discussion on this title by expressing his fear that in practice Spain may have gone "beyond the permissible bounds of justice and religion".[136] When Vitoria's just titles are considered, it is difficult to consider them apart from the abuse that took place. Nevertheless, he allows the Spanish to use the *ius gentium* rights only under the condition that their use in no way harms the Indians. Likewise, the evangelization is to be guided by Christian charity and under no circumstances may the Indians be forced to convert. Vitoria ended the lecture "On the American Indians" on a pragmatic note by reflecting on the detrimental effects that a Spanish withdrawal would entail. He notes that if all the just titles he had presented "were inapplicable ... the whole Indian expedition and trade would cease, to the great loss of the Spaniards".[137] This leads him to claim that whatever the injustices of the ongoing occupation, "trade would not have to cease".[138] However, Spanish sovereignty would come to an end and the Indians would regain their land and property. How should one value these restraints and notions?[139]

Vitoria delivered the second lecture on the Indian question, titled "On the Law of War", a few months after the first one in the summer of

---

[132]   Ibid., 284.

[133]   Ibid., 285.

[134]   Ibid., 285-286.

[135]   Vitoria, see note 47, "On the American Indians", 286.

[136]   Ibid., 286. Two other Spanish titles relate to evangelization.

[137]   Vitoria, see note 47, "On the American Indians", 291.

[138]   Vitoria, ibid., 292.

[139]   These questions are addressed below.

1539. He raised questions that equally preoccupy the minds of 21st century international lawyers. Who has authority to wage war? What conditions constitute the right to wage war? What means can be used in a just war? Like in everything else, Vitoria's discussion on war owed much to Greco-Roman ideas. The concept of "just war", which stands at the heart of Vitoria's lecture, was coined by Aristotle.[140] Roman scholars took the "just war tradition"[141] further by developing a list of causes which warranted the commencement of hostilities. St. Augustine laid the basis for the Christian concept of just war. His teaching was fundamental in the way it defeated the "early Christian condemnation of war and the associated requirement that military service be refused" and, on the other hand, in the way it "transformed Antiquity's conceptions of just war ... and integrated them into a Christian view of the world".[142] He also forged the conditions for just war that were to remain at the heart of the discussion right up to Vitoria: legitimate authority, just cause, proportionality, last resort and objective of peace.[143] Vitoria answers the question, "whether it is lawful for Christians to wage war?", affirmatively by leaning on Church tradition, Scripture and common sense. No doubt remains, "Christian[s] may lawfully fight and wage war".[144] The integrity of Vitoria's overall theory requires that no war can be just on both sides. Were it not so, the unity and oneness of the divine/natural order would be under threat. The whole idea of a humanity united in its ability to recognize and follow the laws of God would shatter if those laws could be interpreted in various ways. God's universe would fracture into discordant factions. It is the *a priori* divine order that dictates how sovereigns behave both in relation to their subjects and other sovereigns as it assigns each prince a sphere of influence and a set of prerogatives. Vitoria presumes that each prince understands the demands of the natural order and stays within the predetermined limits of his domain. He also presumes that in any conflict only one of the princes has overstepped his jurisdiction. Thus, only when a sovereign transgresses the limits of that divinely instituted domain and infringes the rights of another sovereign, does warfare become an op-

---

[140] F.H. Russell, *The Just War in the Middle Ages*, 1975, 3-4.
[141] This is from the title of James Turner Johnson's book *Just War Tradition and the Restraint of War. A Moral and Historical Inquiry*, 1981
[142] Grewe, see note 100, 107.
[143] C. Tyerman, *God's War. A New History of the Crusades*, 2006, 34.
[144] Vitoria, see note 47, "On the Law of War", 297.

tion;[145] the injured party may commence a justum bellum in order to punish the offender for the impious action. Vitoria's system means that, for instance, difference of religion, "enlargement of empire", or "the personal glory or convenience of the prince",[146] can never be causes for a just war since God proscribes and punishes such motives. A prior injury is always an absolute precondition for the use of force.

Anghie claimed that the Amerindians (and non-Christians in general) "are inherently incapable of waging a just war" and that "the sovereign, the entity empowered to wage a just war, cannot, by definition, be an Indian".[147] He bases his argument on a few sentences in which Vitoria discusses wars waged between Christians and Muslims, and on Vitoria's claim that no war can be just on both sides. Particularly the passage: "the wars of Turks and Saracens against Christians would be justified, since these peoples believe that they are serving God by waging them",[148] is in Anghie's mind crucial. But this argument is based on a textual interpretation that is, ultimately, incompatible with Vitoria's overall theory. Anghie also refers to Vitoria's means of war to further prove his conclusion. The right to use some of the war measures depends on the religious beliefs of the enemy.[149] The first point in which Vitoria treats the enemies unevenly is the enslavement of "innocent non-combatants", which may be carried out against pagan women and children only.[150] Vitoria's brutal statement that it is sometimes "lawful and expedient to kill all the enemy combatants" is an applicable rule in wars against the infidel "from whom peace can never be hoped for on any terms", which means that "the only remedy is to eliminate all of them".[151] However, in wars fought between Christians this is not permissible because "great harm would result for mankind".[152]

While Vitoria speaks of infidels as one group, it is clear that these two Christian rights are targeted against the arch-enemy of his Christianity, the Ottoman Empire, which had already ingested the remains of

---

[145] In Vitoria's words, the sole just cause for waging war "is when harm has been inflicted", ibid., 303.

[146] Ibid., 302-303.

[147] Anghie, see note 26, 26.

[148] Vitoria, see note 47, "On the Law of War", 307.

[149] It should be noted that most of the means of warfare belong equally to all sovereigns whatever their religious beliefs.

[150] Vitoria, see note 47, "On the Law of War", 318.

[151] Ibid., 321.

[152] Ibid.

the Byzantine Empire and was closing in on the very heart of Europe. Vitoria's tone is much more moderate whenever he discusses the position of the Indians. He urges the Spanish to soften their approach towards the natives and only if the latter continue to threaten and intimidate the Spanish, do the extensive rights of war become an option. The overwhelming technological lead of the Europeans made sure that the Amerindians posed no real threat to the former. This divergent treatment is conceptually based on the dichotomy invincible/vincible ignorance with which Vitoria elucidates the basic reasons behind sovereign misbehavior.[153] Invincible ignorance refers to those who have never heard of Christ or the Gospel, such as the Amerindians. They can follow the law of nature, but their unbelief diminishes its force, which makes them susceptible to misunderstanding Spanish intentions and the demands of the natural order more generally. Vincible ignorance refers to those who have heard God's word but still refuse to accept it or twist its meaning, such as the Saracens. When Vitoria states that the Turks and Saracens "believe that they are serving God by waging"[154] war against the Christians, he is referring to their vincible ignorance. In other words, Vitoria's religious conviction made him argue that the wars between Christendom and the Islamic world were invariably commenced by the latter, although Christians had not harmed them in any way. But Vitoria does not mean that Christians could not harm non-Christians in a way which would not justify the latter to wage war against the former. He simply presumes that this has not, historically, been the situation in any of the wars between them. It is the only conclusion that is in line with his overall theory which emphasizes natural law's true universality.

IV. Lessons of Vitoria

A sense of discomfort arises when reading Vitoria's discussion on the above titles. To grant reciprocal rights to the natives feels absurd and condescending given their radically divergent outlook on human life and the realities of the situation. Vitoria's tone has a mixture of empathy and arrogance and his support for the interests of the Spanish colonists, against their European rivals, is more or less explicit. Scott's uncondi-

---

[153] This division originates from Aquinas's Summa, see note 43, 930-933, I.-II., question 76, articles 1-4, and 1207-1218, II.-II., question 10.

[154] Vitoria, see note 47, "On the Law of War", 307.

tional admiration for Vitoria engenders similar sentiments. Anghie's claim that Vitoria's system is structurally tilted in favor of the particular Christian customs and beliefs, is hard to refute. But it is equally hard to label Vitoria as an unqualified supporter of the real-life colonial project. He was well aware of the Spanish excesses as the Dominicans were among the first to send missionaries across the Atlantic. Vitoria refers to this misbehavior occasionally and his frustration is evident. It may seem infuriatingly naïve of Vitoria to write that the colonists should act compassionately towards the natives. Their "willingness to parrot Christian doctrine and profess a Christian morality while continuing to behave like savages"[155] should have forced Vitoria to reconsider the value and relevance of his normative utopia. In Vitoria's ideal world the Spaniards would have behaved in a Christian way and the Indians would have greeted them with brotherly love. They would have established some kind of barter economy that would have benefited both, and the missionaries would have taught the natives the truth about God and the heavenly kingdom. That is what the divine order demanded of the Spaniards. We are unable to concur with his vision as the certainties that undergird his belief system are no longer available and God's judgment seems either too distant to affect human behavior or a baseless idea to begin with. Faith alone does not bring about a just world order. We need sanctions and threats, control and enforcement mechanisms in order to curb the excesses of both states and individuals. And we despair over their absence in the international world.

Despite the fact that Vitoria's system remained unchallenged by "self-governing" sub-disciplines or by competing meta-narratives, the formal perfection of his system did not improve the social conditions of the Amerindians, just as today's declarations of, say, the General Assembly seem to have little relevance for those that remain at the sharp end of world politics. But Vitoria did not settle for mere academic work. In addition to repudiating the official colonial ideology, he made several protests to the Spanish Crown against native exploitation, after hearing the horrible accounts of the Dominican missionaries.[156] Still, this does not take away the ambivalence that circles his work. Vitoria had an unflinching belief in the supremacy of the Christian way. His

---

155 J.M. Coetzee, *Diary of a Bad Year*, 2007, 219.

156 In response, Charles V, The Holy Roman Emperor wrote a letter to Vitoria's home priory in Salamanca and demanded that ecclesiastic measures should be taken to prevent Vitoria from propagating his unloyal views in lecture halls, Grewe, see note 100, 241.

work has an ambiance of bravado to it that is not uncommon today; political rhetoric is saturated with nationalist sentiment and ethos that views the world through black-and-white spectacles. The Christian message of forgiveness and charity is lost in sections where he uncomplicatedly reduces the non-Christian world into a terrain of ignorance, malice and superstition. He rides on a wave of unbridled confidence as his institution and creed represent the unchallenged dogma of the day. This is why he has no need to argue that the Indians should be compelled to accept Christian-European customs; he presumes that once their charitable essence is revealed, the Indians will embrace them voluntarily.

Vitoria's teleology, the idea that God's plan is being carried out and humanity is heading towards better times, is an undertone that much international legal writing shares. Today this undertone is expressed in narratives which tell a story of a progressive discipline (of international law) that has moved from its earlier state-centrism to a phase that now recognizes the individual in the shadow of the state and is committed to promote "a. higher standards of living ... b. solutions of international economic, social, health, and related problems; and ... c. universal respect for, and observance of, human rights ... for all".[157] For many, the coordinated efforts of the United Nations and its Member States are decisive in the quest for global justice, just like the Catholic Church led by its clergy was decisive for Vitoria. What unites Vitoria and a European constitutionalist is the way both claim to have located the benign forces of the world. The United Nations seem to represent and pursue a set of ostensibly universal values and have a toolbox designed precisely to mend the world's injustices and generate global welfare. There is no need to look for alternatives or engage in self-reflection since there already is a framework within which the particular ideals are efficiently protected and promoted. From a pragmatic perspective, such an understanding creates cause for concern. It denotes *excessive* contentment with the *status quo*, with the structures and procedures already in place. It seems there is no need to engage in any analysis over the assumptions, consequences, limits and possibilities of the action employed, since the meta-effect of the United Nations is presumed to be positive and effective. An advocate of the United Nations might think that if only states would pay heed to the wise counsel of the Charter and other seminal international treaties, global problems could be solved or at least mitigated. While such a wish is easy to understand, it leaves unan-

---

[157] Article 55 of the UN Charter.

swered what the genuine role and relevance of the UN institutions and procedures are in the solution of global issues?

An example illustrates the problematic. The AIDS/HIV epidemic has highlighted the tension between patent rights and access to proper medication. The economic incentive needed to facilitate continuous research at pharmaceuticals leads to high-pricing of patented drugs. More than seventy per cent of patients that could benefit from antiretroviral therapy remain outside it according to a recent WHO assessment.[158] While it is easy to argue that access to medication is a human right, the International Covenant on Economic, Social and Cultural Rights acknowledges the "right of everyone to the enjoyment of the highest attainable standard of physical and mental health"[159], it seems far more difficult to understand and affect the opaque processes of global drug distribution as well as to understand the role international law plays. While the global effort has decreased infection rates and increased the number of those properly treated, more resources are needed to gain an edge on the epidemic. What role should international lawyers play in the process? Has the legal profession done its part once the multilateral treaty is signed and the argument for access to medication is available? One small aspect of the global effort is the reporting mechanism established under the Covenant which requires states to submit reports "on the measures which they have adopted and the progress made in achieving the observance of the rights recognized".[160] Based on the reports, the Committee on Economic, Social and Cultural Rights (CESCR) has composed a set of non-binding General Comments designed to clarify what the treaty requires of its Member States. General Comment No. 14 titled "The right to the highest attainable standard of health"[161], lays out highly abstract guidelines and normative demands – such as "[h]ealth facilities, goods and services have to be accessible to everyone without discrimination"[162]; "health facilities, goods and services must

---

[158] *Towards Universal Access. Scaling Up Priority HIV/AIDS Interventions in the Health Sector, Progress Report, April 2007*, WHO, 2007, 5, available at <http://www.who.int/hiv/mediacentre/universal_access_progress_report_en.pdf>.

[159] Article 12 (1) ICESCR.

[160] Article 16 ICESCR.

[161] Committee on Economic, Social and Cultural Rights, *General Comment No. 14*, 2000.

[162] Ibid., para. 12.

also be scientifically and medically appropriate and of good quality"[163]; and "health facilities, goods and services must be affordable for all".[164]

But what is the relevance of the CESCR mechanism or the role of the formal legal argument about the existence of a human right in this respect? Do they affect those decisions by which more resources are given to the fight against HIV/AIDS or dictate the extent to which medical companies are willing to loosen their patents? When one ploughs through the websites of pharmaceuticals and, for instance, their "Corporate Responsibility Reports", it becomes clear that economic considerations along with public image concerns dictate the extent to which pharmaceuticals are willing to relax their intellectual property rights.

No rational person would claim that access to essential drugs is not a fundamental human right. But the tension between patent rights and health rights cannot be solved in any categorical way. While it is intellectually appealing to construct formal legal solutions to right conflicts – along the lines of *lex superior* or *lex specialis* – such constructions fail to reflect the conditions of political life in which the suggested solution has to operate. As has been compellingly argued, "the social meaning of rights is exhausted by the content of legal rights, by the institutional politics that gives them meaning and applicability. From a condition or limit of politics, they turn into an effect of politics".[165] Property and drug accessibility, and rights in general, have to be balanced against each other, case by case as the practice of various human rights bodies, the European Court of Human Rights (ECHR) in particular, has amply demonstrated. But the structural constraints of global resource distribution – here, the robust protection endowed to intellectual property rights – means that the overall picture will remain bleak. That millions of people continue to die of preventable causes every year may evoke moral outrage, but such circumstances are not due to any impersonal evil but are "the product of decisions by people, decisions that are framed, implemented and defended in legal terms".[166] The rights of

[163] Ibid.
[164] Ibid.
[165] M. Koskenniemi, "Human Rights, Politics, and Love", *Mennesker & Rettigheter* 33 (2001), 35.
[166] D. Kennedy, "One, Two, Three, Many Legal Orders: Legal Pluralism and the Cosmopolitan Dream", a keynote address at the International Law Association (British Branch) Spring Conference, SOAS, Brunei Gallery, Lon-

Sub-Saharan HIV/AIDS patients have to yield to the proprietary rights of pharmaceuticals however much it breaches the precepts of the Charter or the Universal Declaration of Human Rights. Pharmaceuticals can always defend their property by equally impeccable legal argument as an advocate of universal drug accessibility. While an argument that prefers property to human life seems detestable, such calculation is at the heart of much international legal talk and will not go away. Vitoria, too, failed to recognize the interests that dictated Spanish colonial policy and denied what Machiavelli knew all along; the Devil had irremediably pervaded the sovereign's soul.

Thus, if we add up the Covenant and the reporting mechanism, a few national cases in which courts have verified that access to essential drugs is a human right[167] as well as the argument that access to "life-saving medication in national health emergencies, particularly in pandemics, subject to progressive realization is part of customary international law"[168] what do we have? A functioning legal regime efficiently safeguarding drug accessibility? A profound insight of the global mechanisms that relate to, regulate and affect access to medication? We have neither. When the focus is solely on the end-products of transnational diplomacy, on multilateral treaties and on UN declarations and procedures, their salient nature is presumed and too much is left out. As David Kennedy has argued, "[m]yriad networks of citizens, commercial interests, civil organizations and government officials are more significant than interstate diplomacy".[169] In other words, if human rights receive "meaning and applicability" through political processes in which public and private actors bargain over interests, resources and benefits, international lawyers should attempt to understand those processes better in order to find new ways to influence the outcome of distributory decisions that affect the enforcement of core human rights.[170] Just like

---

don, United Kingdom, March 4, 2006. Available at <http://www.law.harvar d.edu/faculty/dkennedy/speeches/>.

[167] For these, see H.P. Hestermeyer, "Access to Medication as a Human Right", *Max Planck UNYB* 8 (2004), 101 et seq.

[168] Ibid., 176.

[169] D. Kennedy, "Challenging Expert Rule. The Politics of Global Governance", *Sydney Law Review* 27 (2005), 7 et seq. Kennedy's phenomenal article put into words the intuitions I had about the problems of international legal traditions.

[170] As Kennedy notes, there are three related assumptions and aspects to this "recalibration": "First, the proposition that background norms and institutions are more important in global governance than we have thought. Sec-

Vitoria combined his normative blueprint with practical political action, we should combine the abstract legal argument with a more grass-root understanding and action in order to make the formal law count for something more.

The challenge would be to understand better how drug-related resources are allocated, which norms and institutions are involved, what assumptions drive their work, who influences those that call the shots, and how the impact of the decisions that affect drug allocation could be brought to light, scrutinized and contested, in intellectual and pragmatic terms. Understanding the mechanisms would enable targeted action in particular contexts in which the legal argument might be useful alongside economic and moral considerations. If prevention is considered focal, the forces and factors that contribute to the spreading of the illness should be disclosed and challenged.

For instance, we often hear the claim that excessive pricing of patented drugs is mandatory in order to maintain a resourceful research and development division. But to what extent this is a false "necessity" whose sole purpose is to end the discussion right there? Who could tell? How big a portion of the net sales of a particular pharmaceutical would a "standard" relaxation of a particular patent constitute? Knowledge in statistics and economics would be needed to formulate an argument that could persuade pharmaceutical executives and institutional investors to seriously consider the relaxation. The formal legal argument for access to medication disregards the expectations of various interest groups that tie the hands of pharmaceutical executives or politicians deliberating the content of suggested intellectual property legislation. Are the flexibilities outlined in the TRIPS agreement and the Doha Declaration viable? Their one-sided utilization will probably generate more or less veiled threats on the part of pharmaceuticals and political circles, as recent experiences have shown.[171]

---

ond, the idea that the vocabularies, expertise and sensibility of the professionals who manage these background norms and institutions are central elements in global governance. Third, the proposition that expert work might be reinterpreted and contested in political terms, despite the ubiquity of the conviction among international legal experts that their expert work is not political, ibid., 7.

171 In late 2006 Thailand announced that it aimed to issue several "compulsory licenses" for patents related to AIDS and heart medications. This maneuver was based on the relaxation mechanisms under the TRIPS agreement. In response, Abbott Laboratories, a US based pharmaceutical, "announced that it has withdrawn applications to sell seven new drugs in Thailand in re-

If the mechanisms established under multilateral treaties have no effect on problems they attempt to solve, surely international lawyers should think up something new. What about the fundamentals of public and private drug development? Which rules and regimes govern those questions? Could national parliaments subsidizing medical innovation demand easy accessibility for the end products and which national and international bodies could be used today to take legal action on "drug-related" issues?

To focus on the structures, processes and instruments we already have, leaves too many questions unaddressed and sanctions the opaque mechanisms and background forces whose actions determine the broad outlines of global resource (and drug) distribution. The "conventional", UN-centered mindset creates "a misconception that to the extent someone can do anything about anything, it will be the normal players...[and the existing institutions and instruments of] the political system".[172] Vitoria's vision attempted to bypass the problems of enforcement by presuming their ultimate non-existence, whereas the UN-centered vision attempts to bypass them by viewing social reality from a bird's eye view which fails to detect the ambivalences and causalities of political life that perpetually hamper and deflate the coming of the ambitiously normative UN-led world order. Both visions seem remarkably out of touch with the complexity of forces and rationale that engender violence and conflict between states and groups of humans as

---

sponse to the country's decision to issue a compulsory license for the company's antiretroviral drug Kaletra", excerpt from article "Abbott to stop launching new drugs in Thailand in response to country's compulsory license for antiretroviral Kaletra", available at <http://www.medicalnewsto day.com/articles/65274.php>. Peter Mandelson, the EU Trade Commissioner, wrote a letter to the Thai Minister of Commerce expressing his concern for the detrimental effects the Thai policy would have on "the patent system". While acknowledging the right of WTO members to grant compulsory licenses, the Commissioner was of the view that neither "the TRIPS agreement nor the Doha Declaration appear to justify a systematic policy of applying compulsory licenses wherever medicines exceed certain prices". This was followed by a call for the Thai Government "to engage in direct discussions with the right holders" and to create a "constructive dialogue" which would serve the long-term needs of populations, that is, the Thai Government should pay more compensation for issuing the compulsory licenses. The letter is available at: <http://www.wcl.american.edu/pijip /documents/mandelson07102007.pdf?rd=1>.

[172] Kennedy, see note 169, 9.

well as with the structural inequities of social life and ordinary human experience.

V. Concluding Remarks

Deep cleavages continue to divide peoples horizontally and vertically and the opaque processes of globalization seem to favor the most dominant players. The questions and points raised above are only the tip of the iceberg, a sneak peak at one corner of the operation and problems of the "global governance regime" which operates in the shadow of public politics but fundamentally affects how wealth and power are distributed between groups of humans. No engineer could have matched its complexity but it is nonetheless run by humans and constantly reshaped by the decisions we take. Perhaps some of the questions could be answered instantly or ignored as completely irrelevant. But the point was to highlight the perplexities we have to face today when considering any international issue. Fragmentation is a fait accompli which cannot be wished away by defending the integrity of public international law; such a vision will function properly only in a normative laboratory.

Anghie's idea of a "truly universal international law" that could "further justice … [and] increase the well being of humanity",[173] is something we recognize and desire, just as Vitoria and Scott would have. But it is an overambitious vision. We should move our emphasis, in whichever context we work, from overtly normative blueprints or highly abstract critique to more pragmatic action that could help real people in real need without thinking that today's global establishment already represents general will and is driven by a cosmopolitan undertone. We should understand better the assumptions, effects and limits of our own work and recognize the contingent nature of our forms of action; none of them were or are carved in stone but are the result of a historical process shaped by contingent events. Anghie's idea of universal justice resembles the belief Vitoria had in the blessedness of the life to come. Like salvation, universal justice connotes an idea of complete freedom from the restraints of a divided and unjust world. But justice cannot be institutionalized or captured in a legal code or in some other legal process or technique. The very paradox of the idea that law is the medium towards global justice is the fact that any system of law, at a

---

[173] Anghie, see note 26, 317 and 320.

fundamental level, will continue to promote some interests and out-
looks over others as well as safeguard the prevailing social inequities.

Focus:

The Rule of Law

In August 2004, Secretary-General Kofi Annan issued a report entitled *The Rule of Law and Transitional Justice in Conflict and Post-Conflict Societies.* The Report aimed at articulating a "common language of justice for the United Nations" of key concepts of justice, rule of law and transitional justice.

Later the Secretary-General highlighted the rule of law as the all important framework and pledged to make the United Nation's work to strengthen the rule of law and transitional justice a priority of the United Nations.

The view that international law and the rule of law are the foundations of the international system and that it is therefore imperative to strengthen the rule of law in all its dimensions, e.g. national, international and institutional levels, was instantly commonly shared and ever since the notion rule of law and its content is under consideration and became a fast growing field of activity within the UN system.

For this reason the *Max Planck Yearbook of United Nations Law* felt it was appropriate to include several contributions concerning this issue.

Thomas Fitschen, Stefan Barriga, Alejandro Alday and Konrad Bühler from the Permanent Missions of Germany, Liechtenstein, Mexico and Austria in New York describe this notion and its development throughout the last years from a practitioners point of view, each focusing on a specific subject.

The Focus is completed by an article about the Reform of the Administration of Justice System within the United Nations, being another aspect in the still ongoing debate about the rule of law.

Rüdiger Wolfrum   Armin von Bogdandy

Inventing the Rule of Law for the United Nations

*Thomas Fitschen**

---

*   The views expressed in the article are those of the author and do not necessarily represent those of the Federal Foreign Office.

> *"The rule of law as a concept refers to a principle of governance in which all persons, institutions and entities, public and private, including the state itself, are accountable to laws that are publicly promulgated, equally enforced and independently adjudicated, and which are consistent with international human rights norms and standards. It requires, as well, measures to ensure adherence to the principles of supremacy of law, equality before the law, accountability to the law, fairness in the application of the law, separation of powers, participation in decision-making, legal certainty, avoidance of arbitrariness and procedural and legal transparency".*
>
> (*The Rule of Law and Transitional Justice in Conflict and Post-Conflict Societies*, Report of the Secretary-General to the Security Council, 2004)

I. The Secretary-General's 2004 Report to the Security Council: Rule of Law as Concept and Common Language

When Secretary-General Kofi Annan, in his now famous 2004 report to the Security Council entitled *The Rule of Law and Transitional Justice in Conflict and Post-Conflict Societies* that contained the language above, set out to articulate a "common language of justice for the United Nations,"[1] he quickly found broad acclaim. The report and the concepts developed therein were welcomed as incorporating a "seachange"[2] in the way the United Nations was doing business in sup-

---

[1]   *The Rule of Law and Transitional Justice in Conflict and Post Conflict Societies*, Report of the Secretary-General, Doc. S/2004/616 of 23 August 2004.

[2]   C. Bull, *No Entry without Strategy. Building the Rule of Law under UN Transitional Administration*, 2008, 45; see also R. Kleinfeld, "Competing Definitions of the Rule of Law: Implications for Practitioners", Carnegie Paper No. 55, Carnegie Endowment for Peace, 2005; A. Hurwitz, "Civil War and the Rule of Law: Towards Security, Development and Human

port of strengthening the rule of law, particularly in war-torn societies emerging from years and decades of conflict. The report, in the eyes of many, provided the first formulation of a common concept where no coherent policy direction had existed before.[3]

The report had come in response to activities of the Security Council,[4] which had in a very general way "underline(d) ... the need for respect for human rights and the rule of law" already in its high-level meeting on the occasion of the Millennium Summit in 2000,[5] but discussed the specific role of the United Nations in establishing justice and the rule of law in post-conflict societies for the first time ever, and right at ministerial level, on 24 September 2003. At the end of that meeting the Council noted the "abundant wealth of relevant experience and expertise that exists within the United Nations system and in the Member States", considered that it would be appropriate to examine further "how to harness and direct this expertise", and accepted the offer of the Secretary-General to provide a report that could "guide and inform further consideration" of these matters.[6] In another debate on 26 January 2004, this time on post-conflict national reconciliation, the Council invited the Secretary-General to include the views expressed in that debate in his envisaged report on the previous debate.[7]

Rights, in: A. Hurwitz/ R. Huang (eds), *Civil War and the Rule of Law. Security, Development and Human Rights*, 2008, 1 et seq.

[3]   Bull, see note 2; see also S. Carlson, *Legal and Judicial Rule of Law Work in Multi-dimensional Peacekeeping Operations: Lessons Learned Study*, Department of Peacekeeping, 2006, 2: "a definition that is notable both for its breadth as well as the specificity with which it identifies elements".

[4]   On the role of the Security Council in promoting the rule of law see the article by K. Bühler, in this Focus; see also Letter dated 18 April 2008 from the Permanent Representative of Austria to the United Nations, Doc. A/63/69-S/2008/270 of 7 May 2008, Annex: The UN Security Council and the Rule of Law, Final Report and Recommendations from the Austrian Initiative "The Role of the Security Council in Strengthening a Rules-Based International System" 2004-2008.

[5]   S/RES/1318 (2000) of 7 September 2000, Section I.

[6]   See the statement of the President of the Security Council dated 24 September 2003, Doc. S/PRST/2003/15.

[7]   See the statement of the President of the Security Council dated 26 January 2004, Doc. S/PRST/2004/2.

1. Towards a Common Understanding of the Rule of Law for the United Nations

In his landmark report the Secretary-General pointed out that recent years had seen an increased focus by the United Nations on questions of transitional justice and the rule of law in conflict and post-conflict societies and attempted to "highlight key issues and lessons learned from the organisation's experience". And the report continued:

> "Concepts such as 'justice', 'the rule of law' and 'transitional justice' are essential to understanding the international community's efforts to enhance human rights, protect persons from fear and want, address property disputes, encourage economic development, promote accountable government and peacefully resolve conflict".

But even though these concepts "serve both to define our goals and to determine our methods", there was no agreement on what they meant. Instead, as the report deplored, there was a multiplicity of definitions and understandings even among the UN's partners in the field. What was "essential" in the eyes of the Secretary-General in order to work together effectively, was to achieve a "common understanding of these concepts".[8]

a. Elements of the Rule of Law

Having made the case for developing a common understanding, the Secretary-General embarks on setting out the details. In the "concept" paragraph quoted above the Secretary-General identifies no less than fifteen elements that are decisive for his understanding of the rule of law:

it is a principle of governance in which

- all persons, institutions and entities, public and private, including the state itself, are accountable to laws, which for their part must be
- publicly promulgated,
- equally enforced,
- independently adjudicated,
- in terms of substance they must be consistent with international human rights norms and standards,

---

[8]   Ibid., Fn 1, para. 5.

–   furthermore, the rule of law requires measures to ensure adherence to a number of additional principles, namely:
    –   supremacy of law,
    –   equality before the law,
    –   accountability to the law,
    –   fairness in the application of the law,
    –   separation of powers,
    –   participation in decision-making,
    –   legal certainty,
    –   avoidance of arbitrariness,
    –   procedural and legal transparency.

It should be noted, however, that nowhere in this concept of the rule of law is any reference being made to the particular situation of post-conflict societies. It is clear that here the description supplied by the Secretary-General is general and applies to all societies, whether war-torn and post-conflict or stable and affluent.

The report then sets out briefly the parameters of the other two core concepts ("justice" being described as an "ideal of accountability and fairness in the protection and vindication of rights and the prevention and punishment of wrongs", whereas for the purposes of the report "transitional justice" was meant to comprise "the full range of processes and mechanisms associated with a society's attempts to come to terms with a legacy of large scale past abuses, in order to ensure accountability, serve justice and achieve reconciliation").

b. The Normative Basis for the United Nation's Work on the Rule of Law

Finally, the report does not fail to mention the legal sources of the United Nation's work in these fields:

> "The normative foundation of our work in advancing the rule of law is the Charter of the United Nations itself, together with the four pillars of the modern international legal system: international human rights law; international humanitarian law; international criminal law; and international refugee law. This includes the wealth of United Nations human rights and criminal justice standards developed in the last half-century".

Because these standards are "universally applicable standards adopted under the auspices of the United Nations", they must therefore "serve as the normative basis for all United Nations activities in support of justice and the rule of law".[9]

In 2005 the Secretary-General, in his follow up report to the outcome of the Millennium Summit entitled "In Larger Freedom: Towards Development, Security and Human Rights for All", again made the rule of law a central issue by stating, in a Chapter on the "Freedom to Live in Dignity", that "the protection and promotion of the universal values of the rule of law, human rights and democracy are ends in themselves. They are also essential for a world of justice, opportunity and stability".[10] To improve the coordination of rule of law activities within the organisation, the report proposed the establishment of a special rule of law assistance unit.

c. The Rule of Law at the 2005 World Summit

In the 2005 World Summit Outcome,[11] Member States subscribed to the views of the Secretary-General by recognising "the need for universal adherence to and implementation of the rule of law at both the national and the international levels" and reaffirming their "commitment to an international order based on the rule of law and international law which is essential for peaceful coexistence and cooperation among states". They also supported establishing a rule of law assistance unit within the Secretariat "so as to strengthen United Nations activities to promote the rule of law".[12]

It would be somewhat far-fetched, however, to assume that this has meant any kind of acceptance of the concept of the rule of law as developed by the Secretary-General in his earlier report of 2004. As can be seen from the ensuing debate in the General Assembly's Sixth (Legal) Committee under the new agenda item "The Rule of Law at the National and International Levels",[13] which had been established in the

---

[9] Doc. S/2004/616, see note 1, para. 9.
[10] *In Larger Freedom: Towards Development, Security and Human Rights for All*, Report of the Secretary-General of the United Nations for Decision by Heads of State and Government, Doc. A/59/2005, para. 137.
[11] A/RES/60/1 of 16 September 2005, para. 134.
[12] Ibid.
[13] A/RES/61/39 of 4 December 2006; for the debate see Doc. A/C.6/61/SR.6, 7, 20 and 22; A/RES/62/70 of 6 December 2007, debate in Doc.

wake of the Summit Outcome,[14] and in the various statements submitted by governments for the 2007 report of the Secretary-General to the General Assembly under that agenda item,[15] there is hardly a common understanding of this issue.[16]

As Simon Chesterman has rightly pointed out, the content of the term "rule of law" remains contested over time and geography, and it was exactly a *dissensus* as to the concrete meaning of the "rule of law" that allowed the consensus on this issue at the Summit.[17] The same can probably be said of the drafting of the United Nations Millennium Declaration in 2000 in which the heads of state and government had solemnly resolved to "strengthen respect for the rule of law in international and national affairs" (in the Chapter on Peace, Security and Disarmament) and to "spare no effort to promote democracy and strengthen the rule of law, as well as respect for all internationally recognized human rights and fundamental freedoms" (in the Chapter entitled Human Rights, Democracy and Good Governance).[18]

A/C.6/62/SR.14-16; on the background see also S. Barriga/ A. Alday in this Focus.

[14] For the justification of this new item on the agenda of the 6th Committee see the memorandum submitted by Mexico and Liechtenstein, Doc. A/61/142 of 22 May 2006, Annex, where the co-sponsors of the new item state that "despite the importance attached to the concept of the rule of law in the Summit Outcome (...) the United Nations still lacks the appropriate tools to promote it in a coherent manner", on the background see S. Barriga/ A. Alday in this Focus.

[15] *The Rule of Law at the National and International Levels: Comments and Information received from Governments*, Doc. A/62/121 of 11 July 2007, and Add.1 of 6 September 2007.

[16] For reasons and consequences see R. Mani, "Exploring the Rule of Law in Theory and Practice", in: Hurwitz/ Huang, see note 2, 21 et seq. See also *Promoting the Rule of Law and Strengthening the Criminal Justice System, Working Paper prepared by the Secretariat for the Tenth UN Congress on the Prevention of Crime and the Treatment of Offenders*, Vienna 10-17 April 2000, Doc. A/CONF.187/3, para. 5: "there is no universal agreement as to what the term 'rule of law' actually means".

[17] S. Chesterman, "An International Rule of Law?", *American Journal of Comparative Law* 56 (2008), 331 et seq.

[18] A/RES/55/2 of 8 September 2000.

d. Concept, Definition or Common Language?

The Secretary-General for his part was so far careful enough not to elaborate the issue any further and to leave the character of his description of terms in his 2004 report open. He strictly avoids even to suggest that what he has termed a "concept" for internal use by the United Nations was meant to define the rule of law[19] in a way that could apply also outside the Secretariat. In his subsequent report to the Security Council he has underlined once again the centrality of the rule of law to the work of the organisation while playing down his terminology as nothing more than an attempt to come up with a "common language of justice" for the work of the United Nations that "incorporates", *inter alia*, the concept of the rule of law.[20] In another report, this time on the rule of law and development submitted to the Commission on Crime Prevention and Criminal Justice in 2006, the concept of the rule of law as "defined" in the 2004 report is repeated, but with the explicit *caveat* that "it should be noted, however, that the above explanation is one among many definitions of the rule of law".[21]

Whether or not the Secretary-General has only drafted "language" on the rule of law or has actually defined it,[22] one can say that his 2004 report in response to the request by the Security Council has sparked a lively discussion within and outside the United Nations. By underlin-

---

[19] A report by the UN High Commissioner for Human Rights to the Human Rights Council, however, treats the three concepts in the SG's report as "definitions", *Human Rights and Transitional Justice*, Report of the Office of the United Nations High Commissioner for Human Rights, Doc. A/HRC/4/87 of 23 December 2006, para. 3.

[20] *Uniting our Strengths: Enhancing United Nations Support for the Rule of Law*, Report of the Secretary-General, Doc. A/61/636-S/2006/980.

[21] Commission on Crime Prevention and Criminal Justice, 15th Sess., *The Rule of Law and Development: Strengthening the Rule of Law and the Reform of Criminal Justice Institutions, including in Post-Conflict Reconstruction*, Report of the Secretary-General, Doc. E/CN.15/2006/3, para. 6. For a broader concept the report quotes from R. Kleinfeld, "Competing Definitions of the Rule of Law: Implications for Practitioners", Carnegie Paper No. 55, Carnegie Endowment for Peace, 2005.

[22] S. Carlson, *Legal and Judicial Rule of Law Work in Multi-Dimensional Peacekeeping Operations: Lessons-Learned Study*, Department of Peacekeeping Operations 2006, applauds the paragraph as "a definition of the rule of law that is notable both for its breadth as well as for the specificity with which it identifies the elements encompassed within the term".

ing the centrality of the rule of law for the work of the organisation he has certainly given the rule of law a much higher profile and has taken the conceptual thinking about it to a new level.

The sudden emphasis on the term as such, the precision with which the Secretary-General has outlined its core elements, and the undisputed "centrality" for the very mission of the organisation that the Secretary-General has claimed for the rule of law, stands in sharp contrast to the difficulties that Member States still have in coming to terms with it. In the work of an international organisation such as the United Nations good ideas – or, for that matter, ideas in general – always take time to seep into the system. Progress here is more often a not-so-new idea whose time has come. By referring to the normative foundations of the United Nations work in the field of advancing the rule of law, and by identifying areas of international law that he regards as its pillars, the Secretary-General has already indicated some of the sources of the organisation's new thinking. If indeed the rule of law today is considered to be so central to the United Nation's mission, it may be of interest to trace some of the origins of that concept in the political work of the organisation and to describe how the new language on the rule of law was formed.

II. To Whom it Does Concern: The Rule of Law and Human Rights

1. The Normative Foundation of the Rule of Law in the Universal Declaration of Human Rights, the Covenants and Other Human Rights Instruments

Unlike the UN Charter, the Universal Declaration of Human Rights of 1948 does contain the term "rule of law", albeit only in its preamble. Here the Declaration declares it essential that "human rights should be protected by the rule of law". The term is not defined in the text, but by juxtaposing the desired protection of human rights through law to "tyranny and oppression" – against which man may only have recourse, as a last resort, to "rebellion" – the language seems to suggest that the rule of law is the formal and procedural safeguard against violations of human rights, whereas under the rule of tyrants and oppressors no proper way to seek redress against human rights violations short of rebellion is available. In the operative part the notion is not used any more, but a number of articles do contain, in their outline of the inalienable rights that everyone has, explicit references to the law or laws of a state;[23] other core human rights provisions deal with procedural rights of the individual without such reference. But the key requirement in the preamble that "human rights should be protected by the rule of law" makes it clear that according to the Declaration the other human rights listed therein shall be equally grounded in, and guarded against violations by, (the rule of) law.

Subsequent human rights treaties follow the same logic, although generally without using the term "rule of law". Article 2 of the 1966 International Covenant on Civil and Political Rights requires states parties to adopt such laws or other measures that may be necessary to give effect to the rights recognised in it and to ensure that any person shall have an effective remedy against violations, and that the respective right shall be determined by competent judicial or other authorities. Many other provisions prescribe explicitly that the rights they contain shall be protected by law.[24] Under article 4 of the 1966 International Covenant on Economic, Social and Cultural Rights, states parties may subject the rights contained therein only to such limitations as are determined by law. The Convention on the Elimination of All Forms of Discrimination Against Women of 1979 requires states, in article 2 (a), to embody the principle of the equality of men and women in their constitution or other legislation and to ensure, through law and other appropriate means, the practical realisation of this principle. The International Convention on the Elimination of All Forms of Racial Discrimination of 1965, is based on the consideration, in the preamble, that all human be-

---

[23] Article 6 on the right to recognition as a person before the law; article 7 on equality before the law and on the right to equal protection of the law without discrimination; article 8 on the right to an effective remedy by the competent national tribunals for acts violating fundamental rights granted by the constitution or the law; article 11 para. 1 on the right to be presumed innocent unless proved guilty according to law; article 11 para. 2 on the principle of *nulla poena sine lege*; article 12 on the protection of the law against arbitrary interference of privacy and attacks upon honour and reputation.

[24] See, for example, article 6 on the right to life which shall be protected by law, article 9 para. 1 on the right to liberty and security except on grounds and in accordance with procedures as are established by law; article 14 para. 1 on the right to a fair and public hearing by a competent independent and impartial tribunal established by law; article 16 on the right to recognition as a person before the law; article 15 on the principle of *nulla poena sine lege*.

ings are equal before the law and are entitled to protection of the law
against any discrimination. Article 5 guarantees the right of everyone to
equality before the law, notably in the enjoyment of a number of rights
listed therein. Many other instruments contain similar provisions. It is
interesting to note, though, that despite these numerous references to
national laws as the means through which human rights are being given
effect, none of these instruments has referred to "the rule of law" as
such.

2. The 1993 World Conference on Human Rights in Vienna: Strengthening Institutions that Uphold the Rule of Law

It was not before the World Conference on Human Rights, held in Vienna in June 1993, that language on the rule of law appeared at the
highest official level. A preambular paragraph of the Vienna Declaration
and Programme of Action, adopted by the Conference on 25 June 1993
gives us an indication why: after noting "the major changes taking place
on the international scene and the aspirations of all the peoples for an
international order based on the principles enshrined in the Charter"[25]
– which is a very understated way of referring to the democratic revolu-
tions in Eastern Europe, the end of the East-west confrontation in international relations and in its wake the strong moves towards democratisation in many regions – the Conference lists a large number of aspects that have come back into focus. Among the principles that all
peoples aspire for we find, *inter alia*, the promotion and encouragement
of respect for human rights, peace, democracy, justice, equality, self-
determination, pluralism, development and, finally, "rule of law". In
para. 30 of the operative part of the Vienna Declaration and Programme
of Action, the Conference expresses its dismay at, and condemns, gross
and systematic violations of human rights and other "situations that
constitute serious obstacles to the full enjoyment of all human rights".
The list of such violations and obstacles to the enjoyment of human
rights is long and includes everything from torture and summary executions to arbitrary detention, racism and racial discrimination, apartheid,
foreign occupation, xenophobia, poverty and hunger to terrorism, discrimination against women and then, last but not least, "lack of the rule
of law".

---

[25] World Conference on Human Rights, *Vienna Declaration and Programme
of Action*, Doc. A/CONF.157/23 of 12 July 1993, preambular para. 9.

Based on this analysis, the Vienna Declaration and Programme of Action sets out to recommend measures to change the picture: countries which so request should be assisted to create the conditions whereby each individual *can* enjoy all human rights, and governments and the UN system are urged to increase the resources they provide to programmes aiming at the "strengthening of national legislation, national institutions and related infrastructures which uphold the rule of law and democracy". In the Chapter on cooperation, development and strengthening of human rights, this call is further refined: special emphasis is to be given to the strengthening and building of institutions relating to human rights and for the conduct of elections; "equally important", however, "is the assistance to be given to the strengthening of the rule of law and the administration of justice".[26]

And finally the Conference gives the signal for a broad-based engagement of the United Nations itself in this field, by strongly recommending "that a comprehensive programme be established within the United Nations in order to help states in the task of building and strengthening adequate national structures which have a direct impact on the overall observance of human rights and the rule of law". The task of this programme – to be coordinated by the Centre for Human Rights – was to provide assistance to national projects in reforming penal and correctional establishments, education and training for lawyers, judges and security forces in human rights and "any other sphere of activity relevant to the good functioning of the rule of law".[27]

3. The General Assembly after Vienna: The Rule of Law as Essential Factor in the Protection of Human Rights

The General Assembly reacted immediately to the new emphasis which the Vienna World Conference had laid on the role of the rule of law in securing the full enjoyment of all human rights. In a new resolution en-

---

[26]   The importance of the administration of justice is addressed separately in para. 27 of the Declaration, but unfortunately without a reference to the rule of law: "The administration of justice, including law enforcement and prosecutorial agencies, and, especially, an independent judiciary and legal profession in full conformity with applicable standards contained in international human rights instruments, are essential to the full and non-discriminatory realization of human rights and indispensable to the processes of democracy and sustainable development."

[27]   Vienna Declaration and Programme of Action, see note 25, para. 69.

titled "strengthening of the rule of law" the Assembly expressed its conviction that "as stressed in the Universal Declaration of Human Rights, the rule of law is an essential factor in the protection of human rights" and endorses the recommendations by the Conference to set up a programme which would help states in building and strengthening adequate national structures which have a direct impact on the overall observance of human rights and the maintenance of the rule of law.[28] The Assembly also supports that such programmes should help states to carry out certain projects in the field of penal reforms and training of judges "and in any other sphere of activity relevant to the good functioning of the rule of law".[29] In the following year the General Assembly speaks once again of the rule of law as "an essential factor in the protection of the rule of law" and calls for the support of projects that have a direct impact on "the realization of human rights and the maintenance of the rule of law".[30] Since then, these two elements have become the linguistic backbone of all General Assembly resolutions on the strengthening of the rule of law,[31] which in their remaining parts deal mostly with issues of cooperation and assistance. Here the provisions vary according to the practical needs of the times, as for example the welcoming of contacts initiated by the High Commissioner for Human Rights with other bodies on cooperation in providing assistance for the strengthening of the rule of law in 1995; the call for high priority to be given to technical cooperation provided by the High Commissioner – as the focal point for coordination – with regard to the rule of law in 1996; the taking note of cooperation between the High Commissioner and UNDP in providing technical assistance, at the request of states, in the promotion of the rule of law in 1998; the inclusion of attention to institution-building in the area of the rule of law in 2000; or the welcoming of the assistance given by the High Commissioner in the design of human rights components of UN peace opera-

---

[28] *Strengthening of the Rule of Law*, A/RES/48/132 of 20 December 1993, para. 1; this is an exact quote of para. 69 of the Vienna Declaration and Programme of Action, see note 25.

[29] A/RES/48/132, para. 2, which again is a quote from para. 69 of the Vienna Declaration and Programme of Action.

[30] *Strengthening of the Rule of Law*, A/RES/49/194 of 23 December 1994, paras 5 and 6.

[31] *Strengthening of the Rule of Law*, A/RES/50/179 of 22 December 1995; A/RES/51/96 of 12 December 1996; A/RES/52/125 of 12 December 1997; A/RES/53/142 of 9 December 1998; A/RES/55/99 of 4 December 2000; A/RES/57/221 of 18 December 2002.

tions and in providing advice once they are formed, including in the field of the rule of law,[32] as well as promoting better inter-agency cooperation and complementarity of action concerning assistance to states in strengthening the rule of law in 2002.[33] It is interesting to note that the number of players mentioned in these resolutions with whom the High Commissioner is supposed to cooperate gradually expands, reflecting the growing practical importance of rule of law activities for the United Nations. Towards the beginning of the new millennium the promotion of the rule of law has indeed become a priority in the technical assistance programmes carried out by the High Commissioner, in recognition of the link between the rule of law and the respect for human rights.[34] It is therefore regrettable that the resolution entitled "strengthening of the rule of law" was discontinued at the 59th session in 2004.

4. The Rule of Law as Conceptual and Operational Framework for the United Nation's Human Rights Programme – Another Description of the Rule of Law

This growing importance of the assistance through the United Nations to rule of law activities worldwide prompted another report of the Secretary-General which also came out in 2004 and was somehow overshadowed by the paper that was sent to the Security Council – a report which is even more elaborated on the components of the rule of law and provides a deeper analysis of the characteristics of the "rule of law". In his standard bi-annual report to the Third Committee on "Strengthening the Rule of Law", under the agenda item entitled "human rights questions including alternative approaches for improving the effective enjoyment of human rights and fundamental freedoms", the Secretary-General emphasises that the rule of law provides a:

> "particularly appropriate conceptual and operational framework for the UN's human rights programme, as it equally accommodates

---

[32]   See the new series entitled "Rule-of-Law Tools for Post-conflict States" published by the Office of the High Commissioner, which includes the following titles: Vetting an Operational Framework; Mapping the Justice Sector; Monitoring Legal Systems; Prosecution Initiatives; Truth Commissions, 2008.

[33]   All sources see note 31.

[34]   *Strengthening of the Rule of Law*, Report of the Secretary-General, Doc. A/57/275 of 5 August 2002, para. 1.

both the requirements for implementation of all human rights and concerns itself with the substantive and the procedural, the national level and the international level, and with the quality, content and objectives not only of laws, but also of processes, institutions, practices and values."[35]

Less apodictic and normative in style than the other report, it tries to describe rather than prescribe certain features of a well-run society governed by the rule of law, thus transcending a lot better the fact that the rule of law is not so much a norm or a certain way of organising a justice system, but a many-faceted cultural achievement that also includes certain values and practices in everyday societal life. To be able to appreciate fully the specific tone, a longer quote from the text[36] seems entirely appropriate:

"The rule of law presumes that a law is in place and encompasses its content, particularly its consistency with international human rights standards, its certainty of application, its supremacy in the hierarchy of power, the institutions and procedures for its implementation and enforcement, and the fairness with which it is applied in any given case. A system of government established under the rule of law ensures the availability of mechanisms for conflict resolution, whether judicial or non-judicial, and adequate remedies to address possible violations and transgressions. The system must also ensure that such mechanisms and remedies are accessible to all, function in respect of international standards and are backed by the State's commitment to accountable government. At the institutional core of systems based on the rule of law is a strong independent judiciary, adequately empowered, financed, equipped, and trained to uphold human rights in the administration of justice. Also essential is an effective justice sector including adequate facilities and national training regimes for lawyers, judges, prosecutors, police and prison officials. Ending impunity is a fundamental aspect of furthering the rule of law. (...) The good functioning of the rule of law necessitates a strong legal framework, under the Constitution, which upholds human rights and democracy, and which provides for the effective protection, implementation and redress in key areas at domestic level that relate to all human rights, be they civil, cultural, economic, political or social rights. Transparency of institutions, policies, practices and pro-

---

[35] *Strengthening of the Rule of Law*, Report of the Secretary-General, Doc. A/59/402 of 1 October 2004, para. 4.

[36] Ibid., paras 5-11.

grammes affecting all aspects of life is essential for any properly functioning society. Transparency helps to foster stability and predictability of government. Transparency is essential for the realization of rights, whether they relate to the exercise of emergency powers, the protection of civil and political rights or the allocation of available resources in the context of achieving progressively the full realization of economic, social and cultural rights. Under the transparency principle, society at large is able to monitor a State's compliance with its obligations. This requires a strong civil society and effective non-governmental organizations committed to ensuring respect by the state of human rights standards and vigilant in its demands that the rule of law be rigorously observed".

III. The Rule of Law in the Administration of Justice

1. The Normative Basis: Standards without a Term

As the Secretary-General had pointed out in his 2004 report, one of the normative pillars of the modern international legal system that forms the basis of the United Nation's work for the rule of law is international criminal law, including the wealth of United Nations criminal justice standards developed in the last half-century. These standards, as the Secretary-General had added, "also set the normative boundaries of United Nations engagement (...). United Nations-operated facilities must scrupulously comply with international standards for human rights in the administration of justice".

Based on the principles of the Charter, the Universal Declaration of Human Rights and the other international human rights instruments as far as they relate to criminal justice matters, the United Nations had very early on started to flesh them out and develop standards and norms in crime prevention and criminal justice. These standards cover basically every aspect of criminal justice from the treatment of offenders to the right to remedy for victims of gross violations of human rights. Many of these standards and norms have emanated from the quinquennial UN Congresses on Crime Prevention and the Treatment of Offenders, the first of which was held in 1955; others came from the former Commission on Human Rights or the Commission on Crime Prevention and Criminal Justice; most have been adopted by the General Assembly or the Economic and Social Council. A recent report by the Secretariat of the Eleventh Congress on Crime Prevention and

Criminal Justice, 2005 in Bangkok[37] that looks back at fifty years of standard-setting, lists dozens of such standards in the order in which they were adopted; the full text of the earlier ones can be found in a compendium that was published at the request of the Economic and Social Council[38] in 1992.[39] Many of the standards have also been compiled and re-edited for specific topical training purposes in the area of human rights.[40] The standards do not impose enforceable obligations on Member States; they embody a common ideal of how the criminal justice system should be structured and how criminal policy strategies should be devised, by providing practical guidance to states.

What is of interest for the purpose of this article is the question whether and to what extent these standards, or the bodies that have adopted them, have put the standards themselves or any of their considerations explicitly in a larger context of the rule of law, which would allow us to deduce from there an eventual common understanding of the latter concept. It is striking that this was almost never the case. In the cover resolutions whereby the standards were adopted and in the standards themselves one finds all kinds of cross-references to human rights concerns, the Universal Declaration and the international human rights instruments as well as the Charter and the principles for the administration of justice embodied therein, but the concept of "rule of law" simply does not appear.[41]

---

[37] Eleventh United Nations Congress on Crime Prevention and Criminal Justice, *Making Standards Work: Fifty Years of Standard-Setting in Crime Prevention and Criminal Justice*, Working Paper prepared by the Secretariat, Doc. A/CONF.203/8 of 1 April 2005.

[38] E/RES/1989/69 of 24 May 1989.

[39] *Compendium of United Nations Standards and Norms in Crime Prevention and Criminal Justice*, United Nations publication, Sales No. E.92.IV.1 and Corr. 1.

[40] Office of the High Commissioner for Human Rights, *Human Rights in the Administration of Justice. A Manual on Human Rights for Judges, Prosecutors and Lawyers*, Professional Training Series No. 9, 2003; *Human Rights and Pre-Trial Detention: A Handbook of International Standards Relating to Detention*, Professional Training Series No. 3, 1994; *Human Rights and Law Enforcement: A Manual on Human Rights Training for the Police*, Professional Training Series No. 5, 1996.

[41] See for example the *Code of Conduct for Law Enforcement Officials*, adopted by A/RES/34/169 of 17 December 1979; the *UN Standard Minimum Rules for the Administration of Juvenile Justice*, adopted by A/RES/40/33 of 29 November 1985; the *Declaration of Basic Principles of*

One attempt to have the rule of law in this context confirmed by the General Assembly was made in 2005 when the Basic Principles and Guidelines on the Right to a Remedy and Reparation for Victims of Gross Violations of International Human Rights Law and Serious Violations of International Humanitarian Law, which had been adopted by the Commission on Human Rights[42] and had been endorsed by the Economic and Social Council,[43] were sent to the General Assembly for adoption. Whereas the text that was recommended to the Assembly contained a paragraph "recognizing that, in honouring the victims' right (...) the international community (...) reaffirms the international legal principles of accountability, justice and the rule of law", the respective part in A/RES/60/147 of 16 December 2005 reads differently: here the General Assembly, after equally recognizing the victims' rights, went on simply to reaffirm "international law in this field".

2. The General Assembly and Human Rights in the Administration of Justice: The Rule of Law as Latecomer to the Scene

Besides the resolutions whereby the General Assembly had taken note of the outcomes of the various UN Crime Congresses and adopted the standard rules on criminal justice proposed by them, the Third Committee had run for a long time a resolution entitled "human rights in the

---

Justice for Victims of Crime and Abuse of Power, adopted by A/RES/40/34 of 29 November 1985; the *Body of Principles for the Protection of All Persons under Any Form of Detention or Imprisonment*, adopted by A/RES/43/173 of 9 December 1988; the *Basic Principles for the Treatment of Prisoners*, adopted by A/RES/45/111 of 14 December 1990; the *UN Guidelines for the Prevention of Juvenile Delinquency (The Riyadh Guidelines)*, adopted by A/RES/45/112 of 14 December 1990; the *UN Standard Minimum Rules for Non-Custodial Measures (The Tokyo Rules)*, adopted by A/RES/45/110 of 14 December 1990; the *United Nations Rules for the Protection of Juveniles Deprived of their Liberty*, adopted by A/RES/45/113 of 14 December 1990; the *Model Treaty on Extradition and Model Treaty of Mutual Assistance in Criminal Matters*, adopted by A/RES/45/116 and 45/117 of 14 December 1990; the *International Code of Conduct for Public Officials*, A/RES/51/59 of 12 December 1996, annexed to the Resolution.

42 CHR/RES/2005/35 of 19 April 2005.
43 E/RES/2005/30 of 25 July 2005.

administration of justice", i.e. criminal justice. Early resolutions had always referred extensively to the standard rules and other decisions concerning criminal law and procedure as well as various sources for human rights norms, but just as in the resolutions mentioned above, the rule of law as reference point was not to be found in any of them.[44] That changed in 1993, precisely after the Vienna World Conference on Human Rights. Resolution 48/137[45] made the inroad by recognising, for the first time in this series of resolutions, "that the rule of law and the proper administration of justice are prerequisites for sustainable economic and social development". In the next resolution, two years later, that part read a little different and came out somewhat bolder: in its resolution 50/181, the rule of law and the proper administration of justice are "important elements" for development "and play a central role in the promotion of human rights".[46] Another four years later the text receives further improvement when the preamble of resolution 54/163 makes the rule of law and human rights concrete and equal goals: this time the General Assembly is "mindful of the importance of establishing the rule of law and promoting human rights in the administration of justice, in particular in post-conflict situations, as a crucial contribution to building peace and justice".[47] In the 2001 version that preambular paragraph takes in a cross-reference to the growing importance in the work of the United Nations on the fight against impunity ("... crucial contribution to building peace and justice and ending impunity").[48] Furthermore a paragraph is added saying that "the right to access to justice (...) forms an important basis for strengthening the rule of law through the administration of justice" – so here it is the other way round: certain features in the administration of justice strengthen the rule of law. And for the first time ever the rule of law appears also in

---

[44] See *Human Rights in the Administration of Justice*, A/RES/40/146 of 13 December 1985; A/RES/41/149 of 4 December 1986; A/RES/42/143 of 7 December 1987; A/RES/43/153 of 8 December 1988; A/RES/44/162 of 15 December 1989; A/RES/45/166 of 18 December 1990; A/RES/46/120 of 17 December 1991.

[45] *Human Rights in the Administration of Justice*, A/RES/48/137 of 20 December 1993.

[46] *Human Rights in the Administration of Justice*, A/RES/50/181 of 22 December 1995.

[47] *Human Rights in the Administration of Justice*, A/RES/54/163 of 17 December 1999.

[48] *Human Rights in the Administration of Justice*, A/RES/56/161 of 19 December 2001, preambular para. 5.

the operative part, where the General Assembly underlined the "importance of rebuilding and strengthening structures for the administration of justice and respect for the rule of law and human rights in post-conflict situations" and suggested certain reforms "in order to establish and maintain stable societies and the rule of law in post-conflict situations".[49] These four paragraphs remain basically unchanged in resolution 60/159.[50] The latest text of 2007, however, loses most of the earlier gains through a dramatic shortening of both parts of the resolution. Only the preambular paragraph on the "importance of ensuring respect for the rule of law and human rights in the administration of justice, in particular in post-conflict situations, as a crucial contribution to building peace and justice and ending impunity" was kept.[51] On the whole the question arises whether the trend towards focusing solely on questions of the rule of law in post-conflict situations does the concept any good – as if the general obligation to uphold human rights and the rule of law in the administration of justice was somehow not a permanent challenge for *all* states.

3. Close Encounter: The Tenth UN Congress on Crime Prevention and Criminal Justice in Vienna 2000

The political changes during the nineteen-nineties finally allowed also the Congresses on Crime Prevention and Criminal Justice to approach the rule of law. When the General Assembly decided, in 1997, upon a recommendation of the UN Commission on Criminal Justice, to include in the agenda of the Tenth UN Congress on Crime Prevention and Criminal Justice to be held in Vienna in the year 2000 an item entitled "promoting the rule of law and strengthening the criminal justice system", it did so because developments during that decade seemed to allow to take a "fresh look"[52] at the issue. At a time where many states all over the world had embarked on processes of constitutional reform,

---

49 A/RES/56/161 of 19 December 2001, paras 13 and 14.
50 *Human Rights in the Administration of Justice*, A/RES/60/159 of 16 December 2005.
51 *Human Rights in the Administration of Justice* A/RES/62/158 of 18 December 2007, preambular para. 2.
52 Tenth United Nations Congress on the Prevention of Crime and the Treatment of Offenders, *Discussion Guide*, Doc. A/CONF.187/PM.1 of 22 September 1998, para. 7.

promotion of and respect for human rights and democracy, and where widespread transition to a market economy happened in Eastern European states and Asia, the time seemed ripe for the development of new activities aimed at the strengthening of the rule of law.[53] A preparatory paper noted that in the past decade the international community, aware of the importance of a stable legal framework for development, had increasingly included activities focusing on justice and the rule of law in its development assistance. Now that a debate between Western and the Socialist countries over the rule of law would no longer turn into "a battleground of the cold war",[54] the discussion of the topic at the Congress was expected to centre on efforts to strengthen the rule of law and criminal justice systems "under new conditions".[55]

a. Some Elements or Requirements of the Rule of Law: A Working Paper by the Secretariat to Stimulate Discussions

In order to stimulate the discussion about the rule of law and criminal justice, the Secretariat produced a most remarkable working paper[56] that attempted to lay out a modern understanding of the rule of law in criminal justice. In it we find many of the elements which later turned up in the 2004 report of the Secretary-General. But whether this extensive background paper had any influence at all on the delegations who negotiated the outcome of the Congress is hard to tell.

At the very outset of its Chapter on the "nature of the rule of law" the paper emphasises that indeed "there is no universal agreement as to what the term rule of law actually means". The paper then goes on to describe the rule of law as a "system of principles that relate to the legal governance of societies, but is not in itself primarily a legal system". The rule of law "anchors and stabilizes legality" without freezing it in any given state; to the contrary, it allows change and adaptation of the law to changing legal practices. What the paper considers "essential" for the rule of law is not only a developed legal infrastructure, but also "social and cultural traditions of legitimacy, acceptance of legal authority

---

53 On the background see Tenth United Nations Congress, see note 52.
54 Tenth United Nations Congress on the Prevention of Crime and the Treatment of Offenders, *Promoting the Rule of Law and Strengthening the Criminal Justice System: Working Paper prepared by the Secretariat*, Doc. A/CONF.187/3, para. 2.
55 Working Paper, see note 54, para. 9.
56 Working Paper, see note 54.

and respect for law". The paper then develops "some elements of the rule of law" – freely formulated and without any references or legal sources – as follows:

"A. The law must be comprehensive

The essence of judicial decision-making is that it involves the application of legal rules and not other less-tangible considerations to whatever facts are at hand. To replace purely ad hoc decision-making, the law must provide rules on which decisions can be based. (...)

B. The law must be clear, certain and accessible

Criminal law must be sufficiently clear to guide both executive and judicial decision-making. It must also be understood by the general population, which is generally presumed to know it and expected to comply with it. (...) Accessibility is also a requirement for legislative and judicial proceedings. Openness and transparency in legislative proceedings support the popular legitimacy of the legislation that results. The same is true for judicial proceedings in which precedents are set or law is made. (...)

C. The law must be legitimate: consent and compliance

In any society, the rule of law depends on the fact that the majority of people confronted with legal rules, whether in official functions or private life, will comply with them, thereby keeping the cases of non-compliance within manageable levels. This depends to a large degree on what has been described as the "legitimacy" of the law, which in turn depends on several key factors, including:

(a) Legislative legitimacy (...)

(b) Legitimacy of policy (...)

(c) Legitimacy of application (...)

(d) Legitimacy of support structures (...)

D. The law must balance stability and flexibility

The rule of law elements such as accessibility and legitimacy also depend to some degree on a satisfactory balance between stability and flexibility in both laws and law-making. (...)

E. Equality before the law

Originally, equality before the law meant that individuals and the State must be equal before the law. This remains an important principle, but modern concepts[57] have expanded it to encompass the general equality of everyone concerned with the law. What is important for the rule of law is that everyone should be equal before the law, regardless of power, wealth, individual or corporate status or other characteristics not directly relevant to the issues at hand. In individual-State matters, the State and its officials should be bound by their own laws, subject to the same scrutiny and sanctions for non-compliance, and stand on an equal footing with individuals in legal disputes between the two. (...) Equality is essential to ensuring that legal determinations are made on the basis of legal rules as opposed to the status of the parties involved.

F. Institutional independence and the separation of powers

The integrity of the rule of law and legal structures is commonly protected by distributing powers among disparate actors or agencies that can then act as controls on one another. (...)

The rule of law is itself a form of power dispersion because it sets up legal principles as a control on social, economic or other pressures in society and vice versa.

G. Legal rights as elements of the rule of law

Human rights in general can be distinguished from the rule of law, but some legal rights are necessary elements. Laws can govern behaviour and settle disputes only if those who have legal concerns have meaningful access to accurate information and competent advice about the law. Individuals can use the rule of law as a control on State acts only if those affected have meaningful access to the courts and effective remedies against the state. (...) Legal rights that are important to ensuring the rule of law in criminal justice systems include the following:

(a) The right not to be prosecuted for offences that did not exist in law when committed or that are too vague or uncertain to inform individuals as to what is a crime and what is not;

(b) The right to be informed about the nature and substance of any criminal charges and the status of criminal proceedings;

(c) The right to competent and independent counsel and, more generally, the right to mount a full and fair defence to criminal charges;

---

[57]   Here and elsewhere throughout the text the reader would have appreciated a reference.

(d) The right not to be subject to arbitrary arrest, detention, search or seizure in the course of criminal proceedings;

(e) The right of access to independent courts, in interim proceedings, at trial and while incarcerated, in order to question actions taken by the State;

(f) The right to effective remedies, including meaningful appeals, against the State, in interim and final proceedings and while incarcerated;

(g) The right to have proceedings dealt with expeditiously, in particular if liberty of other significant interests are prejudiced or curtailed while proceedings are pending or ongoing. (...)"

b. The Congress Debates

The agenda item on promoting the rule of law was discussed in Congress Committee I, and from the Committee's report it is not quite clear whether in the debate delegations actually referred to the paper, but a number of its key findings actually reappear in the report and the conclusions of the Committee. The report notes that in the discussions a number of key components of the rule had been identified, including the following:[58]

"law should conform to the standards enshrined in the Universal Declaration of Human Rights and other international instruments; law should be applied fairly and equally to all and should be accessible to all; law should respect the separation of powers of different branches of government; law should be capable of being accepted and obeyed; law should be drafted clearly and comprehensively".

And since delegations were aware that the mere adoption of laws alone does not necessarily result in the desired changes in the criminal justice system, it was also said that law needed "effective implementation whereby the law would be accepted and respected by both civil society and those administering criminal justice". In addition, "a balance between the efficiency of administering the criminal justice system and the protection of the basic rights of those involved in the criminal process, such as fairness and equality before the law", needed to be maintained. Having made all these observations, the report boils them down,

---

[58] Tenth United Nations Congress on the Prevention of Crime and the Treatment of Offenders, *Report of Committee I on Topic I, Conclusions*, Doc. A/CONF.187/L.3 of 14 April 2000, paras 13-23.

with almost aphoristic brevity, to no more than "two prerequisites for the rule of law: an effective and impartial justice system, and open, transparent and accountable government". These key components identified in the Chairman's summary are fairly sketchy, but they do contain a number of the factors that keep returning in later work on the issue, both substantive and procedural; and the references to the separation of powers and accountability of governments in general go even beyond the mere internal procedures within a justice system.

c. The "Vienna Declaration on Crime and Justice": A Missed Opportunity

But for reasons that could not be ascertained in the context of this article, none of this survived the level of Committee discussions and made it into the final document of the Congress. The "Vienna Declaration on Crime and Justice: Meeting the Challenges of the 21st Century"[59] which was supposed to lead the work of the United Nations in the criminal justice field into the next century, is completely silent on the rule of law. Despite the fact that it had been one of the four substantive items on the agenda, the text does not mention the term "rule of law" even once. It does reaffirm, however, the goal of "more effective and efficient law enforcement and administration of justice, respect for human rights and fundamental freedoms, and the promotion of highest standards of fairness, humanity and professional conduct" as well as the "responsibility of each state to maintain a fair, responsible, ethical and efficient criminal justice system"[60] – both of which captures at least some of the requirements of the rule of law that had been identified by the Committee and the working paper. But the very notion of the rule of law is absent from the text.

---

[59] Tenth United Nations Congress on the Prevention of Crime and the Treatment of Offenders, *Vienna Declaration on Crime and Justice: Meeting the Challenges of the Twenty-first Century*, Doc. A/CONF.187/4/Rev.3 of 15 April 2000.

[60] Ibid., para. 2-3.

4. Rule of Law as a Prerequisite for Successful Crime Prevention: The Eleventh UN Congress on Crime Prevention and the Treatment of Offenders

When international experts on crime prevention met for the Eleventh Congress in 2005 in Bangkok, Thailand, the rule of law was again one of the points of reference for their work that could not be ignored. But due to the traditional reluctance to refer to the rule of law in this area, the reference were rather non-committal. In the debates it was pointed out that key principles of strengthening the rule of law, respect for human rights and good governance were "basic ingredients for effective crime prevention". The rule of law was said to be "a prerequisite for the trust of people in the state and its institutions". Rule of law and integrity of the justice system were also qualified as "prerequisites to ensuring the development of fair, effective and efficient criminal justice systems", which had to enshrine due process, the independence of the judiciary and an effective and impartial police and prison system and also to provide for transparency and public participation.[61] In the Declaration adopted at the end of the Congress[62] states declare their conviction that "upholding the rule of law and good governance and proper management of public affairs and public property at the local, national and international levels are prerequisites for creating and sustaining an environment for successfully preventing and combating crime" and their commitment to the "development and maintenance of fair and efficient criminal justice institutions". It becomes clear that the crime prevention and criminal justice experts see no need any more to define or further develop the concept of the rule of law for their purposes. By downgrading the rule of law to a "prerequisite" or "ingredient" for the effectiveness of national criminal justice systems, the concept loses its normative character.

---

[61] Report of the Eleventh United Nations Congress on Crime Prevention and Criminal Justice, Bangkok 18-25 April 2005, Doc. A/CONF.203/18, para. 84-85.
[62] *Bangkok Declaration, Synergies and Responses: Strategic Alliances in Crime Prevention and Criminal Justice*, in: Report of the Eleventh United Nations Congress, see note 61, pp. 1-6.

IV. The Road not Taken: Rule of Law and Democracy

Another field of activity that was opened up only after the political changes in the early nineteen-nineties was democracy. The Vienna World Conference had mentioned both the rule of law and democracy as some of the factors necessary for the full enjoyment of human rights, and with all the calls for transparency of judicial procedures the link between the two seems to be evident. The Second International Conference of New and Restored Democracies in Managua, Nicaragua in 1994, which had adopted a Declaration and an Action Plan,[63] called for the support of governments struggling to promote and consolidate new or restored democracies, and the United Nations was of course one of the key sources for that kind of support. In Resolution 49/30 of 7 December 1994 the General Assembly requested the Secretary-General to submit a comprehensive report on the ways the United Nations system could support such efforts by governments. In his report that was forwarded to the General Assembly in the following year the Secretary-General identified three areas of United Nations support,[64] and one of the four items in the Chapter entitled "building institutions for democracy" was called "enhancing the rule of law". Here the rule of law is set out not as a goal in itself, but as a necessary precondition for democracy: "For democracy to become a reality, the rule of law must prevail."

The proposals that follow, however, are rather procedural and vague, still a far cry from the comprehensive lists of elements we find in later years:

"Policies and regulations should be developed and implemented according to an institutionalized process with opportunities for review. The use of discretion must not result in arbitrary and capricious exercise of power. In short, a set of rules must be known in advance, rules must be enforced and should provide room for conflict resolution, and known procedures for amending the rules must exist".[65]

---

[63]   Text in Doc. A/49/720, Annexes I and II.

[64]   Promoting a Democratic Culture, Electoral Assistance, Building Institutions for Democracy, see *Support by the United Nations System of the Efforts of Governments to Promote and Consolidate New or Restored Democracies,* Report of the Secretary-General, Doc. A/59/332 of 7 August 1995.

[65]   Ibid., para. 94.

One year later the Secretary-General submitted, again at the request of the General Assembly,[66] yet another report in which, once more under the heading "enhancing the rule of law", he repeated his view that the rule of law was one of the conditions conducive to democracy, but with a slight twist: now it is "democratization", i.e. the process rather than – as in the previous report – "democracy" as the final goal or a given state of things, that needs the rule of law to become a reality: "Political pluralism cannot prosper until efficient legal institutions are established". The report leaves it open, however, in what sense those legal institutions ought to be efficient. It again takes a purely technical approach to the rule of law by stating that in order to function effectively a legal system must include not only "adequate legislation", but also an "efficient institutional infrastructure for the design of and administration of the law" – institutions and procedures that can "ensure the proper conception, administration and enforcement of legislation".[67] The report continues by recalling that "efforts to enhance the rule of law" for their part would only "prove effective if they are undertaken in tandem with measures that ensure the provision of security, through adequate crime control and effective justice".[68]

Later that year saw the appearance of another document by the Secretary-General on democracy that was submitted under the same agenda item, but on the Secretary-General's own initiative in the form of a letter addressed to the President of the General Assembly: Boutros Ghali's famously ill-fated "Agenda for Democratization".[69] Encouraged by the success of his two earlier concept papers – his "Agenda for Peace",[70] submitted in 1992 at the request of the Security Council, and

---

[66] A/RES/50/133 of 20 December 1995.

[67] *Support by the United Nations System of the Efforts of Governments to Promote and Consolidate New or Restored Democracies,* Report of the Secretary-General, Doc. A/51/512 of 18 October 1996, paras 44 – 45.

[68] Ibid., para. 47.

[69] *Support by the United Nations System of the Efforts of Governments to Promote and Consolidate New or Restored Democracies,* Letter dated 17 December 1996 from the Secretary-General to the President of the General Assembly, Doc. A/51/761 of 20 December 1996.

[70] *An Agenda for Peace, Preventive Diplomacy, Peacemaking and Peace-Keeping,* Report of the Secretary-General pursuant to the Statement adopted by the Summit Meeting of the Security Council on 31 January 1992, Doc. A/47/277-S/24111 of 17 June 1992.

the 1994 "Agenda for Development"[71] at the request of the General Assembly, Boutros Ghali had ventured to come up with a third "agenda" in the form of a supplement to the two earlier reports, but with an entirely different structure and political content. Submitted, in the absence of a specific request by any main organ of the United Nations, in the form of a letter by the Secretary-General to the President of the General Assembly, and characterised by Boutros Ghali himself as not much more than "a paper", it was meant to complete his earlier reflections in the other two submissions and to offer a "deeper consideration of the idea" of democratization "in all its ramifications and possibilities", including almost philosophical considerations on the linkage between peace, development and democracy that no other United Nations organ had ever undertaken. The fate of this – probably Boutros Ghali's most audacious – effort to find a response to the massive political changes in the 1990s needs no discussion in the confines of this article. For the purpose of our topic it may suffice to note that the rule of law has obviously not played any role whatsoever in his thinking. Apart from a factual statement that democratic countries are "more likely to respect the rule of law"[72] and a short reference to the work of certain United Nations departments in this field, the term is nowhere to be found.

When the General Assembly took the item up again in its 52nd session 1997, it had before it the first report on the item under the new Secretary-General Kofi Annan, who took a different approach and distanced himself clearly from his predecessor. The new paradigm was now good governance, and the Chapter on the rule of law disappears. The three reports of the former Secretary-General, in the words of the new one, "contribute significantly to the process of providing a solid foundation for the eventual formation of a new and flexible framework for the United Nations system in the fields of democratization and governance, two key concepts which I believe should stand together."[73]

---

[71] *An Agenda for Development,* Report of the Secretary-General, Doc. A/48/935 of 6 May 1994.

[72] Letter, see note 69, para. 17.

[73] *Support by the United Nations System of the Efforts of Governments to Promote and Consolidate New or Restored Democracies,* Report of the Secretary-General, Doc. A/52/513 of 21 October 1997, para. 6.

In the following report[74] the Chapter on "enhancing the rule of law" stages a short comeback as the chapeau for some information on UN activities "for establishing or re-establishing a fair, effective and efficient justice system based on the rule of law". But the report to the 54th session of the General Assembly is again completely silent,[75] whereas its successor report at least recalls, in passing, that good governance "promotes the rule of law and equal justice under the law".[76] In the report to the 56th session of the General Assembly the rule of law is once again called "another essential element of democracy", but the reasoning is somewhat opaque:

> "Democracy must encompass those principles, rules, institutions and procedures that ensure representation and accountability and protect the individual or groups against arbitrary behaviour, injustice or oppression by the State or other actors".[77]

And finally, in the report to the 58th session, a Chapter heading "enhancing the rule of law" gets coupled with "accountable public administration", but actually no rule of law activities are being reported.[78]

V. Rule of Law in Peacekeeping Operations

The changing character of UN peacekeeping in the past fifteen years or so – away from the classical blue helmet type of "keeping the peace" and towards, in many local conflicts, a more complex challenge of building or rebuilding the peace, whether in support of a government or as part of the entire takeover of the administration of a country by

---

[74] *Support by the United Nations System of the Efforts of Governments to Promote and Consolidate New or Restored Democracies*, Report of the Secretary-General, Doc. A/53/554 of 29 October 1998.

[75] *Support by the United Nations System of the Efforts of Governments to Promote and Consolidate New or Restored Democracies*, Report of the Secretary-General, Doc. A/54/492 of 22 October 1999.

[76] *Support by the United Nations System of the Efforts of Governments to Promote and Consolidate New or Restored Democracies*, Report of the Secretary-General, Doc. A/55/489 of 13 October 2000, para. 14.

[77] *Support by the United Nations System of the Efforts of Governments to Promote and Consolidate New or Restored Democracies*, Report of the Secretary-General, Doc. A/56/499 of 23 October 2001, para. 26.

[78] *Support by the United Nations System of the Efforts of Governments to Promote and Consolidate New or Restored Democracies*, Report of the Secretary-General, Doc. A/58/392 of 26 September 2003, para. 18.

the United Nations[79] – has given rise to numerous questions about the
goals to be pursued and the guidelines to be followed. The Panel of Experts on United Nations Peace Operations, in its report of 2000 ("Bra-
himi Report"), had deplored a limited understanding of the role of UN
civilian police and judicial experts in peacekeeping missions and called
for a better focus on the strengthening of rule of law institutions; it recommended a:

> "doctrinal shift in the use of civilian police, other rule of law ele-
> ments and human rights experts in complex peace operations to in-
> flect an increased focus on strengthening rule of law institutions and
> improving respect for human rights in post conflict environ-
> ments".[80]

Current peace operations try to include rule of law elements in their activities, but often on an *ad hoc* basis and without precise guidance from
the Security Council as to what exactly needs to be done in a given
situation, and how.[81] The Security Council has been called upon to give
greater weight to establishing or re-establishing the rule of law[82] and to
include rule of law elements more consistently in his mandates. The
Council has responded by stating that it considers "the enhancement of
the rule of law activities as crucial in the peacebuilding strategies in
post-conflict societies."[83] There is, as the Security Council itself has
stated in his debate in September 2003, such a wealth of experience –
but unfortunately often buried in internal studies and reports of the
various peacekeeping operations – that it was impossible in the confines
of this article to search for definitions or concepts there.[84] This is what

---

[79] On this see the articles on the topic *Restructuring Iraq, Possible Models
     based upon Experience gained under the Authority of the League of Na-
     tions and the United Nations*, in: *Max Planck UNYB* 9 (2005).

[80] *Report of the Panel on United Nations Peace Operations*, Doc. A/55/305-
     S/2000/809 of 21 August 2000, paras 39-41 and 47.

[81] Bull, see note 2, 2-8; see also B. Oswald, *Addressing the Institutional Law
     and Order Vacuum: Key Issues and Dilemmas for Peacekeeping Opera-
     tions*, Department of Peacekeeping Operations, 2005; Carlson, see note 22.
     C.L. Sriam, "Prevention and the Rule of Law: Rhetoric and Reality", in:
     Hurwitz/ Huang, see note 2, 71 et seq.

[82] Letter dated 18 April 2008, see note 4, Recommendation 3.

[83] Statement by the President of the Security Council of 22 June 2006, Doc.
     S/PRST/2006/28.

[84] For two recent overviews see International Society of Military Law and
     Law of War (ed.), *La règle de droit dans les opérations de la paix / The rule
     of law in peace operations*, 2006; J. Howard/ B. Oswald (eds), *The Rule of*

the Secretary-General's report of 2004 has tried to synthesize.[85] The recent establishment of the Office of Rule of Law and Security Institutions within the Department of Peacekeeping Operations in September 2007, was meant to make the Department more responsive and agile in providing support in the areas of police, justice and corrections, mine action and security sector reform, and is proof of the growing role and responsibility of United Nations peace operations in this area. It's Criminal Law and Judicial Advisory Section covers legal and judicial systems and corrections or prison systems – two distinct rule of law areas that are of immediate practical relevance to peace operations on the ground.

But the rule of law is a concept that applies to *all* states, so we can probably assume that what has been developed in the other areas will also serve as a yardstick and guideline in the field of peace operations, at least in principle. It is thus quite correct that the Secretary-General, in his 2004 concept paper, does not differentiate between two groups of states – post-conflict states on the one hand and all others on the other – without denying, however, the huge differences in practice.

VI. Conclusion

With the two concept papers submitted by the Secretary-General – or three, if we also count in the Working Paper submitted to the Tenth Crime Congress – the Secretariat now has indeed a wealth of conceptual thoughts at hand on which to base its activities. As the United Nations is duty-bound to apply and follow the normative standards in the areas of human rights, criminal law and other fields of international law which serve – as the Secretary-General has put it – as the normative basis for all United Nations activities in support of the rule of law, all three concepts follow a rights-based approach and represent not merely procedural, but deeply political and normative concepts of the rule of law.[86] Whether all Member States of the United Nations, despite the

---

Law on Peace Operations: A Conference of the "Challenges of Peace Operations" Project, Conference 2002; cp. also Department for Peacekeeping Operations, *Primer for Justice Components in Multidimensional Peace Operations: Strengthening the Rule of Law*, 2006.

[85] For issues involving the Security Council see the article by K. Bühler in this Focus.

[86] Bull, see note 2, 44-46.

myriad of general references to the importance of the rule of law in protecting human rights and strengthening the administration of justice in
the resolutions of the General Assembly, would subscribe to all or even
most of the elements provided in those reports, remains doubtful. It is
therefore probably wise for the Secretariat and all "friends of the rule of
law" among Member States not to force the General Assembly as the
main political organ of the United Nations to recognise or "adopt" any
of the concepts in circulation within the Secretariat, or to suggest that
these are a "definition" that is somehow indicative or even binding for
activities outside the United Nations in this field. Pragmatically applied
as "common language" or conceptual framework, they and the numerous standards and instruments on which they draw may indeed serve as
a most welcome guidance and be used by those who work "on the
ground" and those who support their activities. In this sense the rule of
law as laid out by the Secretary-General may indeed be considered to
have established its proper place among the guiding principles of the
work of the United Nations.[87]

---

[87]   Mani, see note 16, 22.

The General Assembly and the Rule of Law: Daring to Succeed?

– The Perspective of Member States

*Stefan Barriga and Alejandro Alday**

I. Introduction

On 13 September 2006, the General Assembly decided to include in its agenda the item entitled *The Rule of Law at the National and International Levels*. The decision was taken without a vote and with broad support by Member States from all regions. There seemed nothing controversial about the proposition that the General Assembly was "uniquely positioned to [...] promote universal adherence to the concept of the rule of law, in particular at the international level".[1] In fact,

---

*   The views expressed in this article are the authors personal views only.
1   See Doc. A/61/142 of 22 May 2006, *Request for the Inclusion of an Item in the Provisional Agenda of the Sixty-First Session, The Rule of Law at the National and International Levels*, Letter dated 11 May 2006 from the

it seemed rather surprising that the rule of law had not already for many years been a formal item on the agenda of the General Assembly, given the role assigned to the Assembly under Article 13 of the United Nations Charter for the progressive development of international law and its codification. However, addressing the rule of law as a comprehensive concept is a rather recent phenomenon for the General Assembly.[2] This development received a decisive boost with the adoption of the World Summit Outcome (WSO)[3] on 16 September 2005, following many months of lengthy negotiations. The WSO contains numerous references to the rule of law as well as to international law, and provided a springboard for Member States interested in the rule of law to follow-up on those ideas in the context of the General Assembly. The Sixth Committee's work under the agenda item *The Rule of Law at the National and International Levels* would serve as the center of gravity for these activities.

This article intends to shed some light on the positions of United Nations Member States regarding the rule of law, with particular emphasis on the rule of law at the international level. It examines the General Assembly's work on this issue from the preparations for the 2005 World Summit to the present, as reflected in various debates, negotiations and resolutions. It outlines the extent to which Member States agree on the concept of the rule of law at the international level, and on measures to strengthen the role of the United Nations in this area. Finally, the authors submit some recommendations for the future work of the General Assembly under this agenda item, calling on Member States to focus on the opportunities rather than on the risks of a deeper engagement in rule of law issues.

II. Recent General Assembly Decisions regarding the Rule of Law

1. The World Summit Outcome Document

History has taught us that every successful system of nations requires a strong anchorage in international law for the achievement of the pur-

---

    Permanent Representatives of Liechtenstein and Mexico to the United Nations addressed to the Secretary-General, Annex, para. 7.

2   For some of the history in that regard see T. Fitschen, in this Focus.

3   A/RES/60/1 of 16 September 2005.

poses and ensuring the values that inspired its establishment. Whatever the fashion or the recipe has been, international law is the fundamental ingredient. The United Nations cannot be the exception.

The 2005 World Summit was not just another high level meeting. It was originally programmed as a major event to follow up on the Millennium Declaration[4] and review its implementation, but it was also conceived as a unique opportunity to refresh and update a sixty-year old organization for the 21st century. In fact, the World Summit was the starting point for a reform process that touches each and everyone of the United Nations' components, from the institutional structures to operations on the ground, and even reaching the realm of new ideas and concepts. The only limitation during that process was to preserve and build upon the core values and principles of the United Nations Charter.

In this context, on 21 March 2005, then Secretary-General Kofi Annan proposed a comprehensive framework for consideration by Member States in preparation of the summit, aimed at strengthening the protection and promotion of universal values like democracy, human rights and the rule of law. In Chapter IV of his report *In Larger Freedom*,[5] entitled "Freedom to Live in Dignity", the Secretary-General proposed to take concrete steps and stronger action to translate the concept of rule of law into a more powerful tool for the international community, having in mind governments as well as individuals, particularly the most vulnerable ones. That freedom to live in dignity would entail the realization of human rights for all; bringing justice to societies emerging from conflict or other violent experiences; real deterrence against future atrocities; and the peaceful settlement of disputes among states, to mention just a few examples.

The course of action suggested by the Secretary-General included many elements, among them: universal participation in multilateral conventions and their proper implementation at the internal level; the creation of more effective domestic legal and judicial institutions; the continuous development of the United Nations' potential in providing rule of law assistance and capacity building to Member States; full cooperation by all states with international tribunals, such as the International Criminal Court and other international and mixed tribunals; and

---

[4]   A/RES/55/2 of 8 September 2000.
[5]   *In Larger Freedom: Towards Development, Security and Human Rights for All*, Doc. A/59/2005.

a greater use of the ICJ through wider recognition of its compulsory jurisdiction, but also through greater use of its advisory powers.[6]

This was the basic rule of law framework proposed for advancing peace and security, development and human rights – a formula to be coined by the heads of state and governments as the three pillars of the whole UN system.[7] In addition, one element of the Secretary-General's report deserves a special mention: the proposal to finally fill the gap between the international community's commitments and the bleak reality, when it comes to protecting civilians from mass atrocities. The Secretary-General endorsed the concept of the Responsibility to Protect,[8] proposed by the International Commission on Intervention and State Sovereignty and subsequently taken up by the High-level Panel on Threats, Challenges and Change.[9] He called on the wider membership of the United Nations to embrace that Responsibility to Protect and, when necessary, to act on it, based on the principles of international law and the United Nations Charter. A bold call for action, whose chances to succeed would depend greatly upon the balance between questions of security, development and human rights that could eventually be achieved in the final outcome document.

In preparation of the summit, the General Assembly engaged for several months in protracted negotiations. The Secretary-General's recommendations for the advancement of the rule of law were negotiated under the coordination of the Permanent Representatives of Bangladesh and Slovenia as part of the so-called "Cluster III".[10] The process

---

[6]   Ibid., paras 133 to 139.

[7]   WSO, see note 3, para. 9.

[8]   The rationale provided by the Secretary-General is that this responsibility lies, first and foremost, with each individual state, whose primary *raison d'être* and duty is to protect its population. But if national authorities are unable or unwilling to protect their citizens, then the responsibility shifts to the international community to use diplomatic, humanitarian and other methods to help protect the human rights and well-being of civilian populations. When such methods appear insufficient, the Security Council may out of necessity decide to take action under the Charter of the United Nations, including enforcement action, if so required.

[9]   Note of the Secretary-General transmitting the *Report of the High-level Panel on Threats, Challenges and Change, A More Secure World: Our Shared Responsibility*, Doc. A/59/565 of 2 December 2004, para. 203.

[10] In preparation of the Summit, the General Assembly worked in thematic clusters to consider the report of the Secretary-General *In Larger Freedom*, see note 5.

showed how difficult it can be to agree on language dealing with such a comprehensive concept as the rule of law. Keeping aside the Responsibility to Protect, which contained numerous ingredients for controversy (innovation, politicization, relation to the use of the powers of the Security Council), many Member States reacted positively to the recommendations for action within the United Nations, in particular the proposal for the establishment of a special unit to coordinate UN activities in this field. The real challenges arose when this purely legal approach confronted its ubiquitous opponents: the political interests (from different states, groups and regions), the special status of the permanent members of the Security Council (P-5), and the internal struggles of the organizations' bureaucracy. It is important to underline that for the great majority of countries the structure proposed and the approach taken by the Secretary-General were very welcome. Those countries most interested in and most committed to the issue considered it a particularly strong signal that the rule of law was framed as a special section of the report, and referred to both its national and international dimension. This was also perceived as an excellent invitation for identifying areas for further development and strategies for the better implementation of international law.

The recommendations of the Secretary-General on the rule of law were divided into two big groups of issues. The first one considered the existing link between democracy, human rights and the rule of law. The second group encompassed the traditional notion of the international dimension of the rule of law, including international criminal justice, the role of the ICJ and to some extent, the work and the powers of the Security Council.

For the first set of issues the debate turned out to be balanced. On the one hand, developed countries promoted the need to strengthen the rule of law domestically for the full realization of human rights and consolidation of democracy. They argued that the improvement of these areas at the national level, beyond the domestic benefits, would contribute to the prevention of conflicts at the international level. Furthermore, this would also have a positive impact on the rule of law as an indispensable component for post-conflict situations. On the other hand, developing countries emphasized the link between international cooperation and the rule of law at the national level. From their perspective, international assistance and support are needed to build appropriate domestic institutions to deliver justice and promote human rights. The capacity to fulfill their international obligations, such as those emanating from multilateral treaties, is seen as closely related to the right to development. Eventually, these two approaches to the rule of law proved to be reconcilable and translated into cross-regional support for the establishment of a rule of law unit within the Secretariat.[11]

As for the second group of issues, the diverging views of Member States were more difficult to turn into actionable recommendations. The role of the ICJ is a good example. Of course all states praised the work of the ICJ highlighting its role in the maintenance of peace and security; some also suggesting improvements in its work methods. But while a significant part of the membership advocated for strong language in the WSO urging more states to recognize the compulsory jurisdiction of the Court, and encouraging greater use of its advisory jurisdiction, the final text remained on the soft side. It calls upon states "that have not yet done so" to simply "consider" accepting the ICJ's jurisdiction, which can also be read to mean that those that have already thought about it need not think about it again. The ICJ's advisory powers did not receive any mention at all.[12]

As regards the rule of law within international organizations, the discussions were mainly focused on what happens in the Security Council and provided another lesson of *Realpolitik*. A small group of states took up the issue of human rights (due process of law) *vis-à-vis* the sanctions regimes (especially in the area of counter-terrorism), arguing on the basis of a simple moral logic: since the United Nations is promoting the universal values of human rights worldwide, common sense dictates that its principal organs should equally abide by them. A second set of countries urged the Security Council to cease its legislative decision-making, and demanded that its resolutions must be clearly based on international law. The countries argued that the Council's competences must be exercised with utmost diligence, especially in light of Member States' agreement to accept and carry out decisions of the Security Council according to Article 25 of the Charter. In the same vein, concern was expressed about the Council developing or reinterpreting international law on a case by case basis, given its political nature and limited composition.

Agreeing on concrete language for the WSO on such controversial issues proved to be an almost impossible task. Permanent members of the Security Council in particular could not accept any text references to the way the Security Council exercises its function under the United Nations Charter, almost to the point where the discussion itself was

---

[11]   WSO, see note 3, para. 134 (e).
[12]   Ibid., para. 134 (f).

seen as incompatible with the Council's authority. It was all the more remarkable that the negotiators found a compromise formula for the issues of sanctions and due process. The solution was to avoid the word "due process", which would have evoked notions of procedural guarantees as they are required under criminal law. Instead the WSO called for "fair and clear procedures" for placing individuals and entities on sanctions lists and for removing them.[13] Ever since the World Summit, this phrase has provided the basis for an extensive discourse on how to design targeted sanctions in a manner that is compatible with rule of law requirements. And while that process is still ongoing, it has strongly highlighted the need for the Security Council to embrace rule of law principles, such as legality, respect for human rights and transparency, in particular when dealing with the rights of individuals.

The WSO negotiations underlined that in the area of the rule of law, the Member States, as with many other topics, are walking at different speeds. The good news in that respect is that the vast majority of countries perceive the strengthening of the rule of law through the United Nations as an opportunity, linked to the achievement of important goals such as development and human rights. The World Summit prepared the ground for important institutional arrangements for the promotion of the rule of law, and generated much needed food for thought on the issue. The summit also showed that the international community can make some progress on the rule of law, and it paved the way for the more permanent engagement of the General Assembly on this issue, as will be described next.

2. Inclusion of the Agenda Item *The Rule of Law at the National and International Levels*

In the aftermath of the 2005 World Summit, an informal cross-regional group of delegations at UN Headquarters in New York, led by the Permanent Representative of Austria, continued its efforts to promote rule of law activities within the United Nations through awareness-raising and lobbying.[14] This group, among other activities, generated

---

13 Ibid., para. 109. See also Kanetake in this Volume.

14 The group was purely informal in nature and composed of the Permanent Representatives of Angola, Austria, Bahamas, Belgium, Canada, Cape Verde, Finland, Germany, Latvia, Liechtenstein, Mexico, Morocco, Pa-

the idea of creating a universal and generic discussion forum about the rule of law by including this topic on the agenda of the General Assembly. On 11 May 2006, two member delegations of the group, Liechtenstein and Mexico, addressed a letter to the Secretary-General requesting the inclusion in the provisional agenda of the 61st session of the General Assembly of an item entitled *The Rule of Law at the National and International Levels*. The request was approved by the General Committee[15] and on 13 September 2006 by the plenary of the Assembly itself by consensus.[16] This was a logical next step derived from the prominent place accorded to the rule of law in the Summit Outcome, and generally welcomed by Member States in the first debate on the item.[17] The explanatory memorandum annexed to the letter outlines the rationale for the request, mainly by referring to the WSO, and explains in particular the reference to both the national and international level:

"The international and national dimensions of the rule of law are strongly interlinked. The international legal order serves not only as a framework for peaceful relations and source of rights and obligations for States and other actors, but also as a source of inspiration for the development of national legal standards, in particular in the field of human rights. The strengthening of the rule of law at the international level thus has a direct impact on the rule of law at the national levels."[18]

Earlier informal discussions among members of the group had revolved around the question whether such an item should be limited to the international dimension of the rule of law.[19] While the wording of the agenda item eventually chosen treats both dimensions equally, the request itself places particular emphasis on the international dimension of the rule of law. This is explained with the major improvements already achieved by the United Nations in its rule of law work at the national level, in particular in post-conflict situations, while a considerable

nama, Papua New Guinea, Paraguay, Romania, Senegal, Slovakia, Slovenia, Singapore, Spain, Sweden, Switzerland, and the United Kingdom.

[15] See the Committee's report, Doc. A/61/250.
[16] See Doc. A/61/PV.2, page 17.
[17] See the official records, Docs A/C.6/61/SR.6, SR.7 and SR.20.
[18] Liechtenstein/ Mexico, see note 1, Annex, para. 2.
[19] See for example a discussion paper submitted by Switzerland on 14 March 2006 to the Council of Europe, Committee of Legal Advisers on Public International Law, CAHDI (2006) 11.

gap remains with regard to the international level. The request concludes that the:

> "General Assembly, as the United Nations' chief deliberative, policymaking and representative organ, with its central role in the area of development and codification of international law, is uniquely positioned to fill that gap and to promote universal adherence to the concept of the rule of law, in particular at the international level".[20]

The General Assembly also followed the request by Liechtenstein and Mexico to allocate the item "in view of the legal nature of the issue" to the Sixth Committee. This rationale was, albeit not explicitly, also intended to serve as a self-fulfilling prophecy. The potentially extremely broad scope of the agenda item should receive some "natural" delimitations by placing the discussion in the context of the work of the Assembly's legal Committee. By and large, this prophecy proved to be accurate during the first two years of the Assembly's consideration of the item.[21] Most importantly though, the inclusion of the agenda item provided the Assembly with a permanent forum in which issues related to the rule of law can be discussed and pertinent initiatives be advanced without first having to overcome procedural hurdles. The resolutions subsequently adopted under this agenda item, which *inter alia* provided material support to the establishment of the Secretariat's Rule of Law Unit, serve as a case in point and will be considered in the following.

3. General Assembly Resolutions negotiated in the Sixth Committee

During the first two years of its consideration of the item *The Rule of Law at the National and International Levels*, the Sixth Committee recommended two draft resolutions that were subsequently adopted by the General Assembly in plenary meetings. The first resolution was adopted following relatively short negotiations chaired by Ambassador Juan Manuel Gómez-Robledo, then Deputy Permanent Representative of Mexico to the United Nations and Chairman of the Sixth Committee at the 61st session.[22] Despite the broad scope of the topic, resolution

---

20 Liechtenstein/ Mexico, see note 1, Annex, para. 7.

21 See the Chapter on the Sixth Committee debates below.

22 A/RES/61/39 of 4 December 2006, adopted upon recommendation by the Sixth Committee (see the Committee's report Doc. A/61/456 of 17 November 2006).

A/RES/61/39 ended up being remarkably short, with only six preambular paragraphs and five operative paragraphs.

A look at the preambular part, which in the General Assembly's practice usually reflects the conceptual framework of a resolution, reveals that the delegations negotiating the text strived to remain on safe ground: these paragraphs contain to the greatest extent language taken from the WSO which can be considered of direct relevance to the rule of law, and they also take up some relevant Charter principles. The General Assembly reaffirmed, *inter alia*, its "commitment to the purposes and principles of the Charter of the United Nations and international law";[23] it reaffirmed "that human rights, the rule of law and democracy are interlinked and mutually reinforcing and that they belong to the universal and indivisible core values and principles of the United Nations";[24] it reaffirmed "the need for universal adherence to and implementation of the rule of law"[25] and its "solemn commitment to an international order based on the rule of law and international law".[26] The preamble further emphasizes the link between the rule of law, development, human rights and international security,[27] it reaffirms the duty of all states to refrain from the "threat or use of force in any manner inconsistent with the purposes and principles of the United Nations"[28] and to "settle their international disputes by peaceful means in such a manner that international peace and security, and justice, are not endangered"[29], and it also calls upon states to consider accepting the jurisdiction of the ICJ.[30] The only genuinely "new", though equally not revolutionary, statement is contained in the last preambular paragraph, which reads:

> "Convinced that the promotion of and respect for the rule of law at the national and international levels, as well as justice and good gov-

---

23   A/RES/61/39, see note 22, preambular para. 1; based on the WSO, see note 3, para. 2.
24   Ibid., preambular para. 2; based on the WSO, see note 3, para. 119.
25   Ibid., preambular para. 3; based on the WSO, see note 3, para. 134.
26   Ibid., preambular para. 3; based on the WSO, see note 3, para. 134 (a).
27   Ibid., preambular para. 4; based on the WSO, see note 3, paras 11 and 7.
28   Ibid., preambular para. 5; based on the WSO, see note 3, para. 5 and on the United Nations Charter, Article 2 para. 4.
29   Ibid., preambular para. 5; based on the United Nations Charter, Article 2 para. 3.
30   Ibid., preambular para. 5; based on the WSO, see note 3, para. 134 (f).

ernance, should guide the activities of the United Nations and of its Member States".

The preamble is remarkably short and general, particularly in light of the resolution's character as an "omnibus" resolution which should – theoretically – deal with all aspects of the item under consideration in one text. This can to some extent be explained by the approach chosen by the chairman and supported by the Committee to focus on uncontroversial elements which can be adopted by consensus, since the Sixth Committee traditionally adopts its draft resolutions without a vote.[31] The rather focused conceptual framework of the resolution should, however, not necessarily be interpreted as a lack of ambition. It can at least to some extent also be attributed to the fact that the Sixth Committee finds itself only at the beginning of a concerted effort to deal with the promotion of the rule of law. Therefore, the resolution does not address conceptually more challenging questions such as the scope of the term "rule of law", despite the fact that the Secretary-General had previously provided thorough analysis on the issue which states could have used as the basis for their discussion.[32]

The final outcome of the negotiations on the resolution's preamble was considered to be very "balanced" by all delegations, which explains why this part remained essentially unchanged the following year in resolution A/RES/62/70.[33] Furthermore, there was a general understanding that the General Assembly's work on the promotion of the rule of law was only at the very beginning, and that more substantive considerations could only be agreed upon after a detailed analysis of the United Nations' work in this area was available, and once a more thorough discussion on the issue had taken place.

This understanding also explains the rationale for the operative parts of resolutions A/RES/61/39 and A/RES/62/70, which in essence require the Secretariat and Member States to provide, over the course of two sessions, the necessary input with a view to a more substantive consideration of the issue at the 63rd session in fall 2008. The basis of that exercise would be an "inventory of the current activities of the

---

[31] See Historical and Analytical Note on the Practices and Working Methods of the Main Committees, Doc. A/58/CRP.5, para. 75.

[32] For an extensive analysis of the Secretary-General's 2004 report on the rule of law see T. Fitschen, in this Focus, there under I.

[33] A/RES/62/70 of 6 December 2007, adopted upon recommendation by the Sixth Committee (see the Committee's report Doc. A/62/454 of 20 November 2007).

various organs, bodies, offices, departments, funds and programmes within the United Nations system devoted to the promotion of the rule of law at the national and international levels", mandated for submission by the Secretary-General at the 63rd session.[34] An interim report on this mapping exercise was submitted at the 62nd session, and it contains information on the rule of law activities of forty United Nations entities.[35] At the time of writing, the Secretariat had just published its final inventory of over 150 pages. The wealth of information listed in the inventory shows the challenge of properly categorizing a myriad of projects and ongoing activities which are difficult to compare in size and scope.[36] The General Assembly will hopefully make good use of the wealth of information contained in the report, even though it deliberately omits information on the activities undertaken by intergovernmental bodies.[37]

The Secretary-General was further mandated to submit a report:

"identifying ways and means for strengthening and coordinating the activities listed in the inventory (...) with special regard to the effectiveness of assistance that may be requested by States in building capacity for the promotion of the rule of law at the national and international levels."[38]

At the time of writing of this article, these recommendations were about to be finalized by the Secretariat. However, one crucial measure aimed at coordinating the United Nations' rule of law activities was already undertaken shortly after the initial request of resolution A/RES/61/39 was made: the Secretary-General, in a report not mandated by the Sixth Committee but submitted as follow-up to the Security Council's work on the rule of law, announced the establishment of

---

[34] A/RES/61/39, see note 22, para. 2. This request was reiterated in A/RES/62/70, see note 33, para. 2.

[35] Doc. A/62/261, para. 10.

[36] In this sense see also the statement by Guatemala, Doc. A/C.6/62/SR.14, para. 48.

[37] Doc. A/63/64, para. 3. It was in response to this approach, which had already been explained in the interim report, that the Sixth Committee included a paragraph in its subsequent resolution on the rule of law asking the ICJ, UNCITRAL and the ILC to comment, in their next reports to the General Assembly, on their current roles in promoting the rule of law, A/RES/62/70, see note 33, para. 3.

[38] A/RES/61/39, see note 22, para 3. This request was reiterated in A/RES/62/70, see note 33, para. 2.

the *Rule of Law Coordination and Resource Group*, which took up its work only a short time thereafter.[39] That report was submitted on 14 December 2006, and thus only a few days after the General Assembly formally adopted resolution A/RES/61/39. The request for recommendations to be submitted two years later, during the 63rd session, was therefore, at least to some extent, almost immediately overtaken by new events. The Secretary-General's decision to establish the *Rule of Law Coordination and Resource Group* – a system-wide consultation and coordination process on rule of law matters – without interfacing with Member States through the Sixth Committee was not without risks, given that resolutions A/RES/61/39 and A/RES/62/70 had envisaged a two-year process of analysis and consultation, with the leading role to be played by Member States: after all, the Secretary-General was asked, in general terms, to "seek the views of Member States on matters pertaining to the issues addressed in the present resolution",[40] and more specifically to submit his report on strengthening and coordinating rule of law activities "after having sought the views of Member States".[41]

The procedural disconnect between the Secretary-General's initiative and the Sixth Committee process on the rule of law could have caused serious problems for the negotiations of the second rule of law resolution. In the end, however, the view prevailed that the establishment of the *Rule of Law Coordination and Resource Group* was a sound response to the needs of the United Nations system in this area. Delegations took a pragmatic approach and noted "with appreciation" the Secretary-General's report, and explicitly expressed their support for the group.[42] One of the arguably most important structural reforms in the United Nations relating to the rule of law was thus endorsed by the General Assembly with relatively little controversy, already at half-time of a process aimed at improving the rule of law architecture. This is an achievement that will be difficult to replicate in the near future.

Finally, the General Assembly also used the two resolutions as vehicles to bring progress to the establishment of the Rule of Law Unit in the Secretariat, mandated to give professional support to the *Rule of Law Coordination and Resource Group*. The establishment of that Unit had already been endorsed by the WSO, but subsequently faced persis-

---

[39] *Uniting our Strengths: Enhancing United Nations Support for the Rule of Law*, Report of the Secretary-General, Doc. A/61/636/-S/2006/980.

[40] A/RES/61/39, see note 22, para. 1.

[41] A/RES/61/39, see note 22, para 3; and A/RES/62/70, see note 33, para. 3.

[42] A/RES/62/70, see note 33, para. 4.

tent bureaucratic obstacles in the Secretariat. Resolution A/RES/62/70 put the ball back in the Secretariat's court, demanding the Secretary-General to provide a report about budgetary implications "without delay" for consideration during the spring 2008 sessions of the Fifth Committee (budgetary and administrative matters). At the time of writing, more than half a year later and following further internal problems in the Secretariat, that report had just been issued; too late for consideration before fall 2008.[43]

The United Nations Secretariat is not alone in experiencing difficulties in the establishment of new structures and procedures aimed at promoting the rule of law. The Sixth Committee itself evidenced a certain degree of uneasiness with the multi-faceted nature of the topic, precisely when trying to make the issue more accessible. Resolution A/RES/61/39 recommended that the Sixth Committee shall, as from the 62nd session and after consultations among Member States, "annually choose one or two sub-topics to facilitate a focused discussion for the subsequent session, without prejudice to the consideration of the item as a whole".[44] This provision was intended to allow the Committee to bring at least some degree of focus to its annual debates on the item, and was modeled after the practice of the General Assembly in matters pertaining to the law of the sea.[45] The informal consultations on the choice of topic which took place in October 2007 brought about a great number of suggestions for topics to be chosen for the subsequent session, ranging from the practical (e.g. "Strengthening the Rule of Law through Technical Assistance and Capacity Building") over the conceptual (e.g. "Identification of the Scope of the Rule of Law at the National and International Levels") to a number of more specific sub-areas of rule of law activities (e.g. "Strengthening Criminal Justice at the National and International Levels").[46] However, the Sixth Committee

---

[43] Doc. A/63/154.

[44] A/RES/61/39, see note 22, para. 5.

[45] See most recently A/RES/62/215 of 22 December 2007, para. 141, regarding the United Nations Open-ended Informal Consultative Process on Oceans and the Law of the Sea.

[46] The informal consultations on the draft resolution, including those on the choice of topic, were coordinated by the authors of this article. The following topics were identified in the course of these consultations, and clustered by the coordinators as follows: Cluster 1 – Strengthening the Rule of Law through Technical Assistance and Capacity Building: a) Strengthening the Rule of Law through Technical Assistance and Capacity Building; b) Better Coordination of UN Assistance Programs in the Rule of Law Area; c) Im-

proved unable to meet the challenge of choosing one or more of the topics suggested for consideration at the subsequent session. The major bone of contention in that respect was the suggestion to discuss the "scope" of the rule of law at the national and international levels. This suggestion was perceived by some to mark the beginning of a process aimed at defining the term "rule of law" and therefore objectionable. Eventually, the Sixth Committee ended these informal consultations without agreement on a topic and without result. Nevertheless, it must be noted that the topic *Strengthening the Rule of Law through Technical Assistance and Capacity Building* was, in any event, expected to be the main focus of the subsequent Sixth Committee session. After all, the comprehensive inventory of United Nations rule of law activities and the report on ways and means to better coordinate and strengthen these

---

plementation of International Obligations through Technical Assistance and Capacity Building; Cluster 2 – Promoting a Common Understanding of the "Rule of Law at the National and International Levels": a) Identification of the Scope of the Rule of Law at the National and International Levels; b) Means to respect the Sovereignty of States over their Territory and their Right to choose the Optimal Legal Regime, based on the General Principles of International Law; c) Means of Achieving Democracy at the International Level; Cluster 3 – Promoting the Rule of Law at the International Level: a) The Observance of the International Rule of Law; b) Laws and Practices of Member States in implementing International Treaties; c) Principles followed by Member States in their Interpretation of International Treaties and their Practices in this Regard; d) Peaceful Settlement of Disputes; e) The Impact of Failure to implement the Principle of Equality of All before the Law on Non-Compliance with Resolutions of International Organizations; f) Principle of Territoriality of National Laws and the Effects of a State Imposing its Jurisdiction on Citizens of another State for Crimes committed beyond its Territory, without Support from International Conventions or the Principles of International Law; Cluster 4 – The Rule of Law and Transitional Justice in Conflict and Post-Conflict Societies: a) International Criminal Justice (in particular Legacy Issues); b) Strengthening Criminal Justice at the National and International Levels; c) Development of National and International Criminal Systems to end Impunity; d) The Role of International Tribunals; e) Transitional Justice; f) Transitional Justice at the National Level; Cluster 5 – Strengthening the Rule of Law through International Organizations: a) Acceptance of the Jurisdiction of the ICJ; b) The Impact of Failure to implement Resolutions of International Organizations and the Judgments of the ICJ; c) Methods of Work and Adoption of Resolutions by International Organizations to ensure the Application of the Principles of International Law; d) The United Nations as a Rules-Based Organization.

activities was to be submitted at that session, thus presenting a natural focus for the debates. It was also understood that the efforts to choose a topic for subsequent sessions would be continued at the 63rd session.

In sum, the General Assembly's first two resolutions on the rule of law have provided a cautious beginning for what should become, at a later stage and on the basis of the Secretariat's analysis, a stronger involvement of Member States in the process of strengthening United Nations activities for the promotion of the rule of law.

III. Sixth Committee Debates on the Rule of Law

While the Sixth Committee resolutions on the rule of law, as illustrated above, address a rather limited number of substantive issues, the two Sixth Committee debates under this agenda item reflect in more detail the views of Member States on how the General Assembly should promote the rule of law. 32 delegates speaking on behalf of individual states or groups of states, representing over 90 Member States, participated in the first such debate held at the 61st session in fall 2006.[47] 50 delegates, representing around 160 Member States, participated in the second debate held one year later.[48] In between these two debates, 15 delegations

---

[47]   See the summary records of these meetings, Doc. A/C.6/61/SR.6, SR.7 and SR.20. Statements were made by the representatives of Finland (on behalf of the European Union as well as Bulgaria, Romania, Turkey, Croatia, the former Yugoslav Republic of Macedonia, Albania, Bosnia and Herzegovina, Serbia, Iceland, Norway, Ukraine and Moldova), New Zealand (also on behalf of Australia and Canada), Pakistan, Liechtenstein, the Sudan, Switzerland, Mexico, Guyana (on behalf of the Rio Group), Ethiopia, Malaysia, Japan, China, Cuba, Sierra Leone, Zimbabwe, Trinidad and Tobago, South Africa, Tanzania, Thailand, the Republic of Korea, Israel, India, Belarus, Algeria, the Russian Federation, Zambia, the United States, Indonesia, Syria, Iran and Egypt.

[48]   See the summary records of these meetings, Doc. A/C.6/62/SR.14, SR.15 and SR.16. Statements were made by the representatives of New Zealand (also on behalf of Australia and Canada), the Dominican Republic (on behalf of the Rio Group), Portugal (on behalf of the European Union as well as Turkey, Croatia, the former Yugoslav Republic of Macedonia, Albania, Bosnia and Herzegovina, Serbia, Iceland, Ukraine, Moldova, Armenia and Georgia), Cuba (on behalf of the Non-Aligned Movement), Benin (on behalf of the African Group), Liechtenstein, Switzerland, China, Myanmar, Libya, Guatemala, Sudan, Mexico, India, Vietnam, Indonesia, Mozambique, Egypt, Bangladesh, Colombia, Cuba, the Democratic Republic of

submitted their views on this issue in writing.[49] The areas of conceptual agreement during these two debates can easily be identified by reverting to the preambular language of the two resolutions discussed above. Many delegations introduced their statements by pledging their commitment to the United Nations Charter and to an international order based on the rule of law, by emphasizing the rule of law as an indispensable prerequisite for international peace and security, development and human rights, by referring to basic principles of international law such as *pacta sunt servanda* and the prohibition to invoke internal law as justification for failure to perform a treaty, by stressing Charter principles such as the peaceful settlement of disputes and the obligation to refrain from the threat or use of force, and by acknowledging that the national and international dimension of the rule of law are interdependent and complementary. These areas of commonality are – at least at the conceptual level – of such basic and undisputed nature that these references, while obviously welcome as reaffirmation of the core principles of international law – have little to offer in terms of analytical value. In the following, emphasis will therefore be placed on issues which appear to be more controversial among Member States, namely the question of the scope of the rule of law at the international level, and the issue of the rule of law within the United Nations.

1. Defining the *International Rule of Law*

While the Secretariat has made great strides in developing at least a "common language" of the rule of law,[50] Member States have so far not embarked on a coordinated exercise of defining the term, and are unlikely to do so in the foreseeable future. Some states cautioned pub-

---

the Congo, Nigeria, Sierra Leone, Malaysia, Singapore, Thailand, Chile, Algeria, Venezuela, Tanzania, Japan, Tunisia, Republic of Korea, Kenya, South Africa, the United States, Kuwait, Norway, Israel, Pakistan, Iran, El Salvador, the Russian Federation, Morocco, Albania, Syria, Latvia, the Holy See (Observer) and the International Development Law Organization (Observer).

[49] Doc. A/62/121 and A/62/121/Add.1. These include a number of observations by members of the European Union that did not express themselves in the debates due to the common EU statement.

[50] See T. Fitschen, in this Focus, there under VI.

licly against attempts aimed at defining the term,[51] while others did so in the context of the closed Sixth Committee consultations on the choice of topic for subsequent debates. Nevertheless, the Sixth Committee debates also showed a desire by a great number of countries from different regions to encourage at least a debate about the definition,[52] and to put their own views about the concept of the rule of law on record. Some of those who favored the attempt of a definition acknowledged, however, that it could only encompass some common denominators and would not be exhaustive.[53] These statements are particularly interesting with regard to the rule of law at the international level, or the "international rule of law", as some delegations put it.[54] The question of defining the rule of law at the national level will not be considered separately in this article. Indeed, some delegations considered that even in the absence of any kind of formal agreement, the rule of law was well-defined at the national level.[55]

---

[51]   See e.g. comments submitted by France, Doc. A/62/121, page 16, para. 4: "Given the great diversity of issues addressed under the rubric of 'the rule of law' in various organs of the United Nations, it would certainly be useful to examine more closely the notion of 'rule of law'. France is of the opinion, however, that given the complex theoretical concepts to which this notion has given rise and which have been affirmed in various ways in the different legal systems, it would be best to adopt a pragmatic and practical approach to the question". See also statement by New Zealand (also on behalf of Australia and Canada), Doc. A/C.6/61/SR.6, para. 93.

[52]   Non-Aligned Movement, Doc. A/C.6/62/SR.14, para. 17; statement by the Dominican Republic (on behalf of the Rio Group), Doc. A/C.6/62/SR.14, para. 19; statement by Switzerland, Doc. A/C.6/61/SR.7, paras 9 and 14, suggesting that the Secretary-General could provide analysis and suggest a definition of the concept of the rule of law at the international level; statement by Egypt, Doc. A/C.6/62/SR.14, para. 69; statement by Iran, Doc. A/C.6/62/SR.16, para. 68; comments by the Netherlands, Doc. A/62/121, page 27, para. 2.

[53]   Statement by Switzerland, Doc. A/C.6/62/SR.14, para. 32; statement by Mexico, Doc. A/C.6/62/SR.14, para. 51; statement by Iran, Doc. A/C.6/62/SR.16, 68.

[54]   Statement by Switzerland, Doc. A/C.6/61/SR.7, para. 14; statement by Colombia, Doc. A/C.6/62/SR.15, para. 3; statement by the Dominican Republic on behalf of the Rio Group, Doc. A/C.6/62/SR.14, para. 18; statement by China, Doc. A/C.6/62/SR.14, para. 41.

[55]   See e.g. statement by Switzerland, Doc. A/C.6/1/SR.7, para. 9; statement by Mexico, Doc. A/C.6/62/SR.14, para. 51.

The following are some of the more concrete statements made about the definition of the international rule of law: Mexico suggested to define the rule of law as a common denominator of civilized international society, akin to the general principles of law recognized by civilized nations referred to in Article 38 para. 1 (lit.c) of the Statute of the ICJ. At the international level, the rule of law called for "an international order based on compliance by States with international law".[56]

Colombia stated that the basis of the international rule of law was:

"an international legal system that recognized the legal equality of States and set limits on the exercise of power through checks and balances in order to avoid excesses and arbitrariness".[57]

Singapore stressed that, at its most basic level, the law set out legitimate expectations of what was "acceptable conduct and what was not". The rule of law meant that no party, whatever its status or interests, could act in an arbitrary manner.[58]

Austria, in a comment not explicitly framed as part of a definition of the rule of law, referred to "clear and foreseeable rules, adherence to these rules and a system to prevent or sanction violations of rules".[59]

Iran suggested to identify some common elements based on general principles of international law such as:

"States' obligation to refrain from the threat or use of force in their international relations, to comply with the principles of universal respect for human rights and fundamental freedoms for all, to respect the equal rights and self-determination of peoples, and the sovereign equality and independence of all States, and not to interfere in the domestic affairs of other States".[60]

Egypt suggested that a definition of the rule of law must:

"rely on the general principles of law consistent with the foundations of justice, democracy, human rights, the equality of all before the law, respect for State sovereignty, safeguarding the right of legitimate self-defence, avoidance of the misuse of that right, the prohibition of the use of force or the threat thereof and also the safe-

---

[56] Statement by Mexico, Doc. A/C.6/61/SR.7, para. 15.
[57] Statement by Colombia, Doc. A/C.6/62/SR.15, para. 3.
[58] Statement by Singapore, referring to both the national and international dimension of the rule of law, Doc. A/C.6/62/SR.15, para. 24.
[59] Comments by Austria, Doc. A/62/121, page 2, para. 2.
[60] Statement by Iran, Doc. A/C.6/62/SR.16, para. 68.

guarding of the principle of balance between rights and obligations in accordance with the principles of the aforementioned law".[61]

Germany submitted a number of detailed elements which can be summarized as follows: respect for the sovereign equality of all states and for self-determination of peoples; the principle that states must act in good faith and settle any disputes peacefully and must refrain from the threat or use of force in any manner inconsistent with the Charter; the duty of states to fulfill their obligations under international law; an effective multilateral system so as to prevent or sanction violations of international law; full respect for and effective protection of human rights and fundamental freedoms; and the obligation of international organizations to act in accordance with international law.[62]

For Sweden:

"the international rule of law means that international law constitutes the foundation of international relations, that sovereign equality and the right of self-determination are respected, that States abide by their obligations under treaty law and general international law in good faith, that disputes are settled peacefully, that States have recourse to effective remedies before international institutions, that international organizations and other institutions monitor the implementation of obligations and take effective action, if necessary, that international obligations are fully implemented at the national level, including through effective legal mechanisms, and that the rule of law and human rights prevail nationally."[63]

Switzerland suggested that at the international level, the rule of law was based "mainly on international law as the cornerstone of relations between States",[64] and later on submitted in writing a detailed catalogue of elements of the international rule of law which also refers to elements related to the Responsibility to Protect as part of the international rule of law.[65]

While there has not been any effort by the Sixth Committee to compile elements such as those cited above and to negotiate an agreed definition, or at least some core elements of the rule of law at the inter-

---

[61]   Comments by Egypt, Doc. A/62/121, page 11, para. 3.
[62]   Comments by Germany submitted in its national capacity, Doc. A/62/121, page 18.
[63]   Comments by Sweden, Doc. A/62/121, page 31, para. 2.
[64]   Statement by Switzerland, Doc. A/C.6/62/SR.14, para. 32.
[65]   Comments by Switzerland, Doc. A/62/121/Add.1, page 3, para. 8.

national level, the commonalities of these elements, raised by delegations from different regions and with different political interests, are rather striking. Many of these elements are indeed and indisputably core rules of international law, based on the United Nations Charter, general principles of international law, customary international law and treaty law, and have been reaffirmed by Member States on many occasions, including in the World Summit Outcome and, in a more focused manner, in the General Assembly's two rule of law resolutions discussed above. They have also been referred to by a wide range of states from different regions in the Sixth Committee debates. If a synthesis of these elements were to be made, the list of core elements of the international rule of law, as seen through the lens of the General Assembly, should include:

- The commitment to an international order based on international law, in particular the Charter of the United Nations;
- the duty of all states to refrain from the threat or use of force and the duty of all states to settle their disputes by peaceful means;
- the principles of sovereign equality of all states and of self-determination of peoples;
- the principle of *pacta sunt servanda* and the duty of all states to fulfill their obligations in good faith;
- the principle of the supremacy of international law obligations over domestic law;
- the promotion and protection of human rights and fundamental freedoms.

This would, at first sight, support the notion that an agreed definition of the "international rule of law" would not be impossible to achieve, should the General Assembly decide to embark on such an exercise. After all, the real divisions regarding all of the above-mentioned rules and principles relate to their interpretation and application in practice rather than to the realm of ideas and concepts. Nevertheless, it seems inevitable that a number of disputes currently existing between some Member States that raise questions about the non-selective interpretation and application of international law[66] would enter the discus-

---

[66]   In that sense see statement by Viet Nam, Doc. A/C.6/62/SR.14, para. 58.

sion, once the stakes would be raised from a mere debate to an exercise of finding a definition of the rule of law.[67]

Indeed, and rather surprisingly, the first two debates on the rule of law in the Sixth Committee saw remarkably few direct expressions of concrete political grievances, framed as violations of the rule of law.[68] Instead, political grievances occasionally appeared as subtext of statements, usually evidenced by the choice of rule of law principles mentioned most prominently, such as the principle of non-interference in domestic affairs or the rejection of unilateral measures.[69] It is quite likely that such political divisions would rather quickly jeopardize any negotiations aimed at defining the "international rule of law", and even if they were successful, such negotiations would only lead to a catalogue of rules and principles which are beyond dispute and well-known.

The protection of human rights and fundamental freedoms could probably be included in such a definition of the international rule of law, however the emerging rule of the Responsibility to Protect might not stand the test of such a delicate exercise. Similarly, another element which would be difficult to agree upon would be the suggestion that the international rule of law requires "effective remedies"[70] at the inter-

---

67   The extremely difficult negotiations on what has been phrased the "definition of terrorism" in the context of the Sixth Committee's work on a draft comprehensive convention on international terrorism are a case in point. For further details on that process see M. Hmoud, "Negotiating the Draft Comprehensive Convention on International Terrorism – Major Bones of Contention", *Journal of International Criminal Justice* 4 (2006), 1031 et seq. Another example for a negotiation process heavily influenced by major political events and grievances concerns the definition of the crime of aggression as foreseen in article 5 (2) of the Rome Statute of the International Criminal Court. For the current status of that process see the upcoming report of the Special Working Group on the Crime of Aggression, ICC-ASP/6/20/Add.1.

68   See e.g. statement by Zimbabwe, Doc. A/C.6/61/SR.7, condemning the detention of prisoners at Guantánamo Bay.

69   See e.g. statement by Venezuela, Doc. A/C.6/62/SR.16, para. 18; statement by Cuba (on behalf of the Non-Aligned Movement), Doc. A/C.6/62/SR.14, para. 14; statement by Sudan, Doc. A/C.6/62/SR.14, para. 49; statement by Iran, Doc. A/C.6/62/SR.16, para. 71.

70   Comments by Sweden, Doc. A/62/121, page 31, para. 2. Similar suggestions were made by Switzerland, Doc. A/62/121/Add.1, page 3, para. 8, referring to "the possibility for every State to have effective recourse against violations of its rights before an appropriate international institution"; and

national level against violations of international law. The precise scope of such an element would certainly be subject to heated debates, given the reluctance of many states to be subject to international adjudication – an obvious precondition to a system of effective remedies at the international level. This is also reflected in the rather weak language on the ICJ contained in the WSO, which merely calls upon states to "consider accepting" the jurisdiction of the court in accordance with its statute,[71] and which does not refer to the ICJ's advisory powers at all.[72]

These few examples make it clear that overall the chances of successfully negotiating a "definition" of the international rule of law, going beyond a limited number of well-established core elements, are rather slim. This is not to say that the scope of the international rule of law should not be discussed, quite to the contrary. However, the fear that an open discussion would be the first step toward a negotiation process has, until now, somewhat restricted the debate in the General Assembly on this important question. This trend will hopefully be reversed in future debates.

2. The Rule of Law and Human Rights within the United Nations

While some core elements of the concept of an "international rule of law" are clearly established and undisputed as far as relations between states are concerned, a number of delegations used the Sixth Committee debates to take the road less traveled, airing their views on what could be called the "rule of law at the institutional level".[73]

To a great extent, these interventions focused on the question of the powers and competences of the United Nations' principal organs, in particular the Security Council, and the balance between the Security Council and the General Assembly. Much of that discussion, however,

---

by Germany, Doc. A/62/121, page 18, referring to "an effective multilateral system so as to prevent or sanction violations of international law".

[71] WSO, see note 3, para. 134 (f).

[72] The absence of any reference to the Court's advisory functions can to some extent be explained as a reaction to some controversial advisory opinions rendered by the ICJ, in particular *Legal Consequences of the Construction of a Wall in the Occupied Palestinian Territory*, 2004 *ICJ* (9 July 2004).

[73] See comments by Austria, Doc. A/62/121, page 6, para. 26; statement by Iran, Doc. A/C.6/62/SR.16, para. 71.

was prompted by concern over the "legislative" and "quasi-judicial"[74] activities of the Security Council in the area of counter-terrorism and non-proliferation in recent years,[75] but also by the equally recent phenomenon of thematic Security Council activities, such as debates on "Natural Resources and Conflict"[76] or "Energy, Security and Climate"[77] and other thematic work.[78] Especially states members of the Non-Aligned Movement posited that the Security Council's "encroachment on the traditional areas of competence of the General Assembly and the Economic and Social Council was a cause for concern".[79] This ongoing dispute, however, relates in most of the cases to the nuances of the intended balance of activities between the General Assembly and the Security Council rather than to the legal question whether and to what extent the decision-making of these organs is limited by rules of international law. In this context, respect for the mandates and competences of the various United Nations organs as defined in the Charter was frequently demanded[80] – in itself certainly not a controversial concept, beyond the concrete political context in which such demands are made.

While it is firmly established that the United Nations as an international organization (and thus its organs) are subject to certain rules of international law, in particular its constituent instrument, the United Nations Charter, as well as customary international law (including *jus*

---

[74] See most recently I. Johnston, "Legislation and Adjudication in the UN Security Council: Bringing Down the Deliberative Deficit", *AJIL* 102 (2008), 275 et seq. See statement by Cuba, Doc. A/C.6/62/SR.15, para. 9.

[75] Though that was criticized as well, e.g. statement by Cuba, Doc. A/C.6/62/SR.15, para. 9; statement by Iran, Doc. A/C.6/62/SR.16, para. 71.

[76] Security Council Open Debate on 25 June 2007.

[77] Security Council Open Debate on 17 April 2007.

[78] See e.g. statement by Algeria, Doc. A/C.6/61/SR.7, para. 90, criticizing the Security Council's "frequent recourse to thematic resolutions which were inconsistent with the Council's chief prerogatives as set forth in the Charter of the United Nations".

[79] Statement by Cuba (on behalf of the Non-Aligned Movement), Doc. A/C.6/62/SR.14, para. 14.

[80] E.g. statement by Sudan, Doc. A/C.6/61/SR.7; statement by Cuba, Doc. A/C.6/61/SR.7, para. 51; statement by Iran, Doc. A/C.6/62/SR.16, para. 71. South Africa suggested to examine the "limits of the powers vested in the Council under Chapter VII", Doc. A/C.6/61/SR.7, para. 61.

cogens) and general principles of international law,[81] the scope of the rule of law within the United Nations becomes less clear when entering the area of human rights. Simon Chesterman diagnosed "a surprising degree of uncertainty as to whether the organization is bound by, for example, the human rights treaties for which it has been the primary vehicle".[82] This question has received increasing attention in the work of delegations at UN Headquarters, in particular in the light of recent internal reform efforts regarding the UN's internal justice system[83], and with respect to the Security Council's targeted sanctions regimes. Not surprisingly though, these discussions were dominated by policy considerations rather than by an analysis of the extent of the organization's legal obligations, and could only scratch the surface of this vexing question. In the context of the Sixth Committee debates on the rule of law, the Rio Group suggested that the question of the "subjection of international organizations to the rule of law" should be part of future focused discussions on the "observance of the international rule of law".[84]

While it was frequently observed in rather general terms that the United Nations organs were also subject to the rule of law,[85] hardly any statements addressed the question of the precise extent to which United Nations organs are bound by international law *beyond* its Charter. Colombia stated that all organs of the United Nations, without exception, were "subject to the principle of legality and to *jus cogens* norms".[86]

---

[81] See P. Sands/ P. Klein, *Bowett's Law of International Institutions*, 2001, 441 et seq.

[82] S. Chesterman, *An International Rule of Law?*, NYU Law School, Public Law Research Paper No. 08-11, 27.

[83] See on this topic the article by A. Reinisch and C. Knahr in this Focus.

[84] Statement by the Dominican Republic (on behalf of the Rio Group), Doc. A/C.6/62/SR.14, para. 19.

[85] E.g. statement by Switzerland, Doc. AC.6/61/SR.7, para. 8; statement by Chile, Doc. A/C.6/62/SR.16, para. 9; statement by Colombia, Doc. A/C.6/62/SR.15, para. 4; statement by Cuba, Doc. A/C.6/62/SR.15, para. 9; statement by Iran, Doc. A/C.6/62/SR.16, para. 71.

[86] Statement by Colombia, Doc. A/C.6/62/SR.15, para. 4. The Colombian delegation also expressed "serious reservations about the theory of implicit powers, which could weaken the principle of legality and result in ultra vires actions taken by international organizations, one of the more common and sometimes subtle ways of undermining the rule of law", ibid. The Court of First Instance of the European Communities has equally argued that the Security Council was bound by *jus cogens*, see *Yassin Abdullah Kadi* v. Council of the European Union and Commission of the European

Austria commented that "strengthening the rule of law at the institutional level requires that rules are fully respected within and by the
United Nations and its organs, as well as other international organizations". Germany submitted that the rule of law entails the "obligation
of international organizations to act – internally and in their relations
vis-à-vis Member States and the international community – in accordance with, and showing full respect for, international law".[87]

Such statements hint at, but do not clearly answer the question to
what extent United Nations organs are bound by rules of international
law beyond the Charter. Further clarifying interventions could have
been expected in the context of the reform process of the United Nations' internal administration of justice, which is driven by Member
States' desire to provide UN staff with a system of justice that lives up
to the standards of international human rights. In that process, however, no clear statements have been made to the effect that the internal
justice system should be improved in order to abide by an international
legal obligation, rather than as a matter of good policy and moral consistency.[88]

In the context of ongoing discussions[89] about the Security Council's
sanctions listing practice, some Member States have been slightly more
outspoken in arguing that the Security Council needs to respect human
rights.[90] Once again, however, these statements do not clearly establish
that United Nations organs such as the Security Council should respect
human rights as a matter of an international legal obligation,[91] despite

---

Communities, Case T-315/01, *OJ* (2002), C 56/16 et seq. See in this respect
also the article of M. Kanetake in this Volume, pages 152 et seq.

[87] Comments by Germany, Doc. A/62/121, page 19, para. 3.

[88] In the words of the Secretary-General, the United Nations should "practice what it preaches", see Doc. A/61/758, para. 5 (b). See also statement by
Chile, Doc. A/C.6/62/SR.16, para. 8.

[89] This discussion took place largely outside the framework of the Sixth
Committee's work on the rule of law, though some states did refer to this
question in the context of the rule of law debate, see statement by Pakistan,
Doc. A/C.6/61/SR.6, para. 99; comments submitted by Austria, Doc.
A/62/121, page 7, para. 29.

[90] Such as the right to be informed, the right to be heard, the right to review
and an effective remedy; see the Secretary-General's Letter on this topic reflected in Doc. S/PV.5474, page 5.

[91] See for example a discussion paper on this topic submitted to the Security
Council by Denmark, Germany, Liechtenstein, the Netherlands, Sweden
and Switzerland, Doc. A/62/891-S/2008/428, which argues mainly on the

some Member States being mindful of the very question.[92] It seems that the General Assembly's future work on the rule of law could benefit from a thorough debate of this question. The Sixth Committee debates on *The Rule of Law at the National and International Levels* would be the logical forum.

IV. Conclusion

Over the last few years, the General Assembly has re-established itself as a key forum for an international policy debate on the rule of law, as well as for concrete initiatives aimed at strengthening the United Nations' performance in that area. In this respect, the General Assembly has now caught up with the Security Council, which seems to have passed its peak in its thematic work on the rule of law.

At the same time, the General Assembly is only at the beginning of a more concerted effort to discuss and promote the rule of law, and many delegations are still grappling with the large dimension of this undertaking, which is underscored by the massive amount of information contained in the Secretary-General's inventory on rule of law activities.

Nevertheless, the General Assembly has given new impetus to this work and its institutional position in the United Nations. With the new agenda item *The Rule of Law at the National and International Levels*, the General Assembly now has a permanent procedural anchor for further policy discussions and initiatives. There should be no illusions as to how difficult it would be to make further progress on the concept of the Responsibility to Protect, or on agreeing on a definition of the rule of law or some of its sub-sets, such as the international rule of law or the rule of law at the institutional level.

At the same time, the General Assembly remains the one forum of universal membership that bestows unique legitimacy on policy debates and their outcomes. It is therefore hoped that more and more Member States will consider these debates as an opportunity rather than a risk and not shy away from addressing sometimes difficult legal concepts. With the right amount of courage and engagement from delegations, the

---

basis of the World Summit Outcome's commitment to ensure "fair and clear procedures" for sanctions listings (see Doc. A/60/1, para. 109), rather than on international human rights law.

[92] See statement by Liechtenstein in the Security Council Open Debate of 22 June 2006, Doc. S/PV.5474 (Resumption 1), page 9.

General Assembly still has much to contribute to the promotion of the rule of law worldwide.

The Austrian Rule of Law Initiative 2004 - 2008

– The Panel Series, the Advisory Group and the Final Report on the UN Security Council and the Rule of Law

*Konrad G. Bühler**

I. Introduction

The year 2004 marked the beginning of an unprecedented renaissance of the rule of law at the United Nations, which was ignited by then UN Secretary-General Kofi Annan and spurred by initiatives of several like-

---

*   The views expressed in this article are the author's personal views only and cannot be attributed to the Permanent Mission of Austria or the Austrian Federal Ministry for European and International Affairs.

minded UN Member States. Five years later, the rule of law has become a very popular term at the United Nations and a fast-growing field of activity of the UN system.

In August 2004, Secretary-General Kofi Annan issued a Report entitled *The Rule of Law and Transitional Justice in Conflict and Post Conflict Societies*,[1] which aimed at articulating a "common language of justice for the United Nations" of the key concepts of justice, rule of law and transitional justice. In addition, on 21 September 2004, in his much-acclaimed address to the 59th UN General Assembly,[2] Kofi Annan highlighted the rule of law as the all-important framework and pledged to make the United Nations' work to strengthen the rule of law and transitional justice a priority for the remainder of his tenure.

While it is true that the rule of law was not a new idea at the United Nations,[3] it is only since a few years that the United Nations has started to develop comprehensive common concepts, coordinate, and give coherent policy direction to the manifold activities of the UN system in the field of rule of law. Until then, the rule of law activities of the United Nations followed a piecemeal approach, were limited in scope (e.g. only in conflict and post-conflict situations or in the field of human rights) and lacked coordination and a coherent policy.

The present article is an attempt from a practitioner's point of view to shed light behind the scenes of the above-mentioned developments in the field of rule of law at the United Nations during the past five years, focusing in particular on the Austrian Rule of Law Initiative.

II. The Austrian Rule of Law Initiative

In her speech at the 59th UN General Assembly,[4] then Austrian Foreign Minister Benita Ferrero-Waldner warmly welcomed Secretary-General Kofi Annan's address and his pledge to make the strengthening

---

1   *The Rule of Law and Transitional Justice in Conflict and Post Conflict Societies*, Report of the Secretary-General, Doc. S/2004/616 of 23 August 2004.

2   See UN Press Release SG/SM/9491 – GA/10258 dated 21 September 2004.

3   See the article by T. Fitschen in this Focus.

4   Statement by H.E. Dr. Benita Ferrero-Waldner, Federal Minister for Foreign Affairs of the Republic of Austria, at the 59th Session of the UN General Assembly, 23 September 2004, at <http://www.un.org/webcast/ga/59/statements/auseng040923.pdf>.

of the rule of law a priority of the United Nations. She stressed that in particular for smaller and medium sized countries an international order based on the rule of law was of paramount importance. As a contribution to the Secretary-General's efforts, Ferrero-Waldner announced to launch a discourse on the role and function of the Security Council in the strengthening of a rules-based international system.

This announcement was the starting point of the Austrian Rule of Law Initiative, which consisted of the following three main prongs:

- First, a series of seven panel discussions from 2004 to 2008 on the role of the Security Council in strengthening a rules-based international system and a retreat of experts at Alpbach, Austria, in August 2007.

- Second, the establishment of an Advisory Group, which over the years has become the Group of "Friends of the Rule of Law" at the United Nations in New York.

- Third, the publication of the Final Report and Recommendations on "The UN Security Council and the Rule of Law", reflecting the outcome of the four years' panel series.

1. The Panel Series and the Alpbach Retreat

Starting in November 2004 during the first International Law Week[5] at the United Nations, the Austrian Permanent Mission in New York, in cooperation with the Institute for International Law and Justice at New York University School of Law,[6] convened a series of panel discussions on various aspects of the central theme of "The Role of the Security Council in Strengthening a Rules-Based International System" at the Dag Hammarskjöld Library Penthouse at United Nations Headquarters in New York.

---

5   Based on an Austrian proposal, on 9 December 2003 the General Assembly had decided that the first week in which the report of the International Law Commission is discussed in the Sixth Committee should henceforth be known as "International Law Week". See A/RES/58/77 of 9 December 2003, op. para. 11 and preambular para. 7.

6   The author would like to take this opportunity to thank Professor Simon Chesterman, Professor Benedict Kingsbury and Professor Thomas Franck at New York University School of Law for the excellent cooperation.

The panel discussions, which brought together experts from both theory and practice, including representatives of the diplomatic, United Nations and academic communities and civil society, focused on questions such as "The Security Council as World Legislator?" (4 November 2004), "Who needs Rules?" (5 May 2005), "The Security Council as World Judge?" (27 October 2005), "The Security Council as World Executive?" (26 October 2006) and "The Security Council and the Individual" (27 March 2007).[7] The panels enjoyed great interest and wide participation of United Nations Member States.

The topics were also analyzed in depth at a retreat of key experts (including many members of the Advisory Group, see below under Chapter II. 2.) at Alpbach, Austria, on 25 – 27 August 2007, which was organized by the Austrian Federal Ministry for European and International Affairs and the Permanent Mission of Austria in conjunction with the European Forum Alpbach, as well as a public panel discussion on "The Security Council and the Rule of Law" at the Alpbach Conference Centre (27 August 2007).[8] Some preliminary conclusions and recommendations that emerged from the panel series and the Alpbach Retreat were publicly presented and discussed at a wrap-up panel in New York during the International Law Week 2007 (1 November 2007).

As a result of this process, the Rapporteur of the Austrian Initiative, Dr. Simon Chesterman, Global Professor and Director of the New York University School of Law Singapore Programme, prepared a Final Report, which reflected the discussions and the recommendations that emerged on how the Council could support the rule of law in its various fields of activity in order to strengthen an international system based on rules. The Final Report and Recommendations on "The UN Security Council and the Rule of Law" were presented by Austrian State Secretary Dr. Hans Winkler and the Rapporteur Dr. Simon Chesterman at United Nations Headquarters in New York on 7 April 2008 (see below under Chapter II. 3.).

---

[7] For further information on the panel series, including the agendas and lists of speakers see Doc. A/63/69 – S/2008/270, Appendix I. Electronic copies of reports of the panel discussions can be downloaded from the website of the Austrian Mission at <http://www.bmeia.gv.at/newyorkov>.

[8] See Doc. A/63/69 – S/2008/270, Appendix II.

2. The Advisory Group – the Group of "Friends of the Rule of Law"

In order to supplement the panel series, at an inaugural meeting on 25 January 2005 a small Advisory Group was established, which was composed of Permanent Representatives of United Nations Member States from all regional groups and high-ranking officials from the UN Secretariat. The members of the Group, who all served in their personal capacity, informally met three to four times a year to provide strategic guidance to the initiative, discuss and analyze the topics of previous and future panels, and make substantive contributions to the work of the Rapporteur.

In the following years the personal and material scope of the Advisory Group was gradually expanded. In the beginning, the Group was rather small, but its personal scope was later enlarged when a number of members expressed their interest to participate in its work. Membership in the Group was always handled in an open, informal and flexible manner, while strictly maintaining its cross-regional balance and high-level participation. In the light of the personal character of the membership, some members resigned when they left New York or moved to new positions. In sum, during the past four years, representatives of more than 30 United Nations Member States[9] from all regional groups have participated in meetings and supported the work of the Advisory Group.

Although the Advisory Group had initially been established to only deal with topics related to the Austrian panel series, it soon expanded its material scope and became a forum of like-minded United Nations Member States to discuss and take joint initiatives regarding various issues in the field of rule of law. Thus, over the years, the Advisory Group developed into an informal Group of "Friends of the Rule of Law" at the United Nations in New York, who all shared the view that international law and the rule of law are the foundations of the international system and that it is therefore imperative to strengthen the rule of

---

9   These UN Member States included Angola, Austria, Bahamas, Belgium, Canada, Cape Verde, Colombia, Costa Rica, Finland, Germany, Ghana, Jordan, Kenya, Latvia, Liechtenstein, Mexico, Morocco, Panama, Papua New Guinea, Paraguay, Romania, Republic of Congo, Republic of Korea, Senegal, Singapore, Slovakia, Slovenia, Spain, Sweden, Switzerland and the United Kingdom.

law in all its dimensions, i.e. at the national, international and institutional levels.

Among the many rule of law issues considered by the Advisory Group, the following three topics merit particular attention.

a. The 2005 World Summit Outcome

After Secretary-General Kofi Annan in his address in September 2004 had highlighted the rule of law as the all-important framework of the United Nations and pledged to make the strengthening of the rule of law a priority for the organization (see above under Chapter I.), many were disappointed that in their December 2004 Report the High-level Panel of eminent persons, who had been asked by the Secretary-General to make recommendations for strengthening the United Nations in preparation of the 2005 World Summit, failed to call attention to the strengthening of the rule of law among the means to address the current threats to peace and security.[10]

In order to raise awareness to the importance of the rule of law as a precondition for lasting peace and stability, in early 2005 the Permanent Mission of Austria prepared a non-paper[11] on the Report of the High-level Panel with recommendations on the strengthening of the rule of law. The non-paper was circulated and discussed among the members of the Advisory Group and transmitted to Secretary-General Kofi Annan on 1 March 2005. Not least as a result of this input, the Secretary-General in his March 2005 Report *In Larger Freedom* devoted a whole chapter to the rule of law, in which he *inter alia* announced his intention to create a special rule of law assistance unit (see below under Chapter II. 2. c.).[12]

---

[10] See *Report of the High-level Panel on Threats, Challenges and Change, A More Secure World: Our Shared Responsibility*, Doc. A/59/565 of 2 December 2004. The High-level Panel had been asked to assess current threats to international peace and security; to evaluate how existing policies and institutions have done in addressing those threats; and to make recommendations for strengthening the United Nations so that it can provide collective security for all in the twenty-first century.

[11] See Austrian Non-Paper of 11 February 2005 (not published, on file with the author).

[12] See *In Larger Freedom: Towards Development, Security and Human Rights for All*, Doc. A/59/2005, Report of the Secretary-General, paras 133-139.

In the ensuing informal consultations and negotiations of the General Assembly to prepare the 2005 World Summit, the group of like-minded United Nations Member States through their statements[13] and by submitting concrete drafting suggestions[14] continued their lobbying for the inclusion of language on the rule of law in the outcome document. As a consequence of these joint efforts, a number of specific references to international law and the rule of law were included in the World Summit Outcome adopted by the heads of state and government on 16 September 2005.[15] In particular, in para. 134 the World Summit Outcome:

- Recognized the need for universal adherence to and implementation of the rule of law at both the national and international levels (Chapeau);

- Reaffirmed the commitment to the purposes and principles of the Charter and international law and to an international order based on the rule of law and international law, which is essential for peaceful coexistence and cooperation among states (lit. a); and

- Supported the idea of establishing a Rule of Law Assistance Unit within the Secretariat, in accordance with existing relevant procedures, subject to a Report by the Secretary-General to the General Assembly, so as to strengthen United Nations activities to promote the rule of law, including through technical assistance and capacity-building (lit. e).

---

[13] See informal thematic consultations of the General Assembly to discuss Cluster III (Freedom to live in Dignity) contained in the report of the Secretary-General (*In Larger Freedom*): cf. Statement by H.E. Ambassador Gerhard Pfanzelter, Permanent Representative of Austria to the United Nations, 20 April 2005, at <http://www.bmeia.gv.at/en/austrian-mission/austrian-mission-new-york/news/statements-and-speeches/2005/informal-thematic-consultations-of-the-general-assembly-on-reform-cluster-freedom-to-live-in-dignity.html>; Statement by H.E. Ambassador Christian Wenaweser, Permanent Representative of the Principality of Liechtenstein to the United Nations, 19 April 2005, at <http://www.liechtenstein.li/en/pdf-fl-aussenstelle-newyork-dokumente-uno-04-19-2005-statement-cluster-3.pdf>.

[14] Informal papers with drafting suggestions on the rule of law were submitted, *inter alia*, by Austria, Liechtenstein, Mexico and Switzerland.

[15] World Summit Outcome, A/RES/60/1 of 16 September 2005. For further details see also the article by S. Barriga/ A. Alday in this Focus, there under II. 1.

The inclusion of these references in the 2005 World Summit Outcome was the first important achievement in the efforts of the "Friends of the Rule of Law" to strengthen the rule of law at the United Nations.

b. The New General Assembly Agenda Item on *The Rule of Law at the National and International Levels*[16]

While the idea of a new agenda item on the rule of law had already emerged in the spring of 2005 during the preparations for the World Summit,[17] it did not materialize until a meeting of the Advisory Group on 8 December 2005, in which the follow-up to the 2005 World Summit Outcome in the field of rule of law was discussed. At that meeting the Group endorsed the idea of a new General Assembly agenda item on the rule of law and agreed that the Permanent Missions of Liechtenstein and Mexico would take the lead to prepare the necessary steps for inclusion of this new item in the agenda of the next General Assembly, whereas the Permanent Mission of Austria would focus on the implementation of the World Summit regarding the establishment of the Rule of Law Unit.

Based on various suggestions made during the discussions in the Group, Liechtenstein and Mexico prepared a draft explanatory memorandum regarding the inclusion of the new item in the agenda of the 61st session of the General Assembly, which was circulated to all members of the Advisory Group on 1 March 2006. By a letter dated 11 May 2006 the Permanent Representatives of Liechtenstein and Mexico formally submitted the request for inclusion of the new agenda item on

---

[16] For further details see also the article by S. Barriga/ A. Alday in this Focus, there under II. 2.

[17] Cf. e.g. the Statement by the Austrian Ambassador Gerhard Pfanzelter on 20 April 2005, see note 13, in which he *inter alia* proposed the following: "In order to reflect the importance of the rule of law for the work of the UN, we believe that during the International Law Week, when Legal Advisers of the Member States are present, the Sixth Committee should hold a general debate on a new agenda item on 'The state of the rule of law and international law' on the basis of a report prepared by the Secretariat"; see also the statement by the Liechtenstein Ambassador Christian Wenaweser on 19 April 2005, ibid.

The Rule of Law at the National and International Levels[18] with an explanatory memorandum to the Secretary-General.[19]

At a meeting of the Advisory Group on 6 June 2006 future steps regarding the proposed new agenda item were discussed and coordinated among the members of the Group, including ideas regarding a Report of the Secretary-General analyzing the concept of the rule of law, an inventory of all rule of law activities of the United Nations and the selection of an annual sub-topic to focus the debate, some of which were later also discussed and adopted by the Sixth Committee of the General Assembly. The members of the Group also agreed to lobby for broad support of the initiative of Liechtenstein and Mexico in their own regional groups.

The subsequent inclusion of the new item on *The Rule of Law at the National and International Levels* in the agenda of the General Assembly in the fall of 2006 marked another important achievement in the efforts of the "Friends of the Rule of Law".

c. The Establishment of the Rule of Law Unit

In his March 2005 Report *In Larger Freedom*, Secretary-General Kofi Annan for the first time announced his intention:

> "to create a dedicated Rule of Law Assistance Unit, drawing heavily on existing staff within the United Nations system, in the proposed Peacebuilding Support Office [...] to assist national efforts to re-establish the rule of law in conflict and post-conflict societies."[20]

During the preparations of the 2005 World Summit the group of like-minded United Nations Member States strongly supported the Secretary-General's intention and stressed the need for a new coordinating unit for all rule of law activities of the United Nations with a broad mandate that would not be limited to conflict and post-conflict situations.[21]

---

[18] For further details see also the article by S. Barriga/ A. Alday in this Focus, there note 16.

[19] See Doc. A/61/142 of 22 May 2006 and Annex.

[20] Doc. A/59/2005, see note 12, para. 137.

[21] See Statement by the Austrian Ambassador Gerhard Pfanzelter on 20 April 2005, see note 13, advocating a broad approach of the rule of law: "We welcome the proposal to create a Rule-of-Law Assistance Unit in the Peacebuilding Support Office. However, the numerous other important efforts of the United Nations to promote the rule of law in national legal systems

As a consequence, the 2005 World Summit Outcome, while keeping the term "Rule of Law Assistance Unit" proposed by the Secretary-General, did no longer refer to the placement of the Unit in the Peace-building Support Office and to conflict and post-conflict situations, but followed the broad approach and supported:

> "the idea of establishing a Rule of Law Assistance Unit *within the Secretariat* [...] so as to strengthen *United Nations activities to promote the rule of law*, including through technical assistance and capacity-building."[22]

In the fall of 2005, as a contribution to the follow-up and implementation of the World Summit Outcome in the field of rule of law, the Permanent Mission of Austria prepared a non-paper on the establishment of the Rule of Law Assistance Unit, which was discussed at the meeting of the Advisory Group on 8 December 2005. At that meeting the Group endorsed the non-paper and tasked Austria to draft a joint letter to the Secretary-General on the basis of the non-paper and the various comments and suggestions made during the discussions.

The joint letter dated 31 January 2006, which was signed by 13 Permanent Representatives to the United Nations,[23] was sent to Secretary-General Kofi Annan with a number of concrete proposals regarding the future role and mandate of the Rule of Law Assistance Unit. In that letter the group of like-minded countries reaffirmed that the Unit should have a broad mandate that is not limited to conflict and post-conflict

---

irrespective of a conflict situation should not be neglected. Such measures include national capacity-building to strengthen domestic criminal law systems and international legal cooperation to counter transnational threats, technical assistance to ratify and implement international treaties for the fight against terrorism, organized crime, drugs and corruption or the drafting of model legislation for the harmonization of national legislation. Given the wide range of activities and the involvement of various organizations and UN-bodies, we believe that there is a need for better coordination and streamlining of the rule of law assistance activities of the UN in general. In order to promote synergy, efficiency and coherence it would thus be useful to identify all UN-bodies active in this field and establish a coordinating unit for their assistance activities." Cf. also the statement by the Liechtenstein Ambassador Christian Wenaweser on 19 April 2005, ibid.

22 A/RES/60/1, see note 15, para. 134 (e) (italics added).

23 The joint letter dated 31 January 2006 was signed by the Permanent Representatives of Austria, Canada, Costa Rica, Finland, Germany, Jordan, Liechtenstein, Mexico, Morocco, Slovenia, Spain, Sweden and Switzerland. For the text of the joint letter see Annex I to this article.

situations. Moreover, its mandate should include the coordination and streamlining of all UN activities to promote the rule of law, the facilitation of technical assistance (it should, however, not provide technical assistance itself), making of recommendations and cooperation with other organizations, funds and programs. Finally, the Unit should be established at an adequately high level in the Secretariat in order to effectively coordinate among the various departments, funds and programs of the UN system.

However, while the idea of the establishment of such a new Unit enjoyed wide-spread support among the UN membership, it met with unexpected skepticism and opposition within the Secretariat of the United Nations. At a meeting on 6 June 2006 the Advisory Group was informed that the joint letter had been received by the Secretary-General as a most welcome contribution, but that the Executive Office of the Secretary-General was faced with serious difficulties and delays to establish the Unit due to internal turf battles and disputes regarding competences and mandates between various parts of the UN system.[24]

In the light of the lingering stalemate within the UN Secretariat, on 25 October 2006 the Permanent Mission of Austria arranged for a personal meeting of 11 Permanent Representatives with Secretary-General Kofi Annan,[25] in which they expressed their concern that more than a year after the 2005 World Summit the establishment of the Rule of Law Assistance Unit still remained to be implemented. Reminding the Secretary-General of his pledge at the 59th General Assembly, the Group reiterated its call for the establishment of the Unit as outlined in the joint letter without any further delay. In addition, in the Sixth Committee of the General Assembly, the members of the Group pressed for the inclusion of a paragraph in General Assembly resolution 61/39 on *The Rule of Law at the National and International Levels*, urging the Secretary-General, as a matter of priority, to submit the Report on the establish-

---

[24] Apparently, some of the concerns were caused by the name "Rule of Law *Assistance* Unit", as originally proposed by the Secretary-General, which had given rise to the impression that the new Unit itself would provide technical assistance. However, according to the proposals of the group of like-minded countries, it was always envisaged that the Unit would only have a coordinating role and rather serve as a "Rule of Law *Coordination* Unit". Thus, in order to avoid any misunderstandings, the expression "Rule of Law Unit" was subsequently used.

[25] The meeting on 25 October 2006 was attended by the Permanent Representatives of Austria, Costa Rica, Finland, Germany, Liechtenstein, Mexico, Morocco, Slovenia, Spain, Sweden and Switzerland.

ment of a Rule of Law Assistance Unit within the Secretariat, in conformity with para. 134 (e) of the 2005 World Summit Outcome.[26]

As a result of these persistent calls, on 14 December 2006, only a few days before the end of his tenure, Secretary-General Kofi Annan issued his long-awaited Report *Uniting our Strengths: Enhancing United Nations Support for the Rule of Law*[27], in which he highlighted the centrality of the rule of law to the work of the United Nations and announced his decision to establish a Rule of Law Coordination and Resource Group within the Secretariat, chaired by the Deputy Secretary-General and supported by a small Secretariat Unit, to act as focal point for coordinating system-wide rule of law activities.

While the establishment of the Rule of Law Coordination and Resource Group and the Rule of Law Unit can be seen as a crowning achievement of the efforts of the Group of "Friends of the Rule of Law" to strengthen the rule of law at the United Nations, two issues that were left open in the Secretary-General's Report have continued to require the attention of the Group:

  – First, the Report left open the decision as to where the Rule of Law Unit would be located, noting that this would be addressed by the incoming Secretary-General. However, given the broad remit of the new entity, the Report also noted that it would not be appropriate to place it within the Peacebuilding Support Office.[28]

  – Second, the Unit was established "within existing resources" without any funding from the regular UN budget. According to the Report, during the initial phase the staff of the Unit of up to four professionals would be seconded from key United Nations actors.

With regard to the question of the location of the Unit, at a meeting on 13 February 2007 to discuss the follow-up to the above-mentioned Report, the Advisory Group tasked Austria to draft another letter addressed to the new Secretary-General to state its views on this matter. In a joint letter dated 26 February 2007 addressed to Secretary-General Ban Ki-Moon, which was signed by 24 Permanent Representatives to

---

[26] A/RES/61/39 of 4 December 2006, op. para. 4.

[27] Doc. A/61/636–S/2006/980 of 14 December 2006.

[28] Ibid., para. 49.

the United Nations,[29] the "Friends of the Rule of Law" expressed their strong support for the establishment of the Rule of Law Coordination and Resource Group and its Secretariat Unit and reaffirmed that in order to effectively coordinate all rule of law activities of the UN system the Unit would be best located at the highest level in the Secretariat, i.e. the Executive Office of the Secretary-General.

Since this issue nevertheless remained undecided,[30] a passage was included in A/RES/62/70 of 6 December 2007 on *The Rule of Law at the National and International Levels*, which expressly referred to "the rule of law unit in the Executive Office of the Secretary-General".[31] In the end, more than a year after the issuance of the December 2006 Report, the question of the location of the Unit in the Executive Office was finally settled in the spring of 2008.

On the other hand, the question of staffing and funding from the regular UN budget remains a serious challenge for the future of the Rule of Law Unit. Since according to the above-mentioned Report of the Secretary-General, during the initial phase, the Unit was set up "within existing resources" with staff seconded from other UN entities, no provision has been made in the regular UN budget for posts, adequate offices and appropriate financial, technical and administrative resources of the Unit. The absence of a budget line has seriously hampered the Unit's ability to fulfill its mandate and become fully operational. In order to ensure the sustainability of the Unit and to enable it to properly carry out its functions, the "Friends of the Rule of Law" have repeatedly requested to provide the Unit with staffing and funding from the regular UN budget.[32]

---

[29]   The joint letter dated 26 February 2007 was signed by the Permanent Representatives of Angola, Austria, Bahamas, Belgium, Canada, Cape Verde, Finland, Germany, Latvia, Liechtenstein, Mexico, Morocco, Panama, Papua New Guinea, Paraguay, Romania, Senegal, Singapore, Slovakia, Slovenia, Spain, Sweden, Switzerland and the United Kingdom. For the text of the joint letter see Annex II to this article.

[30]   Reportedly, the Executive Office of the Secretary-General was hesitant to host the Rule of Law Unit, since this would entail an increase of 5 to 7 staff in the Executive Office, contrary to the Secretary-General's declared goal to maintain a small Executive Office.

[31]   A/RES/62/70 of 6 December 2007, para. 4.

[32]   In its views submitted to the Secretary-General pursuant to General Assembly resolution 61/39 in the spring of 2007 Austria called "upon the Secretary-General and Member States to provide all the necessary assistance and support to the Unit, including through voluntary contributions and

By a letter dated 22 October 2007 addressed to all members of the
Advisory Group the Austrian Permanent Representative appealed to all
"Friends of the Rule of Law" to make a statement in the Sixth Committee calling for adequate staffing and funding of the Unit from the regular UN budget and supporting the inclusion of a respective paragraph
in the annual rule of law resolution. Although this view enjoyed very
broad support, no consensus could be reached on this issue.[33] After difficult negotiations chaired by Liechtenstein and Mexico, it was finally
agreed that the General Assembly in A/RES/62/70 of 6 December 2007
would request:

> "the Secretary-General to provide details on the staffing and other
> requirements for the unit without delay to the General Assembly
> for its consideration during the sixty-second session in accordance
> with existing relevant procedures."[34]

While, initially, it was intended that the requested Budget Report on
the Rule of Law Unit would be considered by the Fifth Committee at
its resumed session in spring 2008 during the 62nd session of the General Assembly, due to internal discussions within the Executive Office
of the Secretary-General and the Controller's Office the Budget Report
was delayed. Thus, on 28 May 2008, six months after the request by the
General Assembly, the Permanent Mission of Austria arranged for a
personal meeting of 16 Permanent Representatives[35] with Secretary-
General Ban Ki-Moon. At that meeting the "Friends of the Rule of
Law" expressed their concern that the UN Secretariat had failed to

---

the secondment of personnel and, after the initial phase, financing from the
regular budget, in order to ensure that it can fulfil its important functions
in a proper and sustainable manner." See *The Rule of Law at the National
and International Levels: Comments and Information received from Governments*, Report of the Secretary-General, Doc. A/62/121 of 11 July 2007,
para. 35. In November 2007 Austria was the first country to make a voluntary contribution of USD 55,000.- to the budget of the Unit and is currently financing an Associate Expert/Junior Professional Officer in order
to help alleviate the staffing situation of the Unit.

[33] The United States and Japan were opposed to any additional funding from
the regular UN budget.

[34] A/RES/62/70, see note 31. This paragraph was a joint proposal by the
Member States of the European Union and the Non-Aligned Movement.

[35] The meeting on 28 May 2008 was attended by the Permanent Representatives of Angola, Austria, Bahamas, Canada, Cape Verde, Finland, Liechtenstein, Mexico, Morocco, Panama, Papua New Guinea, Paraguay, Senegal,
Slovenia, Spain and Switzerland.

meet the deadline set by the General Assembly and expressed their hope that the Budget Report requested by the General Assembly would soon be issued. It was further agreed that the "Friends of the Rule of Law" would continue an informal exchange of views with the Secretary-General on rule of law matters on a periodic basis. The long-awaited Budget Report was finally issued on 21 July 2008[36] and will be considered by the Fifth Committee during the 63rd session of the General Assembly in the fall of 2008.

3. The Final Report on *The UN Security Council and the Rule of Law*

Apart from the panel series and the achievements of the Advisory Group, the most important outcome of the Austrian Rule of Law Initiative was the Final Report on *The UN Security Council and the Rule of Law*,[37] which was presented in New York on 7 April 2008. The Report, which was prepared by the Rapporteur of the Austrian Initiative, Dr. Simon Chesterman, reflects the discussions that emerged during the Austrian panel series from 2004 to 2008 and contains 17 concrete recommendations how the Security Council could support the rule of law in its various fields of activity in order to strengthen an international system based on rules.

The recommendations contained in the Report are intended to be pragmatic and realistic, although some might be more difficult to implement than others. They attempt to take into account the interests of all states, large and small, developing and developed, as well as permanent and non-permanent members of the Security Council. The Report should contribute to further discussions to support the role of the Security Council in promoting a rules-based international system and maintaining international peace and security under the rule of law.

---

[36] *Revised Estimates Relating to the Programme Budget for the Biennium 2008-2009 related to the Rule of Law Unit*, Report of the Secretary-General, Doc. A/63/154 of 21 July 2008.

[37] *The UN Security Council and the Rule of Law: The Role of the Security Council in Strengthening a Rules-based International System*, Final Report and Recommendations from the Austrian Initiative, 2004-2008, at <http://www.bmeia.gv.at/newyorkov/rolreport> (printed English version) or Doc. A/63/69 – S/2008/270 (translated in all official UN languages).

The following Chapter gives a brief summary of the Final Report and recommendations.[38] The full text of the set of recommendations is reproduced in Annex III to this article.

a. The International Rule of Law[39]

Many high-level documents, including the 2005 World Summit Outcome[40] and the Millennium Declaration[41], contain references to the rule of law at the national and international levels. This consensus on the rule of law is possible in part because of relative vagueness as to its meaning.[42] Within national legal systems, in common law and civil law systems and other legal traditions, there are significant differences of what is understood by the rule of law. Further complications arise when one applies the rule of law to the international level. In a national legal order, the sovereign exists in a vertical hierarchy with other subjects of law; at the international level, however, sovereignty remains with states, existing in a horizontal plane of sovereign equality.

From the definition of the rule of law in the 2004 Report by Secretary-General Kofi Annan[43] and a survey of legal traditions, the Report identifies three basic elements of the rule of law: (i) a government of laws; (ii) the supremacy of the law; and (iii) equality before the law. The "international rule of law" may be understood as the application of these rule of law principles to relations between states, as well as other subjects and objects of international law. Not all concepts will translate directly, however. Applying the rule of law to the international level thus requires an examination of the functions that it is intended to serve. Strengthening a rules-based international system by applying these principles at the international level would increase predictability of behavior, prevent arbitrariness, and ensure basic fairness.

---

[38]   This Chapter is based on the Final Report on *The UN Security Council and the Rule of Law* prepared by Professor Simon Chesterman. Due to space constraints, several parts of the report have been considerably shortened. For a full picture of the issues involved it is therefore highly recommended to read the Final Report in its entirety.

[39]   See also generally S. Chesterman, "An International Rule of Law?", *American Journal of Comparative Law* 56 (2008), 331 et seq.

[40]   A/RES/60/1, see note 15, para. 134.

[41]   A/RES/55/2 of 8 September 2000, para. 9.

[42]   See also the article by T. Fitschen in this Focus.

[43]   Doc. S/2004/616, see note 1, para. 6.

Applying these principles to the Security Council, the Report recommends that the Security Council should emphasize the importance of the rule of law in dealing with matters on its agenda, including by reference to upholding and promoting international law, and ensuring that its own decisions are firmly rooted in that body of law (Recommendation 1). Moreover, as part of a commitment to the rule of law, the Council should adopt formal rules of procedure rather than continuing to rely on provisional rules (Recommendation 2).

b. Strengthening the Rule of Law within States

Supporting the rule of law when it breaks down within states is an important function of the Security Council. Apart from a preambular reference in relation to the Congo in 1961,[44] the Council first used the words "rule of law" in S/RES/1040, referring to "national reconciliation, democracy, security and the rule of law in Burundi".[45] Many peacekeeping operations have subsequently had important rule of law components (e.g. Guatemala, Democratic Republic of the Congo, Liberia, Côte d'Ivoire and Haiti), with broad mandates calling for the "re-establishment" or "restoration and maintenance" of the rule of law. In practice, activities have included the training of police, justice, and prison personnel; assisting institution-building; advising on law reform issues; and monitoring the judicial sector and human rights law. In Kosovo and East Timor the United Nations has had direct responsibility for the administration of territory, including control of police and prison services and the administration of the judiciary.

In addition to traditional post-conflict peacebuilding, more recently the Security Council has also promoted the rule of law as a tool for preventing or resolving conflicts. The Security Council has created international criminal *ad hoc* tribunals for the former Yugoslavia and Rwanda. The Special Court for Sierra Leone was set up at the "request" of the Council in S/RES/1315 (2000) of 14 August 2000, while the Special Tribunal for Lebanon was established with Council authority substituting for agreement of one of the parties.[46] The Council has also exercised its power under the Rome Statute to refer a matter to the International Criminal Court, as it did in March 2005 with respect to the situation in

---

[44]   S/RES/161 B (1961) of 21 February 1961, preamble.
[45]   S/RES/1040 (1996) of 29 January 1996, para. 2. Note that the French text rendered rule of law as "*le rétablissement de l'ordre*".
[46]   S/RES/1757 (2007) of 30 May 2007.

Darfur, Sudan.[47] The preparedness of the Council to act in support of law within states was also endorsed at the 2005 World Summit, which embraced the Responsibility to Protect.[48]

In the light of these developments, the Report recommends that when establishing UN operations, the Security Council should give greater weight to establishing or re-establishing the rule of law, including transitional justice mechanisms and mechanisms for peaceful resolutions of disputes (Recommendation 3). The Security Council should, working together with the Peacebuilding Commission,[49] the Rule of Law Coordination and Resource Group and the Rule of Law Unit, pay particular regard to ensuring the sustainability of rule of law assistance measures after the end of a UN operation (Recommendation 4). Moreover, the Council should support criminal justice mechanisms and confirm its opposition to impunity. Where local institutions are unwilling or unable to prosecute those responsible for international crimes, the Council should consider appropriate measures to encourage or compel prosecution, including referral of a matter to the International Criminal Court as foreseen under the Rome Statute, as well as to ensure cooperation in order to bring perpetrators to justice (Recommendation 5). The Council should also be prepared to act for the international community in exercising the Responsibility to Protect, as stated at the 2005 World Summit (Recommendation 6).

In addition, the Report recommends that the Security Council should draw more effectively on two sets of actors in supporting its efforts to prevent conflict or establish peace: first, the Council should seek to strengthen its cooperation with regional arrangements and organizations, such as the African Union, the OSCE, and the Council of Europe, that can support the rule of law at the regional level (Recommendation 7).[50] Second, the Council should pay special attention to the impact of armed conflict on women and their important role in conflict resolution, including peace negotiations and peacebuilding, and ensure the more effective and coherent implementation of S/RES/1325 (2000) of 31 October 2000 on Women, Peace, and Security. The Council should reiterate its call upon the Secretary-General to appoint more

---

[47]   S/RES/1593 (2005) of 31 March 2005, para. 1.
[48]   A/RES/60/1, see note 15, para. 139. See also S. Barriga/ A. Alday in this Focus, there note 8.
[49]   A/RES/60/180 of 20 December 2005, para. 16.
[50]   Cf. S/PRST/2007/7.

women as Special Representatives or Special Envoys, including as heads of UN operations (Recommendation 8).[51]

Finally, the rule of law must also apply to those who intervene. Abuses by those who are sent by the Security Council to protect vulnerable populations have seriously undermined the credibility of the United Nations. After-the-fact investigations of misconduct of UN personnel are an important element to strengthen accountability, but remain an inadequate response if not complemented by appropriate preventive action and measures to support the victims. The Council has an interest in ensuring the existence of effective institutions and procedures to prevent and prosecute abuse and, while ensuring appropriate safeguards are in place to protect the rights of both victim and accused, to offer effective remedies against individuals who do wrong.

The Report therefore recommends that the Security Council should ensure that all UN efforts to restore peace and security themselves respect the rule of law. When authorizing a UN operation the Council should take appropriate measures to support the implementation of the Secretary-General's zero-tolerance policy on sexual exploitation and abuse by UN personnel, the recommendations in the Comprehensive Strategy to Eliminate Future Sexual Exploitation and Abuse in United Nations Peacekeeping Operations[52] as well as the Comprehensive Strategy on Assistance and Support to Victims of Sexual Exploitation and Abuse[53] (Recommendation 9).

c. The Security Council as a Creature of Law

The Security Council has played a central role in the expansion of the rule of law as an instrument at the international level, a role that raises the question of how the rule of law might apply to the Council itself. The Council is a creature of law but there is no formal process for reviewing its decisions; the ultimate sanctions on its authority are political. The Council today does not act as a world government, but its powers have grown significantly through practice. It is generally ac-

---

[51]   Cf. S/PRST/2007/40. The first female special representative of the Secretary-General (SRSG) was appointed in 1992. In 2002 the Secretary-General set a target of fifty percent of women in high-level positions (cf. Doc. S/2002/1154, para. 44). By 2005 there were two female SRSGs. In late 2007 there was only one.

[52]   Doc. A/59/710.

[53]   A/RES/62/214 of 21 December 2007; cf. also Doc. A/62/595 (2007).

knowledged that the Security Council's powers are subject to the UN Charter and norms of *jus cogens*.

Despite the absence of formal review mechanisms, the Report identifies some checks on the Council's expansive interpretation of its powers: these include (i) the Council's own voting rules, (ii) challenges to the Council's authority by the General Assembly through a censure resolution, by requesting an advisory opinion of the International Court of Justice or curtailing the Council's actions through its control of the UN budget, (iii) incidental questions in cases before national and international courts (e.g. the *Lockerbie* case, the *Tadic* case or the *Yusuf* and *Kadi* cases); and, ultimately, (iv) individual or collective refusal to comply with the Council's decisions.

The Report recommends that the Security Council should limit itself to using its extraordinary powers for extraordinary purposes. The exercise of such powers should be limited in time and it should be subject to periodic review; as a rule the Council should allow for representations by affected states and, where possible, individuals. In general the Council should not decide that which does not need to be decided; it should err on the side of provisional responses rather than permanent solutions (Recommendation 10).

d. The Security Council as Legislator[54]

The tension between effectiveness and legitimacy of Security Council actions plays out most clearly in the passage of quasi-legislative resolutions. The most prominent of such resolutions were adopted in response to a specific crisis, but drafted in language of general application: S/RES/1373 (2001) of 28 September 2001 on terrorism was passed in response to the 11 September 2001 attacks on the United States; S/RES/1540 (2004) of 28 April 2004 on proliferation of weapons of mass destruction came after revelations concerning the A.Q. Khan network.

---

[54] See also generally A. Marschik, *The Security Council as World Legislator?: Theory, Practice & Consequences of an Expanding World Power*, IILJ Working Paper 2005/18; id., "Legislative Powers of the Security Council", in: R. St. John Macdonald/ D.M. Johnston (eds), *Towards World Constitutionalism*, 2005, 457 et seq.; E. Rosand, "The Security Council as 'Global Legislator': Ultra Vires or Ultra Innovative?", *Fordham Int'l L. J.* 28 (2005), 101 et seq.

Legislation by Council decisions under Chapter VII of the UN Charter is a tantalizing short-cut to law. Years of negotiations over international instruments related to the prevention and suppression of international terrorism and the proliferation of weapons of mass destruction may be contrasted with the swift adoption of resolutions 1373 (2001) and 1540 (2004). The same holds true for the Rome Statute establishing the International Criminal Court as compared to the swift creation of the International Criminal Tribunal for the former Yugoslavia and its counterpart for Rwanda, or the establishment of the Special Tribunal for Lebanon.[55]

The temptations of legislation by the Security Council must be balanced, however, by a recognition that implementation depends on compliance by Member States. And if the effectiveness of the implementation of Council decisions depends on participation by Member States, the legitimacy of those decisions may depend on participation by Member States through their involvement in the decision-making process. As the Council is not a representative body, any "legislative" resolution should be adopted only after a process that seeks to address the legitimate concerns of the wider membership of the United Nations. Any such resolution should, moreover, be acknowledged by the Council as an exception to the normal law-making process.

The Report therefore recommends that when the Security Council adopts a resolution of a legislative character that is general rather than particular in effect, the legitimacy of and respect for that resolution will be enhanced by a process that ensures transparency, participation, and accountability, which should include (i) the holding of open debates on any such proposals; (ii) wide consultation with the membership of the United Nations and other specially affected parties; and (iii) a procedure to review the resolution within an appropriate timeframe. (Recommendation 11). Moreover, as any "legislative resolution" is an exceptional matter, it should, as a rule, terminate after a period of time set by the Council in the resolution (a "sunset clause") unless there is an affirmative decision by the Council to renew it (Recommendation 12).

---

[55]   S/RES/1757 (2007) of 30 May 2007 provided for the Lebanon Tribunal to be created by Council authority under Chapter VII in the event that Lebanon did not execute within eleven days an "agreement" with the United Nations to establish that tribunal.

e. The Security Council as Judge

As the Security Council's powers have expanded it is arguable that it has also taken on judicial functions: the Council has established international tribunals with criminal jurisdiction over individuals, created exceptions to the jurisdiction of the International Criminal Court, ruled on border disputes between Iraq and Kuwait and established a compensation commission to award damages, and set up an international criminal investigation commission. This increasing scope of powers raises questions of competence, applicable safeguards, and the Security Council's relationship to other organs.

While the UN Charter establishes the ICJ as the "principal judicial organ" of the United Nations, the Charter is not conclusive as to whether the Security Council, in carrying out its specific duties under its primary responsibility to maintain international peace and security, might also assume judicial functions, or as to its relationship to international courts. The lack of a separation of powers in the Charter is compounded by the fact that each United Nation organ determines the scope of its own competence under the Charter. The International Criminal Tribunal for Yugoslavia confirmed in the 1995 *Tadic* case the Security Council's competence to create a tribunal of its kind; today it is generally accepted that the Security Council has the power to establish such tribunals.

The need for a swift and effective response to a threat to international peace and security might preclude the application of the same safeguards that would apply to domestic courts. Questions of legitimacy are raised when the Council intercedes in the exercise of jurisdiction by duly constituted tribunals and when the Council itself acts in a manner that affects the rights and obligations of individuals or states. Distinct problems arise when considering the relationship between the Security Council and its creations. Once a judicial tribunal comes into being, it enjoys certain powers of its own that make it independent of the organ that created it. Other concerns relate to the International Criminal Court, set up as a separate international organization, whose independence was tested by efforts by the Security Council to create exemptions from its jurisdiction through the operation of S/RES/1422 (2002) of 12 July 2002 and 1487 (2003) of 12 June 2003.

The tendency to create new, *ad hoc* judicial institutions has been inefficient and has contributed to the fragmentation of international law. There are existing institutions to which the Security Council could turn, but precedents for the Council drawing on such institutions are scarce: only once the Council referred a matter to the ICJ (S/RES/22 (1947) of 9 April 1947 regarding the Corfu Channel case), requested an advisory opinion from the ICJ (S/RES/284 (1970) of 29 July 1970 on Namibia); and referred a matter to the International Criminal Court (S/RES/1593 (2005) of 31 March 2005 on Darfur, Sudan).

In the light of the above, the Report recommends that the Security Council should support and draw more frequently on existing judicial institutions of international law, including by (i) promoting peaceful settlement of disputes before the ICJ; (ii) requesting advisory opinions from the ICJ; and (iii) referring matters to the International Criminal Court (Recommendation 13). Furthermore, the Council should establish *ad hoc* judicial institutions only in exceptional circumstances in order to avoid the proliferation of costly new courts and tribunals and the fragmentation of international law (Recommendation 14).

f. The Security Council and Individual Rights

One area of particular concern in relation to Security Council action has been the use of targeted sanctions against individuals. While such measures successfully reduced the humanitarian consequences of sanctions, they have been criticized for the manner in which individuals were selected without transparency or the possibility of formal review. Challenges have arisen in national and regional courts, most prominently the *Yusuf* and *Kadi* cases currently on appeal before the European Court of Justice.[56]

In the 2005 World Summit Outcome, Member States called upon the Security Council, with the support of the Secretary-General, to ensure that "fair and clear" procedures exist for the listing and delisting of individuals and entities on targeted sanctions lists.[57] Secretary-General Kofi Annan responded in June 2006 with a non-paper, in which he

---

[56]   Cf. *Ahmed Ali Yusuf* and *Al Barakaat* International Foundation v. Council of the European Union and Commission of the European Communities (Court of First Instance of the European Communities, Case T- 306/01, 21 September 2005); *Yassin Abdullah Kadi* v. Council of the European Union and Commission of the European Communities (Court of First Instance of the European Communities, Case T-315/01, 21 September 2005). See also the Opinion of Advocate General Poiares Maduro regarding the case of *Yassin Abdullah Kadi* v. Council of the European Union and Commission of the European Communities (Case C-402/05 P, 16 January 2008).

[57]   A/RES/60/1, see note 15, para. 109.

noted four basic elements as minimum standards required to ensure fair and clear procedures:[58]

(a)   A person against whom measures have been taken by the Security Council has the right to be informed of those measures and to know the case against him or her as soon as, and to the extent, possible. The notification should include a statement of the case and information as to how requests for review and exemptions may be made. An adequate statement of the case requires the prior determination of clear criteria for listing.

(b)   Such a person has the right to be heard (via submissions in writing) within a reasonable time by the relevant decision-making body. That right should include the ability to directly access the decision-making body, possibly through a focal point in the Secretariat, as well as the right to be assisted or represented by counsel. Time limits should be set for the consideration of the case.

(c)   Such a person has the right to review by an effective review mechanism. The effectiveness of this mechanism will depend on its impartiality, degree of independence and ability to provide an effective remedy (lifting of the measure and/or, under specific conditions to be determined, compensation).

(d)   The Security Council should, possibly through its committees, periodically review on its own initiative "targeted individual sanctions", especially the freeze of assets, in order to mitigate the risk of violating the right to property and related human rights. The frequency of such review should be proportionate to the rights and interests involved.

Subsequent Security Council resolutions marked significant progress towards achieving the goal set by the World Summit. S/RES/1730 (2006) of 19 December 2006 strengthened procedural safeguards to protect the rights of individuals by establishing a focal point to receive delisting requests, and adopted specific procedures to govern the handling of delisting requests.[59] In S/RES/1732 (2006) of 21 December 2006 the Council welcomed the recommendations and best practices in the Re-

---

58   The unpublished letter by the Secretary-General dated 15 June 2006 addressed to the President of the Security Council was referred to in the Security Council debate on 22 June 2006, Doc. S/PV.5474 (2006), page 5.

59   Doc. S/2007/178.

port of the Informal Working Group on General Issues of Sanctions.[60] S/RES/1735 (2006) of 22 December 2006 and, most recently S/RES/1822 (2008) of 30 June 2008, further improved procedures for listing and delisting of the Al-Qaida/Taliban sanctions committee established pursuant to S/RES/1267 (1999) of 15 October 1999.

It has been questioned, however, whether these measures have satisfied the need for "fair and clear procedures" in this area. Recent and pending cases in national and regional courts will prove instructive to future implementation of targeted sanctions and the protection of individual rights. The alternative is that sanctions will become ineffective and not be applied rigorously. The fact that some states are hesitant to submit names to be included on sanctions lists and others are not seeking formal humanitarian exemptions may be evidence that this is happening already.[61]

There has been much discussion inside and outside the United Nations of possible mechanisms to review listing and delisting decisions of the Council. Such a mechanism could, theoretically, take numerous forms.[62] Given the political sensitivities involved, however, in practice the establishment of an independent quasi-judicial or administrative review seems difficult to achieve. In the short term, the most likely advance would be to support the decision-making process of the relevant sanctions committees in conducting their own review of listing and delisting decisions. This might include establishment of a small panel of experts to examine delisting requests and make a recommendation to the Security Council committee.[63]

The Report recommends that the Security Council should be proactive in further improving "fair and clear procedures" to protect the rights of individuals affected by its decisions, which should include, as

---

[60] Doc. S/2006/997.

[61] See e.g. Doc. S/2007/677, para. 26; Doc. S/2006/154, Annex, para. 57.

[62] See generally Watson Institute for International Studies (ed.), *Strengthening UN Targeted Sanctions Through Fair and Clear Procedures*, 30 March 2006 at <http://www.watsoninstitute.org/TFS>.

[63] Cf. e.g. the Discussion Paper on improving the implementation of sanctions regimes through ensuring "fair and clear procedures" submitted by Denmark, Germany, Liechtenstein, the Netherlands, Sweden and Switzerland, Doc. A/62/891–S/2008/428 of 2 July 2008. An earlier version of the Discussion Paper with Supplementary Guidelines for the Review of Sanctions Committees' Listing Decisions and Explanatory Memorandum was presented at a Roundtable in New York on 8 November 2007.

minimum standards, the four basic elements listed in the above-mentioned 2006 non-paper of the Secretary-General (Recommendations 15 and 16). Finally, building on recent innovations, such as the creation of the focal point, the Council should invite the Secretary-General to present it with options to further strengthen the legitimacy and effectiveness of sanctions regimes, paying particular regard to the need to protect sources and methods of information, as well as to protect the rights of individuals by upholding the minimum standards, including the right to review (Recommendation 17).

The Report concludes that the Security Council is most legitimate and most effective when it submits itself to the rule of law. Though the Council does not operate free of legal limits, the most important limit on the Council is self-restraint. Member States' preparedness to recognize the authority of the Council depends in significant part on how responsible and accountable it is – and is seen to be – in the use of its extraordinary powers. All Member States and the Security Council itself thus have an interest in promoting the rule of law and strengthening a rules-based international system.

III. Conclusion

As was outlined in the previous Chapters, the Austrian Rule of Law Initiative has in many ways contributed to the recent developments in the field of rule of law at the United Nations:

- First, the series of seven panel discussions from 2004 to 2008 and the Alpbach Retreat in August 2007 have stimulated a lively and fruitful discourse among experts from both theory and practice, including representatives of the diplomatic, United Nations and academic communities and civil society, on various aspects of the role of the Security Council in strengthening a rules-based international system. In addition, the panel discussions have contributed to the revitalization of the discussions during the International Law Week.

- Second, the Advisory Group of the Austrian Initiative, which over the years has become the Group of "Friends of the Rule of Law" at the United Nations in New York, through its joint efforts and initiatives, has contributed to many important achievements to strengthen the rule of law at the United Nations, such as the inclusion of specific references to international law and the rule of law in the 2005 World Summit Outcome, the inclusion of a new General Assembly agenda item on *The Rule of Law at the National and International Levels* and the establishment of the Rule of Law Unit.

- Third, the Final Report on *The UN Security Council and the Rule of Law* with its 17 concrete recommendations, which reflects the manifold discussions, ideas and proposals that had emerged during the four years' panel series, the Alpbach Retreat and the meetings of the Advisory Group, has set a fundamental yardstick for Security Council action to support the rule of law and to strengthen an international system based on rules.

While the panel series and the Final Report on *The UN Security Council and the Rule of Law* were concluded in 2008, the Austrian Rule of Law Initiative remains an ongoing process. For the "Friends of the Rule of Law" much work lies still ahead, be it the implementation of the recommendations of the Final Report, the debates under the General Assembly agenda item, or the staffing and funding of the Rule of Law Unit from the regular UN budget.

Finally, and most importantly, the Austrian Rule of Law Initiative has always been a truly joint project of all "Friends of the Rule of Law" at the United Nations who have accompanied and supported the initiative since its inception. Their loyal friendship, continuous interest and invaluable contributions have propelled the initiative over the years. Thus, the words of Austrian State Secretary Dr. Hans Winkler on the occasion of the presentation of the Final Report in New York on 7 April 2008 hold true not only for the Final Report, but for the entire initiative:

"The report prepared by Professor Chesterman has many authors and represents the outcome of a collective effort. And that had always been our goal. The rule of law is not an 'Austrian' issue. And although we are proud of having taken this initiative, the result reflected in this report is as much a global effort as the United Nations has ever seen. It includes the input of delegates from States large and small, of experts from the UN and civil society, and of renowned academics. This report not only has many fathers – and mothers – it has a family tree rooted in our shared values and beliefs."[64]

---

[64] Statement by State Secretary Dr. Hans Winkler on the occasion of the Presentation of the Final Report and Recommendations from the Austrian Initiative 2004-2008 on "The UN Security Council and the Rule of Law", New York, 7 April 2008, at <http://www.bmeia.gv.at/en/austrian-

In this spirit, all "Friends of the Rule of Law" are "parents" of the initiative and it is hoped that they will continue to foster their child and join their forces to strengthen the rule of law at the United Nations and promote an international order based on the rule of law and international law.

---

mission/austrian-mission-new-york/news/statements-and-speeches/2008/presentation-final-report-the-security-council-and-the-rule-of-law-state-secretary-winkler.html>.

Annex I:

Joint Letter dated 31 January 2006 signed by the Permanent Representatives to the United Nations of Austria, Canada, Costa Rica, Finland, Germany, Jordan, Liechtenstein, Mexico, Morocco, Slovenia, Spain, Sweden and Switzerland addressed to Secretary-General Kofi Annan

Excellency,

The undersigned Permanent Representatives to the United Nations have the honor to share with you the following ideas and suggestions regarding the implementation of the World Summit Outcome in the field of international law and the rule of law:

1. In our view, the strengthening of the rule of law is an important element of United Nations reform. It is essential that the international system is governed by international law and the rule of law. Clear and foreseeable rules and a system to prevent or sanction violations of rules are preconditions for lasting peace and security. It is therefore imperative that the rule of law is strengthened in all its dimensions, i.e. on a national, international and institutional level.

2. We are pleased to note the special attention given to international law and the rule of law in the World Summit Outcome Document adopted by the Heads of State and Government on 16 September 2005. We welcome that in order to strengthen the United Nations activities to promote the rule of law, including through technical assistance and capacity-building, the Heads of State and Government supported the idea of establishing a rule of law assistance unit within the Secretariat (World Summit Outcome, paragraph 134 (e)).

3. It has been suggested to create such a rule of law assistance unit in the new Peacebuilding Support Office. Thereby, the mandate of the new unit would be limited to conflict and post-conflict situations. In our view, however, the efforts of the United Nations promoting the rule of law are much broader in nature and irrespective of a conflict situation. The rule of law assistance unit should therefore have a broad mandate that is not limited to conflict or post-conflict situations. This mandate should encompass the following functions

   – Coordination and streamlining of all rule of law assistance of the United Nations;

- Facilitation of technical assistance in the field of rule of law;
- Making of recommendations to strengthen the rule of law; and
- Cooperation with other organizations, funds and programs active in this field.

4. The broad mandate of the rule of law assistance unit is particularly warranted in view of the variety of rule of law activities by the United Nations and its organs, bodies, departments, funds and programs, such as the International Court of Justice and other international courts and tribunals, the Sixth Committee of the General Assembly, the International Law Commission, the Office of Legal Affairs, the Department of Peacekeeping Operations, the UN Office on Drugs and Crime, the UN Development Program, the UN High Commissioner for Human Rights, etc.

5. Through its mandate, the rule of law assistance unit could assist in further strengthening and promoting the rule of law, particularly in the following areas:

- Provide and facilitate technical assistance to Member States to implement international rules, emanating from treaties or custom, mandatory decisions adopted by United Nations organs, in their national legal systems (e.g. implementation in the field of counterterrorism and sanctions, etc.), as well as decisions of international courts and tribunals (e.g. ICJ, ITLOS, ICC, etc.).

- Support the strengthening of domestic legal systems, especially the establishment of an independent judiciary, in post-conflict situations, situations of "new democracies", new successor States and in the context of development.

- Prepare guidelines and model legislation to enhance the uniform implementation of international rules.

- Prepare and disseminate digests of State practice (national legislation, judicial decisions, etc.) of the core international legal instruments to facilitate more consistency in their interpretation and application.

- Disseminate information, including decisions and advisory opinions, of international courts and tribunals (ICJ, ITLOS, ICC, etc.) to all UN organs, other organizations and bodies in the UN system and Member States.

- Promote peaceful settlement of disputes by recourse to international courts and tribunals.

- Build national capacity for the implementation of international law through establishment of best practices and training and exchange programs for government officials, judges, prosecutors, lawyers, etc.

- Promote global dissemination, education and outreach programs to gain grass roots understanding, support and involvement by civil society and NGO's for the strengthening of the rule of law, including education programs at universities and schools.

6. We believe that the rule of law assistance unit should be established at an adequately high level in the Secretariat in order to effectively coordinate among the various departments, funds and programs of the UN system, taking into account the central role and function of the United Nations Office of Legal Affairs in this field to advise the United Nations on substantive legal matters.

7. We are convinced that the creation of a rule of law assistance unit as outlined above would be the best way to implement the World Summit Outcome and increase the visibility of the determination of the United Nations to make the strengthening of the rule of law a priority of the organization.

We hope that you might find the above ideas useful and
worth considering.

Please accept, Excellency, the assurances of our highest consideration.

[Signatures]

Annex II:

Joint Letter dated 26 February 2007 signed by the Permanent Representatives to the United Nations of Angola, Austria, Bahamas, Belgium, Canada, Cape Verde, Finland, Germany, Latvia, Liechtenstein, Mexico, Morocco, Panama, Papua New Guinea, Paraguay, Romania, Senegal, Singapore, Slovakia, Slovenia, Spain, Sweden, Switzerland and United Kingdom addressed to Secretary-General Ban Ki-Moon

Excellency,

1. The undersigned Permanent Representatives to the United Nations represent a group of like-minded countries from various regional groups. We all share the view that international law and the rule of law are the foundations of the international system. It is essential that the international system is governed by international law and the rule of law. Clear and foreseeable rules and a system to prevent or sanction violations of rules are preconditions for lasting peace and security. In our view, it is therefore imperative to strengthen the rule of law in all its dimensions, i.e. at the national, international and institutional levels.

2. We warmly welcome the specific references to international law and the rule of law in the World Summit Outcome Document adopted by the Heads of State and Government on 16 September 2005. In order to strengthen the United Nations activities to promote the rule of law, including through technical assistance and capacity-building, the World Summit supported the idea of establishing a Rule of Law Assistance Unit within the Secretariat (paragraph 134 (e)).

3. Over the past years, we have repeatedly called for the establishment of a Rule of Law Unit within the Secretariat with a broad mandate for the coordination, streamlining and promotion of all activities of the United Nations system to strengthen the rule of law. We were therefore very pleased that at the end of last year the Secretary-General in his Report "Uniting our strengths: Enhancing United Nations support for the rule of law" (UN Doc. A/61/636–S/2006/980) highlighted the centrality of the rule of law to the work of the United Nations and announced his decision to establish a Rule of Law Coordination and Resource Group within the Secretariat, chaired by the Deputy Secretary-General and

supported by a small Secretariat Unit, to act as focal point for coordinating system-wide rule of law activities.

4. The undersigned Permanent Representatives would like to take this opportunity to express their strong support for the establishment of the Rule of Law Coordination and Resource Group and its Secretariat Unit. We consider the establishment of the Group and Unit an important step to implement the World Summit Outcome, which demonstrates the determination to make the strengthening of the rule of law a priority of the United Nations. We hope that the Group and the Unit will soon become fully operational.

5. In this context, we note that the question as to where the Group and its small Secretariat Unit will be located was not decided in the above-mentioned Report. We believe that in order to effectively coordinate all rule of law activities of the UN system, the Group and the Unit would be best located at the highest level in the Secretariat, i.e. the Executive Office. This seems most practical, since the Group and the Unit will be chaired and supervised by the Deputy Secretary-General, and would also show the importance which the United Nations attaches to this matter.

6. In order to raise awareness and garner support among the wider membership and the general public, we believe it might be useful to organize an informal briefing of the General Assembly, preferably before the end of March, following the model of the recent launching of the Online Counter-Terrorism Handbook, in which you and the Deputy Secretary-General might wish to present the above-mentioned Report and the steps envisaged or already undertaken by the Secretariat to implement it. At this initial stage, however, before the Group and the Unit have started their work, it would seem premature to hold a General Assembly debate or consider a General Assembly Resolution on this matter.

7. We hope that you might find the above suggestions worth considering. We fully trust that you will lend your full support to the Group and the Unit and will continue to make the strengthening of the rule of law as a key priority of the United Nations.

Please accept, Excellency, the assurances of our highest consideration.

[Signatures]

Annex III:

The UN Security Council and the Rule of Law
Final Report and Recommendations from the
Austrian Initiative, 2004-2008
(UN Doc. A/63/69 – S/2008/270)

Summary of Recommendations

Recommendation 1.

The Security Council should emphasize the importance of the rule of law in dealing with matters on its agenda. This embraces reference to upholding and promoting international law, and ensuring that its own decisions are firmly rooted in that body of law, including the Charter of the United Nations, general principles of law, international human rights law, international humanitarian law, and international criminal law.

Recommendation 2.

Acknowledging that the Council's powers derive from and are implemented through law will ensure greater respect for Council decisions. As part of a commitment to the rule of law, the Council should adopt formal rules of procedure rather than continuing to rely on provisional rules.

Recommendation 3.

When establishing UN operations, the Council should give greater weight to establishing or re-establishing the rule of law. Such efforts may include transitional justice mechanisms but also efforts to build mechanisms for peaceful resolutions of disputes. In a period of transition, it may be necessary to establish temporary institutions to combat impunity, prevent revenge killings, and lay the foundations of more sustainable order.

Recommendation 4.

The Council should, working together with other parts of the UN system, in particular the Peacebuilding Commission, the Rule of Law Coordination and Resource Group, and the Rule of Law Unit, pay particular regard to ensuring the sustainability of rule of law assistance measures after the end of a UN operation.

Recommendation 5.

When taking measures to maintain international peace and security, the Council should support criminal justice mechanisms and confirm its opposition to impunity. Where local institutions are unwilling or unable to prosecute those responsible for international crimes, the Council should consider appropriate measures to encourage or compel prosecution, including referral of a matter to the International Criminal Court as foreseen under the Rome Statute, as well as to ensure cooperation in order to bring perpetrators to justice.

Recommendation 6.

The Council should be prepared to act for the international community in exercising the Responsibility to Protect. As stated at the 2005 World Summit, this should be in accordance with the Charter, including Chapter VII, on a case-by-case basis and in cooperation with relevant regional organizations as appropriate, should peaceful means be inadequate and national authorities are manifestly failing to protect their populations from genocide, war crimes, ethnic cleansing and crimes against humanity.

Recommendation 7.

In order to prevent conflict, as well as to stabilize a post-conflict environment, the Council should seek to strengthen its cooperation with regional arrangements and organizations that can support the rule of law at the regional level.

Recommendation 8.

The Council should pay special attention to the impact of armed conflict on women and their important role in conflict resolution, including peace negotiations and peacebuilding, and ensure more effective and coherent implementation of resolution 1325 (2000) on Women, Peace, and Security. The Council should reiterate its call upon the Secretary-General to appoint more women as Special Representatives or Special Envoys, including as heads of UN operations.

Recommendation 9.

The Council should ensure that all UN efforts to restore peace and security themselves respect the rule of law. When authorizing a UN operation the Council should take appropriate measures to support the implementation of the Secretary-General's zero-tolerance policy on sexual exploitation and abuse by UN personnel, the recommendations in the Comprehensive Strategy to Eliminate Future Sexual Exploitation and Abuse in United Nations Peacekeeping Operations as well as the Comprehensive Strategy on Assistance and Support to Victims of Sexual Exploitation and Abuse. In particular:

(i) the Council should encourage Member States contributing or seconding personnel to take appropriate preventative action, including the conduct of pre-deployment training, and to be in a position to hold their nationals accountable for criminal conduct;

(ii) the Council should support the Secretary General's efforts to seek formal assurances from troop contributing countries (TCCs) that they will exercise jurisdiction over their personnel;

(iii) the Council should affirm its commitment to put victims at the centre of its attention by expressing its support for the Comprehensive Strategy on Assistance and Support to Victims of Sexual Exploitation and Abuse.

Recommendation 10.

The Council should limit itself to using its extraordinary powers for extraordinary purposes. The exercise of such powers should be limited in time and it should be subject to periodic review; as a rule the Council should allow for representations by affected States (such as under Articles 31 and 32 of the UN Charter) and, where possible, individuals. In general the Council should not decide that which does not need to be decided; it should err on the side of provisional responses rather than permanent solutions.

Recommendation 11.

When the Council adopts a resolution of a legislative character that is general rather than particular in effect, the legitimacy of and respect for that resolution will be enhanced by a process that ensures transparency, participation, and accountability. This should include:

(i) the holding of open debates on any such proposals;

(ii) wide consultation with the membership of the United Nations and other specially affected parties; and

(iii) a procedure to review the resolution within an appropriate time-frame.

Recommendation 12.

As any "legislative resolution" is an exceptional matter, it should, as a rule, terminate after a period of time set by the Council in the resolution (a "sunset clause") unless there is an affirmative decision by the Council to renew it.

Recommendation 13.

The Council should support and draw more frequently on existing judicial institutions of international law. This includes:

(i) promoting peaceful settlement of disputes before the International Court of Justice (ICJ);

(ii) requesting advisory opinions from the ICJ; and

(iii) referring matters to the International Criminal Court.

Recommendation 14.

The Council should establish ad hoc judicial institutions only in exceptional circumstances in order to avoid the proliferation of costly new courts and tribunals and the fragmentation of international law.

Recommendation 15.

The Security Council should be proactive in further improving "fair and clear procedures" to protect the rights of individuals affected by its decisions. These should include, as minimum standards:

(i) the right to be informed of measures taken by the Council and to know the case against him or her, including a statement of the case and information as to how requests for review and exemptions may be made;

(ii) the right to be heard (via submissions in writing) within a reasonable time by the relevant decision-making body and with assistance or representation by counsel; and

(iii) the right to review by an effective, impartial, and independent mechanism with the ability to provide a remedy, such as the lifting of the measure or compensation.

Recommendation 16.

The Council should itself, on its own initiative, periodically review targeted individual sanctions, especially the freezing of assets. The frequency of such review should be proportionate to the rights and interests involved.

Recommendation 17.

Building on recent innovations, such as the creation of the focal point, the Council should invite the Secretary-General to present it with options to further strengthen the legitimacy and effectiveness of sanctions regimes, paying particular regard to the need to protect sources and methods of information, as well as to protect the rights of individuals by upholding the minimum standards, including the right to review.

From the United Nations Administrative Tribunal to the United Nations Appeals Tribunal – Reform of the Administration of Justice System within the United Nations

August Reinisch and Christina Knahr[*]

---

[*]   The authors would like to thank Philipp Bocking und Edward Flaherty for their valuable comments on an earlier draft of this paper.

I. Introduction

Since the 1990s the internal justice system of the United Nations as well as other international organizations, providing for the settlement of disputes between the employer organizations and their staff, has been intensively criticized, by staff associations, legal practitioners and academics.[1] Over the last few years different panels of experts have addressed this issue, identified major weaknesses, and made recommendations for improving the current system, regarding both the informal and the formal system of staff dispute settlement. Already in the late 1990s, reform proposals concerning the ILO Administrative Tribunal (ILOAT)[2] were high on the agenda,[3] however, they did not result in any concrete changes. Ten years later, the debate has reached the United Nations and the reform suggestions put forward by the so-called Redesign Panel in 2006 have led to a follow-up process that is likely to create a completely new system of internal dispute settlement within

---

[1]   See e.g. A. Reinisch/ U. Weber, "In the Shadow of Waite and Kennedy – The Jurisdictional Immunity of International Organizations, the Individual's Right of Access to Courts and Administrative Tribunals as Alternative Means of Dispute Settlement", *International Organizations Law Review* 1 (2004), 59 et seq.; E.P. Flaherty, "Legal Protection for Staff in International Organisations – a Practitioner's View", Paper presented at the Conference "Accountability for Human Rights Violations by International Organizations", in Brussels 16-17 March 2007; R. Boryslawska/ L. Martinez Lopez/ V. Skoric, "Identifying The Actors Responsible For Human Rights Violations Committed Against Staff Members Of International Organizations: An Impossible Quest for Justice?" *Human Rights & International Legal Discourse* 1 (2007), 381 et seq.

[2]   Statute of the Administrative Tribunal of the International Labour Organization, adopted by the International Labour Conference, 9 October 1946, amended 29 June 1949, 17 June 1986, 19 June 1992 and 16 June 1998, <http://www.ilo.org/public/english/tribunal/stateng.htm>.

[3]   See e.g. London Resolution of the ILO Staff Union, 28 September 2002, <http://www.ilo.org/public/english/staffun/info/iloat/londonres.htm>. See also Legal Opinions on ILOAT Reform by Ian Seiderman, <http://www.ilo.org/public/english/staffun/info/iloat/seiderman.htm>; as well as Geoffrey Robertson, <http://www.ilo.org/public/english/staffun/info/iloat/robertson.htm>, and by Louise Doswald-Beck, "ILO: The Right to a Fair Hearing Interpretation of International Law", under <http://www.ilo.org/public/english/staffun/info/iloat/doswald.htm>.

the United Nations and the specialized agencies that have accepted the statute of the United Nations Administrative Tribunal (UNAT).[4]

This article will start by providing an overview of the deficiencies of the current internal justice system of the United Nations and will then analyze the recommendations for reform and their chances for success.

II. Criticism of the Current System

Discussions about improving the system of administration of justice at the United Nations are not new. Already since the 1970s attempts have been made to reform the system,[5] which has been established in the late 1940s and is thought not to conform to current international standards in a number of respects. Previous attempts have, however, remained largely unsuccessful. Only minor changes have been made to the original 1949 UNAT Statute.[6] Due to continuing and increasing criticism the General Assembly established the so-called *Redesign Panel on the United Nations System of Administration of Justice* in 2005.[7] This group of experts examined and analyzed the current system and issued a report in which it harshly criticized the system as a whole and identified a number of problems that were particularly urgent and in need of reform. In its report[8] the Panel found, *inter alia*, that,

---

[4]   Statute of the Administrative Tribunal of the United Nations, as adopted by A/RES/351 A (IV) of 24 November 1949 and amended by A/RES/782 B (VIII) of 9 December 1953, by A/RES/957 (X) of 8 November 1955, by A/RES/50/54 of 11 December 1995, by A/RES/52/166 of 15 December 1997, by A/RES/55/159 of 12 December 2000, by A/RES/58/87 of 9 December 2003, and by A/RES/59/283 of 13 April 2005, <http://untreaty.un. org/UNAT/Statute.htm>. Pursuant to article 2 of its statute, UNAT has jurisdiction over employment disputes between United Nations staff and the organization; in addition, staff disputes within IMO, ICAO, and those concerning the staff of the ICJ and the ITLOS Registry and the International Seabed Authority may be heard (article 14 UNAT statute).

[5]   For an overview see Administration of Justice at the United Nations, Report of the Joint Inspection Unit, Doc. JIU/REP/2000/1, Geneva 2000, paras 2-12.

[6]   Statute of the Administrative Tribunal of the United Nations, see note 4.

[7]   A/RES/59/283 of 13 April 2005, paras 47 et seq.

[8]   Report of the Redesign Panel on the United Nations System of Administration of Justice, Doc. A/61/205 of 28 July 2006, para. 5.

"the administration of justice in the United Nations is neither professional nor independent. The system of administration of justice as
it currently stands is extremely slow, under resourced, inefficient
and, thus, ultimately ineffective. It fails to meet many basic standards of due process established in international human rights instruments. For all these reasons, staff of the Organization have little
or no confidence in the system as it currently exists."

Similarly strong wording was also used in the conclusions of the report, where the Redesign Panel stated that,

"the dysfunctional system of administration of justice that currently
exists is outmoded and inconsistent with the principles and aspirations of the United Nations, and needs to be replaced."[9]

This criticism was also reflected in General Assembly resolutions
which recognized,

"that the current system of administration of justice at the United
Nations is slow, cumbersome, ineffective and lacking in profession-
alism, and that the current system of administrative review is
flawed."[10]

A functioning internal justice system is, however, particularly important since, due to the jurisdictional immunities enjoyed by the
United Nations,[11] staff members do not have any recourse to the domestic legal systems of the United Nations Member States.

The current system provides for formal as well as informal settlement of disputes. One major point of criticism, however, is that the in-

---

[9]   Ibid., para. 150.

[10]   Administration of Justice at the United Nations, A/RES/61/261 of 4 April
       2007, Preamble.

[11]   According to Article 105 (1) UN Charter, "[t]he Organization shall enjoy
       in the territory of each of its Members such privileges and immunities as
       are necessary for the fulfilment of its purposes." Article II Section 2 of the
       Convention on the Privileges and Immunities of the United Nations, 13
       February 1946, GAOR 1st Sess., 1st Part, Resolutions adopted by the Gen-
       eral Assembly from 10 January to 14 February 1946, 25 et seq., makes clear
       that this functional immunity, in fact implies an absolute immunity from
       suit: "The United Nations, its property and assets wherever located and by
       whomsoever held, shall enjoy immunity from every form of legal process
       except insofar as in any particular case it has expressly waived its immunity.
       It is, however, understood that no waiver of immunity shall extend to any
       measure of execution." See in detail A. Reinisch, *International Organiza-
       tions before National Courts*, 2000, 332 et seq.

formal system is too weak and would need to be strengthened. This deficiency has already been identified by the Joint Inspection Unit (JIU) in its report in 2000,[12] in which it recommended the establishment of the position of an Ombudsman. This suggestion was implemented and led to the creation of a United Nations Ombudsman's Office.[13] In order to improve the informal means of dispute settlement the Redesign Panel in 2006 suggested structural changes within the Office, in particular the creation of a Mediation Division, which should provide formal mediation services, and the establishment of regional Ombudsmen, who should have jurisdiction over all matters arising in their respective region.[14]

In addition, a number of deficiencies can be identified regarding the formal system of dispute settlement. A very significant one is the lack of a possibility for appealing decisions of the UNAT. For a certain period of time, there was a possibility of making a reference to the ICJ for an Advisory Opinion that was available to UNAT and ILOAT.[15] Currently, however, there is no option available for a staff member to appeal to a second instance to have a judgment of the UNAT reviewed. This situation seems unsatisfactory and is thus one of the central points of the current debate on reform. Already in 2000, the JIU recommended that further consideration should be given to a possible establishment of a higher instance for appeal.[16] In its report in 2006 the Redesign Panel emphasized the need for a second instance and suggested the establishment of a two-tier system of administration of justice in the United Nations as one of the cornerstones of the current reform efforts. A *United Nations Dispute Tribunal* (UNDT) should be created and serve as the first instance, whereas the existing UNAT should be re-

---

12   Report of the Joint Inspection Unit, see note 5.
13   Doc. ST/SGB/2002/12 of 15 October 2002.
14   See text at note 45 below.
15   In 1955, the UNAT statute was amended by A/RES/957 (X) of 8 November 1955, making provision in its new article 11 for a limited review of UNAT judgments through the power of a special committee to request Advisory Opinions from the ICJ. That system was abolished in 1996 by A/RES/50/54 of 11 December 1995. See also P. Sands/ P. Klein, *Bowett's Law of International Institutions*, 5th edition, 2001, 427 et seq.; J. Gomula, "The International Court of Justice and Administrative Tribunals of International Organizations", *Mich. J. Int'l L.* 13 (1991), 83 et seq.
16   Report of the Joint Inspection Unit, see note 5, p. ix.

named *United Nations Appeals Tribunal* and have the primary function of hearing appeals of decisions of the UNDT.[17]

Furthermore, the current inequality of arms between the organization and its staff members in disputes is problematic. While the United Nations is supported by well trained experts in the legal service department of the organization, staff members can only rely on – frequently not legally qualified – staff counsel. This situation has already been pointed at by the JIU in 2000, which found that staff is at a disadvantage in this respect compared to the administration[18] and recommended that the *Office of the Coordinator of the Panel of Counsel* should be strengthened by appointing a Coordinator, who would have to possess a sound legal background.[19] The Redesign Panel also criticized that the Panel of Counsel was under-resourced and not professionalized[20] and that there was no requirement for legal qualifications in order to serve on the Panel of Counsel.[21] The Redesign Panel thus recommended the creation of a professional *Office of Counsel*, which should consist of persons demonstrating legal qualifications and be adequately resourced.[22]

Another procedural issue that has been identified as being in need of reform is the lack of oral hearings. Currently the proceedings are in written form only. This fact has been heavily criticized by staff unions arguing that this violates the right to a fair trial as provided for in human rights treaties.[23] While the JIU suggested that the possibility of

---

[17]   See text at note 55 below.

[18]   Report of the Joint Inspection Unit, see note 5, paras 136-143.

[19]   Ibid., para. 144.

[20]   Report of the Redesign Panel, see note 8, para. 100.

[21]   Ibid., para. 105.

[22]   Ibid., paras 107-111.

[23]   With regard to the ILOAT practice of denying oral hearings it has been remarked that "all human rights treaties require a 'fair and public hearing' for disputes concerning civil obligations: a fortiori they are breached by a Tribunal which offers no hearings at all. There may be cases where the facts are not in dispute and the legal issues can be satisfactorily adumbrated on paper, and there may be cases where the use of personally sensitive data calls for in camera measures. But to deprive all complainants of a hearing to which they are presumptively entitled cannot be justified. The very fact that ILOAT has adopted a 'blanket refusal' policy in respect of hearing applications, thereby contravening the spirit of its statute and rules, demonstrates the need for a new written rule which makes pellucidly clear that any party is entitled to an oral hearing on request, which may only be re-

holding oral hearings should be subject to further study,[24] the Redesign Panel emphasized the importance that oral hearings be in fact implemented.[25]

A further point of criticism is the lack of independence of certain United Nations bodies within the administration of justice system. For example, the Secretariat of UNAT is under the aegis of the Office of Legal Affairs, whereas the Registry of the ILOAT is independent from the organization's legal service, however, staff of both bodies are selected and report to the executive head of the organizations. In most cases these executive heads are parties to the cases heard by the administrative tribunals. There has also been substantial criticism of the process by which members of the tribunals are selected and re-elected.[26] This led the JIU to emphasize the importance that *all* bodies concerned with the administration of justice be independent.[27] Also the *Administrative Law Unit* has the problematic double function of advising whether a decision should be reviewed and later defending the position taken in an appeal.[28] Moreover, the independence of the members of the *Joint Appeals Boards* (JAB) and the *Joint Disciplinary Committees* (JDC) has been questioned due to the increase in fixed-term contracts relative to permanent contracts.[29] In order to guarantee a truly independent system of justice the Redesign Panel suggested the establishment of an *Office of Administration of Justice* as well as an *Internal Justice Council*, which should monitor the formal justice system.[30]

---

fused in limited and defined circumstances and with a reasoned decision that such circumstances exist." Robertson Opinion, see note 3, para. 13.

[24] Report of the Joint Inspection Unit, see note 5, p. ix.

[25] Report of the Redesign Panel, see note 8, paras 10 and 92.

[26] For criticism in the context of ILOAT see e.g. E.P. Flaherty, "Legal Protection for Staff in International Organisations – a Practitioner's View", Paper presented at the Conference "Accountability for Human Rights Violations by International Organizations", Brussels, 16-17 March 2007.

[27] Reform of the Administration of Justice in the United Nations System: Options for Higher Recourse Instances, Report of the Joint Inspection Unit, Doc. JIU/REP/2002/5, p. vi.

[28] Report of the Redesign Panel, see note 8, para. 112.

[29] Ibid., para. 64.

[30] Ibid., paras 124-127 and also at note 76 below.

III. Current Reform Steps

The Redesign Panel made a number of recommendations for improving and reforming the current system. It took up a number of the points previously made by the JIU and other bodies, emphasized the urgent need for reforms and made concrete system-altering suggestions for improving the *status quo* of the administration of justice at the United Nations.

In fact, the Panel did not simply suggest minor adaptations. Rather, it suggested a complete overhaul of the current system. Aside from maintaining the dual system of informal and formal dispute settlement, not much should remain the same. Significant changes are envisaged within both the informal and formal system. The deficiencies identified above should be remedied through the establishment of new institutions (United Nations Dispute Tribunal, Office of Administration of Justice, Office of Counsel, Internal Justice Council), the transformation of existing ones (United Nations Administrative Tribunal to United Nations Appeals Tribunal), the abolishment of existing institutions (Joint Disciplinary Commission, Joint Appeals Board, Panels on Discrimination and Other Grievances) and the endowment of specific existing institutions (Office of the Ombudsman) with new or increased competences.

In April 2007, the General Assembly acted upon the report of the Redesign Panel by deciding to establish a new internal system for the settlement of disputes with the United Nations as employer along the suggested reform plans.[31] The resolution also indicated some of the policy rationales and management motivations behind this reform agenda by "*[a]ffirming* the importance of the United Nations as an exemplary employer"[32] and "*[r]eiterating* that a transparent, impartial, independent and effective system of administration of justice is a necessary condition for ensuring fair and just treatment of United Nations staff and is important for the success of human resources reform in the Organization."[33] The importance of the latter aspect was underlined in the wording of the operative part of the resolution expressing the General Assembly's decision to establish a new system of the administration of justice.

---

[31]   Administration of Justice at the United Nations, A/RES/61/261 of 4 April 2007.

[32]   Ibid., preambular para. 3.

[33]   Ibid., preambular para. 2.

The new system should be "consistent with the relevant rules of international law and the principles of the rule of law and due process."[34] Although neither the Redesign Panel nor the General Assembly made clear which rules were meant, it appears obvious that such fundamental rights as the right to a fair trial, as expressed in article 10 of the Universal Declaration of Human Rights,[35] would provide a guideline for the shaping of an adequate mechanism of settling disputes involving the United Nations as a party.[36]

In February 2008, the General Assembly endorsed the basic framework of the new system of the administration of justice at the United Nations, deciding to establish the proposed two-tiered justice system within the United Nations.[37] The General Assembly requested further information on a number of issues from the Secretary-General includ-

---

34   Ibid., para. 4 ("Decides to establish a new, independent, transparent, professionalized, adequately resourced and decentralized system of administration of justice consistent with the relevant rules of international law and the principles of the rule of law and due process to ensure respect for the rights and obligations of staff members and the accountability of managers and staff members alike").

35   Article 10 of the Universal Declaration of Human Rights (A/RES/217 (III) of 10 December 1948) provides: "Everyone is entitled in full equality to a fair and public hearing by an independent and impartial tribunal, in the determination of his rights and obligations and of any criminal charge against him."

36   Doswald-Beck suggests that the standards declared by human rights instruments are so similar that they may be presumed to be part of customary international law. Referring to article 14 of the ICCPR, article 6 of the ECHR, article 8 of the ACHR, and arts 7 and 26 of the African (Banjul) Charter, Doswald-Beck states, "[t]hese texts are very similar and, even more significantly, so is the jurisprudence of the treaties' supervisory bodies. Therefore, we can speak of principles of customary law", L. Doswald-Beck, "ILO: The Right to a Fair Hearing Interpretation of International Law", in: L. Doswald-Beck/ R. Kolb, *Judicial Process and Human Rights: United Nations, European, American and African Systems: Text and Summaries of International Case-Law*, 2004, 119 et seq. On the applicable law issue see also A. Reinisch, "Accountability of International Organizations According to National Law", *NYIL* 36 (2005), 119 et seq.; Reinisch/ Weber, see note 1.

37   Administration of Justice at the United Nations, A/RES/62/228 of 22 December 2007, para. 39 ("*Decides* to establish a two-tier formal system of administration of justice, comprising a first instance United Nations Dispute Tribunal and an appellate instance United Nations Appeals Tribunal as from 1 January 2009").

ing the proposal for statutes for the two tribunals to be established. The Secretary-General responded by a note which contained detailed information as to the available dispute settlement possibilities for staff and non-staff against the United Nations and which included Draft Statutes for the proposed tribunals.[38]

In April 2008, the Secretary-General issued a report which contained the Draft Statutes of both the United Nations Dispute Tribunal and the United Nations Appeals Tribunal.[39] It presented the new system "as an integral part of the Secretary-General's quest for greater accountability in the Organization."[40] The Draft Statutes had also been discussed by an *Ad Hoc Committee on the Administration of Justice at the United Nations*, established by the General Assembly in December 2007.[41]

The following comments are based on an analysis of the provisions of the Draft Statutes of the two tribunals as contained in the April 2008 report of the Secretary-General.[42] They also take into account various preliminary materials as well as the considerations of the *Ad Hoc Committee* of April 2008.[43] As of June 2008, it is likely that the statutes of the tribunals will be adopted by the General Assembly in autumn 2008 in order to enable the tribunals to commence operation, as planned, in January 2009. However, it is also to be expected that some aspects of the Draft Statutes may be revised before they are adopted. One issue that appears unclear with this approach is how judges will be recruited in time between General Assembly approval and January 2009. This appears to suggest that recruitment of judges and a number of other administrative matters will need to be addressed prior to General Assembly approval. Particularly with regard to the appointment of

---

[38] Administration of Justice: Further Information Requested by the General Assembly, Note by the Secretary-General, Doc. A/62/748 of 14 March 2008.

[39] Administration of Justice, Report of the Secretary-General, Doc. A/62/782 of 3 April 2008, Annex I, Draft Statute of the United Nations Dispute Tribunal, Annex II, Draft Statute of the United Nations Appeals Tribunal.

[40] Administration of Justice, Report of the Secretary-General, see note 39, para. 98.

[41] General Assembly Decision 62/519 of 6 December 2007.

[42] Administration of Justice, Report of the Secretary-General, see note 39.

[43] Letter dated 29 April 2008 from the President of the General Assembly addressed to the Chairman of the Fifth Committee, 30 April 2008, Doc. A/C.5/62/27, Annex II and Annex III.

judges, it is not clear how any appointments can conform to the statute if selection commences prior to formal agreement, since the qualification and appointment procedures may still change.[44]

1. Recommendations Concerning the Informal System

a. Strengthening the Position of Ombudsmen

According to the Redesign Panel the informal system of dispute settlement already in place should be strengthened. In particular, the Ombudsmen should play a more important role. Currently there are three Ombudsmen, i.e. the United Nations Ombudsman, an Ombudsperson for UNDP, UNICEF, UNFPA and UNOPS (United Nations Office for Project Services), and a UNHCR Mediator.[45] According to the report of the Redesign Panel, one of the central goals of the system of justice should be to have in place an Ombudsman office that combines a monitoring function, on the one hand, and the mediation of disputes on the other hand.[46] Therefore, the Panel proposes that the existing Office of the Ombudsman should be reformed insofar as to have two components, the Ombudsmen and a Mediation Division.[47] Moreover, the office should receive significantly more powers and competences to ensure its independence.

The General Assembly endorsed the Panel's suggestion concerning reforms of the Office of the Ombudsman. As proposed by the Redesign Panel, the General Assembly decided to establish a Mediation Division located at Headquarters within the Office of the Ombudsman.[48] Its purpose will be to provide formal mediation services for the

---

[44] The posts for judges of the United Nations Dispute Tribunal and the United Nations Appeals Tribunal have recently been advertised. According to the job announcement, "[p]ersons applying to serve as judges of the Tribunals should be of high moral character. In the case of the UNDT, candidates should have at least 10 years, and in the case of UNAT, 15 years of judicial experience in the field of administrative law, or the equivalent within one or more national jurisdictions.", announcement available under <http://www.un.org/reform/pdfs/UN%20inviting%20applications%20for %20Judges.pdf>

[45] Report of the Redesign Panel, see note 8, para. 40.

[46] Ibid., para. 44.

[47] Ibid., para. 49.

[48] A/RES/61/261 of 4 April 2007, para. 16.

UN Secretariat, funds and programs.[49] The General Assembly also emphasized again the importance of informal conflict resolution within the United Nations administration of justice system.[50]

b. Abolishment of the Joint Appeals Boards and Joint Disciplinary Committees

A second major change to the existing system that has been suggested by the Redesign Panel is the abolishment of the two advisory bodies, the JAB and the JDC. According to the Panel, these institutions do not function as they were supposed to.[51] It has been criticized that these bodies are composed of staff members, who frequently lack legal qualifications. Moreover, disciplinary proceedings are protracted and due to the fact that both bodies share one secretariat there are significant delays in proceedings of the JABs. The Redesign Panel therefore suggested that these bodies should be dispensed with for the benefit of a true two stage administrative process, with the new to be created United Nations Dispute Tribunal serving as the first instance and the United Nations Appeals Tribunal being the second instance reviewing the judgments of the United Nations Dispute Tribunal.[52]

The suggestions of the Redesign Panel to abolish the advisory bodies indeed found support within the General Assembly. In 2007 it decided to replace the existing advisory bodies, including the JABs and JDCs, by the United Nations Dispute Tribunal.[53] The General Assembly, however, requested the Secretary-General to ensure that the advisory bodies as well as the existing UNAT should continue to function until the new system was operational in order to clear all cases that were currently pending before them.[54]

---

[49]   Ibid.

[50]   Ibid., para. 11, and A/RES/62/228 of 22 December 2007, para. 22.

[51]   Report of the Redesign Panel, see note 8, paras 63-69.

[52]   See text at note 55 below.

[53]   A/RES/61/261 of 4 April 2007, para. 20.

[54]   Ibid., para. 29.

2. Establishment of a New Formal System of Dispute Resolution

a. United Nations Dispute Tribunal and United Nations Appeals Tribunal

The perhaps most radical change to the existing system will be the establishment of a new two-tiered system of formal justice.

The establishment of a second instance was already considered by the JIU, which in its 2002 report made concrete suggestions as to the composition of an *ad hoc* Panel that should be endowed with this function, as well as on the application criteria for a review of judgments.[55] The report also included the views of a number of organizations within the United Nations system on this issue. It indicated that not all of them were in favor of such a second instance.[56]

In 2006, the Redesign Panel recommended that a United Nations Dispute Tribunal (UNDT) should be created, which should replace, as mentioned above, the JABs and JDCs. The existing UNAT should be transformed into a United Nations Appeals Tribunal and be competent to hear appeals of decisions rendered by the UNDT. As indicated below,[57] the jurisdiction of this new tribunal should be significantly broader in scope then that of the UNAT.

A possibility to appeal judgments of administrative tribunals has been requested by many staff representatives supported by human rights groups which argued that the right to appeal formed a standard of the administration of justice of which an organization like the United Nations should not fall short of.[58]

---

[55]   Reform of the Administration of Justice in the United Nations System: Options for Higher Recourse Instances, Report of the Joint Inspection Unit, Doc. JIU/REP/2002/5, p. vii.

[56]   Ibid., paras 52-66.

[57]   See below at III. 2. e.

[58]   With regard to the lack of appellate procedures before the ILOAT Ian Seiderman argued: "The fact that a complainant does not have a right to appeal not only impairs his or her direct interests, but also may have adverse implications for the independence of the judiciary. An appellate body serves the function of providing a check on the lower tribunal to make sure it correctly administers the substantive law and adheres to proper procedures. With the knowledge that their decisions are not subject to review,

b. Composition of the New Tribunals – Qualifications for Judges

Traditionally, members of UNAT have often been academics or persons who had served as state representatives to international organizations or worked within such organizations.[59] The original UNAT statute did not provide for any substantive qualifications for UNAT judges but the prestige that came with this job ensured that there was always enough interest in it. Over the years concerns have been voiced about the judicial and, in particular, the administrative law qualifications of judges serving on administrative tribunals[60] and also the terms and conditions of service and the manner of their appointment.[61] It has been pointed out that the selection process plays a significant role in order to ensure the appointment of individuals with the highest qualification as well as to safeguard the independence of the judges.[62]

Within UNAT this led to changes of its statute at a relatively late stage. In 2000, the substantive qualifications were inserted into the statute for the first time which then required from UNAT judges "the requisite qualifications and experience, including, as appropriate, legal qualifications and experience."[63] Through another amendment to the statute in 2003, these requirements were made more precise. In its new version the statute demanded "judicial or other relevant legal experience in the field of administrative law or its equivalent within the member's national jurisdiction."[64] In 2005, another change was made and since

---

judges may be more prone to abuse their discretion, or at least give the appearance of acting in such a manner." Seiderman, see note 3.

[59] See P. Pescatore, "Two Tribunals and One Court – Some Current Problems of International Staff Administration in the Jurisdiction of the ILO and UN Administrative Tribunals and the International Court of Justice", in: N. Blokker/ S. Muller (eds), *Toward More Effective Supervision by International Organizations*, Vol. 1 (1994), 219 et seq. (220).

[60] Pescatore, see note 59, 236.

[61] The Judicial Independence of the Administrative Tribunal of the International Labour Organization (ILOAT): Potential for Reform, April 2007, 32-67, <www.suepo.org/rights/public/archive/iloat.independence.ailc.final.02.06.07.pdf>.

[62] Ibid., 32.

[63] Article 3 (1) UNAT statute, see note 4, as amended by A/RES/55/159 of 12 December 2000, para. 1 (a).

[64] Article 3 (1) UNAT statute, see note 4, as amended by A/RES/58/87 of 9 December 2003.

then the UNAT statute has required "judicial experience in the field of administrative law or its equivalent within their national jurisdiction."[65]

The proposal for the new internal justice tribunals for the United Nations reaffirms this break with the old tradition by providing for the appointment of professional administrative law judges as members of the two new tribunals. While the Redesign Panel recommended only "relevant professional experience", the Draft Statutes require ten, respectively 15, years of "judicial experience in the field of administrative law, or the equivalent within one or more national jurisdictions."[66] Though it may not be quite clear what kind of experience will be regarded as "equivalent", the focus on administrative law judges with considerable experience clearly indicates the intended "target group" of future members of the proposed new tribunals. Despite the improvement that these formal requirements represent, it should nevertheless be remembered that the nature of the cases before such tribunals is more closely related to employment disputes. It would therefore seem restrictive to limit membership to persons with administrative law experience, where employment law would be more appropriate.

In practice, it remains to be seen whether the new requirements will lead to problems of recruitment. Under the current system, where the tribunals sit in sessions of a relatively short duration, membership in administrative tribunals is manageable for a larger group than will be the case if the tribunals become permanent in character. While the United Nations Appeals Tribunal will continue this tradition,[67] the new United Nations Dispute Tribunal is intended to function in permanent

---

[65]   Article 3 (1) UNAT statute, see note 4, as amended by A/RES/59/283 of 13 April 2005, para. 40.

[66]   Article 4 (3)(b) of the proposed UNDT statute, see note 39, provides: "To be eligible for appointment as a judge, a person shall [...] possess at least 10 years of judicial experience in the field of administrative law, or the equivalent within one or more national jurisdictions." Similarly, article 3 (3)(b) of the proposed United Nations Appeals Tribunal statute, see note 39, provides: "To be eligible for appointment as a judge, a person shall [...] possess at least 15 years of judicial experience in the field of administrative law, or the equivalent within one or more national jurisdictions."

[67]   Cf. article 4 (1) of the proposed United Nations Appeals Tribunal statute, see note 39, provides: "The Appeals Tribunal shall hold ordinary sessions at dates to be fixed by its rules, subject to the determination of the President that there is a sufficient number of cases to justify holding the session."

session.[68] The non-renewable term-limits of seven years, coupled with the exclusion from any comparable subsequent posts within the United Nations system,[69] is unlikely to be attractive for committed mid-career administrative law judges from national jurisdictions, or for academics, since in both cases it would require abandoning their current career. These criteria therefore appear to be focused on late-career judges, or those who have already reached pensionable age.

c. Independence – Appointment Procedure

Criticism has been voiced over the fact that many administrative tribunals enable members to be reappointed for office.[70] It was argued that this could lead to a pro-organization bias since the decision to be reappointed or to be nominated for re-appointment would be made by the defendant organization or its officers.[71] Thus, there was unanimity that the re-appointment possibility should be eliminated which was combined with a prolongation of the terms of office of individual members of the two new tribunals. The recommendation of the Redesign Panel to appoint members for five year-periods only was slightly modified in

---

[68]   Article 5 of the proposed UNDT statute, see note 39, provides: "The three full-time judges of the Dispute Tribunal shall normally perform their functions in New York, Geneva and Nairobi, respectively. The Dispute Tribunal may decide to hold sessions in other duty stations, as required by the caseload."

[69]   Pursuant to article 4 (6) of the proposed UNDT statute, see note 39, "[a] former judge of the Dispute Tribunal shall not be eligible for any subsequent appointment within the United Nations, except another judicial post."

[70]   Article 3 (2) of the original 1949 UNAT statute simply provided that members "may be re-appointed".

[71]   Cf. C.F. Amerasinghe, *Principles of the Institutional Law of International Organizations*, 1996, 455. See also the criticism of Robertson with regard to the re-appointment possibility for ILOAT judges: "the Tribunal members are 'contract judges', whose well-remunerated employment is contingent upon the regular approval of the very body which is a defending party to their proceedings. This position is plainly incompatible with the rule that requires the judiciary to be independent, and which is breached by any arrangement which offers an inducement to the judges to decide cases in ways which will not upset the re-appointing body," Robertson, see note 3, para. 6.

the proposed statutes for a new UNDT and a United Nations Appeals Tribunal to seven year terms of service.[72]

A related issue regarding the independence of judges concerns the appointment procedure itself. Currently, most statutes of administrative tribunals provide for the election of its judges by the plenary organ of an organization. In this fashion also UNAT judges are currently elected by the General Assembly after nomination by Member States.[73] The fact that it is an organ of the organization against which complaints are brought that appoints the judges sitting over such complaints has raised doubts about the formal independence of such judges.[74] However, it is difficult to envisage an appointment procedure for administrative tribunal judges without any role for the organs of the organization to be served. A relatively high degree of independence may be seen in the case of those international organizations which have accepted the jurisdiction of the ILOAT and UNAT without having had any possibility to influence the composition of these tribunals. Given the concerns about the independence of UNAT judges, which led to the suggestion of non-renewable terms, it was to be expected that also the appointment procedure would aim at a procedure reducing the potential influence of the organization.

It is against this background that parts of the proposal of the Redesign Panel came as a surprise. While United Nations Appeals Tribunal judges will continue to be appointed by the General Assembly, it was suggested that judges on the UNDT would be appointed by the Secretary-General.[75] Though in both cases the appointments would be made

---

[72] Articles 3 (4) of the proposed UNDT/United Nations Appeals Tribunal statutes, see note 39, provides: "A judge of the Dispute/Appeals Tribunal shall be appointed for one non-renewable term of seven years."

[73] Article 3 (2) UNAT statute, see note 4, provides: "The members shall be appointed by the General Assembly for four years and may be reappointed once."

[74] Administration of Justice: Harmonization of the Statutes of the United Nations Administrative Tribunal and the International Labour Organization Administrative Tribunal, Report of the Joint Inspection Unit, Doc. JIU/REP/2004/3, Geneva 2004, 2; G. Robertson/ R. Clark/ O. Kane, *Report of the Commission of Experts on Reforming Internal Justice at the United Nations*, 2006, para. 51.

[75] Report of the Redesign Panel, see note 8, para. 128 provides: "The judges of UNAT should be appointed by the General Assembly from the list prepared by the Internal Justice Council and submitted by the Secretary-General. The judges of the United Nations Dispute Tribunal should be ap-

from a list prepared by a newly created Internal Justice Council.[76] Still the fact that appointments to UNDT were to be made by the Secretary-General who represents the defendant organization in staff disputes remained irritating. This suggestion has been corrected, however, in the Draft Statutes which now provide in both cases for appointment through the General Assembly.[77] Notwithstanding this correction, the need for both transparency and parity in the appointment of judges should not be underestimated. The elimination of bias is not limited to the body which formally appoints the judges. The nomination procedure of ILOAT judges has been criticised and in particular the virtual monopoly that the executive head of the ILO has in proposing members to the ILO governing body.[78]

d. Three Member Panels or Single Judges

The current UNAT, composed of seven judges, decides individual cases in panels of three members.[79] This collegiate form of adjudication corresponds to the practice of other administrative tribunals.[80]

Obviously for cost-saving purposes, it has been suggested that UNDT should operate through three individual full-time judges sitting

---

pointed by the Secretary-General from the list prepared by the Internal Justice Council."

[76] The Internal Justice Council, suggested by the Report of the Redesign Panel, see note 8, para. 127, was established by the General Assembly by A/RES/62/228 of 22 December 2007, para. 36. It consists of "a staff representative, a management representative and two distinguished external jurists, one nominated by the staff and one by management, and chaired by a distinguished jurist chosen by consensus by the four other members."

[77] Arts 4 (2)/3 (2) of the proposed UNDT/United Nations Appeals Tribunal statutes, see note 39, provide: "The judges (of the Appeals Tribunal) shall be appointed by the General Assembly from a list of candidates compiled by the Internal Justice Council established pursuant to General Assembly resolution 62/228."

[78] The Judicial Independence of the Administrative Tribunal of the International Labour Organization (ILOAT): Potential for Reform, April 2007, 41, in particular footnotes 216-218, <www.suepo.org/rights/public/archive/iloat.independence.ailc.final.02.06.07.pdf>.

[79] Article 3 (1) UNAT statute, see note 4.

[80] See article III ILOAT statute, arts IV, V statute of the World Bank Administrative Tribunal.

in New York, Geneva and Nairobi assisted by two half-time judges.[81] This suggestion was followed in the Draft UNDT Statute which explicitly provides that "[t]he Dispute Tribunal shall be composed of three full-time judges and two half-time judges."[82] The fact that they are supposed to fulfill their duties as single judges can be derived from the mandate that they "shall normally perform their functions in New York, Geneva and Nairobi, respectively"[83] and is expressly addressed in article 10 (8) of the Draft UNDT Statute which provides that "[j]udgements by the Dispute Tribunal shall normally be rendered by a single judge."[84] Although the same paragraph provides that "[t]he Dispute Tribunal may decide to refer a case to a panel of three judges to render a judgement" it is unclear in which situations panels would be formed. In his report, the Secretary-General suggested, among others,

"cases involving (a) a contested administrative decision relating to appointment, promotion or termination; (b) an allegation of harassment or discriminatory treatment supported by substantiated evidence; or (c) a situation where the potential exists for substantial financial damages for the Organization."[85]

However, this recommendation did not find its way into the Draft Statute. It thus remains to be seen how practice will evolve.

The appointment of administrative law judges from diverse national jurisdictions who will decide cases as individual judges sitting in geographically distant places carries with it the danger of a fragmentation of the case-law of the UNDT. Any international dispute settlement body that functions as a collegiate body is more likely to develop a coherent case-law than single judges. Given the fact that the Redesign Panel lamented the partially incoherent case law of the UNAT,[86] it ap-

---

81 Report of the Redesign Panel, see note 8, para. 76: "New York, Geneva and Nairobi should each have a full-time judge, while Santiago and Bangkok should each have a half-time judge. There should be regular monthly sittings at each of the three headquarters registries and every two months in Santiago and Bangkok."

82 Article 4 (1) of the proposed UNDT statute, see note 39.

83 Article 5 of the proposed UNDT statute, see note 39.

84 Article 10 (8) of the proposed UNDT statute, see note 39.

85 Administration of Justice, Report of the Secretary-General, Doc. A/62/782 of 3 April 2008, para. 66.

86 Report of the Redesign Panel, see note 8, para. 72: "The decisions of UNAT are not always consistent, and its jurisprudence is not well developed."

pears particularly ironic that the new design of the UNDT may actually increase such incoherence.

It remains to be seen whether the United Nations Appeals Tribunal, which will "continue" to function as a collegiate body,[87] will be able to fulfill its harmonizing function.

e. Scope of Jurisdiction *ratione materiae*

Administrative tribunals are regularly competent to decide upon alleged violations of employment contracts or terms of appointment of staff members of international organizations.[88] The latter regularly include their internal staff rules and regulations. This is also true with regard to the UNAT. Since its establishment the UNAT statute has provided,

> "The Tribunal shall be competent to hear and pass judgement upon applications alleging non-observance of contracts of employment of staff members of the Secretariat of the United Nations or of the terms of appointment of such staff members. The words 'contracts' and 'terms of appointment' include all pertinent regulations and rules in force at the time of alleged non observance, including the staff pension regulations."[89]

This limited subject-matter jurisdiction has been criticized as creating *lacunae*.[90] The restrictive interpretation of administrative tribunals, taken together with the general practice of international organizations not to waive immunity, and national courts reluctance to hear cases, raises a number of questions with regard to the ability of staff members to effectively defend their rights.[91]

Among others, the restriction to the individual employment contracts and terms of appointment as well as internal staff rules and regulations precludes any findings of accountability for issues such as har-

---

[87] Article 10 (1) of the proposed UNDT statute, see note 39, provides: "Cases before the Appeals Tribunal shall normally be reviewed by a panel of three judges and decided by a majority vote."

[88] C.F. Amerasinghe, *The Law of the International Civil Service*, Vol. I (1994), 72.

[89] Article 2 (1) UNAT statute, see note 4.

[90] Boryslawska/ Martinez Lopez/ Skoric, see note 1.

[91] See also Reinisch, see note 36 "Accountability".

assment, discrimination, health and safety or more fundamentally claims of violation of basic human rights.[92]

Thus, the Redesign Panel suggested in its report to include the power of the new tribunals to hear allegations concerning not only violations of internal administrative rules, but also, among others, "of the duty of care, the duty to act in good faith or the duty to respect the dignity of staff members, that infringes their rights, including the right to equality."[93]

The Draft Statute of the new UNDT has not incorporated this suggestion. Rather, it limits the tribunal's competence to hearing appeals against administrative decisions alleged to be in non-compliance with the "terms of appointment" or the "conditions of employment."[94] This omission would be harmless if the suggested obligations were included. However, it is questionable whether the suggested obligations such as a "duty of care" or a "duty to respect the dignity of staff members" are regarded as implicit obligations of an international organization by administrative tribunals.[95]

In addition, the insertion of the words "to appeal administrative decisions" may lead to a further restriction of the rights of staff members and other potential claimants to bring their grievances to the new inter-

---

[92] K.J. Webb/ A. van Neck, "The Non-compliance of the International Labour Organisation Administrative Tribunal with the Requirements of Article 6 ECHR", 3 August 2005, <http://www.suepo.org/rights/public/archive/ailc-suepo_article6_echrandiloat.pdf>.

[93] Report of the Redesign Panel, see note 8, Annex I: "The Tribunal shall be competent to hear and to pass final and binding judgement in the following matters: [...] (iii) Alleging prejudicial or injurious conduct that does not conform to the Staff Rules and Regulations or administrative instructions, that involves a breach of the duty of care, the duty to act in good faith or the duty to respect the dignity of staff members, that infringes their rights, including the right to equality, or was engaged in for an improper purpose, including reprisal for seeking the assistance of the Ombudsman's Office or for bringing action before the Tribunal."

[94] Article 2 (1) of the proposed UNDT statute, see note 39, provides: "The Dispute Tribunal shall be competent to hear and pass judgement on an application filed by an individual, as provided in article 3(1) of the present statute, against the United Nations, including separately administered United Nations funds and programmes: (a) To appeal an administrative decision that is alleged to be in non-compliance with the terms of appointment or the conditions of employment."

[95] See text at note 117 below.

nal justice system. A literal reading of this jurisdictional requirement implies that complainants will no longer be able to bring claims before the UNDT where no formal administrative decision has been taken. Thus, *de facto* violations of terms of appointment or the conditions of employment through acts or omissions of the United Nations may be outside the scope of UNDT's jurisdiction.[96]

f. Persons Entitled to Access the New Internal Justice System

Traditionally access to administrative tribunals of international organizations was limited to staff members. Only very reluctantly, some administrative tribunals have cautiously broadened the scope of personal jurisdiction by including single cases of non-staff members where such persons would not have had any legal recourse against the defendant organization elsewhere.[97]

The Redesign Panel suggested a new, much wider range of persons who should be able to access the internal justice system of the United Nations by providing a new definition of the "staff" of the organization. According to the Panel, staff should include, in addition to real staff and "former staff and persons making claims in the name of deceased staff members",

> "all persons who perform work by way of their own personal service for the Organization, no matter the type of contract by which they are engaged or the body or organ by whom they are appointed but not including military or police personnel in peacekeeping operations, volunteers, interns or persons performing work in conjunction with the supply of goods or services extending beyond

---

[96] The issue of unwritten decisions was addressed by the UNAT in its *Andronov* judgment, where it found that not only express, but also implied administrative decisions could be appealed to the UNAT; see *Andronov v. Secretary-General of the United Nations*, UNAT, 30 January 2004, Judgment No. 1157. It remains to be seen how the UNDT will deal with this question.

[97] See *Teixera v. Secretary-General of the United Nations*, UNAT, 14 October 1977, Judgment No. 230; *Irani v. Secretary-General of the United Nations*, UNAT, 6 October 1971, Judgment No. 150; *Zafari v. UNRWA*, UNAT, 10 November 1990, Judgment No. 461. See also, in more detail, A. Reinisch, "The Immunity of International Organizations and the Jurisdiction of Their Administrative Tribunals", *Chinese Journal of International Law* 7 (2008), 285-306.

their own personal service or pursuant to a contract entered into with a supplier, contractor or a consulting firm."[98]

This suggestion has been taken up by the Secretariat. In the Draft Statute of the UNDT, the group of persons who will have access to the new tribunal is significantly enlarged. In addition to staff members, former staff members as well as persons making claims in the name of an incapacitated or deceased staff member article 3 (1)(d) includes,

"Any person performing work by way of his or her own personal service for the United Nations Secretariat or separately administered United Nations funds and programmes, no matter the type of contract by which he or she is engaged, with the exception of persons in the following categories:

(i) Military or police personnel in peacekeeping operations;

(ii) Volunteers (other than United Nations Volunteers);

(iii) Interns;

(iv) Type II gratis personnel (personnel provided to the United Nations by a Government or other entity responsible for the remuneration of the services of such personnel and who do not serve under any other established regime); or

(v) Persons performing work in conjunction with the supply of goods or services extending beyond their own personal service or pursuant to a contract entered into with a supplier, contractor or consulting firm."[99]

The expansion of the scope of jurisdiction of the new tribunal is certainly remarkable. If implemented, this would constitute a significant enlargement in particular in comparison to the jurisdiction *ratione personae* of the present UNAT, which does not have jurisdiction over those working for the United Nations on a purely contractual basis. The new language would cover a significant number of employees of the United Nations who are not permanent staff but usually work for the organization for a certain period of time on a contractual basis. It will include consultants and individual contractors, United Nations

---

[98] Report of the Redesign Panel, see note 8, Annex I.

[99] Administration of Justice: Further Information Requested by the General Assembly, Note by the Secretary-General, Doc. A/62/748 of 14 March 2008, Annex I, Draft Statute of the United Nations Dispute Tribunal, article 3 (1)(d).

volunteers,[100] as well as officials other than Secretariat officials, such as members of the JIU.[101] Experts on mission who do not receive remuneration, such as members of the ILC, are not considered to hold a remunerated post and will thus not be able to access the new UNDT.[102] Such experts on mission holding consultant contracts may avail themselves of the dispute settlement clause provided for in the respective contract. Otherwise, there are no known established or specified recourse mechanisms or procedures applicable to experts on mission.[103]

The proposed enlargement of the personal jurisdiction of the United Nation's internal justice system is to be welcomed. It closes a lack of legal protection for some of those persons who did not have access to the UNAT and who often just had a theoretical possibility to demand arbitration against the United Nations. Contracts with the United Nations routinely provide for arbitration pursuant to the UNCITRAL Arbitration Rules,[104] but such method of dispute settlement is often prohibitively costly and lacks due regard for the special character of employment disputes. Thus, the ability of non-staff members to have access to the United Nation's internal justice system will not only contribute to the effective redress of their grievances but also assist the United Nations in effectively fulfilling its duty under the Convention on the Privileges and Immunities of the United Nations to,

"make provisions for appropriate modes of settlement of [...] disputes arising out of contracts or other disputes of a private law character to which the United Nations is a party."[105]

It should, however, be noted that there remain some persons who will continue to be denied access to the United Nation's dispute resolu-

---

[100] Administration of Justice, Report of the Secretary-General, Doc. A/62/782 of 3 April 2008, para. 22: "United Nations Volunteers are individuals who work with United Nations agencies and governmental and non-governmental organizations on a voluntary and short-term basis."

[101] Ibid., paras 8-42.

[102] Ibid., para. 33.

[103] Ibid. para. 34. Military observers and civilian police personnel in peace-keeping missions are also considered being such experts on mission, ibid., para. 32.

[104] UNCITRAL Arbitration Rules, approved by the General Assembly on 15 December 1976, GAOR, 31st Sess., Suppl. No. 17, Chap. V, Sec. C, Doc. A/31/17, 1976, *ILM* 15 (1976), 701 et seq.

[105] Article VIII Section 29(a) of the Convention on the Privileges and Immunities of the United Nations, see note 11.

tion mechanisms; most notably these are United Nations job applicants and other third parties who neither have an employment relationship, nor a contract with the United Nations.[106]

g. Standing for Staff Associations

Staff associations play an important role in protecting the interests of staff members of international organizations. The Redesign Panel's suggestion to expressly include a *jus standi* of staff associations before the new tribunals[107] has been endorsed by the Secretariat in its Draft Statutes.[108] The Draft UNDT Statute as formulated by the Secretariat,

---

[106] See *Darricades v. United Nations Educational, Scientific and Cultural Organization (UNESCO)*, Judgment ILO Administrative Tribunal No. 67, 26 October 1962, dismissing a complaint upon a finding that the complainant was only a "casual employee" of the United Nations Educational, Scientific and Cultural Organization and that it therefore lacked jurisdiction under the ILOAT statute to hear her complaint; *Liaci v. EPO*, Judgment No. 1964, 12 July 2000, and *Klausecker v. EPO*, Judgment No. 2657, 11 July 2007, (both cases were job applicants which were provided no access to a tribunal). The decisions can be downloaded under <www.ilo.org/public/en glish/tribunal/fulltext>.

[107] Report of the Redesign Panel, see note 8, Annex I: "The Tribunal shall be competent to hear and to pass final and binding judgement in the following matters: [...] (b) Applications by a staff association against the Organization or its funds and programmes: (i) To enforce the Staff Rules and Regulations or associated administrative instructions; (ii) On behalf of a particular class of its members affected by a particular administrative decision."

[108] Article 2 (3) of the proposed UNDT statute, see note 39, provides: "The Dispute Tribunal shall be competent to hear and pass judgement on an application filed by a staff association, as provided in article 3(3) of the present statute, against the United Nations or separately administered United Nations funds and programmes:
(a) To enforce the rights of staff associations, as recognized under the Staff Regulations and Rules;
(b) To appeal an administrative decision that is alleged to be in non-compliance with the terms of appointment or the conditions of employment, on behalf of a group of named staff members who are entitled to file such application under article 2(1) of the present statute and who are affected by the same administrative decision arising out of the same facts; or
(c) To support an application filed by one or more staff members who are entitled to appeal the same administrative decision under article 2(1)(a) of the present statute, by means of the submission of a friend-of-the-court brief or by intervention."

however, not only refined but also limited the scope of cases potentially brought by staff associations. Whereas the Redesign Panel suggested endowing staff associations with a right to bring a complaint "to enforce the Staff Rules and Regulations or associated administrative instructions", the Draft Statute merely provides for standing to "enforce the rights of staff associations, as recognized under the Staff Regulations and Rules."[109]

Further, the Redesign Panel clearly envisaged situations where individual staff members are reluctant to bring complaints in their own name.[110] Through the suggested broad power to file applications "to enforce the Staff Rules and Regulations" staff associations would have had the power to act on behalf of individual applicants. This appears no longer possible under the Draft Statute which limits the right of staff associations to enforce "their own rights", to bring complaints on behalf of a "group of staff members" and to file *amicus curiae* briefs in cases brought by staff members. Though this latter aspect embodies a modest expansion of the Redesign Panel's suggestions it seems clear that the Draft Statute does not allow staff associations to act on behalf of individual members.

The possibility for staff associations to file *amicus curiae* briefs has existed at the ILOAT since 2005 where a number of staff associations were permitted to file observations related to cases.[111] However, in

---

[109] Article 2 (3)(a) of the proposed UNDT statute, see note 39.

[110] Report of the Redesign Panel, see note 8, para. 82: "Because staff members are sometimes reluctant to enter the formal justice system for fear of reprisals, it is considered necessary to give staff associations an independent right to bring action to enforce the Staff Rules and Regulations."

[111] In 2005 the ILOAT began to accept *amicus curiae* briefs from staff associations. *Burchi et al v. FAO*, Judgment No 2420, 2005 (Consideration 7. "The Association of Professional Staff has submitted an *amicus curiae* brief. Although the possibility of gathering the observations of an association or union representing staff interests is not envisaged under its Statute, the Tribunal considers that it can only be beneficial to extend that possibility, as do other international administrative tribunals, to associations and unions wishing to defend the rights of the staff members whom they represent in the context of disputes concerning decisions affecting the staff as a whole or a specific category of staff members. Indeed, the Organization has raised no objection to the Tribunal's examination of the submissions in question, which are not, however, to be equated with the brief of an intervener, and which are simply intended to clarify certain points raised by the complaints with the Tribunal"). See also *Bebron and Lodesani v. FAO*, Judgement No.

practical terms the possibility to do so is limited since all ILOAT cases remain private until the judgment is pronounced. It also appears strange that staff associations will not receive the right to file a case which is consistent with such staff associations having a legal personality. This legal personality has been recognized as a fundamental right under the freedom of association.[112] The failure to recognize this right and provide appropriate access to administrative tribunals would appear problematic, since the organization's immunity prevents other forms of redress.

h. Legal Advice to and Representation of Applicants

A further significant problem that has been identified is the current inequality of arms between staff members and the organization in a dispute. Already the JIU recommended providing for adequate legal representation for staff in disputes with the organization.[113] This point has also been raised by the Redesign Panel and seems particularly important to staff unions. The latter have emphasized the need for adequate representation of staff also by external counsel and rejected the argument that this has not been implemented since external lawyers would have difficulty navigating through United Nations reports and circulars.[114] It is certainly problematic that while the organization is repre-

---

2421, 2005; *Connolly and Russell v. IAEA*, Judgment No. 2422, 2005; *Dexter And Koretski v. WMO*, Judgment No. 2423, 2005; *Plaisier v. FAO*, Judgement No. 2590, 2007; *Giorgi (NO.4), Lacsamana and Perera v. WIPO*, Judgment No 2672. 2008. All judgments can be downloaded under <www.ilo.org/public/english/trib unal/guidefj.htm>.

[112] ILO Convention No. C87 – Freedom of Association and Protection of the Right to Organise (1948), UNTS Vol. 68 No. 881, article 7, "The acquisition of legal personality by workers' and employers' organisations, federations and confederations shall not be made subject to conditions of such a character as to restrict the application of the provisions of Articles 2, 3 and 4 hereof." ILO Convention No. C151 Labour Relations (Public Service) Convention, UNTS Vol. 1218 No. 19653, article 9, "Public employees shall have, as other workers, the civil and political rights which are essential for the normal exercise of freedom of association, subject only to the obligations arising from their status and the nature of their functions."

[113] Reform of the Administration of Justice in the United Nations System: Options for Higher Recourse Instances, Report of the Joint Inspection Unit, Doc. JIU/REP/2002/5, p. viii.

[114] G. Robertson/ R. Clark/ O. Kane, *Report of the Commission of Experts on Reforming Internal Justice at the United Nations*, 2006, paras 56-58.

sented by the legal advisors office, staff members can only rely on the support of frequently not highly qualified staff counsel in the form of the Panel of Counsel comprised of volunteers.[115]

In the current situation, representation through external counsel is problematic since many organizations do not permit such representation during informal stages. The right of appropriate representation is part of fundamental rights.[116] The bi-lingual nature of administrative tribunals and the multi-lingual nature of the international organizations themselves raise issues as to how the right of representation can be achieved. The current proposals do not appear to address this, in particular the needs of translation and interpretation.

i. Applicable Law – In Particular Fundamental Rights

In the past, administrative tribunals have been criticized[117] for the way how they reasoned their awards and what they considered to form the legal basis of their decisions, i.e. the applicable law. Administrative tribunals often limited their reasoning to the terms of employment contracts as well as the applicable staff rules and regulations without taking into account fundamental rights guarantees.

Although some administrative tribunal decisions have come close to recognizing the relevance of fundamental rights as general principles of law to be respected by them,[118] the case-law of most of them makes

---

115 Report of the Redesign Panel, see note 8, para. 100: "The Panel of Counsel, which was formally established in 1984 and which has the responsibility to provide legal assistance and representation to United Nations staff members in proceedings within the internal justice system, is extremely under-resourced and is not professionalized. [...] As a result, the current structure of and resources available to the Panel are fundamentally inconsistent with the goal of an efficient and effective administration of justice in the United Nations."

116 See note 36.

117 See notes 36, 78, 90, 92.

118 See *Waghorn v. ILO* [1957] ILOAT Judgment No. 28, holding that it is "bound [...] by general principles of law." See also *Franks v. EPO,* [1994] ILOAT Judgment No. 1333, in which the ILOAT included alongside "general principles of law" also "basic human rights." Similarly, the World Bank Administrative Tribunal held that sexual discrimination or harassment violated "general principles of law", *Mendaro v. IBRD*, World Bank Administrative Tribunal Reports, Judgment No. 26 [1981] at 9.

clear that they are not formally bound by any human rights instruments.[119]

This lack of protection of individual rights was also acknowledged by the Redesign Panel.[120] However, the Redesign Panel failed to expressly call for the inclusion of an applicable law provision which would have included fundamental rights among the obligatory rules for the United Nations. Also the proposed Draft Statutes for the new tribunals fail to specifically identify the applicable law. In many other statutes of international courts and tribunals applicable law clauses are standard features. Given the past controversy over the applicability of human rights law[121] and the express intention to improve the international justice system it is remarkable that no rules on the applicable law have been included. As can be seen from other contexts the United Nations is bound by customary international law including principles of human rights law.[122]

j. Remedies – The Issue of Specific Performance

Compared to the ILOAT, the potential remedies available from UNAT are limited.[123] Although the present UNAT statute provides for the tribunal's power to order specific performance, this power is severely limited in practice by the fact that it also has to fix the amount of compensation to a maximum of two years' net base salary and that the Secretary-General may choose to grant compensation only.[124] In practice, the

---

[119] G. Hafner, "The Rule of Law and International Organizations", in: K. Dicke et al. (eds), *Weltinnenrecht. Liber Amicorum Jost Delbrück*, 2005, 307 et seq. (310); A. Pellet, "La Grève des Fonctionnaires Internationaux", *RGDIP* 79 (1975), 932 et seq.

[120] Report of the Redesign Panel, see note 8, para. 72: "Thus, there is a widespread view, which is largely correct, that the formal justice system affords little, if any, protection of individual rights, such as the right to a safe and secure workplace or the right to be treated fairly and without discrimination."

[121] Reinisch, see note 36, 156; Reinisch/ Weber, see note 1.

[122] See A. Reinisch, "Developing a Human Rights and Humanitarian Law Accountability of the UN Security Council for the Imposition of Economic Sanctions", *AJIL* 95 (2001), 851 et seq.

[123] Amerasinghe, see note 88, 480.

[124] Article 10 (1) of the UNAT statute, see note 4, provides: "If the Tribunal finds that the application is well founded, it shall order the rescinding of the decision contested or the specific performance of the obligation in-

Secretary-General almost always opts for compensation instead of changing the (wrongful) decision. According to a 2004 report of the JIU, the fact that it is *de facto* the Secretary-General and not UNAT who decides whether specific performance will be required or damages will be paid "undermines staff confidence in the Tribunal and raises questions regarding the independence and fairness of the process."[125] This contrasts clearly with the case of ILOAT which decides itself whether rescission or specific performance "is not possible or advisable",[126] in which case it awards monetary compensation. According to UNAT itself, this discrepancy "represents a glaring example of injustice and discrimination between the two categories of staff members working under the United Nations system."[127]

It has been argued that the two years limitation may often amount to inadequate compensation.[128] Also the Redesign Panel has been highly critical of this situation[129] and recommended that the new

---

voked. At the same time, the Tribunal shall fix the amount of compensation to be paid to the applicant for the injury sustained should the Secretary-General, within thirty days of the notification of the judgement, decide, in the interest of the United Nations, that the applicant shall be compensated without further action being taken in his or her case, provided that such compensation shall not exceed the equivalent of two years' net base salary of the applicant. The Tribunal may, however, in exceptional cases, when it considers it justified, order the payment of a higher indemnity. A statement of the reasons for the Tribunal's decision shall accompany each such order."

[125] Administration of Justice: Harmonization of the Statutes of the United Nations Administrative Tribunal and the International Labour Organization Administrative Tribunal, Report of the Joint Inspection Unit, Doc. JIU/REP/2004/3, Geneva 2004, 2.

[126] See article VIII ILOAT statute: "In cases falling under article II, the Tribunal, if satisfied that the complaint was well founded, shall order the rescinding of the decision impugned or the performance of the obligation relied upon. If such rescinding of a decision or execution of an obligation is not possible or advisable, the Tribunal shall award the complainant compensation for the injury caused to him."

[127] Letter dated 8 November 2002 from the President of the United Nations Administrative Tribunal addressed to the Chairman of the Fifth Committee, Doc. A/C.5/57/25 of 20 November 2002, Annex II, para. 2.

[128] Robertson/ Clark/ Kane, see note 74, para. 53; Administration of Justice: Harmonization of the Statutes of the United Nations, see note 125, 3, 4.

[129] Report of the Redesign Panel, see note 8, para. 71: "The power of the Secretary-General to choose between specific performance and the payment of limited compensation can, and sometimes does, result in inadequate com-

UNDT have far-reaching powers to order specific performance.[130] The Draft Statute of the new UNDT is much more reserved. Since the subject matter jurisdiction is limited to challenges to administrative decisions[131] the primary remedy envisaged is the rescission of such decisions.[132] However, the Draft Statute retains the organization's right to choose compensation rather than specific performance, and again this is limited in general to two years' net base salary.[133]

Also the Redesign Panel's suggestion to allow for punitive damages in exceptional cases[134] was expressly rejected in the Draft Statute of the new UNDT.[135] This rejection is remarkable when considering that the possibility to award punitive damages already forms part of the case law of the ILOAT.[136]

---

pensation, particularly in cases of wrongful termination or non-renewal of contract."

[130] Report of the Redesign Panel, see note 8, para. 83: "The United Nations Dispute Tribunal should have power to grant final and binding relief by way of: (a) Specific performance, injunction and declaratory decree, including the order that an appointment be set aside; […]."

[131] See note 94.

[132] Article 10 (4) of the proposed UNDT statute, see note 39, provides: "Where the Dispute Tribunal determines that an application is well founded, it may order one or more of the following:
(a) Rescission of the contested administrative decision or specific performance, provided that, where the contested administrative decision concerns appointment, promotion or termination, the Dispute Tribunal shall also set an amount of compensation that the respondent may elect to pay as an alternative to the rescission of the contested administrative decision or specific performance ordered;
(b) Compensation, which shall not normally exceed the equivalent of two years' net base salary of the applicant. The Dispute Tribunal may, however, order the payment of a higher indemnity in exceptional cases and shall provide the reasons for that decision; […]."

[133] Article 10 (4)(b) of the proposed UNDT statute, see note 39.

[134] Report of the Redesign Panel, see note 8, para. 83: "The United Nations Dispute Tribunal should have power to grant final and binding relief by way of: […] (b) Compensation and damages, including, in exceptional circumstances, exemplary or punitive damages".

[135] Article 10 (6) of the proposed UNDT statute, see note 39, provides: "The Dispute Tribunal may not award exemplary or punitive damages."

[136] *D.J.G. v. ITU*, Judgement No. 2540, 12 July 2006, (Damages: 10,000.- SFR, Moral Damages: 25,000.- SFR, Punitive Damages: 25,000.- SFR, Costs: 10,000.- SFR); *Magrizos and Skelly (NO.3) v. EPO*, Judgement No. 2418, 9

k. Transparency: Amicus Curiae Briefs, Oral Hearings and the Publication of Judgments

As with other international courts and tribunals there are a number of possibilities how to increase transparency. One is the option for judicial bodies to admit so-called *amici curiae* as non-parties to file briefs that may inform the decision makers on the legal issues involved.

This possibility is by now well established practice, e.g. in the context of the WTO and in international investment arbitration. Although the option for non-disputing parties to make written submissions is not expressly provided for in the WTO Dispute Settlement Understanding (DSU),[137] the Appellate Body established early on that panels as well as the Appellate Body itself had the power to accept and consider unsolicited *amicus curiae* briefs from NGOs or other non-state actors.[138] In the context of investment arbitration calls for increased transparency have equally become louder in recent years and did not remain without consequence. In 2004 the NAFTA Free Trade Commission clarified that it was permissible for non-disputing parties to file written submissions with a tribunal.[139] In 2006 the ICSID Arbitration Rules were amended to provide, among others, for the possibility for non-disputing parties to make written submissions to arbitral tribunals.[140]

October 2003, (Damages: 2,000.- Euro, Punitive Damages: 5,000.-Euro, Costs: 2,000.- Euro). Both judgments are available at <http://www.ilo.org/public/english/tribunal/guidefj.htm>.

[137] Understanding on Rules and Procedures Governing the Settlement of Disputes, Marrakesh Agreement Establishing the World Trade Organization, Annex 2, *ILM* 33 (1994), 1226 et seq.

[138] See *United States – Import Prohibition of Certain Shrimp and Shrimp Products*, Report of the Appellate Body, WT/DS58/AB/R (12 October 1998); *European Communities – Measures Affecting Asbestos and Asbestos-Containing Products*, Report of the Appellate Body, WT/DS135/AB/R (12 March 2001). See, in more detail, C. Knahr, *Participation of Non-State Actors in the Dispute Settlement System of the WTO – Benefit or Burden?*, 2007.

[139] NAFTA Free Trade Commission: Statement of the Free Trade Commission on Non-Disputing Party Participation, *ILM* 44 (2005), 796 et seq.

[140] Amendments to the ICSID Rules and Regulations and the Additional Facility Rules, effective 10 April 2006, <http://www.worldbank.org/icsid/basicdoc/CRR_English-final.pdf>. See, in more detail, C. Knahr, "Transparency, Third Party Participation and Access to Documents in International Investment Arbitration", *Arbitration International* 23 (2007), 327 et seq.

Though the Redesign Panel recommended the possibility of *amicus curiae* briefs,[141] it was not expressly incorporated into the Draft Statutes of UNDT or the United Nations Appeals Tribunal. While the statutes provide for the tribunals' powers to regulate interventions by non-parties "whose rights may be affected by the judgement"[142] such intervention is unlikely to include *amici curiae* who are – by definition – not affected by the outcome of litigation.

One of the most heavily criticized practices of almost all administrative tribunals, including UNAT, was the *de facto* absence of any oral hearings[143] although their statutes regularly provide for oral proceedings to be held in public as the general rule.[144]

This practice has been strongly attacked by staff unions and outside counsels representing staff members.[145] They argue that the lack of any direct personal impression of the judges, in particular with regard to factual disputes, would make a proper administration of justice very difficult and that, as a result, tribunals often unquestioningly assumed the correctness of the findings made by the organization during the internal stage of dispute settlement, despite the fact that these internal means are advisory in character and do not meet minimum guarantees of impartiality and independence required of a tribunal.[146]

The Redesign Panel thus emphasized that the newly to be created UNDT should hold oral hearings "in any case involving disputed issues

---

[141] Report of the Redesign Panel, see note 8, para. 84: "It should also have power to make its own rules, including with respect to interveners and *amici curiae* (friends of the court)."

[142] Article 7 (2)(d) of the proposed UNDT statute, see note 39, provides that the rules of procedure, to be adopted by UNDT, should include provisions concerning: "Intervention by persons not party to the case whose rights may be affected by the judgement."

[143] See Amerasinghe, see note 88, 608; Robertson/ Clark/ Kane, see note 74, para. 52; K. Wellens, *Remedies against International Organisations*, 1992, 83; E.P. Flaherty, "Legal Protection for Staff in International Organisations – a Practitioner's View", Paper presented at the Conference "Accountability for Human Rights Violations by International Organizations" in Brussels, 16-17 March 2007; see also Reinisch/ Weber, see note 1, 108.

[144] Article 8 of the UNAT statute, see note 4, provided since 1949: "The oral proceedings of the Tribunal shall be held in public unless the Tribunal decides that exceptional circumstances require that they be held in private."

[145] See text at note 23.

[146] See note 92.

of fact."[147] However, this clear mandate in favor of oral hearings was not expressly incorporated into the Draft Statutes. Although the statutes provide that oral hearings should in principle be held in public,[148] that the tribunals may require the personal appearance of the applicant[149] and envisage more detailed provisions concerning oral hearings in the respective rules of procedure of the two tribunals,[150] there is no express rule that would require them to hold oral hearings. It will thus remain within the discretion of the two new tribunals whether or not to do so. Given the practice of the current administrative tribunals not to hold oral hearings[151] it is difficult to see how sufficient guarantees of applicants' rights[152] will be provided.

Public scrutiny is an important element of creating confidence in any judicial system. This requires access to sufficient information to form a reasonable opinion that justice is being served. Such information includes not only the judgments but also information as to the details of the cases, and how the court deals with these matters. Currently, the UNAT statute only provides for the communication of judgments to the parties in the case and that copies may be made available to "interested persons" upon request.[153] In practice, UNAT has created a web-

---

[147] Report of the Redesign Panel, see note 8, para. 92: "The proposed United Nations Dispute Tribunal must have power to hold oral hearings and should be required to do so in any case involving disputed issues of fact. The hearings should be public, including by videoconference if necessary."

[148] Article 9 (3) of the proposed UNDT statute, see note 39: "The oral proceedings of the Dispute Tribunal shall be held in public unless the Dispute Tribunal decides, at its own initiative or at the request of either party, that circumstances require the proceedings to be closed." Equally, article 8 (4) Draft Statute of the United Nations Appeals Tribunal.

[149] Article 9 (2) of the proposed UNDT statute, see note 39: "The Dispute Tribunal shall decide whether the personal appearance of the applicant is required at oral proceedings and the appropriate means for satisfying the requirement of personal appearance." See also article 8 (2) Draft Statute of the United Nations Appeals Tribunal.

[150] Article 7 (2)(e) of the proposed UNDT statute, see note 39. Equally, article 6 (2) Draft Statute of the United Nations Appeals Tribunal.

[151] See notes 90, 92.

[152] See note 36.

[153] Article 11 (5) of the UNAT statute, see note 4, provides: "A copy of the judgement shall be communicated to each of the parties in the case. Copies shall also be made available on request to interested persons."

site on which all its judgments dating back to 1950 are publicly available.[154]

Such an increased level of transparency has also been recommended by the Redesign Panel. It suggested that judgments of the dispute and the appeals tribunal should be delivered in public and published on the internet in English and in French.[155] The Draft Statutes of the new tribunals, while not expressly referring to the internet, codify the existing practice and provide for the publication of their judgments.[156] This will ensure more openness of the system and access of interested individuals or the public at large to information about the proceedings.

l. Grounds for Appellate Review

The central element of a two-tier formal system of administration of justice within the United Nations is the scope of review possible by the second instance tribunal. There are various models current in international and national judicial practice, from restricted types of review limited to questions of law to full reassessments of both law and facts. The Redesign Panel recommended broad appellate powers for the United Nations Appeals Tribunal.[157] The Draft Statute of the United Nations Appeals Tribunal provides as follows:

"The Appeals Tribunal shall be competent to hear and pass judgement on an appeal filed against a judgement rendered by the United Nations Dispute Tribunal, in which it is asserted that the Dispute Tribunal has:

(a) Exceeded its jurisdiction or competence;

(b) Failed to exercise jurisdiction vested in it;

(c) Committed a fundamental error in procedure that has occasioned a failure of justice;

(d) Erred on a question of law; or

---

[154]   See UNAT website <http://untreaty.un.org/UNAT/main_page.htm>.

[155]   Report of the Redesign Panel, see note 8, para. 94.

[156]   Article 11 (6) of the proposed UNDT statute, see note 39: "The judgements of the Dispute Tribunal shall be published and made generally available by the Registry of the Tribunal." See also article 10 (9) Draft Statute of the United Nations Appeals Tribunal.

[157]   Report of the Redesign Panel, see note 8, para. 96: "As UNAT will have power to make orders that should have been made by the Dispute Tribunal, there will be no limitation on its appellate powers."

(e) Erred on a question of material fact."[158]

The issue of whether the United Nations Appeals Tribunal should also be competent to hear appeals on facts has been controversial during the negotiations. Fear exists that such an expansion of the powers of the envisaged tribunal would significantly increase the number of appeals and possibly overstretch the tribunal's capacity.

IV. Conclusion

An examination of the proposed changes to the currently existing administration of justice system of the United Nations shows that what is suggested is far more than minor adaptations; it is a completely new system. One of the most significant reform steps is certainly the establishment of a two-tier system of administrative justice with the creation of the United Nations Dispute Tribunal as the first instance and the United Nations Appeals Tribunal as the second instance. A number of other reforms are targeted at improving the administrative proceedings, among them providing adequate representation for staff or ensuring proper qualification and independence of the judges. Further, the reform efforts aim at strengthening the options for informal dispute settlement.

If implemented as planned, the new system seems to benefit staff members as well as the organization. United Nations staff will most likely welcome the new possibilities for appealing first instance decisions and other procedural improvements flowing from the reform.

In light of the radical nature of the proposed changes and the considerable additional costs of the new system, however, one can expect hesitance or even reluctance on the part of some United Nations members to actually implement the changes as they are currently on the table. Further, even if the measures are not opposed, it seems doubtful that the present time-schedule can be maintained and the new system will be fully up and running as planned by January 2009.

While some issues already seem to have been solved satisfactorily through this reform, the devil lies in the detail and a number of questions, particularly regarding the statutes of the two tribunals, has remained open and still needs to be looked at more closely. Nonetheless

---

[158] Article 2 (1) of the Draft Statute of the United Nations Appeals Tribunal, see note 39.

the decision taken by the General Assembly to put in place this new system of administration of justice at the United Nations certainly reflects a major reform step.

The LL.M. thesis being published below is the fourth in a series written in connection with a project introduced in 2004, by the Faculty of Law of the University of Heidelberg and the Universidad de Chile with scientific support from the Max Planck Institute for Comparative Public Law and International Law and the Institute for International Studies at the Universidad de Chile.

The project offers a one year Ph.D. course (International Law – Trade, Investments and Arbitration).

Chairs of the project are Prof. Rüdiger Wolfrum and Prof. Maria Theresa Infante.

Intellectual Property and the Protection of Traditional Knowledge, Genetic Resources and Folklore: The Peruvian Experience

University of Heidelberg, Max Planck Institute for Comparative Public Law and International Law and the University of Chile, March 2007

Rosa Giannina Alvarez Núñez

Table of Contents

I. Introduction

The present work tries to find a solution to the questions originating around the idea of the protection of traditional knowledge, genetic resources and folklore developed by indigenous peoples. Protection of the traditional knowledge of indigenous peoples and communities is necessary for two reasons. First, it is important for the conservation and maintenance of diversity; and second, the knowledge contributes to the industrial innovation process.

> "It is known that traditional knowledge has been used in many industries as starting point for new product development, in sectors such as food and beverages, pharmaceuticals, agriculture, horticulture and personal care and cosmetics, and it remains a significant resource for many commercial research and development programs."[1]

These industries have used it without giving a compensation or obtaining authorisation and, or even worse, in many cases, they have obtained intellectual property rights, without having fulfilled the inventive or novelty requisite.

Cases such as the neem tree, ayahuasca, or quinoa are good examples to show how intellectual property rights are granted to individuals or research companies, in spite of the fact that the use and knowledge about these plants was originally developed by indigenous communities in developing countries. In most cases, there was no rigorous assessment regarding novelty and inventiveness, and the research institutions appear as the owners of such knowledge, and make money out of it, without sharing the benefits with the respective communities.

Furthermore, the knowledge, innovations, and practices of indigenous and local communities, developed and passed on for centuries through traditional culture, are also closely linked to the protection of the biodiversity. The communities know how to use their resources without depredating them. In fact the *Convention on Biological Diversity* recognises the importance of traditional knowledge for enhancing the conservation and sustainable use of biodiversity. Article 8 (j) of the Convention requires countries to respect, preserve and maintain the

---

[1]   G. Dutfield, "Developing and Implementing National Systems for Protecting Traditional Knowledge: Experiences in Selected Developing Countries", in: S. Twarog/ P. Kapoor (eds), *Protecting and Promoting Traditional Knowledge: Systems, National Experiences and International Dimension*, 2004, 141 et seq.

knowledge, promote its wider application and encourage the equitable sharing of benefits derived from the use of such knowledge.

Article 8 (j) is considered to be of a very broad scope and in fact "does not recognize, and even less create, a property right in favour of indigenous peoples over their traditional knowledge."[2] It does, however, establish a number of underlying principles of respect, responsibility and equity, which are guiding the implementation of article 8 (j).

The protection of traditional knowledge, genetic resources and folklore has provoked a long and interesting debate between developed and developing countries. Developed countries have used arguments such as, traditional knowledge is in the public domain and there is no such thing as "biopiracy". They consider that developing countries use these arguments for getting concessions under the TRIPS agreement. On the other hand, developing countries argue that the actual intellectual property rights system leads to unfair situations, such as misappropriation of traditional knowledge, "biopiracy" and an unsustainable use of biodiversity. They claim the requisite of disclosure of origin, benefit sharing and even the necessity of an amendment of the TRIPS agreement.

The respective parties have started to work at national and regional levels, and, in many cases, the search for a new system to protect possible rights stemming from traditional knowledge has it main focus on the general framework of the intellectual property rights regimes. However, it is widely recognised that the prevailing intellectual property rights regime is not sufficient in order to protect traditional knowledge, or provide a means to ensure that the benefits from the use of such knowledge are shared equitably. Therefore, efforts to protect indigenous peoples' rights over traditional knowledge are now increasingly focusing on the development of alternative or *sui generis* rights regimes.

WIPO has become actively involved in the protection of traditional knowledge. In 2000 it created the Intergovernmental Committee on Intellectual Property, Genetic Resources, Traditional Knowledge and Folklore (IGC) with the mandate of discussing a.) access to genetic resources and benefit sharing b.) protection of traditional knowledge and c.) protection of expressions of folklore. WIPO's work has focused on the possible development of a *sui generis* regime for traditional knowl-

---

2   B. Tobin/ K. Swiderska, *Speaking in Tongues: Indigenous Participation in the Development of a sui generis regime to Protect Traditional Knowledge in Peru*, 2001, 11 et seq.

edge, but no serious analysis has been made in respect of the standards for the patentability applied by WIPO members (for example the standard applied in the United States with regard to inventions disclosed in non-written form within and outside the country), which allow the patenting of genetic resources and traditional knowledge.

According to Rosemary Coombe, "intellectual property rights are not merely technical matters."[3] And in the present authors opinion they involve crucial questions concerning not only economic questions but also the environment, food security, ethics and international human rights issues. It is necessary to use the issue of intellectual property to reduce the poverty and to balance unfair situations. National and international recognition of traditional knowledge is very important for many developing countries, especially Peru, whose geographical setting places it among the ten countries with the most extensive biodiversity in the world, also known as "mega diverse country", because of its range of ecosystems, species, genetic resources and indigenous cultures with valuable knowledge. The Peruvian government, along with those of other "mega diverse" countries[4] is concerned about the existing patent system, which gives rise to unfair situations by granting intellectual property rights for inventions based directly or indirectly on genetic resources of Peruvian origin or traditional Peruvian knowledge. As a consequence in Peru national as well as regional legislation has been developed in order to protect genetic resources and traditional knowledge of Peruvian origin.

At the national level, Peru has developed Law 27811, establishing a protection regime for the collective knowledge of indigenous people derived from biological resources. At the regional level, the Andean Community (Peru, Bolivia, Colombia, Ecuador) has adopted Decision 391, which requires the prior informed consent of indigenous, afro-American and campesino communities as a condition for access to, and use of, their knowledge. Peru consistently advocates mandatory inclusion of disclosure of origin and legal provenance of traditional knowl-

3   R.J. Coombe, "The Recognition of Indigenous Peoples' and Community Traditional Knowledge in International Law", *St. Thomas Law Review* 14 (2001), 275 et seq.

4   The Group of Like-Minded Megadiverse Countries was officially set up in February 2002 as a policy coordination area for the main megadiverse countries (Cancún Declaration, Mexico). The Group has the following members: Brazil, Bolivia, China, Colombia, Costa Rica, Ecuador, India, Indonesia, Kenya, Madagascar, Malaysia, Mexico, Peru, Philippines, Venezuela.

edge in the patent system and has maintained its position in the different intergovernmental negotiating fora, where the subject has been addressed, i.e. the CBD, the WTO and WIPO.[5] The Peruvian experience provides a salutary lesson for any national authority or regional organisation seeking to develop legislation for the protection of traditional knowledge and genetic resources.

II. General Issues Relating to the Protection of Traditional Knowledge, Genetic Resources and Folklore

1. Definitions

Traditional knowledge is a very broad term referring to various knowledge systems, encompassing a variety of areas, held by traditional communities or to knowledge acquired in a non-systematic way. They embrace different aspects and forms of information's expressions, making it difficult to agree on a legally and scientifically acceptable definition. For that reason there is no official or agreed definition of the term. For Carlos Correa "the different types of knowledge could be distinguished by the elements involved, the knowledge's potential or actual applications, the level of codification, the individual or collective form of possession, and its legal status."[6]

From the interest generated by these items, much literature and many proposals, both for regulation and for action at the national and international level, have emerged.

Precisely how the term traditional knowledge is defined has important implications for the kind and scope of a possible protection regime. According to Christoph Beat Graber and Martin A. Girsberger, there are several characteristics that can be attributed to this knowledge, de-

---

5   Doc. IP/C/W/447 of 8 June 2005, Communication from Peru to the WTO TRIPs Council.

6   C. Correa, *Traditional Knowledge and Intellectual Property. Issues and Options surrounding the Protection of Traditional Knowledge.* A discussion paper commissioned by the Quaker United Nations Office (QUNO), 2001, 4 et seq.

spite the lack of a clear terminology.[7] These characteristics, also used in the WIPO papers are[8]:

– Traditional knowledge consists in innovations, creations and practices originated and used by indigenous and local communities
– It is transmitted from generation to generation
– It is transmitted in oral form
– It is usually held in common by the community
– It is constantly being improved and adapted to the changing needs of its users

WIPO referred to traditional knowledge as:

"... tradition-based literary, artistic or scientific works; performances; inventions; scientific discoveries; designs; marks, names and symbols; undisclosed information; and all other tradition based innovations and creations resulting from intellectual activity in the industrial, scientific, literary or artistic fields."[9]

"Tradition-based" refers to knowledge systems, creations, innovations and cultural expressions which have generally been transmitted from generation to generation; are generally regarded as pertaining to a particular people or its territory; and, are constantly evolving in response to a changing environment. Categories of traditional knowledge could include: agricultural knowledge; scientific knowledge; technical knowledge; ecological knowledge; medical knowledge, including related medicines and remedies; biodiversity-related knowledge; expressions of folklore in the form of music, dance, songs, handicrafts, designs, stories and artwork; elements of languages, such as names, geographical indications and symbols; and, movable cultural properties.

From the definition given above it can clearly be seen that the concepts of traditional cultural expressions/folklore and traditional knowledge are mixed. However, in discussions about intellectual property and

---

7   C. Graber/ M. Girsberger, "Traditional Knowledge at the International Level", *Recht des ländlichen Raums* 11 (2006), 243 et seq.
8   Doc. WIPO/GRTKF/IC/3/7 of 6 May 2002, Document of the WIPO Intergovernmental Committee on Intellectual Property, Traditional Knowledge, Genetic Resources, and Folklore. Doc. WIPO/GRTKF/IC/4/8 of 30 October 2002, Document of the WIPO-Intergovernmental Committee on Intellectual Property, Traditional Knowledge, Genetic Resources, and Folklore.
9   Doc. WIPO/GRTKF/IC/3/9 of June 2002.

its rights both terms have to be analysed in a distinct way, in order to facilitate better and more efficient discussions. This experience has shown that different tools are needed to protect specifically traditional knowledge and traditional cultural expressions or expressions of folklore; the latter one for example involves a cultural policy and, unlike the more technical traditional knowledge, involves legal doctrines close to copyright and related rights systems.

According to WIPO, traditional knowledge "focuses on the use of knowledge such as traditional technical know-how, or traditional ecological, scientific or medical knowledge. This encompasses the content or substance of traditional know-how, innovations, information, practices, skills and learning of traditional knowledge systems such as traditional agricultural, environmental or medical knowledge. These forms of knowledge can be associated with traditional cultural expressions (TCEs) or expressions of folklore, such as songs, chants, narratives, motifs and designs."[10]

On the other hand, *traditional cultural expressions/expressions of folklore* mean items consisting of characteristic elements of the traditional artistic heritage developed and maintained by a community or by individuals reflecting the traditional artistic expectations of such a community, in particular:[11]

- Verbal expressions, such as folk tales, folk poetry and riddles, signs, words, symbols and indications; musical expressions, such as folk songs and instrumental music;
- Expressions by actions, such as folk dances, plays and artistic forms or rituals; whether or not reduced to a material form; and,
- Tangible expressions, such as:
  - productions of folk art, in particular, drawings, paintings, carvings, sculptures, pottery, terracotta, mosaic, woodwork, metal ware, jewellery, basket weaving, needlework, textiles, carpets, costumes;
  - crafts;
  - musical instruments;
  - architectural forms.

---

[10]   WIPO Booklet No. 2, *Intellectual Property and Traditional Knowledge*, 17.
[11]   WIPO, ibid.

Professors Lowenstein and Wegbrait have given more precise definitions[12] of the three main items which encompass the general term traditional knowledge, including: traditional knowledge, genetic resources and expressions of folklore. *Traditional knowledge* is understood as the group of practices acquired by a community through the observation and coexistence with the ecosystem in which it lives. (Free translation from Spanish). *Genetic resources* are the existing biological materials in a certain ecosystem, that are used, for example, in agriculture and medicine. It is possible to emphasise that these resources are related to a traditional knowledge. *Expressions of folklore* are understood as the accumulation of fixed and unfixed cultural expressions of a community, such as artistic works, handicrafts, designs, dances and musical and dramatic performances (Free translation from Spanish).

But, one important characteristic of this traditional knowledge is, that although it has been developed in the past, it still continues to develop. "Traditional knowledge is not static, it evolves and generates new information as a result of improvements or adaptation to changing circumstances."[13]

To summarise: it is possible to identify a general tendency to characterise traditional knowledge as information which has been developed in ancestral times among indigenous people from generation to generation, and actually is subject to improvement and adaptation, without necessarily being codified, and as being primarily collective in nature. It may possess commercial value depending on its potential or actual use. An important aspect to be taken into account, which makes the definition of traditional knowledge even more complex, is the distinction between traditional knowledge and what has been termed indigenous knowledge. Indigenous knowledge has been defined as knowledge "that specifically belongs to indigenous peoples." On the other hand, traditional knowledge is defined more broadly and includes the knowledge held by both indigenous peoples and non-indigenous peoples or local communities living within a geographical boundary or region.[14]

---

[12] V. Lowenstein/ P. Wegbrait, "La Protección de los conocimientos tradicionales, recursos genéticos y folklore", *Cuadernos de Propiedad Intelectual* 2 (2005), 149 et seq.

[13] Correa, see note 6.

[14] WIPO, *Intellectual Property Needs and Expectations of Traditional Knowledge Holders: WIPO* Report on Fact Finding Missions on Intellectual Property and Traditional Knowledge, (1998- 1999), 2001, 23.

These kinds of distinctions are very important and relevant in order to confer rights, seek prior informed consent for the use of traditional knowledge, deal with benefit-sharing arrangements and commercialisation activities. "This may imply a need to establish a classification system of traditional knowledge to distinguish indigenous or traditional knowledge and other categories of information entered into any database or register."[15]

2. An Overview of the International Debate

The *Convention on Biological Diversity* (CBD) is the only international treaty that directly recognises the value of traditional knowledge, establishing a general requirement of protection for the parties of the Convention.

Article 8 (j) of the CBD specifically provides that each Contracting Party shall, as far as possible and as appropriate:

"Subject to its national legislation, respect, preserve and maintain knowledge, innovations and practices of indigenous and local communities embodying traditional lifestyles relevant for the conservation and sustainable use of biological diversity and promote their wider application with the approval and involvement of the holders of such knowledge, innovations and practices and encourage the equitable sharing of the benefits arising from the utilization of such knowledge, innovations and practices."[16]

The CBD was a first step to take into consideration the protection of traditional knowledge and since it entered into force in 1993, this topic has been acknowledged as an important factor in the search for sustainable development. However, this knowledge, including grain species, traditional medicines, traditional art images, music, rituals among others, has been part of an international debate, which has focused primarily on the need to control the actions of the scientific and commercial sector and particularly the unapproved and uncompensated use of such knowledge. This has especially been the case with regard to the use that the pharmaceutical and agricultural industries have made of traditional knowledge (and biological and genetic resources) in their re-

---

15   Report of the United Nations University – Institute of Advanced Studies, *The Role of Registers and Databases in the Protection of Traditional Knowledge*, 2004.

16   Convention on Biological Diversity of 5 June 1992.

search and development processes, most particularly when intellectual property rights have been granted for the product of such research and development activities.[17] In this context, the concept of "biopiracy" emerges, and it is articulated "as the process through which the rights of indigenous cultures to genetic resources and knowledge are erased and replaced by those who have exploited indigenous knowledge and biodiversity."[18] The protection of traditional knowledge, genetic resources and folklore has provoked wide and interesting debate between developing and developed countries. A number of particular points will be analysed in the following.

a. Developed Countries' Arguments

aa. *Traditional Knowledge in Public Domain*

Some objections to the protection of traditional knowledge with regard to the public domain are not necessarily motivated by bad faith. "To some critics, the creation of a traditional knowledge regime would represent the removal from the public domain of a very large body of practical knowledge about the biosphere including solutions to health, agricultural and environmental problems affecting many people. Since the existence of a large public domain is good for everybody such removal, it is argued, would be a bad thing."[19]

Actually, there exists the presumption that traditional knowledge is in the public domain, encouraging the idea that nobody is harmed and no rules are broken when research institutions and corporations use it freely. "In fact this presumption is not only false but the implications of its wide acceptance may be detrimental for traditional peoples and communities."[20] According to Coombe[21] traditional knowledge is threatened, but when it is supported, rewarded, and encouraged, a revitalisation of it can be seen. Many of these communities when they are not protected, tend to migrate and as a logical consequence there exists

---

[17] United Nations University – Institute of Advanced Studies, see note 15, 10.

[18] S. Vandana/ J. Afsar/ B. Gitanjali / R. Holla Bhar, *The Enclosure and Recovery of the Commons*, 1997, 31 et seq.

[19] G. Dutfield, *Protecting Traditional Knowledge. Pathways to the Future*, 2006. 8 et seq.

[20] Id., "TRIPS related Aspects of Traditional Knowledge", *Case W. Res. J. Int'l L.* 13 (2001), 238 et seq.

[21] Coombe, see note 3, 279.

the possibility of the disappearance of an important source of traditional knowledge and of biological diversity.

bb. Developing Countries Use Traditional Knowledge for Obtaining Concessions under the TRIPS Agreement

Many developing countries use the protection of traditional knowledge, as an argument against developed countries in the WTO, promoting its recognition as a TRIPS related issue, but, they do very little at the national level (with notable exceptions).[22] In fact, many commentators consider that developing countries use this argument for wielding pressure over developed countries without a legitimate interest in the protection of traditional knowledge. According to Dutfield[23] the possible explanations for developing countries pursuing this issue at the WTO could be either that developing countries have identified several problems with the TRIPS agreement, namely that it promotes the piracy of traditional knowledge. They propose ways to be found to eradicate the problems. Or developing countries are using this issue to look for concessions in regard to the TRIPS agreement from developed countries, without a true sense of justice on behalf of their traditional peoples and communities.

cc. The Disincentive Effect

The industry is also of relevance. Indeed, it has been stated that since the emergence of synthetic chemistry, natural products are not necessary for the development of drugs. It has also been said, in a very contemptuous way, that pharmaceutical industries have little, if any, interest in the "jungle pharmacy", and alternative drug discovery might be more promising, if researchers did not have to comply with complex traditional knowledge protection regimes and benefit sharing. According to Dutfield, "it is hard to know if these concerns are genuine or are groundless scaremongering."[24]

One publication by the Pacific Research Institute deserves notoriety. This paper purports to scientifically determine the losses of the pharmaceutical and biotechnology industries in 27 countries up to 2025 in

---

[22]   Dutfield considers the following countries as notable exceptions: The Philippines, Peru, India and Costa Rica.

[23]   Id., see note 20.

[24]   Id., see note 20, 23 et seq.

terms of reduced capital stocks resulting from declining research and development investments caused by the establishment of what the authors call – without any clarification whatsoever – a "patent-based ABS regime" (access and benefit sharing regime).[25] The US government and US biotech industry have openly promoted this propaganda, which gives its opinions little credit.

b. Developing Countries' Arguments

According to Document IP/C/W/370/Rev.1 drawn up by the Secretariat of the Council for Trade Related Aspects on Intellectual Property Rights,[26] the principal concerns expressed about the protection of traditional knowledge and folklore at the international level made by developing countries as owners of these kinds of resources are:

- concern about the granting of patents or other intellectual property rights covering traditional knowledge to persons other than those indigenous peoples or communities who have originated and legitimately controlled the traditional knowledge;
- concern that traditional knowledge is being used without the authorisation of the indigenous peoples or communities who have originated and legitimately controlled it and without proper sharing of the benefits that accrue from such use. The reasons why international action should be taken to remedy these problems can be summarised as follows:

aa. Equity

Many proposals which emerge for the protection of traditional knowledge are based on equity considerations. It is said that, given the important economic value of traditional knowledge, the holders of this should be considered in the economic benefit sharing derived from that knowledge. Also it is said that if the TRIPS agreement requires developing countries (with traditional and indigenous communities) to provide intellectual property rights for a broad range of subject-matters including biological material and computer software, it is equitable that tradi-

---

[25] T.A. Wolfe/ B. Zycher, *Biotechnological and Pharmaceutical Research and Development Investment under a Patent-based Access and Benefit Sharing Regime*, 2001.

[26] Doc. IP/C/W/370/Rev.1 of 9 March 2006. Note made by the Secretariat of the WTO TRIPs Council, 3.

tional knowledge should have legal recognition.[27] An example can be found in genetic resources linked to traditional knowledge. Traditional farming developed varieties of genetic resources through planting, seed production and selecting the best adapted varieties. In addition to these efforts, these people know the qualities of the product, which could be very useful in different fields such as medicine. However, this knowledge is collected by researchers or investigators who can obtain intellectual property rights for this knowledge and benefit from its commercial use. The farmers, on the contrary, who contributed to the developing of the resource are not compensated. The basic point is that traditional/ indigenous peoples are not paid for the value they deliver, nor is there any later compensation or sharing of benefits with them. A similar argument applies to other intangible components of traditional knowledge.[28]

bb. Environment

The traditional knowledge of indigenous peoples and local communities is central for their ability to operate in an environmentally sustainable way and to conserve genetic and other natural resources. Protection of traditional knowledge is therefore closely linked to the protection of the environment.[29]

cc. Avoiding "Bio-Piracy" and ensuring Benefit Sharing

According to Christoph Beat Graber,[30] the term "bio-piracy" encompasses a variety of circumstances, including:
- The acquisition of genetic resources or traditional knowledge without permission of their holder;
- Cases where benefits arising from the commercial use of genetic resources or traditional knowledge are not shared with the provider of these resources or knowledge;

---

27 Doc. IP/C/W/165 of 3 November 1999, Communication from Bolivia, Colombia, Ecuador, Nicaragua and Peru to the WTO TRIPs Council.

28 Correa, see note 6, 5.

29 Doc. IP/C/M/30 of 1 June 2001, Communication from the Secretariat of the WTO TRIPs Council.

30 Graber/ Girsberger, see note 7.

– Cases where traditional knowledge is protected by intellectual property rights, primarily patents. The holders of these rights have not been innovative themselves, but have simply copied this knowledge.

In some cases the recognition of positive rights in respect to traditional knowledge is not the only objective. Rather, the prevention of unauthorised appropriation ("bio-piracy") and ensuring benefit sharing, as provided under arts 8 (j), 15, 16 and 19 of the CBD are the main objectives of the protection. The granting of patents, which cover traditional knowledge, may be prevented by improving the information available for patent offices with regard to the examination of novelty and inventiveness.

dd. Coherence of International and National Law

International recognition of traditional knowledge should be in conformity with the obligation "to respect, preserve and maintain knowledge, innovations and practices of indigenous and local communities," provided for in article 8 (j) of the CBD.[31] Without the existence of an international mechanism, national and regional laws, which acknowledge the collective rights of indigenous and local communities over their traditional knowledge and folklore, could be undermined.[32] Moreover, legal protection of traditional knowledge would improve confidence in the international intellectual property system.[33]

ee. National Economies Benefit

The trade with traditional knowledge and traditional cultural expressions, as handicrafts, medical plants, agricultural products and non wood forest products in both domestic and international markets is an important source of profit for exporter countries. It is a fact that traditional knowledge is frequently an input into modern industries such as pharmaceuticals, botanicals, cosmetics among others, but, in most cases, companies based in developed countries that are capable of scientific,

---

[31] Doc. IP/C/W/165 of 28 May 2003, Submission by Brazil, Bolivia, Cuba, Dominican Republic, Ecuador, India, Thailand, Peru and Venezuela to the WTO TRIPs Council.

[32] Doc. IP/C/W/404 of 24 June 2003, Communication from Bolivia, Brazil, Cuba, Dominican Republic, Ecuador, India, Peru, Thailand, Venezuela to the WTO TRIPs Council.

[33] See note 26.

technological and marketing evolution capture much more of the added value. This situation must be addressed so that developing countries can benefit more of the added value.

According to Dutfield "it seems that protecting traditional knowledge has the potential to improve the performance of many developing country economies by enabling greater commercial use of their biological wealth and increasing exports of traditional knowledge related products."[34] It is important not to overestimate the economic potential of traditional knowledge, because as we have seen, research institutions claim that they can develop drugs with synthetic chemistry and they are not interested in natural products. In the long run, this would reduce the interest in natural product research. The value of traditional knowledge must not be measured in purely economic terms; however, there are other important reasons, such as environmental or cultural factors that emphasise the importance of its protection.

c. Other Points of the Debate

aa. Existing Intellectual Property Rights and sui generis Systems

On the one hand, there is a continuing controversy over whether intellectual property could be a tool to protect traditional knowledge of indigenous and local communities. On the other hand, "many indigenous people's representatives and commentators complain that existing intellectual property systems are inadequate to protect indigenous intellectual and cultural property rights ... there is a concern that IPRs systems encourage the appropriation of traditional knowledge for commercial use without the fair sharing of benefits." But, many commentators consider that the conventional intellectual property systems "create effective incentives for innovative use of biodiversity, which in turn creates profits on which innovators can draw in negotiating benefit sharing arrangements with the holders of traditional knowledge and biodiversity."[35]

According to WIPO there are many examples of traditional knowledge that are or could be protected by the existing intellectual property rights system. However, there have been many suggestions that modify

---

[34]   Dutfield, see note 1, 143.
[35]   D. Downes, "How Intellectual Property could be a Tool to Protect Traditional Knowledge," *Columbia Journal of International Law* 25 (2000), 253 et seq. (257 et seq.).

and use new property right tools to improve the actual intellectual property system in order to protect traditional knowledge in a better way.[36] These debates have in turn prompted international and national efforts to find appropriate legal mechanisms through which traditional knowledge can be provided with the respective recognition and protection.

bb. International or National Actions?

Currently there has been much discussion about the necessity of international protection of traditional knowledge and folklore. Many countries, like Peru, consider it necessary to amend the TRIPS agreement.[37] National action is not enough as it only creates rights, which cannot be claimed and enforced in third countries. On the other hand the European Community, for example, sees "no reason to amend article 27.3(b) as it now stands. The TRIPS Agreement allows Members sufficient flexibility to modulate patent protection as a function of their needs, interests or ethical standards."[38]

Authors, like Carlos Correa consider that efforts to develop an international framework may deviate attention from the resolution of important domestic problems. He also considers that is better to develop a national regulation first in order to have better negotiations at the international level with large countries. Nothing, however, prevents the search for an international framework at an early stage.[39]

III. The Actions of WIPO

1. The World Intellectual Property Organization (WIPO)

Since 1998, WIPO has taken actions and has been involved in the protection of traditional knowledge. In that year a Global Intellectual Property Issues Division was created, and its duty was to undertake several studies on traditional knowledge and, in particular, to organise

---

[36] WIPO, see note 14.

[37] See note 26.

[38] Doc. IP/C/W/383 of 17 October 2002, Communication from the European Community.

[39] Correa, see note 6, 17

fact finding missions to identify concerns of traditional knowledge holders.[40]

The creation of the already mentioned Intergovernmental Committee on Intellectual Property and Genetic Resources, Traditional Knowledge and Folklore (the IGC)[41] was an idea suggested by the WIPO Secretariat at its 25th session. The document that was prepared by the Secretariat invited all Member States to constitute a forum with three themes which it had envisioned during the consultations. Many developing countries supported the idea, which then was approved without formal opposition from any member. The IGC met for the first time on 30 April – 2 May 2001, with the mandate of discussing:

– access to genetic resources and benefit sharing;
– protection of traditional knowledge, whether or not associated with those resources;
– the protection of expressions of folklore.

During the first few years following its inception, this committee focused on defensive protection, principally the improvement of the availability of patent examiners of traditional knowledge. In addition, many discussions developed in regard to the disclosure of origin of genetic resources and/or related traditional knowledge in patent applications. This topic will be analyzed further.

However, in the past few years, positive protection has been considered an important matter because many countries have found that defensive protection is not enough and it is necessary to confer some rights to traditional knowledge holders in order to give them an effective protection. In this regard, in 2002, WIPO prepared a paper focusing on the developing of *sui generis* systems.[42] In 2003 the WIPO General Assembly decided that IGC would focus on the international rec-

---

40   Doc. WIPO/RT/LDC/1/4 of 30 September 1999, *High-Level Interregional Roundtable on Intellectual Property for the Least Developed Countries (LDCs)*.

41   Doc. WIPO/GA/26/6 of 25 August, Matters Concerning Intellectual Property and Genetic Resources, Traditional Knowledge and Folklore.

42   Doc. WIPO/GRTKF/IC/3/8 of 29 March 2002, Complete Document made by the Secretariat of the WIPO-Intergovernmental Committee on Intellectual Property, Traditional Knowledge, Genetic Resources, and Folklore.

ognition of the subject.[43] The United States questioned the desirability of establishing international rules on genetic resources, traditional knowledge and folklore, while other delegations indicated the need for further analysis of the subject. Many delegations have presented measures that have been taken at a national level to protect traditional knowledge and TCEs. Generally, these countries do not agree with the idea of using current intellectual property rights and many of them have developed *sui generis* systems (Peru, Panama, Costa Rica, Venezuela, among others).

Throughout the various sessions, developed and developing countries have had several discussions about the international recognition and amendment of the TRIPS agreement; but in the fifth session of the IGC (7–15 July 2003), both groups discussed the committee's mandate. On the one side, developed countries aimed to prolong the current mandate, which was limited to technical analysis, for another two-year period or more. The United States in particular, proposed to prolong the current mandate unchanged for another four years. On the other side, the African Group demanded an immediate start of negotiations for legally binding international instruments on genetic resources, traditional knowledge and folklore. Developing countries from Asia and Latin America suggested an action-oriented agenda, "aiming at 'norm-setting' of some kind, in particular about biopiracy and misappropriation of traditional knowledge."[44]

The WIPO General Assembly (22 September – 1 October 2003) decided to prolong the mandate of the committee. The new tasks of the committee would be to focus on the international dimension of intellectual property and genetic resources, traditional knowledge and folklore. Pressure by developed countries caused the agreed-upon language to be vague, without the establishment of clear objectives. The new mandate also foresaw the possibility that the discussions by the committee should be conducted without prejudice, and go to another forum, particularly the WTO. This was a concession made to the developing countries to avoid blockades by relying on the argument that studies on these issues are still pending in the WIPO. With this new mandate, developing countries have the opportunity to examine the provisions in

---

[43] Doc. WIPO/GA/30/8 of 1 October 2003, Report made by the WIPO General Assembly.

[44] C. Correa, *Update on International Development relating to the Intellectual Property Protection of Traditional Knowledge including Traditional Medicine*, 2004.

patent laws which allow misappropriation, and many of them have noted that "IGC has become very useful for developed countries that wish to confine these subject to a single forum well away from those forums and processes dealing with intellectual property rule-making and standard-setting."[45]

2. Provisions for the Protection of Traditional Knowledge

These are the provisions for the protection of traditional knowledge,[46] and the provisions for the protection of TCEs[47] developed by the IGC. The text of the provisions is as follows:

"I.   POLICY OBJECTIVES

(i)   Recognize value

(ii)   Promote respect

(iii)   Meet the actual needs of traditional knowledge holders

(iv)   Promote conservation and preservation of traditional knowledge

(v)   Empower holders of traditional knowledge and acknowledge the distinctive nature of traditional knowledge systems

(vi)   Support traditional knowledge systems

(vii)   Contribute to safeguarding traditional knowledge

(viii) Repress unfair and inequitable uses

(ix)   Concord with relevant international agreements and processes

(x)   Promote innovation and creativity

(xi)   Ensure prior informed consent and exchanges based on mutually agreed terms

(xii)   Promote equitable benefit-sharing

(xiii) Promote community development and legitimate trading activities

---

45   Dutfield, see note 19.

46   Doc. WIPO/GRTKF/IC/9/5 of 9 January 2006, Document made by the Secretariat of the WIPO-Intergovernmental Committee on Intellectual Property and Genetic Resources, Traditional Knowledge and Folklore.

47   Doc. WIPO/GRTKF/IC/9/4 of 9 January 2006.

(xiv) Preclude the grant of improper intellectual property rights to unauthorized parties

(xv)   Enhance transparency and mutual confidence

(xvi) Complement protection of traditional cultural expressions

CORE PRINCIPLES

II. GENERAL GUIDING PRINCIPLES

(a) Responsiveness to the needs and expectations of traditional knowledge holders

(b) Recognition of rights

(c) Effectiveness and accessibility of protection

(d) Flexibility and comprehensiveness

(e) Equity and benefit-sharing

(f) Consistency with existing legal systems governing access to associated genetic resources

(g) Respect for and cooperation with other international and regional instruments and processes

(h) Respect for customary use and transmission of traditional knowledge

(i) Recognition of the specific characteristics of traditional knowledge

(j) Providing assistance to address the needs of traditional knowledge holders

III. SUBSTANTIVE PRINCIPLES

1. Protection against Misappropriation

2. Legal Form of Protection

3. General Scope of Subject Matter

4. Eligibility for Protection

5. Beneficiaries of Protection

6. Fair and Equitable Benefit-sharing and Recognition of Knowledge Holders

7. Principle of Prior Informed Consent

8. Exceptions and Limitations

9. Duration of Protection

10.   Transitional Measures
11.   Formalities
12.   Consistency with the General Legal Framework
13.   Administration and Enforcement of Protection
14.   International and Regional Protection."

3. Provisions for the Protection of Traditional Cultural Expressions

The text of the provisions is as follows:

"I. OBJECTIVES

(i)   Recognize value

(ii)   Promote respect

(iii)   Meet the actual needs of communities

(iv)   Prevent the misappropriation of traditional cultural expressions/expressions of folklore

(v)   Empower communities

(vi)   Support customary practices and community cooperation

(vii)   Contribute to safeguarding traditional cultures

(viii)   Encourage community innovation and creativity

(ix)   Promote intellectual and artistic freedom, research and cultural exchange on equitable terms

(x)   Contribute to cultural diversity

(xi)   Promote community development and legitimate trading activities

(xii)   Preclude unauthorized IP rights

(xiii)   Enhance certainty, transparency and mutual confidence

II. GENERAL GUIDING PRINCIPLES

(a)   Responsiveness to aspirations and expectations of relevant communities

(b)   Balance

(c)   Respect for and consistency with international and regional agreements and instruments

(d)   Flexibility and comprehensiveness

(e)   Recognition of the specific nature and characteristics of cultural expression

(f)   Complementarity with protection of traditional knowledge

(g)   Respect for rights of and obligations towards indigenous peoples and other traditional communities

(h)   Respect for customary use and transmission of TCEs/EoF

(i)   Effectiveness and accessibility of measures for protection

III. SUBSTANTIVE PRINCIPLES

1.   Subject Matter of Protection

2.   Beneficiaries

3.   Acts of Misappropriation (Scope of Protection)

4.   Management of Rights

5.   Exceptions and Limitations

6.   Term of Protection

7.   Formalities

8.   Sanctions, Remedies and Exercise of Rights

9.   Transitional Measures

10.   Relationship with Intellectual Property Protection and Other Forms of Protection, Preservation and Promotion

11.   International and Regional Protection."

IV. Strategies for Protecting Traditional Knowledge and TCEs/ Folklore

Given the diversity surrounding traditional knowledge and TCEs/folklore, there is no form of legal protection that can replace the complex social and legal systems that sustain traditional knowledge and TCEs/folklore within the indigenous communities. One form of protection is the application of laws to prevent the unauthorised or inappropriate use of traditional knowledge by third parties beyond the traditional circle. This is a sort of recognition of the need to prevent third parties from misusing traditional knowledge. This has been achieved in many different ways by the use of national laws though not necessarily by creating property rights, although this approach has been taken in some cases. A common threat has been the need to refocus existing laws or to create new ones to clarify and strengthen the legal constraints against various forms of misuse or misappropriation of traditional knowledge.

1. Protection of Traditional Knowledge and TCEs/Folklore

As we have already seen, some indigenous communities have felt outraged by the appropriation of parts of their traditional knowledge, including plant materials for agricultural and pharmaceutical purposes, by big companies and corporations under the intellectual property rights system. The cases of the neem tree (US Patent 5124349), ayahuasca (US Plant patent 5751) and quinoa (US Patent 5304718), among others, illustrate situations where the communities have claimed for protection against misappropriation. "Although the Convention on Biological Diversity acknowledges the rights of indigenous communities to their knowledge, there are no regulations to enforce the protection of these rights."[48] Many proposals made by academics and NGOs respond to such demands, while some go further in seeking the development of more comprehensive systems of protection. These proposals include options like the disclosure of origin and legal provenance of traditional knowledge, among others, which have been the most controversial issues in international discussions, especially the political and legal viability of these requirements. Despite the continuing controversy there are several areas where useful work could be done to enhance the sharing of benefits related to intellectual property rights with indigenous and local communities and could meet the objective of article 8 (j) of the CBD. On the other hand, article 27.3 of the TRIPS agreement establishes a life patenting exception and a *sui generis* clause for developing *sui generis* systems to protect plant variety.

Commentators like Downes consider "that it is necessary for governments to maintain and extend the flexibility provided in this article in order to protect and promote traditional knowledge, and to experi-

---

[48]   A.M. Pacón, "The Peruvian Proposal for protecting Traditional Knowledge", in: Twarog/ Kapoor, see note 1, 176 et seq.

ment with sui generis regimes."[49] This provision allows countries to exclude plants and animals from patenting and provides for the development of *sui generis* systems for plant variety protection. Downes is of the opinion that "maintaining this discretion is essential to preserve the flexibility needed to experiment with various approaches to the protection of traditional knowledge, and to allow for further evaluation of other complex ethical and socioeconomic issues. In contrast, requiring all countries to uniformly recognize life patenting and mandating uniform systems of plant variety protection would block countries from gaining the experience needed to implement article 80 of the CBD effectively."[50]

2. Forms of Protection

The two important demands on traditional knowledge protection that have arisen with the debate are:

-   First, the call for recognition of the rights of traditional knowledge holders relating to their traditional knowledge, and,
-   Second, concerns about the unauthorised acquisition by third parties of intellectual property rights over traditional knowledge. In this regard, two forms of protection have been developed and applied. These two approaches should be undertaken in a complementary way.
-   Positive protection: giving traditional knowledge holders the right to take action or seek remedies against certain forms of misuse of traditional knowledge; and
-   Defensive protection: safeguarding against illegitimate intellectual property rights being taken by others over traditional knowledge subject matters.

---

[49]   Downes, see note 35, 266.
[50]   Downes, see note 35.

3. Positive Protection – Recognition of Intellectual Property Rights in Traditional Knowledge

"Positive protection requires legal recognition of rights over traditional knowledge, either under existing IPR regimes or sui generis regimes."[51]

As we have already seen, the existence of a diversity of knowledge within traditional communities makes it impossible to have a single solution which fits with all the needs of these communities in all countries. Instead, effective protection may be found in a co-ordinated "menu" of different options for protection. These options could be underpinned by international common objectives and principles which could form part of a legal framework The key is to provide traditional knowledge holders with an appropriate choice of forms of protection, in order to let them participate in their own interests and choose their own directions for the protection and use of their traditional knowledge. The definition of the objectives at international level would define and shape the protection system inside a country, and for that reason the implementation of such objectives would require a degree of flexibility at the national level, in order to satisfy the diversity and the needs of traditional knowledge holders. Protection of traditional knowledge, like the protection of intellectual property in general, is not undertaken as an end in itself, but as a means to broaden policy goals.

The kind of objectives that traditional knowledge protection is intended to serve include:

- Recognition of value and promotion of respect for traditional knowledge systems
- Responsiveness to the actual needs of holders of traditional knowledge
- Repression of misappropriation of traditional knowledge and other unfair and inequitable uses
- Protection of tradition-based creativity and innovation
- Support of traditional knowledge systems and empowerment of traditional knowledge holders
- Promotion of equitable benefit-sharing from use of traditional knowledge
- Promotion of the use of traditional knowledge for a bottom-up approach to development.

---

[51]   United Nations University – Institute of Advanced Studies, see note 15.

The options for positive protection include:
- Existing IP laws and legal systems (including the law of unfair competition),
- Extended or adapted IP rights specifically focused on traditional knowledge (*sui generis* aspects of IP laws), and
- New, *sui generis* systems which give specific rights.

Other non-intellectual property options could form part of the overall menu, including trade practices and labelling laws, the law of civil liability, the use of contracts, customary and indigenous laws and protocols, regulation of access to genetic resources and associated traditional knowledge, and remedies based on such torts as unjust enrichment, rights of publicity, and blasphemy.[52] Peru and Panama e.g. have recognised rights over traditional knowledge holders in a different way. The declaratory regime established in Peru, recognises that rights over traditional knowledge derive from ancestral rights rather than an act of government. Rights over traditional knowledge do not stem from the inclusion in declarative registers. However, registration may provide the benefit of giving notice to the authorities of the existence of such knowledge for benefit–sharing purposes and for the purposes of challenging patents, etc.

In Panama, the situation is different because relevant legislation establishes a regime granting exclusive property rights over traditional knowledge. A constitutive register is part of such a regime, and registration puts the public on notice of the existence of rights over traditional knowledge.

Both Panama and Peru in their respective legislation on folklore and collective traditional knowledge of biological diversity have recognised traditional knowledge to be the cultural patrimony of indigenous peoples. This kind of recognition, as cultural patrimony being recognised as inalienable and indefeasible establishes obligations between the state and the indigenous peoples, and creates an effective measure of protection against third parties. As cultural patrimony may not be alienated, it cannot be commercialised in a manner giving monopolistic rights to third parties. Furthermore, it requires, that all benefits received, be util-

---

[52]   Doc. WIPO/GRTKF/IC/5/7 of 7 May 2003, Document prepared by the Secretariat of the WIPO-Intergovernmental Committee on Intellectual Property and Genetic Resources, Traditional Knowledge and Folklore.

ised by the recipient indigenous peoples in order to strengthen and protect their knowledge in a manner which secures equitable sharing.[53]

a. Application of Existing Intellectual Property Rights

The possibility of applying the existing modes of intellectual property rights protection to different components of traditional knowledge has been extensively explored. The policy debate about traditional knowledge and the intellectual property rights system has underlined the limitations of the existing intellectual property rights laws in meeting all the needs and expectations of traditional knowledge holders. Even so, the already existing laws have been successfully used to protect against some forms of misuse and misappropriation of traditional knowledge, including the use of patents, trademarks, geographical indications, industrial designs, and trade secrets. Some of the drawbacks of the use of the actual intellectual property rights system to protect traditional knowledge and traditional cultural expressions are:

- traditional knowledge is often held collectively by communities, rather than by individual owners – this is often cited as a drawback in protecting traditional knowledge
- Communities' concerns about traditional knowledge typically span generations, a much longer timeframe than the duration of most intellectual property rights
- There are also concerns that the costs of using the intellectual property rights system is a particular obstacle for traditional knowledge holders. This has led some to explore capacity building, evolution of legal concepts to take greater account of traditional knowledge perspectives, the use of alternative dispute resolution, and a more active role for government agencies and other players.

---

[53] Peruvian Law No. 27811, 2002, *article 9. Role of Present Generations:* The present generations of the indigenous peoples preserve, develop and manage their collective knowledge for their own benefit and that of future generations.
Article 10. Collective Nature of the Knowledge: The collective knowledge protected under this regime belongs to one or several indigenous peoples. It does not belong to any specific individual who is a member of any such towns. These rights are independent from those that might be generated inside the indigenous peoples in which case traditional systems can be enforced in the distribution of benefits.

In the next few sections possible applications of the actual intellectual property rights system and its principal drawbacks will be discussed.

aa. Unfair Competition and Trade Practices Laws

This system permits actions against false or misleading claims that a product is authentically indigenous, or has been produced or endorsed by, or otherwise associated with, a particular traditional community.

bb. Copyright

As is known, for many years indigenous peoples and communities have claimed that outsiders frequently neglect to ask permission to reproduce their fixed and unfixed cultural expressions such as artistic works, handicrafts, designs, dances, and musical and dramatic performances. They also fail to acknowledge the source of the creativity, passing off the works as authentic. At an international level there has been concern about these matters since 1960, when the idea of applying copyright law to protect traditional knowledge emerged. At that time the term applied to traditional knowledge was "folklore". "The possibility of protecting folklore by means of copyright was raised at the Diplomatic Conference of Stockholm in 1967 for the revision of the Berne Convention. While this issue was not fully resolved, some unsatisfying provisions were included in the Stockholm Act of the Convention, and retained in the most recent revision adopted in Paris in 1971."[54]

In the case of unpublished works where the identity of the author is unknown, but where there is every reason to presume that he is a national of a country of the Union (in respect of article 1 of the Berne Convention), it shall be a matter for legislation in that country to designate the competent authority, which shall represent the author and shall be entitled to protect and enforce his rights in the countries of the Union.[55] In a document presented to WIPO, a group of countries from Latin America and the Caribbean, considers that copyright can be used to protect the artistic manifestations of traditional knowledge holders, especially artists who belong to indigenous and native communities, against unauthorised reproduction and exploitation.

---

[54] Dutfield, see note 19, 249.

[55] Article 15 (a) of the Berne Convention for the Protection of Literary and Artistic Works of 9 September 1986.

"It could include works such as: literary works, (tales, legends and myths), traditions, poems; theatrical works; pictorial works; textile works (fabrics, garments, textile compositions, tapestries, carpets); musical works; and, three-dimensional works (pottery and ceramics, sculptures, wood and stone carvings, artefacts of various kinds). Related rights to copyright, such as performing rights, could be used for the protection of the performances of singers and dancers and presentations of stage plays, puppet shows and other comparable performances."[56]

However, copyright has some fundamental limitations in the folklore context, since it excludes some expressions from eligibility for copyright protection,

– as Copyright requires an identifiable author, and the notion of authorship is a problematic concept in many traditional societies.[57] Traditional knowledge and practices are often handed down from generation to generation, and have no clearly identifiable author. For that reason intellectual property rights are considered as not being suitable. They do not recognise collective rights, they just protect knowledge created by individuals. In this sense, copyright law emphasises the role of individuals in knowledge creation and fails to reward those communities which provided the raw material for the later protected work. According to this view, one might think that copyright might undermine the interests of indigenous peoples rather than promote them, but although this is probably true, some authors consider that this is not a reason to discount copyright completely. Downes thinks that the problems regarding traditional knowledge, especially those arising from collective authorship, are generalisations. In reality, he argues, there are more complicated circumstances. He considers that "within a communal system, individuals in local or indigenous communities can distinguish themselves as informal creators or inventors separate from the community, so discussion of IPRs and traditional knowledge should draw more on the diversity and creativity of indigenous approaches to IPRs issues."[58] In the works of UNESCO and WIPO, there are Model Provisions for National Laws for the Protection of Expres-

---

[56]   Doc. WIPO/GA/26/9 of 14 September 2000. *Documents prepared by the Group of Countries of Latin America and the Caribbean (GRULAC)*, Annex II, 3.

[57]   Dutfield, see note 19, 250.

[58]   Downes, see note 35, 259.

sions of Folklore against Illicit Exploitation and other Prejudicial Actions.[59] This framework provides a possibility for the protection of traditional knowledge. The Model Provisions attribute rights not only to individuals, but also to communities, and allow the protection of ongoing or evolutionary creations.

– *Copyright just gives temporary protection and has a time limit.*[60] But for many communities their knowledge is an important element of their identity and history. They think that this knowledge should not be released into the public domain, at least not to the extent that others are free to do with it whatever they like.

– *Copyright normally requires works to be fixed.*[61] However, most traditional knowledge expressions are not fixed and are passed on orally from generation to generation.

All these arguments exclude such expressions from eligibility for copyright protection, although, as we have seen there were some efforts from WIPO and developing countries for protecting them through the current intellectual property rights system.

Ricardo Antequera, in his recent work, considers that "despite the attempts to safeguard folklore in a legal way through copyright, none of them has satisfied the expectations,"[62] because, as we have seen, traditional cultural expressions have their own characteristics, especially in terms of collective property, which is opposed to the classical principles of copyright.

cc. Patents

The patent system could be used for the protection of technical solutions that are industrially applicable and universally new and involve an inventive step. For example, patents may be given for products isolated, synthesised or developed from genetic structures, micro-organisms and plants or animals or organisms existing in nature. Carlos Correa considers that some elements of traditional medicine may be protected under patents. Patents have been granted for natural components, as well

---

59   Dutfield, see note 19, 250.
60   Id., see note 19, 251.
61   Id., see note 19.
62   R. Antequera, *"La tutela del Folklore en el marco de los derechos intelectuales", (algunas reflexiones sobre la protección Sui Generis)*, 2007, 505 et seq.

as on combinations of plants for therapeutic use[63] for example the European Patent EP 0519777 on formulations made from a variety of fresh plants.[64] There are, however, several major obstacles to afford patent protection to existing traditional medical knowledge. Some such obstacles stem from the legal standards established to acquire patent rights in national laws. An invention usually needs to meet the requirements of absolute novelty (previously unknown to the public), inventive steps, and being capable of industrial application (or being useful for it). Patents may be granted for all types of processes and products, including those related to primary production, namely agriculture, fishing or mining. However, since most of the traditional knowledge is not contemporary, but rather has been used for long periods, the novelty and/or inventive step requirement of patent protection may be difficult to meet. As for the novelty requirement, it is considered that patent law cannot be used to protect community knowledge acquired and shared over several generations. It is virtually impossible to call such knowledge new, for one cannot say which part is new. One could argue that all the discrete components of the knowledge were new when they were created, but one can think of a holistic body of knowledge extant at a given point in time, none of which is new. Dutfield[65] lists the main objections for a patent regime over traditional knowledge as follows:

– *Traditional knowledge is collectively held and generated while patent law treats inventiveness as an achievement of individuals*

    Traditional knowledge is, in many cases developed and spread throughout the indigenous community, which makes it very difficult, if not impossible, to identify unequivocally the inventor. According to Dutfield[66] the treatment of inventiveness as an achievement of individuals does not easily fit for patents, because lately research corporations have considered the idea of a unique inventor to be inconvenient. As a consequence, nowadays it is difficult to get a "one man invention".

– *Patent specification must be written in a technical way that examiners can understand*

---

63   Correa, see note 6.
64   C. Correa, "Protection and Promotion of Traditional Medicine: Implications for Public Health in Developing Countries". Paper prepared for WIPO, 2000.
65   Dutfield, see note 19.
66   Id., see note 19, 250.

It is difficult for an indigenous group to complete a patent specification; they do not have the ability to describe the phenomenon in e.g. the language of chemistry or molecular biology.

- *Applying for Patents and enforcing them once they have been awarded is expensive*

The poverty often surrounding indigenous groups and communities could make it very difficult to register a patent. Likewise, the costs of litigation make it almost impossible to enforce patent rights. In the words of Ana María Pacón,[67] another consideration is that patents confer only temporary protection. Once the time frame expires, inventions are in the public domain and freely available. Given the unique characteristics of traditional knowledge, such as its transgenerational nature, not only present but also future generations should benefit from meaningful protection. The type of protection available under patents would lead to communal and intercommunal tensions arising from inexorable competition for the commercial benefits deriving from the knowledge. Another concern with regard to patents is that the United States for example does not recognise undocumented knowledge. Therefore, it is legal to copy this knowledge and apply for a patent. A good example for this is the Ayahuasca case.[68]

Ayahuasca (*Banisteriopsis caapi*) is a plant used for many medical and ritual purposes. Ayahuasca is the vernacular name among the Amazon Quichua people, in whose language ayahuasca means "vine of the spirits". It is a sacred plant for many indigenous peoples of Amazonia. In 1986, after research in Ecuatorian Amazonia, a US scientist was granted a patent on ayahuasca (US Plant patent No. 5751). The US Patent and Trademark Office (USPTO) revoked it in November 1999. It based its decision on the fact that publications describing *Banisteriopsis caapi* were "known and available" prior to the filing of the patent application. The USPTO's decision came in response to a request for reexamination of the patent by the Coordinating Body for the Indigenous Organisations of the Amazon Basin, the Coalition for Amazonian Peoples and their Environment, and lawyers at the Center for International Environmental Law.[69] But on appeal the patent was re-established. Later, the USPTO revoked the patent again on the basis that documents presented by the Indigenous Organisations of the Amazon Basin

---

67 Pacón, see note 48, 176.
68 See under <http://www.ciel.org/Biodiversity/BiodiversityIntellectualPrope rty.html>.
69 Correa, see note 6, 18.

showed that the plant was not distinctive or new. However, if that body had been unable to present written evidence refuting the patent, then the USPTO would not have cancelled the ayahuasca patent. As long as it seems normal to assume that indigenous knowledge has always been free for taking until its "discovery" and subsequent "privatization" by explorers, scientists, governments, corporations, etc. there will be no sufficient protection for the indigenous communities.

dd. Trade Secrets

Trade secrets have been used to protect non-disclosed traditional knowledge, including secret and sacred traditional knowledge. Under this modality, all information is protected against unauthorised acquisition or use by third parties.[70] In many societies it is normal for some healers or shamans to protect through secrecy the knowledge they do not want to share. Holders of this knowledge may be protected against disclosure through registration or other formalities but very often this is not asked for. Most laws require, as a condition for protection, that the person in control of the information adopts the steps necessary, under the relevant circumstances, to keep the information confidential. In other words, there should be deliberate acts aimed at protecting, as secret, the relevant information. The principal criterion for this system is that the information needs to be confidential and, as the knowledge of the communities is diffused among various members of a community, it is difficult to gain protection through this method. But if the information is kept only by one person, as in the case of shamans, then this system may work.

ee. Geographical Indications

Geographical indications may, in some cases, be a suitable mechanism to enhance the value of agricultural products, handicrafts and other traditional knowledge-derived products. Several developing countries within the WTO have indicated their interest in an enhanced protection. Geographical indications, however, do not protect a specific technology or knowledge as such, but only prevent the false use of the geographical indication.

Geographical indications, especially appellations of origin, may be used to enhance the commercial value of natural, traditional and craft

---

[70] Pacón, see note 48, 176.

products of all kinds, if their particular characteristics may be attributed to their geographical origin. A number of products that come from various regions are the result of traditional processes and knowledge implemented by one or more communities in a given region. The special characteristics of those products are appreciated by the public, and may be symbolised by the indication of the source used to identify the products. A better exploitation and promotion of traditional geographical indications would make it possible to afford better protection of the economic interests of the communities and regions where such products originate from.

ff. Trademarks/Trade Names and Industrial Designs[71]

Trademarks may also be used to protect signs or symbols of commercial interest for local and indigenous communities.

Industrial designs could protect the design and shape of utilitarian craft products such as furniture, receptacles, garments and articles of ceramics, leather, wood and other materials.

Trademarks may protect all goods manufactured and services offered by manufacturers, craftsmen, professionals and traders in native and indigenous communities. Similarly, the bodies that represent them or in which they are grouped (cooperatives, guilds, etc.), may be differentiated from each other with trademarks and service marks. The *trademark* is an essential element in the commercial promotion of goods and services both at national and international level.

Trade names may protect any manufacturer, craftsman, professional person or trader in a native or indigenous community, and may also be used to identify the bodies that represent such persons or in which they are grouped (cooperatives, guilds, etc.). The trade name is also used to promote the activities of the person or entity that it identifies, both within and beyond the borders of the country of origin.

Nevertheless, in conclusion, taking into account the reality of these communities, whether intellectual property rights exist or not, indigenous communities are likely to face serious obstacles in the process of acquiring and enforcing such rights when protecting a certain component of traditional knowledge. The cost of acquisition of rights (when registration is required such as in the case of patents, industrial designs and trademarks) and, the costs of enforcement of the relevant rights

---

[71] See note 57.

might preclude these people from taking advantage of these rights. Administrative and judicial procedures are often long and costly. "The availability of IPRs protection for traditional knowledge may be, therefore, of little or no real value to those who may claim rights in traditional knowledge."[72]

b. Adaptations of Existing Intellectual Property through *sui generis* Measures

Many countries have adjusted existing intellectual property rights systems to the specific needs of their communities through *sui generis* measures. For example "New Zealand's trade mark law has been amended to exclude trademarks that cause offence, and this applies especially to Indigenous Maori symbols. India's Patent Act has been amended to clarify the status of traditional knowledge within patent law. The Chinese State Intellectual Property Office has a team of patent examiners specializing in traditional Chinese medicine."[73]

- Use of sui generis Exclusive Rights

Many countries, such as Peru, have considered that the actual intellectual property rights system, even with some modifications, is not adequate to protect the unique character of traditional knowledge. This is the reason for the adoption of a *sui generis* regime. "What makes an IP system a sui generis one is the modification of some of its features so as to properly accommodate the special characteristics of its subject matter, and the specific policy needs which led to the establishment of a distinct system."[74]

The *sui generis* regime of Peru established by Law No. 27811, has positive and defensive protection. The objectives are to promote fair and equitable distribution of benefits, to ensure that the use of the knowledge takes place with the prior informed consent of the indigenous peoples, and to prevent misappropriation. Protection is afforded for collective knowledge of indigenous peoples associated with biological resources. The law grants indigenous peoples the right to consent to the use of traditional knowledge. The law also foresees the payment of equitable compensation for the use of certain types of traditional

---

[72]   Correa, see note 6, 13.
[73]   See note 10.
[74]   See note 10.

knowledge into a national Fund for Indigenous Development or directly to the traditional knowledge holders.

4. Defensive Protection

Defensive protection is used to prevent the granting of patents over traditional knowledge, although this does not amount to a recognition of actual rights of ownership over traditional knowledge in favour of indigenous peoples. According to WIPO defensive protection can be valuable and effective in blocking illegitimate intellectual property rights, but it does not stop others from actively using or exploiting traditional knowledge.[75] Some form of positive protection is needed to prevent unauthorized use. Carlos Correa proposed a misappropriation regime which would allow national laws to determine the appropriate measures to avoid the misappropriation (including the obligation to stop using a knowledge or to pay a compensation for such use). "This regime should have three important points: documentation of traditional knowledge, proof of origin or materials, and prior informed consent". [76] This will be analysed further.

According to Carlos Correa, two United Nations documents implicitly support the misappropriation proposal: Decision V/16 of the CBD's Conference of the Parties, and the Principles and Guidelines for the Protection of the Heritage of Indigenous Peoples. Paragraph seventeen of the first document states,

> "Request[ed] Parties to support the development of registers of traditional knowledge, innovations and practices of indigenous and local communities embodying traditional lifestyles relevant for the conservation and sustainable use of biological diversity through participatory programmes and consultations with indigenous and local communities, taking into account strengthening legislation, customary practices and traditional systems of resource management, such as the protection of traditional knowledge against unauthorized use."[77]

The second document, Principles and Guidelines for the Protection of the Heritage of Indigenous Peoples, elaborated in 1995 by Erica-

---

[75]   See note 10.

[76]   Correa, see note 6, 18.

[77]   Decision V/16 of the Fifth Conference of the Parties to the Convention on Biological Diversity. Nairobi, Kenya (15-26 May 2000).

Irene Daes, then Special Rapporteur of the former UN Sub Commission on the Prevention of Discrimination and Protection of Minorities,[78] establishes in paras 26 and 27 the following,

> "National laws should deny to any person or corporation the right to obtain patent, copyright or other legal protection for any element of indigenous peoples' heritage without adequate documentation of the free and informed consent of the traditional owners to an arrangement for the sharing of ownership, control, use and benefits.

> National laws should ensure the labelling and correct attribution of indigenous peoples' artistic, literary and cultural works whenever they are offered for public display or sale. Attribution should be in the form of a trademark or an appellation of origin, authorized by the peoples or communities concerned."

The WIPO Intergovernmental draft provisions for the protection of traditional knowledge contain an article on protection against misappropriation.[79] It states as follows,

> "*Article 1*

> *Protection against Misappropriation*

> 1.   Traditional knowledge shall be protected against misappropriation.

> 2.   Any acquisition, appropriation or utilization of traditional knowledge by unfair or illicit means constitutes an act of misappropriation. Misappropriation may also include deriving commercial benefit from the acquisition, appropriation or utilization of traditional knowledge when the person using that knowledge knows, or is negligent in failing to know, that it was acquired or appropriated by unfair means; and other commercial activities contrary to honest practices that gain inequitable benefit from traditional knowledge.

> 3.   In particular, legal means should be provided to prevent:

> (i)   acquisition of traditional knowledge by theft, bribery, coercion, fraud, trespass, breach or inducement of breach of contract, breach or inducement of breach of confidence or confidentiality, breach of fiduciary obligations or other relations of trust, deception,

---

[78]   ECOSOC, Principles and Guidelines for the Protection of the Heritage of Indigenous Peoples of 21 June 1995.

[79]   Doc. WIPO/GRTKF/IC/8/5 of 8 April 2005, Document prepared by the Secretariat of the WIPO- Intergovernmental Committee on Intellectual Property, Traditional Knowledge, Genetic Resources, and Folklore.

misrepresentation, the provision of misleading information when obtaining prior informed consent for access to traditional knowledge, or other unfair or dishonest means;

(ii) acquisition of traditional knowledge or exercising control over it in violation of legal measures that require prior informed consent as a condition of access to the knowledge, and use of traditional knowledge that violates terms that were mutually agreed as a condition of prior informed consent concerning access to that knowledge;

(iii) false claims or assertions of ownership or control over traditional knowledge, including acquiring, claiming or asserting intellectual property rights over traditional knowledge-related subject matters when those intellectual property rights are not validly held in the light of that traditional knowledge and any conditions relating to its access;

(iv) if traditional knowledge has been accessed, commercial or industrial use of traditional knowledge without just and appropriate compensation to the recognized holders of the knowledge, when such use has gainful intent and confers a technological or commercial advantage on its user, and when compensation would be consistent with fairness and equity in relation to the holders of the knowledge in view of the circumstances in which the user acquired the knowledge; and

(v) wilful offensive use of traditional knowledge of particular moral or spiritual value to its holders by third parties outside the customary context, when such use clearly constitutes a mutilation, distortion or derogatory modification of that knowledge and is contrary to ordre public or morality.

4.   Traditional knowledge holders should also be effectively protected against other acts of unfair competition, including acts specified in article 10bis of the Paris Convention. This includes false or misleading representations that a product or service is produced or provided with the involvement or endorsement of traditional knowledge holders, or that the commercial exploitation of products or services benefits holders of traditional knowledge. It also includes acts of such a nature as to create confusion with a product or service of traditional knowledge holders; and false allegations in the course of trade which discredit the products or services of traditional knowledge holders.

5.   The application, interpretation and enforcement of protection against misappropriation of traditional knowledge, including deter-

mination of equitable sharing and distribution of benefits, should be guided, as far as possible and appropriate, by respect for the customary practices, norms, laws and understandings of the holder of the knowledge, including the spiritual, sacred or ceremonial characteristics of the traditional origin of the knowledge."

Paragraph 1 of the following article states that,

"1. The protection of traditional knowledge against misappropriation may be implemented through a range of legal measures, including: a special law on traditional knowledge; laws on intellectual property, including laws governing unfair competition and unjust enrichment; the law of contracts; the law of civil liability, including torts and liability for compensation; criminal law; laws concerning the interests of indigenous peoples; fisheries laws and environmental laws; regimes governing access and benefit-sharing; or any other law or any combination of those laws. This paragraph is subject to article 11(1)." [80]

Arguably, such a misappropriation regime could and probably should incorporate: (1) the concept of unfair competition; (2) moral rights; and (3) cultural rights.[81]

a. The Disclosure of Origin and Legal Provenance of Traditional Knowledge

The disclosure of origin as an option to protect the misappropriation of traditional knowledge can be defined as "the obligation to identify, where necessary, the origin of resources covered by IPRs claims."[82] This would allow protection of any rights of the countries supplying the materials and the application, if appropriate, of the benefit-sharing principle contained in the CBD. For example, Decision No. 391 of the Andean Community establishes that any intellectual property rights or other claims to resources shall not be considered valid if they were obtained or used in violation of the terms of a permission for access to biological resources situated in any of the Andean countries, as regulated under that Decision.

---

[80] "Eligibility for protection of traditional knowledge against acts of misappropriation should not require any formalities."

[81] Dutfield, see note 19.

[82] Correa, see note 6, 19.

There are several reasons for considering disclosure of origin and legal provenance an important question,

– *Economic* (genetic resources and traditional knowledge have economic significance and it is necessary to ensure the possibilities of their commercial exploitation and industrialisation),
– *Legal* (the need to grant "good" patent rights and the need for complementarities between legal regimes at the international level),
– *Cultural* (the need to respect the beliefs and rights of indigenous peoples) and
– *Political* (the need to safeguard countries' interests with regard to sovereign rights over their resources).[83]

The group of megadiverse countries rich in biodiversity, which have historically been suppliers of genetic resources (and traditional knowledge), takes the view that the only way to enforce disclosure requirements is to ensure that they are recognised by the authorities of the countries in which most patents are granted.

Diverse international fora, such as the CBD, WTO and WIPO have been scenes of interchange of opinion between the developed, developing and megadiverse countries, which have been discussing the subject of the disclosure of genetic resources origin and its relation or entailment with intellectual property. Thus within the framework of the CBD the megadiverse countries, among them Peru, raised the suggestion of tying the disclosure of origin of the genetic resource and the right to equitable distribution of the benefits to the intellectual property question. Countries opinions are divided between:

– those that oppose the inclusion of this type of requirement in the patent system (at the international or national level) represented by the TRIPS agreement,
– those that are considering the possibility of such inclusion, albeit on a voluntary basis and one that is limited (to disclosure of origin) and
– those including Peru, which advocate mandatory inclusion so as to guarantee the more efficient and secure implementation of TRIPS itself and generate a situation of positive synergy between TRIPS and the CBD.[84]

---

[83] See note 5.
[84] See note 5.

b. Prior Informed Consent (PIC)

This principle establishes that traditional knowledge holders should be consulted before their knowledge is accessed or used by third parties and an agreement should be reached on appropriate terms. Given the close relationship between genetic resources and some forms of traditional knowledge, this same principle is also used in a number of national laws concerning access to and use of traditional knowledge (like in the case of Peru, where the presentation of a written agreement with a community is necessary to use a certain knowledge). It is important to point out that the concept of disclosure of origin and legal provenance presupposes the existence of prior informed consent and of fair and equitable benefit-sharing.

c. Documentation of Traditional Knowledge

One mechanism with much potential as a tool of protection for traditional knowledge is its documentation in databases and registers. Once published in this format, novelty in respect of the disclosed information could not be claimed.

Within WIPO and the IGC, databases and registers have been discussed as mechanisms for both defensive and positive protection of traditional knowledge. These databases demonstrate the wide variety of objectives, scopes, procedures, rights, benefits and enforcement mechanisms which have been employed by different actors in order to secure varying levels of protection of traditional knowledge. The studies show a tendency for all databases and registers to play a role in the preservation of traditional knowledge. This may be primarily the case for the benefit of indigenous peoples themselves. Although, databases and registers have been used in an interchangeable way when describing existing experiences in documenting traditional knowledge, there is a substantial difference between the two, which is necessary to avoid confusion for all those trying to find mechanisms to protect traditional knowledge from misappropriation. According to Downes a registry is not merely a list or database designed to provide information to users. It is a list or database into which people put information in order to gain legal rights relating to that information. "Registering something in a registry, puts it on the record and puts the public on notice that the registrant asserts a claim."[85]

Databases would be an important source of information for authorities reviewing patent applications in order to determine whether they achieve the required levels of novelty and inventiveness. This has led to proposals for incorporating traditional knowledge already in the public domain into more accessible databases for the purpose of aiding patent authorities. Despite the potential of defensive protection provided by compilation of traditional knowledge into open access databases, there exists some criticism which considers that a database increases access to traditional knowledge for the private sector, without increasing indigenous peoples' rights. These circumstances have led to the establishment of confidential registers. As a result important sources of prior art including local community registers, indigenous peoples and other confidential registers including the confidential register under the Peruvian legislation, as well as the registers for oral traditional knowledge maintained by elders, wise men and women, are effectively excluded from the remit of prior art investigations.

Placing traditional knowledge in the public domain as a condition for recognising it as prior art has positive and negative consequences. It may be seen as requiring a renunciation by indigenous peoples of their rights to control their traditional knowledge by placing it in the public domain in order to prevent weakness in the intellectual property rights regimes.

"Strict application of the principle of the public domain to traditional knowledge may therefore lead to inequities for indigenous peoples. To attempt to redress these inequities measures may be sought of to provide some form of compensatory scheme for use of traditional knowledge in the public domain. In Peru, for instance, legislation on collective knowledge requires payment of compensation for use of traditional knowledge in the public domain."[86]

This tool could act in connection with the disclosure of origin because the requirement of disclosure of origin in patent applications would assist patent authorities in their direct searches of prior art in the country of origin. Incorporating local and indigenous peoples' registers within the framework of a national register of traditional knowledge

---

[85] D. Downes/ S. Laird, *Community Registers of Biodiversity related Knowledge: Role of Intellectual Property in Managing Access and Benefit Sharing*, 1999.

[86] United Nations University – Institute of Advanced Studies, see note 15, 6.

would extend the remit of potential sources of evidence of prior art for the purposes of defensive protection.

5. The sui generis Protection of Folklore

On this point, it is interesting to note that the existing legislative formulas are not uniform when they refer to the object of a "sui generis protection". Some of them talk about the protection of single literary and artistic works,[87] others extend it to the folklore that includes musical instruments, languages, traditions or beliefs. However, although in the beginning copyright constituted a way for the protection of folklore, the reality has demonstrated that the problems arising considerably exceed those benefits. It has also been indicated that copyright should acknowledge the principles of the rights of authors to safeguard folklore.[88]

The Panamanian Law of 2000 and the related Decree of 2001 establish a special intellectual property regime in respect of the collective rights of the indigenous peoples. This law aims at protecting the collective intellectual property rights and knowledge of indigenous communities through the registration, promotion, commercialisation and marketing of their rights in such a way as to give prominence to indigenous socio-cultural values and cultural identities and for social justice. Another key objective is the protection of the authenticity of crafts and other traditional artistic expressions (Preamble and article 1 of the Law; Preamble of the Decree). This law gives the indigenous communities a preponderant role concerning the defence of the use and cultural commercialisation of the art, crafts and other manifestations.

---

[87] For example the Copyright Law from Bolivia. In Bolivia, the Copyright Law of 1992 provides, in article 21, that "... folklore being understood in the strict sense of the body of literary and artistic works created within the national territory by unknown or unidentified authors presumed to be nationals of the country or of its ethnic communities, which are handed down from generation to generation and thereby constitute one of the fundamental elements of the traditional cultural heritage of the nation."

[88] Antequera, see note 62.

V. From Theory to Practice: The Peruvian Experience

1. The Peruvian Position

In June 2005, Peru proposed a modification of article 27.3 of the TRIPS agreement, advocating mandatory inclusion of disclosure of origin and legal provenance of genetic resources within the patentability exceptions. Peru suggests that TRIPS should include a new type of exception (27.3.c) for patents or products, which include genetic resources which do not fulfil the international and/or national legislation. This would guarantees a positive synergy effect between TRIPS and the CBD.[89] In the Communication No. IP/C/W/441 before the Council for Trade-related Aspects of Intellectual Property Rights, the Peruvian government manifested its position that "ensuring protection at the domestic level is not sufficient, and therefore the international recognition of traditional knowledge as protectable intellectual property will give the beneficiaries legal standing to assert their rights in other countries."

Peru's main suggestions are:

i) the disclosure of origin and the legal provenance of genetic resources (or traditional knowledge) as a condition for the patent request; and

ii) the genetic resources and the traditional knowledge must be incorporated in a database system which allows a correct evaluation of the novelty requirements. One of the reasons of this exposition is to prevent "biopiracy".

From the Ministerial Declaration of Doha to that of Hong Kong, ample debates have taken place regarding the obligatory requirement of disclosure of origin for genetic resources. On 29 May 2006, Peru and other countries proposed a draft that would establishes a new article 29B in the TRIPS agreement. This proposal contains 5 parts. According to it a request for a patent referring to genetic resources and traditional knowledge, has to state i) the name of the country which provides the resources or knowledge, ii) the name of the person from whom it is obtained in the supplier country and iii) the fulfilment of the prior informed consent principle and the right to equitable distribution of the benefits. A further requirement is that the Member States establish procedures for the effective observance of their legislation in this respect. This proposal will not be discussed until 2009, as the negotiations have been suspended because of discrepancies in the agriculture sector.

---

[89] See note 5.

2. The Peruvian Regime

a. Introduction

The Peruvian government has been concerned with traditional knowledge for a long time. In 1993, it mentioned the necessity to regulate, at an Andean level, the access to genetic resources. This was obtained in 1996, through the Andean Community of Nations, Decision 391.[90] Later, in 2003 and 2004, together with other countries, Peru proposed the obligation of disclosure of origin for biological resources, including the uses associated with traditional knowledge. Additionally, in 2005, Peru sustained the necessity of introducing the subject of disclosure of origin. Already in 1996 Peru, responding to calls from national interest groups and mindful of its obligations under the Andean Community's regional legislation, tried to explore possible options for protecting and regulating traditional knowledge and controlling access to genetic resources. In that year, the government formed five consultation groups, whose tasks were to:

- Determine the forms of organisation used by indigenous communities in Peru and the mechanisms they used for benefit sharing
- to compile an inventory of genetic resources in Peru
- Regulate access to genetic resources
- Protect traditional knowledge
- Develop information material; and a strategy for training indigenous communities.[91]

Members including representatives of the government, from NGOs, the academia and the indigenous communities decided that a "sui generis" protection would be suitable. Although in the first and formative phase, indigenous people's participation was minimal, it became increasingly clear that many complex issues could be addressed only with indigenous participation. Despite its shortcomings, the process surrounding the elaboration of a proposal and a law to protect traditional knowledge has been successful, and Peru has rightly obtained an influential voice in international fora, where measures are being sought of to protect the rights of indigenous peoples over their traditional knowledge.

---

[90] Decision 391 of the Andean Community of 2 July 1996, *Common Regime on Access to Genetic Resources*.

[91] Pacón, see note 48, 176.

Drafts were discussed at a first meeting in Lima (26-27 April 1999) with the leaders of the indigenous communities, and at a second in Cusco (10-12 May 1999) with the leaders and representatives of groups of indigenous communities. Finally, an international seminar (19-21 May 1999) was organised by the National Institute for the Defence of Competition and the Protection of Intellectual Property and WIPO. Representatives of the government, the private sector, NGOs, the academia and indigenous communities also participated, as well as representatives from other countries, in particular Brazil and other Andean countries. After these talks, the National Institute published a proposal in October 1999 to invite comments from all interested parties. Through national and international workshops and seminars, it had been possible to disseminate the proposal widely. In August 2000, a second proposal reflecting comments, obtained so far, was published.[92]

The Peruvian government has been concerned about the protection of traditional knowledge, as well as the avoidance of "biopiracy". Its proposals and the regime adopted within the country cover only traditional knowledge associated with biodiversity, different from "Panama for example, which has an interesting legislation for protecting collective intellectual property rights and traditional knowledge of indigenous peoples over creations such as inventions, models, drawings and designs, innovations contained in images, symbols, graphics and others; and cultural elements of their history, music, art, traditional artistic expressions, all of which might be susceptible to commercial use through a special system of registers."[93] In Peru, all these items mentioned, are out of the regime's scope. The government continues to work closely with the indigenous communities and has successfully introduced a law concerning a protection regime for the collective knowledge of indigenous peoples derived from biological resources.[94]

---

[92]   El Peruano newspaper of 21 October 1999.

[93]   The Law No. 20 of 26 June 2000 from Panama creates the Special Regime for Intellectual Property over Collective Knowledge of Indigenous Peoples for the Protection and Defense of their Cultural Identity and their Traditional Knowledge.

[94]   Law No. 27811 of 24 July 2002.

b. Developments in Respect of Public Policy and Legislation in the Andean Region

At the Andean level, all member countries that have subscribed to the CBD have been concerned about the protection of biological diversity and its sustainable use, regulating access to genetic resources to ensure equitable benefit-sharing. In 1993, in Decision 345, the Third Transitory Disposition, established a term to regulate access to genetic resources, which was confirmed in Decision 391 in 1996. In 2000, Decision 486 established a legal industrial property framework applicable in the countries of the Andean region.

aa. Decision 391 – Common Regime on Access to Genetic Resources (2 July 1996)

As a result of formal proposals made by Peru and Colombia at the negotiating meetings on the Andean regime on access to genetic resources, Decision 391 provided for the adoption of legal requirements at a regional level. It directly linked the access regime to intellectual property.[95] This decision just makes general regulations, which means, that every country has to adopt its own legislation. The regime incorporated provisions which link the authorities of intellectual property with those with access to genetic resources. It applies only when it is certain that an invention, is the subject of an intellectual property right (the decision does not refer specifically to patents), has been obtained or developed through genetic resources or products derived from such resources and denies intellectual property rights in the absence of compliance with regulations on access. The second and third supplementary provision establish as conditions for granting an intellectual property right that there be compliance with requirements under the access to genetic resources regimes.

The second supplementary provision of Decision 391 provides that:

"The Member Countries shall not acknowledge rights, including intellectual property rights, over genetic resources, by-products or synthesized products and associated intangible components [including traditional knowledge], that were obtained or developed through an access activity that does not comply with the provisions of this Decision. Furthermore, the Member Country affected may request nullification and bring such actions as are appropriate in

---

95   See note 5.

countries that have conferred rights or granted protective title documents."

In more specific terms, the third supplementary provision provides that, "The competent national offices on intellectual property shall require the applicant to give the registration number of the access contract and supply a copy thereof as a prerequisite for granting the respective right, when they are certain or there are reasonable indications that the products or processes whose protection is being requested have been obtained or developed from genetic resources or their by-products originating in any one of the Member Countries. The competent national authority and the competent national offices on intellectual property shall establish systems for exchanging information about the authorized access contracts and intellectual property rights granted."

bb. Decision 486 – Common Industrial Property Regime (14 September 2000)

This decision establishes the legal industrial property framework (patents, designs, utility models, marks, etc.), linking biodiversity with industrial property. Thus, article 3 of Decision 486 assures that industrial property rights granted by members will be made in a way that respects and protects the biological and genetic patrimony of its indigenous, Afro-American or local communities. Specifically, in the patents system, these rights will only be granted in case of proper acquisition of genetic resources in accordance with international, communitarian and national legal ordering.

"This article ties the principles of the CDB with traditional knowledge and genetic resources; joining these orderings with the patents."[96] (free translation from Spanish). Consolidating the idea of disclosure of origin and legal provenance, this decision incorporated the rules on this subject for the first time in a standard-setting intellectual property enactment of regional scope *per se*. Article 26 (h) and (i) of the Decision provides that applications for patents shall contain:

"(h) if applicable, a copy of the access contract, where the products or processes for which a patent application is being filed were ob-

---

[96] M.C. Arana, *La propiedad intelectual y la protección de la diversidad biológica en los convenios internacionales y la ley nacional*. 2007. Available at <www.latn.org.ar>.

tained or developed from genetic resources or by-products originating in any one of the Member Countries;

(i) if applicable, a copy of the document certifying the licence or authorization to use the traditional knowledge of indigenous, African American or local communities in the Member Countries, where the products or processes whose protection is being requested were obtained or developed from such knowledge originating in any one of the Member Countries, in accordance with the provisions of Decision 391 and the amendments and regulations thereto currently in force."

Article 75 (g) and (h) of Decision 486 goes a little further by providing that a patent shall be declared null and void if the applicant has failed to submit a copy of the access contract or the document certifying the licence or authorisation for the use of traditional knowledge.

cc. Peruvian Legislation

Peru has its own legislative framework with respect to Intellectual Property and Biodiversity. It only covers traditional knowledge associated with biodiversity. It does not cover other kinds of traditional knowledge. This legislative framework is an indicator of the enormous importance that genetic resources have for Peru. The Peruvian legislator has been incorporating principles and obligations contained in the CBD, establishing a legal institutional base both for taking advantage of genetic resources, and for protecting them in the best possible way.

Law 27811 – Regime for Protection of the Collective Knowledge of Indigenous Peoples relating to Biological Resources

Law 27811, published on 10 August 2002, which establishes the Regime for Protection of the Collective Knowledge of Indigenous Peoples related to Biological Resources, is the first comprehensive effort by a developing country with a large indigenous population to establish a *sui generis* regime for the protection of rights over traditional knowledge. "Through a system of registers, licenses and compensatory mechanisms it is hoped to achieve a degree of legal protection of the traditional knowledge of Peru's indigenous peoples."[97]

The law was the product of a protracted development process spanning almost six years, which adopted a range of strategies to engage in-

---

97   See note 5.

digenous peoples, and incorporated the participation of national and international experts in its preparation.[98] The Protection Regime recognises that the traditional knowledge of the indigenous peoples helps to conserve and make sustainable use of the components of biodiversity. It establishes a *sui generis* system to give adequate protection to those possessing traditional knowledge.

The present law, besides offering definitions of "Collective Knowledge" and "Biological Resource" in article 2,[99] establishes in article 5 as one of its objectives, the avoidance of the granting of patents for inventions obtained or developed from collective knowledge of the indigenous communities of Peru, without taking into account the pre-existence of this knowledge when examining the novelty and inventive level of the inventions. The proposed regime recognises the indigenous people's ownership and associated rights over their traditional knowledge, as well as their right to decide how it should be used. A voluntary register is to be set up within the National Institute for the Defence of Competition and the Protection of Intellectual Property. The law also states that indigenous peoples may enter into "knowledge licensing contracts", which specify the terms for the use of their knowledge. One requirement for access to knowledge that is not within the public domain is prior informed consent by the people possessing the knowledge. An innovative and extremely important feature of the regime is the creation of a Fund for the Development of Indigenous Peoples. It will receive 10 per cent out of the sales resulting from the marketing of products, developed on the basis of traditional knowledge.[100]

The existing law has been recognised as being merely the first step in adopting an effective regime for traditional knowledge protection; moreover there exist some proposals for the modification of the law by indigenous peoples "including calls to broaden its scope to include not only knowledge, but also their innovations and practices relating to

---

[98] United Nations University- Institute of Advanced Studies, see note 15, 24.

[99] Article 2 – Definitions:
b) Collective knowledge - Accumulated and trans generational knowledge developed by the towns and indigenous communities with respect to the properties, uses and characteristics of the biological diversity;
e) Biological resources - Genetic Resources, organisms or parts of them, populations, or any other type of the biotic component of the ecosystems of real or potential value or utility for the humanity.

[100] Doc. WTO/CTE/W/176 of 27 October 2000. Communication from Peru to the WTO.

biodiversity and for increased protection over traditional knowledge in the public domain."[101]

dd. Main Points of the Peruvian Law

– Scope of Protection

This legal regime focuses on the protection of traditional knowledge as it specifically relates to the characteristics, uses and properties of biodiversity.

– Objectives of the proposed regime (article 5)

The objectives of the Peruvian regime are very ambitious:

- To promote respect for the protection, preservation, wider application and development of the collective knowledge of indigenous peoples;
- To promote the fair and equitable distribution of the benefits derived from the use of that collective knowledge;
- To promote the use of the knowledge for the benefit of the indigenous peoples and mankind in general;
- To ensure that the use of the knowledge takes place with the prior informed consent of indigenous peoples;
- To promote the strengthening and development of the potential of indigenous peoples and of the machinery traditionally used by them to share and distribute collectively generated benefits under the terms of this regime;
- To avoid that patents are granted for inventions made or developed on the basis of collective knowledge of the indigenous peoples of Peru without any account being taken of the fact that this knowledge is prior art, and not having undertaken any examination of the novelty and inventiveness.

– Title holding

The rules and regulations of the proposal will apply only to collective knowledge. In cases where two or more communities posses specific knowledge, they will become co-holders (article 10).

---

[101] Tobin/ Swiderska, see note 2.

– Prior Informed Consent

As a basic principle, any interested party who seeks to use traditional knowledge for scientific, commercial or industrial purposes needs the prior informed consent of the respective organisation of indigenous peoples (article 6). Traditional knowledge will be protected through a series of inter-related instruments: contracts (licences for the use of traditional knowledge for commercial or industrial ends), trade secrets, registers and unfair competition administrative regulations. Authorisation for research is different from authorisation for exploitation. For the former, prior informed consent is required; for the latter, additionally a licensing agreement must be obtained.

– Traditional Knowledge in the Public Domain

Traditional knowledge is considered to be in the public domain when it has been established that people not belonging to the indigenous community have acquired this knowledge through media sources (e.g. newspapers or television broadcasts) and perhaps personal contacts with the indigenous community (article 13). Once this knowledge has been disseminated, even if unintentionally, it is considered to be in the public domain, so that its exploitation does not require either intellectual property rights or a licensing agreement. The law establishes an important precedent in recognising rights of indigenous peoples in order to share the benefits derived from the use of such traditional knowledge in the public domain. This right is limited in two aspects, first it relates only to traditional knowledge which entered the public domain in the last twenty years, and second, it only allows for a right to compensation and not to restrict or otherwise control access to or use of such traditional knowledge.

– Duration of rights

These rights are not limited. They are the property of the National Patrimony and will be passed on from generation to generation. (arts 11 and 12).

– Registers

The registers are intended to preserve the knowledge of the communities. They are created basically to preserve traditional knowledge and safeguard existing rights of communities over them, as well as to provide the National Institute with information which might allow to de-

fend indigenous peoples' interests in respect of their traditional knowledge (article 16). These registers are not compulsory. However, it brings
about certain advantages: the patenting of traditional knowledge listed
in the registers is only permitted upon application for and granting of
authority from the National Institute. The Institute is also of assistance
to potential bioprospectors in order to locate various sources. The Peruvian law provides for three types of traditional knowledge registers: a
National Public Register, a National Confidential Register and local
registers. The National Registers will be administered by the National
Institute, the National Authority for Consumer Affairs, and the respective intellectual property rights do apply.

– The National Public Register

The National Public Register will incorporate traditional knowledge
which is in the public domain (article 15). It will basically serve to assist
in providing centralised and organised information relevant for patents
prior art searches and to challenge patents and other intellectual property rights granted in conflict with rights over traditional knowledge.
The public register will be open and available to interested parties.

The National Public Register of Collective Knowledge lists the
knowledge in books as well as the Internet. According to article 17 this
information is accessible to any user who enters the National Institute's
website.[102] Giving the name of the entries, and their equivalent in the
original languages or other usual denominations. Further information
can be asked for, like for example the description of the resource or its
use (nutritional, medical, etc.), but this additional information is only
accessible if it is requested by the National Institute in order of investigation or, a patents office needs to know the status of a technique or to
determine the novelty of the patent that is in transaction.[103]

The information which appears in the National Public Register can
be seen in the next examples:

---

[102] See under <www.indecopi.gob.pe>.
[103] See note 96.

Maca[104]
Other denominations: Maca, maka, maca-maca, maino, ayak chichira, ayak willku ; English: maca, Peruvian ginseng.

Uña de gato[105]
Other denominations: Uña de gato, Garabato, Samento, Unganangui, Garabato amarillo, Kug Kukjaqui, Paotati - mosha, Misho-mentis, Tua juncara (Colombia), Bejuco de agua (Colombia).

– The National Confidential Register

This register contains detailed information of the knowledge, but, according to article 18, this is not accessible to the public. Information may not be disclosed, and only those who have authorisation from the communities can access it. The knowledge for this register is obtained from this communities, which through a representative of their organisation can register it at the National Institute. The exact role of this kind of register is still unclear. Some commentators consider that a local register for a confidential valuable secret of traditional knowledge might be safer and better than a national register because it is difficult to envisage the incentives that indigenous peoples would have to register traditional knowledge confidentially.[106]

– The Local Registers

According to article 24, the indigenous communities can organise their own collective local registers, according to their uses and customs. The local registers will be developed and administered by the communities themselves (article 15). The law provides that the National Institute may provide technical assistance, if required, to assist with design, development, and implementation of these registers. The law makes no specific provisions for the recognition of such local registers as sources of prior art and it is unclear what exactly the relationship, if any, will be between the local registers and the national one. [107]

---

[104] See under <http://www.indecopi.gob.pe/portalctpi/RegistrosExistentes.jsp?pLetra=M&lng=1>.

[105] See above.

[106] United Nations University - Institute of Advanced Studies, see note 15, 25.

[107] The national registers and their protective nature are closely related to the Andean Community Decision 486 on Common Industrial Property, which

– Procedure for Registration

Indigenous peoples, through their representative organisation will register their traditional knowledge in the public or confidential register administered by the National Institute. Applications for registering traditional knowledge will include: identification of indigenous peoples, identification of representatives, indication of the biological resource to which traditional knowledge is related, uses of biological resource, clear description of traditional knowledge subject to registration, formal agreement by which indigenous people agree to register their traditional knowledge. The application could include a sample of the relevant biological resource or, if this is not possible in practice, photographs which enable the National Institute to identify the resource under consideration and submit it to an taxonomical analysis (article 20). In terms of procedure, the application should be registered within ten days after its entry. If a prerequisite is missing, indigenous peoples are given up to six months to complete the application form. In case they do not, the whole procedure has to be restarted (article 21). To further promote the registration of traditional knowledge, the National Institute will send out officials in order to register traditional knowledge (article 22).

Registration in either the public or confidential register may be cancelled by the National Institute if the registration does not comply with the overall provisions of the law or if the information and data included are proved to be false or not being exact (article 34).

– Licensing Agreement

The representative organisation of indigenous peoples will be able to grant licences for the respective traditional knowledge to third parties but only in written form, in their native as well as in the Spanish language. The period covers a term of no less than one year and no more than three years (article 26). The agreement must stipulate the payment of royalties to the communities for the use of their knowledge (article 27 C). The registration of the licensing agreement at the National Institute is obligatory (article 25).

---

requires patent applicants to provide evidence for legal access to genetic resources and traditional knowledge, used in the development of inventions. INDECOPI could use these registers to assess patent applications in relation to their novelty and inventiveness.

– Justifiable Compensation

The first money has to be paid once the licensing agreement is entered into. This payment is obligatory and can take the form of money or goods (e.g. building schools, clinics, communication centres and so on). The moment benefit has been obtained from the exploitation of traditional knowledge further money has to be paid. The minimum payment is 10 per cent of the gross sales (article 8).

– Development Fund

Given that a large part of the knowledge is shared by more than one community, and given that it is impossible for all of them to consent to the execution of the licence to use the respective knowledge, a Development Fund should be created. The details have to be sorted out by a committee existing of representatives from the respective communities and the government. The law establishes so far an indigenous fund to be managed by indigenous peoples. The fund will take ten per cent of all transactions involving traditional knowledge. The purpose of the fund is to promote more equitable sharing of benefits amongst the nation's indigenous peoples (article 37).

– Disclosure of origin and legal provenance

In the matter of disclosure of origin and legal provenance, the Second Supplementary Provision of Law 27811 provides that:[108]

"In the event that an invention patent - related to products or processes obtained or developed from certain collective knowledge - is required, the applicant must present a copy of the license contract as a previous requirement to be granted the corresponding right, unless it is a collective knowledge in the public domain. Non compliance with this requirement will provide grounds for denial or for nullity for the patent at issue."

This provision supplements at the national level the provisions of Decision 486, specifically with regard to the disclosure of origin and legal provenance of traditional knowledge that could form part of an invention.

---

[108] Law establishing the Regime for the Protection of the Collective Knowledge of Indigenous Peoples Relating to Biological Resources.

LAW 28216. Protection of Access to Peruvian Biological Diversity and to the Collective Knowledge of the Indigenous Peoples (1 May 2004)

Article 1 establishes the objective of the law, which is the protection of access to Peruvian biological diversity and to the collective traditional knowledge of the indigenous people.

Article 2 establishes the creation of the National Commission for the Protection of Access to Peruvian Biological Diversity and to the collective knowledge of the indigenous peoples (hereinafter the National Anti-Biopiracy Commission) whose functions are defined in article 4.

The National Anti-Biopiracy Commission has the task of developing actions to identify, prevent and avoid acts of "biopiracy" with the aim of protecting the interests of the Peruvian state. Its main functions are:[109]

a) to establish and maintain a register of biological resources and traditional knowledge;

b) to provide protection against acts of "biopiracy";

c) to identify and follow up patent applications made or patents granted abroad that relate to Peruvian biological resources or collective knowledge of the indigenous peoples of Peru;

d) to make technical evaluations of the above-mentioned applications and patent grants;

e) to issue reports on the cases studied;

f) to lodge objections or actions for annulment concerning the above-mentioned patent applications or patent grants;

g) to establish information channels with the main intellectual property offices around the world;

h) to draw up proposals for the defence of Peru's interests in different forums.

The third and final supplementary provision of the law defines "biopiracy" as access to and unauthorized use of biological resources or traditional knowledge of the indigenous people by third parties without compensation, without the necessary authorization and in contravention of the principles established in the Convention on Biological Diversity and the existing rules on the subject. This appropriation may

---

[109]   See note 5.

come to light through physical inspection, through ownership rights in products incorporating such illegally obtained elements or, in some cases, through the invocation of such rights.

Since its creation, the Commission has developed a series of actions to identify and to prevent acts of "biopiracy" with the purpose of protecting genetic resources. Its efforts began in August 2004 and still continue to date. One of its main activities has been to identify potential cases of "biopiracy" involving genetic resources and traditional knowledge.

According to a report produced by the Commission, it is known that 149 patents linked to Peruvian biological resources have been requested or granted in the United States, the European Union and Japan. The following table shows the number of requested or registered patents linked to six resources of Peruvian origin:[110] Hercampuri, Camu Camu, Yacón, Caigua, Sacha Inchi and Chancapiedra.

---

[110] This table was made with information obtained from Doc. IP/C/W/441.

NUMBER OF REQUESTED OR REGISTERED PATENTS LINKED TO RESOURCES OF PERUVIAN ORIGIN			
Countries / Resources	USA	EU	JAPAN
	N° of linked patents	N° of linked patents	N° of linked patents
Hercampuri *Gentianella alborosea* (Gilg) Frabris	1	2	11
Camu – Camu Myrciaria dubia	2	1	16
Yacón Smallanthus sonchifolius	15	--	50
Caigua Cyclanthera pedata L	1	--	--
Sacha Inchi Plukenetia volúbilis L	8	--	--
Chancapiedra Phyllantus niruri	22	6	14
Total of Patents per country	49	9	91

As a final remark, it is important to note that the regulation of the rights of the indigenous communities does not in any way hamper the obtaining of intellectual property rights. "The two systems of protection must be linked. For this reason, the Peruvian Protection Regime stipulates that if an invention has been developed based on the knowledge of an indigenous community, its patenting is not possible unless authorisation for its use is given. A similar disposition regarding access to genetic resources can be found in the norms on access to Andean genetic resources (Decision 391) and in the regulation law for Peruvian access. At the same time, a norm with the same terms has been included in the Andean Decision on IP."[111]

c. The US-Peru Trade Promotion Agreement

The United States – Peru Trade Promotion Agreement was signed on 12 April 2006. It has not entered into force because it is still pending ratification by the US government. The chapter concerning intellectual property was one of the toughest to negotiate. However, an important understanding between both countries regarding biodiversity and traditional knowledge was reached.

Before the negotiations, there was some fear about a clear position of the United States with regard to traditional knowledge and genetic resources. The United States insisted on the live organisms' patents favouring the American companies that are developing biotechnology programs and as a logical consequence need patents on genetic resources. In order to obtain their objectives the companies need the genetic resources of other countries and will try to obtain them. Consequently Peru had a certain strategy and achieved some of its aims with regard to this issue.

Next to the principal text of the agreement, there is a specific document annexed regarding traditional knowledge and biodiversity. This Understanding recognises the importance of traditional knowledge and biodiversity and their potential contribution to cultural, economic and social development. The parties also recognise the importance of the following:

(1) Obtaining prior informed consent from the appropriate authority prior to accessing genetic resources under the control of such authority;

---

[111] A.M. Pacón, *The Peruvian Proposal for Protecting Traditional Knowledge*, 2004. And page 178 in Twarog/ Kapoor, see note 1.

(2) Equitably sharing of benefits arising from the use of traditional knowledge and genetic resources; and

(3) Promoting quality patent examination to ensure that the conditions for patentability are satisfied.

The parties recognise that access to genetic resources or traditional knowledge, as well as the equitable sharing of benefits that may result from the use of those resources or that knowledge, can be adequately addressed through contracts that reflect mutually agreed terms between users and providers. Each party shall endeavour to seek ways to share information that may have an impact on the patentability based on traditional knowledge or genetic resources by providing (a) publicly accessible databases that contain relevant information; and (b) an opportunity to give written notice, to the appropriate examining authority of existing prior art that may have an influence on patentability.[112]

This Understanding represents an important step forward for the Peruvian government which has always tried to protect these items, because the United States government undertakes to respect and collaborate now in the protection of traditional knowledge and genetic resources.

VI. Conclusions

– Traditional and indigenous knowledge has been used for centuries by indigenous and local communities, and the importance of its protection has been recognised by the CBD. Nevertheless, diverse forms of traditional knowledge have been appropriated under intellectual property rights by researchers and commercial enterprises, without any compensation.

– The protection of traditional knowledge has become a very complex matter, since there are broad discrepancies regarding the definition of the subject matter, the rationale for protection, and the means for achieving this. However, the difficulty in defining it should not be an obstacle for developing some form of protection.

– The current intellectual property rights system can be useful for the protection of some forms of traditional knowledge, such as TCEs

---

[112] This understanding can be found in English and Spanish on the following websites <http://www.ustr.gov/Trade_Agreements/Bilateral/Peru_TPA/Section_Index.html> and <http://www.tlcperu-eeuu.gob.pe>.

through copyright law. However, it has been demonstrated that this alone is not enough. It is necessary to develop *sui generis* forms of protection in order to satisfy the different needs of the respective communities, each with their own characteristics. Given the diversity of cultures and resources, it is impossible to have a single system of protection; there must be a diversity of options to protect traditional knowledge.

– WIPO, through the IGC has established principles to guide the development of *sui generis* regimes, and has formed fact-finding missions on intellectual property and traditional knowledge. However, given the limited mandate of WIPO as an organisation aiming to promote intellectual property protection, it failed in respect of undertaking a serious analysis of the standards for patentability applied by WIPO members.

– Peru, as one of the most megadiverse countries, advocates mandatory inclusion of disclosure of origin and legal provenance, to guarantee the more efficient and secure implementation of TRIPS itself and generate a situation of positive synergy between TRIPS and the CBD.

– At the regional level, the Andean Community (Peru, Bolivia, Ecuador, Colombia) has adopted two important decisions (Decisions 391 and 486), that take into consideration the disclosure of origin and legal provenance as requisites to undertake research and make use of Andean origin's resources and related knowledge. Both of them are highly controversial issues in international discussions on the relationship between biodiversity, traditional knowledge and intellectual property.

– The Peruvian government is one of the few that has developed a *sui generis* system for the protection of collective traditional knowledge of indigenous peoples derived from biological resources. It has been considered an important example and a lesson for governments looking for models from which they can develop their own traditional knowledge protection system. However, the scope of such regime does not include expressions of folklore, which have been considered in other national law undertakings, such as in the Panamanian law.

Book Reviews

Alan Boyle/ Christine Chinkin: The Making of International Law
Oxford University Press, 2007, XXX + 338 pages, ISBN 978-0-19-924819-3

International law is of fundamental importance for a globalised world. Climate change, transnational organised terrorism, the despoliation of the environment, gross human rights violations, and the spread of deadly diseases, arms and drugs across national borders, among other problems, require solutions in the form of rules, standards and procedures and, thus, law-making on an international level.

The book of Alan Boyle, Professor at the University of Edinburgh, and Christine Chinkin, Professor at the London School of Economics and Political Science, explains vividly how international law is made. It does not give a formalistic account on the traditional – and untraditional – sources and theories of international law but identifies the actors, instruments, and processes by whom and through which international law is generated. This new approach unites norm creation with the interpretation, application, and development of international law.

In a succinct Introduction, which already forms the first Chapter, Boyle and Chinkin point to the fight against terrorism as an illustrative example of current international law-making. Moreover, they clarify the concept of legitimacy, which they define as "the normative belief that a rule or institution ought to be obeyed" (p. 24). The authors distinguish between process legitimacy and system legitimacy. They rightly argue that process legitimacy could not be used as a substitute for legality where the designated and accepted procedures had not been followed, or where substantive laws had been breached.

The notion of system legitimacy is used with regard to the role and actions of the most powerful states. Traditionally, these states had a hegemonic position in the formation of international law. But recently there has been some change in both customary international law and treaty-making processes. The practice of a large number of states may outweigh that of a smaller number of more powerful states, as has happened in the case concerning the extent of the territorial sea and the determination of the preferential fishing zones, or more generally economic zones. Furthermore, the multilateral law-making processes leading to the adoption of the Rome Statute of the International Criminal Court, the Convention on the Prohibition of the Use, Stockpiling, Production and Transfer of Anti-Personnel Mines and on Their Destruction (Landmines Convention), the Convention on Climate Change and the Kyoto Protocol show that even the dissenting United States, the world's only remaining superpower, cannot assume that it will be able to dictate the outcome against the will of the majority.

The second Chapter of the book deals with the participants in the process of international law-making. Boyle and Chinkin acknowledge that states continue to dominate the international law-making agenda and the allocation of resources, but they also hold that it would be short-sighted to insist on the classical view of states as the sole makers of international law. Hence, the authors examine in detail the involvement of non-state actors in international law-making , in particular those that are variously termed civil society, transnational advocacy networks, social movements, and, above all, in an institutionalised form, non-governmental organisations (NGOs).

The participation of NGOs is regarded as not being unproblematic. Boyle and Chinkin urge that caution is required in assuming that it democratises international law-making, since NGOs were "often non-democratic, self-appointed, may consist of only a handful of people and determine their own agendas with an evangelical or elitist zeal. There is no guarantee that the views expressed by even high-profile NGOs are representative, either generally, or with respect to their claimed constituencies" (p. 58). The authors first analyse the NGOs strategies both for participation in treaty-making and for influencing institutional law-making. They refer, on the one hand, to the Convention against Torture, the Landmines Convention, the Rome Statute, the UNIDROIT Convention on Mobile Equipment, and the Multilateral Agreement on Investment as examples, and on the other hand, to the UN General Assembly and the UN Security Council, which have allowed only very limited access to NGOs through the so-called Arria Formula (see for further information on this procedure, the article of C. Breen in this Volume), and global summit meetings. Then they turn to NGO monitoring, norm generation and advocacy. They explain that the interactive processes between international institutions, states, regional and local authorities, which function as "interpretative communities", since they "give meaning to and incorporate international instruments into their own local regimes through a mix of their own narratives, experiences, values, visions and dreams", and NGOs are "potentially law-making insofar as they generate state practice as a basis for customary law, help establish general principles of law, or constitute evidence for the interpretation and application of existing norms and principles" (pp. 82-83).

The third Chapter outlines the variety of international processes which exist for the negotiation and adoption of treaties, decisions, and soft law instruments. The authors in this context return to the concept of legitimacy. Instead of the notion of democratisation as a suggested perspective on legitimacy, they argue in favour of a "more cosmopolitan notion of participation in international law-making [... as] a possible solution, exemplified by the election of parliamentary organs in international institutions such as the Council of Europe, the Nordic Council or the Organisation for Security and Co-operation in Europe" (p. 101). Moreover, they state that the equal participation of all sovereign states in the process of law-making could be viewed as inherently democratic, particularly when the negotiating power of individual states, however small, was strengthened by consensus negotiating procedures. Regarding the future, they suggest that "the present international law-making 'system' – in reality more a bric-a-brac than system – should evolve into something closer to the European Union, the only functioning model of a multilateral legislative system currently available. On that model the UN General Assembly might become the Parliament, the Security Council would be the equivalent of the Council of Ministers, and the Secretariat would perform the functions of the European Commission" (p. 102).

Then the authors shed some light on law-making by the United Nations, namely by the Security Council, which has the power, albeit of dubious legitimacy, to make legally binding obligations on questions of law of a kind that are typically made by courts and to override both customary law and applicable treaties. Thereafter, they examine the law-making by the Food and Agriculture Organization, the World Health Organization, the International Maritime Organization, and the World Trade Organization, as well as by international conferences such as the Third UN Conference on the Law of the Sea and the Rome Diplomatic Conference for an International Criminal Court, and by intergovernmental and human rights treaty bodies. Boyle and Chinkin make an assessment concerning law-making by consensus, which cannot always be interpreted as approval. Consensus negotiating procedures inevitably generate a greater need to engage in diplomacy, to listen and to bargain than decisions being taken by majority. As the negotiations of the 1982 UNCLOS and the Climate Change Convention have demonstrated, these procedures tend to democratise decision-making by diminishing disparities in power among states; no participating state can be ignored, every state has to consent. Furthermore, the adoption of a consensus package-deal can have a powerful law-making effect; securing widespread support, not only legitimising and promoting consistent state practice, but makes it less likely that other states will object to immediate implementation. Consequently, new customary law may come into being very quickly.

In the fourth Chapter, the authors turn to the codification and progressive development of international law. They portray in detail the work of the ILC, which could, according to their view, with better guidance from the 6th Committee of the General Assembly and a much closer relationship with states, assist but not lead the process of shifting the focus of international law-making away from the codification of existing law towards the negotiation of new law. Boyle and Chinkin find it is slightly surprising that the multilateral treaty has been the ILC's preferred instrument for the codification of international law since a treaty runs the risk of securing only a relatively small number of parties and referring the draft articles to a diplomatic conference might re-open debates on a text which already rests on a delicate compromise between differing views. They propose that the ILC should evolve and make greater use of soft law instruments in future.

This proposal leads to, and also predetermines the structure of, the fifth Chapter dealing with the instruments employed by international law-making processes. The authors do not start their explanations by focussing on treaties but on soft law, a term which they hold to be a convenient description for a variety of non-binding instruments used in contemporary international relations. They point out that substance and intent are categories for the distinction between hard law and soft law; "the label attached to the instrument is not decisive" (p. 213). Soft law instruments can represent an alternative to law-making by treaty for four reasons: firstly, it may be easier to reach agreement when the form is not binding; secondly, it may be easier for some states to adhere to non-binding instruments since they can avoid the domestic treaty ratification process; thirdly, soft law instruments are more flexible since they are normally easier to supplement, amend or to replace than treaties; fourth and finally, they may provide more immediate evidence of international support and consensus than a treaty whose impact is heavily qualified by reservations and the need of ratification and entry into force. Furthermore, soft law instruments are often used as mechanisms for authoritative interpretation or amplification of the terms of a treaty. They may contain general principles and have effects on customary international law, providing evidence for existing law, or of the *opinio juris* or state practice that generates new law. Thereafter, the authors turn to UN Security Council resolutions, which can over-ride treaty-law and general international law, and to treaties themselves, which do not, as the authors stress, *per se* make general international law but can, not unlike soft law, contribute to the process by which new customary law is created and developed. They briefly explain how treaties can have legal effects for non-parties, how they can be maintained as evolving regimes, and how different law-making treaties interact.

The last Chapter gives an overview of the role international courts and tribunals play with regard to the making of international law. The authors argue that "[i]n a decentralized system without a legislative body or authoritative law-making process and where unwritten law is developed through the amorphous processes of state practice and *opinio juris*" (p. 268) international courts and tribunals, in particular the ICJ, do more than simply apply the law; they are part of the process of making it. In some cases this involves affirming the law-making effect of multilateral agreements, UN resolutions, ILC codifications or other outputs of the international law-making processes. In other cases, judges have drawn upon a much broader legal basis for their decisions, and articulated, not least in the case of gaps in written international law, rules and principles of law that can only be described as novel and are not necessarily supported by evidence of general state practice or *opinio juris*. Moreover, international courts take over the task to address the problems of coherence and fragmentation and try to find solutions pointing to an integrated concept of international law.

In sum, the book of Boyle and Chinkin is an excellent insight in, and analysis of, the genesis and development of contemporary international law. The authors often deviate from the established paths of the foundations of the international legal order and give hints to a modern understanding, thereby taking a critical stand towards American foreign policy and mainstream scholarship. The authors use a mixture of inductive and deductive methods, refer to countless examples, and present their results in clear language. The book should have a firm place in international law discussions.

Dr. Diana Zacharias, Senior Research Fellow at the Max Planck Institute for Comparative Public Law and International Law, Heidelberg

Holger Hestermeyer: Human Rights and the WTO – The Case of Patents and Access to Medicines
Oxford University Press, 2007, XXXVI + 369 pages, ISBN 978-0-19-921520-1

Conflicts between the liberal economic principles of the global trading regime established by the Agreements entered into under the umbrella of the World Trade Organization (WTO) and non-economic concerns such as human rights, protection of the environment or development policies have been at the forefront of the debates about "harnessing globalisation" for quite some time. In recent times, the case of patents and access to medicines has probably received the greatest attention in both political circles and also in academia. Publications on the question to what extent the compulsory licensing of patents for pharmaceuticals desperately needed to fight pandemic diseases such as HIV/AIDS infringe or do not infringe the WTO Agreement on Trade-related Aspects of Intellectual Property Rights (TRIPs) have multiplied over the last few years (see for example, the monographs by Gamharter, Access to Affordable Medicines: Developing Responses under the TRIPS Agreement and EC Law, 2004; von Kraack, TRIPs oder Patentschutz weltweit – Zwangslizenzen, Erschöpfung, Parallelimporte, 2006 and Rott, Patentrecht und Sozialpolitik unter dem TRIPS-Abkommen, 2002).

The present work of Holger Hestermeyer, Senior Research Fellow at the Max-Planck-Institute for Comparative Public Law and International Law in Heidelberg, will nevertheless find a wide and interested readership, not least because of being written in English and being published by one of the best-known and most prestigious publishing houses world-wide Oxford University Press. The book is based on Hestermeyer's doctoral thesis, which was written under the supervision of Rüdiger Wolfrum and accepted by the University of Hamburg in 2006.

According to its own description in the Introduction (xxxiii – xxxvi), the study treats "the conflict between patent law obligations under the [...] TRIPS-Agreement and access to medicine, a conflict that is, at its core, a conflict between the law of the [...] WTO and human rights law." Against this backdrop, one may question the wisdom of choosing

"Human Rights and the WTO" as main title for the work (presumably for reasons of better marketability) and putting the reference to "Access to Medicines" only in the subtitle. Readers who expect a wider treatment of the conflict between WTO law and human rights, which raises many more questions than the one related to TRIPs (see e.g. Cottier/ Pauwelyn/ Bürgi (eds), Human Rights and International Trade, 2005), might – quite understandably – be disappointed. From the point of view of scientific and scholarly culture, it begs once more the question whether the "German way" of publishing genuine academic work – the author has to pay for the production costs of the book, but will enjoy more leeway as regards the substance and title of the publication – is not preferable to the anglo-american way that obviously is to some extent driven by market considerations.

After the already mentioned short introduction, Hestermeyer lays the foundation of the treatment of the specific conflict by introducing the background of the debate (Chapter 1, pages 1 -17), namely the legal disputes that arose in connection with the pricing policy for the AIDS medicine AZT and with the South African Medicines Act. Chapter 2 (pages 18 – 75) describes and analyses the international rules on patents, their underlying concepts and rationales and their rather new application to pharmaceuticals as a consequence of the TRIPs. Chapter 3 (pages 76 – 136) delineates access to medicine as a human right protected under different instruments of public international law. According to Hestermeyer, this includes a right of individuals *vis-à-vis* their governments to receive financial support for the purchase of medicines needed or alternatively a right to receive the medication from the government directly (which would have to buy the pharmaceuticals then), or, again alternatively, a right to a legally guaranteed "adequate level of the price of the medicine." (p. 136)

This is a crucial point. Hestermeyer bases his argument regarding the first two alternatives on the states' obligation to "fulfil", regarding the latter on the obligation to "protect" the right to life and access to medicines. However, it clearly makes a difference if a state fulfils its obligations by spending public money for the purchase of pharmaceuticals on the market or if it restricts the enjoyment of (intellectual) property rights of (typically foreign) individuals in order to fulfil its obligations. Given the importance of the argument for the overall aim of the study, one would have appreciated a more comprehensive elaboration of this structural difference (but see later pages 153 – 158). Moreover, it seems a somewhat short-sighted interpretation of a right to access to medicine to include only the pharmaceuticals already developed and not a right to the development of essential medicines in the future. A state would then not only be under an obligation to create a legal order in which access to life-saving medicine is guaranteed, but also research and development (Hestermeyer discusses this matter at pages 158 – 166).

However, Hestermeyer comes to the conclusion that patents for pharmaceuticals in developing countries generally interfere with the access to medicine without a justification (page 166). In Chapter 4 (pages 137 – 206), Hestermeyer's bottom-line argument is the following: human rights law is fundamentally based on morality and thereby deserves normative superiority to the utilitarian and instrumental WTO legal order. It is worth recalling at this point, that Hestermeyer rejects practically any human rights foundation of intellectual property (which he considers to be only functional). From that perspective, private traders' market access rights are indeed a mere reflex. Not only Ernst-Ulrich Petersmann presumably disagrees with this approach (as Hestermeyer realises himself, see page 197 et seq.). I do also. Human rights conventions do create rights of individuals directly and not "as a mere reflex" of horizontal state-to-state obligations since they predominantly affect the relationship between states and their own citizens. Hence, there will be no nation state that could exercise diplomatic protection and the individuals must thus be empowered themselves. In contrast, trade treaties typically deal with obligations of states *vis-à-vis* nationals of other states, which are usually construed as obligations towards the foreign state. This logical *constructional* difference does not suffice to justify a *fundamental normative hierarchical claim*, nor does the lack of a globally protected individual right to property, which is largely due to the political division of the world until 1989. Using Fukuyama's picture of that time, it seems that in Hestermeyer's reasoning "history strikes back."

In Chapter 5 (pages 207 – 292), Hestermeyer addresses the ultimate question of how access to medicine affects the interpretation of the relevant obligations under the TRIPs. He correctly points out that it may not as such be relied upon in WTO dispute settlement in order to justify an infringement of the obligations deriving therefrom. Notwithstanding that it serves as an argument for a broad interpretation of the flexibilities inherent in the TRIPs (page 229 – 250). Not surprisingly, Hestermeyer finds access to medicines to constitute an argument mitigating in all cases in favour of freedom of choice for WTO members (regime of exhaustion, compulsory licences etc.). However, all interpretative efforts cannot overcome the clear wording of article 31 (f) TRIPs that makes compulsory licences for exports impossible, a possibility indispensable for countries without sufficient manufacturing capabilities to produce the generics themselves (pages 250 – 253).

The last part of the analysis is devoted to the three different legal instruments that were adopted by the WTO in response to the disputes about the legal limits to WTO members' compulsory licensing policies. Hestermeyer describes the negotiating history and content of all of them in great detail (page 256 – 276) and analyses their respective legal status (page 276 – 287). The latter is far from clear and undisputed and the WTO membership has made extremely creative use of its limited power to create "secondary" WTO law. Despite these efforts, access to medicines remains impaired by the TRIPs, Hestermeyer argues. Even the solution for compulsory export licensing will not be able to remedy the situation, since the necessary investment for manufacturing capacities in countries like India will no longer pay off, if it can only be used for exports to very small LDCs (and not also for the huge domestic Indian market). The practice following the August 2003 export licensing waiver indicates its own practical insufficiency or irrelevance: only one export licence has been granted on this basis so far.

In the final pages of his study, Hestermeyer discusses possible solutions for the underlying systemic conflict between WTO law and human rights. Given the political unlikelihood of any amendments to the WTO agreements that provide for a greater role of human rights obligations inside the WTO legal system, Hestermeyer demands a more active role of WTO dispute settlement organs in the "importation of human rights into the WTO legal order" and points to the example of the European Court of Justice in the 1970s (page 288 et seq.). However, the differences between the two systems, partly admitted by Hestermeyer himself, are too large to make the European Union an example. The key difference between the two legal systems is the fact that the European Community exerts genuine sovereign rights in a way very similar to that of a Nation State. The same is by no means true for the WTO. The European Court of Justice initially imported fundamental rights considerations into the EC legal order to restrict this law-making power of the EU's institutions, not to relativise the obligations of the Member States in any way. The latter has taken place only very recently, when the European Court of Justice accepted fundamental rights to qualify as important public concerns justifying *prima facie* infringements of the fundamental freedoms.

Notwithstanding the criticism expressed above, which is to some extent admittedly a question of normative paradigm, the book is an extremely thoughtful, knowledgeable, comprehensive and well-written contribution to a discussion of fundamental importance for the future development of the global trading system. Whether it is also a suitable "comprehensive introduction to the debate for non-specialists", as it claims to be (page xxxiii), is a different question.

Dr. Christoph Herrmann, Munich/Vienna